PELICAN BOOKS

THE JAPAN READER 1
IMPERIAL JAPAN: 1800–1945

Jon Livingston read Japanese studies at Harvard
University. He is co-editor of *China Yesterday and Today*
and a staff member of the Bay Area Institute of San
Francisco.

Joe Moore has been a congressional assistant and has
studied at the University of Wisconsin. He specializes in
modern Japanese history and is, at present, teaching in
California.

Felicia Oldfather read Asian studies at Washington
University, St Louis, and at the University of California,
Berkeley. She is an editor of *China! Inside the People's
Republic.*

The Japan Reader

VOLUME ONE
IMPERIAL JAPAN
1800–1945

Edited, annotated, and with introductions
by Jon Livingston, Joe Moore,
and Felicia Oldfather

Penguin Books

Penguin Books Ltd,
Harmondsworth, Middlesex, England
Penguin Books,
625, Madison Avenue, New York, New York 10022, U.S.A.
Penguin Books Australia Ltd,
Ringwood, Victoria, Australia
Penguin Books Canada Ltd,
41 Steelcase Road West, Markham, Ontario, Canada
Penguin Books (N.Z.) Ltd,
182–190 Wairau Road, Auckland 10, New Zealand

First published in the U.S.A. by Random House 1973

Published in Great Britain in Pelican Books 1976

Made and printed in Great Britain by
Richard Clay (The Chaucer Press) Ltd, Bungay, Suffolk
Set in Linotype Times

Acknowledgments

Grateful acknowledgment is made to the following for permission to reprint previously published material:

George Allen & Unwin Ltd.: For "A Political History of Japan During the Meiji Period," "The Sino-Japanese War," and "The Political System in Japan" by Walter McLaren, excerpted from *A Political History of Japan During the Meiji Period* by Walter McLaren.

Appleton-Century-Crofts and Barrie & Jenkins Ltd.: For "Economic Movements" by G. B. Sansom, excerpted from *Japan: A Short Cultural History,* by G. B. Sansom. Copyright 1943 by D. Appleton-Century Company, Inc., © 1962 by Appleton-Century-Crofts, Inc. (Appleton-Century-Crofts, New York; the Cresset Press, London).

Harumi Befu: For "Village Autonomy and the State" by Harumi Befu. Abridged and excerpted with deletion of footnotes from his article "Village Autonomy and Articulation with the State: The Case of Tokugawa Japan," which originally appeared in the *Journal of Asian Studies,* 25:1 (1965), pp. 19–32.

Cambridge University Press: For "The Japanese Family Storehouse or the Millionaires' Gospel Modernised" by Ihara Saikaku, excerpted from *The Japanese Family Storehouse or the Millionaires' Gospel Modernised* by Ihara Saikaku, translated by G. T. Sargent (Cambridge University Press, 1959).

Columbia University Press: For excerpts from pages 234–49, 245–8 of *Japan's First Modern Novel, Ukigumo of Futabatei Shimei,* translated with critical commentary by Marleigh Grayer Ryan (Columbia University Press, New York, 1967); for "Tokugawa Administration" and "Modernity, Culture, and Religion" by Joseph Kitagawa, excerpted from *Religion in Japanese History* by Joseph Kitagawa (Columbia University Press, 1966).

Cornell University Press and Oxford University Press: For "Landlords and Village Society" and "The Power Structure of the Hamlet" by Fukutake Tadashi, excerpted from *Japanese Rural Society* by Fukutake Tadashi.

The East Asian Institute of Columbia University: For "Attitudes Toward Asia and the Beginnings of Japanese Empire" by Marlene Mayo, excerpted from Grant Goodman, comp., *Imperial Japan and Asia—A Reassessment.*

Harper & Row Publishers, Inc.: For "The Emperor's Birthday" by Sydney Greenbie, excerpted and abridged from pages 394–5 in *Japan: Real and Imaginary* by Sydney Greenbie (Harper & Row, 1920).

Harvard University Press: For "Student Enthusiasts" by Peter Duus, excerpted from *Party Rivalry and Political Change in Taisho Japan* by Peter Duus. Copyright © 1968 by the President and Fellows of Harvard College; for "The Tenant Movement" by Wakukawa Seiyei, excerpted from "The Japanese Farm-Tenancy System" by Wakukawa Seiyei, from *Japan's Prospect,* edited by Douglas G. Haring. Copyright 1946 by the President and Fellows of Harvard College.

Hawthorn Books, Inc., and John Murray Publishers, Ltd.: For "The Most Exacting Crop in the World" by J. W. Robertson Scott, excerpted from *The Foundations of Japan* by J. W. Robertson Scott (1922). All rights reserved.

Holt, Rinehart & Winston, Inc.: For "A Japanese Husband" and "Are Miners Human Beings" by Baroness Shidzue Ishimoto, excerpted from *Facing Two Ways* by Baroness Shidzue Ishimoto. Copyright 1935, © 1963 by Shidzue Ishimoto.

The Johns Hopkins University Press: For "Evolution of the Family," "Itagaki and the Movement Towards a Parliament," and "Ito and the Constitution" by Ike Nobutaka, excerpted from *Beginnings of Political Democracy in Japan* by Ike Nobutaka. Copyright 1950 by The Johns Hopkins University Press.

Iowa State University Press: For "Japan—Land and Men" by Lawrence Hewes, excerpted from *Japan—Land and Men* by Lawrence Hewes. Copyright © 1955 by the Iowa State University Press, Ames, Iowa.

Japan Publications, Inc.: For "The Samurai Family and Feudal Ideology," "Riots in the Cities," "Social Change and the City," "Civil Law and the Family" by Yazaki Takeo, excerpted from pages 205–9, 230–3, 258–9, 262–4, 358–63 of *Social Change and the City in Japan* by Yazaki Takeo.

René Juillard: For "Tokyo Burns" by Robert Guillain, excerpted from *Le Peuple japonais et la guerre* by Robert Guillain (René Juillard, 1947).

Alfred A. Knopf, Inc., and Martin Secker & Warburg Ltd.: For "Fires on the Plain" by Ooka Shohei, excerpted from *Fires on the Plain* by Ooka Shohei, translated by Ivan Morris. Copyright © 1957 by Alfred A. Knopf, Inc.

J. B. Lippincott Company and Ann Elmo Agency, Inc.: For "The Way of the Gods" by Helen Mears, excerpted from *The Year of the Wild Boar* by Helen Mears. Copyright 1942 and renewed 1970 by Helen Mears.

McGraw-Hill Book Company: For excerpts from *Japan's Economic Progress— The Progress of Industrialization* by John Orchard (McGraw-Hill Book Company, New York, 1930).

Oxford University Press: For "Tenancy and Aggression" and "War and the Rural Areas" by R. P. Dore, excerpted from *Land Reform in Japan* by Ronald P. Dore, published by Oxford University Press under the auspices of the Royal Institute of International Affairs.

Pacific Affairs and The University of British Columbia Press: For "The Kiheita," and "Conscription and the Opposition to It," by E. H. Norman, excerpted from *Soldier and Peasant in Japan* by E. H. Norman (International Secretariat, Institute of Pacific Relations, New York, 1943); for "Early Industrialization," "Peasant Protest and the Land Tax," and "Parties and Politics" by E. H. Norman, excerpted from *Japan's Emergence as a Modern State* by E. H. Norman (International Secretariat, Institute of Pacific Relations, New York, 1940); for excerpts from "The Genyosha: A Study in the Origins of Japanese Imperialism,".by E. H. Norman, *Pacific Affairs*, XVII:3 (September, 1944).

Pacific Affairs, The University of British Columbia Press, and T. A. Bisson: For "Japan as a Political Organism" by T. A. Bisson, from *Pacific Affairs* XVII (Dec. 1944), pp. 392–420; for "Increase of Zaibatsu Predominance in Wartime Japan" by T. A. Bisson, from *Pacific Affairs* XVIII (March, 1945) pp. 55–9; for "The Zaibatsu's Wartime Role" by T. A. Bisson, *Pacific Affairs* XVIII (Dec. 1945) pp. 355–64.

Paragon Reprint Corp.: For "Peasant Uprisings in Japan of the Tokugawa Period" by Hugh Borton, excerpted from *The Transactions of the Asiatic Society of Japan*, 2nd Series, Vol. XVI (1968).

Penguin Books Ltd.: For "After a Fruitless Argument" and "Rather Than Cry" by Ishikawa Takuboku, from *The Penguin Book of Japanese Verse*, translated and edited by Geoffrey Bownas and Anthony Thwaite. Copyright © 1964 by Geoffrey Bownas and Anthony Thwaite; for "Change in Tokugawa Society" by Richard Storry, excerpted from *A History of Modern Japan* by Richard Storry. Copyright © 1960, 1961, 1968 by Richard Storry.

Praeger Publishers, Inc., and George Weidenfeld and Nicolson: For "Japan in the Early Nineteenth Century" and "Town Life and Tokugawa Culture" by W. G. Beasley, excerpted from *The Modern History of Japan* by W. G. Beasley. Copyright © 1963 by W. G. Beasley.

Princeton University Press: For "National Defense and the Consolidation of Empire, 1907–1913" and "Japan's Quest For Autonomy" by James Crowley, excerpted from *Japan's Quest For Autonomy: National Security and Foreign Policy 1930–1938,* by James Crowley, with the deletion of all footnotes. Copyright © 1966 by Princeton University Press; for "Zaibatsu and the War" by Eleanor Hadley, excerpted from *Antitrust in Japan* by Eleanor Hadley. Copyright © 1970 by Princeton University Press; for "The Great Combines," "Japan's Economy in Transition," and "Trade, Armament, Industrial Expansion, 1930–38" by William Lockwood, excerpted from *The Economic Development of Japan* by William W. Lockwood (expanded edition, Princeton University Press, 1968; second Princeton Paperback Printing, 1970).

G. P. Putnam's Sons: For "Japanese Labourers" by Matsukata Kojiro, excerpted from *Japan to America—A Symposium of Papers by Political Leaders and Representative Citizens of Japan on Conditions in Japan and on the Relations Between Japan and the United States* (G. P. Putnam's Sons, under the auspices of the Japan Society of Americans, 1914).

Thomas C. Smith: For "The Japanese Village in the Seventeenth Century" by T. C. Smith, excerpted from *Studies in the Institutional History of Early Modern Japan,* edited by Hall and Jansen (Princeton University Press, 1968).

Stanford University Press: For "Motivation to Industrialize" and "Agrarian Distress and Taxation" by T. C. Smith, excerpted from Chapters 3 and 4 of *Political Change and Industrial Development in Japan: Government Enterprise, 1868–1880* by Thomas C. Smith. Copyright © 1955 by the Board of Trustees of the Leland Stanford Junior University; for "Wartime Local Government" by Kurt Steiner, excerpted from *Local Government in Japan* by Kurt Steiner. Copyright © 1955 by the Board of Trustees of the Leland Stanford Junior University.

Teachers College Press, Teachers College, Columbia University: For "Mori Arinori" and "The Japanese Educational System" by Herbert Passin, excerpted from *Society and Education in Japan* by Herbert Passin. Copyright © 1965 by Teachers College, Columbia University.

Charles E. Tuttle Co., Inc.: For "Shank's Mare" by Ikku Jippensha, excerpted from *Shank's Mare* by Ikku Jippensha (Charles E. Tuttle Co., Inc., Tokyo & Vermont, 1960).

University of Arizona Press and James Crowley: For "From Closed Door to Empire" and "Creation of an Empire, 1896–1910" by James Crowley, excerpted from *Modern Japanese Leadership,* edited by Bernard Silberman and Harry Harootunian (University of Arizona Press, Tucson, 1966).

The University of Chicago Press: For "Suye-Mura—The Life History of the Individual" by John Embree, excerpted from *Suye-Mura—A Japanese Village* by John Embree (University of Chicago Press, 1939).

University of North Carolina Press: For "Hunger in the Mountains" by Gwen Terasaki, excerpted from *Bridge to the Sun* by Gwen Terasaki (University of North Carolina Press, 1957).

University Press of Hawaii: For "Labor, Repression, and the Public Police Act" and "Labor's Lot in the War Period" by Ayusawa Iwao, excerpted from *A History of Labor in Modern Japan* by Ayusawa F. Iwao. Copyright © 1966 by East-West Center Press, Honolulu.

Van Nostrand Reinhold Company: For "Imperial Rescript, 1879" and "Educational Rescript, 1890," excerpted from *Modern Japan: A Brief History* by A. Tiedmann. Copyright © 1955 by Litton Educational Publishing, Inc.

The World Publishing Company: For "Zone of Emptiness" by Noma Hiroshi, excerpted from *Zone of Emptiness* by Noma Hiroshi. Copyright © 1956 by The World Publishing Company.

The Yale Review: For "Japan's Aristocratic Revolution" by T. C. Smith, from *The Yale Review* L:3 (Spring 1961), pp. 370–83. Copyright © 1961 by Yale University Press.

Yale University Press: For "The Early Socialist Movement," "The New Labor and the Japan Communists" and "Social Democratic Reactions toward War and Totalitarianism" by George Totten, excerpted from *The Social Democratic Movement in Prewar Japan* by George Totten (Yale University Press, 1966).

To my parents

J.L.

To my parents and my wife, Tomoko

J.M.

To my parents

F.O.

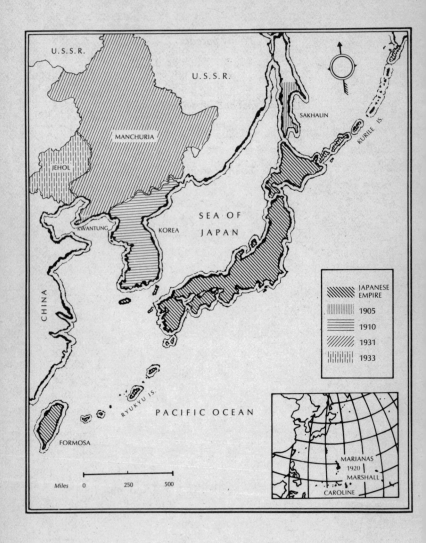

U.S.S.R.

U.S.S.R.

MANCHURIA

JEHOL

SAKHALIN

KURILE IS.

KWANTUNG

KOREA

SEA OF JAPAN

CHINA

JAPANESE EMPIRE
1905
1910
1931
1933

RYUKYU IS.

PACIFIC OCEAN

FORMOSA

Miles   0   250   500

MARIANAS
1920
MARSHALL
CAROLINE

Contents

Preface   xvii

PART I: Japan's Feudal Origins: 1800–1868   3

1. IMPRESSIONS OF FEUDAL JAPAN   6

CAPTAIN VASILII GALOWNIN: *Memoirs of a Captivity in Japan*   7

2. FEUDALISM AND ITS DECLINE   13

JOSEPH KITAGAWA: *Tokugawa Administration*   14

W. G. BEASLEY: *The Samurai Tradition*   15

RICHARD STORRY: *Change in Tokugawa Society*   19

G. B. SANSOM: *Economic Trends*   21

3. THE PEASANTS   26

J. W. ROBERTSON SCOTT: *The Most Exacting Crop in the World*   26

HARUMI BEFU: *Village Autonomy and the State*   34

T. C. SMITH: *The Japanese Village in the Seventeenth Century*   42

HUGH BORTON: *Peasant Uprisings in Japan of the Tokugawa Period*   49

4. SAMURAI, MERCHANTS, AND TOWNSMEN   56

YAZAKI TAKEO: *The Samurai Family and Feudal Ideology*   57

W. G. BEASLEY: *Town Life and Tokugawa Culture*   63

JIPPENSHA IKKU: *Shank's Mare*   64

IHARA SAIKAKU: *The Japanese Family Storehouse or the
    Millionaires' Gospel Modernized*   72

YAZAKI TAKEO: *Riots in the Cities*   80

5. THE DISCOVERY OF THE WEST AND THE MEIJI
   RESTORATION   83

TAKASUGI SHINSAKU: Yūshu Niroku (*Shanghai Diary*)   83

MAKI IZUMI: Bakumatsu Shishi no Tegami (*Letters from
    a Patriot in the Last Days of the Shogunate*)   85

E. H. NORMAN: *The Kiheitai of Chōshū*   87

T. C. SMITH: *Japan's Aristocratic Revolution*   91

PART II: Meiji Japan—Foundations for Empire:
         1868–1890   105

1. ECONOMIC CHANGES: THE DECISION TO
   INDUSTRIALIZE   108

T. C. SMITH: *Motivation to Industrialize*   108

E. H. NORMAN: *Early Industrialization*   116

2. THE COUNTRYSIDE AND THE CITIES   123

E. H. NORMAN: *Peasant Protest and the Land Tax*   124

T. C. SMITH: *Agrarian Distress and Taxation*   129

YANAGIDA KUNIO: *From the Village to the Factory*   132

YAZAKI TAKEO: *Social Change and the City*   135

FUTABATEI SHIMEI: Ukigumo (*Floating Cloud*)   138

3. IDEOLOGY FOR THE NEW SOCIETY   147

HERBERT PASSIN: *Mori Arinori*   148

*Imperial Rescript: The Great Principles of Education,
    1879*   151

Imperial Rescript on Education, 1890   153

JOSEPH KITAGAWA: *Modernity, Culture, and Religion*   154

NOBUTAKA IKE: *Evolution of the Family* 159

YAZAKI TAKEO: *Civil Law and the Family* 162

4. POLITICS AND THE MILITARY 165

JAMES CROWLEY: *Formation of the Meiji
Military Establishment* 166

E. H. NORMAN: *Conscription and the Opposition to It* 171

NOBUTAKA IKE: *Itagaki and the Movement Toward a
Parliament* 176

E. H. NORMAN: *Parties and Politics* 181

NOBUTAKA IKE: *Itō and the Constitution* 186

**PART III: Industrialization and Imperialism:
1890–1929** 199

1. POLITICS, THE MILITARY, AND FOREIGN POLICY 202

WALTER MCLAREN: *A Political History of Japan
During the Meiji Era* 203

MARLENE MAYO: *Attitudes Toward Asia and the
Beginnings of Japanese Empire* 212

WALTER MCLAREN: *The Sino-Japanese War* 221

JAMES CROWLEY: *Creation of an Empire, 1896–1910* 225

JAMES CROWLEY: *National Defense and the
Consolidation of Empire, 1907–1913* 231

WALTER MCLAREN: *The Political System in Japan* 235

2. AGRICULTURE 240

FUKUTAKE TADASHI: *Landlords and Village Society* 240

FUKUTAKE TADASHI: *The Power Structure of the
Hamlet* 245

WAKUKAWA SEIYEI: *The Tenant Movement* 251

3. EDUCATION AND THE POSITION OF WOMEN 256

SYDNEY GREENBIE: *The Emperor's Birthday* 256

HERBERT PASSIN: *The Japanese Educational System* 257

ISHIKAWA TAKUBOKU: *After a Fruitless Argument*   271

PETER DUUS: *Student Enthusiasts*   272

ISHIKAWA TAKUBOKU: *Rather Than Cry*   274

SHIDZUÉ ISHIMOTO: *A Japanese Husband*   275

4. LABOR AND INDUSTRY   285

WILLIAM LOCKWOOD: *The Great Combines*   285

AYUSAWA IWAO: *Labor, Repression, and the Public
    Police Act*   291

GEORGE O. TOTTEN, III: *The Early Socialist Movement* 298

JOHN ORCHARD: *Japan's Economic Position—The
    Progress of Industrialization*   305

MATSUKATA KŌJIRŌ: *Japanese Laborers*   311

SHIDZUÉ ISHIMOTO: *Are Miners Human Beings?*   313

JOHN ORCHARD: *The Effects of the World War on
    Industrialization*   318

ARTHUR YOUNG: *The Rice Riots of 1918*   322

GEORGE O. TOTTEN, III: *The New Labor and the
    Japanese Communists*   327

JOHN ORCHARD: *Government Suppression of the
    Labor Movement*   332

5. THE TWENTIES AND BEYOND   336

WILLIAM LOCKWOOD: *Japan's Economy in Transition*   336

T. A. BISSON: *Japan as a Political Organism*   342

**PART IV: Depression, Militarism, and War:
           1929–1945**   349

1. POLITICAL ECONOMY, 1929–1936   353

E. H. NORMAN: *The Genyōsha: A Study in the
    Origins of Japanese Imperialism*   355

JAMES CROWLEY: *Japan's Quest for Autonomy*   368

Contents

WILLIAM LOCKWOOD: *Trade, Armament, Industrial Expansion, 1930–1938*   371

G. C. ALLEN: *The Concentration of Economic Control*   378

2. LABOR, PEASANTS, WOMEN, CONSCRIPTION, REPRESSION   384

GEORGE O. TOTTEN, III: *Social Democratic Reactions To War and Totalitarianism*   385

JOHN K. EMMERSON: *The Japanese Communist Party*   397

COMMUNIST INTERNATIONAL, 1932: *The Japanese Situation and the Duty of the Japanese Communist Party*   405

AYUSAWA IWAO: *Labor's Lot in the War Period*   410

HELEN MEARS: *The Way of the Gods*   413

HANI SETSUKO: *The Japanese Family System as Seen by a Japanese Woman*   424

R. P. DORE: *Tenancy and Aggression*   431

JOHN EMBREE: *Suye Mura—The Life History of the Individual*   439

KURT STEINER: *Wartime Local Government*   445

LAWRENCE HEWES: *Japan—Land and Men*   449

R. P. DORE: *War and the Rural Areas*   450

3. POLITICAL ECONOMY, 1936–1945   452

ELEANOR HADLEY: *The Zaibatsu and the War*   452

T. A. BISSON: *Increase in Zaibatsu Predominance in Wartime Japan*   456

T. A. BISSON: *The Zaibatsu's Wartime Role*   458

4. THE JAPANESE PEOPLE AND THE WAR   465

GWEN TERASAKI: *Hunger in the Mountains*   465

ROBERT GUILLAIN: *Tokyo Burns*   475

NOMA HIROSHI: *Zone of Emptiness*   485

ŌOKA SHŌHEI: *Fires on the Plain*   489

Chronology: 1600–1945   495

Further Reading   497

Notes on Contributors   499

Index   503

About the Editors   519

Preface

THERE ARE numerous translations of modern Japanese fiction and
beautiful books about Japanese art and architecture. In recent
years, there has also been a growing number of books on modern
Japanese history. Yet ironically this sheer quantity is becoming an
obstacle to understanding, making it hard to know even where to
begin. To most Americans Japan remains unknown or paradoxical—the United States' westernized partner in Asia, a startlingly
beautiful country with highly developed aesthetic tastes, and a new
"yellow peril," flooding markets with "made in Japan" trademarks
and threatening American jobs. *The Japan Reader* is designed to
bring together in an introductory and readable form information
essential to understanding Japan now scattered among a myriad
of books and publications. Particular emphasis is placed on
Japanese social and economic questions, two of the most important, if little understood, aspects of modern Japan.

Japan emerged from centuries of isolation, rapidly industrialized, fought and lost a world war, and then recovered to take a
position as a world power—all in a brief hundred years. Yet after
this enormously varied period of historical upheaval and change,
Japan is often viewed simply as the "success story of Asia"—the
only nonwhite nation to become a powerful, industrialized, modern state. Numerous writers, determined to discover how Japan
broke from the supposed Third World norm, compare it with
China, Latin America, India, and even Israel. Others view Japan
as a successful "imitator" and duplicator of Western methods, an
Oriental stepchild of the Western world.

In these volumes we seek not only to understand "how," but to
raise the issue of "success" itself. Because the Japanese achievement has been an ambiguous one, we have sought to clarify the
costs as well as the gains.

The problem is partly one of vantage point. Having sought and won parity with the Western imperial powers at the close of the nineteenth century, Japan itself became imperialist. It succeeded in industrialization, partially at least, at the expense of its weaker Asian neighbors, and its perceptions of strategic and economic needs ultimately led it into World War II. Can the Japan of late August 1945, the conclusion of Volume I, be called a modern-day success story?

Viewing Japan as a successful modernizer, moreover, raises at least as many problems as it clarifies. If the establishment of a dynamic industrial state and strong army constitutes modernization, then Japan was as modern as most of the Western nations in this century. Yet often when Westerners apply this perspective to Japan, they envision a state with social, intellectual, and institutional structures comparable to those of an advanced Western capitalist nation. Whatever falls outside this idealized model is viewed as quaint or exotic, or dismissed as anachronistic or "dysfunctional." Thus much of the richness and significance of Japan's road to economic development is lost, the roots of its social conflicts distorted, and its culture crudely simplified.

Postwar Japan has been touted as the only successful implantation of Western-style democracy in Asia. Such claims are usually made largely on the strength of Japan's parliamentary and political party system without questioning how such institutions really function in Japanese society, or considering where and how economic and political decisions are made. Knowledge of the historical origins of the present system is crucial, for power today is still largely restricted to the descendents of prewar parties with their strong ties to the bureaucratic and business elites.

About Japan's postwar "economic miracle" there are few apparent doubts: Japan has managed to sustain a growth rate of around ten percent in its Gross National Product for more than twenty years. Yet this economic expansion also has unattractive features: pollution of staggering proportions, glaring economic inequalities, poor working conditions. Control over the Japanese economy by the zaibatsu conglomerates remains powerful, and Japan's industry, finance, and trade are today as much as ever the preserve of a tightly knit oligopoly. In this reader we pose questions about the cost to Japan of this economic surge, and explore new political challenges to the status quo emerging in popular movements around issues of ecology, education, and militarism.

The Japan Reader is arranged chronologically in six major sections, four in Volume I and two in Volume II. There are topical divisions within each section so that, for example, one can turn to a section on the Japanese labor movement during the American occupation period. The first volume ends with 1945: Japan met the West, achieved her goal of *fukoku kyōhei*—"rich country, strong army"— and finally lost a war when she tried to include China in her empire and challenged America's Pacific power. The second volume begins with the American occupation after World War II, and moves through the economic resurgence of the past two decades.

In assembling selections for the book, we sought materials that illustrated the central issues of modern Japanese history. We have used contemporary accounts, fiction, and documents, as well as more academic writing, including the work of such men as E. H. Norman and T. A. Bisson, whose lives and reputations were damaged by McCarthyism. The book is composed mainly of writings by Westerners and the best Japanese works available in English. Although, for reasons of time and resources, we decided against an anthology entirely of new translations from Japanese, we have included newly translated materials when nothing suitable could be found in English.

American readers should be reminded that in Japanese names the surname is followed by the given name. In the introductions to our selections we have used this order, but unfortunately there was no way to standardize names in the selections themselves. In each volume, we have included a chronology, a brief bibliographical guide to further reading, and notes about the authors of our selections. Most selections have been abridged and footnotes have been removed. We thank all those who have given permission to include their writings.

Finally, we wish to acknowledge that the origins of this book lie in the Committee of Concerned Asia Scholars, to which the three of us belong. This is our first full-length effort dealing with Japan, but it is obviously only a beginning in our effort to understand Japan, whose future is crucial for Southeast Asia and China, as well as for the United States.

I.
Japan's Feudal Origins
1800–1868

❀ WHEN FEUDAL JAPAN was forced by Commodore Perry to open itself to foreign shipping and trade, it had passed through more than two centuries of official, self-imposed isolation from the rest of the world. In the early 1600s, to insure the peace, Tokugawa Ieyasu (1542–1616) instituted a strict caste system. The samurai, the military caste, were separated from the land, and lived in the castle towns as administrators for their lords, the daimyō. These daimyō in turn were loyal to the head of the Tokugawa house, who ruled over his own lands as well. Ideologically, the samurai warrior and his military code held the highest position. Beneath them were the great mass of the people, the peasantry. Since Tokugawa society was based on rice cultivation, the peasant was valued above the merchants and artisans, whose economic roles were considered unproductive. After consolidating its rule over other feudal lords at the end of the sixteenth century, the Tokugawa clan had forced out almost all foreigners—in particular the troublesome Christian missionaries. Only the Dutch were allowed to maintain a trading outpost at Nagasaki, after promising they would not attempt to convert anyone.

The long period of Tokugawa peace turned the samurai into civilian administrators, paid in stipends of rice. They thus had no use for their military skills, and an income which made them dependent on rice merchants. Centered on large trading towns, the economy developed rapidly, producing a highly artistic, lively, and sometimes bawdy culture in which money was valued more than the warrior ethic. Due to their financial power, the merchants developed a symbiotic relationship with even the highest-ranking samurai. The merchants needed the samurai, for they lacked official status, and the samurai needed the merchants, to whom they traded their rice and gradually became indebted. Even though daimyō could use their social position to cancel debts to merchants, this was not an effective long-range solution to the growing impoverishment of the military caste.

In the countryside, too, economic growth was modifying traditional divisions and creating others. Increased commercialization and improvements in agricultural technology increased social divisions within the village and combined with taxation policies to spark frequent peasant uprisings. However, the peasants' weak organizations and their lack of opposing ideology kept such rebellions manageable by the elite. Enterprising peasants who became wealthy invested in rural industries and in spite of their low social status were richer than many samurai.

In the early nineteenth century the Japanese elite sought solutions against this backdrop of peasant unrest and recurrent economic crises. Some sought a refuge in traditional feudal values, while others pursued studies seeking a unique Japanese character in her historical development. Some far-sighted intellectuals, perceiving a future need for Western skills to defeat the West, engaged in "Western learning," even though this was carefully controlled by the Tokugawa shogunate.

Through the Dutch, knowledge of Western technology gradually spread, and Japan learned of the fate of China as she succumbed to the military power of the Western imperialists. The rule of the Tokugawa clan was badly shaken by the growing awareness that Japan was not strong enough to hold off the Western barbarians. After Commodore Perry forced his way into Japan in 1853, he was soon followed by other Westerners, and Japan was forced to sign unequal treaties officially reflecting her weakness. The debates among the Japanese elite over what to do about the foreigners began to divide the country, loosening the bonds of the Tokugawa peace. The positions taken were sometimes inconsistent, and often extreme, but it was agreed that Japan's weakness could no longer be ignored. Some samurai planned and carried out assassinations of foreigners and government officials, who were held responsible for Japan's dangerous condition. Others argued that Japan had to tolerate the foreigners until it was stronger. The Tokugawa shogunate, placed in the unenviable position of having to yield to the barbarians, was open to serious attack for the first time in 250 years. Its legitimacy was based on its claim to rule for the emperor, whose court had been maintained as a powerless figurehead throughout the Tokugawa period. Thus, when the government was shown to be impotent, its opponents also couched their complaints against it in terms of loyalty to the emperor.

Japan faced a twofold threat: internally, the *bakufu* was weak and near financial disaster; externally, the foreigners were forcing themselves on Japan. A few of the samurai, who believed that the Tokugawa shogunate was unable to meet this challenge, sought a solution in adopting Western military techniques. Without sanction of the Tokugawa government they shelled Western shipping in 1863 from forts commanding the narrow Strait of Shimonoseki. In retaliation, British and French warships destroyed the forts and the town of Shimonoseki. The lesson was clear: more than piecemeal application of foreign techniques was needed.

In the following years disorder and confusion continued until a group of young samurai, foreshadowing new institutional developments, organized a mixed militia of peasants and commoners, and finally defeated the Tokugawa shogunate militarily. The new leaders of Meiji Japan realized that to solve the foreign and domestic crises drastic change was required.

1. Impressions of Feudal
Japan

❀ WHEN JAPAN WAS "opened" by Commodore Perry in 1854, it had been cut off from the rest of the world by a deliberate policy of self-isolation. This policy lasted over 200 years, during the feudal regime of the Tokugawa government, and came to an end only under the threatening guns and warships of the Western imperialist powers in the 1850s and 1860s.

Communication during the period was not completely absent, for the Japanese had already experienced over a century of contacts with Portuguese and other European missionaries. However, when the Japanese authorities decided that the missionaries were determined to overturn the feudal order, they were expelled. Only the Dutch, who scrupulously refrained from such activities in favor of commerce, were allowed to maintain a small trading colony in Nagasaki. Other contacts were strictly forbidden by the feudal government and the only foreigners seen were occasional shipwrecked sailors.

In 1806–1807 Nikolai Rezanov, a Russian Imperial official, ordered raids on Japanese villages after his attempts to establish relations with the feudal regime were rebuffed because of the exclusion policy. Later, in retaliation, Captain Vasilii Galownin and the crew of his survey ship were taken prisoner. Galownin's memoirs during three years of confinement on the northern island of Hokkaido are excerpted here.

His observations do not suffer from the usual Western preoccupation with Japanese quaintness and peculiarity. They are notable rather for their attempt to analyze and describe the feudal system of Tokugawa Japan, its class structure, and important economic changes. There is major discrepancy between Galownin's description and the actual feudal order in the number and rank of classes, but he must be given credit for noticing the rise of commercial influences. During this period the power of the samurai military class began to be challenged and feudalism itself began to crumble. One of the main factors in the downfall of feudalism was the increasingly central role of money and the consequent rise of merchant influence, despite the feudal ethic which relegated them to a lower social status. Thus Galownin's observations, though inaccurate on details, are remarkably perceptive concerning the major changes occurring in late feudal Japan.

CAPTAIN VASILII GALOWNIN*
Memoirs of a Captivity in Japan

The inhabitants of Japan are divided into eight classes:

1. Damjo [daimyō], or reigning princes.
2. Chadamodo [hatamoto], or nobility.
3. Bonzes, or priests.
4. Soldiers.
5. Merchants.
6. Mechanics.
7. Peasants and laborers.
8. Slaves.

FIRST CLASS.—The reigning princes do not all enjoy the same rights and privileges: some have greater or smaller advantages above the others, founded on conventions and agreements. . . . These privileges are different not only in things of consequence, but they even extend to the most insignificant circumstances of

* Captain Vasilii Galownin, *Memoirs of a Captivity in Japan in the Years 1811, 1812, and 1813* (London: Henry C. Colburn Co., 1824), pp. 82–94, 202–203.

etiquette and ceremony. Some princes, for instance, have the right to use saddle cloths of beaver skin when they ride on horseback; others have them of panther skins, etc. But the greatest privilege of them all consists in their governing their principalities as independent sovereigns, as far as the general laws of the empire allow, and as is consistent with the welfare of the other parts of the empire.

The dignity of all the reigning princes is hereditary, and properly always belongs to the eldest son; but a laudable and useful ambition in the princes, to have only worthy successors, frequently causes them to break through this rule. If the eldest son is incapable of supplying the place of his father, the ablest of the younger sons obtains the right of succeeding him. It not unfrequently happens that a prince, induced by the incapacity of all his children, deprives them of the succession, and adopts the most worthy of the younger sons of another prince, has him educated under his own eye, and leaves him his title and his possessions. The consequence of this measure is that the reigning princes, in Japan, are almost always sensible men, well versed in public affairs: hence, too, they are so formidable to the emperors, as they can always restrain his power within the due bounds.

SECOND CLASS.—The nobility, also, enjoy very important privileges in Japan. All the places in the second council, or senate, all the important offices of state, and the posts of governors in the imperial provinces, are filled up entirely from their body alone. If a war breaks out, the commanding generals are chosen from among the reigning princes or the nobility. Every noble family has a particular distinction, and the right to keep a train of honor, which is made use of by the eldest of the family. The nobility is also hereditary, and descends to the eldest son, or, according to the will of the father, to the most worthy. If the father judges his legitimate unworthy of this dignity, he may adopt a son from another family; hence, a good-for-nothing nobleman is a rare phenomenon, which only the too great love of a father for an unworthy son can render possible.

THIRD CLASS.—The ecclesiastics, who consist of priests and monks, are very numerous in Japan, and divided into several classes, which have their particular privileges in the different sects: the principal of them are not indeed sanctioned by the laws, but enjoyed by the ecclesiastics among all nations: I mean idleness and luxury, at the expense of others.

FOURTH CLASS.—In the class of soldiers, the higher military officers must not be included, because in Japan these are chosen out of the nobility, or another class, and such as have already filled public offices in the civil departments. Everybody who is in the service of the emperor or the princes must learn the art of war, that he may be fit, in case of war, to be employed against the enemy. As the Japanese consider war merely as a temporary concern, they will not dedicate their whole lives to the service. Besides, the situation of the empire, and the pacific policy of the government, often make it impossible for a whole series of generations, from the grandfather to the great-grandson, to serve their country in this line. Every Japanese of distinction, therefore, endeavors to obtain a civil appointment, and learns besides the art of war, in order, in case of need, to command the troops which are in garrison in the fortresses, or are distributed in other places to maintain order and tranquility among the people.

The profession of the inferior military officers, and of the privates, is hereditary, and therefore they form a distinct class. No soldier, however old or weak, obtains his discharge till he can bring a son to supply his place, who must have already thoroughly learned everything belonging to the service. The boys are capable of bearing arms at the age of fifteen. If a soldier has more than one son, he is at liberty to dedicate all of them, or only one, to the military profession; but as in Japan the service is easy, and the maintenance good, soldiers generally let all their sons follow the profession and serve themselves till their death. If a soldier has no sons, he may adopt one, educate him, and let him supply his place. The laws allow both the soldiers and the other classes to adopt three children, but if these die, no more can be adopted, as it is presumed to be against the will of the gods.

The military profession is held in great honor in Japan. The common people, and even the merchants, give the soldiers in conversation the title of *sama* (sir) and show them all possible respect. I have spoken before of the privileges which the Imperial soldiers possess above those of the princes: Europeans who have visited Japan have always taken the common soldiers for people invested with high offices; and this is very natural, because when

European ships arrive they generally put on rich silk dresses, embroidered with gold and silver, receive the Europeans proudly, and remain sitting, and smoke tobacco while they speak with them. At the beginning of our imprisonment we were in the same error: we believed that the Japanese feared us greatly, since they appointed officers to guard us. But when we became better acquainted with these supposed officers, we found that they were soldiers. . . .

All the soldiers have the right to wear a saber and dagger, like the first officers of the empire. In almost every village are two or three soldiers, whose business it is to preserve order, and to keep a watchful eye on the police officers. To deprive a soldier . . . of his profession is the greatest punishment that can be inflicted on him. The oldest soldier, or subaltern officer, who was on guard over us when we escaped was degraded, but afterwards obtained the rank of a common soldier again: during this time he suffered his hair, beard, and nails to grow, and showed in this manner his profound affliction. The Japanese soldiers have such a sense of honor that they frequently fight duels with each other in consequence of being affronted.

FIFTH CLASS.—The class of merchants, in Japan, is very extensive and rich, but not held in honor.* The merchants have not the right to bear arms: but though their profession is not respected, their wealth is; for this, as in Europe, supplies the place of talents and dignity and attains privileges and honorable places. The Japanese told us that their officers of state and men of rank behaved themselves outwardly with great haughtiness to the merchants, but, in private, are very familiar with the rich merchants and are often under great obligations to them. We had with us, for some time, a young officer who was the son of a rich merchant, and who, as the Japanese said, owed his rank not to his own merit but to his father's gold: thus, though the laws do not favor the mercantile

---

* [It is said] that the merchants are the only individuals who can become rich, sometimes amassing very large fortunes: yet the most wealthy are as much despised as the poorest, the general opinion being that a man who makes money by trade must have done it by dishonorable means, and by the oppression of his fellow citizens. In Japan, a merchant can never rise into the rank of gentility.

profession, yet its wealth raises it; for even in Japan, where the laws are so rigorously enforced, they are often outweighed by the influence of gold.

SIXTH CLASS.—The Japanese seem not yet to be acquainted with the difference between mechanics and artists*; therefore the architect and the carpenter, the sculptor and the brazier, etc., belong, among them, to one class: their rights and privileges are almost the same as those of the merchants, except those which the latter acquire by their riches.

SEVENTH CLASS.—The peasants and laborers are the last class of the free inhabitants of Japan. In this class are included all those who go into the service of others to gain their livelihood; for Japan is so populous, that everybody who possesses the smallest piece of land does not cultivate it himself, but hires persons who are quite indigent to do it for him. We had soldiers among our guards who possessed gardens, and paid laborers to cultivate them; they themselves went hunting in their leisure hours and sold the game they had caught. In this class they also reckon sailors, whom the Japanese call Fäkscho-Sschto [hyakushō no hito], i.e., "laborers." The lower classes in general are denominated by the Madsino-Sschto [machi no hito], literally translated, "people who carry on their business in the streets."

EIGHTH CLASS.—The last class of the inhabitants of Japan are slaves; they are descended from the prisoners taken in ancient times in China, Korea, etc., and from children who were sold by their parents as slaves, from poverty and inability to bring them up. This trade in children is still carried on; but the law to make prisoners slaves has been also abolished since the time that the Christian religion was extirpated: at present prisoners are kept in confinement for life, as one of the most ancient laws prescribes; by this means the Japanese have the advantage that the prisoners

* The tanners are considered as the lowest class of people in Japan, because it is not only their trade to skin the dead cattle, most of which die a natural death, as little animal food is eaten, but also to serve the office of hangman, and they are not permitted to mix with other classes of society, but live in small spots assigned to them in the vicinity of the places of execution.

cannot communicate their religion or their manners to the people.
The slaves are entirely in the power of their masters.

I could not learn from our Japanese acquaintance to what class
the civil officers, who are not nobles, the physicians, the literati,
and the younger children of the nobles belonged? They told us that
these persons were respected in the state, had titles suitable to their
rank, but formed no particular class. The literati and physicians
wear a saber and a dagger, like all persons in office, and are on an
intimate footing with them: but the Japanese could not tell us
whether they possess a civil rank or any dignity answerable to it;
we only heard that the eldest among the two hundred physicians of
the temporal emperor was equal in rank with the governor of
Matsumae.

The commercial spirit of the Japanese is visible in all the towns
and villages. In almost every house there is a shop, for more or
less important goods; and, as we see in England the magnificent
magazine of a jeweler next door to an oyster shop, so we see here a
rich silk merchant and a mender of straw shoes live and carry on
their business close to each other. In their regard to order, the
Japanese very much resemble the English; they love cleanliness
and the greatest accuracy. All goods have in Japan, as in England,
little printed bills, on which are noted the price, the use, and the
name of the article, the name of the maker, or manufactory, and
often something in their praise. Even tobacco, pomatum, tooth
powder, and other trifles are wrapped up in papers, on which a
notice of the quality and the price is printed. In packing up goods,
they observe the same order as in Europe. Rice and other grain
they pack in sacks made of straw. They have no casks for liquids;
but keep them, as Sotschio [shōchū], Sagi [sake], Soja [shōyu], etc.
in tubs which hold three or four pailfuls. These tubs have only
wooden hoops, and are broader above than below; in the top board
there is a small hole, generally square. The best kind of sagi is
kept in large earthen jars. Stuffs of all kinds, tea, etc., are packed
up in chests. Silk goods are laid in pieces, in separate chests which
are made of very thin boards, and have an inscription indicating the
article, the name of the maker, the measure, and the quality.

2. Feudalism and Its Decline

❃ THE FOUNDATIONS OF the feudal system were laid in the early seventeenth century by Tokugawa Ieyasu, the founder of the military family that ruled Japan until 1868. The military government (called the shogunate or *bakufu*) centered on the head of the Tokugawa clan, who was called shōgun, "chief barbarian-quelling generalissimo." Beneath him came lords, daimyō, with their own feudal domains, and finally their military retainers, in all cases samurai. There were various types of daimyō and a complicated administrative machine, but the military ruling elite never comprised much above five percent of the total population. In theory, the four classes in society were arranged in a strictly organized four-tier system: samurai, peasants, artisans, and merchants.

From the beginning, this ranking system was more a legal fiction than a reality, and the gap between feudal theory and Tokugawa society widened drastically in the eighteenth and nineteenth centuries. With a rising population and rapid growth in agriculture, merchants gradually assumed a position of greater importance, as Beasley and Storry show below. The new money economy and the "conspicuous consumption" life style of the military elite forced many samurai into debt—inevitably to the merchants, who profited from the lavish expenditures of the feudal court. The money economy was not only disadvantageous to the samurai, but also had serious effects on the peasants' livelihood. They lived in a system in which rice prices could change rapidly, to their detriment, and were also plagued by numerous crop disasters and bad weather. The result for peasants under the feudal system, as Sansom points out, was extreme hardship.

Overall, the Tokugawa feudal system was facing severe strain by the time the first Westerners appeared. The samurai had been pacified, bureaucratized, and impoverished—ideally they were honored, but they were separated from the land, and their warrior ethic was dissipated in the high life of the huge commercial metropolis of Edo (Tokyo). Merchants, on the contrary, found that they could flourish under such a system, even though they were condemned to remain beyond the pale socially. The system as a whole was changing rapidly under the blows of this new commercial tide.

JOSEPH KITAGAWA*
Tokugawa Administration

... What Ieyasu attempted was the establishment of permanent martial law, as it were. Geographically, Japan under the Tokugawa regime was divided into over 250 fiefs of different sizes and values. The Tokugawa ruler was both the shōgun and the most important daimyō; as the latter he directly controlled nearly one-fourth of Japan. The remaining parts of Japan were divided into fiefs of two main types—inner and outer zones. For the most part, the inner zone was given to the *fudai daimyō* or hereditary lieges of the Tokugawa family who held responsible posts in the regime but had comparatively little income, while the outer zone was given to the *tozama daimyō* (literally, "outside daimyō," referring to those who came under the Tokugawa's influence after 1600) who received a fairly sizable income but were excluded from positions of influence. In addition, the so-called *shimpan* (relatives of the Tokugawa family) were placed in key spots, for they were considered the most trustworthy allies of the shogunate. The shōgun,

* Joseph Kitagawa, *Religion in Japanese History* (New York: Columbia University Press, 1966), pp. 135–136.

with the assistance of advisory bodies consisting of the elders (*toshiyori* or *rōjū*), the junior elders (*wakadoshiyori*), the bannermen (*hatamoto*), and the chamberlains (*sobashū*), ruled his territory directly, and other parts of the nation indirectly, through the daimyō. There were also many administrative posts, such as those of the commissioners of temples and shrines (*jisha-bugyō*), of finance (*kanjō-bugyō*), and of cities (*machi-bugyō*), as well as censors (*metsuke*). Each daimyō's realm (*han*), supposedly autonomous though strictly controlled by the central regime, had its own administrative machine modeled on a smaller scale after the example of the shogunate in Edo. As the Tokugawa regime imposed its system of hostages and of alternate attendance on all the daimyō, the families of the daimyō were kept in Edo, while the lords themselves were compelled to live alternately in their realms and in Edo. These measures not only kept the daimyō in line but also facilitated commerce, transportation, and communication systems on a national scale, even though the costs proved to be a hardship for many. . . .

W. G. BEASLEY*
The Samurai Tradition

In earlier periods the samurai had been a farmer-warrior, tilling the land in times of peace and following his lord into battle in times of war; but with the increasing scale and complexity of warfare in the fifteenth and sixteenth centuries fighting had tended to become a specialist activity, so that the functions of the samurai and the farmer became distinct. In the end the farmer was forbidden to carry arms, the samurai was incorporated into something very like the garrison of an occupied territory, living in a strongly defended castle from which the surrounding countryside was governed. It was in this way that the typical domain of the Tokugawa period took shape. It was large and geographically compact. Within its frontiers the lord brooked no rival to his authority over

* W. G. Beasley, *The Modern History of Japan* (New York: Praeger, 1963), pp. 9–13.

men and land, whether from the once-powerful shrines and temples or from his followers, only a few of whom were allowed to retain fiefs of their own. These were subject to a system of control which was a replica in miniature of that which the shōgun imposed on Japan at large. Ordinary samurai for the most part lost their land entirely. Required to be in attendance on their lord and live in or around his castle, they were no longer able to supervise in person either cultivation or the collection of dues, these rights being assumed by the feudal lord acting through officials. In return, the samurai was granted a stipend from the domain treasury, its value determined by the estimated annual yield of the piece of land from which it was nominally derived. Many lost even this final link with the village: their stipends were fixed arbitrarily, in extreme cases at a sum payable in cash.

The transformation of the samurai was carried a stage further by the Tokugawa success in restoring and then maintaining law and order after centuries of civil war. Peace made the samurai less needed as a soldier. On the other hand, the nature of the new domains made him all the more important as an administrator. In every castle-town there was a multitude of posts to be filled, their duties ranging from the formulation of policy to the government of a rural district, from control of finance or achives to service as attendants, guards, and messengers. All were filled by samurai, usually samurai of a specified rank. So great was the preoccupation with civil office that a famous scholar, Yamaga Sokō, writing toward the end of the seventeenth century, was able to describe the life of a samurai as follows:

> In minor matters, such as dress, food, dwelling, and all implements and their uses, he must live up to the best samurai traditions of good form. . . . Among major matters there are the maintenance of peace and order in the world; rites and festivals; the control of feudal states and districts; mountains and forests, seas and rivers, farms and rice fields, temples and shrines; and the disposition of suits and appeals among the four classes of people.

. . . In a society where every man knew his place, it is not surprising that the ruling philosophy was of a kind calculated to keep him in it. The Confucian ideas associated with the name of the Sung philosopher, Chu Hsi, were admirably suited to this purpose, for they emphasized the subordination of wife to husband, of son to father, of subject to ruler, in a manner which in Tokugawa

Japan brought about a natural alliance between feudal authority and Confucian scholarship. The duties of loyalty and service were expounded in official schools maintained by the shōgun's government and feudal lords. To them went almost all samurai of middle and upper rank to learn the duties of their station, to learn above all that a man's own welfare counted for less than that of the group, whether family or domain, to which he belonged. The attitude was reinforced by the pervading social and religious concept of obligation. . . . This brought together strands from Buddhist as well as Confucian thought, emphasizing that man's primary task was to live in such a way as would constitute a return for favors received: to the deity for his blessings, to the universe which supported life, to parents for their love, to political superiors for their protection. Thus loyalty and filial piety came together and were given religious sanction.

These ideas, in association with elements from an older tradition, became part of bushidō, the code of the warrior class. In its Tokugawa form this was as much a code of the bureaucrat as of the soldier. Death in the service of one's lord remained the ultimate expression of loyalty, bringing something not far short of salvation in a religious sense; but if this could not be, then dutiful service and honest advice were not to be despised. Learning and scholarship were also to be valued for the training they gave, though it was a training more appropriate to administration than the battlefield. Even the time-honored military virtues of austerity and frugality were given a new gloss. Diligence and economy were the form in which they were now enjoined, the one to ensure the maximum contribution in service, the other the minimum consumption by way of recompense. This, too, was a kind of loyalty.

Ideals of behavior which the ruling class prescribed for itself were readily adopted by the rest of society. In this sense, bushidō influenced all groups, at least all those which sought social recognition. On the other hand, this did not make its rules any easier to observe, especially where they ran counter to economic change. Frugality was one of them. Peace and the growth in agricultural production had contributed to a rapid development of commerce in the seventeenth century, making possible a rise in standards of living which was enjoyed in most parts of the country. Even in remote castle-towns one could now obtain products from as far afield as Kyushu and Hokkaido. In the great cities of Edo, Kyoto, and Osaka luxuries abounded. Edo, especially, played a major part in samurai life, since feudal lords, accompanied always by a large retinue of followers, were required to live there for half the year. Here were many temptations by way of goods and entertainment, temptations which most found it impossible to resist. Unfortunately, they had to be paid for, usually in cash. For samurai—of whatever rank—who received their incomes in rice, the provision of money to be spent in Edo became a serious problem, one which could be solved only with the help of the merchant and financier. The improvident soon found that their new habits had left no margin to meet the sort of unexpected expenditure or loss of income which might be occasioned by fire or flood. For them the merchant became moneylender, making advances against future income. Others, who were more careful, were eventually caught in the same web despite themselves, for city prices rose faster than crops increased and it was easier to acquire expensive tastes than to lose them. By 1700 the whole samurai class was in a state of chronic debt.

In the eighteenth century samurai indebtedness continued to grow, despite efforts which feudal rulers made to check it. Moreover, since the Tokugawa and domain governments faced the same difficulties as did individuals, they were rendered unable to help their retainers to any great extent and were often forced to levy new imposts on them. These levies, euphemistically described as loans, might amount to half a samurai's stipend. They caused great discontent, the tenets of bushidō notwithstanding. In many domains this led the middle samurai, blaming their troubles on the incapacity of their superiors, to agitate for, and sometimes obtain, a larger share in administration. Lesser samurai, whose case was far worse, also tended to become supporters of reform movements of various kinds, while many sought personal solutions outside the existing feudal framework altogether, relinquishing their samurai status to become farmers or merchants, or using the devices of marriage and adoption to bring wealth into the family in return for social standing. This process, familiar enough among impoverished aristocracies at any time or place, helped to induce a greater degree of social mobility at the lower levels of the ruling class, to which officialdom contributed by engaging in what was virtually a sale of rank. It was the merchants and a new class of rural landlords who largely benefited.

RICHARD STORRY*
Change in Tokugawa Society

... [I]n spite of the Tokugawa determination to preserve a static hierarchical society, very important changes, mostly undesired by the shogunate, were taking place within this society. Their origin was the spread of money in a country that was organized from above on the basis of a rice economy. The official standard of wealth was rice. The status of a daimyō was expressed in terms of the assessed rice crop in his domain. The samurai class as a whole received its income, from shōgun or daimyō, in bales of rice. And rice at the beginning of the Tokugawa age was the principal means of exchange. But during the long years of internal peace, and with the growth of such cities as Osaka and Edo (having a population of over half a million by the early eighteenth century), the use of such cumbersome material as rice as a means of exchange gave way to money.

Silver and copper coins had been in very limited circulation for several hundred years, but it was not until the fifteenth century that they began to resemble, if faintly, what we understand as a currency. However, foreign trade in the sixteenth and early seventeenth centuries promoted greater circulation of coins, since the main export from Japan in the vessels of the Portuguese, Spanish, Dutch, and English was gold and silver. This naturally encouraged the development of mining and the minting of coins. The convenience and use of these were complementary; and, as the seventeenth century progressed, more and more of the samurai class traded their rice for cash with merchants in Osaka, who soon developed into a very rich, though still socially inferior, community. As Edo grew, becoming the headquarters of a very large population of nonproductive warriors, so the merchant class there multiplied in numbers and in wealth.

On the other hand the samurai class steadily lost economic power. For it was the boast of the samurai that he was indifferent

* Richard Storry, *A History of Modern Japan* (Baltimore, Md.: Penguin Books, 1961, rev. ed.), pp. 73–76.

to money or, rather, to the details of acquiring and holding money. He looked down on the merchants, for they were, after all, the lowest of the four broad social classes in the land—warriors, peasants, artisans, and merchants, in that order.

By the early years of the eighteenth century the warriors of Japan, daimyō and retainers alike, were in debt to the merchant class. This class, now enriched, contrived to develop for itself in the cities of Edo and Osaka a manner of life that was vigorous and sophisticated at the same time. It is reflected in most of the color prints depicting Edo life, in the novels of Saikaku, and in the plays of Chikamatsu; for it was in this period that the Kabuki theater, in spite of intermittent restrictions placed upon it by a disapproving *bakufu,* flourished as a bourgeois form of art. From time to time the government would try to prune the affluence of the city merchant class. There would be cancellations of samurai debts, or the outright confiscation of the property of some over-ostentatious rice broker; and earnestly phrased injunctions were issued time and again from Edo Castle against extravagance in dress and behavior among the merchant class.

Yet these measures had little effect; and while in the country-side, especially after 1700, the conditions of all but a few usurers and rich farmers grew more rigorous—the rural samurai class often living in a state of defiant but uncomfortable indebtedness—there prevailed in cities such as Edo a robust, pleasure-seeking life, predominantly bourgeois in tone. Still, the merchants were unable, and were indeed perhaps unwilling, as merchants, to acquire the social prestige that usually accompanies economic power. To some extent their position may be compared with that of the wealthier Armenian subjects of the Ottoman empire; but the parallel cannot be pushed too far. For the lot of the Japanese merchant under the later Tokugawa shōgun was, in reality, a good deal happier. In practice the Japanese class structure was rather less formidably rigid than would appear at first sight. Social mobility, it is true, was very slight; but it was not entirely nonexistent. From time to time wealthy and ambitious merchants achieved samurai rank through adoption or marriage. Conversely, impoverished warriors were glad, sometimes, to enter the merchant class. There is no doubt, too, that financial power enabled individual merchants to wriggle themselves into important political positions within certain fiefs. One Japanese of the Tokugawa period has recorded—it may be with a touch of exaggeration—that the anger of the rich merchants of Osaka could strike terror into the hearts of the daimyō. In course of time some of the more powerful brokers and money-lenders became in effect bankers to the great feudatories. The house of Mitsui, for example, was famous in this field long before it built up its supremacy as a huge capitalist combine in modern Westernized Japan.

The rise and efflorescence of this capitalist class was not really compatible with the continued existence of a feudal society; and indeed, by comparison with early Tokugawa Japan, the country in the late eighteenth and early nineteenth centuries can hardly be described as truly feudal except in a rather formal sense. It may be said that under the *bakufu* Japan remained scientifically, indus-trially, and politically backward. But commercially there took place on a small scale in Japan, during the seventeenth and eighteenth centuries, the same development that was seen in contemporary England, France, and Holland—namely, the growth of mercantilism. In other words, in Tokugawa Japan the city was the monopolistic "mother country" and the surrounding country-side was the Japanese substitute for the overseas colony. There was of course no industrial revolution, but handicraft manufactur-ing was diverse and well developed, often catering to a national market; and there was considerable mining both of metals and coal. There was a good deal of regional specialization, much encouraged by enterprising daimyō. One area, for example, would concentrate upon the manufacture of porcelain, another on silk, and so on. On the whole, however, these handicrafts were the products of part-time, household industry, supplementing the ex-tremely meager livelihood of rice-growing peasants. Most of the capital that was accumulated piled up in the hands of the numeri-cally small merchant class—the traders and the moneylenders.

G. B. SANSOM*
Economic Trends

The Tokugawa government, calling in the aid of philosophers, attempted to solve their numerous difficulties by treating them as if

* G. B. Sansom, *Japan: A Short Cultural History* (New York: Appleton-Century-Crofts, 1943), pp. 513–518.

they were mainly ethical problems, and most of their efforts were directed toward preserving unchanged the existing class divisions. But they were in reality faced with economic conditions which could not be remedied on such lines. Fundamentally their problem was an economic problem, the perennial problem of food supply; and this they could never solve so long as they refused to change the social institutions over which they presided. During the years from 1600 to 1725 the population of Japan increased, agriculture taken as a whole prospered, industry made moderate advances, and methods of distribution were improved; so that the country was able to support a general rise in the standard of living. But further progress was checked by a number of obstacles. . . . The substitution of money for rice as a medium of exchange, while it caused a decline in the power of the samurai which was disturbing to the *bakufu,* had an even more serious effect in that it reduced the productive power of the farmers. A mere transfer of wealth from one unproductive class to another, from soldiers to merchants, would doubtless have caused an unpleasant derangement of the social order; but this might have been adjusted without much difficulty, particularly as many of the *chōnin* [townspeople] rendered services to the community in the carriage of goods, the investment of capital, and the manufacture of essential commodities. The sufferings of the farmers, however, their poverty and their tenancy troubles, in a word the agrarian problem, struck at the foundation of the state.

The agrarian problem in Japan under the Tokugawa regime, though complicated in its details, can at very little expense of accuracy be stated in the following terms. The life of the peasant, wretched at the best of times, was rendered almost unbearable by fluctuating prices of rice and by the rising standard of living among all classes but his own. Since no surplus was left to him by the tax collector, he could profit little by a good crop, while a bad crop left him on the verge of starvation. These misfortunes affected the farming class in various ways, but nearly always to their increasing disadvantage. Some got into debt to the few slightly more prosperous cultivators than themselves or to usurious townspeople; and for a peasant to get into debt was to be on a steep road down to destruction. Some migrated to other districts, in the hope of making a fresh start. Some absconded and became vagrants. Some made their way to the towns in search of employment as domestic servants or day laborers. Those who remained on the land found themselves short of workers for their fields, and unable to support their families. And meanwhile the daimyō and their retainers, pressed by the merchants and moneylenders, turned the screw on the already tortured peasants, so that (to quote from a work written before 1750) the farmers were treated by officials and taxgatherers "as a cruel driver treats an ox or a horse, when he puts a heavy burden on the beast, and lashes it mercilessly, getting all the angrier when it stumbles and whipping more violently than ever, with loud curses."

Peasants were often compared to seeds, like sesame, which were pressed for their oil, because "the harder you press the more you squeeze out." Such testimony to the misery of farmers is to be found throughout Tokugawa literature—naturally, since the position of agriculture was so desperate that it could not escape the notice of the most callous observer. Nor can it be said that the rulers of Japan were blind to these abuses. They tried to remedy them, and to understand them within the limits of their knowledge. Indeed it is one of the most striking features of the intellectual activity of the age that its leading scholars concerned themselves with economic problems, and its learned literature consists largely of treatises on agriculture, currency, and similar topics. The greatest Confucian scholars paid the closest attention to such problems. . . . It is remarkable that, at least until the early part of the nineteenth century, even the most penetrating minds among them failed as a rule to grasp the truth, that the wealth of Japan was adequate neither in amount nor in distribution to the needs of her society. Some of them saw it dimly, but most of them proposed only neat ethical solutions of the terrible equation of supply and demand. Peasants must work hard and respect their betters, merchants must be honest and content with small profits, and samurai must not be extravagant.

Meanwhile the decrease in the farming population, which may be looked upon as having set in from about 1725, reacted further upon the condition of the peasants, accentuating their already severe distress and giving still greater speed to movements that tended to diminish food supply or to cause disastrous fluctuations in prices. These movements cannot be described fully here, but some idea of their nature can be gained from the following disconnected account of the more spectacular features of agrarian distress. It should be premised that not all farmers were impoverished. There were a few who prospered, usually by getting a hold on the land of other men and working them like slaves, so that a writer on social topics (circa 1800) could say: "For one man who makes a fortune there are twenty or thirty reduced to penury." Such impoverishment made it impossible for the peasants to support children, and they resorted freely to abortion and infanticide. There are traces of these practices before Tokugawa times. Then they seem to have been sporadic and to have followed natural calamities like famine and plague; but by the middle of the eighteenth century they were prevalent throughout Japan, and had reached such alarming dimensions that they were prohibited by official edict in 1767. Naturally such decrees had no success. Infanticide was regarded as a quite proper process, and was known as *mabiki,* which is the word used of thinning a row of vegetables by uprooting. Conversely, in order to secure a supply of children for work in the fields without the expense of bringing them up, farmers were known to buy children kidnapped in the large towns by regular traffickers known as "child merchants."

While infanticide and abortion kept down the numbers of the agricultural population, there was also a constant drain upon farm labor owing to the influx of peasants into the towns. City life offered a refuge from the endless struggle on the land, to the young a delightful prospect of pleasures and excitements, to their parents a relief from oppression, for as *chōnin* they were untaxed and received a money wage which they could spend as they chose. Even as early as 1712 the decrease of the rural population began to cause concern, and the Tokugawa government decreed that all peasants must return to their native villages. Decrees of this kind were repeated at intervals until as late as 1843, when forcible measures were taken to send migrators back to their provinces from Edo. Nothing, however, could stop men from deserting their farms, since hardly any punishment could be worse than the life they had to lead in the country. There is no means of knowing exactly the movements of population during this period, but it may be safely assumed that the number of agricultural workers remained almost stationary even if it did not actually decrease. It appears that there was, generally speaking, an increase in the area of land under cultivation, thanks to reclamation in certain parts of Japan, and methods of cultivation tended to improve, if only to meet the exactions of landlords. But most of this advantage was offset by abuses. In northern and eastern Japan large tracts were abandoned by farmers because the land would not produce enough to satisfy the taxgatherer. At the other extreme there were good farms which were so productive that the officials marked them down for absurdly high assessment, with the fantastic result that their owners relinquished them to poor peasants, who even in some cases had to be given a sum of money to induce them to accept the gift. Into the question of tenancy we need not enter here, but it is worth observing that the poverty of the peasants forced them, in many instances, to surrender their land by sale or pledge to creditors, and there were thus brought into existence two new classes, one of persons who owned land which they did not farm, the other of persons who farmed land which they did not own. This created new hardships for agriculturalists and a clash of interests between tenant farmers and landowners (other than feudal lords). The most curious anomalies arose, as for example when a landowner reproved his tenant for producing too much rice, because taxation increased in proportion to the yield, while the tenant objected that unless the yield were high there was no surplus for his own subsistence. Tenant disputes continued throughout the eighteenth and nineteenth centuries, and in some parts of Japan they have recurred in quite recent years.

As if the peasantry were not sufficiently oppressed by human greed and stupidity, Nature took a hand in completing the tale of their miseries. There were frequent epidemics of pestilence, while famine raged from 1732 to 1733 and again from 1783 to 1787. The loss of life through plain starvation, and the lowering of the power of resistance of the ill-fed classes, reduced the population by over 1,000,000 in the years between 1780 and 1786. . . .

3. The Peasants

✿ RICE AND PEASANTS were traditionally the twin pillars of Japanese society. Peasants made up the vast majority of the population until well into the modern period, and rice remained the main agricultural product. The selection below, written about Japan in the early part of the twentieth century, describes the traditional methods of growing rice—the backbreaking work of intensive wet paddy farming. It was this meticulous rice cultivation that supported Japanese feudalism and eventually made possible Japanese industrialization. The yield figures, of course, are much higher now, but the main point is still accurate: rice is the highest yield crop possible for a peasant society with limited arable land.

J. W. ROBERTSON SCOTT*
The Most Exacting Crop in the World

The vast difference between Far Eastern and Western agriculture is marked by the fact that, except by using such a phrase as shallow pond—and this is inadequate, because a pond has a sloping bottom and a rice field necessarily a level one—it is difficult to describe a rice field in terms intelligible to a Western farmer.

. . . Many of us have seen rice growing in Italy or in the United States. But in Japan the paddies are very much smaller than any-

* J. W. Robertson Scott, *The Foundations of Japan* (New York: Appleton, 1922), pp. 68–71, 73–79.

thing to be seen in the Po Valley and in Texas. Owing to the plentiful water supply of a mountainous land, cultivation proceeds with some degree of regularity and with a certain independence of the rainy season; and there has been applied to traditional rice farming not a few scientific improvements.

There is a kind of rice with a low yield called upland rice which, like corn, is grown in fields. But the first requisite of general rice culture is water. The ordinary rice crop can be produced only on a piece of ground on which a certain depth of water is maintained.

In order to maintain this depth of water, three things must be done. The plot of ground must be made level, low banks of earth must be built round it in order to keep in the water, and a system of irrigation must be arranged to make good the loss of water by evaporation, by leakage, and by the continual passing on of some of the water to other plots belonging to the same owner or to other farmers. The common name of a rice plot is paddy, and the rice with its husk on, that is, as it is knocked from the ear by threshing, is called paddy rice. The rice exported from Japan is some of it husked and some of it polished.

Some ninety percent of the rice grown in Japan is ordinary rice. The remaining ten percent is about two percent upland and eight percent glutinous—the sort used for making the favorite *mochi* (rice flour dumplings, which few foreigners are able to digest). It would be possible to collect in Japan specimens of rice under 4000 different names, but, like our potato names, many of these represent duplicate varieties. Rice, again reminding us of potatoes, is grown in early, middle, and late season sorts.

Just one-half of the cultivated area of Japan is devoted to paddy, but there is to be added to this area under rice more than a quarter million acres producing the upland rice, the yield of which is lower than that of paddy rice. The paddy and upland rice areas together make up more than a half of the cultivated land. The paddies which are not in situations favorable to the production of second crops of rice (they are grown in one prefecture only) are used, if the water can be drawn off, for growing barley or wheat or green manure as a second crop.

It is not only the Eastern predilection for rice and the wet condition of the country, but the heavy cropping power of the plant . . . that makes the Japanese farmer labor so hard to grow it.

Intensively cultivated though Japan is, the percentage of cultivated land to the total area of the country is, however, little more than half that in Great Britain. This is because Japan is largely mountains and hills. Level land for rice paddies can be economically obtained in many parts of such a country by working it in small patches only. There is no minimum size for a Japanese paddy. I have seen paddies of the area of a counterpane and even of the size of a couple of dinner napkins.

The problem is not only to make the paddy in a spot where it can be supplied with water, but to make it in such a way that it will hold all the water it needs. It must be level, or some of the rice plants will have only their feet wet while others will be up to their necks. The ordinary procedure in making a paddy is to remove the topsoil, beat down the subsoil beneath, and then restore the top soil—there may be from five to ten inches of it. But the best efforts of the paddy-field builder may be brought to nought by springs or by a gravelly bottom. Then the farmer must make the best terms he can with fortune.

Paddies, as may be imagined from their physical limitations, are of every conceivable shape. There is assuredly no way of altering the shape of the paddies which are dexterously fitted into the hillsides. But large numbers of paddies are on fairly level ground. There is no real need for these being of all sizes and patterns. They are what they are because of the degree to which their construction was conditioned by water-supply problems, the financial resources of those who dug them, or the position of neighbors' land. And no doubt in the course of centuries there has been a great deal of swapping, buying, and inheriting. So the average farmer's paddies are not only of all shapes and sizes but here, there, and everywhere.

. . . It is because more than half the paddies are always under water that rice cultivation is so laborious. Think of the Western farm laborer being asked to plow and the allotment holder to dig almost knee-deep in mud. Although much paddy is plowed with the aid of an ox, a cow or a pony, most rice is the product of mattock or spade labor. There is no question about the severity of the labor of paddy cultivation. For a good crop it is necessary that the soil shall be stirred deeply.

Following the turning over of the stubble under water comes the clod smashing and harrowing by quadrupedal or bipedal labor. It is not only a matter of staggering about and doing heavy work in sludge. The sludge is not clean dirt and water but dirty dirt and water, for it has been heavily dosed with manure, and the farmer is not fastidious as to the source from which he obtains it. And the sludge ordinarily contains leeches. Therefore the cultivator must work uncomfortably in sodden clinging cotton feet and leg coverings. Long custom and necessity have no doubt developed a certain indifference to the physical discomfort of rice cultivation. The best rice will grow only in mud, and, except on the large uniform paddies of the adjusted areas, there is small opportunity for using mechanical methods.

One day when I went into the country it happened to be raining hard, but the men and women toiled in the paddies. They were breaking up the flooded clods with a tool resembling the "pulling fork" used in the West for getting manure from a dung cart. On other farms the task of working the quagmire was being done by two persons with the aid of a disconsolate pony harnessed to a rude harrow. The men and women in the paddies kept off the rain by means of the usual wide straw hats and loose straw mantles, admirable in their way in their combination of lightness and rain-proofness. . . .

Planting time arrives in the middle of June or thereabouts, when the paddy has been brought by successive harrowings into a fine tilth or rather sludge. It is illustrative of the exacting ways of rice that not only has it to have a growing place specially fashioned for it, it cannot be sown as cereals are sown. It must be sown in beds and then be transplanted. The seed beds have been sown in the latter part of April or the early part of May, according to the variety of rice and the locality. The seeds have usually been selected by immersion in salt water and have been afterwards soaked in order to advance germination. There is a little soaking pond on every farm. By the use of this pond the period in which the seeds are exposed to the depredations of insects, etc., is diminished. The seed bed itself is about the width of an onion bed, in order that weeds and insect pests may be easily reached. The seed bed is, of course, under water. The seed is dropped into the water and sinks into the mud. Within about thirty or forty days the seedlings are ready for transplanting. They have been the object of unremitting care. Weeds have been plucked out and insects have been caught by nets or trapped. There is a contrivance which, by means of a wheel at either end, straddles the seed bed and is drawn slowly from one end to the other. It catches the insects as they hop or fly up.

... At transplanting time every member of the family capable of helping renders assistance. Friends also give their aid if it is not planting time for them too. The work is so engrossing that young children who are not at school are often left to their own devices. Sometimes they play by the ditch round the paddies and are drowned. Five such cases of drowning are reported from three prefectures on the day I write this. The suggestion is made that in the rice districts there should be common nurseries for farmers' children at planting time.

The rate at which the planters, working in a row across the paddy, set out the seedlings in the mud below the water is remarkable. The first weeding or raking takes place about a fortnight after planting. After that there are three more weedings, the last being about the end of August. All kinds of hoes are used in the sludge. They are usually provided with a wooden or tin float. But most of the weeding is done simply by thrusting the hand into the mud, pulling out the weed and thrusting it back into the sludge to rot. The backbreaking character of this work may be imagined. As much of it is done in the hottest time of the year the workers protect themselves by wide-brimmed hats of the willow-plate pattern and by flapping straw cloaks or by bundles of straw fastened on their backs.

A sharp lookout must be kept for insects of various sorts. In more than one place I saw the boys and girls of elementary schools wading in the paddies and stroking the young rice with switches in order to make noxious insects rise. The creatures were captured by the young enthusiasts with nets. The children were given special times off from school work in which to hunt the rice pests and were encouraged to bring specimens to school.

There is no greater delight to the eye than the paddies in their early green, rippled and gently laid over by the wind. (One should say greens, for there is every tint from the rather woebegone yellowish green of the newly planted out rice to the happy luxuriant dark green of the paddies that have long been enjoying the best of quarters.) As harvest time approaches, the paddies, because they are not all planted with the same variety of rice, are in patches of different shades. Some are straw color, some are reddish brown or almost black. A poet speaks of the "hanging ears of rice." Rice always seems to hang its head more than other crops. It is weaker in the straw than barley, but rice frequently droops not only because of its natural habit, but because it has been over-manured or wrongly manured or because of wind or wet.

Beyond wind, insects, and drought, floods are the enemies of rice. When the plants are young, three or four days' flooding do not matter much, but in August, when the ears are shooting, it is a different matter. The sun pours down and soon rots the rice lying in the warm water. Sometimes the farmer, by almost withdrawing the water from his paddies, raises the temperature of the soil with benefit to the crop.

. . . Western farmers are hard put to it when their grain crops are beaten down by wind and rain; Japanese agriculturists, because they gather their harvest with a short sickle, do not find a laid crop difficult to cut. But these harvesters are very muddy indeed. When the rice is cut and the sheaves are laid along the low mud wall of the paddy they are still partly in the sludge. We know how miser-able a wet harvest is at home, but think of the slushy harvest with which most Japanese farmers struggle every year of their lives. The rice grower, although year in and year out he has the advantage of a great deal of sunshine, seldom gets his crop in without some rain. How does he manage to dry his October and November rice? By means of a temporary fence or rack which he rigs up in his paddy field or along a path or by the roadside. On this structure the sheaves are painstakingly suspended ears down. Sometimes he utilizes poles suspended between trees. These trees, grown on the low banks of the paddies, have their trunks trimmed so that they resemble parasols.

When the sheaves are removed in order to be threshed on the upland part of the holding, they are carried away at either end of a pole on a man's shoulder or are piled up on the back of an ox, cow, or pony. The height of the pile under which some animals stagger up from the paddies gives one a vivid conception of "the last straw."

Threshing is usually done by a man, woman, girl, or youth taking as many stems as can be easily grasped in both hands and drawing the ears, first one way and then another, through a hori-zontal row of steel teeth. The flail is not used for threshing rice but is employed for barley. Another common way of knocking out grain is by beating the straw over a table or a barrel. There are all sorts of cheap hand-worked threshing machines. After the threshing of the rice comes the winnowing, which may be done by the aid of a machine but is more likely to be effected in the immemorial way, by one person pouring the roughly threshed ears from a basket or skep while another worker vigorously fans the grain. The result is what is known as paddy rice. The process which follows winnowing is husking. This is done in the simplest possible form of hand mill. Before husking, the rice grain is in appearance not unlike barley and it is no easy matter to get its husk off. The husking mill is often made of hardened clay with many wooden teeth on the rubbing surface. After husking there is another winnowing. Then the grains are run through a special apparatus of recent introduction called *mangoku doshi,* so that faulty ones may be picked out. The result is unpolished rice.

It looks gray and unattractive, and unfortunately the unprepossessing but valuable outer coat is polished away. This is done in a mortar hollowed out of a section of a tree trunk or out of a large stone. One may see a young man or a young woman pounding the rice in the mortar with a heavy wooden beetle or mallet. Often the beetle is fastened to a beam and worked by foot. Or the polishing apparatus may be driven by water, oil, or steam power. Constantly in the country there are seen little sheds in each of which a small polishing mill driven by a water wheel is working away by itself. After the polishing, the *mangoku doshi* is used again to free the rice from the bran. This polished rice is still further polished by the dealer, who has more perfect mills than the farmer.

The farmer pays his rent not in the polished but in the husked rice. At the house of a former daimyō I saw an instrument which the feudal lord's bailiff was accustomed to thrust into the rice the tenants tendered. If when the instrument was withdrawn more than three husks were found adhering, the rice was returned to be recleaned. There are names for all the different kinds of rice. For instance, paddy rice is *momi;* husked rice is *gemmai;* half-polished rice is *hantsukimai;* polished rice is *hakumai;* cooked rice is *gohan.*

A century ago the farmer ate his rice at the *gemmai* stage, that is, in its natural state, and there was no beri-beri. The "black sake" made from this *gemmai* rice is still used in Shinto ceremonies. In order to produce clear sake the rice was polished. Then well-to-do people out of daintiness had their table rice polished. Now polished rice is the common food. Half-polished rice may be prepared with two or three hundred blows of the mallet; fully polished or white rice may receive six, seven, or eight hundred, or even, it may be, a thousand blows.

❀ LIFE for the Japanese peasantry under the Tokugawa feudal regime was harsh, and the question arises of how the military elite managed to retain successful control over the large rural population. The two selections here provide details of the administration of the local village and the various social controls which sought to assure the smooth functioning of the agricultural economy at the local level. Strong economic controls, moreover, also acted to ensure peasant submission to authority.

Befu is concerned with the links between the government and the local village elite, while Smith explores the class structure of the village—landlords and tenants. Village autonomy and solidarity, whose functions were mainly to benefit the well-being of and provide protection for the village, were used by the feudal government as means of control. As both Smith and Befu show, the peasants had relatively few rights, power in the village was the preserve of a few wealthy landowners, and these figures were delegated authority by the government. It was a very tightly organized society, and Befu notes a tendency for relationships to be defined in familial terms. Smith also argues that, unlike in China, in Japan the peasant remained somewhat passive under conditions favoring revolt.

HARUMI BEFU*
Village Autonomy and the State

When village communities exist in the context of a larger political system, understanding of the system of control at the village level requires analysis both of the system of control imposed on the village by the state and also of that which has evolved within the community through centuries of its existence. These two systems, of course, cannot operate altogether independently of each other but must somehow be articulated with one another. . . .

. . . What areas of peasant life did these governments attempt to control and why? How was the indigenous political structure of the village organized in relation to the government? Questions such as these are not easy to answer. For most students of Tokugawa political structure have almost exclusively discussed the political institutions of the military government, ignoring the native village political structure. And those who have analyzed the indigenous village political system have emphasized the autonomous and corporate character of the village, with little regard for the role of imposed government institutions. Consequently, how one is related to the other, how the powerful military government dealt with the supposedly semi-autonomous village has never been made clear.

. . . The administrative machinery of the shogunate and daimiate governments consisted, at the village level, of the headman, . . . the elders, . . . the delegates, . . . and the five-man groups. . . . Among these the headman was without question the most important official both in terms of the power delegated and the responsibilities assigned by the government. The government held him responsible for keeping accurate and detailed records of the village census, reporting any changes in the village population (through birth, death, migration, marriage, divorce, etc.), apportioning to individual families rice tax levied on the village, collecting the tax in full

* Harumi Befu, "Village Autonomy and Articulation with the State," in John W. Hall and Marius B. Jansen, eds., *Studies in the Institutional History of Early Modern Japan* (Princeton, N.J.: Princeton University Press, 1968), pp. 301–306, 308–314.

and on time, maintaining public works in the village, adjudicating disputes arising within the village, reporting any violation of the law, and finally in general assuming the role of the father figure for the village. In addition, he was responsible for the conduct of his villagers, *i.e.,* punishable for their crimes.

There were three or four elders in most villages and it was their duty to assist the headman. The delegates were presumably representatives of ordinary peasants and . . . were supposed "to keep an eye on the conduct of the village officials, to give counsel and admonition, and generally guard and promote the best interest of the village."

. . . The power which the officials needed to execute their responsibilities was derived from the government and tradition of the village. The government empowered the officials to carry out their assigned duties and gave them the right to arrest and report to the magistrate any criminal offenders. But it is important to note at the same time . . . that the officials' ability to carry out their duties effectively was supported by the fact that they represented families which were respected by villagers because they were old, often being among the founding families of the village.

. . . In addition to the officers of the headman and his assistants, the government instituted the *gonin-gumi,* or five-man group, system for additional security. Though called five-*man* group . . . the basic units of the group were always families rather than individuals. The size of the group, although supposedly five families, varied a great deal, from one or two to more than ten. In most villages only the propertied peasants were the full-fledged members of the group, tenants and their families being usually included in the family of their landlord. All peasants were thus required to belong to one five-man group or another (with the exception of village officials, who were sometimes excluded from membership). The group had its head, generally called *kumigashira.* . . .

The political significance of this institution for control of the peasantry is that it was the unit of group responsibility. A crime committed by a member was a crime of all the others, and concealment of a crime committed by a fellow member was also a crime of all the others. On the other hand, an informer who would report a violation of law by a fellow member of his five-man group was given a lighter punishment than the others, or sometimes even rewarded.

... The government capitalized on the indigenous solidarity of the village in instituting group responsibility. For example, levying a lump sum tax on the village, as was usually done, was a far more effective way of collecting the full amount of tax than levying tax to individual families, some of which in any village were too poor to meet the quota. In lump-sum taxation, wealthier peasants paid more than their share to help the poorer neighbors. Group responsibility, however, had its negative effects, too. The same sense of solidarity—to help and protect one another—impeded the policing function of the group, because villagers were more likely to connive with one another against the government rather than blackmail a fellow villager.

It may be helpful to review briefly the regulations which the government imposed on peasants. To appreciate the types of regulations and their details, we should note several assumptions on which the shogunate and daimiate governments based their philosophy of ruling the peasantry. First, the state manifestly existed for the benefit of the ruling class, and therefore other classes, including the peasants, existed to support the ruling class. Hence the oppressive measures to keep the peasants at the bare subsistence level, taking away every bit of surplus they produced. Second, the peasants were considered by nature stupid, needing detailed regulations for conduct. Third, the society was conceived of in absolutely static terms in which the peasantry had a definite position defined by the ruling elite: hence the numerous regulations aimed at maintaining and emphasizing the status relation of the peasants to other classes, especially to the ruling class. Fourth ... to Tokugawa administrators law and morals were both bound up in the concept of government. Hence the moralistic admonitions intermingled with legal codes and the moralistic tone of legal codes.

... The village was a corporate body, a legal entity which owned, bought, and sold property; loaned and borrowed money; and sued, was sued by, and entered into agreements with other villages. The fact that the village had such corporate qualities is important. It indicates the degree of commitment by village members toward the village as a unit and the degree of solidarity they expressed. It is this solidarity which enabled villagers to enforce their self-made laws and invoke sanctions against any members who transgressed them.

The solidarity of this corporate body is best expressed in village codes. These codes contain rules and regulations evolved in the village through centuries of collective living; their purpose was to maintain peace in the village by forbidding disruptive acts and requiring collective defense. The important point is that these codes are a pact agreed upon by all villagers and not something forced upon them from above. Village codes, written in the village codes book, are followed by a statement of oath by all members of the village assembly to abide by the codes.

Whereas the book of the five-man group generally included scores of clauses, sometimes more than one hundred, a book of village codes usually included approximately ten clauses and rarely more than twenty. The great length of the former resulted from the fact that government administrators simply piled edict upon edict, and most of them became incorporated into the book of the five-man group regardless of whether they applied to the village. The village codes, on the other hand, tended to contain only essential items of law.

. . . Village codes covered such topics as taxation, agriculture, policing, adjudication, civil records (e.g., property transaction), sumptuary regulation, and intervillage agreement. This listing might give the impression that these codes simply reiterate regulations promulgated by the state. To a certain extent they do. For example, there are clauses dealing with handling of the tax levied by the government. Sumptuary regulations, too, seem to be almost direct copies of government edicts.

These regulations were included in the village codes because they were relevent to village life in one way or another. . . . This is obvious for the government tax. Sumptuary laws, too, made sense to peasants, simply as a means of making ends meet in their tight subsistence economy, although not as a means of maintaining and expressing status symbols as the government intended.

In the areas of policing and security, again village codes overlap with government regulations. . . . While the government law aimed to promote the welfare of the ruling elite, the village codes were designed primarily for the welfare of the village. For example, whereas government laws aimed primarily at increasing production, through encouraging reclamation, maximum use of land, etc., village codes aimed to reduce internal conflicts and disputes by regulating those areas of village life (such as management of communal land, irrigation system, and property boundaries) in which disputes and conflicts were likely to occur. The corporate village is also of prime significance in codes concerned with external affairs. In dealing with higher authorities for such matters as filing of grievances against the district magistrate or in settling disputes with neighboring villagers, villagers were required to present a solid front; anyone who acted contrary to the interest of the village received the severest penalty. . . .

Compared with the corporate welfare of the village, individual problems seem to have been relatively unimportant. Matters concerning families or individuals, such as marriage or inheritance, were not generally codified.

. . . Thus two bodies of law regulated the life of the peasant. But they did so in somewhat different spheres of life because their ultimate objectives were different. The state's objectives were maximum exploitation of the peasants and maintenance of a static and stratified society through both moral and legal legislation. The village wanted primarily to maintain internal peace and protect the village as a corporate entity. The village, of course, was subject to state regulations insofar as peasants were useful in helping the state achieve its goal. This meant that compliance to state law was most important in fiscal matters and status relations and of secondary importance in policing and morality. But the village codes emphasized policing as well as some other aspects of village life which the state did not stress. The next question is how the village executed its own law.

The major political institution for the enactment and enforcement of village codes was the village assembly. In addition, the elite families of the village and the age-grade organization performed important political roles in the village.

The village assembly was the governing body of the village. Although we are not always told who had the right and duty to attend the assembly, it seems that each family—at least the propertied families . . . —was represented in it. The assembly met from time to time, though not at any regular intervals, for such purposes as drawing up new village codes, selecting village officials (if it had this function), indicting misbehaving officials, deliberating on violations of village codes, and discussing disputes with neighboring villages.

Punishments the assembly decreed varied according to the

nature of the crime, but they also varied from village to village for the same crime. Those commonly mentioned in the village codes . . . are village ostracism, banishment, fine, and the demanding of verbal or written apology to the assembly. The best-known to present-day scholars of rural Japan is village ostracism, or *mura hachibu,* which is still in use. In *mura hachibu* villagers agree not to associate with the culprit's family except possibly in case of fire or death. In these cases villagers would help only in putting out the fire or in conducting funeral services. But in some villages even these occasions are not excepted. *Mura hachibu* was the punishment for such crimes as disclosing secret agreements made among villagers; supporting someone who had been purged from office; being incorrigibly intractable; or dissenting from a decision made by the village as a whole.

Banishment from the village probably was more severe punishment than *mura hachibu.* Village codes prescribed banishment for such crimes as stealing lumber from the communal land, stealing crops from the field, harboring gamblers, and committing arson. . . .

In addition to the corporate force of the village bearing on individual wrongdoers, one sees the influence of the government-instituted concept of joint responsibility being utilized by the village. The fellow members of a law-breaker's five-man group were usually, though not always, punished along with him for crimes such as gambling and theft. In another form of joint responsibility, the next-door neighbors on both sides and the three families directly across the street were held punishable in some villages for a crime such as gambling, regardless of whether these families belonged to the five-man group of the culprit.

Although village codes are an agreement of the entire village, a close examination reveals that the actual control, at least some of the time, lay with the elite of the village rather than among all members equally. . . .

Elite control of the village is best illustrated in the religious organization known as *miyaza,* or "shrine association." Its membership was limited to old, established families of the village. While *miyaza* was expressly a religious association connected with the village shrine, its members enjoyed many privileges and exercised much power beyond religious functions. For example, it was this organization that chose the village officials; and officials had to be chosen from among its members. In economic spheres, too, members of the *miyaza* had privileges, for example, in possessing exclusive access to the village-owned land.

... It is important to note that the headman and other officials were members of the village rather than administrators sent into the village from outside, such as the warrior was, and that they were elite members of the community. The government, in other words, relied on locally influential individuals to enforce its law. From the point of view of the village, selecting as its head and its representative of the government a man who wielded influence in the village, entirely apart from whatever power he acquired as an agent of the government, meant a positive acceptance by the village of the unchallengeable authority of the government. More-over, the fact that the village officials were normally chosen by the village elite—propertied peasants of the village—meant that the acceptance of the authority of the state could be forced upon the rest of the village through the indigenous political structure.

One last institution to be mentioned in connection with the internal system of control of the village is the age-grade system. Commonly one entered the group sometime in the teens and remained a member until he married or reached some set age in the late twenties or early thirties; membership was compulsory for all those of appropriate ages. Separate groups were organized for the two sexes, the female group being under the strict control of the male group.

The group had an internal hierarchy in which older mem-bers enjoyed higher status and much authority over younger members, demanding strict obedience from the younger ones. Just as the village elite, rather than the headman, held power in village politics, actual authority in the age group lay in a group of elder and more respected members, the leader of the youth group simply being one among them. This council of elders arbitrated disputes among members, made all important decisions regarding activities of the group, and judged violations of group norms.

The youth group was a powerful control group. There were written and unwritten rules and regulations which everyone was to abide by. These codes concerned gambling, drinking, relations with the opposite sex, etiquette toward the elders, one's work habits, mutual help, and relations with outsiders, particularly women of other villages. The male group possessed exclusive sexual access to the unmarried women of the village. Neither the women themselves nor their parents had the right to deny this right to the group, and no men outside the village were to have access to these women. Conversely, no member of the youth group was allowed to flirt with or marry a woman of another village. Violators of these rules met with some of the severest sanctions. Any commission of severe crimes was publicly punished by the group as a whole, and in extreme cases the culprit was expelled from the group and members were forbidden to associate with him in any way whatsoever. It may be noted that this sanction parallels the *mura hachibu* discussed above, for here one sees the village youth practicing roles they were to play in adulthood. Incorrigible members of the age group were sometimes turned over to the village elders. For less severe cases, lighter punishments were meted out, such as temporary expulsion of the culprit from the group (the duration depending on the seriousness of the offense), temporarily seating him in the junior position, formal inquisition, monetary fine, corporal punishment, and written apologies.

Although the youth group was primarily concerned with internal discipline, they sanctioned outsiders, too—that is, villagers who were not members of the group. On certain nights of the year or month, the youth groups in some regions would gather in front of an offender's home or some other designated place in the village and enumerate all the wrongdoings the family was responsible for, and shout abuse at the top of their voices.

It may be instructive to consider the basic reasons why the military government could not rely on the indigenous political system of the village and instead had to create its own legal and administrative structure which it imposed upon the village. The reasons lie in the differences in the goals of the two polities. Village goals were to maintain internal peace and to defend itself against external threat. The goals of the military government, on the other hand, consisted of economic exploitation of the peasants and maintenance of a static society in which the peasantry was given a well defined place. To the village, the welfare of the larger society, of which it was a part, was irrelevant; to the village, too, the exploitative state represented external threat as much as, or even more than, say, a neighboring village trying to steal water.

It is no wonder, seen in this light, that the indigenous village polity, whose goals did not coincide with those of the state, and whose instruments (political structure and codes) were either indifferent or hostile to the goals of the state, was not particularly useful for the implementation of state goals. For this reason the state had to create separate legal and administrative machinery within the village to achieve its goals.

... There was one area in which the state and the village saw eye to eye, so to speak; this was in the matter of maintenance of internal peace. Because both polities were concerned with peace and security of the village—for different reasons, of course—it appears on the surface that the village cooperated with the state in maintaining peace and punishing any criminal who disturbed the peace of the village. But, because the village enforced the law, it usurped the state's prerogative to punish criminals.

The village polity, therefore, was obliged to make a major concession in allowing the state to intrude. This meant that in matters of taxation, status relations, and policing—areas most sensitive to the state—the village was forced to obey the law of the state. In turn, the state permitted the village to deal with internal matters as it pleased. The latter did adopt some of the institutions of the state, for example, in the concept of joint responsibility and made some use of the village officials for sanctioning purposes. But the indigenous political system by and large remained unaffected.

T. C. SMITH*
The Japanese Village in the Seventeenth Century

Everywhere in seventeenth-century Japan the peasant population was divided into those who held land and those who did not. This was more than a purely economic distinction, for it ordinarily implied rights and obligations of different kinds. Only peasants listed in the village land register—that is, *hyakushō,* or landholders —had the privileges and duties that went with membership in the

* Thomas Smith, "The Japanese Village in the Seventeenth Century," in John W. Hall and Marius B. Jansen, eds., *Studies in the Institutional History of Early Modern Japan* (Princeton: Princeton University Press, 1968), pp. 265–275, 278–281.

village. Since taxes of all kinds were laid on land rather than on
persons, only *hyakushō* were responsible for payment of the various dues the village collectively owed the lord. In return, they
alone could participate in a village assembly, hold village offices,
draw shares of the common lands of the village, address the village
headman on official business, or take part in a legal act of the
village such as the sale or acquisition of water rights. The rest of
the population of the village was without public rights and duties,
aside from the general obligation to abide by the law. Indeed, the
local and higher officials rarely took cognizance of them at all
except in criminal cases. Such people were completely dependent,
in one form or another, on some *hyakushō* who used their labor on
his holding; for most purposes he stood between them and the law,
and their obligations and rights were defined primarily by their
relations with him rather than with any public authority. But this
class will be considered later; here we are concerned only with the
hyakushō.

The land registers are the basic economic document on landholding in the village. Since they were compiled for the purpose of
allocating taxes of all kinds, they list the names of the *hyakushō*
and give a description of the holding of each. Too few registers
from the seventeenth century have yet come to light to permit nice
generalizations about the distribution of land among holders. . . .
But even the few registers we have leave very little doubt concerning the general picture of inequality among holdings. Although
they come from widely separated areas, they all show holdings of
less than one-half *chō**—some of them little better than gardens—
or holdings whose annual yield was valued at less than five *koku*
(one *koku* = 4.96 bushels) of hulled rice alongside holdings ten,
twenty, or thirty times as large or productive. Not infrequently
we encounter *peasant* holdings that can only be described as
estates. For example, we find a village headman in Iyo Province
in 1682 holding 34 *chō* with an annual yield of 165 *koku*. . . .

It is not surprising that such extremes of wealth and poverty
among *hyakushō* of the village were accompanied by marked
social distinctions. We may pass over differences of dress, food,
and housing, which directly reflected economic well-being, to distinctions of education and family with one comment. Two contrary

* One *chō* equals 2.45 acres.

complaints about the peasantry run through the economic writings of the whole Tokugawa period and, not infrequently, through the works of a single author. On the one hand, it is said that the peasants lived like beasts in the field; on the other, that they lived with the reckless extravagance of the merchant. Since these are views persistently expressed by contemporaries who knew of what they spoke, they cannot be ignored; and they can only be reconciled if we understand them as comments on the way of life of two rather distinct economic classes among the peasantry.

Although the law bound them to the land and treated them in other respects like ordinary peasants, the rich landholding families were not purely peasant in origin. Many could trace their ancestors back not many generations to petty warriors, some of whom collected taxes and administered justice in the village and, on occasion, even demanded military service from the peasants under them. In the century of anarchy before Nobunaga's time [that is, roughly from the middle of the fifteenth century to the middle of the sixteenth] there had been no clear distinction between soldier and landholder; the very possession of land implied arms to defend it. "No arms, no land," the saying went. Hence, Hideyoshi and the other barons had found no satisfactory distinction at hand for prying warrior and peasant apart when they sought to separate the two at the end of the sixteenth century, with the result that nearly everywhere a backwash of warrior families was left among the peasantry.

. . . The economic and social dominance of the larger *hyakushō* in the village was supported by a tight monopoly of local administrative and political power. Invariably the headman and his lieutenants came from this class, and their monopoly of office was almost impossible to break—short of rebellion. Often the office of headman was hereditary in a single family, and at best it rotated among a few qualified families, each holding office for a generation. In rare instances, it is true, at least in the late Tokugawa, the headman was elected by the *hyakushō* of the village; but given the unequal stacking of the cards in other respects, it is not very difficult to guess how these elections ordinarily turned out.

The practice of restricting local office to the larger holders was not new. By the Tokugawa period it was already so firmly established in custom that legal enactments to support it would have been superfluous. . . .

Thus far we have been considering only the *hyakushō:* that is, those peasants who were listed in the land registers. Until recent years it was believed that the land registers accounted for the whole peasant population and, accordingly, that the Tokugawa village was a community of small holders who were the virtual owners of the land they worked. Tenantry, so characteristic a feature of modern Japanese agriculture, could be explained, therefore, as the result of capitalism having invaded the village, thrusting this peasant up and that one down.

This view is no longer tenable. . . .

Although the evidence available on the ratio of tenants to *hyakushō* in our period is too scanty to permit precise conclusions, tenants must have comprised a substantial part of the total population. In some areas the percentage of tenants runs very high indeed. . . . This much seems certain: tenantry was already characteristic of Japanese agriculture in the seventeenth century before capitalism had invaded the countryside in any considerable force. . . . Moreover, the overtones of personal dependence associated with tenant status suggest something more than a purely economic contract between the tenant and his landlord.

The tenant did not share any of the public rights and duties of the landholder. . . . His rights and duties, for the most part, were private in nature and . . . they were governed by his relationship to his landlord (for so we may now call the larger *hyakushō* whose holdings were worked wholly or in part by tenants). Although this was a customary and private relationship, it was respected and supported by the political authorities. There seems to have been no general legislation in the period regulating it, and administrative interference by the local magistrate, which did occur infrequently, was resisted by landlords as an invasion of a domain that was their exclusive concern.

Certainly tenantry involved an economic dependence on the landlord that was very nearly complete. Although custom gave the tenant some measure of protection in his holding, he had no legal claim to the land he worked. The only right acknowledged by the village register, and consequently by the lord and his officials, was that of the landlord. The landlord sold or mortgaged or passed on to his heirs both land and tenants, without consulting the latter's wishes. No doubt in most cases he could also dispossess his tenants without cause or compensation if only he were prepared to risk the censure of his neighbors. Everywhere the plots assigned tenants were too small to have permitted them to accumulate any significant capital of their own. There is good reason, moreover, to believe that when favorable economic or political factors, such as increased productivity or a low tax rate, made a higher income for the tenant possible, the landlord took the increment in higher rents. But the tenant was dependent on the landlord not only for access to land; the house in which he lived and the tools with which he worked often belonged to the landlord. And he had access to the common forest and wastelands of the village, which provided much of the fertilizer and all the fuel and building materials so essential to the economy of the peasant household, only because the landlord drew a share of the common as a village *hyakushō* and permitted the tenant the use of it.

The personal relations of the tenant and landlord reflected the generally accepted criteria of the time for dealings between unequal parties. All relations of this kind in Tokugawa society between employer and employee, teacher and pupil, lord and vassal tended to approximate the Confucian ideal of family relationships. All had their peculiar features, but all had in common distinctions of worth between the two parties and reciprocal but different sets of obligations—obedience and loyalty on the one side and benevolence and protection on the other—that ideally obtained between father and son. To the tenant the landlord was *oyakata* or "parent"; to the landlord the tenant was *kokata* or "child."

This system of values inevitably tended to turn economic dependence into intense personal subordination. There are a few scraps of evidence that throw some direct light on this aspect of the tenant's position. The tenants of Shinano Province, in addition to performing labor services for the landlord, were all subject to a class of obligations that seem more a signification of personal dependence than an economic payment. Some tenants were required to send their sons and daughters as unpaid servants to the landlord for a fixed term; others to deliver firewood to the landlord, or to provide a meal for him on specified occasions, or to attend him on occasions of personal sorrow or rejoicing; and still others to deliver a small quantity of rice and wine or such things as a wooden bucket or a piece of cloth at certain seasons of the year.

... High as the figures ... on the ratio of tenants to *hyakushō* seem to be, they by no means show the whole peasant population that stood outside the land registers. Entirely omitted in these figures are the hereditary servants that were often found in the households of rich peasants. This group appears in the documents under a variety of names, but perhaps the most common and certainly the most descriptive is *genin* or "low person." It is impossible to guess how numerous the *genin* were, but there can be no doubt that they were an important source of agricultural labor under the older system of landlord management. ...

Like the tenant, the *genin* had no public standing in the village, and his rights were defined by his relations to his master. Although he was handed down in a single family from father to son like any other piece of property, it is the opinion of one of Japan's outstanding social and legal historians that he could not be transferred to a new master against his will. Perhaps the best way of describing the *genin*'s position is as an inferior member of the master's family. One of the distinctive features of the Japanese family is its capacity for almost indefinite expansion to include not only remote relatives within its lines of authority, but persons having no blood or marriage relationship to the family at all. Indeed, not infrequently the *genin* was formally incorporated in the family: he worshiped the family ancestors, owed loyalty and obedience to the head of the family, and in return received such protection as the family accorded members of inferior standing.

... The peasants were not the homogeneous class depicted by the Confucianists. Peasant society itself was a pyramid of wealth and power and legal rights that rose from the tenant and *genin* at the bottom through small and middling landholders to what might be called a class of wealthy peasants at the top. Nor was this pyramid a recent structure, the work of capitalism in placing one peasant over another. Rather it was the survival from an earlier age in which men were raised and lowered in society by force of land and arms, not by the power of money.

... The persistent docility of the peasantry, in a country where peasants even today number almost half the population, is a fact of obvious and immense significance. Most students would agree, I believe, that this political and social passivity has provided an extraordinarily solid base for authoritarian government and support for social policies of the most conservative order for the past four centuries at least. To inculcate and enforce such discipline among peasants who, in general, have been held consistently at the ragged edge of starvation implies some extremely efficient system of social and political control. I would suggest that this system was composed in part of the following elements. (1) The peasantry was divided against itself by arrangements in which one peasant exploited the labor of another and in which the upper layer of the peasantry was in fact an adjunct of the ruling class, sharing in the economic benefits of the regime and in the administration of the country so that any prospective peasant uprising would find this group—the wealthy and literate families of the village—aligned solidly against it. (2) This group sprang partly from the warrior class: in its ranks were many men who had run local affairs by a combination of land and arms for centuries; and although it was disarmed at the end of the sixteenth century, its local authority was by no means weakened, for it was now supported by the armies of a feudal lord. (3) Despite the spectacular changes effected in other spheres, the Meiji restoration passed over the village without disturbing the distribution of power or the system by which land was exploited. Thus, the Japanese landlords of modern times, taken as a whole, were not a new and precariously dominant group thrown up by the impact of capitalism on the village but a class whose habit of power goes back to the formative period of Japanese feudalism.

♣ OUTLETS for the expression of grievances were few for the peasants. Though agricultural productivity rose during the period and more land was brought under cultivation, few of the peasants benefited. Occasionally, in times of extreme distress, they rose in large-scale riots and violent disorders known today as *nōmin ikki,* described here by Hugh Borton. The outcome, however, seldom resulted in more than minor concessions by the authorities, given the overwhelming military strength of the feudal government. These jacqueries lacked both ideology and sustaining organization. None led, as rebellions sometimes did in China, to the overturning of regimes, but they nonetheless show that the peasants were not always passive. They took

vengeance in these risings, even if only temporarily, on those
they felt responsible for their plight—the rich merchants, landlords, and corrupt administrators.

HUGH BORTON*
Peasant Uprisings in Japan of the Tokugawa Period

In studying the various peasant uprisings under the Tokugawa
bakufu, whether chronologically or geographically, it is difficult to
determine the exact number of disturbances. However, most recent
calculations show a total of 1153 cases having occurred between
1603 and 1867 with increasing frequency as the period progressed.
For the first hundred years there were only 157 cases distributed
fairly evenly throughout the century, but for the next fifty years
alone (1703–1753), 176 cases appear showing an increase of
over 100 percent, with fifty-one of these uprisings falling between
1743 and 1753. For the last one hundred and fifteen years of this
period there was an average of over six uprisings a year. . . .

The cycle through which most of the peasant uprisings of the
Tokugawa period passed was as follows. As a direct result of
some grievance, natural disaster, or displeasure on the part of the
peasants, they would assemble into a party or "mob" (*totō*) for
the purpose of presenting an appeal (*esso*) to the authorities concerned, against the prevailing grievance. If the appeal was presented by the mob as a whole in the form of a "mob appeal,"
(*gōso*), before the castle of their lord, it was usually accompanied
by destruction of property of the wealthy or the officials representing the fief, as the mob approached the castle town. After the
appointment of an intermediary, the demands were then presented
to the proper authorities for their consideration. If the uprising was
successful, and the demands were granted, the peasants would
return to their villages. If unsuccessful, they were often dispersed
by the soldiers. In either case, an investigation of the affair followed and the leaders were usually severely punished, either

* Hugh Borton, *Peasant Uprisings in Japan of the Tokugawa Period*
(Transactions of the Asiatic Society of Japan, Second Series,· Vol. XVI,
Tokyo, May 1938), pp. 39, 16–19, 21–32, 60–62, 78–80.

crucified, decapitated, or banished. Though several of the uprisings
. . . did not pass through all these stages, though some of them were
dismal failures, yet it will appear that as the central government
became weaker, as the conditions of the farmers became more
pitiable, and as the foundation of the whole feudal structure
became unsteady, many of the demands of the farmers were accepted. . . .

By far the majority of uprisings of the Tokugawa period,
however, are of a type having direct relationships between the
peasants and the governing class that controlled them. From an
economic standpoint, they were against the landowners and their
policies, similar to modern tenancy disputes. They became local-
ized in many cases due to the fact that taxation was a joint
responsibility of each village, and often arose from the demands of
the authorities to open new lands which brought with them increased taxation, for it was by this process that the warriors could
most easily increase their income and they were officially encouraged by the *bakufu* itself. In situations where wealthy merchants
had become landowners due to their appropriation of land which
they had acquired in exchange for money and goods borrowed by
the peasants, it was easy for the discontented peasant, especially if
he were impelled by crop failures and famine as in 1783–1787, to
direct his wrath against these merchants. From a social standpoint,
the uprisings were directed against the village officials, who, as the
attorneys and representatives of the controlling class, collected the
taxes, spied upon the plans of the farmers for insurrection, and
added special taxes for their own profit. . . .

A feature of Japanese feudalism, allowing officials to act arbitrarily, with an uprising of the farmers as an only check, was
absentee ownership. Moreover, this situation was greatly aggra-
vated by the system of "alternate attendance," *sankin kōtai*, which
required that every daimyō not only come to Edo at specified
intervals and remain there, but also leave his wives and children
there as a sort of hostages, to assure his good conduct when he
returned home to his fief. This "alternate attendance" not only
impoverished the daimyō and made them less formidable enemies
of the Tokugawa *bakufu,* but also persuaded many daimyō to
remain in the capital and have their fiefs governed as their officials
willed. An excellent example of uprisings resulting from this situation is that in the province of Echigo in the fief of the Makino

family at Nagaoka. Here six different uprisings arose between
1828 and 1868, directly the result of the maladministration of the
fief and the heavy taxes imposed upon the peasants by officials
who administered with a free hand as their lord always remained
in Edo.

Additional underlying causes of uprisings, usually accompanied
by other causes, included ignorance on the part of the peasant, the
increasing difference in wealth between the rich and poor, the
isolation of fiefs by distance and mountains as in the provinces
of Echigo, Sado, and Shinano, and a disproportion of the population, with men predominating, as in the case of Mimasaka. On the
economic side, there was an ever-increasing demand on the part of
the *bakufu* and the officials of the various domains for the extension in the area of cultivated land. That their efforts were effective
becomes obvious from the fact that in 1600 there were 5,000,000
acres under cultivation while in 1868 this figure was more than
doubled to 11,500,000 acres. Along with this fact was a population which remained practically stationary, which meant that the
burden of labor of the peasant in the amount of land he was
supposed to cultivate had doubled; and, since many of his former
fellows had escaped to the towns, it made it practically impossible
for those that remained on the land to carry the burden alone.

With these primary causes as the underlying forces in many of
the uprisings, although not specifically mentioned as such, the
more immediate or motivating causes are easier to determine. In
the first place, they readily fall into economic, financial, or administrative causes, of which the first was of supreme importance.
Among these economic motivating causes, first to be mentioned
are the effects of natural calamities, whether volcanic eruptions,
drought, floods, or frost, ruining the crops and directly affecting
the farmers whose livelihood and very existence was dependent
upon the rice crop. . . . Closely connected with crop failure and
directly dependent upon it was the increase in price not only of
rice, but of other commodities as well. This was largely responsible
for the rice riots in Edo and Osaka in 1787, rice riots again in
1837, and for a total of 101 uprisings due to high prices throughout the Tokugawa period.

Among the financial causes as a motive for peasant uprisings
oppressive taxes must be mentioned first. Although the tax was
generally fifty percent following the establishment of the *bakufu,*

with the villages taking joint responsibility for its payment, not only the regular taxes gradually increased but special taxes were added. Uprisings resulting from this fact alone comprise over twenty-five percent of the total and amounted to 295 incidents, largely occurring after the middle of the seventeenth century. . . .

Another motivating financial cause for disorders and appeals on the part of the farmers came as a by-product of the financial distress of the *bakufu* itself. To overcome any deficit the central government might have acquired, or to aid in the reconstruction of the Imperial or Edo castle after fire or earthquake, it began the policy of ordering special "forced levies" (*goyōkin*), not only upon the rich merchants in Osaka and Edo, but also upon the daimyō in proportion to their incomes. To pay for this extraordinary levy, the daimyō in turn taxed the farmers, which resulted in various uprisings. . . .

Closely connected with both the economic and financial causes for uprisings were the various administrative motives; the unlawfulness of the village officials, the corruption of the direct representatives or special envoys of the *bakufu,* the arbitrary actions of the representatives of the government of the various domains, the failure of universal governmental administration, and finally changes in the relations of villages to the domains. In the first place, by far the most common administrative cause for insurrection was the action of the local officials and representatives of the daimyō. This was an outcome, of course, of the whole situation created by absentee ownership, and a total of sixty-two uprisings are recorded throughout the entire Tokugawa period as a result of the maladministration of the village officials alone. . . .

And lastly there remain those uprisings which arose from what might be called social causes. Although not the only motivating cause, they were a definite factor in several incidents. Before mentioning these, however, a fuller explanation of these social conditions is necessary. There were throughout the Tokugawa period an increasing number of rōnin, lordless warriors, the result of the fief of their lord having been confiscated or the daimyō having been transferred or having died without issue. They formed a certain discontented element in society and their influence was definitely to be felt at the time of the restoration of 1868, but the surprising thing to note is not the frequency with which they allied themselves with the farmers, leading them in revolt for their own ends, but the opposite. The reason for this doubtless lies in the disdain with which they considered the farmers as in a class of society far below them, and the lack of common grievances of the two groups. There were, however, uprisings in which rōnin took part. . . .

The foregoing reference to types and causes of uprisings has dealt largely with what are usually classed as positive forms of resistance of the peasants. There were, however, a sufficient number of disturbances which had primarily a negative form. Their causes were similar to those already mentioned but rather than following the usual procedure of forming a mob, destructive advance upon the castle town, and "mob appeal," they developed into desertions. Originally, individuals would secretly desert into a neighboring village or fief to avoid some specific grievance or hardship, but gradually the habit developed into an organized group of one or more villages leaving en masse. If the villagers crossed into the neighboring fief or province, they would petition the lord of that fief that they either be allowed to remain within his domain, or that he intervene on their behalf. . . .

There also developed after the middle of the Tokugawa period, and increasing in intensity even up to most recent times, a series of farm tenancy disputes. As these are a special type of disturbance and concern more modern times, they will not be dealt with at length here. However, in spite of a law against division of farms into sections less than one *chō* (2.45 acres), or the sale in perpetuity of cultivated fields, it was inevitable that the land fall into the hands of the propertied class, that the farmers become tenants, and that tenancy disputes result. . . .

It was among the tenants that the most deplorable conditions developed and their disputes with their landlord became prevalent after about 1730. They were directly related to peasant uprisings in cases where the tenants formed groups in their own village out of which an uprising might start. . . .

Likewise, as there had been no harvest in the province of Izumo, on the southwestern coast of Japan, in 1783, a severe disturbance developed there in the fief of Matsudaira Harusato, lord of the castle of Matsue, an uprising breaking out in the villages of Ōzu, Mitoya, and Takuwa, in Kando and Iishi districts. The previous year a new tax of three *koku* [1 *koku* = 4.96 barrels] on each ten *chō* of rice fields and five *koku* on each ten *chō* of dry lands had been ordered, as well as a *fumai* tax or duty of villagers to provide money for the work to be done in the lord's mansion in the city. There had also been levied a *sunshimai,* or special rice tax to be collected in the fourth instead of the sixth month. One of the elders of the fief, therefore, appealed several times for relief, but the lord merely complained of the increase in expenses. In Kando district, the price of rice had risen since the first of the year, and the people were wandering about demanding rice gruel. A strange person appeared and ordered everyone to appear the next day at Ōzu *machi* [village] to make a mob appeal, the doctors, townsmen, acupuncture doctors, and heads of the shrines coming to the support of the peasants. On the night of the nineteenth of the first month, several thousand men, beating on the doors with split bamboo sticks and calling out with loud voices demanding the people to come out and join them, came from the west of Ōzu, dressed in sandals and with towels wrapped around their heads for the occasion. They then broke into the home of Morihiroya Gampei, breaking down the walls of his home, entering his garden, and pulling down the out-buildings, tearing off and destroying the storm doors, and entering the house with muddy feet. Taking out all of his furniture and movable goods, they broke them into bits; and opening his godown, they distributed some 533 bales of rice. The rioters then demanded that Morihiro Ikuta be their mediator and present their appeal to the officials, leaving him the alternative of having his own place ruined, and thus precipitating his quick departure for Matsue on their behalf. The demands of the farmers, to which they added the terse comment: "If you do not listen to our appeal, all the farmers in the district will rise up and attack the castle. This is important!" included the following:

1. They be freed from an increase in taxes.
2. They be allowed five years in which to pay back any borrowed money.
3. They be allowed a loan of ten *koku* on every 100 for food to be paid in five years.
4. The abuses of the villages be changed and help be given the starving.
5. The sale and manufacture of sake (Japanese rice wine) cease.
6. They be lent money for the purchase of livestock.

7. There be restrictions on payment of *yōmai,* or rice paid in lieu of wages.

Meanwhile a similar uprising had broken out in Iishi district, being joined by farmers from Nita district, making a total of at least 7000 participants. This group ruthlessly destroyed the property of a rich merchant in Mitoya village, who had profiteered on the change in the prices of rice. Bursting open some 1000 wine kegs in his storehouses, they drank profusely and left a pool of sake as deep as one's knees.

4. Samurai, Merchants, and Townsmen

❀ UNDER THE FEUDAL Tokugawa system, the essential role of the samurai changed from sword-bearing warrior to that of the bureaucrat based in a castle town or in the capital of Edo (today's Tokyo). During the 250-year *Pax Tokugawa,* the fierce civil wars of the Japanese Middle Ages gave way to peace. Under the new regime samurai found themselves in jobs that were largely unrelated to their military training. Yet the decline in usefulness of such martial skills could also lead to challenges of feudal authority. To forestall such threats and to reinforce the feudal structure, the shogunate placed heavy emphasis on the feudal class hierarchy. This strict ranking of classes in society, based on idealized Confucian values, thus served as the main rationale for the rule of the samurai class.

In the passages below Yazaki describes the samurai family as a reflection of feudal ideology. Absolute obedience to the male head of the household was maintained and then put forth as the ideal for other classes. Yazaki also outlines the feudal administrative machinery which governed cities and towns. City governments were headed by the *machi-bugyō,* magistrates who along with the village headman, the *nanushi,* represented the authority of the Tokugawa feudal government. The hierarchy of classes, propagation of the Confucian family ideal, and harsh governmental regulations all served to bolster Japanese feudalism as it was increasingly challenged in the eighteenth and nineteenth centuries.

YAZAKI TAKEO*
The Samurai Family and Feudal Ideology

Inasmuch as the basis of the stratified feudal structure was the military and political authority of the daimyō, it was absolutely essential that the common people be completely obedient to their masters. Relations were reciprocal only in the sense that gaining the master's favor was utterly dependent upon the unswerving loyalty of all subordinates. Individuals were bound within a family-type social system of stratification based on the specific status of each person. In all interpersonal relationships it was imperative to have all lines of authority firmly fixed.

Warriors were differentiated from all other peoples both by titles and by the sword-bearing privilege which symbolized their right to govern all classes of farmers, artisans, and merchants. If their authority was questioned or their honor insulted by any non-warrior, they were free to kill them on the spot, a custom known as *kirisutegomen.* Martial arts, *budō,* were promoted as the primary expression of the warriors' morality. Each warrior family had its own special norms to observe, according to its relative place in the hierarchy. Their authority was protected against threats from other classes by manifest and strict adherence to their own specific norms, and behavior permissible among the warriors was thus highly restricted.

The family system of the warrior class had developed in conjunction with the evolution of the feudal order. Hence, the regulations and laws of the *bakufu* and domains had strong implications for that family system. The basic thrust was focused in the family as a whole as the norm for all human relations within it. Under the overarching authority of the head of the family, each member had his designated place, according to sex and age. Every member was expected to live each day in such a way as to guarantee the continued existence of the family.

* Yazaki Takeo, *Social Change and the City in Japan* (Tokyo: Japan Publications, 1968), pp. 205–209, 230–233.

In this system the head of the household held absolute authority over every single component member, in much the same formalized way that a feudal lord governed his domain. Predominance over other members by the head of the family was symbolized by the places of authority of the father, husband, and eldest son. The wife, other sons, and all daughters were to obey the family head, such obedience constituting the highest moral code for their lives. This morality was articulated for the wife's role by Kaibara Ekken in his work "Great Learning for Women" (*"Onna daigaku,"* sometimes rendered "University for Women") as follows: "Approach your husband as you would heaven itself; for it is certain that, if you offend him, heaven's punishment will be yours." Not only was the eldest son heir to the family property, but men in general were treated more favorably than women throughout all society. According to the feudal code the propagation of the household always took precedence over the individual. Therefore, parental relations were accorded priority over marital ones, a priority reflected in the saying, "The womb is a thing borrowed [for begetting heirs]" (*hara wa karimono*).

Sons other than the eldest were regarded as impositions on the household. Some of them were offered for adoption to other families. A few were given employment by the master over the household if they possessed suitable talents. Given no such alternatives, lesser sons were forced to remain as life-long dependents (*heyazumi*) in the household of the eldest son, bothersome boarders who could not pay their own way.

Each household was a basic unit in the stratified social structure geared to status. Individuals as such were neglected. The character and worth of a particular household depended upon its relative place in the social stratification. Occupations were transmitted by inheritance just as faithfully as family property. Even a warrior's stipend, *karoku,* was a kind of household property for successive transmission to descendants. A family's honor was guarded with the same sort of concern for continuity. The tradition, precepts, and behavioral code of a family were nurtured for transmission to its heirs generation after generation. The ancestors of each family were enshrined in the household, serving to integrate all members into the larger family and giving final sanctification to the primacy of the total household over each individual member.

Marriage was not between individual persons but, rather, between households and, even then, within the limits defined by their status. There were official regulations fixing these limits. Marriages between warriors and nonwarriors, whether farmers, artisans, or merchants, were prohibited. Marriages between residents of different domains were prohibited. Regulations forbade the formation of power cliques through marriage arrangements. Marriage proposals had to be cleared with the proper authorities, and marital negotiations between two households had to be conducted by officials whose own status was commensurate with that of the families concerned. . . .

If sons or daughters exceeded the bounds of family precepts in love affairs, they were punished by the household head with scoldings or beatings. In extreme cases, they were disowned by the head of the family. Divorces resulted more often from dissatisfaction with a wife's deportment on the part of the husband's parents, than from initiatives taken by the husband himself. The wife's position in the home was exceedingly weak as she was forced to be subservient to her husband's entire household.

From youth the warriors were nurtured in the cultural forms and norms formalized in their special status and family system. They constituted the ruling elite of the feudal order and represented its power and authority before the common people. They were expected to lead exemplary lives. . . .

The neo-Confucianist philosophy known as *shushigaku,* based on the ideas of a medieval Chinese Confucian scholar, Chu Hsi, was authorized as the basic content of education in the *bakufu* and no other schools of thought were presented. One of the principles of *shushigaku* was that a person's fate and fortune were determined by the social conditions of his birth. No one could, nor should he try to, alter his inherited station in life, a notion uniquely tailored for the stabilization of authority in a feudal social order.

. . . The status strata motif of society resulted in many differences in living conditions of the warriors. This was evident in the style of houses, areas allowed for residential lots, and even the locations of residences, not to mention actual incomes and the different levels of culture enjoyed. If this was true within the warrior class, how much more pronounced were the differences between them and the lower classes of farmers, artisans, and merchants. Preservation of the varying social and cultural levels appropriate to each class, and to each grade within the classes, depended upon main-

tenance of the radical differences in political and economic power
that existed between the warriors and their inferiors. Only when
changes occurred in the economic structure did cracks appear in
the stratified edifice of status that so clearly separated the rulers
from the ruled.

. . . [I]t is necessary to explore further the reasons for the effective rule by so small a corps of leaders.

First of all, the thorough penetration of the feudalistic morality
into all layers of society must be underscored. Through its application to family life, to life in the neighborhoods and townships, and
to occupational structures, the people were domesticated so as to
follow the lead of the feudal authority. In Edo society one could
not observe any emerging freedom of the individual based on the
rising power of people from the bottom. There was lacking among
the people any strong critical spirit or thought pattern based on
respect for individual worth. The norms imposed by the ruling
class were accepted passively. Parallel to such conformity, and as
if to assist the process voluntarily, organizations were formed by
and among the citizens which facilitated the governing processes
imposed from above.

Under the overall supervision of the *machi-bugyō* of the central
government, the ranking townsmen were three elders (*machi-
doshiyori*) operating under the inherited family names of Taruya,
Naraya, and Kitamura. These men were superior to the elders of
particular towns. . . .

The elders were descended from former vassals of Tokugawa
Ieyasu who had good records of service and had been appointed
to office when Ieyasu set up his government in Edo. Endowed
with their own lands, their residences served also as their offices.
Their incomes ran from 550 *ryō* to 600 *ryō* per year, coming from
rents due on their lands but going into expenses incurred in the
fulfillment of their positions. Though townsmen, their status was
highly esteemed and they were permitted to wear swords. The fact
that they were granted audiences with the shōgun suggests the
character of their roles as semi-officials of the *bakufu*. . . .

Official notices relayed through the top three elders were posted
at the police lookouts in townspeople's communities. It was the
town head's [*nanushi*] responsibility to see that due attention was
given the notices. To restrict influx from rural areas the town

heads investigated any unfamiliar persons in their communities. To support the national government's intensified campaign to control public morality, the *nanushi* also checked on observance of obligations for loyalty and filial piety.

. . . Residents of a township could appeal to the *bakufu* if dissatisfied with decisions of the *nanushi,* but the appeal document had to have the official seal of the town head. Actually it was impossible for townsmen to avail themselves of this legal right. The *nanushi* became petty dictators among the citizens.

The *nanushi*'s office usually passed to his heirs by hereditary rights, though formal procedures of "recommendation" were enacted. The formula of recommendation remained through later ages. Whenever an heir was to succeed to office, and especially when a new town head was to be appointed, he was formally recommended by joint action of the landowners, *yanushi,* of the town, who were the effective bosses of local communities. Formal appointment was made by the *machi-bugyō* after receiving the recommendation of the *yanushi.* . . .

The *yanushi* were landowners of both lands and houses for rent in their towns but . . . hired bosses (*oya*) to handle concrete business details. The hired agents represented their employers in public rights and duties, which were neither few nor light. For instance, the landowner could be held liable if a criminal was found among residents in his houses. Therefore, the *yanushi* took extreme care in checking the background and behavior of their tenants, or *tanako.* The latter could do virtually nothing without first consulting the landlords. The relationship was a paternalistic one that was almost absolute. If a tenant had the misfortune to be under a tyrannical landlord, legally he had the right to petition the town head for dismissal of the landlord. But, as town heads (*machi-nanushi*) and *yanushi* worked hand in hand to maintain stability and security in their town, the tenants were quite helpless.

The organs of local government in Edo were designed to strengthen and sustain the hierarchical structures of complete obligation on the part of inferiors by organizations of mutual responsibility at every level. Controls over the warriors were strict. Even more so were the townsmen prevented from taking individual or group initiatives among themselves, as is common in modern times. The organizations of government tied the behavior of every class of citizens to the sufferance of immediate superiors, all the way to the very top of the warrior-dominated feudal order.

❀ PARTLY BECAUSE OF the extreme rigidity of the social structure, economic and social changes brought new challenges to the stability of the regime. The most prominent expression of these changes was visible in the merchant culture which sprang up in Edo in the wake of economic prosperity. The city scene produced novels, plays, and poetry which often posed attacks on feudal authority. Though such sentiments were usually expressed indirectly, they were indicative of the changes occurring.

An example of this boisterous and unrestrained cultural trend is *Shank's Mare* (1802), a rambunctious satirical tale of two supposed religious pilgrims traveling the Tōkaidō road, the main commercial highway from Edo to Kyoto made famous in woodblock prints. On their way to the temples of Kyoto, the heroes Yaji and Kita manage to insult both the warrior ethic and Buddhism. In the first two selections they mockingly imitate a samurai (a crime punishable by death) to wangle a cheap ferry passage across a river. Then they taunt a poor swordless samurai, who has only a piece of lath for a sword. These actions were equivalent in feudal values to stamping on a cross, but no less so than the antireligious behavior shown when Yaji and Kita have great fun at the expense of a Buddhist priest. Upon arriving in Kyoto, they go to a temple and begin mockingly chanting *"Namu Amida Butsu"*—the prayer supposed to gain salvation for the Buddhist faithful—until run off by annoyed priests. Finally, in a horrendous mistake, they eat the ashes of a Buddhist pilgrim's dead wife (he is taking them on a religious trip to the monasteries of Mount Kōya)—yet they are completely undisturbed by their sacrilegious actions. Among the lower classes such disregard for feudal and religious officialdom was widespread during the middle and late Tokugawa period.

W. G. BEASLEY*
Town Life and Tokugawa Culture

Town life in the Tokugawa period, especially that of Edo and Osaka, contributed a new element to Japanese culture. It was an element of noise and turbulence and color, quite unlike the restraint proper to a long-established aristocracy, and it derived from that part of the population which might be described as *nouveaux riches*, the great merchants and their households. To cater to their whims and those of their feudal overlords, there developed what contemporaries called *ukiyo,* the floating world: a world ... "of fugitive pleasures, of theaters and restaurants, wrestling-booths and houses of assignation, with their permanent population of actors, dancers, singers, story-tellers, jesters, courtesans, bath-girls and itinerant purveyors, among whom mingled the profligate sons of rich merchants, dissolute samurai and naughty apprentices." It was with this world that much of the period's art and literature were concerned. Color prints depicted actors and famous courtesans, as well as street scenes in busy commercial quarters. The theater, especially the puppet drama, found its themes in subjects which the townsmen loved: the clash between feudal loyalty and personal inclination—typical of Tokugawa Japan and popular because it took its audience into high society—or the fortunes, good and bad, of rich merchants and poor journeymen, of their mistresses and wives. Novels and short stories followed the same course. It was not a literature for the prudish, but it was bursting with life. By comparison, the verse and landscapes of the Chinese tradition seemed anemic and artificial.

* W. G. Beasley, *The Modern History of Japan* (New York: Praeger, 1963), p. 15.

JIPPENSHA IKKU*
Shank's Mare

Continuing their journey they came to the River Ōi and were met at Shimada by a ferryman.

"Do you gentlemen wish to cross the river?" he asked.

"Are you the ferryman?" said Yaji. "How much for the two of us?"

"The river has only been passable since this morning," said the man, "and it would be dangerous to carry you across. If you have a raft it will cost you eight hundred coppers for the two."

"That's an awful price," said Yaji. "We're not in Echigo or Niigata. Eight hundred's too much."

"Well, how much will you give?" asked the waterman.

"Never mind what we want to give," replied Yaji. "We can get over by ourselves."

"Well, the temple will only charge two hundred coppers for burying you if you're carried away by the current and drowned," said the waterman, "so it's cheaper that way. Ha-ha-ha!"

"Fool!" said Yaji. "I'll go and talk to your master. Look here, Kita," he added as they walked on, "it's a nuisance having to bargain with these men. Let's go and see the headman. Just lend me your dirk."

"Why?" asked Kita. "What are you going to do?"

"I'm going to become a samurai," said Yaji. He took Kita's dirk and put it in his girdle with his own, pulling down the scabbard so as to make it appear that he was wearing two swords, a long one and a short one.

"There," he said. "Don't I look like a samurai now? You carry the bundles and follow behind."

"Now we'll have some fun," said Kita. He took Yaji's bundle, tied it up with his own, and put them on his shoulder. Soon they came to the headman's office.

"Ah, are you the head ferryman?" asked Yaji, pretending to

* Ikku Jippensha, *Shank's Mare* (*Hizakurige*) (Tokyo and Rutland, Vt.: Charles Tuttle Co., 1960), pp. 98–100, 135–136, 261–263, 320–322.

speak like a samurai. "I'm on very important business for my lord. Just call your men to put me across."

"Certainly, your honor," said the headman. "How many are there in your suite?"

"Eh?" said Yaji. "My suite?"

"Yes. Is your honor traveling in a *kago* [palanquin] or on horseback? How many packloads of baggage have you?"

"There are three horses fully laden," said Yaji, "and fifteen horses with lighter loads, but as they impeded my progress I left them outside Edo. Instead I am traveling in a *kago* with eight tall fellows to carry it. Just take a note of that."

"Yes, your honor. And your attendants?"

"There are twelve of them," said Yaji, "besides spearmen, sandal-bearers, and those carrying my lacquered boxes and stilts— altogether, from the highest to the lowest, over thirty persons."

"Ay, ay!" said the headman. "But where are these attendants?"

"Well," said Yaji, "they were all with me when I set out from Edo, but they caught the measles at one time or another, so I had to leave them at different stages and there's only two of us to cross the river. How much will a raft be?"

"For the two of you a raft will be four hundred and eighty coppers," said the man.

"That's rather high," said Yajo. "Can't you reduce it a bit?"

"We don't make any reduction in our charges," said the man. "You'd better go on instead of standing there talking like a fool."

"Eh?" said Yaji. "How dare you address a samurai in that way?"

"Ha-ha-ha!" laughed the man. "A fine sort of samurai!"

"You insult a knight?" cried Yaji. "It is unpardonable."

"A fine knight you are," said the man. "Look at the tip of your sword."

Yaji turned round to look and saw that the tip of his sword had struck against a post, and as it was only the scabbard it had bent in two. Then everybody burst into laughter and Yaji was struck dumb with shame.

"Where did you ever hear of a samurai with a broken sword?" said the man. "You came here to deceive us, but we are not to be taken in."

"I'm a descendant of Minoya Shirōtoshi," said Yaji. "That's why I wear a broken sword."

"If we have any more of your insolence," said the headman, "we'll tie you up."

"It's no use, Yaji," said Kita. "You can't settle it that way. Let's go."

He took Yaji's hand and drew him away and they both sneaked off.

"Ha-ha-ha!" laughed the ferrymen. "What idiots they are!"

"I didn't make a hit that time," grumbled Yaji. "Botheration!"

Laughing, they hastened to the bank of the river, where they found the ferry crowded with people of all ranks. Amid the sound of many disputes they settled the price for the raft and started to cross. . . .

They started off again and by and by came to the town of Futagawa, where all the teahouse girls were in the street calling to the travelers to come in. "Come in and try our hot soup," they called. "Try our raw fish and sake."

Then a carrier who was standing by the corner of the teahouse called to the men who were carrying Yaji and Kita: "Hi, Hachibei, you'd better go home and look after your wife. There's bad goings on in your house."

"Fool," replied one of Yaji's carriers. "Don't you know your father's hung himself, you old dirt-eater? Ha-ha-ha!"

Yaji and Kita alighted in front of the *kago* house and walked on. A daimyō's train was taking a short rest at this stage, his palanquin being set down in front of the hostel and a number of samurai and retainers gathered round the entrance, while the contractors for carrying the baggage were hurrying about.

"Halloa, the master of the house wears two swords also," said Kita.

"You think everybody's the owner as long as they are wearing a *hakama*," said Yaji.

"Look at that *kago*," went on Kita. "Look how the cushions are piled up on it."

"Of course," replied Yaji. "Look at the persons who ride in them. They're all *fukusuke*. Ha-ha-ha! Look out, there's a horse."

"Hin-hin-hin!" whinnied the horse, and "Oh, oh, oh!" yelled Yaji. "What an awkward place to put a *kago*."

Hearing Yaji grumbling, a man who looked like some sort of upper retainer began to revile him. "What do you mean by treading on the *kago* with your muddy foot?" he demanded. "I'll knock your head off."

"Ha-ha-ha!" laughed Yaji. "You've got to do it first."

"What's that?" said the man. "Do you want me to cut you down?"

"Do you think your rusty sword would cut anything?" jeered Yaji.

"If you speak like that I must cut you down," said the man. "Here, Kakusuke, lend me your sword."

He began pulling at his companion's sword, but the man resisted. "If you want to cut anybody down," he said, "why don't you use your own sword?"

"Don't make such a fuss," replied the other. "What does it matter whose sword it is?"

"No, no," said Kakusuke. "You can't have mine."

"What a stingy chap you are," said the other. "Just let's have it for a moment."

"No, no," said Kakusuke. "What an obstinate fellow you are. You know the spearman Tsuchiemon took my real sword for the two hundred coppers I owed him."

"Oh, ah!" said the other. "I'd forgotten. Well," he added, turning to Yaji, "I'll forgive you this time. You can go."

"Go?" said Yaji, pushing up against him. "I shan't go. Why don't you cut me down?"

At this the retainers who stood round began to laugh and seemed too amused at the scene to think of interfering.

"Well, then, there's no help for it," said the retainer. He drew his sword, but as it proved to be only a piece of lath Yaji caught hold of him and threw him down, whereupon the fellow began to bawl loudly, "Murder! Murder! Help! Help!"

But the daimyō was now leaving his lodgings and the signal for the train to form was given. The quarrel thus ended, and fortunately Yaji was able to get away with Kita.

"Ha-ha-ha!" laughed Yaji. "That was a funny quarrel."

. . . Soon they came to the Kiyomizu temple, in the main hall of which stands the Eleven-Faced Thousand-Handed Kannon. Yaji and Kita rested here awhile and then wandered round the precincts till they came to where an old priest, standing by a table on an elevated piece of ground, was calling to the crowd of pilgrims.

"A picture of the holy Kannon of this temple may be obtained here," he cried. "Try its wonderful virtues. It makes the blind to talk and the dumb to hear. The cripples who have walked all the way here are able to walk all the way home again. Those who worship it just once, even though they are strong and healthy, enter Paradise immediately. The devout who desire salvation should not leave without receiving one of these pictures. Offerings may be made to any amount. Are there no believers here?"

"What a chattering old priest," said Kita. "By the way, Yaji, I've heard a story about people jumping off from this place."

"From ancient times," said the priest, "those who have made a vow to Buddha have jumped from here in perfect safety."

"They'd be smashed to pieces if they did," said Yaji.

"Do they ever do it now?" asked Kita.

"Yes," said the priest. "Even naturally timid people have been known to come and jump off here. There was a young girl jumped off here the other day."

"What happened to her?" asked Kita.

"She jumped and fell," said the priest.

"Yes, but what happened after she fell?" asked Kita.

"What an inquisitive person you are," said the priest. "Well, as she was full of sin, the Buddha, for punishment, made her turn up her eyes."

"Didn't her nose turn up too?" asked Kita.

"Well, she hadn't got any nose when she started," replied the priest.

"Did she lose her senses?" asked Kita.

"Yes, she became unconscious," answered the priest.

"And what happened then?" asked Kita.

"What a persistent fellow you are," said the priest. "What do you want to know all this for?"

"It's a bad habit of mine," said Kita. "I'm never satisfied till I hear everything to the end."

"Well, I'll tell you," said the priest. "When the girl got to the ground she went mad."

"Dear me," said Kita. "And what did she do then?"

"She began reciting the million prayers," said the priest.

"And what then?" asked Kita.

"She struck the bell."

"And what then?"

"*Namu Amida Butsu.*"

"And after that?"

"*Namu Amida Butsu.*"

"And what came next?"

"*Namu Amida Butsu.*"

"Yes, but what came after that?"

"*Namu Amida Butsu.*"

"Yes, yes, yes, but what came after the prayers?"

"Well, you must wait till she's finished. She's got to say it a million times."

"What?" cried Kita. "Have I got to wait till she's done reciting the prayer a million times? How awful!"

"Well, you said you liked to hear about everything to the end," said the priest, "so if you have patience you'll know. If you get tired of waiting you might help her say the prayers."

"Ah, that would be interesting," said Kita. "You help too, Yaji. *Namu Amida Butsu. Namu Amida Butsu.*"

"You must strike the bell too," said the priest. He struck the bell loudly while he recited the prayer. "*Namu Amida Butsu.*" (Chan-chan.) "*Namu Amida Butsu.*" (Chan-chan.)

"This is quite amusing," said Kita.

"Here, just hold the bell a minute. I've got to go somewhere," said the priest.

He thrust the bell into Kita's hand and went off. Kita took the bell and went on praying, "*Namu Amida Butsu. Namu Amida Butsu.*" (Chan-chan. Chiki-chan-chan. Chiki-chan-chan.)

"You don't strike the bell properly," said Yaji. "Give it here."

"What?" said Kita. "Don't I do it properly?"

He began striking the bell so loudly and making such a row that a priest came out of the temple and fell into a terrible passion when he saw what was going on.

"Here," he cried. "What are you doing at the holy shrine? Don't you know any better than to behave in that uncouth manner in a sacred place?"

"The priest in charge went away," said Kita, "so we thought we'd just keep things going."

"Don't make any of your silly jokes here," said the priest. "Where do you think you are?"

"This is Kiyomizu, Atsumori's place, ain't it?" said Kita.

"You must be mad," said the priest.

"Yes, that's why we're saying the million prayers," replied Kita.

"Nonsense," said the priest. "Go away at once. This is a holy place of prayer."

The priest got so angry and spoke in such a loud voice that many more priests came running out of the temple, and as they looked very threatening Yaji and Kita slunk down the hill.

"That comes of being too clever with the bell," said Kita.

It was now four o'clock, and the two thought they had better set off for Sanjō to look for an inn for the night. . . .

Laughing over the incident they tumbled into bed, and the Tamba man was soon fast asleep and snoring. The other two lay talking for some time longer. They could hear the sound of dogs barking in the fields at the back of the inn and the noise of someone splitting bamboo. Then the drum beat for the hour of midnight.

"What's that rustling sound, Yaji?" asked Kita, lifting his head.

"I couldn't sleep," said Yaji, "and I was tumbling about when I found this."

From the bedclothes he pulled out a small chip box.

"Why, isn't that the box the old chap brought out before?" said Kita. "The one with the sugar candy in it, I mean."

"Don't speak so loud," said Yaji. "It must have dropped out of his wicker basket. I've had my eye on it for a long time."

"Let's have a bit," suggested Kita.

"Wait a minute," said Yaji. The lantern was so far away he could not see very well, but he took the lid off and put some of the contents into his mouth. "It's hard," he said.

"Let's see," said Kita, snatching the box away. He also put some in his mouth and chewed it.

"Whatever is it?" he said. "It's like ashes."

"It's not sugar candy," said Yaji, "What a strong smell it has."

Then he began to feel rather sick and to retch, whereupon the Tamba man opened his eyes at the noise and jumped up astounded when he saw what they were doing.

"What are you doing?" he cried. "What are you eating my wife for?"

"What do you mean by your wife?" asked Yaji.

"What do I mean?" exclaimed the Tamba man. "It's sacrilege. That is my dear wife. Look on the lid of the box."

Yaji jumped up and went over to the lantern with the box.

There he saw written on the lid "Shūgetsu Myokwo Shinnyō."
"Then the box contains the ashes of your wife?" he asked.

"What? The ashes?" cried Kita. "This is dreadful. That's why I feel so queer."

"You may feel bad but I feel worse," said the man. "I'm carrying those remains from my village to Mount Kōya. It's desecration for you to eat it. You can't be real men. You must be devils or beasts. Whatever shall I do? Whatever shall I do?"

Here he hid his face in his sleeve and began to cry.

"What a terrible thing!" said Yaji, although he was secretly rather amused. "When you opened your wicker basket it fell out and got tumbled about without anybody knowing what it was. That was your fault. My fault was in mistaking it for sugar candy. So as there were faults on both sides there's nothing to quarrel about."

"No, no," cried the Tamba man. "Put it back as it was before. Put it back."

Thereupon he began to wail and cry again, till Kitahachi managed to soothe him with many excuses and he became appeased.

Then, the matter settled, they sank to sleep again, but not for long, for the dawn came to disturb them in their dreams, and the servant came from the kitchen to awaken them. . . .

☘ THE RISE of the merchants to a position of wealth and considerable influence led to the full flowering of the carefree, definitely unpuritanical culture typified for Westerners by woodblock prints and Kabuki drama. The "floating world" of Edo, a city with vast areas devoted to entertainment and pleasures, was the exact opposite of the samurai–Confucian ideal promoted by the government, and it was continually attacked by the authorities. The Tokugawa regime tirelessly issued decrees and promulgated "sumptuary regulations"—the edicts mentioned in Saikaku below, forbidding extravagance in food, dress, and expenditures generally—but to no avail. This flourishing culture was based in the growing commercial trade and was a reflection of the decline of feudalism.

The selections below by Ihara Saikaku, a famous novelist

and dramatist, well illustrate the dominant cultural tone in elegant and witty stories. "Ancient On-Account and Modern Cash-Down" shows samurai doing their best to keep up with fashion. One of the great modern industrial combines, Mitsui, makes its appearance here as the world's first department store, dealing in expensive tailor-made clothing on a cash-on-the-barrelhead basis. The message of "A Dose of What the Doctor Never Orders" is that to be poor is to be sick. A remedy, however, is prescribed: with cleverness and hard work anyone could become rich. In stories like these Saikaku expresses the distinctly unmartial tone of Edo's urban world of merchants and artisans.

IHARA SAIKAKU*
The Japanese Family Storehouse or the Millionaires' Gospel Modernized

ANCIENT ON-ACCOUNT AND MODERN CASH-DOWN

Ancient simplicity is gone. With the growth of pretense the people of today are satisfied with nothing but finery, with nothing but what is beyond their station or purse. You have only to look at the way our citizens' wives and daughters dress. They can hardly go further. To forget one's proper place is to invite the wrath of heaven. Even the august nobility are satisfied with clothes of nothing more splendid than Kyoto *habutae* silk, and in the military class the formal black dress of five crests is considered ill-suited to none, from minor retainers to the greatest daimyō. But of recent years, ever since some ingenious Kyoto creatures started the fashion, every variety of splendid material has been used for men's and women's clothes, and the drapers' sample books have blossomed in a riot of color. What with delicate *ukiyo* stencil patterns, multicolored "Imperial" designs, and dappled motifs in wash-

* Ihara Saikaku, *The Japanese Family Storehouse or the Millionaires' Gospel Modernised* (Cambridge, England: Cambridge University Press, 1959), pp. 26–29, 59–63.

graded tints, man must now seek in other worlds for an exotic effect, for every device on earth has been exhausted. Paying for his wife's wardrobe, or his daughter's wedding trousseau, has lightened the pocket of many a merchant, and blighted his hopes in business. A courtesan's daily parade of splendor is made in the cause of earning a living. Amateur beauties—when they are not blossom-viewing in spring, maple-viewing in autumn, or being married—can manage well enough without dressing in layers of conspicuous silks.

Not long ago, in a tailor's shop set back a little from Muromachi Street, and displaying on its curtains the crest of a fragrant citron, there was a craftsman who tailored stylish clothes with even more than the usual Kyoto dexterity. Such piles of silk materials and cotton wadding were deposited with him that he enjoyed a constant prospect of the "Mount of Clothes" without stirring a step from his shop. Though it was always a rush to remove the tacking stitches and apply the smoothing iron in time, each year on the first day of the fourth moon, in readiness for the season's "Change of Clothes"—even as the impatient cuckoo sounded its first notes in the skies above Mount Machikane—he had ready in his shop a fresh array of splendidly colored summer kimonos. Among them one might have seen garments of three distinct layers—scarlet crepe enclosed within translucent walls of delicate white silk—and garments with sleeves and neckpieces stiffened with padding. Such things had been unheard of in former days. One step further and we might have been wearing imported Chinese silks as working clothes. The recent clothing edicts were truly for the good of every one of us, in every province in the land; and, on second thought, we are grateful. A merchant wearing fine silks is an ugly sight. Homespun is not only more suited to his station, but he looks smarter in it.

With samurai, of course, for whom an imposing appearance is essential in the course of duty, it is not desirable that even the most servantless among them should dress like an ordinary person. In Edo, where peace reigns changeless as the pine, on foundations as firm as the ageless rocks of Tokiwa Bridge, drapers' establishments were recently opened in Honchō to cater for the great lords. They were branches of Kyoto firms, and proudly advertised their crests in all the "Guides to Trade." Managers and clerks, in single-minded devotion to duty, applied their united efforts to the task of securing orders from the various great mansions which favored them with patronage. Never relaxing for a moment from matters of business, they displayed eloquence and finesse, judgment and ingenuity. Expert in accountancy, and never deceived by a dubious coin, they would gouge the eyes from a living bull for profit. To pass beneath the Tiger Gate in the darkness of the night, to prowl a thousand miles in search of custom—such things they accepted as no more than necessary duties; and early next day, while the stars were still shining overhead, they would be hard at work in the shops, checking weights on the rods of their scales. From dawn till dusk they courted the favor of customers—but things were no longer as they used to be. The broad and fertile plain of Musashi was still there, but every inch of the ground had been exploited, and there were no easy pickings left. Formerly, on the occasion of a lord's wedding or a distribution of presents, it had been possible for the contractor—with the friendly cooperation of the lord's chamberlain—to do a little trade on satisfactory terms, but nowadays, with tenders invited from all sides, the expectation of profit was meager, and the incidental expenses more than balanced it. The true condition of these businesses was a sad story, and orders were supplied to the great households for prestige only. Not only that, but the greater part of the sales were on credit, and accounts remained unsettled year after year. Such money would have been more profitably invested even with a Kyoto banker. The shops were in constant difficulty over the shortage of ready cash to negotiate new bills of exchange, and as a result and also because it was unthinkable suddenly to close down businesses which had only just been opened, they were obliged to limit themselves to small-scale transactions only. But, do what they might, the accounts balanced no better, and before long the main shops in Kyoto were closed and only the Edo branches remained, with their losses running into hundreds and thousands of *kamme*. Each firm began devising methods of cutting expenses while the position was still retrievable. But other ways of trade existed, had they known.

In Suruga-chō—a name which brings back memories of the gleam of old *koban*—a man called Mitsui Kuroēmon, risking what capital he had in hand, erected a deep and lofty building of eighteen yards frontage and eighty yards depth, and opened a new shop. His policy was to sell everything for cash, without the inflated charges customary in credit sales. There were more than forty skilled clerks in his service, constantly under the master's watchful eye, and to each he assigned full charge of one type of cloth: one for gold brocades, one for Hino and Gunnai silks, one for *habutae,* one for damask, one for scarlets, one for hempen overskirts, one for woolen goods, and so on. Having divided the shop into departments in this manner, he willingly supplied anything which his customers asked for, however trifling—a scrap of velvet an inch square, a piece of imported damask suitable for the cover of an eyebrow tweezer, enough scarlet satin to make a spearhead flag, or a single detachable cuff of *ryūmon* silk. Whenever a samurai required a formal waistcoat for an immediate audience with his lord, or someone was in urgent need of a gown for a dress occasion, Kurōemon asked the messenger to wait, marshaled a score or so of the tailors on his staff, manufactured the garment on the spot, and delivered it immediately to the customer. By such means the business flourished, and the average daily sales were said to amount to one hundred and fifty *ryō*. The shop was a marvel of convenience to all. To look at, the master was no different from other men—he had the usual eyes, nose, hands, and feet—but in his aptitude for his trade a difference lay. He was the model of a great merchant.

Neatly folded in the alphabetically arranged drawers of his shop were all the materials of Japan and countries overseas, a varied selection of antique silks, Lady Chūjō's homespun mosquito net, Hitomaro's Akashi crepe, Amida's bib, a strip of Asahina's "flying-crane" kimono, the mattress which Daruma Taishi used for meditation, Rin Wasei's bonnet, and Sanjō Kokaji's sword sheaths. Absolutely nothing was missing. A firm with such well-filled stock books is indeed fortunate!

A Dose of What the Doctor Never Orders

For each of the four hundred and four bodily ailments celebrated physicians have produced infallible remedies, but the malady which brings the greatest distress to mankind—to even the wisest and cleverest of us—is the plague of poverty.

"Is there a treatment to cure this?" a poor man asked a gentleman of great wealth.

"My dear fellow," the rich man replied, "if you have lived till now without knowing such things, you have wasted precious years.

In matters of health the best time to take preventive measures is before you reach the wrong side of forty, and you have left this consultation until rather late. However, I observe certain factors which may yet pull you through—your custom of wearing deer-skin socks, for example, and bamboo clogs with thick leather soles. If that indicates your approach to life, we may even make a moderately rich man out of you. I have, it so happens, an excellent nostrum called 'The Millionaire Pill,' and I shall give you the prescription:

Early rising	5 parts
The family trade	20 parts
Work after hours	8 parts
Economy	10 parts
Sound health	7 parts

Grind the ingredients thoroughly, use common sense to get the proportions correct, mix carefully, swallow, and inwardly digest twice daily—and there is no reason why you should not become a millionaire. However, during treatment it is imperative to abstain from certain noxious things:

(1) Expensive foods, expensive women, silken suits for day-to-day wear.

(2) Private palanquins for wives; private lessons in music or poemcards for eligible daughters.

(3) A professor of percussion for the sons of the house.

(4) Kickball, miniature archery, perfume appreciation, and poetry gatherings.

(5) A craze for the tea ceremony, and for remodeling the best rooms on tea principles.

(6) Flower-viewing, boating excursions, baths in the middle of the day.

(7) Evenings out with friends, gambling parties, playing *go* or backgammon.

(8) Classes for townsmen in sword-drawing and dueling.

(9) Temple-going, and preoccupation with the next world.

(10) Getting involved in others' troubles, and standing surety.

(11) Lawsuits over reclaimed land, and meddling in new mining projects.

(12) Sake with supper, excessive pipe-smoking, unnecessary journeys to Kyoto.

(13) Backing sumō contests for charity, and giving too generously to temple funds.

(14) Carving knickknacks during business hours, and collecting fancy sword accessories.

(15) Familiarity with Kabuki actors, and with brothel quarters.

(16) Borrowing money at a monthly rate of more than eight in
the thousand *momme*.

"All these things are more deadly than blister-fly drugs or
arsenic. I need hardly say, of course, that to taste any one of them
is fatal—but the very idea of them must never enter your head."

He bent close to his questioner's ear—a little ear, full of the
promise of poverty—and the man listened enraptured, accepting
every word as a drop of pure gold. He resolved to follow this
wealthy person's advice, and to work unremittingly from morn till
night.

But this was Edo, unfortunately, where the competition would
be stiff in whatever trade he chose. He would do well to select
some line of business which was a little out of the ordinary. With
this in mind, seeking inspiration, he stood for one whole day, from
early dawn, at the southern end of Nihon Bridge. Truly, this was
the place where all the provinces of Japan rubbed shoulders. The
bridge was a mountain which moved, and no crowds at the Gion
festival in Kyoto, nor at Osaka's Temma carnival, were ever more
tightly packed. Day after day brought new prosperity to Edo, and
age after age the power of its lord and the breadth of its highways
grew. But even this great road of Tōri-chō, recently widened to
twenty-four yards from side to side, was already too narrow. On
the bridge itself, at any moment of the day he might have counted
at least one horseman, one priest, and one halberdier. But no one
dropped anything of value, and, screw his eyes though he might, he
could not detect a single *zeni*. Reflecting on this, he came to appreciate the true value of the coin: it was not a thing to be lightly
spent.

"The only way is to try luck at a trade," he told himself. "But if
you start with empty hands these days—unless you're a wrestling
instructor or a midwife—there's no hope of making money. I've
never heard of a *koban* nor even a *zeni* sprouting from seedless
soil. Can there be no way of making something out of nothing, I
wonder?"

He was still looking about him and racking his brains when, back from the day's work at the various daimyō mansions, walking in their separate groups—now two hundred, now three hundred strong—came a procession of carpenters and roof thatchers, chattering loudly and discordantly, sidelocks falling over ears, heads comically disheveled, kimonos dirty at the collar, waistbands tied outside their coats, sleeves frayed at the cuff. Some brandished two-yard measures as walking sticks. Most walked with hands in pockets and shoulders hunched. He needed no signboard to tell him their employment. Behind them they had apprentice boys to carry shavings and wood-ends, but if precious scraps of cypress were dropped and wasted, no one bothered. It must indeed be the castle-town of castle-towns, he thought, where even workmen are as liberal as daimyō. Keeping his eyes about him and picking up the dropped pieces one by one, he followed along from the Suruga-chō crossroads to Sujikai Bridge in Kanda, and in that distance collected as much as he could safely carry in one load across his shoulders. He sold the pieces just as they were, and made a clear profit of two hundred and fifty *zeni*. It irked him to think that he had overlooked till now opportunities which lay at his very feet, and every day thereafter, waiting impatiently for nightfall, he kept a lookout for the homeward-bound carpenters and picked up whatever they left in their wake. His catch was never less than five full loads. On days when it was too wet to do anything else he carved the wood scraps into chopsticks, and then sold them wholesale to the grocers' stores in Suda-chō and Setomono-chō. He became famous along Kamakura bank as Chopstick Jimbei, and gradually acquired a considerable fortune. Later, when the scraps in which he dealt had grown to trees, he bought a large mansion in Timber Merchants' block, where he employed more than thirty clerks alone, and he bought up forest land no less extensive than the holdings of Kawamura, Kashiwagi, or Fushimiya. Next—his ambition boundless as the ocean, his fortune's sails set square to the winds of trade—he stocked his timber yard with tall ships' masts, and sold them all at prices merchants dream about. In a mere forty years he made a hundred thousand *ryō*. All this was the result of taking millionaire pills in his younger days.

Now that he was well past his seventieth year he judged that a little relaxation of the treatment would do no harm, and for the first time in his life he changed into a complete outfit of Hida

homespun silk, and even cultivated a taste for the marine deli-
cacies of Shiba. On his way back from regular morning worship at
the Nishi Honganji temple in Tsukiji he dropped in at theaters in
Kobiki-chō, and in the evenings he played go at home with groups
of friends. While snow fell outside he held social gatherings to
mark the opening of the winter's first tea jars, and as soon as the
early daffodils were in bloom he set out tasteful flower arrangements in the impressionist manner. Exactly when he had learned
all these refinements is not clear—but money makes everything
possible.

There are people who draw no distinction between the beginning
and the end, and who remain close-fisted all their lives; but Jimbei,
who knew that even if he saved a Mount Fuji of silver his body was
nevertheless destined to be smoke above Hashiba and dust on
Musashi plain, had wisely set aside a portion for his declining
days, and with this he thoroughly enjoyed himself. When he
reached eighty-eight all who knew of his good fortune begged him
to cut them lucky bamboo rice-levels and to choose names for
their new-born children. At last, weary of the ways of men, craving
no further earthly honors, he died as a saint might die, in a spiritual
state conducive to the immediate attainment of Nirvana, and
people felt all the more admiration and envy at the thought that he
might fare no worse in the next world than in this.

The golden rule for men is to save in youth and spend in old
age. It is impossible to take your money to heaven, and it is
essential to have it on earth.

❀ WHILE THE CLOSE of the Tokugawa era saw the impoverishment of much of the samurai class, as merchants grew
steadily richer, the lot of ordinary city dwellers remained
largely unchanged. Like their counterparts in the countryside,
the poor residents of Edo and other cities were strongly affected
by changes in the prices of foodstuffs, by natural disasters, and
by higher taxes. In a number of major riots, described below by
Yazaki, city residents rose against the feudal government and
the rich merchants, expressing their anger by attacking ware-
houses and shops. Such rebellions came to be a characteristic

feature of the late Tokugawa and were viewed by some at the time as a clear sign of moral decay in the feudal scheme.

YAZAKI TAKEO*
Riots in the Cities

The discontent caused by poverty and social discrimination smoldered until it finally came to a head. Antagonism focused primarily on the constantly increasing tax burdens. Action on the part of the poor was precipitated, though, when rice prices skyrocketed because of poor crops. Riots broke out in which the poor attacked the homes of rich merchants favored by *bakufu* officials. Houses of the wealthy were destroyed, and their possessions, rice and other goods, were stolen. The rioters had at last chosen to press their political demands upon the officials by force. In the beginning there existed some antagonism between farmers and townsmen. These differences were later resolved and they were able to stand together in organized resistance against the government and upper-class citizens. A few riots provoked others on a larger scale, and they became increasingly political in character. The ruling class was forced to retreat and make concessions to the enraged citizens. The influence of the general populace gained strength and signaled the approaching downfall of feudal power and authority.

... [T]here occurred over two hundred riots in the cities between the end of the eighteenth-century and the fall of the Tokugawa *bakufu*. There were only ten riots in the first half of the eighteenth century, concentrated in the Kyōhō era (1716–1736). When a famine in the Temmei era (1781–1789) drove the price of rice sky-high, more than sixty riots erupted throughout the country. Similar conditions provoked a similar number of riots in the first half of the nineteenth century. During the Tempō era (1830–1844) over forty-five urban uprisings followed sharp rises in rice prices due to successive years of crop failures. Some thirty-five riots were mounted in the last twenty years of the *bakufu*'s exis-

* Yazaki Takeo, *Social Change and the City in Japan* (Tokyo: Japan Publications, 1968), pp. 258–259, 262–264.

tence, half of them occurring in a single three-year period of desperation over tax and rice price advances.

... Social unrest and rioting occurred frequently in Osaka. Considerable confusion in 1755, and riots in 1782, 1787, and 1789, followed upon the heels of sudden rises in rice prices. Poor crops precipitated further rioting in 1833, 1834, and 1836. The most serious uprising in Osaka was one in 1837 centering in the leadership of a former police guard named Ōshio Heihachirō. Its significance lay in exposing clearly the defects in the administrative system of the Tokugawa *bakufu.*

Ōshio had served in the east office of the Osaka town commissioner. He was learned in literature and skilled in martial arts, as well as a recognized scholar of the Wang Yang-ming (*Ōyōmei* in Japanese) school of Confucian philosophy. The commissioner and police often sought his opinion on many things concerning Osaka affairs, both public and private. Ōshio became quite sensitive to the poverty that increasingly plagued the lives of the poorer classes in Osaka and submitted a recommendation to the commissioner's office that the rice reserves of the government be used to alleviate the people's sufferings. The commissioner turned down this plea.

The wealthy merchants could not be persuaded to give succor; their concern for huge profits for themselves was their reason for buying up rice, thereby aggravating price increases. Ōshio took things in his own hands and sold his own books, distributing the proceeds to 10,000 people. He then penned and distributed among the people a declaration accusing the town commissioner of irresponsible, selfish deeds against the people. The declaration also decried the guilt of rich men who looked only to their own interests at the expense and sacrifice of countless poor people. After proclaiming publicly the guilt of social and governmental elite alike, he laid a plan to instigate a rebellion and set about rounding up firearms and ammunition.

Before Ōshio could get his uprising under way, one of his comrades lost heart and informed the town commissioner. Ōshio was forced to begin his attack on the troops of the *bakufu* without adequate preparation. His forces included three hundred low-class warriors and farmers of means from Osaka's suburban areas. They attacked Tōshōgu and Temma shrines with guns. Kōnoikeya, Tennōjiya, Hiranoya, and Masuya were set aflame with *hiyahō* (guns shooting flaming arrows) and *rokudama* (primitive hand grenades). Gold and silver coins were looted from the merchants' shops for distribution among poor people. Fires were set in many places throughout Osaka. The rebellious troops drew close to the castle of Osaka.

The troops of the *bakufu,* under the town commissioner's command, were poorly trained for actual fighting. It took them quite some time to put down the rioters. When defeat finally came, Ōshio committed suicide together with his own son. All those who had participated in the rebellion were severely punished.

How broad Ōshio's actual base of support among the citizens was is not altogether clear. It is certain, though, that he represented a wide feeling of complaint and unrest. The attempted revolt lasted only for a day. But it pinpointed accurately the injustices of administration and the greedy extravagance of the wealthy. It also dealt a heavy blow to the *bakufu* by demonstrating the weakness of the government for all to see in the major commercial city of the age.

5. The Discovery of the West and the Meiji Restoration

⚙ As CONTRADICTIONS IN feudalism deepened in the 1840s and 1850s, threats also appeared for the first time from abroad. Western ships were sighted off Japan's coast regularly, and it quickly became apparent that the *bakufu* did not have the military strength to prevent the imperialist powers from gaining a foothold in Japan as they had elsewhere in Asia. The seriousness of the foreign threat was soon illustrated by the gradual subjugation of neighboring China, first through trade concessions and finally by virtual occupation by foreigners. In both of these brief selections, the example of China is foremost. Takasugi Shinsaku (1839–1867), a samurai from the Chōshū domain, traveled on a Japanese mission to Shanghai in 1862 and recorded these impressions in his diary. They show a high consciousness of the effects of imperialism in China, also illustrated in a letter from samurai Maki Izumi to his wife.

TAKASUGI SHINSAKU*
Yūshu Niroku (*Shanghai Diary*)†

May 7. From the land, the sounds of rifles have come echoing and tearing through the dawn sky across which the day has not broken yet. According to everyone I have talked with, this must be the

---

* In Naramoto Tatsuya, *Takasugi Shinsaku* (Tokyo: Chūō Kōronsha, 1965).
† Translated by Tomoko Moore.

sounds of the rifles with which the Imperial Army and the Taiping rebels are fighting. If they are right, I will be able to see the real fight. I could not hide my excitement. . . . I heard that the place where our ship is anchored is called Shinko. The width of the river has become very narrow and the distance between the banks is only a few *chō*. Muddy water is swiftly flowing. According to a British sailor, the few thousand ships which have been anchored here and the Chinese who live on the land are all using this muddy water as their drinking water. Near dusk, a small ship passed by our ship flying a flag which said "munitional duty." The flurry of the war made me restless. . . .

May 21. During the morning, I walked around an antique shop and saw some paintings. I have come to think about the city, Shanghai, all day long today. Here most of the Chinese have become the servants of foreigners. When English and French people come walking, the Chinese give way to them stealthily. Although the main power here is Chinese, it really is nothing but a colony of England and France. Peking is said to be 300 *ri* [1. *ri* = 2.44 miles] away from here—the traditional China of the past must remain there. I really hope that is so. I wonder, what would those Chinese think of if they saw this city? However, turning to the situation in our country and thinking of the case of Japan, we'll have been forewarned—who can be sure the same fate will not visit our country in the future? . . .

May 23. In the morning, I visited the English missionary (Muirhead) with Godai. The missionary has come to Shanghai to propagate the Christian religion. The place where he lives serves both as a church and as a hospital. I heard it is called Shii-in. When Europeans propagate their religion in foreign countries, they always bring a physician with them. At the Shii-in they help to cure people who are down with sickness and then convert them to Christianity. We will have to be prepared for such things too in Japan.

*MAKI IZUMI**
Bakumatsu Shishi no Tegami (*Letters from a Patriot in the Last Days of the Shogunate*)†

The foreigners have been planning and plotting various things for some years. But the government officials in the east (Tokyo) do not like to fight, and they are doing only what the foreigners want. So the Imperial Court has gotten mad at them and has often ordered them to send the foreigners away and not let them in as in the past. Despite this, however, they have been managing things badly, and this is why such an incident as *"Sakurada Mongai no Hen"* of March last year happened.

However, the Westerners, while things are going their own way, have asked the government favors, such as to build barriers in Osaka, Sakai, and Hyōgo. I understand that it has gotten to the point that they are ready to start construction in August of next year. If this comes through like they say, I think Japan will be divided in two, the eastern part and the western part, and the Imperial Court will be pushed under their foot.

As you know, I have concerned myself with the emperor at the sacrifice of my life since childhood. This is why I have come to think the situation right now is dangerous, and in any case I can not idle the time away. People know my spirit and beliefs. And there are even some people who are from Satsuma, Chikuzen, and Hizen who have heard about me and have come to ask various things.

You should not worry about it. If this country is taken over by the foreigners, there will be no use in living and no other way for my whole family than to die.

It was not very long ago, about twenty years ago in China during the *Ahen Sensō* [the Opium War], that England started to take over and did various things to humiliate the women. In August last year, they finally took over China.

* Maki Izumi, letter, in Naramoto Tatsuya, ed., *Bakumatsu Shishi no Tegami* (Tokyo: Chūō Kōronsha, 1969), pp. 106, 115.
† Translated by Tomoko Moore.

Though Japan is a warriors' country, it is a small country and the situation has become quite dangerous. From now on we have to steady ourselves, and women too have to be prepared.

After you finish reading this letter, please burn it and throw it away immediately.

❀ THE FEUDAL GOVERNMENT remained unable to deal with the recurring economic crises and with the Western military threat as both problems grew in importance. By the 1860s, the clear need for some response to the West encouraged plots and antifeudal military groups in some of the more isolated domains of western Japan. There had been experimentation in two of these areas, Chōshū and Satsuma, in Western military technology, and small groups of samurai within these domains began equipping local military forces along Western lines. Led by younger men and by rōnin (masterless samurai), they organized militias composed partly of peasants and outcasts and trained them in Western methods and with Western arms. Such peasant armies (*nōhei*) later helped defeat the old-fashioned armies of the feudal regime.

One pioneer in adopting Western military techniques was Takasugi Shinsaku, whose career is described by E. H. Norman, a Canadian diplomat and an accomplished scholar of modern Japanese history. The most important social fact of the new armies was the recruitment of peasants—a direct contradiction of feudal codes which decreed that only samurai could bear arms. The changeover to a Western-style military, whose effectiveness had already been proved, was a logical step in Japan's emergence from feudalism.

E. H. NORMAN*
The Kiheitai of Chōshū

Our last and most interesting example of clan *nōhei* is the case of the *kiheitai* of Chōshū. As the *bakufu* entered its last decade of rule, the men of Chōshū, most aggressive and hostile to the *bakufu* of all clans, were engaged in intrigues, plots, and violent *émeutes* directed against the *bakufu*. The leaders in the anti-*bakufu* movement were rōnin and the lower samurai, restless and impoverished men whose feverish activity in Kyoto culminated in the bloody street fighting of 1865, after which the *bakufu* secured an Imperial decree outlawing them from the capital and compelling their lord to retire in disgrace, and to live for a year or more under voluntary house arrest.

Before this, however, there had been brewing within Chōshū itself a crisis in clan politics between a radical party of younger samurai and the dominant clique of older clan bureaucrats. These conservative clan counselors, more compromising in their policy toward the *bakufu*, were purged in a *coup de main* in which several of them were assassinated, and the radical party of younger officials then dominated the clan government. The elder lord of Chōshū, Mori Takachika, realizing that the growing intransigence of his clan would soon draw down upon it the armed wrath of the *bakufu*, decided to entrust the reorganization of his army to the younger, more daring and imaginative samurai. To this end he summoned the brilliant strategist Takasugi Shinsaku, then only twenty-five years of age. This Chōshū samurai had studied under Japanese masters of Dutch learning at Edo and acquired a considerable knowledge of gunnery and Western military science. Like other younger Chōshū samurai, he was a violent partisan of the *sonnō jōi* movement. (Literally, "revere the emperor, expel the barbarian." It was under this slogan that the anti-Tokugawa movement outmaneuvered and finally overthrew the *bakufu*.) Takasugi's interview with his lord took place on June 6, 1863, and

* E. H. Norman, *Soldier and Peasant in Japan* (New York: International Secretariat, Institute of Pacific Relations, 1943), pp. 27–30, 32–35.

he secured virtually a free hand from Mori in order to reform the clan army. His views as recorded in one of the clan histories were very radical; he did not hide his contempt for the samurai of his day. His actual words were: "The stipendiary samurai have become soft and indolent through years of peace and idleness. Their martial prowess has been dulled, and to reinvigorate an army one must recruit volunteers with spirit, courage, and skill regardless of their class, whether they be samurai, peasant or artisan." . . .

With his lord's permission, Takasugi at once set on foot the creation of a band of troops called the *kiheitai* (literally, "surprise troops") who were allowed to enlist regardless of social status. . . . In his first order of the day, Takasugi set forth his plans for the *kiheitai*. He stated that volunteers would be accepted only if they were brave and had initiative and without regard as to whether they were rear-vassals (*baishin*) or clan samurai. In accord with the saying that even the most humble person cannot be deprived of his ambition, there would be no discrimination against persons of lowly origin. The only qualifications were skill, daring, and obedience to the commander who would punish and reward each man according to his merits. Both Japanese and Western arms would be used in fighting but special opportunity for acquiring familiarity with Western arms would be given. A historical analogy that comes to mind both in the sobriety and the strict discipline of the leader, together with his daring experiments in military matters, is Cromwell. Takasugi's words quoted above are almost an echo of Cromwell's: "I had rather have a plain russet-coated captain that knows what he fights for and loves what he knows, than that which you call 'a gentleman' and is nothing else."

. . . Chōshū was perhaps the most intransigently anti-*bakufu* clan; its *kiheitai* not unexpectedly was antifeudal insofar as it recognized the need of freeing peasants from the feudal yoke and utilizing their released energies in the anti-*bakufu* struggle. Thus the *kiheitai* represents a kind of peasant revolt controlled *from above* and directed against the *bakufu;* history has recorded how formidable a weapon was this small but intrepid army. A contemporary chronicler writing as a *bakufu* partisan admits the strength of this army. "The rebels of Bocho [*i.e.* Chōshū] are truly most skilled in the use of Western arms; from reports received it seems scarcely credible [literally, "human"] the way they advance and retreat along mountains and precipices; indeed theirs is a formidable power. But when the allied clans [*i.e.* the *bakufu* and its allies] attack, they use old-fashioned types of gun, notably the matchlock [*hinawaju*]. In this way from the very start the rebels gain the advantage and the attacking side shows its weakness, and for this reason the *bakufu* infantry must ever be going to the aid of the allied troops."

In a letter from Matsudaira, Lord of Hōki (one of the clans allied to the Tokugawa), written in July 1865 to two officials of the *bakufu,* Itakura and Inaba, the writer describes the preparations being made by the *bakufu* for its punitive expedition against Chōshū; the levies and demands made of clans allied to the *bakufu;* the half-hearted and indifferent response with which these requests were met; the antiquated weapons used by the *bakufu;* the use by the Chōshū *nōhei* of the most up-to-date rifle, the Minie, which was even supplied to outcasts (*eta*) who fought with the Chōshū irregulars with the result that the *bakufu* troops were continually routed. . . .

Although the rank and file of the *kiheitai* were comparatively raw troops in years of service compared to the Tokugawa armies, they constantly outfought the Tokugawa soldiers, displaying far greater skill particularly in their use of Western arms. We might cite a Western journalist, then living in Japan, on the superiority of these Chōshū troops. "One circumstance that always appears to me worthy of notice with regard to Satsuma and Chōshū is that both of them practically acknowledged the superiority of foreign appliances in war, by obtaining rifles and ammunition, and largely arming their men with them, adopting, at the same time as far as they could, foreign drill and discipline. But in the fight with Chōshū that was about to take place, many of the samurai [*i.e.,* of the Tokugawa Army] to whom rifles were offered refused to use them, or to undergo the new drill, preferring to trust to the old bows and arrows, the trusty sword, and the tactics of Old Japan."

. . . More than this, the *kiheitai* was led by men of the highest talent, certainly among the best brains in the country. . . . Ōmura Masujirō deserves perhaps more than any other one man the title of founder of the modern Japanese army. He studied Dutch under the famous scholar Obata Kōan, knew and admired von Siebold, acted as guardian and teacher of the latter's daughter, Ine. He studied English from an American in Shinagawa. He read widely in science, including medicine, economics, and foreign studies; in 1864 he translated from the Dutch a work on strategy written from the standpoint of German military theory which was then under the spell of Napoleonic influence. It is thus of some interest that, in the final campaign against the *bakufu,* the *kiheitai* under Ōmura and his companions made use of contemporary European military strategy. A man of strong character, Ōmura had come to entertain such disgust at the cramped military system of feudalism that a story is told of his refusing to talk to a close companion at arms who offended him by wearing his long samurai sword during a conference. . . . With his ideas of sweeping social reforms as a prerequisite for a national army, and particularly with his plan for general conscription which struck at the very citadel of samurai privilege, Ōmura roused the fierce resentment of the clan reactionaries. He was assassinated in 1869 when, as Vice-Minister of War, he had begun to enforce the first steps toward the goal of general conscription, and the modernization of the Japanese army, leaving behind him a group of disciples such as Yamagata Aritomo, Yamada Kenji, and Kido Kōin, who lived on to complete his work.

❀ THE MEIJI "restoration" of 1868, a political *coup d'état* carried out in the name of the emperor, was a watershed in Japanese history. Led by young samurai revolting against the backwardness of the Tokugawa regime and its inability to meet the imperialist Western threat, the restoration rapidly proceeded to destroy much of the old feudal society and then to build a thoroughly revamped modern structure on the old foundations. Japanese feudalism was carefully dismantled by a group of men who were themselves of samurai rank. It is this anomaly—of a class destroying its privileges—that T. C. Smith seeks to explain below.

T. C. SMITH*
Japan's Aristocratic Revolution

Japan's warrior class, a feudal aristocracy though it differed from European aristocracies in crucial respects, did not merely surrender its privileges. It abolished them. There was no democratic revolution in Japan because none was necessary: the aristocracy itself was revolutionary.

Consider the bare outlines of the case. Until 1868, Japan was ruled by a class of knights who alone had the right to hold public office and bear arms and whose cultural superiority the rest of the population acknowledged. A party within this aristocracy of the sword (and swagger) took power in 1868 and embarked on a series of extraordinary reforms. Where there had before been little more than a league of great nobles, they created an immensely powerful central government: they abolished all estate distinctions, doing away with warrior privileges and throwing office open to anyone with the education and ability to hold it; they instituted a system of compulsory military service, although commoners had previously been forbidden on pain of death to possess arms; they established a system of universal public education; and much else. The result was a generation of sweeping and breathless change such as history had rarely seen until this century. I believe, though of course I cannot prove, that these decades brought greater changes to Japan than did the Great Revolution of 1789 to France.

Why was the Japanese aristocracy—or part of it—revolutionary? Why did it abandon the shelter of its historic privileges for the rigors of free competition, which, incidentally, many warriors did not survive? . . . I wish to discuss three such ways that any satisfactory explanation of the aristocratic revolution, as I will call it, would have to take into account. One has to do with the relations of the warrior to the merchant class; another with social and

* T. C. Smith, "Japan's Aristocratic Revolution," *Yale Review,* L:3, (Spring 1961), pp. 370–373, 375–383.

economic distinctions within the warrior class; and the third with the relations of the warrior class to land and political power.

My earlier statement that there was no democratic revolution in Japan because the aristocracy was revolutionary has an important corollary: had there been a democratic revolution, the aristocracy would not have been revolutionary. Nothing unites an aristocracy so quickly and firmly in defense of its privileges as an attack from below, by classes in which it can perceive neither distinction nor virtue.

Unlike the Western bourgeoisie, townsmen in Japan never challenged aristocratic privileges, either in practice or theory. They were seemingly content with a secondary political role, finding apparent satisfaction in money-making, family life, and the delights of a racy and exuberant city culture. This political passivity is puzzling. It is not to be explained by numerical weakness (Tokyo was a city of a million people in the late eighteenth century, and Osaka was only slightly smaller); nor by poverty, nor illiteracy, nor political innocence. Least of all is it to be understood as reflecting an absence of resentment at the warriors' smug and strutting pretensions. There was resentment aplenty and there were many instances of private revenge; but for some reason resentment never reached the pitch of ideology, never raised petty private hurts to a great principle of struggle between right and wrong. For whatever reasons, townsmen acknowledged the political primacy of the warrior, leaving him free to experiment without fear that to change anything would endanger everything.

But, one may suppose, no ruling group ever launches on a career of radical reform merely because it is free to do so; there must be positive incentives as well. In the Japanese case these incentives were in part born of differences within the aristocracy. Such differences were not unique to Japan, of course, but they can rarely have been more pronounced anywhere.

On the one hand were a few thousand families of superior lineage and very large income, with imposing retinues and magnificent houses, who in practice, though not in law, monopolized the important offices of government; some offices in effect became hereditary. On the other hand was the bulk of the warrior class, numbering several hundred thousand families, who were cut off from high office and lived on very modest incomes; many in real poverty, pawning their armor and family heirlooms, doing industrial piecework at home to eke out small stipends, and resorting to such pitiful tricks as sewing strips of white cloth to the undersides of their collars so people might take them to be wearing proper undergarments. As warrior mothers proudly taught their children, a samurai might have an empty belly but he used a toothpick all the same.

But it was not so much the contrast between his own and the style of life of his superior that moved the ordinary warrior to fury. It was, rather, the impropriety of the merchant's wealth. Surely it was a perversion of social justice, that the warrior, who gave his life to public service, should live in want and squalor, while men who devoted themselves to money-making lived in ease and elegance, treated him with condescension and even rudeness, and in the end not infrequently found favor with the lord.

The merchant himself was not to blame since he merely followed his nature. Though he was feared and hated for that, ultimate responsibility lay with the effeminate high aristocrats who, through idleness or incompetence, failed to use their inherited power for the proper ends of government. No secret was made of the failure, either. Political writings were full of charges of the incompetence and corruption of government, of the fecklessness and indifference of princes; and the only remedy, it was said, lay in giving power to new men—men of lower rank, who were close to the people and whose characters had been formed by hardship. This was no revolutionary doctrine. It called for a change of men, not institutions; but the men it helped to power were in fact radical innovators.

This brings me to the final difference—or rather to two differences—between the Japanese warrior class and European aristocrats. Japanese warriors did not own land, and their political power was to a greater extent bureaucratic. . . .

The warriors who manned the bureaucracy exercised far more power over the rest of the population than warriors ever had before; but it was a new kind of power. Formerly power was personal and territorial: it pertained to a piece of land and belonged to a man as inherited right. Now it was impersonal and bureaucratic: it pertained to a specialized office to which one must be appointed and from which he might be removed.

There is unmistakable evidence of the increasingly bureaucratic nature of power in the more and more impersonal criteria for selecting officials. However writers on government might differ on other matters, by the late eighteenth century they were in astonishingly unanimous agreement that ability and specialized knowledge should take precedence over lineage and family rank in the appointment and promotion of officials. To this end they devised tests for office, job descriptions, fitness reports, official allowances, salary schedules, and pensions.

It was only in the lower ranks of officials that the ideal of impersonality came close to realization. Nevertheless, men of low rank were sometimes promoted to high office; merchants and occasionally even peasants with specialized qualifications were ennobled that they might hold office; and promotion in the bureaucracy became for warriors an important means of improving status. If the highest offices usually went to certain well-placed families, this was looked on as an abuse rather than proper recognition of rank, and an abuse that struck at the very foundations of good government. Moreover, many families of high rank were without office, and office rather than rank or wealth gave power.

Thus a group of young samurai who met on the morrow of Perry's first alarming visit to Japan, to consider what they might do for their country, were exhorted by their leader to do what they could *even though none held office*. One cried out: "But what *can* we do without office!" No one, it seems, complained of the lack of age, wealth, or high rank in the group.

. . . The relationship between vassal and lord was slowly, silently, and profoundly transformed. It had been an intimate, intensely emotional relationship, based in no small part on the personal qualities of the lord, a relationship which existed between men who had fought side by side, grieved together at the loss of comrades, whose safety and families' safety depended on their keeping faith. During the centuries of peace and urban living, however, the relationship lost much of its emotional significance. It became distant and formal; it was hedged about by ceremonies and taboos; the vassal came to look on his lord less as a leader in war (for there was no war) than as an administrative head.

One sees this change in the changing concept of the ideal warrior. Once a strong, stout-hearted fellow, quick and warm in his sympathies, generous to the weak and unyielding to the strong, he becomes a man whose native intelligence has been disciplined in the classroom, who gets on harmoniously with his colleagues, who deals with matters within his jurisdiction without fear or favor. Loyalty is still the highest virtue for him; but, where once it had meant willingness to follow the lord to death, now it meant giving the lord disinterested advice and conducting oneself in a way reflecting credit on his administration. Qualities of the ideal bureaucrat had come to be viewed as the very essence of the warrior.

Moreover, the power of the lord as administrative head increasingly became merely symbolic; actual power passed to lower echelons of officials. Partly this was a result of the growing complexity of government, but in greater measure it was because the lord's position was hereditary and as time passed fewer and fewer of his breed were men of force and intelligence, fit for the top job. Vassals who still looked on the lord with awe were likely to be men who regarded him from a distance; those who saw him closer, despite all outward deference, could often scarcely conceal their contempt.

Indeed some hardly tried. An anonymous author, writing about 1860, calls the lords of his day time-servers; men brought up by women deep in the interior of palaces where no sound of the outside world penetrated; surrounded from childhood by luxury and indulged in every whim, they were physically weak and innocent of both learning and practical experience. But it was not revolution that was called for, only better education for rulers, that they might choose better officials. "The secret of good government," the writer confidently declared, "lies in each official discharging his particular office properly, which in turn depends on choosing the right man for the right job."

To summarize up to this point: the two and a half centuries of peace after 1600 brought great changes to the warrior class. They brought a change in the warrior's relationship to the land, which became purely administrative; in his relationship to political power, which became bureaucratic; and in his relationship to his lord, which became distant and impersonal.

I should like now to show, as concretely as I can, the connection between these changes and some aspects of the economic and social transformation of the country after 1868—my so-called aristocratic revolution.

Consider the creation in the years immediately after 1868 of a highly centralized government. This was a brilliant achievement which permitted the new leaders who came to power to formulate for the first time a national purpose and to call up energies that did not before exist. Political power had lain scattered in fragments over the map, each lord collecting his own taxes, maintaining his own army and navy, even following an independent foreign policy. Then, with astonishing speed the fragments were pulled together; a central government created; the entire country subjected to a single will. Feudal lords and their miniature kingdoms were swept away and one bureaucratic empire emerged in their place.

This change was possible in part because warriors had long since been removed from the land and stripped of seignorial rights. Had these interests remained, the warrior must first have been dispossessed of them—the base of his power and source of his pride. Whoever might eventually have succeeded in this would not likely himself have been a warrior, nor have accomplished the feat without a long and bitter struggle. As it was, only the great lords had to be deprived of their power, and the deed was sooner done because their powers had come to be exercised, in fact, by officials who might trade them for similar powers within a vastly larger organization.

But what of the vaunted loyalty of the samurai? One would think this must have prevented liquidation of the great territorial lords by their own vassals. The unconditional loyalty to the lord as war leader, however, had shrunk to the conditional loyalty of the administrative subordinate to his chief—a loyalty valid only so long as the chief performed his duties efficiently. That the great lords had long ceased to do this was known to all. Meanwhile a new and higher loyalty emerged, sanctioning—indeed, those who prevailed thought, demanding—the transfer of all power to a central government. This was loyalty to the emperor, in whose name the aristocratic revolution was carried out. Nor was the emergence of this new loyalty unconnected with the decline of the older one: one suspects that men brought up in the cult of loyalty to the lord, as an absolute obligation and the noblest of human ideals, needed some escape from the disloyalty they felt in their hearts.

Second, consider how the new central government used its power to liquidate the four estates of which society was legally composed. Each estate—warrior, peasant, artisan, and merchant —was theoretically closed, and subject to detailed restrictions concerning occupation, residence, food, and dress peculiar to itself. The new government swept away such restrictions, and endowed men with extensive civic, though not political, rights. Henceforth anything that was legally permissible or obligatory for one was permissible or obligatory for all; moreover, a system of free public schools very soon gave this new legal dispensation concrete social meaning. The warrior lost his privileges and immunities and was forced to compete in school and out with the sons of tradesmen and peasants. Even his economic privileges were done away with. Warrior stipends were commuted into national bonds redeemable in twenty years, after which time warriors, as such, had no claim on the national income.

Now, how is one to explain a ruling class thus liquidating its privileges, and not by a series of forced retreats but at a single willing stroke? Surely part of the answer lies in warrior privileges not being bound up with the ownership of land. To restrict or even abolish them, therefore, did not arouse fears for the safety of property, or stir those complicated emotions that seem to attach peculiarly to land as a symbol of family continuity and an assurance of the continuing deference of neighbors. Few ruling classes have ever been so free of economic bias against change. Warrior power was based almost exclusively on office-holding, and this monopoly was not immediately in danger because no other class had yet the experience, education, and confidence to displace warriors in administration. The striking down of barriers between estates, on the other hand, opened up to warriors occupational opportunities formerly denied them, a not insignificant gain in view of the large number of warriors who, with more than normal pride but neither property nor important office, were nearly indigent.

This brings me to a third aspect of the revolutionary transformation of Japanese society after 1868: the explosion of individual energies that followed the sudden abolition of status distinctions. Until then opportunity was very limited; men looked forward to following the occupations of their fathers, and even to living out their lives in their same villages and towns and houses. After it, everything seemed suddenly changed, and young men strove with leaping hope and fearful determination to improve their characters, to rise in the world, to become something different from their fathers.

For warriors the abolition of status restrictions meant finding new occupations and new roles in society. Few had enough property after the commutation of stipends to live without work, and not all could continue in the traditional occupations of soldier, official, policeman, and teacher. A very large number were forced either to suffer social eclipse or become merchants, industrialists, lawyers, engineers, scientists; or they saw in these occupations exciting new opportunities for wealth and fame.

In any case, there was a grand redirection of warrior talent and ambition. Despite the traditional warrior aversion to money-making and the merchant's love of it, for example, most of the first generation of modern entrepreneurs, above all the earliest and most daring, came from the warrior class. Nor is this to be explained merely by the occupational displacement of the warrior. Part of the explanation lies in the warrior's aristocratic background—his educational preferment under the old regime, his cult of action, and (at his best) his intense social idealism. . . .

Other classes were scarcely less affected than warriors. Finding themselves suddenly free to become whatever wishes, effort, and ability could make them, with not even the highest positions in society closed to competition, they responded with a heroic effort at self-transcendence. Freedom of this kind must always be heady; but one wonders if it is not especially so when it comes suddenly, in societies with a strong sense of status differences, where the social rewards of success are more finely graded and seem sweeter than in societies less schooled to such distinctions.

In a charming little anecdote in his autobiography, Itō Chūbei, the son of a peasant who became a leading industrialist, gives some hint of the poignancy of the hopes for success he shared with other peasant boys of his generation. Upon graduating from elementary school not long after 1868, the first boy in his village to do so, Itō called on the headmaster to take leave. He was not surprised to meet with an angry scolding, since he had been far from the model boy. After the master finished his scolding, however, he spoke glowingly of Itō's future and predicted that, despite his rebelliousness, he would be a success. "You will make your mark in the world, I know it!" he exclaimed. And at this the young boy, unable to hold back his tears, wept aloud. Years later, in recounting this incident to a reunion of his classmates, Itō was so affected that he wept again, and his gratitude to his former teacher was no less when, after the meeting, he discovered that all of his classmates had been sent off with exactly the same exhortation!

Such hopes were real because, though not everyone was equal in the competition for wealth and honor, the privileged estate under the old regime had no prohibitive or enduring advantage. In respect to income, for example, warriors were at no advantage over the rest of the population, and though they were the most literate class in society, literacy was very widespread among other classes as well, and it rapidly became more so through the new schools. But most important, perhaps, warriors could not for long claim a cultural superiority, compounded of superior education, elegance, and taste, to act as a bar to the achievement of others, or to divert others from achievement in the pursuit of aristocratic culture. Indeed, by the twentieth century, one can scarcely speak of an aristocratic culture in Japan, despite the peerage created by the government in 1885. Whether a young man came of warrior family could no longer be reliably told from his speech, manners, or social ideas; moreover, his origins were far less important to his self-esteem and the good opinion of others than whether he had a university diploma and where he was employed.

. . . I should like now to suggest, very briefly, some of the ways in which Japanese society seems to be different because its modern revolution was aristocratic rather than democratic.

First, a point so obvious it need only be mentioned in passing: the aristocratic revolution, despite the civil equality and economic progress it brought, has not made for a strong democratic political tradition—but the contrary.

Second, more than any other single factor, perhaps, that revolution helps explain Japan's rapid transition from an agrarian to an industrial society. How different the story must have been had the warriors behaved as one would expect of an aristocracy, if they had used their monopoly of political and military power to defend rather than change the existing order.

Third, as there was no aristocratic defense of the old regime, there was no struggle over its survival; no class or party war in which the skirmish line was drawn between new and old, revolutionaries and conservatives. There was, of course, tension between traditional and modern, Japanese and Western, but not a radical cleavage of the two by ideology. All parties were more or less reformist, more or less traditional, and more or less modern; excepting perhaps the Communists, whose numbers were insignificant, no prewar party thought of the past, as such, as a barrier to progress. It was a barrier in some respects, in others a positive aid. Modernization therefore appeared to most Japanese who thought about it at all, not as a process in which a life-or-death confrontation of traditional and modern took place, but as a dynamic blending of the two. I wonder if this does not account in large part for what has seemed to many people the uncommon strength of tradition in the midst of change in modern Japan.

Fourth, status-consciousness is relatively strong in Japan in part because there was no revolutionary struggle against inequality, but for that reason class-consciousness is relatively weak. These attitudes are by no means contradictory. The nervous concern of Japanese for status is quite consonant with their relatively weak feeling about classes—higher-ups to some extent being looked on as superior extensions of the self.

. . . [S]ince warriors were never thrown on the defensive by the hostility of other classes, they never felt the need to make a cult of their peculiar style of life, either as evidence of virtues justifying their privileges or as compensation for loss of them. One wonders if Western aristocracies did not put exceptional value on leisure, gambling, dueling, and lovemaking, as aspects of the aristocratic way of life, in good part because they were a dramatic repudiation of bourgeois values.

In any case the warrior did not have the means of supporting a leisurely and aesthetic style of life. The revolution found him separated from the land, living on a government salary rather than on income from property; he therefore carried no capital inheritance from his privileged past into the modern age. He had no country estates, no rich town properties, no consols to spare unbecoming compromises with the crass new world of business. On the contrary, warriors were the chief makers of this world and they scrambled for success in it to escape social and economic oblivion.

Then, too, this new world was irrevocably bound up with Western culture, whence came (with whatever modifications) much of its technology and many of its conventions. Success in it had very little to do with traditional skills and tastes, and much to do with double-entry bookkeeping, commercial law, English conversation, German music, French painting, and Scotch whiskey. Traditional arts were not forgotten, but they were never identified with a particular social class, least of all perhaps the upper class. . . . In respect to such things all classes of Japanese, during the first generation or two after 1868, were born cultural equals. One could not learn of these things at home, any more than one could learn there a foreign language or the calculus. Such subjects were taught only in the schools, and the schools were open to anyone.

II.

Meiji Japan—
Foundations for the Empire
1868–1890

❀ THE FIRST PRIORITY of the young samurai who restructured Japanese society after the Meiji restoration of 1868 was to make Japan a strong and wealthy state capable of renegotiating the unequal treaties with the West. Aware that broad changes were needed in their society to do this, they looked to Western nations for models. They wanted to be able to compete with the West, and they believed that no Asian nations were capable of resisting unless they were radically reformed. This choice of priorities ultimately meant a choice for empire beyond the borders of Japan. Equality with the West was judged to require competition for colonies; and industrialization to require secure sources of raw materials as well as trade.

Initially, the Meiji leaders were able to consolidate their domestic political position, ensuring them broad freedom of action. The decision to move from a feudal society and an agricultural economy toward industrialization became apparent at once, especially in key governmental decrees in 1873. The beginning of a conscript army meant the eventual end of military service as the exclusive preserve of samurai warriors, though many ex-samurai quickly came to dominate the key positions in the army. Moreover, a modern army assumed general literacy, and at about the same time universal education was begun.

The Meiji leaders, seeking a steady, predictable source of revenue for the great sums needed to industrialize Japan and consolidate their new national administration, ultimately had but one significant source to turn to: agriculture. They quickly found it necessary to change from the old land tax assessed in crop yields to a high and rigidly fixed money tax. This was a hardship to the peasantry, for the tax was both constant and payable only in money, and it did not take into account bad harvests, low market prices, or other peasant problems. A rapid increase of tenancy followed the introduction of the new taxation system. Revolts over taxation policies, land rents, and conscription in the early Meiji period shook the government, but they ultimately failed because of their scattered nature and the increasing effectiveness of the conscript army.

The conscript army's first important role was not in defense of Japan against external attack, but in suppression of the final efforts of some samurai to assert themselves. Most samurai, of course, were not included in the new scheme of power; bureaucratic positions were available for only a few thousand former samurai. In the new society the majority of warriors who had supported the restoration found that they had no military role, and their own social privilege—the right to wear a sword—was abolished in 1876, symbolizing the state's monopoly of force. Their stipends were finally abolished, too, leaving them poor and forcing them to seek other sources of income. They were an anachronism in changing Japan.

The income from the agricultural tax and a favorable situation in the international silk market provided the resources and independence for the beginnings of Japanese industrialization. The Meiji leaders played a key role here in providing capital for the early enterprises. In addition, they brought foreign technicians to teach their technology. Concern with the foreign threat also led to an early emphasis on military techniques, continuing the armament development begun by some samurai in the last years of the Tokugawa shogunate.

In February 1889 the Meiji constitution was presented to the Japanese people as a gift from the emperor. In retrospect, it is not clear why the Meiji leaders chose to draft a Western-style constitution at all. They may have seen constitutionalism as part and parcel of the successful Western state—somehow the *sine qua non* of modern powers. In addition, they may have wanted to show the Western states that they were "modern" in order to argue for revision of the unequal treaties. They studied the Western models and were acutely aware of their differences. They purposely chose those elements providing for the most stable, elitist rule, relying largely on the Prussian example. Seeking to strengthen the state, they had no interest in theories of natural law or in any meaningful democratic participation.

During the writing of the constitution some opposition leaders organized movements that called for greater democracy, and the eruption of violent protest in the mid-1880s indicates powerful currents of dissent with government policy. But the actions of other leaders indicated more interest in gaining power than in changing the political system. While some Japanese political leaders have been accused of opportunism for leaving these opposition political groups when offered government posts or stipends, this is misleading. It is more helpful to view several of these competing political party organizations as factions within the elite rather than disputes over ideas of theory or government organization.

As the last decade of the nineteenth century began, Japan was economically, politically, and militarily developing. Though elements of her feudal heritage remained relatively unaffected by the Meiji reforms, they were not as obvious as Japan's new strengths. They nonetheless had important implications for the future. In the countryside living standards were improving, but tenancy was also rising. Institutionally, the old feudal system had been destroyed, but in personal and social relationships hierarchy prevailed. Legally, the family structure remained rigidly patriarchal. Especially after the Educational Rescript of 1890, children were taught ultimate loyalty to the emperor and the idea that society was merely the family writ large, with the emperor at its head.

Politically the new constitution left little room for grassroots political action. Voting requirements kept the great majority of people from voting. Government was structured to be responsible to the desires of the elite—whose goals always included Japan's ability to compete in the arena of imperialist nations.

1. Economic Changes:
The Decision to Industrialize

☘ THE SUCCESSFUL *coup d'état* of 1868 against the feudal Tokugawa regime was probably the easiest step in Japan's transformation into an industrial power. Immediately after taking power, the band of Western-oriented samurai faced a series of formidable problems. Treaties with the Western powers had opened Japan's economy to foreign imports, which stimulated losses in Japan's balance of payments and attacked the rural handicrafts industries; the samurai class, which stood to lose most from the abolition of feudalism, was restive and had to be pacified; and the new elite decided very early that rapid and thorough industrialization would have to be undertaken, but it had little background for this except for the widespread development of government-owned arsenals in the Bakumatsu period. Below T. C. Smith discusses the critical nature of the problems facing the new regime and how the former samurai improvised policies to deal with them.

*T. C. SMITH**
Motivation to Industrialize

By commercial treaties negotiated in 1858 and 1866, Japan was thrown open to foreign trade, almost without restriction. Her

* T. C. Smith, *Political Change and Industrial Development in Japan* (Stanford, Calif.: Stanford University Press, 1955), pp. 25–27, 30–31, 33–35, 39–41.

tariffs were placed under international control and set at levels that exposed her backward agrarian economy to the full impact of the dynamic industrial West, matching in unequal competition the power and precision of the machine with the strength and skill of human hands. Trade on these terms started the same disastrous cycle in Japan that it had elsewhere in Asia—a cycle that led through ruined handicrafts and financial instability to foreign political encroachment. Loss of specie was the first signal that the cycle was under way in Japan and its meaning was understood. . . .

The steady loss of specie had a disturbing effect on the currency and brought serious financial problems in its wake. While specie reserves were falling, the government had been forced to issue paper currency to meet the extraordinary expenditures described below. By 1880 the government held only five million yen in specie against more than 135 million in outstanding notes; this compared with fifteen million in specie against sixty-five million in notes in 1874. Since in the intervening years there had been no significant increase in productivity, the value of notes fell rapidly. The price of gold in terms of notes almost doubled between 1873 and 1881, and the price of rice in Tokyo rose from an annual average of 5.70 yen per *koku* in 1877 to 9.40 yen in 1879 and to 12.20 yen in 1880.

Currency depreciation embarrassed the government in ways described in more detail later on; it will be enough to mention three of them here. First, about seventy-eight percent of the ordinary revenue of the government in the period 1868–1880 came from the land tax; and, since the land tax was a money payment that remained constant from year to year, any depreciation in the value of money meant a corresponding loss of revenue to the government. Second, since any depreciation in the value of money reduced the peasant's land tax relative to his income, it tended to increase his purchasing power and encourage imports, contributing to a further loss of specie and a further depreciation in the value of paper money. Third, rising prices had the effect of reducing samurai income, an important part of which consisted of interest on government bonds and consequently was fixed in terms of money. The effect of inflation on the samurai was particularly dangerous since this class was already under severe economic pressure and in some parts of the country in open rebellion against the government.

For all these reasons members of the government were alarmed by the inflationary spiral and, rightly or not, regarded the loss of specie as its primary cause—or at least the only significant one the government could do anything about. . . .

Since Japan's tariffs were under international control and could not be raised, there was but one way of reducing the flow of imports into the country. That was by driving foreign manufactured products, which accounted for the bulk of Japan's imports, out of the domestic market through competition, and to do this was one of the major aims of industrial policy throughout the early Meiji period. In 1875 Matsukata expressed the hope of the government in the new enterprises it was founding to compete for control of the home market.

> If we henceforth make every effort to increase production and reduce imports, we may confidently expect such growth of industrial production that after a decade financial stability will be achieved as a matter of course. If we fail to do this, however, and continue to buy imported goods with specie, our government and people may give the appearance of making progress but the reality will be quite different.

Falling species reserves were perhaps less serious than what they portended—the ruin of Japan's handicraft industry through foreign competition. The bulk of imports . . . consisted of consumer's goods that competed more or less directly with domestic handicraft products, and the competition was most unequal. Machine-made cotton yarn, for example, was not only stronger and more uniform (and therefore more easily woven) than domestic handicraft yarn, it was also much cheaper. . . . Similarly, sugar imported from China was superior to domestic sugar; kerosene was less expensive and more efficient than vegetable oils and candles for lighting; imported woolens were cheaper and warmer than domestic silks.

The encroachment of imports on the market for domestic handicraft products is reflected in the changing consumption habits of the Japanese people. By the first decade of the Meiji period, Western dress, food, and even architecture were common in Tokyo. A British consular official reported that in 1872 "The consumption in Edo (Tokyo) of foreign goods appears to be very considerable. Almost in every street a certain number of shops may be seen where nothing but foreign articles are offered for sale." . . .

That the early years of the Meiji period, when foreign imports were reaching flood tide, were a time of troubles for the peasantry hardly needs saying. Nor were the baleful effects of agrarian depression confined to agriculture. But the government could not work miracles: it could not, as the peasantry demanded, save handicrafts doomed by the machine. The government heard the demand, however. In the first decade of Meiji there were over two hundred peasant uprisings, more by far than in any ten years of the Tokugawa period, and these uprisings tested the mettle of the government. All that saved the government was the social gulf between samurai and poor peasant. Had the discontent of the two classes flowed in one channel toward a single objective, there would have been little to remember of the Meiji government but its good intentions.

If the government could not work the miracle of reviving old industries, it could at least build new ones. Matsukata warned the Dajōkan in 1874 that if it did not the people would "lose their industries and fall into poverty and starvation," and he added gloomily that Japan would become a producer of raw materials for the industrial West. Whom Matsukata meant by "the people" he did not explain, but we can guess. At the end of the seventies, no less than seventy percent of the population was still engaged in agriculture as a *primary* occupation, and this was the part of the population that was most directly hit by the falling off of handi-craft employment. It is difficult to single out motives for founding particular enterprises, but there can be no doubt that the hope of bringing relief to the hard-pressed peasantry was often among them. The Mombetsu sugar refinery, for example, was founded not only to help check the importation of sugar from China but to provide local growers with a market for their crop. The Tomioka spinning mill, the government announced, was built to provide employment, to encourage private spinners to mechanize their operations by showing them how, and so "to profit the people." Here the meaning of "people" is clear beyond doubt, since the spinning of raw silk was almost entirely a rural industry. Still another example of concern for agrarian interests is the Aichi cotton-spinning mill. When, in 1878, it was proposed to found a modern cotton-spinning mill in western Japan, it was decided to locate the mill in Aichi prefecture because the need was greater there than in other cotton-producing areas in the west.

A third problem that Meiji industrial policy was designed in part to solve was adjusting the samurai to a new society that had no room for a hereditary military class. The problem was at bottom economic and it was not new. It dates roughly from the seventeenth century when the samurai began to feel the adverse effects of commercial development. Rising prices and new luxurious tastes combined with ineptitude in handling money rapidly pushed the samurai into debt and, by the end of the Tokugawa period, the situation of the entire class was desperate. What commercial development had left undone was completed by the restoration, which samurai hoped would bring them relief. The new government not only swept away samurai political privileges and most of their social honors, but also added injury to insult by liquidating their claims against the government with little more than token compensation. . . .

There was earnest discussion of the plight of the samurai in government circles from the restoration until after 1880, and, so far as the written record shows, no one so much as hinted that the samurai simply be left to their fate. They were an elite too valuable to the nation to be allowed to suffer demoralization and economic eclipse if these could be avoided. As Iwakura, who among important leaders was perhaps the most strident champion of the samurai, put it: "Except for this noble kind of men, our people will not be able to compete with foreigners for another twenty or thirty years or more." And again: "Without the samurai our nation cannot embark on the road to progress, but must decline like Korea and China. Whether our nation prospers or not depends above all on the fate of the samurai."

Iwakura's direst prediction of what catastrophes neglect of the samurai class would bring did not strike other members of the government as fanciful; almost to a man they were samurai, and they believed as resolutely as Iwakura in the unique qualities of their class. They were all aware, too, of the immediate political danger of samurai discontent; indeed, the danger was on them before they had more than a taste of political power. Between 1873 and 1877 there were four major uprisings among samurai, all aimed at overthrow of the government; and the government very nearly did not survive the last and largest of these, the Satsuma Rebellion. The fighting ended nevertheless in a victory for the government so decisive that samurai did not again venture to challenge it with arms. Samurai opposition to the government did not cease, however; it now took the no less dangerous form of a political movement shrilly demanding a constitution and representative government.

Since the samurai problem was essentially economic, it called for an economic solution, as every government document on the problem stressed. There were but two possible economic solutions, broadly speaking: either the government had to support the samurai as it had in the past on a kind of dole, or it had to expand the economy sufficiently to make room for them as producers. The first of these alternatives was not seriously considered since it would have saddled the government with a terrible financial burden and forced it to abandon the ambitious program of modernization to which it was fully committed; expansion of the economy, on the other hand, was not only compatible with this program but essential to it. Solution of the samurai problem, therefore, was constantly linked in official memoranda with industrial and agricultural development, particularly the former. "In trying to create employment for the samurai," Iwakura wrote, "we must give first importance to the development of industry." Fortunately this was a task for which it was thought the samurai were particularly suited. Indeed, "With their strength of spirit nurtured through generations, the samurai are equal to any task." It must not be thought, however, that the samurai were merely to manage the new industry, they were to provide part of the working force too, and this was not idle talk: over half of the workers employed in the government's Tomioka silk mill in 1872 were of samurai rank. "Let those samurai with some capital be given financial aid by the government, those with ability be placed in charge of the new enterprises, those with physical strength be employed as workers, and within a few years production in different parts of the country will be sufficiently increased that all the samurai now idle will be useful producers." So wrote Iwakura in support of a program of government loans to samurai, but the stress on solving the samurai problem through industrial development suggests that this was one of the chief aims of government industrial policy as a whole.

As revolutionary leaders are likely to be, the Meiji leaders were desperately harassed men. They had come to power by destroying old institutions and impairing old loyalties, and, until these were replaced, their grip on power was necessarily nervous and insecure. But if their destructive work deprived them of the support of part of the past, it also saved them from the illusion that trapped Chinese leaders: that the past could be preserved intact. Having burned bridges, they had to go forward—to find new solutions rather than refurbish old ones. In essence their problem was to make the transition from a traditional to a modern society: to find a new synthesis that would bring a new social and political stability. There is no evidence in their writings that the Meiji leaders had any clear, preconceived solution to this problem, but they were committed to finding a solution because they were committed to remaining in power; indeed, having used power violently in revolution against others, they could not safely relinquish it. And they discovered their solutions piecemeal, by answering the specific questions history asked of them. The old society, already fatally weakened by their revolt against it, was being steadily undermined by external forces, and the evidence and dangers of the process were clear. Imports exceeded exports, handicrafts were being ruined, the samurai class was dangerously discontent. It was in solving such immediately pressing problems as these that the government's industrial policy was hammered out. . . .

Before the commutation of pension bonds in 1876, almost all of the private wealth sufficiently liquid to have been channeled into industrial investment was in the hands of merchants. One of the reasons it did not flow into this investment field was the generally conservative outlook of its owners. This outlook is well reflected in the "house laws" of merchant families, which ordinarily consisted of a series of rules designed to promote the prosperity of the house. As one would expect, these laws extolled thrift, sobriety, honesty, kindness to customers, and so on, but surprisingly they also extolled conservative virtues generally. For example, the merchant was warned to be ever modest in dress and demeanor and to eschew anything that might be interpreted as socially presumptuous. Not only was he not told to be alert to new business opportunities; he was in effect warned against them. He must not depart from the business practices of the past handed down through generations, and there was the hint that to do so would be disrespectful to his ancestors. Frequently he was explicitly warned against venturing into new lines of business, and he was always warned, usually in the first article of the "house laws," to stay safely within the limits of the law. We would not expect breaking the law to be recommended, of course, but the prominence given this caveat suggests something more than respect for the law and ordinary caution. It reflects a fear of taking risks, of venturing anything uncertain, which seems to have been the cardinal principle of the merchant class. With this outlook it is no wonder the merchant did not break new ground for industry.

Another factor that kept the merchant from investing in machine industry was ignorance. Machine industry placed business in a new context that required new kinds of knowledge—of technology and production, of foreign tastes and markets, of shipping and landing and warehouse charges outside Japan, of international financial practices. The merchant knew almost nothing of these things, and he could not readily learn them. There was little in the traditional lines of business to help him, and he could not learn from books until the government had issued specialized texts for his benefit. Knowledge of foreign languages as well as foreign travel, which was already assuming significant proportions by 1875, was confined almost exclusively to the samurai class. It was no wonder, then, that as late as 1884 Japan's foreign trade was still amost entirely in the hands of foreign traders. . . .

It was clear from the first years of the Meiji period that the many obstacles to Japan's industrial development could not be surmounted without government action of some kind. As Ōkubo Toshimichi expressed it: "Our people are particularly lacking in daring: to encourage them to overcome this weakness and to study industry and overcome its difficulties is a responsibility the government must assume." Two general courses of action were open to the government: (1) it could develop modern industry directly through government enterprises, or (2) it could encourage private investment in industry by extending to investors various forms of state aid including technical assistance, subsidies, and easy credit. Actually both courses were tried during the first decade of the Meiji period, but the second—state aid to private interests—proved almost entirely ineffective. The unsuccessful attempt to build railways with private capital was but one of many failures with this method. . . .

❀ THE HEADLONG PLUNGE into industrialization was not free of obstacles, nor was the proper course entirely clear to the Meiji elite. First attempts to stimulate private investments in industry met with general failure—both because of the conservatism of the old merchant families and because of the immense sums required. The government then adopted the policy that was to prove successful: subsidies for basic investments in industry, initially publicly owned but eventually sold off to private investors at below cost. According to E. H. Norman, though a subject of much debate, one of the noteworthy characteristics of the program was the order of industrial development—from heavy to light industries and from military to consumer goods—revealing a very early preoccupation with the military–strategic importance of industrialization.

E. H. NORMAN*
Early Industrialization

The feverish haste of the Meiji leaders to accomplish in a generation what had taken other nations a century or more to do was now to be checked by the gulf which separated Japanese primitive feudal technique from the industrial technique of the most advanced nations. To leap over this gulf, rather than to plod along the intervening valley road taken by pioneer nations, would require time to train a great body of skilled labor and to amass a large store of capital. Japan still lacked the former in the early Meiji era, and, as for the latter, only a very few wealthy families

* E. H. Norman, *Japan's Emergence as a Modern State* (New York: International Secretariat, Institute of Pacific Relations, 1940), pp. 110–111, 125–133.

had a sufficient accumulation to enter the field as entrepreneurs in factory industries, a condition which incidentally favored monopoly or highly centralized capital right from the beginning of Japanese capitalism. But these few financial magnates who were . . . very close to the government showed hesitation in risking their capital in enterprises which demanded at the very outset such an immense outlay of capital, and before there was any clear indication of the profitability of such undertakings. The lag in distance between primitive Japanese technique and the best Western methods of production created very hard conditions for the genesis and growth of private capital in industry. Although a wide field for industrial investment lay fallow, the merchant princes were reluctant to become pioneers in working this field; so the government with the aid at first of *goyōkin* (loans) from these same magnates and together with its limited revenues, chief of which was the land tax, had itself to develop industry. Thus, early Japanese capitalism may be described as a hothouse variety, growing under the shelter of state protection and subsidy. Big private capital preferred to remain in trade, banking and credit operations, particularly in the safe and lucrative field of government loans, while small capital had no inducement to leave the countryside where trade, usury, and, above all, high rent—averaging almost sixty percent of the tenant's crop—prevented capital invested in agriculture from flowing into industrial channels.

. . . [I]n Japan, because of this concern with strategic industries, the normal order of the starting point and succeeding stages of capitalist production was reversed. In the classical type of capitalist development the starting point is the production of consumer goods, chiefly by light industries such as the great textile mills of Lancashire which began to be important in the first quarter of the eighteenth century. Only when the light industries are nearing maturity does the production of capital goods become significant. Heavy industries in England did not assume importance comparable to the light branch until the invention of the lathe at the end of the eighteenth century. This normal order of transition from light to heavy industry was reversed in Japan. Before the first introduction of cotton spinning machines in Japan in 1866, even before the importation of foreign fabrics, engineering works and arsenals had been established. Cannon were cast as early as 1844 in Mito, and engineering works were established . . .

in 1856 for military and naval purposes in southern Japan. Reverberatory furnaces, arsenals, foundries, and shipyards were built in Satsuma, Saga, Chōshū, and also in the *bakufu* domain in the fifties. The first silk mills to be equipped with modern machinery were not built until 1870 with the filature of Maebashi, on the Italian model, and the French model mill at Tomioka in 1872, with Italian and French technical supervisors.

This reversed order brought about a certain deformity in Japanese technological growth. From the first the strategic military industries were favored by the government, and technologically they were soon on a level with the most advanced Western countries. . . . [T]he arsenals in Nagasaki were originally under Dutch supervision, the Yokosuka shipyard arsenal and iron works under French, and other shipyards under English care. These foreign technicians trained the Japanese—so that in time native workers were technically as literate as their foreign tutors. In the textile industries foreign managers and assistants were also employed: English in the Kagoshima spinning mill, French in Tomioka and Fukuoka, Swiss or Italian in the Maebashi filatures. For training in engineering, government technical schools were established with foreign instructors, while the best Japanese students were sent abroad to master the most up-to-date technique, to replace foreign advisers on their return. In this way the military key industries were technically advanced while those industries which were not of strategic value, or did not compete against foreign articles in the international or home market, were left in their primitive handicraft stage of development.

It was the Meiji policy to bring under government control the arsenals, foundries, shipyards, and mines formerly scattered among various han [fief] or *bakufu* domains, then to centralize and develop them until they reached a high level of technical efficiency, while at the same time initiating other strategic enterprises such as chemical industries (sulphuric acid works, glass, and cement factories); and the last step was to sell a large portion of these industries to the handful of trusted financial oligarchs. But control over the most vitally strategic enterprises, such as arsenals, shipyards, and some sectors of mining, was kept in government hands. . . .

This peculiarity in early Japanese industrialization—the predominance of state control over industrial enterprise—is reflected in the manner in which the government, while retaining and strengthening its control over the key industries, disposed of the peripheral or less strategic industries by selling them into private hands. This change in government industrial policy from direct control to indirect protection was symbolized in the promulgation of the *Kōjō Haraisage Gaisoku* (Regulations or Law on the Transfer of Factories) on November 5, 1880. The reason given by the government for the change of policy appears in the preamble. "The factories established for encouraging industries are now well organized and business has become prosperous, so the government will abandon its ownership (of factories) which ought to be run by the people." Although the preamble expresses the belief that various enterprises created and fostered by the government could now be turned over to private ownership to operate at a profit, it was admitted elsewhere by Matsukata that many projects under direct state control were not at all profitable, but on the contrary threatened to become a drain on the revenue rather than a source of profit for the exchequer. The gradual disposal of government-owned factories, chiefly . . . of enterprises not strictly military, left the government free to devote its finances and administrative energy more exclusively to the military or strategic industries. . . .

The general tendency described above should not be interpreted too strictly, as if the new policy ushered in by the law for the sale of factories divided Japanese industries into two sharply defined groupings, the one related to the armament industries where government control was maintained, and the other embracing all the remaining nonstrategic industries which were suddenly to be exposed to the vicissitudes of pure laissez-faire. The distinction to be made is rather in the *different form* of paternalism adopted by the government after 1880; that is to say, the government retained paternalism as before, both in the military and nonmilitary enterprises after the sale of government factories, but in a form appropriate to each of these two sectors of industry. The *Nōshōmushō* (Department of Agriculture and Commerce), established in April 1881, was the government organ fashioned to realize its new policy.

. . . [T]he first transfers were made in the nonmilitary industries. The model cotton-spinning mills set up by the government in 1881 in Hiroshima and Aichi with the most up-to-date English machinery were sold to Hiroshima prefecture (1882) and to the

Shinoda Company (1886) respectively. The Shinagawa Glass Factory was handed over to the Ishimura Company in 1885, and the Shimmachi Spinning Mill to the Mitsui in 1887 and the Fukuoka filature to the same company in 1883; the Fukagawa Cement Factory was leased to the Asano Company in 1883, and sold outright the following year.

In the sphere of railroad construction, government ownership of lines was partially abandoned in 1880, and the next year the Nippon Railway Company was founded, receiving generous government loans and subsidies during the most active period of railroad construction.

The role of government subsidy is most spectacularly demonstrated in sea transportation. Long before the law for the sale of factories, the government gave gratis to Iwasaki Yatarō, the founder of the Mitsubishi Company, the thirteen ships used for military transport in the Formosan expedition of 1874; and this was soon followed by another stroke of fortune for the company, the purchase of the Yūbin Jōkisen Kaisha, a semigovernmental fleet, for 320,000 yen. In the government's desire to build up a strong mercantile marine it favored this company from the beginning by giving it a yearly subsidy of 250,000 yen, starting from 1875 and lasting for fifteen years. To bolster the monopoly position of this company, the government enacted in 1876 the *Gaikokusen Norikomi Kisoku* (Rules regarding the Boarding of Foreign Ships), thus delivering a crushing blow to the P. and O. hopes of obtaining a monopoly in its newly opened Yokohama–Shanghai service. In the period immediately following the promulgation of the law for the sale of factories the government temporarily abandoned its policy of favoring exclusively the Mitsubishi Company, and with a view to stimulating sea transport through competition, it established a rival line, the Kyōdo Un'yu Kaisha, in 1883, thereby precipitating a bitter struggle with the Mitsubishi. Mobilizing all its financial recources, as well as its widespread political agents and allies, the Mitsubishi succeeded in effecting amalgamation with the Kyōdo Un'yu Kaisha in 1885, forming the world-famous Nihon Yūsen Kaisha. The government now threw its full weight behind this great monopoly firm, granting it a yearly subsidy of 880,000 yen.

After disposing of some of its model factories in the nonmilitary industries, the government gradually turned over some of its mining and shipbuilding enterprises to private hands. Among the most notable transfers in this sphere was the lease (in 1884) and sale a few years later of the great Nagasaki shipyards to the Mitsubishi Company. . . .

One could go on describing the process of transfer of large sections of government-controlled industry into the hands of the financial oligarchy. Among Japanese scholars there is considerable controversy regarding the real motivation of the government in its sale of these industries. But there is no doubt that this policy greatly enhanced the power of the financial oligarchy, especially in view of the ridiculously low prices at which the government sold its model factories. But what is most striking in this process is that, from their favored position as financial supporters of the new regime, a few families, such as the Mitsui, Mitsubishi, Sumitomo, and Yasuda, as well as the lesser Kawasaki, Furukawa, Tanaka, and Asano, have continually strengthened their advantage through such measures as the purchase at low rates of the well-organized government industries. But most important is the position of the smaller circle of financial oligarchs, the zaibatsu, made up of the first four companies in the above list, which, through the tremendous leverage given by their interlocking control over banking on the one hand and industry and commerce on the other, have been able to swallow lesser industrial concerns.

As stated above, the government policy of selling some of its enterprises into the hands of the favored financiers left it free to concentrate on purely military industries which were kept strictly under government control as formerly. After the suppression of the Satsuma Revolt, the government resolutely set about expanding its armament industries; despite retrenchment in other state expenditures in this period (1881–1887) there was a sharp increase (over sixty percent) in military expenditures and (1881–1891) naval estimates (200 percent). . . .

These projects required the import of expensive finished and semi-finished military equipment. But in this sphere of enterprise profit or loss was of no account, and strategic consideration was everything. However, this great expansion in the armament industries had the effect of stimulating the drive for self-sufficiency in Japanese industry. The military industries thus became a mold which shaped the pattern of Japanese heavy industry.

The policy of keeping a tight control upon military industries while maintaining paternalism of appropriate sorts over other types of enterprise has continued down to the present [1940] and is one of the most distinctive characteristics of the history of Japanese industrialization. It can be traced back beyond the days of the restoration to the time when feudal lords took a sudden interest in acquiring modern Western military equipment long before they thought of engaging in other forms of industrial enterprise.

2. The Countryside and the Cities

❀ THE POLITICAL CHANGES of the restoration initially had little impact on the countryside, and the overthrow of feudalism did not entail any immediate benefits or financial relief for the peasants. Despite expectations, tax burdens were not lightened but left at pre-1868 levels. Furthermore, the first reform to have a significant effect in the countryside, the shift in 1873 from taxes in kind to a money land tax, resulted in increased financial difficulties for many peasants, as Norman points out.

Smith examines some of the other undesirable results of the new land tax—a rise in the incidence of rural tenancy and fewer peasants "qualifying" financially to vote or to stand for public office. (This was similar to the American poll tax system, but with eligibility based on payment of a certain minimum land tax.) Though the economic plight of the peasants was related to other factors as well, the land tax was probably the most immediate. Yet the funds necessary for industrialization could only be obtained from agricultural surpluses and the land tax was critical in the program's success, and the wave of peasant rebellions that marked the first decade of Meiji—more than in the last decades of the feudal regime—was firmly suppressed.

E. H. NORMAN*
Peasant Protest and the Land Tax

The peasantry, bewildered by the rapid succession of dramatic events leading up to the restoration, enjoyed no substantial benefit from the new regime. In fact they behaved even more riotously than before, possibly because in some instances vague hopes had been raised by the overthrow of the old regime, hopes that their burden of tribute and debt would be lightened. Promises had been held out by the new government that all state land (except temple lands) would be divided up among the peasants. But they soon discovered that their burden of rice tribute was not to be lessened, nor was there any question of their receiving allotments from state lands. Disappointed in their expectation of release from the yoke of the old regime, suspicious of the purposes and innovations of the new, the peasantry renewed those revolts which had been characteristic of the last decade. Agrarian revolts reached a crescendo of violence and frequency in the year 1873, after which they decreased until by 1877–1878 they became small and inconsequential riots. Thus the year 1877 forms a convenient dividing line in analyzing the significance of peasant revolts in the early Meiji era. Professor Kokushō Iwao makes a striking comparison between the intensity of agrarian unrest in the early Meiji and in the Tokugawa period. He gives the number of revolts in the 265 years of Tokugawa rule as somewhat under 600, while the number for the first decade of the Meiji era (1868–1878) is well over 190. The most arresting feature of these early Meiji uprisings is that they were precipitated by two contradictory forces—one revolutionary, that is to say antifeudal, aimed at the final eradication of feudal privilege over the land and those who worked it, and the other reactionary, in the sense that many of these risings arose from the instinctive opposition of a conservative-minded peasantry toward the innovations of the new government.

* E. H. Norman, *Japan's Emergence as a Modern State* (New York: International Secretariat, Institute of Pacific Relations, 1940), pp. 71–76, 141–144.

Indeed, at first glance, many of these revolts appear to be merely demonstrations of resentment against the many aspects of modernization. Tumult and rioting only too often greeted decrees announcing the reform of the calendar, the abolition of the queue, the legalization of Christianity, the emancipation of the *eta* (outcasts), vaccination, the establishment of government schools, conscription, the land survey, numbering of houses, and the like. Peasants frequently were excited by wild rumors that the numbering of houses was a preliminary measure to the abduction of their wives and daughters; that the phrase "blood taxes" in the conscription decree of 1873 was to be taken literally, so that in joining the army their blood would be drawn and shipped abroad to make dye for scarlet blankets; that the telephone and telegraph lines would be used to transmit the blood; that the children herded into the new schools would also have their blood extracted. But if we look closer we notice that, while these old wives' tales and naïve misunderstandings of the healthy attempt of the government to modernize the nation acted as the *spark* which ignited the uprisings, somehow the *flames* always spread to the quarter of the richest usurer, the land-grabbing village headman, the tyrannous official of the former feudal lord. When the new calendar was introduced, consequent indignation could easily arise from the not unjustifiable fear that moneylenders would take advantage of the reform to juggle accounts to their own advantage. The feeling against the school system arose possibly because government schools might necessitate an increase in the local tax. Conscription meant less hands to help on the farm, and, although it flattered the peasant to be told he was fit to bear arms, it also insulted the samurai who . . . were often in a position to set themselves at the head of a peasant uprising in order to direct its course against the government which dared to infringe upon their exclusive military prerogative. The objection to the land survey is even more obvious, when we learn that, of its total expense of 40,000,000 yen, 35,000,000 yen was paid by the proprietors. The reform whereby local lords yielded political power in their clans and were supplanted by governors appointed by the central government was, like other reforms, received with mixed feelings by the peasantry. If the local lord had a reputation for benevolence, the peasants strenuously objected to his withdrawal in favor of an unknown appointee; but, in those fiefs where the lord was odious to the population, his final departure was a signal for an outburst of joy and relief and even for an assault upon his castle. Other outbreaks, such as those directed against the abolition of the outcast *eta,* against toleration of Christianity, and against vaccination, are clearly manifestations of prejudice which centuries of superstition, medieval bigotry, and Buddhist indoctrination had burned into the consciousness of the people.

According to Professor Kokushō, the fundamental underlying cause of peasant revolt in this period must be distinguished from the casual or accidental, both of which are so closely intermingled. Even such a cursory survey of agrarian unrest before 1877 shows us of what a strange mixture of reaction and revolution, of super- stition and shrewd estimate of class interest it was compounded. Though its weight was in the main thrown against the usurer, the rice-broker, the village headman, or the harsh official representing the lord, in short against all personifications of feudal oppression, it had undeniably the other darker side, that feudal side which many samurai, chagrined at their failure to receive patronage or official position from the government and dreaming of a return to the old warrior-dominated society, were able to exploit in their own campaign against the government, thanks to their knowledge of peasant psychology. What is common to the peasant movement of these ten years was a stubborn antagonism to rent, usury, and exorbitant taxation. The basis for the intrusion of antifeudal revolts from the prerestoration into the postrestoration period can be summed up in this way: the burden of feudal dues and taxation, even after the surrender of the clan land registers to the government in 1869, was still maintained if not actually in- creased, with the result that peasant protest was intensified until the tax reduction in 1877, when the agrarian movement took another path. As far as the peasant was concerned, then, the Meiji government, although holding out hopes of improvement, actually left him untouched for several years after the restoration. In fact we might say that, whereas under feudalism peasant dues to the lord though high were traditional and thus subject to some flexibil- ity (for in bad years a lord might not collect his full quota of the land revenue), in the early years of the Meiji the extremely high rate of exaction which existed under late feudalism—that is, about sixty to seventy percent of the produce—was legalized, standardized on a national scale, and strictly enforced regardless of all circumstances. . . .

The three basic principles of the land tax were: (1) whereas formerly the norm for tax payment had been the harvest, now it was to be the value of land; (2) the rate of taxation was to be three percent of the land value (reduced in 1876 for a short time to 2½ percent) with no increase or decrease for good or bad years, an adjustment possible under the paternalistic feudal regime; (3) the tax was to be collected in money, not as formerly in kind. This tax at three percent of the land value actually meant a reduction from the old feudal tax if the local tax at one percent were not included. But it cut deeper than this: it meant a qualitative as well as quantitative change from the feudal tax system. These points of difference can be summarized as follows: first, the diverse forms of levy which were imposed both arbitrarily and by custom under the *bakufu* and han governments were now unified under a national central government. Secondly, in former days the *direct producers,* irrespective of whether they were tenants or independent cultivators, were the taxpayers, but now only the *landowner,* whether independent producer or absentee landlord, paid the land tax. Thirdly, under the *ancien régime* the tax was fixed according to the yield, or according to the type of soil; but after revision it was fixed at the uniform rate of three percent of the land value without regard to bumper or lean years. Finally, the former payment of the tax in kind, principally in rice, was now changed to a money payment.

The Meiji leaders saw the necessity of taking this step in order to get rid of the fluctuations caused by the variations in the harvest as well as in the price of rice or other agricultural products which had been used as payment for a tax in kind. In other words, by providing for a *constant* source of revenue, they were making possible a modern budgetary financial system. In a country still agricultural and lacking tariff autonomy it was natural that the very considerable burden of military expenditures as well as of capital outlay for model industries and the maintenance of a large body of bureaucrats should be made dependent on the land tax, and it was important that this revenue should not fluctuate. We saw how removing the ban against permanent annexation of land—a measure bound to come in time—logically preceded and blazed the way for the new tax system, because it was absolutely essential for the guarantee of the new tax system that revenue from the land should cease to depend on the paying capacity of each landowner; in other words someone legally identifiable as the owner has to be responsible for the tax on every acre of land regardless of who works it. There is another fundamental difference from the old system. Under feudalism the principle governing the amount of tax paid by the peasant was to appropriate as much as possible, leaving the producer enough for only the barest subsistence, or, in the phrase current in that age, "to see that the peasants had just enough to live on and no more." The system of collection was based upon the group responsibility of the village divided for administrative convenience into teams of five men, and by this method peasant privation was at once deepened and universalized. But under the new government the burden of payment shifted from producer to landholder; the peasants were now freed from the oppressive bondage of feudalism and at the same time deprived of the "paternal" consideration of their lord whose problem it was to see "that they neither died nor lived." In the new society they were free to choose their own fate; to live or die, to remain on the land or sell out and go to the city. In this way the majority of the rural population, while released from the tyranny of feudalism, were not at the same time accorded state protection in the same way as were the landlords by the guarantee of the right to private ownership of land. The position of the small landowner working his own piece of land was precarious in the extreme, subject to all the vicissitudes of nature (bad crops, storms, blight) and of society (fluctuations in the price of rice) and yet unable to escape the responsibility of paying a fixed amount of cash every year to the government as tax. To meet this demand the peasant proprietor could give up the struggle to remain on the land, dispose of his tiny plot by sale, or resort to the village usurer and so enter upon the long uphill path of debt payments, which might end at any time in foreclosure. Furthermore, with the low level of capitalist development prevalent in the countryside, the sudden requirement to turn from twenty-five to thirty percent of his proceeds into money in order to meet the land tax placed a heavy burden on the small isolated cultivator, living off his pigmy-sized farm, who was not yet swept into the main reaches of the national market. By being thrust from a position of comparative self-sufficiency to one of dependence on the market, the peasant was forced to sell his rice as soon as it was harvested, and thus exposed to all the dangers arising from price fluctuations which did not affect to the same extent the position of the large landlords who could store rice in granaries. Here we are speaking of the small producer who owned his land and accordingly paid the land tax himself. The tenant still paid rent, for the most part in kind, to the landlord who, after deducting the amount to be forwarded to the government as land tax, pocketed the remainder as clear profit. . . .

T. C. SMITH*
Agrarian Distress and Taxation

There can be no doubt that the position of the peasant was deteriorating rapidly during the first half of the eighties. One index of this is the sale of agricultural land for nonpayment of taxes. Paul Mayet, a German economist employed by the Japanese government at this time, states that 367,744 holders lost their land for nonpayment of taxes between 1883 and 1890. Since the earliest occupational statistics show a total of 3,121,075 independent holders in 1888, something of the order of eleven percent of all peasant proprietors were dispossessed for nonpayment of taxes in a seven-year period. This, of course, tells but part of the story of agrarian distress. It is probable that only in exceptional cases was land surrendered for back taxes; ordinarily a peasant would borrow, even at the ruinous rates prevailing in rural districts, before letting his land go to the state for a small part of its value, and it seems all but certain that more land was taken by foreclosure than was sold for taxes.

. . . According to Mayet, the proportion of arable land worked by tenants in eighteen prefectures rose from thirty-four percent in 1883 to thirty-nine percent in 1887, and from thirty-nine percent to forty-two percent in sixteen other prefectures during the same period. The trend these figures reveal is confirmed by changes in the number of persons qualified to vote and of persons qualified to be candidates in the election of prefectural assemblies. Suffrage

* T. C. Smith, *Political Change and Industrial Development in Japan* (Stanford, Calif.: Stanford University Press, 1955), pp. 82–85.

was limited to persons who paid a land tax of not less than five yen; in other words, to persons *owning* (tenants did not pay a land tax) land valued at 200 yen or more; and the right of candidacy was limited to persons paying a land tax of not less than ten yen—that is, *owning* land valued at 400 yen or more. The total number of persons in all prefectures who enjoyed suffrage only declined from 846,258 in 1884 to 722,072 in 1886, a decline of fourteen percent in two years. Those who had the right both to vote and to stand as candidates declined from 871,762 to 809,880, or seven percent, in the same period. It is significant that the number of smaller landowners was declining more rapidly than that of the larger, and it seems reasonable to assume that the decline was even more rapid among the class of landowners who did not hold enough land to vote.

The *Kōgyō iken* [an 1884 government report on industrial development] paints a dreary picture of the condition of agriculture at this time. Almost everywhere, the study found, conditions were worse than they had been, and almost everywhere this was blamed on falling agricultural prices, which reflected a hidden increase in the actual rate of taxation. . . .

Behind the statistics of agrarian distress lay the ruin of thousands of peasant families. Gotō Shōjirō, one of the wealthiest businessmen of this period, described agricultural conditions in 1888 as follows:

> Our people [he means the peasantry] are unable to support the burden of taxation. They have been falling into an ever deeper poverty and they have now reached the point where they cannot maintain life. . . . There were 130,000 holders whose land was sold for taxes in 1882; and between 1883 and last year the number has not been less than 100,000 annually. [These figures are far larger than Mayet's.] How many persons may be reckoned to have fallen into the cruelest circumstances as a result? If we count four persons to a family, approximately 400,000 people a year are being deprived of all means of support. . . .

The data we examined . . . seemed to indicate that the Meiji land tax yielded no more but about the same as the Tokugawa land tax, and this was certainly the government's intention. But if there was any considerable difference, it was the Tokugawa tax that yielded more rather than the other way around. Nevertheless the peasantry seems to have been worse off after the new tax was instituted in 1873. This is reflected not only in the confiscation of land for taxes and the growing rate of tenancy, but in some two hundred peasant uprisings recorded for the first decade of the Meiji period—considerably more than for any ten years of the Tokugawa period.

The explanation is probably that the capacity of agriculture to pay taxes declined somewhat between 1870 and 1885. Foreign trade was undermining a broad sector of Japanese handicrafts that competed with imported manufactures, and the land settlement that accompanied revision of the land tax in 1873 deprived many villages of much or all of their common land and so of a source of free fuel, fertilizer, and building materials. Both of these factors reduced the peasant's ability to pay taxes: the first by reducing his income, and the second by increasing his expenses. Moreover, the Meiji land tax made no allowance for good and bad years as had the Tokugawa tax, and this inflexibility ruined many peasant families in bad years.

All things considered, it seems probable that the Meiji land tax was heavier than the Tokugawa land tax; in any case, it was as heavy as the peasantry could bear. There was never any question of increasing the rate of taxation after 1873, badly as additional revenue was needed; indeed, the only change in the rate of taxation was a downward revision by one-half percent in 1877, in an attempt to stop peasant uprisings by lightening the burden on agriculture. To have increased the tax would have entailed a double risk: of cutting into agricultural productivity by overtaxation and so ultimately reducing government revenue, and of driving the peasantry from rebellion to revolution.

Lacking the background of overseas trade, war, and piracy, which created private capital and stimulated private enterprise in the West, Japan was forced to rely on the governmental power to tax and borrow for the financing of industrialization. Despite such limited sources, the Japanese government was able to invest, between 1868 and 1881, something over thirty-four million yen in industrial enterprises directly owned and operated. Though the amount invested was but 5½ percent of total ordinary revenue, it represented a far greater effort than the figure perhaps suggests; at the same time, the government was pushing modernization on other fronts and liquidating the Tokugawa regime at high cost as well. Only in allocating the remaining half of its ordinary income did the government have any real choice.

At a time when the government was engaged in continuous war with armed samurai bands, and the nation was moreover acutely sensitive of military weakness, this same government saw fit to spend nearly thirteen percent of the remaining income for investment in industrial enterprises—almost a third of all combined expenditures on army and navy. Since it was loath to borrow abroad, and had little accumulated wealth at home, most of what the government invested in its enterprises came from currently produced surplus—which is to say, from the agricultural sector of the economy. Without an agriculture capable of producing a sizable surplus year after year, the whole Meiji program, including industrial development, would undoubtedly have been impossible. The entire surplus produced by agriculture had to be taken; the peasant had to be relentlessly exploited for the modernization of the nonagricultural sector of the economy. Since this condemned the peasant to poverty and backwardness, it did much to produce the profound gulf between urban and rural worlds that is so obvious and characteristic a feature of modern Japan.

✻ FROM THE BEGINNING, factories relied heavily on labor recruited or "bought" on contract from the countryside, in particular young women; and the factory dormitory system as a way to control such semi-indentured workers originated in this period. Yanagida Kunio, one of Japan's leading social historians and a specialist in Japanese folk culture, discusses the conditions facing workers in these early industrial enterprises.

YANAGIDA KUNIO*
From the Village to the Factory

The conspicuously low wages that have characterized modern Japanese industry result from a surplus farm population. After the beginning of the Meiji period daughters and younger sons of

* Yanagida Kunio, *Japanese Manners and Customs in the Meiji Era* (Tokyo: Ōbunsha, 1957), pp. 75–76.

farmers were forced to seek work in textile factories, foundries, glass or cement works, and so on. When a new factory was set up in a provincial town, it solicited labor from nearby villages, and the metropolitan factories sent representatives to the rural districts for the same purpose. We might note incidentally that many city enterprises showed a preference for workers of one particular prefecture.

The revision of the tax system affected many landowners adversely, but often they recouped their losses by speculating on rice or simply passed on the taxes to their tenant farmers. The economic gap between landowner and tenant widened, and, when the impoverished tenants heard the bright promises of the labor scouts, they did not long hesitate to send their younger brothers and offspring off to the factories. Those who went boarded the train with high hopes, but they rarely found factory life up to their expectations.

In those days the laborer had no contract with the management. He might be forced to work at any time of the day or night, and he had to manage to live on a pittance. The average worker wanted nothing so much as to pack his bags and go back home, and in the early years of the period the resulting labor turnover was exceedingly high, especially in the textile mills. Those who forced themselves to put up with working conditions sooner or later lost their health and returned to their homes to spread the tuberculosis virus. Even if they managed to get out of the factory while they were still healthy enough to wield a spade, however, they were likely to find that there was no land in which to sink it. Consequently, more and more stayed in the towns. In this connection, we cannot of course overlook that, despite grueling working conditions, many who had had a taste of city life found it difficult to go back to the farm and take up where they had left off.

The textile companies who employed mostly women seem to have had to compete to secure an adequate labor supply. Wily farmers sometimes made contracts for their daughters with labor recruiters from two or three different companies in order to collect the money that was given upon the signing of the agreement, and it is said that the factories thus defrauded had little recourse. In some cases the recruiter, having discovered that a girl had made an arrangement with another company as well as his own, either carried her away virtually by force or used sweet blandishments to coax her into coming to his company. Under the circumstances, once the girls had started working, the company kept a close watch on them, even when they were off duty, for fear that they would run away. Wages were low everywhere, but since the girls were governed by a complicated system of efficiency merits and demerits, they rarely complained even when they were exploited and deceived.

The women textile workers were crowded into dormitories, to which they were unaccustomed, and there they were so jealously supervised that they had no chance to organize themselves into a self-respecting social group. Some reacted to these conditions by becoming wanton and offending against what are called public morals.

As a rule, even when the girls returned home to their parents they became the targets of much criticism. Actually, they had by no means grown accustomed to luxury in the cities, as the country people often said, but they had indeed often grown so unaccustomed to the rhythm of village life that they found it difficult to readjust. Too, they had often missed out on much of the training in housework that a young woman was expected to have received, and it was consequently difficult to find husbands for them.

꩜ AFTER THE GOVERNMENT embarked on its program of adopting wholesale Western technology and ideas, many of the former samurai were quick to follow suit in becoming "modern" in clothes, language, transportation, and outlook. One of the more common cultural mixtures was the half-Japanese, half-Western house, a building of traditional construction with Western-style rooms and imported furniture. Yet significant social patterns, examined here by Yazaki, remained unchanged and essentially feudal; among these was the family, which retained traditional male authority and primogeniture. Business practices, too, kept much that would be called premodern even as commerce was experiencing great expansion along Western lines. The persistence of such feudal structures and values, despite a great deal of superficial change, was a notable feature of the Meiji restoration, partly due to the extraordinary speed with which Japan was transformed from a predominantly agrarian to an industrial society.

YAZAKI TAKEO*
Social Change and the City

... [I]t was the bureaucrats who were most active in introducing new systems from abroad through the acquisition of new knowledge, in business, industry, and society as well as in government. There were genuine and prominent differences between the ruling group and the common people, with respect to general knowledge and social prestige. And the common people paid them the respect they felt due themselves, addressing them as "sir official" (*kaninsama*).

Among the ministers of the new government there were a number of former daimyō, and their salaries reflected their prestige. The prime minister (*dajō daijin*) and other ministers (*sangi*) were paid from 800 to 900 yen per month, a very high salary scale in those days. Even officials of the lowest rank of the ninth class ... were paid fifty yen a month.

Government officials took up residence in homes owned previously by daimyō, *hatamoto,* or *gokenin,* either by directly purchasing the houses, or by making claims on vacated residences. Although such houses were distributed throughout Tokyo, most of them were located in the hills west of the palace. In their new homes the officials managed to adjust with relative ease to a semi-warrior, semi-Western style of living. Enjoying both the prestige and the relative wealth of the upper class of society, the officials worked with a certain enthusiasm to introduce Western ways into their own homes.

Applying their own ideas of what constituted "Western styles," they set about redecorating their daimyō or samurai residences. Modes adopted from different European countries were utilized in a variety of, sometimes ingenious, combinations. In general,

* Yazaki Takeo, *Social Change and the City in Japan* (Tokyo: Japan Publications, 1968), pp. 358–359, 361–363.

though, there was a certain uniformity in the alterations made. A second floor was usually added, carpets put down, and standard furniture such as stuffed chairs, dining tables and chairs, and other items installed. Paper on windows was replaced by plate glass, and stoves were provided in rooms where small braziers had been standard for generations. The basic framework and design of the houses, of course, remained unchanged.

Money was spent lavishly in other areas to acquire Western appearances. Fashionable clothes filled wardrobes, and meats were added to their diets. They took every occasion to speak English, and took carriages when leaving home. Banquets were graced by the best sake and had many geisha in attendance. Not a few kept mistresses in Yanagibashi and other sections. . . .

Among the merchants, whose social positions ranked just below officials, priests, and nuns, the wholesalers were most prominent. Their operations had been modified by the shift from consignments to stocks as the basis of their business, after the loss of their monopoly privileges. Their role in processing products for retail sales diminished even further after large-scale industry developed. But these changes did not occur all at once. Mass production did not emerge on a broad scale until after the Sino-Japanese War (1894–1895), and until that time the wholesalers maintained their influence in commerce through the traditional methods inherited from their ancestors, helping to keep alive strict feudal customs well into the Meiji era.

The position of head of a merchant household was absolute, and family members were bound together under his authority by sacred bonds. Equally as binding as the harsh demands of business on the family head was the obligation to worship the family deities each morning and evening. Within the context of unquestioned authority he treated his employees and servants with benevolence. Those connected with his business were treated as members of the family, were subject to his authority, were recipients of his benevolence, and were bound by the same sacred bonds.

Powerful merchants were extremely proud of the clipped curtains (*noren*) that hung over their entrances, bearing the household name or trademark. They bent every effort to make it a symbol of their own success in accumulating capital and in increasing their reputation among customers. Oriented to the practical goals of business, they were little interested in seeing their sons go off to the newly established schools, least of all to the universities. Their concern was to educate their own sons in successful business practices. . . .

Salaries received by employees in merchant shops were not thought so important to them as the business training they received. The head of a shop took a personal pride in the development of his apprentices. The wishes of master and employee coincided nicely. Employers addressed apprentices by adding the suffix *-don* ("boy") to their names when they first entered a shop at the age of fourteen or fifteen. At age seventeen they were addressed as *chūzō* ("clerk"), after a kind of initiation ceremony performed on New Year's Day, or possibly on the twentieth day of the first month of the year when special prayers (called *ebisu-kō*) were made for prosperity in the coming year. Central to the ceremony was *gempuku,* the celebration of his coming of age, symbolized by his changing to an adult hair style, receiving a half-coat called a *haori* and a tobacco case. From this time on they were called *Kichi* ("lucky") or *Hichi* ("seven"), and were given charge over a younger boy.

Sometime between the ages twenty-one and twenty-five the apprentice-graduates could be promoted to the status of managers (*bantō*), and the suffix *be-e* was added to their names, e.g., *Hichibe-e* or *Kichibe-e.* After completing ten to thirteen years of internship as a manager they were permitted to marry suitable girls and live outside the shop residence. They were outfitted with silk robes and, as responsible managers, could act on behalf of their masters in business matters.

❀ THE RESULTS of major transformations were not all physical, in the form of new factories and ships. The change in social institutions, like the government bureaucracy and business firms, was as rapid as physical industrialization. Along with it came much of the anomie, insecurity, and disillusionment that seem to be common to industrial societies. The process of industrialization yielded in Japan many of the same dilemmas as in the West: the bureaucratic rat race of white-collar work which often leads to bored and unhappy office workers. Scenes like this, which appear to Americans as distinctly Western, were common in Japan, too, with the growth of government and business. Such a personal situation is described below in *Ukigumo* ("Floating Cloud") one of the first modern novels in Japan and significantly one with a social message.

FUTABATEI SHIMEI*
Ukigumo (*Floating Cloud*)

Startled from an unfinished dream by the maid's voice, Bunzō raised his head and saw the reflection of the morning sun piercing obliquely through the shoji. "I've overslept," he thought, but at once the word "dismissed" came to his mind and his heart shrank. He rose stiffly and dressed. Without bothering to fold the bedding, he stuck a toothbrush in his mouth and an old towel in his belt and went downstairs quickly. "Hurry, Bunzō, or you'll be late!" Omasa called. Her voice startled him although it was not especially harsh. He was at a loss for an answer and managed to escape by mumbling something, his words blurred by the toothbrush.

He washed his face quickly and sat down to breakfast. His heart felt stifled; he found it very hard to eat. He had only two bowls of rice instead of his customary three and then modestly put the small table, on which he had eaten, to one side rather than pushing it forward as he usually did. His very body seemed to have grown smaller.

He got up, walked around the house, and furtively looked into the sitting room. Omasa was alone; Osei was not in the room. She was probably in Surugadai for her morning English lesson. Fearfully, Bunzō entered the room.

Omasa was in the midst of polishing the hibachi. She stopped suddenly, obviously startled at Bunzō's appearance. His face was pale and devoid of strength; a mixture of sadness, bitterness, and shame played on his features. "What's the matter? You look terrible."

* In Marleigh Gray Ryan, *Japan's First Modern Novel—Ukigumo of Futabatei Shimei* (New York: Columbia University Press, 1967), pp. 234–240, 245–248.

"Nothing really."

"Well then hurry up. It's almost eight o'clock."

"I—I haven't had a chance to tell you yet, but the fact of the matter is that yesterday—yesterday. . . ." He felt suffocated and cold sweat poured down him. His face became red. He could not speak. After a moment he tried again. "I was dismissed from my job," he declared with an effort. He lowered his head.

The hand holding the polishing rag froze in mid-air. Her body stiffened and Omasa cried out just once in surprise. For a few seconds she sat there, speechless with astonishment, staring at Bunzō. Then she busily put aside the cloth and moved closer to him. "You were dismissed? Why?"

"Why indeed? I don't know. There was some sort of reduction in personnel."

"How terrible. So you lost your job. Isn't that a pity," she said, crestfallen. "Well, in that case," she went on, "what are your plans?"

"I thought I'd have Mother stay in the country a while longer and I'd look for another government opening somewhere. There's nothing else I can do now."

"I suppose it won't make too much difference if you find one easily, but otherwise things will be pretty miserable, won't they? But don't say I didn't warn you. I told you over and over to go and call on your supervisor, but you're so stubborn, you wouldn't go. Now this has happened."

"It surely can't be because of that."

"It must be. If not they would never have let an innocent young man go, no matter how many people they were discharging. Or have you done something wrong?"

"No, I haven't."

"Well then." They were silent for a moment. "What about Noboru?"

"He came through all right."

"You see how everything works out if you're lucky? It's more than luck in his case, though. He's clever and shrewd and he's always alert. I know he goes to call on the supervisor all the time, and that must be why he didn't lose his job. This wouldn't have happened to you either if you had just listened to me and played up to the chief a little. But you never listen to anybody. Now look what's happened."

"That may very well be, but I couldn't possibly do something as disgusting as that."

"Don't be so proud! That's why the chief dislikes you—because you're so proud. Even a man like Noboru doesn't miss a chance to get in his good graces because he's afraid of getting fired. You should have tried twice as hard. If you only had yourself to think about, you could afford to be so superior. But you have your mother to consider."

She realized she had discovered a good instrument of torture. She tapped on the tatami with her pipe. "Don't you feel sorry for your mother? She lost your father early in life and now she has only you to rely on. She must feel so helpless. She could hardly like living down there all alone in the country, but she's patient and lives for your success. If you had thought about what you were doing, you would have realized that you had to make your way in the world no matter what. But you're so vain and selfish. No, you couldn't bear to play up to somebody. Now you've ended up driving your mother to utter destitution. Oh, what a bad day this is. You've brought this all on yourself. You deserve whatever happens to you. But don't you care what happens to your poor mother?" Throughout her tirade Bunzō sat with his head bowed and did not answer.

"Your mother has been waiting and waiting for her chance to be happy. How miserable she'll be when she hears you've lost your job. What hardships she has to endure in her old age."

"I know I've failed my mother. I feel terrible about it."

"I should certainly hope so. You're twenty-three years old and you can't even support your mother decently. What a son!" Feigning indifference, she blew smoke rings.

Bunzō glared at his aunt's profile and was about to explode angrily, but he managed to control himself. He tried unsuccessfully to smile. His voice trembled as he said, "I feel terrible about it, but what's done is done."

"What's that?" She turned slowly toward him. Blue veins stood out on her forehead. The corners of her eyes turned up in fury and her lips became twisted. "What did you say? What's done is done? Who did it? Whose fault is it that you were fired? Isn't it all because of your own stubbornness? You're always causing people trouble and now you're not even sorry that you lost your job. What do you mean by saying that what's done is done? You really are too much. You walk all over people. What do you think I am? You may think I'm an old witch and treat me like a complete stranger, but I'm still your aunt. If I were an outsider, I wouldn't care whether you were fired or not. I wouldn't have to bother with you at all. But we are related. I am your aunt and you are my nephew.

"I've taken care of you all these years all by myself. Maybe I shouldn't have interfered in your life, but I think of you as my own son, even though I have children of my own. Do you know what that means? Not a day has gone by that I haven't thought how much I wanted you to be a success so that you could bring your mother to Tokyo. When you tell me this horrible news, I am naturally upset and worried for your sake, imagining how ashamed it would make you. I'd never feel that way about a stranger. I expected you at least to say you are sorry you lost your job because you haven't listened to my advice. I don't even really care if you don't apologize. But to get fired and then say 'what's done is done'! I just can't believe it. What a waste of sympathy. When I think how I've watched over you and cared for you all these years and you think nothing of it."

"That's not true. I'm very poor at expressing myself, as you perfectly well know, but there are things in my heart which I . . ."

"Oh, no. I won't listen to any excuses. You treat me like a stranger. I'm just an old witch to you. I never dreamed you could be so ungrateful. Here I've been wasting my time worrying about your marriage. I planned to talk to your mother about it. I thought I'd try to find some nice girl for you. I wanted to make all kinds of preparations for your wedding because it was to be my own beloved nephew who was getting married and not some stranger. I've been doing nothing but plotting and planning. I thought I'd stitch up that heavy silk obi and do over the striped crepe and fix up one thing and another. But I should have known better. I don't care so much that you've been fired, but not to feel ashamed of yourself after all I've done for you—to just shrug the whole thing off. I won't say another word. It won't do any good. I'm nothing but a stranger to you.

"And what's more, you should have told me you were fired last night," she went on after a minute. "You never said a word about it and I went to all sorts of trouble to fix lunch for you today. I was worried about you because you work so hard and I decided to put an omelette in your lunch box for a little variety. But Onabe doesn't know how to make it so I had to fix it for you specially myself. The one time I put myself out, this is what I get. I should have kept out of it. Nobody even asked me. Onabe!"

"Yes."

"Throw Bunzō's lunch out!"

Onabe thrust her wide face through the door. She looked very confused.

"Bunzō was fired yesterday."

"Really?"

"These intelligent men are certainly extraordinary." Before Omasa could go on Bunzō got up, white with anger. He walked straight out of the room and returned to his own quarters. He sat down before his desk. Tears of vexation dropped on his knees. He wiped his falling tears away with a handkerchief, but he could not erase the fury that kept swelling up within him. The more he thought about it, the more angry he became, until he was completely lost in resentment and mortification.

His aunt's criticisms were plausible enough, but he knew that they only covered up what she really thought. Her attitude toward him obviously changed just as soon as she learned he had lost his job. The superficiality of her affection came as no surprise; he had endured the knowledge of it before and could do so again. What he could not endure was that she had all but called him a coward to his face. He was too angry to stop to consider why she had jeered at him or why she considered him a coward. He was so furious and so hurt that it seemed his heart would break. "All right then, if that's the way she's going to be. I let her say whatever she wanted because she's my aunt. But if we're going to cut all our ties, I can do whatever I please, just as if I were no relation to her at all. I know what I'll do. I'll move to a boardinghouse just to spite her."

Even as he said this, Osei's image darted before his eyes. He wavered. His hesitation ended when he remembered his aunt's vile face. He became angry once more. "Damn it. Even if she forbids it, I won't stay here!" he declared with rare resolution. The idea of remaining in that house another minute seemed horrible. He began to dislike his room when he thought of it as rented. He was irritated with everything in it, even the firepan with the broken rim, when he realized that nothing was his own.

He looked at the clock. It was already eleven. He decided to pack his belongings at once and move to a boardinghouse that very day. Muttering to himself over and over that he would not stay no matter what his aunt said, he began to assemble things in a great fury. He was searching for something when he happened to open the desk drawer. The photograph of a white-haired woman caught his eye. He stared at it. It was a picture of his mother.

Bunzō loved his mother very much and seeing her photograph forcibly reminded him that he had endured the hardships of the world all this time for her sake as well as his own. All his old feelings of obligation welled up within him and he felt utterly crushed and broken. His determination to leave that hateful house deserted him.

It was three o'clock in the afternoon. The autumn sun began to sink in the sky and the shadow of the tree in the garden grew longer. Omasa sat alone, leaning on the hibachi. She was idly tracing letters in the ashes with a pair of tongs, her mind occupied with her thoughts. She sighed from time to time with annoyance and vexation.

The front door opened with a rattle. Someone entered the house and looked in at the doorway. "Hello," he said. . . .

He was wearing a plain, blue striped kimono of sturdy fabric with a silk pongee *haori* over it. The chain of his pocket watch was coiled around a rather sorry-looking obi of coarse silk. In his hand he carried a Turkish fez. He had obviously changed his clothes after coming from the office.

"Well, this is a rare pleasure. We see so little of you these days. I'm sure you'll be sorry to find just an old lady like me here."

"No, no, that's quite all right. Oh, dear, that sounds terrible, doesn't it? Well, anyway, is Utsumi in?"

"Yes."

"I'll go and talk to him for a minute. Then I'll be right back to get even with you for the last time."

"You may be sorry."

"Maybe." After exchanging a few more words, he went upstairs.

Before he returned, we should have a brief biography of this young man, but unfortunately his past is lost in a haze and we know little of his parentage, the kind of education he received, or

144] IMPERIAL JAPAN: 1800-1945

how he lived as a boy. One set of rumors has it that he lost his parents as a child and drifted about among relatives and friends, a poor, homeless waif, and had been driven to taking employment as a servant. But such idle rumors should be discounted; they rarely prove reliable and are shorter lived than the morning dew. Someone who had actually seen the records reported that the young man was born in Tokyo into a family vaguely connected with the samurai class. This much at least was not a lie.

The young man's name was Honda Noboru. He had been appointed to a post in the lower ranks of the government service two years before Bunzō was hired. With luck he had quickly improved his position. As our story begins, he is in the sixth rank, still a bachelor, and living quite comfortably indeed.

Noboru was what is known as a "clever fellow"; resourceful and proud of his talents. There was no limit to the power of his eloquence; he might, in fact, have rivaled a street entertainer. Unfortunately at times this very gift led him to exaggerate and boast. As for his other talents, he managed to do all sorts of things reasonably well, although it could not be said that he excelled at any one thing. Idleness was his nature and inconstancy his illness.

Suave and charming, Noboru was extremely adept at flattery. He was particularly attentive to people when he first met them, making himself agreeable to everyone, even women and old people. But strangely enough, after he got to know someone better, his cordiality disappeared and he became haughty. He teased his friends and said things which offended them until they grew angry and turned on him. If it was someone less clever than he, Noboru would give another twist to the screw, but if it was someone with more skill, he would laugh it off at the time and wait for a chance to get even later. To express it in a vulgar way, he threw dogs' dung into the face of his enemies.

At any rate Noboru was a clever man and served his chief at the bureau very well.

That worthy gentleman, the chief, had once made a trip abroad. Maintaining that he felt the greatest contempt for the old feudalistic hierarchy, he loudly voiced criticism of the arrogant ways of his fellow bureaucrats. On the other hand, he was known to be a very difficult and unreasonable man himself and would fall into a towering rage over anything that displeased him. In short, he was an old-fashioned despot who made a show of advocating liberalism. This contradiction between the ideas he expressed and his own true nature resulted in tremendous confusion among those who worked with him. Most did not know how to please him.

Only Noboru knew. He copied the gentleman's speech and gestures and even assumed the way he cleared his throat and his manner of sneezing. The imitation was almost perfect, except that the chief laughed in the same way no matter who he was with, while Noboru varied his tone depending on his audience. When the older man spoke to him, Noboru rushed over to his desk and listened respectfully, his head cocked knowingly to one side. After he had finished speaking, the young man would smile broadly and reply most humbly. He maintained just the right tone. He was neither too distant nor too friendly. Everything was done in accordance with the chief's wishes; he was never contradicted. Moreover—and this is the most important point—Noboru took note of the mistakes made by other division heads as a device for praising the man. He, in turn, considered Noboru very promising and was quite partial to him. The other young men in the office did not speak well of Noboru, but he attributed it to their jealousy.

In short, Noboru was a clever man. He went to work diligently and carried out his chores in the office most expeditiously. His face remained pleasant; his manner unruffled. This was particularly impressive because he produced more work in half a day than others could in a full day. Actually, most of his work was done by browbeaten pages and office boys while he merely made a great show of being terribly busy.

At the end of each day he returned to his boardinghouse, changed his clothes, and immediately went out again. He rarely settled down and stayed in his room. On Sunday he would pay his respects at the home of his supervisor and play go with him or run errands.

Once the chief's wife expressed a desire to have a Pekinese for a pet. No sooner said than done. Before a day passed, Noboru had got hold of one and presented it for her inspection. The chief looked at the dog and remarked that it seemed to him to have a rather strange face. Noboru agreed that it indeed had a strange face. The chief's wife suggested that it was considered desirable for a Pekinese to have such a ratlike face. Noboru said that to be sure it was thought to be better if a Pekinese had such a ratlike face, just as the lady had said, and he had complacently patted the dog's head.

Even the talented Noboru makes mistakes at times. They say that once he managed somehow to incur the chief's displeasure, and for a day or two he was so upset that he found it difficult to eat. He soon won the chief's wife over to his cause, and then it was only a matter of a short time until he was able to soothe the anger of the great man himself. How much better he felt when it was all over. He was indeed a young man of considerable talent.

3. Ideology for the New Society

✿ IT WAS RECOGNIZED EARLY by the Meiji elite that Japan would need a modern educational system to provide a literate citizenry for the new industrial society. Under the leadership of Education Minister Mori Arinori this system took shape rapidly and was characterized by a nationalistic tone that encouraged service to the state. Controversies arose between Mori's ideas about education, which were considered too Western or "liberal" by some, and the more traditional Confucian moralism favored by Motoda Eifu, a court official close to the emperor. The argument between the two factions produced much heat (Mori was later assassinated), but it is hard to see really fundamental differences between them on the need for a strong state. In the end the more old-fashioned approach of Motoda won out, and education indoctrinated children in total loyalty to the emperor and in carrying out the vague "mission" of the Japanese people. Yet Mori's initial institution of military training and emphasis on similar nationalistic loyalty had laid the groundwork. One must conclude that the two approaches differed mildly on methods but not in the essential use of education for social control and support for the state.

Higher education was set up explicitly as an elite institution, tied to the bureaucracy, and clearly set apart from the practical education reserved for the lower classes. Government assumed responsibility for practically all areas of education, following a European model, and private institutions were set up only rarely. These were confined to a few colleges set up by Christian churches or by individuals.

The two documents included show the tone of the moral education that was spread throughout the schools. The 1890 Rescript, in particular, was important as an imperially sponsored statement and was taught in most schools.

HERBERT PASSIN*
Mori Arinori

Itō had opposed both the national scholars, who looked to antiquity for the model of what a modern Japanese state should be, and the Confucianists, who were fearful of the effects of Western utilitarianism and "materialism" on morality and public virtue. But this implied no preference for the individual as against the state. The supremacy of the state was a firmly established principle for him, and it had only been confirmed by his long study tour of European constitutional systems. What he wanted was a modern patriotism that would forward the development of national strength. While he was in Paris on his constitutional mission, Mori Arinori, then Minister in England, paid him a visit in September 1882. The two found themselves in such substantial agreement on the role of education in the development of the state that Itō promised Mori privately to make him his Minister of Education. In July 1884 Mori returned home from England.

With the inauguration of the new cabinet system in December 1885, Itō became Japan's first modern Prime Minister. Mori was duly appointed Minister of Education, despite the unrelenting opposition of Motoda and other Confucianists around the Emperor Meiji. Among other things, Motoda charged that Mori was a Christian. Within three months of taking office, Mori carried through the series of ordinances that established the basis of the modern educational system. From then until February 11, 1889, the day of the promulgation of the new constitution, when he was assassinated by a fanatic nationalist youth, he carried on an energetic struggle to entrench his principles in the face of opposi-

* Herbert Passin, *Society and Education in Japan* (New York: Teachers College and East Asian Institute, Columbia University, 1965), pp. 86–91, 226–228.

tion from all sides. In the course of so doing, he left Japanese education with an ambiguous legacy and himself with a controversial historical reputation.

The basic building blocks of his educational structure were laid in short order during March and April of 1886. The Imperial University Decree redesignated the Tokyo University as "Imperial," stipulating its function as the pursuit of higher learning and research in the interests of the nation. Immediately thereafter, the University adopted the official school uniforms and caps that remained for so long a part of the standard equipment of Japanese students. The Elementary School Decree reestablished compulsory schooling at four years (although three years were permitted under certain circumstances). His Middle School Decree made the lower division of the middle school terminal; the upper division was made a distinct unit, eventually becoming, in 1894, the *kōtō-gakkō* (university-preparatory higher school), which continued until the postwar American reform.

The most controversial aspect of Mori's historical reputation is his "nationalism." Once considered pro-Western, almost a foreigner to Japan, he was later considered a leading advocate of militarist nationalism, only to be assassinated in the end by a real nationalist for his purported "disrespect toward the emperor." In 1870, at the age of twenty-three, Mori had written, in a manner reminiscent of Thomas Paine, that "Progress can only be achieved through revolutions and trials. . . ." But in the late 1880s he was also to say: "In the administration of all schools, it must be kept in mind, what is to be done is not for the sake of the pupils, but for the sake of the country."

But the "sake of the country," it will be recalled, implied not only obedience but "training" as well. Obedience might be a necessary, even the basic, civic virtue, but quite clearly it was not likely to bring Japan the new knowledge and techniques she needed to become a major world power. On the other hand, the critical skeptical temper of the West, important though it might be for the development of Japanese science and technology, was a threat to the constitutional absolutism envisioned by the Meiji leaders. Mori's resolution of this dilemma, whatever his true intention may have been, was so ingenious that it remained essentially unchanged until the end of the Second World War.

What he did was to establish a dual system: on the one hand a compulsory sector heavily indoctrinated in the spirit of morality and nationalism; on the other, a university sector for the elite in an atmosphere of the greatest possible academic freedom and critical rationalism. Although the freedom of the university involved a certain degree of risk, Mori felt that it was minimized by the fact that all students would come to it only after a thorough indoctrination in the lower schools. But this was not, it should be noted, the traditional morality demanded by the Confucianists. Mori forbade, during his term of office, the use of morals texts based on Motoda's *Kyōgaku Taishi*. But since he knew that their mere elimination from the schools would not solve the problem, he tried to formulate his own nationalism. This was essentially the same as Fukuzawa's: the need to create a "new" Japanese individual, not "subject" but "citizen," one equipped in education and mentality to accept his personal responsibility for the fate of the country. His willingness to accept the Imperial symbol did not contradict this.

The gap between higher and lower education was to be bridged by the normal school, and here Mori adopted some of his most controversial measures. Normal school students, who were state-supported, were placed in dormitories under strict military-style discipline. Colonel Yamakawa, an officer on active service, was made head of the Tokyo Higher Normal School and military officers were placed in charge of many provincial schools. Six hours of military drill per week were prescribed. The normal school, Mori felt, should place more emphasis on cultivating character than on mere learning. Three virtues were to be pursued: dignity, friendship, and obedience. Mori's solution, whatever his intentions may have been, has resulted in that curious dichotomy between the relative academic freedom of the Japanese university and the severely controlled and indoctrinated system of lower education.

And yet, in spite of appearances, for Mori the essence of the matter was not military training *per se,* but rather physical fitness. In 1879, while still in England, he had written: "Military training must be carried on for the sake of physical development. . . . But I want to make it clear that it is in no sense for the sake of military training itself." Knowledge alone was not enough, he felt. It must be supplemented by unshakable inner strength, which could come only from spiritual and physical discipline. What he aimed at was, in fact, a version of "a sound mind in a sound body." It is not sufficient merely to know the good—one must be able to put it into practice.

These ideas, in spite of their apparent similarity to those of the real nationalists, and even of some of the Confucianists, had come to him from an entirely different, and rather unexpected, quarter. During his year in the United States in 1867, Mori had fallen deeply under the influence of the utopian Christianity of Thomas Lake Harris, a Swedenborgian. Mori, along with several other Japanese students, had actually gone to live in Harris's utopian colony of The Brotherhood of the New Life in Amenia and then Salem-on-Erie, New York. Here, the life of the colonists had been based on the principles of discipline, absolute obedience to God (through absolute obedience to the spiritual master—Harris), and hard physical labor. The slogans, "Dignity, Friendship, and Obedience," which Mori adopted for the normal schools of Japan, were the very slogans of Harris's Brotherhood. It was undoubtedly these ideas that lay behind his ill-chosen physical-fitness methods in the normal schools. The notion that one achieves true freedom only by way of absolute obedience to some transcendental value, or through its earthly representative, made it easier for Mori to accept the notion of absolute obedience to the state and, if necessary, to its symbol, the emperor. The emperor was for him not so much a person or an institution, but rather a remote transcendence that made possible the absolute obedience leading to true liberation.

How much was self-deception, or a deliberate alignment of his views to concord with those of Itō and his companions, it would be hard to say. But the assassin's instinct may very well have been truer than that of his later critics. With Mori's death, the nationalistic resurgence swept to its climax in the Imperial Rescript on Education of 1890.

IMPERIAL RESCRIPT, 1879
Imperial Rescript: The Great Principles of Education, 1879

The Kyōgaku Taishi *was issued as an Imperial Rescript, a form which carried great weight because it presumably embodied the views of the emperor. It was actually written, however, by Motoda Eifu, the controversial Confucian lecturer to the Meiji emperor. In 1878 the emperor had made a tour of the provinces from which he returned alarmed at what he had seen in the schools. Motoda's statement became the center of a continuing controversy that eventuated in the dominance of the conservatives, symbolized by the issuance of the Imperial Rescript on Education on October 30, 1890.*

The essence of education, our traditional national aim, and a watchword for all men, is to make clear the ways of benevolence, justice, loyalty, and filial piety, and to master knowledge and skill and through these to pursue the Way of Man. In recent days, people have been going to extremes. They take unto themselves a foreign civilization whose only values are fact-gathering and technique, thus violating the rules of good manners and bringing harm to our customary ways. Although we set out to take in the best features of the West and bring in new things in order to achieve the high aims of the Meiji restoration—abandonment of the undesirable practices of the past and learning from the outside world—this procedure had a serious defect: It reduced benevolence, justice, loyalty, and filial piety to a secondary position. The danger of indiscriminate emulation of Western ways is that in the end our people will forget the great principles governing the relations between ruler and subject, and father and son. Our aim, based on our ancestral teachings, is solely the clarification of benevolence, justice, loyalty, and filial piety.

For morality, the study of Confucius is the best guide. People should cultivate sincerity and moral conduct, and after that they should turn to the cultivation of the various subjects of learning in accordance with their ability. In this way, morality and technical knowledge will fall into their proper places. When our education comes to be grounded on justice and the Doctrine of the Mean, we shall be able to show ourselves proudly throughout the world as a nation of independent spirit.

Two Notes on Elementary Education

1. All men are by nature benevolent, just, loyal, and filial. But, unless these virtues are cultivated early, other matters will take precedence, making later attempts to teach them futile. Since

the practice has developed recently of displaying pictures in classrooms, we must see to it that portraits of loyal subjects, righteous warriors, filial children, and virtuous women are utilized, so that when the pupils enter the school they will immediately feel in their hearts the significance of loyalty and filial piety. Only if this is done first and then other subjects taught later will they develop in the spirit of loyalty and filial piety and not mistake the means for the end in their other studies.

2. While making a tour of schools and closely observing the pupils studying last autumn, it was noted that farmers' and merchants' sons were advocating high-sounding ideas and empty theories, and that many of the commonly used foreign words could not be translated into our own language. Such people would not be able to carry on their own occupations even if they some day returned home, and with their high-sounding ideas, they would make useless civil servants. Moreover, many of them brag about their knowledge, slight their elders, and disturb prefectural officers. All these evil effects come from an education that is off its proper course. It is hoped, therefore, that the educational system will be less highflown and more practical. Agricultural and commercial subjects should be studied by the children of farmers and merchants so that they return to their own occupations when they have finished school and prosper even more in their proper work.

IMPERIAL RESCRIPT ON EDUCATION, 1890

Know ye, our Subjects!

Our Imperial ancestors have founded our empire on a basis broad and everlasting and have deeply and firmly implanted virtue; our subjects, ever united in loyalty and filial piety, have from generation to generation illustrated the beauty thereof. This is the glory of the fundamental character of our empire, and herein also lies the source of our education. Ye, our subjects, be filial to your parents, affectionate to your brothers and sisters; as husbands and wives be harmonious, as friends true; bear yourselves in modesty and moderation; extend your benevolence to all; pursue learning and cultivate arts, and thereby develop your intellectual faculties and perfect your moral powers; furthermore, advance the public good and promote common interests; always respect the constitution and observe the laws; should any emergency arise, offer yourselves courageously to the state; and thus guard and maintain the prosperity of our Imperial throne, coeval with heaven and earth. So shall ye not only be our good and faithful subjects, but render illustrious the best traditions of your forefathers.

The way here set forth is indeed the teaching bequeathed by our Imperial ancestors, to be observed alike by their descendants and subjects, infallible for all ages and true in all places. It is our wish to lay it to heart in all reverence, in common with you, our subjects, that we may all thus attain to the same virtue.

⚙ SHINTO, the Japanese nature cult, was assigned a central role in the educational system, as described by Kitagawa. Before its elevation to the position of state religion, Shinto had been little more than simple mythology, but Shinto was purely Japanese, unlike Confucianism, and it explicitly acknowledged the position of the emperor as sacred. Thus it fit neatly in a nationalistic outline of history and formed an essential part of the ideology that supported Japanese nationalism and militarism.

Confucianism remained important in defining family roles in the traditional feudal way, but it was secondary to state Shinto. Eventually elements of Confucian thought were absorbed into the Shinto ideology. Both supported the authoritarian tendencies in education, and both were to be increasingly used in fighting the inroads of liberal Western ideas and values.

JOSEPH KITAGAWA*
Modernity, Culture, and Religion

With the establishment of the Meiji regime in 1868, the coalition of National Learning (*kokugaku,* which was equated with the neo-

* Joseph Kitagawa, *Religion in Japanese History* (New York: Columbia University Press, 1966), pp. 253–258.

Shinto movement), Confucian learning (*jugaku,* also called *kangaku* or "Chinese learning"), and Western learning (*yōgaku*) came to an end. In the process of creating a new national image, Shinto was clearly in the saddle, for it alone was equipped to exalt the throne as the legitimate heir to the imperial charisma handed down from the sun goddess, Amaterasu. And the architects of the new regime made full use of the Shinto-inspired rationale of the imperial authority for the unification of the nation. They also encouraged Western learning in order to seek knowledge from all over the world toward the end of maintaining national prosperity and defense (*fukoku kyōhei*). Confucian learning was squeezed out and neglected, or at least so the Confucian scholars felt. Actually, the Confucian tradition was far from being dead. Confucian ethics remained as the only meaningful norm for family and other interhuman relations, and words of Chinese origin which had Confucian connotations were coined to appropriate new ideas introduced from the West. However, Confucianism lost the honors and prerogatives which, as the most influential intellectual tradition, it had enjoyed during the Tokugawa regime, for many of the early Meiji leaders, notwithstanding their indebtedness to Confucian training during their childhood, turned to Western civilization for intellectual and technological assistance in the task of shaping the course of the nation in the modern world.

If Western influence could have been confined to technological and academic spheres alone, as the Meiji regime had hoped, it would not have caused so much anxiety for the government leaders. If that had been possible, Japan could have developed both a highly centralized hierarchical polity and an efficient, "modern" technological civilization. Instead, Western influence resulted in the emergence of a new intelligentsia that demanded liberty, equality, and human dignity. What the Westernized intelligentsia envisaged was not the kind of technological civilization that was merely to serve the political ends defined by a few men who surrounded the throne, but the kind of civilization that "advances the well-being and dignity of man, since man acquires these benefits through knowledge and virtue," to quote Fukuzawa Yukichi, the spokesman of the modernist movement. It is to be noted that the "virtue" advocated by Fukuzawa was not the traditional Confucian virtue, based on that hierarchical relationship in which one is expected to know one's place and to fulfill his obligations with diligence, humility, and obedience. Convinced that all men and women were created equal and furnished with the same dignity without distinction, Fukuzawa and others like him instilled the spirit of "modernity" in the minds of youths who were impatient with the traditional values. Although Fukuzawa had had the usual Confucian training in his childhood, he was critical of the Confucian teachings that stressed trust in the words of ancient Chinese sages. He was against any attempt to look for a model of the new society in the past—in the golden days of Yao and Shun. He went so far as to say: "What the ancients achieved is of their time, what we achieve is of our time. Why study the past to function in the present?" The modernists' influence was strongly felt in the educational philosophy of the early Meiji era, and some of them even favored the adoption of Christianity for practical reasons.

The apparent popularity of the modernist movement, especially among the young people in urban areas, aroused fear and resentment among the conservative elements in government circles. The government leaders realized, however, that Shinto, important though it was as the foundation of the new Japan, lacked the intellectual and moral content that was necessary for the nation. Thus, they soft-pedaled anti-Buddhist measures and also sought the alliance of Confucian scholars. Conversely, both Buddhist and Confucian leaders, alarmed at the penetration of "foreign" influence, rallied behind Shinto and the government leaders. . . . However . . . the government's effort in establishing a new national cult called "Great Teaching or Doctrine" (*Daikyō*), amalgamating Buddhism and Confucianism within the Shinto framework, was doomed to failure. Thus the government resorted to the ingenious measure of creating state Shinto, which was declared to be nonreligious, over and above all religions which were allowed nominal autonomy.

In this situation, Japanese Confucian leaders also attempted to make a comeback. Unfortunately for them, the Confucian college called Shōheizaka Gakumonjo, which had been supported by the Tokugawa regime, was transformed into the government university in 1868. In the same year a group of Confucianists organized the Shiseikai (Association of equality of ideas), but it soon declined. Undaunted, the Confucianists established another society called the Shibun Gakkai (Society for the cause of truth), which, in the opinion of a contemporary scholar on modern Japanese Confucianism, was "the most important Confucian organization in Japan in the years from 1880 to 1918." A number of other Confucian and semi-Confucian organizations also came into being. . . . These organizations were supported by some of the Imperial princes, former court nobles, conservative politicians, and businessmen. While we cannot discuss their activities in detail, we can safely say that they primarily promoted Confucian ethics as the moral foundation of the nation. Their initial attempt at influencing the policies of the Ministry of Education was rebuffed by those who advocated Westernized education. It was through the Ministry of the Imperial Household that the Confucianists influenced the throne, as evidenced in the Confucian contents of the Imperial Rescript on Education. In so doing, they eventually made a decisive impact on the Ministry of Education's educational philosophy.

The promulgation of the constitution (1889) and of the Imperial Rescript on Education (1890) are, as Hugh Borton observes, two sides of the same coin. "That coin was the consolidation in the socio-political-economic life of Japan of a highly centralized authoritarian form of social organization based upon respect for the emperor and the Confucian concept of filial piety. . . . The Imperial Rescript on Education rather than the new constitution was the 'new axis of the new order.' " . . . Significantly, the Rescript made no mention of the Chinese sages. . . . [T]he Confucian virtues are taught as the basic moral principles of Japan, bequeathed to the people of Japan by the Imperial ancestors. . . . The transmutation of Confucianism from a semireligious ethical system, based on the teachings of Chinese sages, into an "indigenous" patriotic ethic enabled Japanese Confucianists in the modern period to pontificate on educational and political questions. For example, a noted Confucianist, Inoue Tetsujirō, championed the cause of the anti-Christian movement on the ground that Christianity, being a "foreign" religion, was incompatible with the spirit of the Imperial Rescript on Education. The most conspicuous influence of the Confucian tradition is seen in the "moral teaching" (*shūshin*), a required subject in the primary and secondary schools until the end of the Second World War. The "moral teaching," which was designed to inculcate "Japanized" Confucian virtues and to strengthen faith in the national polity in harmony with the Imperial Rescript on Education, was considered the basis of education so that boys and girls would become first and foremost faithful subjects of the emperor both in time of peace and in time of war. The transmutation of Confucianism meant, however, that Japanese Confucianism lost its prerogatives as an independent semireligious system, comparable to Shinto and Buddhism. Even the Confucian festival, held at the Confucian temple (*seidō*) at Yushima, Tokyo, in 1907, was conducted with Shinto-style ritual, and the "Conference of the Three Religions," sponsored by the Japanese government in 1912, invited representatives of Shinto, Buddhism, and Christianity, but none from Confucianism, as such, on the ground that Confucianism was a system of nonreligious ethical teachings that were to be practiced by all Japanese nationals regardless of their religious faith. In this situation, "nonreligious" Confucian ethics and state Shinto, which was propagated by government leaders as a "nonreligious" patriotic cult, developed a new coalition.

Once Japanese Confucianism accepted the premise that Confucian ethics were part and parcel of the indigenous, pristine Japanese heritage, it was easy for Confucian scholars to support the ethnocentric pseudo-religion of the state, based on loyalty and filial piety, justifying authoritarianism at home and expansionism abroad. Despite the lofty ethical principles of the Chinese sages, transmitted by the long tradition of Japanese Confucianism, its highest affirmation was now addressed to the throne and to the unique national polity of Japan. . . .

⚙ THE FAMILY was another institution viewed by the Meiji elite as a potential source of social stability and control. With these objectives in mind, the government set about promoting the idealized samurai family organized according to Confucian principles as a model. The sort of family structure desired by the government was even written into law in the civil code of 1898. Moreover, early hesitant steps taken to reshape the family along more modern lines were quickly reversed when the implications of such reforms became apparent, as Yazaki points out. Yet the feudal family model was incompatible with an industrial society, and the ideal family promoted was probably exceptional. What survived, however, was the ideology of "society-as-family" that exalted the emperor and tied all Japanese into a mythology based on theoretically common ancestry in the Imperial family. Even if the feudal model was far in reality from the average family, the family ideal served the important political function of unifying loyalties to the state.

NOBUTAKA IKE*
Evolution of the Family

The evolution of the family, like any other institution, was affected by the character of the restoration settlement. Broadly speaking, in the Tokugawa period there were two types of family system: one prevailing among the samurai class and the other among the plebeian class. To be sure they were not mutually exclusive, since there was a tendency for social inferiors to ape their social betters. At the same time, the samurai class had begun to disintegrate through intermarriage, adoption, and the like. Nevertheless, one might say that among the samurai families the Confucian influence was stronger, the authority of the head of the family was greater, and the relations between the individual members were more formalized than among plebeian families. Among the latter, the family atmosphere was less austere, and the relationship of the members freer and more natural in the sense that there was more display of spontaneous human affection. The samurai, to whom the externals of performance were more important than the spirit in which it was done, thought family life among the commoners was undisciplined, unaffected by rules of propriety and hence "animal-like." . . .

After the Meiji restoration the legal distinctions between classes were abolished. A fluid state of affairs obtained in the early years of the Meiji era; and family organization, if allowed to take its

* Ike Nobutaka, *Beginnings of Political Democracy in Japan* (1950; reprint ed., New York: Greenwood, 1969), pp. 204–208.

natural course of development, very likely would have moved away from Confucian ideals and become more like families in the Western world. . . .

Instead of trying to guide family organization into more democratic paths, the Meiji government took steps to impose the samurai-type of family structure on the entire population. For instance, a decree issued in 1873 by the Dajōkan stated that the commoners should follow the system of primogeniture prevailing among the nobility. "Although no decrees have been issued as yet, with respect to the rights of family succession among commoners, there is no reason why in terms of moral codes a different system of family succession should obtain between the upper and lower classes. Procedure among the commoners should be the same as that among the samurai." The civil code adopted in 1898 contained many provisions which harked back to the feudal period.

An even more effective method of inculcating Confucian ideas on family organization was the indoctrination program carried on in the schools. . . .

It must be said that, on the whole, those who set out to encourage the spread of Confucian family ethics succeeded in their immediate objectives. What they did not foresee was that with the passage of time this type of ethical family code forcibly carried over from a past age would become increasingly incompatible with living realities, thus giving rise to tensions and unresolved conflicts. Speaking of the peculiar nature of disputes in Japan between parents and children, Professor Nakagawa Zennosuke noted: "There is, on the one hand, the Confucian idea of filial behavior which makes filial piety the basis of all action, while, on the other hand, there exists the rather strong individualistic economic life. A great many of the causes [of disputes between parents and children] can be found in the fact that it is not so easy as it used to be to reconcile the two." . . .

Of the various long-range factors contributing to the transformation of the family, urbanization is probably one of the most important.

Census figures show that, as one might expect, the rural areas have a higher birth rate than the cities. Yet the overall rural population has remained relatively stationary. This is brought out by Professor Ueda's figures which show that in the thirty-seven-year period between 1888 and 1925 there was an estimated population

increase of a little over nineteen-and-a-half million. Of this increase, 16,683,000 were living in towns and cities with a population of 10,000 or more. In 1930 one third of the male population
of Tokyo between the ages of fifteen and twenty-four had migrated
to Tokyo within the preceding five-year period.

Owing to the prevalence of the system of primogeniture, it was
generally the second and third sons who migrated to the cities.
There they lived away from their families in dormitories and
boarding houses. A survey made in 1920 in Tokyo revealed, for
instance, that seventy-two percent of the men in the fifteen to
nineteen age bracket and sixty-nine percent of the twenty to twenty-
four bracket were not living with their families. In order to provide
amusement for this large group of young men freed from direct
parental supervision there sprang up in Tokyo in the 1920s a large
number of bars, cafés, taxi dance halls, and other places of
amusement. The well-known phenomena of the *mobo* and *moga* or
the emancipated "modern boy" and "modern girl" were also a
reflection of the cityward movement of young men and women.

Economic independence, city life, sophisticated education—
these were not conducive to the perpetuation of the old Confucian
family system. More and more the young wished to choose their
own mates, and to pursue their own careers. Moreover, with the
acquisition of a new set of values, the old customs became absurd
if not irksome. The brilliant novelist and satirist Natsume Sōseki
caught some of this conflict in his novel, *Kokoro*. After graduation
from a university, the young hero returns home to his parents, who
are extremely pleased at their son's achievement. Then, says the
hero:

> To celebrate my graduation, my parents began to talk about
> inviting our neighbors to a dinner at which we should have *seki-
> han* [mixture of rice and red beans served on happy occasions].
> It was the very thing that I had been secretly dreading since my
> arrival. I at once objected to it, saying, "Please don't make a fuss
> about my graduation."
> I hated country guests. Their only purpose in coming was to
> drink and eat. They were mostly the kind of people who looked
> forward to some event which would make them foregather at
> somebody's house. . . . But I could hardly say to my father and
> mother that they should not make merry with such vulgar people.
> So I only repeated that I did not care for such extravagance.
> "It is not so extravagant, as you think. Your graduation is an
> event which will never occur in your life again. It is reasonable to

celebrate it. You must not refuse," my mother said, who seemed to regard my graduation in the same light as my marriage.

"Of course we can do without it. But you know how people talk," said my father, who disliked other people's backbiting. It was true that these foolish country-people made plenty of ill-natured remarks against people who did not do what they expected.

"The country is different from Tokyo, and very troublesome," he observed again.

"Besides it will affect your father's honor," my mother added.

Other examples from Japanese literature could be easily supplied. Indeed it would be no exaggeration to say that one of the most persistent themes of modern literature is the problem of the individual and the family, and it attests to the severe strains which the family system has been undergoing during the past decades.

YAZAKI TAKEO*
Civil Law and the Family

Just what the family life patterns in the converted warrior dwellings were is not entirely clear. Some insight can be gained from the first three sections of the civil law issued in 1896, and from the fourth and fifth sections of the law of succession of 1898. These laws were drawn up by referring to the standards of households with warrior backgrounds, having little in common with the lives of ordinary people, who were sometimes spoken of as "stupid beasts" by the ruling class. Conditions varied according to the social stratum or province concerned, but these laws are still valuable references for information on family life in the Meiji era.

Enacted first in 1890, the civil law was patterned, in many respects, after French laws, which articulated the basic concept of social equality among people. Consequently, the thoroughgoing discrimination against wives that was customary in the Edo era was modified. The wife's position in the household was made second only to the husband's, displacing male lineage priorities.

* Yazaki Takeo, Social Change and the City in Japan (Tokyo: Japan Publications, 1968), pp. 360–361.

The head of a household was made responsible for younger members within relatively narrow limits. His chief obligation was for their home training and for expenses required in compulsory education. The household head's authority was revised radically. He was not permitted to punish adult children who married without his consent, nor could he punish those who accepted adoption by another family without his consent.

Not only were such ideals unacceptable to many in positions of authority, but in actuality the existing households could not readily absorb such radical reforms. Moreover, the mobilization of all the people required in the programs for increasing national wealth and military strength demanded the cultivation of a populace that readily obeyed authority. A revised civil law was put into effect in 1898, standardizing the family system according to traditional feudal values.

The short-lived attempt to base family life on conjugal (*i.e.*, marriage) relationships, giving the wives better positions, was abandoned. Lineage relationships were reinstated, and family ties were stressed as the basic structure of Japanese society. The centrality of the head of the household was reaffirmed as the one who bears the ancestral spirit of the family. Once again the right of eldest sons to inherit all family properties, and duties, was reinstated.

In the revised civil law the authority of the family head was obviously strengthened. Specifically, his will was determinative in deciding the residential location of all family members. Marriage and adoption plans could be made only with his consent. As conjugal relationships were rejected in favor of lineage relationships, the rights of wives were no longer recognized. While a household was not recognized in the civil law as a legal entity and, hence, family property was not legally recognized, family property rights could be established in some cases. For example, when ownership of property was not clearly established—that is, whether it belonged to the head or to family members—ownership was granted to the head.

Permanent continuation of the family was a strong emphasis of the law. Succession to the headship of the family was limited to males, to the legitimate, eldest son, and he was not permitted to desert his household and proper duty. He was required to venerate his ancestors, performing traditional ceremonies in manifestation of his sincerity. He was the duly authorized guardian of his family's genealogical register, of the ritual equipment of ancestral veneration, and of the family graves.

Family headship and parental authority were formally separated. The father assumed the primary role in parental authority, but the mother's role as next in line was acknowledged. This recognition of the maternal role was a significant step forward in a civil code otherwise reflecting conservative reaction. The law clearly defines the position of men as superior to that of women. A wife was regarded as incompetent to manage her own affairs, and any property she might own was to be managed by her husband on her behalf.

The order of succession strongly favored male heirs. When a family head died, sons and grandsons took precedence over the wife. Only if there were no rightful male heirs could a wife come into ownership of the family property. Such regulations were expressive of the traditional feudal idea that lineage values and relationships took precedence over conjugal ones.

The authority of the head over all members of the family was broadened to cover a wide range of affairs, so as to restore the more familiar elements of feudal society. The actual conditions of family life in the different social classes were not taken into consideration. Rather, the civil law was enacted to mold attitudes and behavior along lines of compliant obedience to authority. The more cooperative patterns of family life and organization among the common people began to disintegrate, especially in the rural districts. In the cities, though, the number of citizens living in small, independent family units increased. These were families formed by marriage that lived on the income earned by the husband, or by the couple jointly. Such families even included some of the former samurai who had gone to work in industry, transportation, or other modernized organs. It is doubtful whether their lives were in complete harmony with the conservative scheme of the family system outlined in the civil law.

4. Politics and the Military

✿ HAVING EMBARKED on the road to industrialization and extensive social reforms, the Meiji leaders very early faced their most serious challenge. Opposition to the course they had chosen, led by tradition-minded samurai, was focused on two immediate national problems: defense against the Western imperialists and the composition of the new modern army.

While there was a strong consensus among all segments of the elite on the need for Japan to become an economically and militarily strong state (summarized in the slogan *fukoku kyōhei* [rich country, strong army]), there were numerous disagreements over how to accomplish this. Controversy centered on the shape of Japan's modern military. The traditionalists led by Saigō Takamori maintained that samurai should constitute the core of the new army, while the majority favored an army raised by conscription in which samurai would be a tiny minority. Saigō urged an expedition against Korea and argued that this would force the internal unity sought by the government.

These foreign and domestic issues became entwined as the majority argued that conscription was useful socially as a means of control and was less adventuristic than occupying Korea, for which Japan was still too weak. Yet their success in molding and equipping a conscript army along Western lines later made possible not only the seizure of Korea but the eventual expansion of Japanese power into China. Moreover, their victory in the debate over what kind of army Japan should have resulted in the permanent disfranchisement of the samurai class as the Meiji oligarchs constructed a peasant army based on conscription and mass literacy.

*JAMES CROWLEY**
Formation of the Meiji Military Establishment

1868–1880: NATIONAL DEFENSE, A MATTER OF TREATY REVISION AND A CIVIL ORDER

With the restoration of the shogunal authority to the emperor, the immediate national security problem was to "strengthen the country" so that Japan could conduct its diplomatic relations on a basis of equality with the Western powers. Two steps seemed essential in this quest: an adequate centralized political system and a strong military establishment. During the first two years of Meiji, there seemed to be no serious degree of incompatibility between organizing a strong national army and an effective national government. As Ōmura Masajirō phrased the initial task, "first prepare against civil disturbances, later, prepare against foreign invasion." To this end, Ōmura, as head of the War Department, envisioned organizing a large army by drawing men from each domain in conjunction with training an officer corps in Western techniques of military organization and command. Although this was to be a national army, Ōmura expected the commoners to constitute the main body of troops, the samurai class to furnish the officer corps. In this manner, Ōmura believed the government could quickly acquire a monopoly of military power and thereby assure domestic order; once this was achieved, the Powers would be compelled to terminate the humiliatingly unequal treaties.

Whether Ōmura would have remained committed to these ideas as he became more familiar with the international scene and with the extremely complex issues associated with training and equipping a national army is difficult to judge. His assassination in 1869

---

* James Crowley, "From Closed Door to Empire," in Bernard S. Silberman and H. D. Harootunian, eds., *Modern Japanese Leadership: Transition and Change* (Tucson, Arizona: University of Arizona Press, 1966), pp 267–268, 269–273.

abruptly terminated this possibility. Still one may say that Ōmura's original policies were not destined to guide the creation of the Imperial army. On the contrary, in the 1870s, when the government resolved in favor of a modest militia and an officer corps open in principle to all men of talent, the strongest adherents of Ōmura's initial program were to be located in the instigators of the rebellions against the new government. The ironic fate of Ōmura's military policies was brought about mainly by two developments: The ability of the new government to assert its political authority throughout the country and to dissolve the han–samurai armies without the necessity of a sizable military force at its disposal; and the acceptance by the senior and junior councillors of the premise that the question of treaty revision and national security could be settled only by comprehensive reforms within Japan. . . .

Without minimizing the significance of these developments, the stability of the new government remained fragile. There was, for example, no real national army. The troops available to the government totaled only 9000 and were drawn almost exclusively from the domains of Chōshū, Tosa, and Satsuma. More fundamentally, it was essentially a collection of warriors, many of whom still gave their primary or personal loyalty to the major military leaders of their former domains, *i.e.*, to Saigō, Itagaki, and Etō. This context was pregnant with grave political dangers, a complication which did not escape the clinical eye of the French military mission.

> "These troops," noted Major Lebon in 1872, "have maintained their clan organization, alongside the new troops recruited indiscriminately in all the provinces of Japan. Today these troops still constitute the Imperial guard for the emperor. However, the central government which they originally served as an instrument and for which they have now become an embarrassment, is seeking to suppress them by dispersing them in a national army."

The efforts to destroy the clan-samurai basis of the new army were, however, hampered by serious dissension in the Council of State. In particular, controversy clustered around the basic approach to the major political and diplomatic problems confronting the government. Should internal unity be sought . . . by posing the national security problem—including domestic order—in terms of a military crisis necessitating the mobilization of all warriors in Japan or should the government initiate comprehensive social, economic, and legal reforms as the best way to achieve a viable political system and to abrogate the "unequal treaties"? Both approaches had their merits, both found articulate and influential proponents among the councillors and administrative departments of the new government. So long as no effective consensus was reached on the basic approach to national problems, the type of military establishment to be developed by the new government remained in doubt.

Originally the War Department had favored the formation of a large national army, one directed by a well-trained officer corps and capable of great expansion by means of a levy *en masse*. This vision, however, soon evaporated as the dimensions of the problems became clearer. In Japan, the French military attaché, Albert Charles du Bousquet, cogently outlined the essential requisites for a national army: a professional military educational system, a literate population so that soldiers could be efficiently taught basic military skills, and an industrial base capable of supplying the necessary supplies and equipment. And, General Yamada, after an intensive survey of the military systems in Europe in 1870, prepared an independent evaluation reinforcing the views of the French attaché. In addition, Yamada stressed the necessity of (1) training a small professional army which could eventually serve as the cadre for a comprehensive conscription army program; and (2) the establishment of a public school system, which would include the rudiments of military training (drill) in the course of study, as the prelude to attempting the implementation of a national conscription program. Yamada's recommendation also embraced another premise, namely, the recruitment of officers theoretically should be open to all citizens.

Obviously, this type of military policy would severely affect the destiny of the samurai. Universal public education would shatter his monopoly of literacy, an officer corps geared to "men of talent" would deny the premise of samurai military leadership, and a small army would preclude a potential military career for most samurai. The result, thought General Torio Koyata, would be rampant civil disorder plus the concomitant evil of enhancing the danger of foreign intervention. Hence, he countered Yamada's views with the argument that all willing samurai be enlisted in the national army and, after this, the army should be reorganized and trained along Western principles. Despite the creditability of these fears, the majority of the staff of the War Department—Yamagata, Nishi, and Yamada—rejected it on two grounds: the government could not afford to equip, feed, and train a force of this size, and there was no imperative strategic necessity for a large army. Hence, the department chose to begin with a very limited conscript program which would provide a national militia capable of preserving civil order.

On January 10, 1873, the government promulgated the first of several conscript laws. Under this program, approximately 10,500 men were to be drafted yearly, with an obligation of three years of active and two years of reserve service. The militia orientation underlying this law is attested to by two of its aspects: (1) it would produce after three years a standing army of 31,680 men and after six years an immediate mobilization potential of 46,350 men; (2) the army was to be comprised of six battalions, located in six military districts. Of most immediate relevance, conscription was first limited to the Tokyo district and, in 1874, applied in the Osaka and Nagoya districts—a maneuver which automatically terminated the hegemony of the warriors from the three major clans in the national army. While the War Department forged ahead with its approach to military affairs, the critics of Yamada's guide temporarily acquired a stronger position in the Council of State.

... The focus on a small army and the commutation of the traditional stipends of the warrior seemed, in Saigō's estimation, to be erroneous on political, military, and ethical considerations. To outflank the reasons justifying these policies, Saigō advanced the famous demand for a Korean military expedition.

> "I need hardly say," Saigō confessed to Itagaki, "that it is at the same time a far-reaching scheme which will divert abroad the attention of those who desire civil strife, and thereby benefit the country. The [adherents of the] former government will lose the opportunity to act, and having to refrain from creating any internal disturbance, will lose the country once and for all."

A Korean campaign, in other words, would sanction Saigō's favorite political-military idea: the immediate formation of a national samurai army as the most efficacious means to promote internal stability.

... [W]hile this famous 1873 controversy—the *seikanron*—was discussed in terms of a Korean War, the central issue at stake was the traditional monopoly of force by the samurai class. Ultimately, with Saigō, Etō, Gotō, and Itagaki dissenting, the councillors vetoed the Korean campaign. The most cogent reason for doing so was articulated by Ōkubo:

> England's influence is particularly strong in Asia. She has occupied land everywhere and has settled her people and stationed her troops thereon. Her warships are poised for any emergency, keeping a silent, vigilant watch, and ready to jump at a moment's notice. However, our country has been largely dependent on England for its foreign loans. If our country becomes involved in an unexpected misfortune [a Korean War], causing our stores to be depleted and our people reduced to poverty, our inability to repay our debts to England will become England's pretext for interfering in our internal affairs which would lead to baneful consequences beyond description.

In effect, by rejecting the Korean campaign the government had finally decided the question which had plagued Japan since the arrival of Perry's gunboats. National defense, whether it be phrased in terms of "expel the barbarian," "open the country," "treaty revision," or *"seikanron,"* was clearly identified as a domestic political problem, one which could not be handled by the time-honored solution: mobilization of the warrior class.

The importance of the 1873 policy decision is difficult to overestimate. It provided the rationale for the subsequent economic and social policies which shattered the privileged social status and economic rights of the samurai class; and it brought about the entrenchment of political power among a handful of men, the famous oligarchy which directed Japan's destiny for the ensuing two decades. Equally important, with the systematic assaults on the traditional privileges of the samurai after 1873, Etō Shimpei rallied the first rebellion against the new government under the trifold banner, "war with Korea," "restoration of the daimyō to their rightful place in the government," and "expel the barbarian." Although this Hizen uprising was squashed easily, the government confronted a greater challenge . . . when Saigō Takamori directed another rebellion under the ideological banner raised initially by the samurai of Hizen [1877]. This conflict, the Seinan War, posed a severe challenge, one which was successfully resolved only after a year of difficult fighting by the entire conscript army. Following this triumph, though, the Meiji oligarchy was able to conduct its foreign relations and to implement political and military reforms without being harassed by the specter of violent civil disorder.

❀ CONSCRIPTION, once in operation, proved to be not only an effective means of social control (peasant draftees were used against rebellions successfully), but one which allowed great opportunities for indoctrinating young conscripts from the countryside. Such inculcation of national values and explicitly racist attitudes towards Koreans and Chinese was to be important later in convincing the average soldier of the necessity of conquering Korea and other areas of Asia. E. H. Norman examines the first decade of conscription and its renewal in 1883, as well as its antidemocratic implications.

E. H. NORMAN*
Conscription and the Opposition to It

. . . The use of naked force to suppress agrarian unrest was not the happiest solution of the problem; it was the last resort which would be used, unflinchingly if necessary, only when other stratagems had failed. And one such stratagem was conscription; first of all, the creation of a unified mass army based on conscription with garrisons stationed at strategic cities and towns would make an uprising in the future much more hazardous and, therefore, unlikely. Thus the mere *threat* of overwhelming force against any local uprising would naturally tend to discourage the resort to violence by the rebellious peasantry. But, looking at it in another way, conscription meant gathering into garrisoned towns large numbers of young and impressionable peasants who, when segregated from their native villages and living under strict military discipline, would no longer be able to hear the complaints of old embittered peasants, nor would be likely to brood over local

* E. H. Norman, *Soldier and Peasant in Japan* (New York: Institute of Pacific Relations, 1943), pp. 46–52.

grievances, or worry over small but pressing problems of domestic economy. In these barracks many of the raw recruits would, especially in the first years of conscription, learn how to read; fresh opportunities for education was one of the by-products of conscription which the more liberal reformers honestly desired. But the government would see to it that the influence which would mould the mind of the recruit would be "safe"; that the reading and instruction in the barracks would emphasize loyalty, unity of the country, the dangers of foreign ideas and particularly of all such seditious concepts as democracy, liberalism, universal suffrage, and, later, socialism and internationalism. Gradually the minds of the conscripts would be turned to safe subjects—such as the need for Japanese expansion, Japan's mission in "freeing" Korea from the tyrannical grasp of China, and finally Japan's role in "liberating" Asia from Western domination. The dominant military figure of modern Japan, whose life spanned both the Meiji and Taishō eras, the man who was, more than any other single individual, the evil genius behind Japan's militarism and black reaction, Field Marshal Yamagata, openly stated that the purpose for the revision and extension of conscription in 1883, with the accompanying enormous increase in military and naval expenditure, was a preparation for war on the continent: "In the meantime the high-handed attitude of the Chinese towards Korea, which was antagonistic to the interests of Japan, showed our officers that a great war was to be expected sooner or later on the continent, and made them eager to acquire knowledge, for they were as yet quite unfitted for a continental war."

It was admitted that the army built up on the basis of the Conscription Act of 1872–1873 was quite sufficient to meet the needs of maintaining internal order, whether to suppress agrarian unrest or pro-feudal rebellion. But after 1877, when the Satsuma Revolt, the last armed stand of feudal reaction, was decisively put down, in the years following 1880 when the great peasant revolts fell off into small infrequent riots, and when there was no real fear of any foreign power attacking Japan, it was precisely at this time that the Japanese government, prodded by Yamagata, initiated the far-reaching military increases mentioned above, which were definitely planned as a prerequisite for future expansion. The historian of the conscription system in Japan quite frankly admits that, after the suppression of the Satsuma Revolt, the expansion of the Japanese army was designed for use abroad: "It is a fact worthy of note that the Satsuma Rebellion was a turning point in the history of the law. Previous to that event, the law had aimed at the maintenance of peace and order at home, but since that time it has always been the object of the law to prepare for emergencies on the continent. This policy of preparedness has ever since been supported by the increase of population at home."

Without understanding the full historical significance of conscription, many farmers, villagers, and townsmen seemed to have instinctively felt some of its implications, because its enforcement in 1873 soon provoked widespread opposition in the form of riots and even armed uprisings. . . .

Conscription with its three years of military service deprived the peasantry for an appreciable period of the strongest hands on the farms, and with no mechanization of agriculture such an absence would be acutely felt. Further, it prognosticated fresh tax burdens, and finally . . . it strengthened the repressive powers of the state.

Even one of the early military leaders, . . . Tani Takeki, noted the fact that the new conscript army was used to suppress agrarian unrest and antifeudal revolt. In describing this counterrevolutionary function of the Japanese army he wrote as follows: "Moreover to our shame there is something which cannot be hidden even if we forcibly tried to gag the mouths of others; and that, as everyone knows, is that the army, created for the purpose of guarding the country against a foreign foe, slaughters the discontented populace of our country; this is truly a disgrace that can hardly be borne."

The incidence of conscription was inequitable, and the historical circumstances in which it was enacted were alarming to those who already feared the increasing autocracy of the government. The Act of 1872–1873, besides providing the usual exemptions for physical and professional reasons, permitted a man to compound for exemption from enrollment by the payment of 270 yen, a sum far beyond the capacity of most commoners. This inequitable incidence has been maintained in less obvious ways until more modern times. . . . "Hence, we may say that the present system of conscription enlists a comparatively greater number of soldiers out of the middle classes, and exempts a great number of the higher classes.

Of course, this circumstance is due to differences of physique, but it is recognized implicitly by all that it is also due *to the discretion of the examiners in the conscript examination."*

Again, young men of well-to-do families with university educations could by the "volunteer" system escape two years of training and at the same time be placed in a favorable position for promotion in case of active service. It is, of course, well known that the senior officers in the army, especially during the Meiji period, came almost exclusively from the famous families of Chōshū and, in the navy, from Satsuma.

In examining the historical circumstances in which conscription was enforced, one should guard against the charge of reckless oversimplification by stating at once that Japanese society was, and still is, a most complex phenomenon, and that it contains what appear to be baffling inconsistencies and inner contradictions. At the time when the military bureaucrats of the early Meiji era were intent on instituting conscription, some of the more obtuse and noisy (hence less dangerous) reactionaries were agitating against it on the ground that the lower classes were unfit to bear arms. On the other hand, Saigō Takamori, the most capable organizer of profeudal reaction, quite characteristically opposed general conscription, advocating instead a permanent standing army of elite professional soldiers. Yamagata, fresh from a study of Western military systems on his return from France in 1870, insisted on general conscription and was supported by the most astute leaders of the day, Ōkubo and Kido.

This digression is merely a warning against the assumption that every opponent of conscription was necessarily a stout champion of democracy and peace. Nevertheless, the more keen-sighted critics of autocracy and reaction saw in conscription, and particularly in its timing, a sinister augury of whither Japanese policy would lead in succeeding years. We have some indication of the politically unnecessary and, therefore, reactionary nature of the early creation of the Japanese conscript army in the words of Ueki Emori, one of the leaders of the left wing of the Liberal Party (Jiyūtō), who wrote in 1879, "An army does not depend on guns and ships but primarily on the feeling of patriotism which is imbued with the true love of liberty."

A fact which must not be overlooked is that both the original law of 1872–1873 and the revised law of 1883, which fixed the pattern of the conscription system for modern Japan, were decreed *before* the establishment of a constitution or of any representative institutions. The conscript army created by the fiat of the Dajōkan (Council of State), where the able but autocratic Meiji bureaucrats issued their decrees unimpeded by the representatives of an assembly or even by the code of a basic constitutional law, became a powerful political weapon in the hands of men who were far too cunning and far-sighted to dull it recklessly by constant or unnecessary use.

▦ THE DISPUTE over conscription and the Korea invasion in 1873 led to the first political splits in the Meiji oligarchy and produced three new groupings: the majority ruling faction, Saigō and the ultraconservative samurai, and the clique led by Itagaki Taisuke. Ike below discusses Itagaki's political career in the early movement for a representative assembly. As the forerunner of the Popular Rights Movement, Itagaki's group was, however, steadfastly aristocratic and as expansion-minded as the rest of the oligarchs (Itagaki had favored the early occupation of Korea).

Liberalism, whose origins in Japan are often traced back to Itagaki's early opposition to his fellow warriors in power, was a movement with no roots in the Japanese tradition. As it developed, especially under men like Itagaki, liberalism's chief trait was opportunism. Japan's first political parties, in fact, were more a reflection of the divisions within the elite than meaningful parties. Norman explores the effects upon the development of parties of their base being in the countryside and from the landlord class.

The government revealed its genuine feelings about democracy in politics by suppressing the radical peasant offshoots of the early parties, which attempted to put life into the rhetoric of Itagaki. Once such subversive groups were weeded out, a politically housebroken Diet (promised for 1890) was guaranteed; and the basic policy was established of encouraging "responsible" political groups while dealing ruthlessly with those that demanded more democratic institutions.

NOBUTAKA IKE*
Itagaki and the Movement Toward a Parliament

The crisis of 1873 marked a great divide in the political history of the Meiji era. The unity of the coalition originally formed to overthrow the Tokugawa was broken. Now that the common enemy was gone, and the confusion attending the first days of reconstruction ended, the restoration began to appear in a different light to different people. To some the partial political revolution, which had been the restoration, had gone too far, while to others it had not gone far enough. The conflicting cross-currents of interest, submerged in the early days of the restoration, at last appeared on the surface. And out of the break that followed there emerged at least three groups where previously there had been but one.

Of these groups the most powerful was the one remaining in control of the government. The roster of this group included virtually all of the names of the leading Meiji political figures—Ōkubo, Kido, Itō, Ōkuma, Yamagata, Iwakura, to mention a few. In matters of basic social and political philosophy these men were in basic agreement. They believed in a program of modernization; but they also attached certain important qualifications. Modernization was to be directed toward the centralization of power, the strengthening of the military arm of the state, and eventual overseas expansion. Opposed to popular control of the government, they aimed to erect an absolute state, using what one writer has called the "mystic quality" of the emperor to bind the various pieces together. Given the agreement on fundamentals, the group naturally possessed a high degree of internal cohesion and formed a tightly knit oligarchy. This internal cohesion, moreover, was reinforced by the fact that almost all of the men were samurai from the two clans of Satsuma and Chōshū. In a time when local sentiment and local loyalties were still very strong, this was a very

* Ike Nobutaka, *Beginnings of Political Democracy in Japan* (1950; reprint ed., New York: Greenwood, 1969), pp. 53–59.

important consideration. The government became something of a private preserve for men from these two areas. Little wonder the critics denounced the government for being a *hambatsu seifu* or "clan government."

The second group, led by Saigō Takamori, consisted of the disaffected samurai. Saigō came from Satsuma, but in his case his dislike of the policy of modernization was strong enough to overcome his sense of loyalty to his fellow clansmen in the central government. After retirement from public office, Saigō returned to his home in Kagoshima, where he organized *shigakkō* or "private schools." In these "schools" which, as an authority puts it, were "really Saigō's own military academy" the samurai were organized, trained, and indoctrinated. Since Satsuma had always formed an *imperium in imperio* and effective control of the central government had never been extended into the province, Saigō was able to carry on his work without much interference. From among the large samurai population (consisting of about one fourth of the total), he recruited many followers. Finally in 1877 Saigō raised the banner of revolt and took the field at the head of some 30,000 men. The Satsuma Rebellion, as this uprising is called, was essentially an attempt to put the clock back and restore the old feudal order. As such it was almost a foregone conclusion that it could not succeed, for Saigō was leading his movement into a historical blind alley. The government immediately dispatched its modern conscript army to do battle with the samurai. The plebeians, armed with rifles, proved more than a match for the samurai elite. After six months of savage fighting, the rebellion was put down. In defeat Saigō, seriously injured, asked one of his officers to put him to death. The Satsuma Rebellion proved to be the last of a series of samurai uprisings. Its failure demonstrated conclusively that the Meiji government was too powerful to be overthrown by force. "It was amply proved," as McLaren has said, "that any criticism of the government must follow a peaceful course, under the guidance of educated public opinion, not the desperate counsel of military fanaticism."

The third group, led by Itagaki Taisuke, is of the greatest interest to us. . . .

In the debate over the Korean question Itagaki had consistently sided with Saigō and had resigned with him when the peace party triumphed. But after leaving the government Itagaki pursued an independent course. While both were opposed to the government, they revealed their opposition in different ways. This can be explained, in part, by the fact that, unlike Saigō, Itagaki's disaffection was mostly that of the "outs" against the "ins." It was a case of a member of a minority clan showing his resentment against the dominance of the Satsuma and Chōshū, or Sat-Chō, faction. For that reason Itagaki's opposition took the form of political action rather than armed uprising.

Itagaki fired his first shot against the Meiji oligarchy a few months after his resignation. His attack took the form of a memorial calling for the establishment of an elective assembly. Since he had been a member of the Dajōkan [Council of State], he must have known about the discussions and research going on within the *Sa-in* [legislative branch] regarding the calling of an assembly and the drafting of a national constitution. It would seem reasonable to assume, therefore, that he decided to steal a march on the government and compel it to agree to the creation of representative institutions. In any case, he discussed the matter with his fellow-clansman, Gotō Shōjirō, who introduced him to Komuro Nobuo and Furuzawa Shigeru, both of whom had just returned from Great Britain. Since Komuro and Furuzawa were anxious to introduce the parliamentary system of government into Japan, they agreed to lend assistance. At Itagaki's request, Furuzawa drafted the memorial. According to some sources, it was originally written in the English language.

On January 17, 1874, the memorial, signed by nine men, including Itagaki and Gotō, was presented to the *Sa-in*. At the same time it was published in the newspapers. This being the first time that a political document of this kind appeared in the press, it aroused considerable interest.

The memorial was a skillfully drawn document. Persuasively written, it effectively exposed some of the weak spots in the government's position. "When we humbly reflect upon the quarter in which the governing power lies," it began, "we find that it lies not with the Crown (the Imperial House) on the one hand, nor with the people on the other, but with the officials alone." The memorial went on to charge that the "administration is conducted in an arbitrary manner, rewards and punishments are prompted by partiality, the channel by which the people should communicate with the government is blocked up and they cannot state their grievances." Since the memorial was being presented by a group of men who had been a minority while in office, this attack on the Meiji bureaucracy was understandable. The memorialists warned that "if a reform is not effected the state will be ruined." In order to avert such a calamity they urged the "establishment of a council chamber chosen by the people. Then a limit will be placed to the power of the officials, and both governors and governed will obtain peace and prosperity."

Next the principle of "no representation, no taxation" was stated. "The people whose duty it is to pay taxes to the government possess the right of sharing in their government's affairs and of approving or condemning. This being a principle universally acknowledged it is not necessary to waste words in discussing it."

Then the memorial attempted to meet some of the objections which the critics were likely to raise to the demand for an elective assembly. To the contention of the government that the people were wanting in "culture and intelligence" and hence it was too early for representative institutions, the memorialists replied that "to give our people culture and intelligence and to cause them to advance into the region of enlightenment, they must in the first place be induced to protect their rights, to respect and value themselves, and be inspired by a spirit of sympathy with the griefs and joys of the empire, which can only be done by giving them a voice in its concerns."

The argument in favor of giving the people a voice in the government was carried a step further. Almost from the very beginning the Meiji government had emphasized everything that would make the nation strong from the military point of view. This attitude was reflected in the well-known slogan, *fukoku kyōhei* or "rich country, strong defense." So now the memorialists asked, "How is the government to be made strong?" "It is by the people of the empire becoming of one mind," they replied. "The establishment of a council chamber chosen by the people will create a community of feeling between the government and the people, and they will mutually unite into one body. Then and only then will the country become strong."

Lastly, the objections to the Japanese suddenly copying foreign institutions were met. Some had argued that parliaments were not formed in the West in one day, but had been developed gradually over a period of many years. The implication, of course, was that the Japanese likewise should gradually evolve a parliamentary system. In reply, the memorial asserted that "The reason why foreigners have perfected this only after the lapse of centuries, is that no examples existed previously and these had to be discovered by actual experience." On the other hand, "If we can select examples from them and adopt their contrivances, why should we not be successful in working them out? If we are to delay the using of steam machinery until we have discovered the principles of steam for ourselves, or to wait till we have discovered the principles of electricity before we construct an electric telegraph, our government will be unable to set to work."

To Itagaki's memorial, the *Sa-in* gave a rather cordial reply. Since it was working on the problem of constitutions and assemblies it may have felt that outside pressure would facilitate its work. It said that the "principle is an excellent one, and this college, having received sanction to a similar proposal made by itself, has drafted a set of regulations. The suggestion, therefore, will be adopted."

But there were others in the government who were not in favor of it. Their spokesman, Katō Hiroyuki, then engaged in giving a series of lectures to the emperor, presented a refutation. . . . Katō's main contention was that the time had not yet come for the establishment of representative institutions in Japan. "Now in establishing a constitution and laws," he said, "it is necessary to observe minutely the state of the country and of public feeling, and to choose such a constitution and laws as are suited to them." In his opinion, the British parliament was "competent to initiate laws and constitutional measures well suited to the wants of the country," but other parliaments were not. Neither Russia nor Prussia, he observed, had been able to establish deliberative assemblies because the people were not advanced enough to share in the government. Katō felt that there was great danger in giving powers to a people whose intelligence was insufficiently developed for "they do not know how to exercise them duly, and hence they fall into license. . . ."

In reply to the passage in the original memorial to the effect that the people would become more enlightened if they had a voice in the government, Katō maintained that it could be better achieved through education. Pointing again to Prussia, he said, "The self-reliant and active character of the Prussian nation at the present day, which has at last raised it to the position of the most powerful nation in Europe, has not been due to the establishment of a deliberative assembly, but to the fact that, since the time of Frederick II, the Prussian government has devoted itself to the cultivation of the people's minds."

A running debate was now begun. The newspapers took sides, some supporting Itagaki, some opposing him. Katō's attack on the memorial evoked several replies, including one by Itagaki, Soejima, and Gotō. It is not necessary to give a detailed account of these replies, except to note one important point made by Itagaki and his friends. In the course of their argument they revealed the kind of assembly they contemplated. "Now if this council chamber be established," they said, "we do not propose that the franchise should at once be made universal. We would only give it in the first instance to the samurai and the richer farmers and merchants, for it is they who produced the leaders of the revolution of 1868."

The true character of the movement initiated by Itagaki now stood revealed. Clearly Itagaki did not intend that the great bulk of the population should enjoy the fruits of self-rule. Only the samurai and the wealthy peasants and merchants were to be represented in the assembly which he proposed. Little wonder that the militarist General Torio Koyata called this *jōryū no minkensetsu* or "upper-class democracy."

E. H. NORMAN*
Parties and Politics

... The point to note is that Japanese liberalism had its roots in the countryside, unlike English liberalism, which was a movement of the cities, especially of the city merchants in opposition to the conservative landed gentry.

The theoretical leaders of the liberal movement were ex-samurai, chiefly from the former Tosa and Hizen clans which no

* E. H. Norman, *Japan's Emergence as a Modern State* (New York: International Secretariat, Institute of Pacific Relations, 1940), pp. 172–174, 180–183, 184–185.

longer shared equally in the fruits of office with Satsuma and Chō-shū. That many of these men were inspired by genuinely liberal ideals is not disputed; their later careers and sacrifices are sufficient testimony to their singleness of purpose. Nevertheless . . . the abolition of the clans had undermined the economic base of feudalism, leaving many discontented samurai, while the failure of the advocates for an expedition to Korea (*seikanron*) had embittered others, and so these ex-samurai were drawn into the liberal movement merely because it was *the antigovernment movement*. Thus individual place-seeking and jealousy of the Sat-Chō monopoly acted as a stimulus for organizing the first political associations in Japan. It was natural that these ex-samurai in opposition to the government should become the acknowledged leaders of the movement which demanded a people's assembly. They enjoyed great prestige as members of the *shizoku* class, and above all as leaders in the restoration of 1868. On this account some Japanese authorities have called them the heirs of the *Kinnō* or *Sonnō* party (loyalists who fought against the *bakufu*) and the true embodiment of the antifeudal struggle.

But the impelling force of the liberal movement came from the great mass of small peasants, tenants, and city poor who rallied to it urging the reduction of taxes, the establishment of representative institutions, even demanding representation in the liberal movement. It was difficult however for the peasants living in outlying, isolated villages to take active part in politics. It was only natural that the most active element in local politics should be the large landowners, while the national leadership tended to be in the hands of ex-samurai or of a few large landlord merchants.

This widespread and loosely connected movement of small landowners and peasants under the leadership of former samurai and big landlord merchants took national form in the Jiyūtō (Liberal party) organized early in 1881. The quality of its leadership inevitably made the political philosophy of the Jiyūtō a rather softened, conciliatory liberalism, a liberalism which strove primarily for democracy, for people's rights, for freedom of enterprise—all for the respectable classes. . . .

Thus from its start Japanese liberalism as embodied in the Jiyūtō was of a moderate, temporizing quality, and later it was to change into its opposite, uncompromising conservatism, when the Seiyūkai was formed from the ruins of the Jiyūtō in 1900. We are not discussing here the extreme left-wing of the Jiyūtō, which later took on almost a revolutionary coloring, but the basic political philosophy of the chief leaders of the Jiyūtō. Despite any vagueness in its program, the Jiyūtō before its split into local grouplets with a right and left wing, because of the enthusiastic backing it received from land-hungry tenants and debt-burdened peasant proprietors, had great *élan* and even revolutionary potentialities. For this reason, as we shall see later, the government in its campaign of suppressing political parties launched its fiercest onslaught against the Jiyūtō.

Even before the dissolution of the parties, with the press effectively muzzled and all political activity stringently suppressed, local branches of the political parties had energetically protested against government suppression and had even turned to insurrection as a means of achieving their end—the overthrow of the autocratic government. Many of the lesser leaders in the Jiyūtō, angered and bewildered by what seemed to them the defection of their chiefs, often supported these ill-starred uprisings. The historical interest of these local incidents arises from the political and economic demands which motivated the rank and file of the liberal movement and the resolution, however misplaced, with which these demands were backed in comparison to the tergiversations of the leaders. One of the shrewdest observers of Japanese national life, Fukuzawa Yukichi foresaw as early as 1881 the tendency for the rank and file in the liberal movement to display a violent impatience with government policy. In writing to Ōkuma, he says, "The *minkenron* [advocacy of people's rights] seems to be more and more favoring direct action. If it goes on in that direction, the antagonism between the government and people will become increasingly embittered, and in the end I fear it will mean unfortunate bloodshed." . . .

Fukuzawa's forebodings were only too accurate. . . . An insurrection occurred in Chichibu (Saitama prefecture) in 1884 in which the Shakkintō or local debtors' party played a leading role, as did also a radical group from the local Jiyūtō. These political leaders were alleged to have stirred up bad feeling among the peasantry and village poor against the local landlords, and when police arrived on the scene the peasants had resisted them forcibly. . . . [W]hat is of interest for our immediate purpose is that this Chichibu uprising symbolizes the great divide in the history of the

Jiyūtō or Liberal party. We have already seen that leadership in this party was in the hands of landowners who were merchants or manufacturers as well; it was this commercial side of their nature which drew them into politics. However, as government repression became intensified to meet the mounting demand for greater democracy, these local branches, which were often in more radical hands than was the national leadership, stirred up such violent popular sentiment not only in favor of representative institutions but also for rent reduction that it terrified many of the more cautious leaders, bringing out the conservative landlord side of their nature, and thus made party dissolution by no means as unpalatable as it might otherwise have been. As one authority writes, "The Jiyūtō and Kaishintō were more or less directly connected with the exhibition of violence in the provinces, though it is not likely that the leaders of either countenanced the measures adopted. To clear itself of the stigma of inciting to rebellion, the Jiyūtō at a general meeting held on October 20, 1884, in Osaka, resolved to disband and wait for an opportunity when society will be prepared for its reconstruction." . . .

Most instructive in this history is the evidence of the fundamental weakness in a liberalism which stemmed *from the country-side*. In other countries victorious liberalism, whether of the Independents or rather the London Presbyterians during the Cromwellian era or of revolutionary Paris, was essentially an urban movement which could draw on the immense financial power of the city merchant and could be propelled by the highly centralized political organization of the city masses. Above all, English and French liberalism, though led by wealthy merchants, lawyers, or even country gentry, was reinforced by the presence in the metropolis of a large and comparatively articulate urban citizenry. This is, of course, equally true of nineteenth-century English liberalism after the Reform Act of 1832, when the Liberal party drew its strength almost exclusively from the city classes. But in Japan a liberalism based on the countryside with its isolated villages, where local issues often absorbed the attention of the neighboring population to the exclusion of all else and where conditions differed widely from one locality to another, inevitably brought inner clashes and final failure. Furthermore the antagonism between the landlord leadership of the Jiyūtō and the rank and file peasant following was bound to force a split in the party.

We have seen how this leadership of the Jiyūtō succumbed more easily to the government offensive after the startling incidents . . . when peasants voiced among other cries the demand for rent reduction. Deprived of all central leadership, the local branches of the Jiyūtō under various names and for various local issues often resorted to violence in order to weaken the grip of government repression. These attempts were too scattered and sporadic, in a word *too local in character* both geographically and politically, to be crowned with even partial success. The government won out all along the line, thanks to the unity of the ruling bureaucracy and its autocratic methods on the one hand, and to the disunity and confusion of the opposition on the other.

The Jiyūtō was reconstituted again with the opening of the Diet in 1890. But the series of successive splits by which the most radical groups within it had been gradually sloughed off, and the very high property qualifications for the electorate (payment of at least fifteen yen in direct national taxes) made the reformed Jiyūtō a chastened and moderate party. Its transformation through various intermediate stages into the Seiyūkai (1900), the party of the landlords, indicates the triumph of that semi-feudal landlord aspect in the leadership of the original Jiyūtō.

❃ THE POPULAR RIGHTS MOVEMENT (*jiyūminken undō*) and the new political parties that arose in the 1870s and 1880s nonetheless mobilized enough public pressure that in 1881 the Meiji oligarchs felt compelled to promise a constitution and eventually a parliament, discussed below by Ike. Popular opposition, led by "out" national and local politicians like Itagaki, was crucial in bringing these changes about; yet within a short time many of the national opposition leaders had been effectively bought off. Although the form of the Diet and the political system were still relatively malleable, the compromises made by Itagaki and others were an important turning point. It is often argued that the growing trends toward democracy that originated in the Popular Rights movement were destroyed or blunted only by full-scale militarism in the

1930s. Yet it is equally plausible that democracy was never solidly established and that its eventual failure was predictable after the early failure to obtain a parliament with significant powers.

The Popular Rights movement was perhaps the most important challenge to the early drift into authoritarianism. Once it ceased effective opposition, the forces arrayed against the oligarchs were scattered, and the trend toward militarism was checked only briefly and temporarily during the 1920s. When Itagaki and others reentered the government, they thereby abdicated responsibility for shaping the new constitutional government in a democratic direction.

The new political system based on the Constitution of 1890 was clearly autocratic and highly centralized. It relegated the Diet to a secondary role and resurrected the Imperial institution to make the emperor the chief symbol of the state's authority (though the emperor himself remained relatively powerless). The oligarchs thus established a regime that would insure their continued control of the developing society in the face of opposition either by former oligarchs like Itagaki or by popular forces. Ike discusses the weaknesses of the opposition in dealing with the antidemocratic trend which was institutionalized firmly in the constitution and which dominated Japanese politics until the end of World War II.

NOBUTAKA IKE*
Itō and the Constitution

In the Imperial Rescript of October 12, 1881, the government solemnly promised to adopt a written constitution and convoke a parliament by the year 1890. In adopting this policy, the government was bowing to popular pressure which had grown to such

* Ike Nobutaka, *Beginnings of Political Democracy in Japan* (1950; reprint ed., New York: Greenwood, 1969), pp. 171–180, 188–191.

proportions as to make continued procrastination in these matters unwise. Somewhat reluctantly the top men in the bureaucracy came to the conclusion that they could no longer hold the line against the democratic movement. But in making concessions to popular demands they saw to it that in return they secured a breathing spell, during which time they could build new dikes to channel the flood.

From the point of view of the government, there was much work to be done. It was necessary that, in the intervening years before 1890, the constitution, election laws, and other basic laws relating to the structure of government be drafted and imposed on the people before public sentiment became even more hostile to the government. There was, therefore, a sense of urgency in high official circles which is clearly revealed in the documents of the period. For instance, in a letter written to Itō Hirobumi in July 1881, Inoue Kaoru pressed for the adoption of a Prussian-style constitution. But he also urged that this be done quickly, giving the following reasons:

> To put into effect a Prussian-style constitution is an extremely difficult task under existing conditions, but at the present time it is possible to carry it out and win over the majority and thus succeed. This is because the English-style constitution has not become firmly fixed in the minds of the people. Among the samurai in the countryside more than one-half, no doubt, have a lingering desire to uphold the Imperial House.
>
> But, if we lose this opportunity and vacillate, within two or three years the people will become confident that they can succeed, and no matter how much oratory we may use it will be difficult to win them back. Most of the political parties will be on the other side rather than ours. Public opinion will cast aside the draft of a constitution presented by the government, and the private drafts of the constitution will win out in the end.

By 1881 the men who formed the inner core of the Meiji government had formulated definite ideas about the character of the constitution which they thought Japan should have. In a memorandum drawn up in July 1881 Iwakura laid down the general outline of the new constitution. Among his more important recommendations were the following: The new constitution should be granted by the emperor. The Imperial House Law should be outside the scope of the constitution. The emperor should take supreme command of the armed forces and should appoint cabinet members, with the Diet having no power to intervene in the organization of the cabinet. There should be a bicameral assembly, with the upper house consisting of peers and Imperial appointees, and the lower house chosen on the basis of restricted suffrage. Only the government should have the right to initiate legislation. In case of failure to approve the annual budget, the budget for the preceding year should be followed.

 ... [T]he keystone in the constitutional arch as Iwakura, Itō, and Inoue envisaged it was the emperor. Throughout the early years of the Meiji era, the architects of the new regime had labored sedulously to build up his political stature. And to a large degree they succeeded. But there are also indications ... that on occasion there was opposition. Perhaps more important, the trend of the times was against them. As Itō frankly states ... there was a "tendency for both the government and the people to slip unknowingly into the spirit of republicanism." To offset such tendencies, Iwakura, in a memorial presented in February 1882, suggested increasing the property held by the Imperial household. Looking ahead to the period after 1890 he anticipated that "the antigovernment views will get stronger and stronger since the extreme democrats always go beyond the proper degree." He was fearful that the provisions of the constitution would be disregarded. "Even the emperor," he stated, "will be controlled by the Diet, and the throne will be as good as gone. The Imperial prerogative will be eventually nullified." He therefore urged that the Imperial household property be increased, making it "sufficient to pay for the cost of the army and navy from its yearly income. If this is done, no matter how radical a view may arise later in the Diet, and again even if the funds for the national treasury are not appropriated, it would be possible to mitigate it."

In short the problem, as it appeared to leaders like Iwakura, was to fit the emperor into the new constitutional structure, while at the same time providing institutional safeguards to buttress his position against democratic influences. ...

As they had done on previous occasions, the Japanese again turned to the West for guidance. In March 1882, Itō Hirobumi, who was the leading figure in the government by now, was appointed head of a mission to study European constitutions. Nine assistants, chosen from the Sat-Chō clique and the court nobility, were also named. The mission set sail on March 14 and proceeded to Europe via the Indian Ocean and the Suez Canal. After arriving in Europe, Itō dispatched Saionji, with some men familiar with the French language, to Paris to study the constitution of the Third Republic. Itō went to Germany with a larger group. Years later, Itō asserted that he took an "extended journey in different constitutional countries to make as thorough a study as possible of the actual workings of different systems of constitutional government, of their various provisions, as well as of theories and opinions actually entertained by influential persons on the actual stage itself of constitutional life." The facts, however, appear to be otherwise.

From the very beginning Itō went to Germany because it had already been decided that Japan should adopt a Prussian-style constitution. In Berlin arrangements were made for the mission to hear lectures by the well known jurist, Rudolf von Gneist. . . .

We can surmise that Itō found Gneist's lectures most gratifying. The German jurist firmly believed that constitutions must be rooted in the history of the country. Itō agreed with him, and in fact later used this argument to reject suggestions that various provisions be borrowed from American, French, and other liberal constitutions. Gneist also had other advice which Itō found easy to accept. Questions of diplomacy, military organization, and similar matters should not be subject to the decisions of the Diet. The legislature should have no power over the property owned by the Imperial household. Ministers should be given great power and the authority of the Diet should be kept down. If the Diet refuses to pass an appropriations bill, the previous year's budget should be used. Gneist also recommended that the suffrage be limited. Lastly, he was opposed to calling a constitutional convention.

At the end of the course under Gneist, the members of the mission moved to Vienna, where they listened to Professor Lorenz von Stein. Like Gneist, Stein gave conservative advice. Being opposed to popular government, he did not approve of universal suffrage, nor of party cabinets. He was also convinced that only the government should have the right to initiate bills. And he thought that the Imperial household should be kept above the constitution.

In his lectures, which began on September 18 and lasted until October 31, Stein covered a wide area of the subject matter of political science. Included among the subjects he discussed were Plato and Aristotle, legislation, political parties, administration,

German administrative justice, diplomacy, and statistics. At the end of each lecture session, Itō asked questions and his assistants took full notes. Itō was much impressed with Stein, and even tried to hire him as an adviser to the Japanese government, but Stein refused the offer.

Altogether Itō spent about seven months studying under Gneist and Stein. He no doubt learned a great deal, but it is also certain that his prejudices were confirmed. "By studying under two famous German teachers, Gneist and Stein," he wrote to Iwakura, "I have been able to get a general understanding of the structure of the state." But he added, "Later I shall discuss with you how we can achieve the great objective of establishing Imperial authority. Indeed, the tendency in our country today is to erroneously believe in the works of British, French, and American liberals and radicals as if they were golden rules, and thereby lead virtually to the overthrow of the state. In having found principles and means of combatting this trend, I believe I have rendered an important service to my country, and I feel inwardly that I can die a happy man."

On the way home, Itō and his party stopped off at Paris and later visited England, where they heard Herbert Spencer lecture on representative government. Itō returned to Japan in the fall of 1883, a little more than a year and a half after his departure from Japan.

Now that the period of preliminary investigation was over, Itō was put in charge of a newly created bureau within the Imperial Household Ministry. This bureau was assigned the task of studying constitutional and administrative reform. The reason for placing it within the Imperial Household was to enable Itō and his assistants to work in secrecy and also to give the illusion that the drafting was being done under the personal supervision of the emperor. Actually, according to Kaneko, little serious work on the constitution was done until 1886. This delay may have been caused in part by the concentration of attention on preliminary matters. Owing to Itō's conviction that a constitution must be rooted in history, his assistants began a restudy of the history of their own country. Also in order to lay the ground work for the new structure, a number of institutional changes were made in the intervening years. In 1884 the nobility was rehabilitated, and five hundred patents of nobility were issued. The following year the old Dajōkan was abolished in favor of a cabinet, headed by Itō and composed of ministers who, in theory, were directly responsible to the emperor. "Great stress," says one authority, "was laid by the oligarchy on the contention that by these changes true personal rule by the emperor had been at last achieved, in order to discourage any popular attack on the regime." The position of the Lord Keeper of the Privy Seal was created. New civil service regulations intended to develop an efficient bureaucracy that would be loyal to the state were also issued.

In 1886 Itō and his staff began the study of constitutional reform in earnest. The work was roughly allocated among three men, although in practice this arrangement was not strictly adhered to. Put in charge of the constitution and the Imperial House Law was Inoue Kaoru. A fellow clansman and trusted friend of Itō, Inoue had once lived in England and had held various important posts in the government. Itō Myōji, also of Chōshū, concentrated his attention on the Law of the Houses. The third member, Kaneko Kentarō, who had attended Harvard Law School, was assigned to study election laws for the House of Representatives.

Itō wrote a memorandum indicating his conception of the scope of legislative power, the responsibility of the cabinet ministers, and related matters. In addition to Itō, Inoue depended on his Prussian adviser, Dr. Carl Friedrich Hermann Roessler, then teaching in the law school of the Tokyo Imperial University. Inoue would write questions in English, and Roessler would reply in English. Then the questions and answers were translated into Japanese for Itō's benefit. Since Roessler was no democrat, his advice no doubt accorded well with the predilections of Itō and Inoue. Roessler was opposed to popular rule; and it was his contention that the ministers should be responsible to the emperor and not the Diet.

On April 30, 1887, Roessler submitted to the group a draft of a constitution written in German. At Itō's request this was translated into Japanese. In May, Inoue followed with two additional drafts of a constitution. It was intended that these drafts would form the basis of further discussion.

About this time, Itō's new summer home in Natsushima, near Yokosuka, was completed. Since a secluded spot like Natsushima afforded greater secrecy, the group moved in June. Owing to the fact that Itō's new home was small, Itō Myōji, Inoue, and

Kaneko stayed in a nearby town. But early in August a briefcase containing Roessler's draft was stolen. After this episode the three men moved into Itō's home for the sake of greater security.

All through the summer of 1887 the staff continued its work, referring from time to time to the only two reference books available in Itō's library, the *Spirit of the Laws* by Montesquieu and the *Federalist*. Finally in September, a fourth draft based on the earlier drafts by Roessler and Inoue was completed. This draft was given to Roessler for his criticisms and suggestions. Starting on October 15, the group began the task of revision. But before the revision was completed, Itō undertook a tour to Kyushu and to Okinawa. Early in 1888 discussions were resumed, and finally in April drafts of the constitution and Imperial House Law were finished. Since no record of the proceedings is available we know very little in detail about the discussions which took place among the four, but we can be sure that there were some differences of opinion over phraseology. We get a glimpse of this in a letter which Itō sent to Inoue. "I have previously argued," wrote Itō, "about the phrase *gikai no shōnin* [consent of the Diet]. In my opinion *sandō* [approval] is the suitable word. But according to Mr. Roessler, 'concurrence' and 'consent' are greatly different in origin. That is to say, 'concurrence' is used between those who are of equal authority, while 'consent' implies recognition of the power of the sovereign, and does not apply to equal status. Accordingly, I supported that view in the end. . . ."

With the draft of the constitution completed, there arose the question of the procedure to be used in ratification. Those in the democratic movement argued in favor of a constitutional convention, while many of the bureaucrats felt that approval by the emperor was sufficient. In the end it was presented to the newly created Privy Council for ratification. Resigning as head of the cabinet, Itō became the president of the Privy Council. His three assistants were appointed secretaries of the Council. Included among the long list of appointments to the Privy Council were two names representing the political opposition, namely Ōkuma and Itagaki. The former, who by this time had been lured back into the government as foreign minister, accepted the appointment, but Itagaki declined. The inclusion of Ōkuma in the Privy Council, however, had no practical effect, since he stayed away from the sessions. For one thing he was busy negotiating with the foreign powers for the revision of the unequal treaties and probably had little time to spare. But one suspects that a more fundamental reason for his boycotting the meetings was his dislike of Itō.

Between May and December 1888, the Privy Council met in forty-one sessions. Three special meetings were also called. All of the sessions except one were held in the presence of the emperor. During these council sessions, elaborate precautions were taken to prevent leakage of information. To make sure that the public was kept in the dark about the provisions of the proposed constitution, no one was allowed to take documents away from the conference room. Those wishing to give further study to the drafts were compelled to remain and work in the presence of a secretary. "This procedure," notes Professor Quigley, "was decided upon after Kaneko discovered that the deliberations of the American constitutional fathers had been in secret."

It is difficult to appraise with any precision the role of the Privy Council in shaping the constitution into its final form, since not all of the documents have been published. We do know, however, that some changes were made. Chapter 3, Article 38, of the Itō draft provided, for instance, that "The Imperial Diet shall deliberate on bills submitted by the government." General Torio Koyata proposed that the Diet also be given power to initiate legislation. Very likely his suggestion was not prompted by liberal impulses, but rather by a realistic analysis of the political situation. He felt that, if the Diet were denied such power, it would soon demand it. Torio's proposal was voted down, but later Itō, having given the matter further study, decided in favor of it. Another clause in the Itō draft provided that "Bills on the budget and other financial matters shall be presented to the House of Representatives first, and after passage shall be sent to the House of Peers. The House of Peers shall only deliberate on the bill as a whole and cannot remove or revise separate sections." After discussion in the Privy Council, this provision was revised to give both houses equal power.

No doubt other suggestions were offered by the Privy Councillors. But in view of the makeup of the Privy Council, it is reasonable to assume that no drastic changes were made in the draft prepared by Itō and his committee. Being composed entirely of conservative and reactionary bureaucrats, the council could hardly be expected to seek a more liberal constitution than that envisaged by Itō. Things having gone this far, only a successful drive to force the government to submit the draft to a constitutional convention for ratification would have produced a democratic constitution. But because ... the democratic movement never fully recovered from its collapse in the mid-1880s, there was little likelihood of such a development.

The history of Japanese politics in the twenty-year period between the restoration and the promulgation of the constitution in 1889 was strongly influenced by the character of the Meiji restoration. The balance of political forces at the end of the Tokugawa era and their peculiar alignment encouraged the subsequent growth of a strong centralized state. The conjunction of two crises in the middle of the nineteenth century, the internal economic crisis and the external pressure of the Western powers, enabled an anti-Tokugawa faction led by a small group of low-ranking but able samurai to effect a political revolution.

The symbols used in this movement, however, were traditionalist rather than revolutionary. The leaders of the restoration gave their actions an aura of legitimacy by appealing to a remote past. The claim was put forward that the shōgun was an usurper and that the emperor was merely being "restored" as the rightful head of the state. From the very beginning steps were taken to make the emperor into an absolute monarch by reviving the ancient mythology which claimed for him divine origins. The throne, it goes without saying, proved to be a useful tool for breaking down local loyalties and for creating a modern nation. Thus, in short, the scales were weighted in favor of the development of a regime in which power would be tightly held by a small group of men.

But ... the group in power did not remain unchallenged. Some disaffected samurai, including a few who had been in the government, organized a popular movement to oppose those in control. From the point of view of the government this was a formidable movement because it had a more than rudimentary party organization and because one of the most important elements in it were the wealthier landowners and rural industrialists who had a firm grip on local government. Furthermore, one of the demands which the popular leaders made was the establishment of a national legislative assembly. The idea of an assembly had a fairly long history in Japan and it was difficult for the government to refuse these demands. In fact it was finally forced to call a Diet in 1890. The crucial issue, however, was the question of the amount of power which this assembly would have. . . . [The more liberal faction proposed a system in which sovereignty rested more clearly in the Diet itself, as a representative elective body.] The center of power would have shifted from the small group of ex-samurai to the newly created Diet consisting chiefly of men from the opposition parties. Since the most prominent of these parties was the Jiyūtō, an important consequence of this might have been a marked change in the tempo of industrialization and modernization, for the landowner-rural industrialists who were influential in the Jiyūtō would have hardly favored voting large appropriations for subsidizing modern urban industries and for building up a huge military establishment. . . .

The fact is, however, that the democratic movement did not succeed in breaking the hold of the Meiji oligarchy; and it may be appropriate to present here some reflections as to why it ultimately failed. One of the most important reasons for its failure was the split within the Jiyūtō. Such a split could have been avoided if the democratic movement had dealt adequately with the question of land reform. But this perhaps would have been asking for the impossible, since the landowners who were powerful in the Jiyūtō surely would have opposed such a move. A conclusion to be drawn from this is that the movement suffered from the lack of a more diversified basis of support. The fact that there existed no important groups of urban merchants and industrialists to join a movement of this kind resulted in serious weaknesses.

The second reason was inadequate leadership. Too often the leaders were willing to abandon the movement to take posts offered by the government. This may have been prompted in part by the persistence of class feeling which led the samurai to look upon themselves as forming a superior class best fitted for governing the nation.

Third, there was the matter of ideology. Although there were some theorists who had a precocious grasp of political theory, the movement was never able to produce an outstanding theorist of its own. In fact it could be said that the theorists for the democratic movement were men like John Stuart Mill, J. J. Rousseau, and Herbert Spencer. A practical consequence of this was the failure to produce new political symbols which could seriously compete with those available to the government, such as the emperor. The

196]   IMPERIAL JAPAN: 1800–1945

advantage which the government enjoyed was that it could point to the Imperial court as a uniquely Japanese institution while those in the opposition could only appeal to universal concepts like natural rights. In a period of rising nationalism, this was an important factor.

This leads to the fourth reason, namely, nationalism. Japan was modernized in a period when the Western powers were enlarging their colonial possessions by the use of military power. Like other Asiatic countries, Japan's sovereignty was impaired by the imposition of unequal treaties. The consequence of this was the growth of an exaggerated form of nationalism; and, given their environment and history, the Japanese quickly learned the usefulness of armed might and began to emphasize military preparedness. Since the leaders of the democratic movement were themselves highly nationalistic, they were unwilling to oppose the principle of a strong state. They could only argue that an ingredient of national power was national unity and that the latter could be best obtained by providing wider representation for the various interests within the nation.

Finally, it is necessary to point to the remarkable ability of the Meiji leaders to grant concessions at the proper moment. Whenever popular pressure became too powerful to be suppressed, they would retreat without giving up the substance of power. They possessed the kind of suppleness which any regime wishing to remain in control must possess. Perhaps an explanation of this is to be found in the fact that these men were able to overthrow the shogunate without having had to acquire a wide popular following. This left them unencumbered with commitments, thus enabling them to act freely as the occasion demanded.

III.

*Industrialization
and Imperialism
1890–1929*

❀ IN 1873, when Saigō Takamori sought to invade Korea with a samurai army to avenge insults to Japan, his anachronistic approach to achieving national honor and empire was rejected. By the 1890s, the Japanese leaders were ready for a Korean expedition. They went not as vengeful samurai, but as an industrializing nation with a professional army seeking to defend what were believed to be its strategic and economic interests. Japan, in other words, was gaining entry into the club of imperialist nations and was amply awarded for her rapid victory in the Sino-Japanese War of 1894–1895 against a disorganized and militarily weaker China. In addition to acquiring the same privileges in China as the Western powers, Japan gained virtually a free hand in Korea and large indemnities. Though humiliated by the Triple Intervention, which forced Japan to return China's Liaotung Peninsula, Japan nevertheless gained more respect from the Western powers. In 1899 the unequal treaties were revised and in 1902 Japan and Britain signed a military alliance. Economically, the Sino-Japanese War was a boost to the modern sector of the economy, particularly to the growing armaments industry.

By 1904 Japan was ready to fight one of the Western powers and fought the Russians over the issue of economic privileges in Manchuria. The stunning victory, both on land and sea and capped by the destruction of the Russian fleet, reaffirmed the growing power. At the Versailles Conference ending World War I, Japan's stature as one of the world's major powers was recognized. However, an ominous note for the future sounded in China during the war. Japan's objectives, expressed in the Twenty-One Demands in 1915, and the successful acquisition of the former German concessions in China, deepened strong Chinese resentment, a resentment which fueled strong resistance to Japanese aggression in the 1930s.

The early twentieth century witnessed in Japan an impressive growth in the industrialization begun by the Meiji government. The wars against China and Russia provided an important stimulus to Japanese shipping, textiles, and strategic industries, and foreign loans provided needed capital. Developments proceeded in the industrial sector, paralleled and made possible by real gains in agriculture, mining, fishing, and forestry. Smaller-scale industry also developed, though not as fast as heavy industry. Most important, Japan continued to have sufficient exports, mainly textiles, to finance imports of foreign machinery without losing control of her economy. The new colonial gains also provided sources of raw materials and opportunities for expanded business activity.

In organization Japanese business diverged sharply from other industrial nations. Initially the Meiji leaders financed direct industrial development by the state. The government later sold off these enterprises to business groups with which it continued to have close ties. These Japanese business houses— called zaibatsu, meaning "financial cliques," and operating under family names and clan rules—came to completely dominate the economy. Through the Second World War four combines played leading roles: Mitsui, Mitsubishi, Sumitomo, and Yasuda. In breadth the zaibatsu resembled modern American conglomerates, but they operated internally more like feudal merchant guilds than modern corporations. Originating in the houses' feudal clan rules, zaibatsu administrative hierarchy and company loyalty mirrored the official government ideology of the state-as-family.

However, the large zaibatsu accounted for only one sector of Japanese manufacturing. Through the 1930s half of the Japanese labor force employed in manufacturing worked in places with less than five employees. Alongside the large factories persisted small cottage industries as well as medium-sized firms, a "dualism" that has only recently been superseded as a distinctive characteristic of Japan's industrialization.

Political parties grew in power in this period, and their leaders joined those from the military, the zaibatsu, and the government bureaucracy in making the key policy decisions for Japan. Working within Japan's circumscribed parliamentary system, the parties enjoyed a brief period of "party government" in the mid-twenties. However, this was hardly a triumph for popular democracy or participation, for the parties' gains were made through compromise and collaboration with key bureaucrats, military leaders, and the zaibatsu. The electoral base, moreover, was so small until universal manhood suffrage in 1925 that candidates did not represent any significant proportion of Japanese peasants and workers. When the mass of the populace could at last vote, they had virtually no influence on important policy decisions or on the way power was exercised. In Japan in the 1920s and 1930s, important issues were not decided openly in the electoral arena, but behind closed doors by the established elites.

Industrialization, imperialism, and the instabilities of the world economy and Japan's own rapidly growing domestic economy brought in their wake dissatisfaction and discontent among workers, peasants, and intellectuals. Although there had been some protest over the Russo-Japanese War and efforts to organize against it, the rice riots of 1918 against high grain prices represented a new level of mass protest in Japan. During the following decade, labor organizations grew in strength alongside socialist and anarchist organizations. In the countryside continuing high tenancy rates and fluctuating prices for farm products contributed to the growth of tenant unions.

The response of the elite to this protest was twofold. Active repression was carried out against the most radical groups. This extended from monitoring meetings to arrests of "extremists," and sometimes to more aggressive actions, such as the murder of radicals by police during the confusion caused by the Tokyo earthquake of 1923. While repressing the far left, the government tolerated moderate unionism and moderate leftist parties, the voting base was extended to all males, and some social legislation was passed. In this fashion dissent was kept under control, although the difficulties of the world economy and the Japanese role in China were soon to make "business as usual" impossible.

1. Politics, the Military, and Foreign Policy

⚛ THE MEIJI administrative and constitutional structure was set up explicitly to achieve the goal of *fukoku kyōhei,* "rich country, strong army." It was not designed for mass participation or for social democracy, but for efficiency and power. In the 1880s the government bureaucracy was tightly centralized, clear limits were set on the powers of local assemblies, and major power for local governmental decisions was put in the Home Ministry.

The Meiji constitution itself was a "gift" from the emperor and contained only minor concessions to popular sovereignty or rights. With supplementary laws, decrees, and administrative procedures, it was designed to perpetuate the rule of the oligarchs with as little interference as possible by the Diet. In fact, the only serious weakness in the document from the oligarchs' perspective was the right of the Diet not to approve the budget, and there were ways to bypass this obstruction.

The clearly nondemocratic nature of the constitutional setup was largely responsible for the attitudes of the opposition parties, the Jiyūtō and Kaishintō, when the first session of the Diet opened. The parties were led predominantly by men who had held power in the post-restoration period and wanted back in, but who also knew that within the constitutional framework their influence was confined largely to blocking legislation and refusing to pass the government's budget. They therefore decided on tactics of disruption. The resulting impasse, which lasted for most of the Diet's first ten years, is described in detail by McLaren, who was in Japan during these events.

WALTER MCLAREN*
A Political History of Japan During the Meiji Era

In 1874 a change of the greatest importance was made in the relations between the local government bodies and the central government. In 1873 the Department of Home Affairs (*Naimushō*) had been created, and in the following year it was given control over the entire local government system. In the rules for the conduct of the business of the *Naimushō* the following powers were specified and granted: to regulate the processes of taking the census; to establish poorhouses and hospitals; to encourage good behavior among the people; to establish agricultural schools and societies; to delimit the boundaries of *ken* and *gun;* to establish, remove, or abolish local government offices; to increase or decrease the expenses of the local government offices and the burden of local taxation; to make roads, embankments, and bridges; to regulate the postal service and merchant ships; to make loans or give charity; to increase or decrease the number of officials; to preserve the records from all parts of the country, as well as places and buildings of historical importance; to investigate the boundaries of towns and villages; to conduct a survey of the land; to revise the organization of towns and villages and change their names, etc. The Minister of Home Affairs had power to rearrange the boundaries of the *ken* and all other local government areas, and he had similarly complete control of the local government organization, the expenditures of any area, and the taxes to be collected from the local people.

The establishment of the Ministry of Home Affairs, which was subject to the control of the Dajōkan in precisely the same degree as any other department of state, although given complete jurisdiction over all local government affairs, helps to account for the peculiarly centralized nature of the Japanese government. From that time till the present every matter of importance which con-

* Walter McLaren, *Political History of Japan During the Meiji Era* (London: George Allen and Unwin/New York: Charles Scribner's Sons, 1916), pp. 94–95, 126–127, 145–147, 130–132, 186, 148–149, 176, 208, 210–213.

cerns a locality has to be brought before the Home Office by the
local authorities, and the action to be taken is decided virtually by
the central government. Thus, if a city wishes to bestow a franchise upon a street-railway company or a gas company, the
consent of the Home Minister must be obtained before any action
can be taken by the city authorities.

The newly created Department of Home Affairs under the
leadership of Ōkubo, who was a man of extremely dictatorial
methods and believed little in consulting the wishes of the people,
began the process of building up the local bureaucracy. . . .

In 1880 elective assemblies were established by the central
government in cities, towns, and villages upon the basis of the
regulations issued two years earlier for the *fu* and *ken.* From that
beginning the system grew, and in 1888 two large bodies of laws,
jointly known as the Municipal Code, were promulgated. These
two laws, containing some 130 articles each, form the basis of the
government of cities, towns, and villages at the present time. The
personnel of the government of the various urban areas is substantially similar in all—an executive official, known in the cities as
shichō or mayor, in the towns as *chōchō* or headman, in the villages as *sonchō* or headman; the deputy mayors and headmen; a
council (originally in the cities only and recently abolished); and
an assembly. All these officials are elective, but according to very
different methods: the members of the assembly directly by the
citizens of the respective areas; the council indirectly by the members of the assembly from among their own members; the headmen
of towns and villages by the members of the assembly from among
the resident citizens of thirty years of age or over, the choice to be
ratified by the governor of the *ken;* the mayors of the cities indirectly by the members of the assembly from among the citizens of
the empire. The election of the mayor is doubly indirect, for the
city assembly nominates three candidates and the emperor, acting
upon the advice of the Home Minister, appoints one of the three or
declines to appoint any of them and calls for a further selection of
candidates. The electorate consists of the citizens of the respective
areas, and the qualifications for citizenship are, in the main, residence and possession of landed property. Eligibility for membership in the assembly, whether of a city, town, or village, is
obtained by qualifying as to age, residence, and the payment of
national taxes. Elections are conducted in the cities on the Prus-

sian three-class system, in towns and villages on a two-class system. The basis of classification in all cases is taxpaying ability. . . .

Above and as the controlling power over the machinery for local government in the urban areas are placed the governors of the *ken,* and in the last resort the Home Minister. In certain matters specified—the issuing of bylaws, raising of loans, imposition of special city taxes, etc.—the Home Minister's consent is necessary and in other matters—the alienation of city property and the imposition of special burdens on any class of the people, whether in the form of taxes or services—that of the governor of the *ken* must be obtained before the assembly's decisions can be enforced. Generally speaking, the governor of the *ken* exercises supervision over the administration of the affairs of every urban area within his jurisdiction. The mayors of cities and the headmen of towns and villages are the representatives in the local areas of the Home Minister or the governor of the *ken.* The power to dissolve an assembly is reserved to the Home Minister.

The development of the representative institutions . . . was significant in the highest degree as illustrating the lines upon which Japanese polity was being gradually reconstructed. There was not the slightest indication of a tendency toward popular government, if by that term is meant responsible government. The assemblies were fitted into a purely bureaucratic system, and to only a slight degree had they power to disturb the equanimity of an absolutist officialdom. . . .

The interest which attaches to the building up of the institutions for local government during this period is centered in two diverse but closely related processes which were going on synchronously, the organization and training of the local bureaucracy and the creation of the elected assemblies. In 1878 it would appear that the central government . . . deliberately set up the provincial (*fu* and *ken*) assemblies as an experiment in representative government in Japan. The local assembly was the forerunner of the national assembly, not only in time but in its constitution and powers also. This method of procedure has often been referred to as a proof of the wisdom of the Japanese statesmen of the day, especially Itō, but the lesson furnished by the *ken* assemblies was far from encouraging. In many of the local areas so little interest was taken in the assembly that some years elapsed before the people could be got to form one, while in other cases educated men would not consent to sit after their election. Also, the assemblies which were created in 1878 and the years immediately following were extremely contentious bodies, in almost constant conflict with the authorities. If any lesson was to be learned from this experiment in democracy, it certainly was not to the effect that the nation was ready for representative institutions, at any rate when coupled with a bureaucracy which was able to thwart the people's wishes at every turn.

... In 1881 the Parliamentary Rescript had to be issued to quell a disturbance in Tokyo, but the oligarchs provided for ample time in which to adjust themselves to the promised regime. How thoroughly they prepared for the establishment of representative institutions we shall see.

The companion process relates to the development of the local bureaucracy. In 1874 the Home Ministry became the center of authority for local government; from that time the efforts of the new department were directed to the creation of an official organization in the provinces, and the bestowal of such powers upon its members as would enable the Home Minister to dominate local administration, even to its minutest details. By a system of inspection, by frequent reports, by strict limitations upon the provincial governor's discretion, by the power of appointment and dismissal of high local officials or removal of governors from one province to another, the central government provided that its will should prevail. As against the people, even as represented in an assembly, the local officials were given ample powers, and the governor's control of the police of the *ken* assured him of protection in any ordinary local disturbance.

If the two processes—the erection of a highly centralized local bureaucracy and the creation of local assemblies—be combined, as they must be in any attempt to understand the period between 1874 and 1885, we can see plainly the policy of the central government. The main purpose of the ruling oligarchy was to extend and consolidate its control over local affairs, and its secondary object was to enfranchise the people in as small a degree as possible—sufficiently to satisfy the popular demand for representation while at the same time not endangering its own supremacy. . . .

The day set for the ceremony of promulgation was the eleventh of February 1889, a date since observed as a national holiday,

Kigensetsu, in honor of the event. Among other preparations made for the occasion was the suppression of practically all the radical newspapers in Tokyo, and the issuance of strict injunctions to the rest of the press that no unfavorable comments were to be made, for the time being, upon the constitution. Apart from two incidents, the events of the celebration occurred without a hitch. The ceremonies were performed at the palace in the presence of high officials, the diplomatic corps, and other invited guests. The streets were gay with flags and bunting, and filled with a holiday crowd who watched, silent, but full of curiosity, as was their habit, the steady stream of carriages and jinrikishas bearing officialdom, in gold lace and cocked hats, to and from the palace. There was no attempt at mirth or frolic: the occasion was a solemn one, and the people behaved accordingly. Neither was there any effort made to include the populace; the constitution was not read in public to the citizens of the capital. The instrument had been framed in secret, ratified by the aristocracy, and promulgated before an audience of officials. It was the government's affair from beginning to end.

... Making allowances for differences in circumstances, the constitutional powers of the Diet are similar to those granted to the various assemblies which we have already considered. The *gikai* [Diet] was fitted into the bureaucratic structure of the central government and subordinated so strictly to the oligarchy that its functions were mainly to consent to laws introduced by the cabinet. Of necessity the setting up of a popular body in the midst of an absolutist system entailed changes, the importance of which has become apparent during the parliamentary regime, but, insofar as it was possible, the oligarchy anticipated those changes and provided against them. In no other way can the constitutional provision for the reapplication of a budget (Article LXXI) be explained than by the bureaucracy's fear that the representatives of the people might attempt to bring the government to terms by refusing supply.

But the significance of the changes made in 1889 can only be estimated when the laws issued in that year are read in connection with an ordinance of 1886 dealing with the organization of the departments of state. That ordinance marked the culmination of the long process of consolidating the administrative organ of the central government. It provided for the standardizing of the various departments of state, both with respect to their official organization and their competency, and for centralizing the whole, nominally in the emperor, but actually in the cabinet. The constitution, by providing that cabinet ministers should be responsible to the emperor (Article LV), made the bureaucracy independent of the Diet, except for the single provision that all measures introduced by the government must receive the consent of the Diet before they could become law. The possibilities of deadlock between the representative and the bureaucratic elements, inherent in the system thus adopted, furnished what little interest there has been in the history of the Japanese parliament, and likewise accounts for the political stagnation of the past two decades. . . .

One other institution must be mentioned . . . and that is the genro, or council of elder statesmen. This body, more or less informally constituted toward the end of Meiji, was not provided for in the constitution; nevertheless, men have been specifically called to it by Imperial order since the era closed; during the reign of the Emperor Meiji, however, the elder statesmen were what the name signified, the surviving members of the original group of samurai who had promoted the restoration and been active in the government through the first thirty years of the reign. The emperor consulted them semiprivately on matters of importance, such as the beginning and termination of hostilities in the Russo-Japanese War. The cabinets of the day also consulted with, or rather submitted to the direction of, the elder statesmen. Their position in national affairs, in short, was the more or less exact counterpart of that of the elders in any ordinary Japanese family council; they are old and therefore wise in experience, and their advice should be followed. . . .

The process of wrecking the constitution and the institutions it created was deliberately entered upon in 1890. Itagaki revived the Jiyūtō, and Ōkuma reestablished his connection with the Kaishintō, the two entering into negotiations the upshot of which was a temporary union of the main opposition parties. The new combination contested the election in July 1890, and when the Diet opened in November it appeared in a solid phalanx, numbering nearly half the membership of the lower house, to oppose the government. . . .

When the lower house of the Diet settled down into working order, the opposition launched its assault against the government, which from the outset it had obviously resolved to make responsible to itself. The attack was directed against the budget, and during the first three sessions and part of the fourth the opposition efforts were concentrated upon that point. But the cabinet, even without the support of a party, was so strongly entrenched on the side of finance that it could not easily be dislodged. Articles LXVII and LXXI of the constitution made a practically impregnable defense, provided the ministers were disposed to be defiant. By the terms of the 67th Article about three fourths of the total annual expenditures were withdrawn from the action of the Diet, and the 71st Article provided that when the houses had not passed the budget the cabinet should carry out the financial arrangements of the preceding year. In spite of these articles, the opposition proposed a sweeping reduction amounting to some 10,000,000 yen in the estimates. The ministers and their delegates protested that the motion was unconstitutional because it exceeded the powers of the Diet, but the opposition remained noisily defiant, and rather than create a complete deadlock at the very outset of the Diet's history a compromise was effected, the ministers yielding two thirds and the opposition one third of their demands, and the estimates were cut by 6,500,000 yen. The session was a long one, marked by great violence of speech and continuous obstruction. The Lower House had forty-nine sittings, but accomplished little. There was, however, a great display of oratory, especially on the subjects of treaty revision and the reduction of taxation. Shimada, Ozaki, and Nakajima earned for themselves an enviable reputation as speakers and debaters. But on the whole the first session gave little comfort to the administration, while it immensely strengthened the determination of the party men to persist in their tactics. Both sides braced themselves, as the Diet closed, for the serious struggle which was to ensue when the House met again toward the end of the year 1891.

But before it reassembled, new capital had been furnished the opposition. To begin with, Yamagata, the Minister President, resigned, and was succeeded by Matsukata, the Finance Minister. The regularity with which the chief office in the cabinet passed back and forth between Satsuma and Chōshū—from 1885 to 1891 the order of succession being Itō, Kuroda, Yamagata, and Matsukata—was not lost sight of by the opposition. Then on May 11 an insane policeman attempted to assassinate the Russian czarevitch, at that time on a tour of Japan. Further, in October a disastrous

earthquake devastated the province of Gifu, and tidal waves
destroyed an immense amount of property in Toyama and
Fukuoka. The consequence of the assault upon the czarevitch was
a series of harshly repressive police regulations, and of the natural
calamities very considerable additions to the estimates, for the
relief of the sufferers. As soon as the Diet opened on November 27
an acrimonious dispute arose over the means adopted by the
government to preserve the peace, the opposition maintaining, with
reason, that it was unnecessary to institute a reign of terror among
the people because one crazy government official had disgraced the
nation by attempting the life of the heir to the Russian throne. To
the government's appeals for the sufferers in the stricken districts
the opposition paid no attention whatever. From this ominous
beginning matters in the Diet grew rapidly worse. The Budget
Committee recommended a reduction of 8,000,000 yen in the
estimates, totally disregarding the provisions of the constitution
with regard to fixed expenditures. Upon every other matter
brought into the House orators poured out floods of oratory or
torrents of abuse. Speeches two hours long were a common occurrence, and they resulted in the total cessation of business. Finally,
the government's patience was exhausted, and it recommended
that the emperor should dissolve the Diet, which was accordingly
done on December 25, 1891.

The members of the opposition regarded the dissolution as a
triumph. With the government obstructed at every turn and compelled to fall back on the constitutional provision for the reapplication of the budget of the previous year, the opposition could claim
that, save for the safeguards inserted into the constitution by the
oligarchy, it was at their mercy. Ōkuma, as was his wont, was
interviewed by the press, and stated that in general the policy of
the opposition was dictated by hostility toward a government
composed of Sat-Chō oligarchs: the monopoly of the administrative and executive offices by the members of the two clans was
intolerable and must be destroyed. But aside from their general
policy of obstruction, the opposition was opposed to the financial
and commercial policy of the government, and especially to the
prevailing corruption and favoritism. Ōkuma openly charged
Inoue with venality in promoting the interests of the Mitsui
family, and in a vague way affirmed that the various members of
the administration derived large sums from their connection with

and the protection they afforded to other commercial houses. Needless to say, Ōkuma made no mention of, nor were his strictures upon Inoue modified in the slightest degree by, the fact that he himself during his term of office had served the interests of the great Mitsubishi Company, owned by the Iwasaki family. On the constructive side, the main items of the opposition's policy, according to the same speaker, were the introduction of party cabinets and the reduction of the land tax.

箓 ALONGSIDE PROGRESS in establishing the bureaucratic and parliamentary system, the military strength of the nation was developing rapidly. In this, as in other areas, the oligarchs looked to Western models. French and German advisers came, and Japanese officials went to Europe. Japan used the Western nations as a model: she wanted, after all, to be at least strong enough to defend herself. Complete equality, even further, perhaps meant the ability to have possessions of her own. By the 1880s, both the military and the cabinet had agreed that independence meant being able to pursue rights and privileges on the Asian continent. More precisely, the "independence" of Korea (from all but Japanese influence) was seen as crucial. This notion was behind the 1895 Sino-Japanese War, a fight between China and Japan for Korea. Marlene Mayo's selection shows how the war was accepted by Japanese leaders and intellectuals of differing persuasions.

The war, as McLaren shows, also served to defuse the stalemate in the new constitutional system. Equally important, it solidified the strength of the military, as well as giving a big boost to the rising industrial corporations, the zaibatsu.

The concern for Korea, and for a foothold on the continent, led in 1904 to war with the Russians. Russia had moved into the Liaotung Peninsula and Manchuria during the suppression of the Chinese Boxer Rebellion, and to the Japanese leaders this was seen as a threat to their security. James Crowley discusses the evolution of Japanese strategic thinking and points out the congruence in attitudes between civil and military leaders.

By the end of the Russo-Japanese War, strategic objectives were set which determined the planning of the Japanese army through World War II, and Japan became the dominant power in the Far East. She had her foothold on the mainland, with Korea, the Liaotung ports, and Japanese-owned railways dominating the trade and industry of Manchuria.

MARLENE MAYO*
Attitudes Toward Asia and the Beginnings of Japanese Empire

. . . Decision-making studies by their very nature may have build-in limitations and conclusions. They all seem to conclude with the same statements that empires grew more by chance and accident than by concerted or sustained effort, that politicians hesitated before choices and did not and could not know ahead of time what was best, that events forced actions, that the demands of a lunatic fringe must not be taken as true popular sentiment or official government policy. This, however, one now expects to be told.

But what were the steady and constant aims, if any, behind the shifts, turns, and feints? If there were no fixed ideologies, no master plans, or well-considered policies, then certainly principles of some sort, broad purposes, ambitions, or attitudes must have guided Japan's actions in times of crisis. Even if the crises were not necessarily of Japan's making, its reactions and explanations of its reactions are significant. The historian cannot always write off a move as merely opportunistic or pragmatic, for in that word alone may be a shade of difference which assists in the creation of an empire. There is something almost as absurd about the vision of poor, orphan Japan in East Asia, a new small nation, fumbling

* Marlene Mayo, "Attitudes Toward Asia and the Beginnings of Japanese Empire," in Goodman, comp., *Imperial Japan and Asia—A Reassessment* (New York: East Asian Institute, Columbia University, Occasional Papers, 1967), pp. 9–17, 19–20.

and stumbling in the dark international jungle, mainly responsive to external forces and pressured by events into aggression and war, as there is about the vision of warlike Japan relentlessly and ruthlessly working out a grand design of conquest.

... Even without ready-made plots, Japan back in 1893 and 1894 may not have been completely unprepared for "various unexpected happenings" in Korea, as Foreign Minister Mutsu Munemitsu labeled the immediate events which led to the outbreak of war. Japan's demand at the peace table for Formosa, in addition to the Liaotung Peninsula, should not be interpreted, I would argue, as a tentative gesture toward colonialism or harmless greed for a half-savage island. Japan was asking for a Chinese dependency (redesignated province in 1887), for a region where there had recently been considerable attempt at reform, for an island with strategic value and commercial potential. If Japan in 1895 as an Eastern nation consciously joined—and was allowed to join— the Western club of great powers engaged in "correct" imperialism, then the step was a momentous one and more should be known about it and the thought of the era. The acquisition of Formosa, even though Japan's rule there was benevolent by comparison with its attitude in Korea, may have as much to tell us about the nature and ideology of Japanese imperialism as the later annexation of Korea. Perhaps diplomatic and intellectual history together can show whether Japan became imperialist out of duty rather than choice, as some now believe, or instead chose to make imperialism its duty. ...

Yamagata Aritomo (1838–1922) was a *Realpolitik* statesman who skillfully practiced both the civil and military arts. In his long life span, he was war minister, chief of the general staff, home minister, prime minister, president of the Privy Council, and genro or elder statesman, at all times a man very much at the center of power. To some he is a sinister figure, the one villain to be singled out from among the Meiji oligarchy for launching Japan upon a militarist road while frustrating the development of parliamentary constitutionalism. Yamagata's reputation has, however, benefited enormously from recent studies. He emerges as an exceedingly cautious statesman, a realist who did not wish to push Japan into adventures beyond its means and who consciously committed the army to overall civilian control, a nationalist but not a jingoist who hoped to reform but not revolutionize Japan.

By 1894, Yamagata, who had on all previous occasions cast a vote against foreign military adventures citing unpreparedness and prematurity, now favored war with China to settle the Korean issue. It would be historical license to give as the only or even main reason the fact that Yamagata, as chief of the general staff, now commanded a modern military establishment capable of offense as well as defense. Japan's decision for war was immensely complicated, and historians, including the revisionists, have not really settled yet whether the preceding twenty years of restraint in foreign policy show the Meiji oligarchy to be in disagreement only over timing, but not over the ultimate goal of expansion.

. . . [I]t was by 1890 that the cabinet and both the armed services had come to believe that Japan could keep its independence only by possessing the ability to join the great powers in demands for rights and privileges in Asia. By 1894, the ability to acquire territories was added. When war broke out that year, the major strategic goal (the army's) was to acquire the Liaotung Peninsula as a guarantee of Korean independence, and the secondary but by no means minor aim (the navy's primarily) was to acquire Formosa as a base from which to control the sea lanes of the China coast and the southern approaches to Japan.

Of all the many memoranda which Yamagata wrote on these problems, I would single out two which provide a key to his thought and a guide to his assimilation of Western theories. The first was begun in 1886 and revised in final form by January 1888, when he was Home Minister in Itō Hirobumi's cabinet; the second was prepared for circulation in March 1890 to his own cabinet. They reveal a pattern of thought which, I think, makes it possible to postulate consistency of purpose or design without having to attribute superhuman foresight or sinister character to the man. It is not necessary to find evidence of a "concerted plan" or of a "substantial plot" to make an important statement about Japanese ambitions in Asia.

It was obvious, Yamagata wrote in the first document, that the existing competition in Asia between Britain and Russia would within a few years cause much trouble in East Asia. The trade and military positions of the two were being revolutionized by plans for the Canadian Pacific Railway and the trans-Siberian railway. Japan must think ahead and build up its arms, for the day would come when the Russian railroad would reach the Pacific, probably in 1911, whereupon Russia would try to dominate Asia. "We know from history," he said, "that the Russians never give up until they realize their ambitions."

When war between Russia and Britain broke out, Japan must be strong enough to decide whether it wished to remain neutral or to take sides. And, if Korea were invaded, which seemed highly likely, how could Japan remain out of danger? "After all, it is our policy to maintain Korea as an independent nation without ties to China and to keep Korea free of the danger of occupation by one of the great nations of Europe." Because of that peninsula's geographic position, whoever occupied it would be in an excellent position to control East Asia and put Japan at a disadvantage. China currently insisted upon treating Korea as a tributary state, and Japan certainly should not remain quiet if China showed any signs of violating the Tientsin Treaty of 1885. It would be a grave mistake to assume that China, once militarily reformed, would not act like a great power. It could conceivably stir up as much trouble in East Asia as either Britain or Russia. In the confused East Asia of the future, Japan should be prepared to contend with multiple adversaries. . . .

In the second document, which appears to be a sounding board for a speech he gave to Japan's first Diet in November 1890 requesting a large military budget, Yamagata asserted that a nation without a plan of self-defense was not a proper nation. If Japan wished to keep its independence, it must draw up a plan of national defense now "before the rain began," to prepare in time of peace for unexpected emergencies, and to make its "direction for the future a definite one." Japan must be ready, first, to defend its line of sovereignty and, then, its line of interest. The first line ran along the frontiers. The second line, he explained, but not too clearly, ran through those neighboring territories or areas which touched upon the axis of Japan's line of sovereignty. All nations had such lines and protected them with diplomacy and armaments. "If we wish to maintain the nation's independence and to rank among the great powers, it is necessary to step forward and defend our line of interest, to be always in a favorable position, and not satisfied to defend only the line of sovereignty." And he added, "our line of interest is really in Korea."

History, Yamagata continued, taught that "power and prosperity" were attained through competition. Since the Japanese lived in an island country, they might mistakenly assume they were isolated from foreign troubles. No country was immune, however, and therefore the martial spirit of the Japanese should be encouraged and stimulated. Diplomacy should be backed by power and should be flexible, always capable of adjusting to the opponent's movements. If in any particular situation Japan saw an advantage to be gained, it should be able to act and to advance. If Japan could make Korea into a Belgium, a Luxembourg, or a Switzerland, it might be able to relax. But if the upper part of East Asia ever came under foreign control—Yamagata's allusion will by now sound very familiar—this would act as a sword over Japan's head. He urged, as in 1888, immediate discussion of these issues. The government must decide now for the next twenty years.

Yamagata's pronouncements in the years that followed were a theme and variations. The specific problems and solutions changed, but the basic fears remained. He spoke somberly of a tough, dangerous, competitive world, in which the means of self-defense were all important. Neither East nor West were to him monolithic; there were weak and strong in both; friend and foe in both. He did not want to see Asia piece by piece become a chain of Western colonies, but neither did he care to have China, always potentially dangerous, dominate the continent.

In these memoranda, Yamagata had displayed a habit of mind, perhaps conditioned by his functions as a military leader, of looking ahead, trying to predict or forecast, trying to determine the "trend of the times," to use a good Japanese phrase, rather than submit Japan to the buffeting of fate. And he would go on worrying and making gloomy predictions. Japan had to understand what the real world was all about, to be prepared to face whatever came, to take advantage of situations—there is a temptation to say "various unexpected happenings."

Yamagata thus did not plot to create an empire; nor did he urge Japan to stir up trouble or stage incidents. He instead talked about security, but the rationale of security—Hilary Conroy would add the "pathology" of security—led him to say there could be no defense without the powers of offense, to support forceful actions in regions outside of Japan's boundaries, and constantly to broaden the perimeter of these actions. In 1888, Korea represented the line of interest. In 1894–1895, Formosa and the Liaotung Peninsula were security requirements. Japan's retention of Formosa generated new concerns, new worries, and new defense plans. Even before the Treaty of Shimonoseki was signed, Yamagata spoke of the need for larger forces to protect Japan's new overseas possessions, and beyond that "to ride the wave of victory, to become the leader in East Asia." He put the case this way:

> Our military preparedness up to this time has been used chiefly to maintain the line of sovereignty. However, if we are to make the result of the recent war something more than a hollow victory and move on to become the leader of East Asia, it will be absolutely necessary to extend the line of advantage. Our present military strength is inadequate for maintaining our new line of sovereignty. It follows that it is inadequate for extending the line of advantage and being dominant in East Asia.

In the summer of 1900, after the Boxer disturbances, Yamagata was counseling the government to bear in mind the old proverb that "a man who chases two rabbits can catch neither." Why not join the Western powers, then hunting in China, and "chase another in the north"—Korea? Some years later during World War I (1915), he wrote with just as much conviction that "Manchuria is for the Japanese the only region for expansion. Manchuria is Japan's lifeline . . . as Asians, the Japanese must of necessity live in Asia." Such expansion was essential for the solution of Japan's population problems and "for the self-protection of Asians and . . . the coexistence of China and Japan."

Thus, Yamagata had begun by talking about security and ended by talking about fulfilling a broader destiny and ambition in East Asia. Empire, even a limited empire, had become a corollary of the quest for security. Although I do not believe there is a straight-line connection between these thoughts and the ideas of the 1930s—the Chinese and Russian revolutions and the Great Depression among other things intervened—Yamagata's realism helps us to see how a preoccupation with security, not even a fixation or obsession, combined with devotion to the emperor's country and a vision of a predatory world, could operate to make control of Formosa, then Korea, Manchuria, Inner Mongolia, China, and Southeast Asia seem necessary to Japan's national interests.

Fukuzawa Yukichi (1835–1901), in contrast to Yamagata, made a point of not serving in the government, but he had enormous influence in the Meiji era as educator, journalist, and public scold. What he has said, thought, and written has assumed for many students of modern Japanese history almost sanctified significance. Fukuzawa, however, is a puzzling figure in his British liberalism and Japanese nationalism and very difficult to categorize. Much of the postwar writing about him has really been a reassessment of the strengths and weaknesses of Japanese liberal thought of the middle-Meiji period. . . . [H]is case illustrates in a Japanese context the truism that historically liberalism has not always been incompatible with either imperialism or authoritarianism.

The question I am asking here is whether the mélange of ideas and feelings associated with contempt for Asia helped ease Japan along the road to aggression. As a young man, Fukuzawa was joyful at his release from the "dregs of Chinese philosophy" and excited by his discovery of the Western world. As a mature man, he remained convinced that the old ways and habits were often enemies of progress and civilization; he supported modernization not just as an aid to preserve Japan's independence but as a means to create a superior society characterized by advances in material and spiritual well-being. He never experienced quite the same anguish as contemporary Chinese Confucians who cared more about preserving the culture of the house than providing for the defense of the land.

In his earlier years, though he vaguely worried about Western intentions in Asia, he argued that nations "must teach and learn from each other, pray for each other's welfare, and associate with each other in accordance with the laws of nature and man." By the late 1870s and early 1880s, however, he was more cynical as he viewed with alarm the renewal of Western imperialism and pondered the significance of Darwinian theories. The principle governing international relations was not, as he had previously in his naïveté thought, benevolent and impartial international law but the law of the jungle, *jakuniku kyōshoku,* the strong devouring the weak. Such behavior, he indicated, was the human condition; all countries struggled for power and profits. This truth was even more worrisome when applied to relations between East and West, since the advanced West had an edge over the backward East. In East Asia, a Western advance would bring in its wake, as elsewhere in the world, humiliation, spiritual oppression, and material destruction.

Fukuzawa offered twofold advice. Japan should build up its military power, for even though a resort to force was primitive behavior, "when others use violence, we must be violent too." Second, Japan must encourage its neighbors to reform but not itself join a combination of Asian countries or conclude a Sino-Japanese alliance. A cogent listing of his reasons was given in an 1881 essay, *Jiji shōgen,* "Commentary on Current Problems," which in subtitle continued as "the necessity of accord within and competition without, and Japan's position in the Orient against Western aggression."

While Japan was making progress in civilization and enlightenment, to use his language, its closest neighbors, China and Korea, gave no thought to reform. How could either possibly hope to remain independent? If China fell, then Japan would be in danger. Since only Japan, among all of the countries of the East, could stand "at the center of civilization" with the West, it should "resolve to make the protection of East Asia" its own responsibility. Fukuzawa did not say that Japan should love East Asia or shoulder a yellow man's burden, but rather work to strengthen Asia for Japan's sake. Reasoning analogically, he told the parable of a man who lived in a stone house but whose neighbor lived in a wooden house. Was the man in the stone house really safe from fire? Only if he could persuade his neighbor to build a stone house too. What if his neighbor remained obstinate? Then, "he is justified in using force to make him" put up a proper house. "If a crisis should be at hand, he is justified in arbitrarily invading his neighbor's land—not because he covets his neighbor's land or hates his neighbor, but simply to protect his own house from fire."

As Fukuzawa saw it, Japan's security required civilized neighbors. He reinforced this argument the following year in another essay, *Heiron,* "On Armaments." If China were to overthrow the Manchu regime, there would be anarchy; the Western powers would yield to temptation, step in and take advantage of the disorder, and partition China. If such a threat materialized, Japan should not stand idly by, hands in sleeves, but join the chase for the prize. In effect, Fukuzawa had shifted his analogy. If outsiders came to live in the wooden house next door, Japan should have a room too. . . .

By 1894, then, it was very much in character for Fukuzawa to come to a vigorous, even exultant defense of the Sino-Japanese war, although the extravagance of his language is a little surprising. On July 29, even before the hostilities had quite become official, he wrote that the war was one "between a country which is trying to develop civilization and a country which disturbs the development of civilization. . . . This is not a war between people and people and country and country, but it is a kind of religious war."

As the war drew to a close, Fukuzawa's voice was neither hysterical with jingoism nor harsh with exacting peace demands, but he constantly emphasized the probable partition of China within a few years. When that happened, Japan must be in a good position to take a profitable and strategic spot, and so should demand at the peace conference territorial concessions sufficient "to extend power in a contest with others." After the war, Fukuzawa's retort to those who again advised Sino-Japanese cooperation was that if two doctors were trying to treat a sick patient and one was scientific and the other from the old school, they could never agree on the diagnosis, let alone the prescription. As long as China was Confucian, as long as the present Ch'ing government existed, there could be no true alliance, cooperation, or kinship.

Fukuzawa's most graphic statement was made in September 1898, just after the collapse in China of the hundred days of reform under K'ang Yu-wei. He conceded the strong historical, cultural, and psychological ties between his country and China. In land and population, Japan was no match for China; and China had for long years been Japan's teacher. But Japan had adopted Western civilization and won a war against China; it could no longer regard China as a teacher and benefactor, or speak of a common culture, or repay an obligation stretching back over a thousand years. His analogy this time was of a dog to an elephant.

In considering ways to help China reform, some Japanese have the opinion that the first step should be a complete change in the Chinese government in Peking. But I cannot help but think it a mistake to apply to China what Japan adopted after the restoration of the emperor's rule. . . . Japan may be compared to a dog and China to an elephant. Whereas a dog begins running at once with all of his might as soon as he hears an order, an elephant cannot move quickly or at will. The slow movement of the elephant is according to the law of nature. Therefore, if it takes one year for Japan to complete a reform, it will take several years for China to do the same. Thus we must be ready to watch patiently while Chinese society moves at a slow tempo. Those who try to estimate Chinese development at the rate of Japanese growth in the past forty years may be considered to have fallen into the error of trying to direct an elephant's movement with a dog's mind.

So much for China—and by extension Asia. Fukuzawa's scorn and lack of sentimentality helped him advocate, then justify aggression. The argument . . . directed that Japan practice the diplomacy of imperialism, and that was precisely what happened as Japan began to participate in the aggressive culture of the West, having already done its share to show how fragile was China's order. Fukuzawa was never an advocate of wanton aggression and never a bombastic nationalist. He was not a "bourgeois spokesman" for financiers or industrialists, but he did believe that life in some mysterious Darwinian way was a brutal struggle for existence and that nations, East or West, which shed the past were the ones to live and advance.

WALTER MCLAREN*
The Sino-Japanese War

The declaration of war [Sino-Japanese War, 1894–95] checked all partisan political activities in Japan. A forward foreign policy had been at last adopted. . . . No grounds of opposition remained except "responsible cabinets" and purely domestic questions of administrative and financial reform, and during a time of war such matters attract little or no attention. Hence it was that the general election of July was as quiet as that held four years previously, and in the brief session of the Diet convoked in October 1894 at Hiroshima, the war capital, each section of the Lower House vied with the others in enthusiastic loyalty to the emperor and the government. Scarcely a murmur against the Cabinet was raised. . . .

The clan oligarchy had played its trump card, and for the time being at least the game was won. During four years and a half,

* Walter McLaren, *A Political History of Japan During the Meiji Period* (London: George Allen and Unwin/New York: Charles Scribner's Sons, 1916), pp. 227–230, 233–236.

after the Diet had begun its sessions, the government had struggled in vain against the opposition. One after another of the clan oligarchs had assumed the responsibility of administration, not one of them with the slightest degree of success. . . . [T]he opposition, if it could not have its way, could at least prevent the government from following its own course, with the result that all progress was stayed, and a veritable deadlock ensued. Development politically and economically was impossible, and the time was rapidly approaching when the abrogation or revision of the constitution would be demanded. . . . Japan in 1894 seemed to have reached a point from which further progress could be made only by some radical changes in her political institutions. The regime of *constitutional monarchy* had broken down. The clan oligarchy's arrangement for the government of the country had failed because it had yielded the *right of consent* to the representatives of the people and withheld substantive powers over the administration. . . .

The China War revived the militarism which had lain dormant since 1873. The ideas and teachings of Yoshida Shōin—that fiery patriot who had appeared in Chōshū in the closing days of the Tokugawa regime—were now brought to light again. His program . . . included the acquisition of the Kurile Islands, Sakhalin, Kamchatka, Formosa, Korea, Manchuria, and large parts of eastern Siberia—in fact, the expansion of the Japanese empire into a great continental Asiatic power. With this prospect . . . Itō consented to quiet the political dissensions of the time. The effect was magical. The voices of the persistent critics of the government were stilled, the hackneyed opposition demands for responsible cabinets, for the destruction of the clans, for financial and administrative reforms, gave place to the cry "On to Peking." . . .

Financially, the war was a failure; instead of improving, it demoralized the government's fiscal arrangements. The actual cost of the various campaigns had been 225,000,000 yen, and, though these expenses were more than reimbursed by the indemnity, the demands of the military services increased; especially after the military party realized that a conflict later with Russia was inevitable did the outlays for armaments become so swollen that the whole of the Chinese indemnity would not have sufficed to liquidate the government's new liabilities. The result was increased taxation, a policy which provided an opportunity of which the opposition politicians were only too eager to make use. . . .

Politically, the war resulted not only in complete cessation of constitutional development, if the unseemly squabbling of the first four years of the parliamentary regime may be dignified by such an epithet, but it also gave the oligarchy the opportunity of acquiring new sources of power over the popular parties. The measures adopted by the clan statesmen were of the most disingenuous character. Against the oligarchs, who had entrenched themselves firmly behind the constitution, as we have pointed out, no action of a strictly legal nature could be taken by the opposition, with any reasonable prospect of successfully accomplishing the downfall of the Sat-Chō combination. Revolution was likewise out of the question, for the nature of the monarchy precluded any such eventuality. But mere obstruction by the opposition had served to destroy one ministry after another, and Ōkuma was not likely to have overlooked the significance of the events of the Diet's history. If the government was strong enough to stay in, it was at the same time powerless to carry out its own plans without the consent of the representatives. The safety of the oligarchy lay in preserving its hold on the administrative offices, and yet that very monopoly of power was dangerous as well as futile. Some device was therefore necessary by which the clans could be strengthened in the popular estimation, but not weakened *vis-à-vis* the opposition. It is manifestly impossible to thrust the emperor constantly into the party arena without destroying his prestige, and seeking shelter behind the provisions of the constitution must inevitably lead to a demand for the revision of that instrument. The simplest way out of the dilemma, as it appears to an outsider, would have been to yield the reins of office to the political parties. But such a course would have been unconstitutional and, moreover, would only have transferred the hostility to the cabinet from the Lower House to the Upper, for the peers were more strongly opposed to party government than were the oligarchs themselves. At least, until a majority of the peers could be brought to accept the principle of responsible government, such a simple expedient was impracticable, even if the constitutional point might be ignored.

The oligarchy's opportunity arrived when, as a result of the war, Japan became the possessor of colonies—Formosa and the Liaotung. Colonial government was a subject of which the people were ignorant, and the appointment of colonial governors not a matter in which they were interested, so, unobtrusively, the Privy Council, under Yamagata's presidency, formulated certain rules for the appointment of governors of colonies, and attached to the list of the offices those of the departments of the Army and Navy. As Formosa refused to be detached from China—or, rather, handed over to Japan—and set up as a republic on its own account, a military occupation of the island became necessary. Under such circumstances nothing was more natural than that the governor-general should be a high officer of the army or navy in active service. Similarly, the nation in its rampant chauvinistic mood felt no inclination to dispute the propriety of having high officers on the active service list of the army and navy as ministers of the military departments of the administration.

From the point of view of the militarist faction in the administration, the importance of these regulations was that they brought under its control Formosa and the various parts of the continent of Asia which were about to be ceded by China to Japan. As more territory was acquired, each additional piece could be used as a base for further encroachment. But that phase of the subject does not interest us so much at present as do the consequences for responsible government of the regulations, in so far as they applied to appointments to the departments of the Army and Navy. So long as a lieutenant-general or some higher officer in active service held the chief post in the War Office would the general staff be in control of that department, and similarly with the navy. Each minister president of state in the future would be under the necessity of applying to the general staff and the Supreme Naval Board for officers to complete his cabinet. Arrangements could then be made by the military party for the support of its policy by the cabinet. If the prime minister refused to comply, then no officers could be obtained to head the military departments and no cabinet could be formed, or if a cabinet, once formed, were unwilling or unable to carry out its covenant with the army and navy, the administration could be destroyed by simply ordering the resignation of the ministers of those services. As Satsuma and Chōshū men, even if they did not completely monopolize the high offices in the two military services, constituted a majority of the members of the general staff and the Supreme Naval Board, the oligarchy was invincible. With this regulation in force, the Sat-Chō combination, in response to popular demands, could well afford to allow party politicians to hold cabinet offices, and, in fact, create what appeared to be a party cabinet, and yet control the policy of the latter through the two nonparty members, the ministers of the army and navy.

JAMES CROWLEY*
Creation of an Empire, 1896–1910

The war with China had been fought for one main strategic objective, control over the Liaotung Peninsula. A secondary aim, advanced by the naval leaders, was the acquisition of Taiwan. With this island, Japan could aspire to controlling the sea lanes of the China trade, as well as the southern approach to the home islands. As is well known, the Tripartite Intervention of 1895 by the Powers deprived Japan of the Liaotung Peninsula, but left Taiwan under Japanese control. In addition, Russia promptly extended herself into Liaotung, thereby replacing China as the primary strategic enemy in army planning. By 1898 the Korean problem was no longer a Sino-Japanese affair, but involved the diplomacy of the Powers. No responsible naval officer could envision challenging British sea power; but the Russian position in Manchuria was another matter. If Russia could be isolated from the European powers in terms of Asian affairs, it might be possible to reassert Japan's position in Liaotung. With this in mind the government in 1896 sanctioned a doubling of the standing army and the imperial fleet. The army was increased to thirteen divisions, giving a mobilization potential of 600,000 men; the navy was ordered to construct a 278,000-ton fleet. Even so, the key to national security, whether seen through the prisms of Meckel's or Mahan's doctrines, was a naval alliance with Great Britain.

... By confining Japan's continental interests to Korea and South Manchuria, it was possible to negotiate the 1902 Anglo-Japanese alliance. While affirming the "independence" of Korea,

* James Crowley, "From Closed Door to Empire," in Bernard S. Silberman and H. D. Harootunian, eds., *Modern Japanese Leadership: Transition and Change* (Tuscon, Arizona: University of Arizona Press, 1966), pp. 279–285.

this treaty recognized Japan's special interest "politically as well as commercially and industrially in Korea." With this alliance, Japan's strategic interests were very well served indeed. Only Great Britain could readily challenge Japanese sea power in the Northeast Pacific; the terms of the alliance reduced a repetition of the Tripartite intervention to a remote possibility; and the naval security of the Anglo-Japanese alliance provided the opportunity to contest Russian control over the Liaotung Peninsula.

Throughout the 1885–1902 period, the "independence" of Korea had provided the starting premise for army policy. Beginning in 1902, however, the Army General Staff concluded that, "for the long-range planning of our country" it was necessary to make "Korea part of the Japanese empire." While the cabinet did not adopt a similar policy for several years, it seems manifest, in retrospect, that the absorption of the Hermit Kingdom was practically dictated by the nature of European rivalries, especially the advance of Czarist Russia into South Manchuria and the projected construction of the trans-Siberian railway. Dictated, that is, insofar as one accepted the basic Meckelian dictum: the Korean peninsula constituted an inherent strategic threat to the Japanese home islands. Of course, if the Korean state were politically stable, and its sovereignty recognized by the powers, theoretically Japan need not directly establish its authority in order to keep any third power from acquiring the handle of the "dagger at the heart of Japan." One suspects that Itō Hirobumi understood the naval (Mahan) strategic approach which feared the potential diplomatic and military implications of an outright continental acquisition. Certainly, as Hilary Conroy indicates, it was Itō who frustrated the army's demand for the annexation of Korea between 1904–1908. That the Imperial navy had formulated a competing version of national defense policy became evident immediately following the Russo-Japanese War.

In appraising the problem of national defense in 1907, the Naval General Staff argued that Japan was an insular nation with insular possessions. Even the development of overseas trade and commerce, particularly the mainland, was a maritime proposition, as testified by the policies of Britain, France, and the United States. Unexpressed, but implicitly conveyed, was the subsidiary premise that Japan need not inevitably commit itself to any continental acquisition. Japan, in fact, had cornered the Korean market and the world's greatest sea power had, in the 1902 Anglo-Japanese Alliance, confirmed a Japanese hegemony over Korea. The central strategic task, judged Japan's naval planners, centered on establishing naval hegemony over the United States in the Western Pacific. Without this, the United States could entrench itself via the Philippines and pursue its "open door" policy, irrespective of the interests or wishes of the Japanese government. More crucially, without a greatly augmented fleet, Japan's national security would be a phantom, a derivative of the alliance with Great Britain. Even the ability to wage war in 1894 and 1904 had been possible, observed the naval staff, only because British seapower had not been employed against Japan. For these reasons, the Imperial navy recommended the ultimate construction of two battle fleets, each headed by eight capital warships. As an immediate goal, it favored the building of twelve capital ships, the eight-four plan. This latter program would guarantee Japanese hegemony over the American fleet; the former proposal would at least furnish the possibility of a successful clash with Great Britain. In view of the Anglo-Japanese alliance, however, Japan's naval leaders did not regard the British fleet with great concern. Only the United States—by its immigration policies and desire to assist in the development of Manchuria—posed an immediate worry. "In 1907," noted Admiral Fukudome, "the Imperial navy made the United States its sole strategic enemy."

The Imperial army, understandably, remained loyal to its earlier commitment that Korea constituted the key to national security. There was no better way to guarantee this security question than by annexation. Within this axiom, Czarist Russia constituted the nation's prime strategic threat. To meet it, the army would need a twenty-five-division standing army, with a mobilization potential of fifty divisions. Moreover, since the army had fought two wars for control over Liaotung and the "independence" of Korea, its officers tended to view the continental scene with proprietary airs. For example, the War Ministry shattered the Foreign Ministry's efforts to encourage American investment in Manchuria; it opposed ending the military governor-generalship over the Liaotung Peninsula—it took the personal intervention of the genro to bring this about; and General Ōyama actually proposed that the "foreign policy of South Manchuria be entrusted completely to the governor-general [Ōyama]." This configuration of army policies and actions conveys how deeply committed the army leaders were to Korea–South Manchuria as essentials of national defense. In effect, by 1907, Japan's military establishment was characterized by a dichromatic approach to national security.

In a country endowed with greater natural resouces and population, the competing views of national defense, the distinctive missions of the army and navy, might not have been so significant. Still, with the annexation of Korea in 1910, Japan had irrevocably committed itself to a continental (army) and oceanic (navy) role. Its military and naval leaders had defined one comprehensive objective: the maintenance of an establishment capable of meeting the strategic threats posed by the Russian army and the American navy. Within the institutional framework of each service, each strategic axiom was a "rational" or "professional" evaluation. It is a moot question whether the Imperial sanction to both views of national defense reflected a comparable phenomenon.

Between 1894 and 1905, Japan astonished the Powers, especially Russia, with its dramatic military and naval victories. In turn these triumphs furnished the Japanese nation with a new set of heroes as well as instilling an undeniable sense of national pride. In the process, the mettle of the Imperial army and navy had been tested and proved adequate to the challenge. Perhaps only in this fashion could a "professional" army and navy have been forged. Even so, it is worthy of note that both Meckel and Mahan had furnished what had been lacking in the han–samurai system of Tokugawa Japan and the national military establishment of the 1870s: a sense of mission divorced from the shores of the home islands. Setting aside the domestic implications of these wars and the appreciable increase in the size of the two services, the concluding observations will focus briefly on: (1) the transformation in the army's rationale for education of conscripts with "love of country" and "reverence for the emperor"; and (2) the role of the "right of supreme command" during the Sino- and Russo-Japanese wars.

During the 1870s, the French military system had furnished the inspiration and guidance for the War Department; and in the 1880s the Prussian model acted as a vital influence in the formation of the Imperial army. This should not be read, however, as one displacing the other. The French concern with "morale" and an "aggressive combat" spirit, as well as French stress on the leadership of the War Minister, were not compromised. After 1880, the military academy continued to be patterned after its French counterpart, and the War Minister still set basic army policies. Phrased differently, the great surge of Prussian influence via Katsura, Kawakami, and Meckel occurred within the framework built in the 1870s. Nevertheless, the purpose behind the training of conscripts was altered significantly, most noticeably after the Russo-Japanese War. Originally, the cultivation of "patriotism" and "loyalty" had been seen as fostering domestic security; but, as the conduct of the war against Russia confirmed, the idealization of "bushidō" also contributed substantially to the combat effectiveness of the troops. Although the direction of campaigns—both in war games and in combat—was monopolized by a highly professional general staff system, the army leaders also became convinced that the ideological aspects of conscript training were as essential as staff planning. What had initially been adopted for political reasons had acquired the sanction of a professional estimate based upon performance in battle. Thus, parallel with the withdrawal of the officer corps from any overt involvement in domestic politics of the 1880s, the army remained committed to indoctrinating the conscripts with the cult of bushidō. Without minimizing the indirect social consequences of this type of education, it would be misleading to regard this indoctrination as a manifestation of "feudalism" within the army.

Finally, much has been written about the theoretical influence of the "right of supreme command," particularly in terms of creating a "dual government" in Meiji Japan. More recently Japanese historians have become intrigued with the bureaucratic aspects of the cabinet system which evolved in the Meiji era. With this approach, the earlier tendency to view the army as a separate institution has been replaced by a focus on rivalries between ministries—for example, the War Ministry and the Foreign Ministry—and to regard the ministers of state as sharing in common the ambition to frustrate any type of effective parliamentary or democratic control over foreign or security policies. The creditability of this approach is supported by the fact that throughout Meiji Japan military planning and policies always remained subordinate to the decisions of the genro and cabinet. . . .

Japan's handling of the Korean and South Manchuria problem during her conflicts with China and Russia mirrored a brilliant coordination of diplomacy and force under astute political leadership. Her conduct of these conflagrations alone belies the clichés that the "right of supreme command" precluded (at least in the Meiji era) viable civilian control over the Imperial army, and that the Meiji military establishment was "feudalistic" in form, possessing only the "shell of military professionalism." Indeed, throughout the 1853–1910 period, Japan's military policies were invariably distinguished by the primacy of political leadership and political considerations, most noticeably in the clusters of decisions and reforms associated with the demise of the "closed door" and with the quest for an empire within the rules sanctioned by the diplomacy of imperialism. The fascinating fusion of political and martial skills evident in the Meiji restoration, in the establishment of a national militia, in the creation of the Meiji state, in the development of a modern army and navy, and in the acquisition of an empire, is too consistent to be accidental, too complex to be neatly explained.

❀ THE VICTORY over the Russians in 1905 left a victorious military establishment eager to sustain its position. But increases in the military budget were controversial and difficult to force through the Diet. Crowley documents the disparate views of the civilian and military bureaucrats, and the resulting clashes.

Yet these struggles in the cabinet and in the Diet over policy and budget were not struggles of the people versus the military. First, the Diet's Upper House, the House of Peers containing aristocrats elected by the elite itself and not by popular vote, was conservative. Second, McLaren argues, the Lower House was exceedingly corrupt and was easily and regularly bought off, not a situation conducive to democratic development. Disagreements ultimately were confined to the civil and military elite, who continued to maintain the same basic goals—economic strength and political order at home, expansion and empire abroad.

JAMES CROWLEY*
National Defense and the Consolidation of Empire

The 1907 strategic calculations of the general staffs were not lacking in validity. The fear of a "war of revenge" by the Czarist government could not be easily discounted; and the world tour of the American fleet of 1906–1907 was, from the viewpoint of Theodore Roosevelt, undertaken to impress upon the Japanese government the power and determination of the American government to exert its influence in Pacific affairs. Although the Japanese and American press promptly expressed belief in the imminence of a Japanese-American conflict, in strategic terms Roosevelt's "big stick" naval diplomacy was really a fragile reed. The Anglo-Japanese alliance precluded any Anglo-American accord against Japan; and the Imperial fleet was approximately equal to that of the United States. Given the cruising range of the warships of the period, this parity invested Japan with a commanding superiority in the Western Pacific. Somewhat belatedly, Theodore Roosevelt realized the Philippines were an "Achilles' heel," indefensible against the power of the Japanese fleet. This perception soon reflected itself in a new style of American diplomacy, in the Root-Takahira and Taft-Katsura executive agreements which tacitly confirmed Japan's special position in Korea and South Manchuria. Parallel with this Japanese-American rapprochement, the Russian and Japanese governments negotiated in 1907 and 1909 an entente by which they recognized each other's position in North and South Manchuria. Finally, in 1910, Japan formally annexed Korea, without any objections or reservations on the part of the Western powers.

This favorable diplomatic context did not alter the strategic axioms of the Japanese general staffs. From their standpoint, the softened tone of Roosevelt's policy was the consequence of Japan's naval strength; and they believed Japan's standing army had forced the reluctant acquiescence of the Russian government. However

* James Crowley, *Japan's Quest for Autonomy* (Princeton, N.J.: Princeton University Press, 1966), pp. 10–15.

well warranted these opinions may have been, the favorable
diplomacy of the postwar period sharply reduced the willingness of
the Japanese political parties to underwrite any major expansion of
the services. In the past, in 1882 and 1896, the genro had only to
formulate comprehensive armament programs and the necessary
funds were allocated; but, between 1907 and 1911, neither the
Diet nor the finance ministry was prepared to champion any significant increase in armament expenditures. This political context
affected the services in strikingly dissimilar ways. Since the navy
was, after the Russo-Japanese War, literally building a fleet of new
ships, it could, by scrapping outdated warships, realize its goal of
twelve capital ships without enlarging its budget. The Imperial
army, in contrast, could not augment the number of standing divisions unless the Diet authorized increased expenditures. Since this
authorization failed to materialize, the army, between 1907 and
1911, remained at nineteen divisions, only one of which was
stationed in Korea. To the army authorities this was intolerable, as
it provided wholly inadequate forces on the mainland for the
defense of Korea and South Manchuria. This frustrating situation
bred a conviction in army circles that the government was not
abiding by its moral and legal obligations to fulfill the estimates of
forces sanctioned by the throne in 1907, a sentiment which boiled
over into a major political crisis.

When Prince Saionji formed his second cabinet in 1911, the
army's hope for an armament increase became bleak. The premier
imposed a program of fiscal retrenchment, forcing a reduction in
the army's existing budget of some six million yen, and in the
naval budget, of some eight million yen. The political basis of this
reduction was beyond dispute: new budgets were the province of
the Diet and Saionji's party commanded a healthy majority in the
Diet. In desperation, the army authorities, with the sanction of
Prince Yamagata, tried to utilize their control over the war minister's portfolio as a club to beat down Saionji's fiscal policies. On
the death of General Ishimoto in May 1912, the army designated
General Uehara as the new War Minister. Moving directly from
his post as chief of the general staff, Uehara confronted the cabinet
with an unequivocal demand: the minimal security needs of the
empire compelled an increase of the army by two divisions, which
were to be stationed in Korea. When Saionji overruled the stipulation, Uehara resigned and the army refused to nominate a new

War Minister. Because his portfolio was confined to officers on active duty, Uehara's action precipitated the resignation of Prince Saionji. The genro, at the insistence of Prince Yamagata, then selected General Katsura to organize a new cabinet, one that would presumably effect an increase of the army by two divisions.

The political strategy of the army authorities, abetted by the covert influence of Yamagata, provoked a crisis of the highest order. Were the budget policies of the government, the legal prerogative of the Diet, to be dictated by a clique of army officers? Could the war minister impose his dictates on the other ministers of state? The challenges posed by Uehara's resignation alienated the political parties and the finance and naval ministers, a situation which temporarily at least forged a bond of political unity between two key ministries and the political parties. The results of this new political configuration were promptly displayed. When General Katsura set out to form his cabinet, he discovered the naval authorities were not prepared to provide a naval minister. This public stance revealed an intense resentment of the army's dictatorial methods and, more pointedly, it acted as a blunt warning that the naval authorities could also play the game of cabinet politics according to army rules. In contrast to Prince Saionji, General Katsura did not yield the point, preferring instead to invoke the aid of the throne and obtain a memorial ordering the appointment of a naval minister. While this maneuver assured the formation of a cabinet, it also intensified the opposition of the majority party in the Diet. Consequently, the Katsura cabinet was unable to enact the desired two-division expansion of the army; and the transparent hostility between the naval ministry and the premier fostered a popular belief that a clique of Chōshū army officers, headed by Yamagata and Katsura, had engineered the downfall of the Saionji government as a means to revive its oligarchical control over governmental policies.

Motivated more by obstinacy than moderation, Katsura retained the premiership for fourteen months. In this interval, he made no serious overtures to ameliorate the conflict between the war ministry and the finance of naval ministries or to seek an accommodation with the Seiyūkai, the majority party in the Diet. As premier, he pressed for an enlarged army budget, only to see his recommendation vetoed by the Diet. Finally the impasse was vividly revealed in the public arena by Ozaki Yukio. On February 5,

1913, in one of Japan's most memorable parliamentary addresses, often regarded as the symbol of the inception of Taishō democracy, Ozaki censured the Chōshū oligarchs for their wanton violation of responsible cabinet government and the vile technique of concealing partisan interests under the mantle of the emperor: "They always mouth 'loyalty' and 'patriotism' but what they are actually doing is to hide themselves behind the throne, and shoot at their political enemies from their secure ambush. The throne is their rampart. Rescripts are their missiles." The vivid metaphor stirred the Seiyūkai to vote a formal censure of the government; and Katsura rashly retaliated with another Imperial rescript requesting the revocation of the censure. This crude stratagem proved his undoing. Defying the rescript, the Seiyūkai affirmed its lack of confidence in the premier; and, once Katsura's behavior had cast the sanctity of the throne in jeopardy, Prince Yamagata added his powerful voice to the demand for a new government. The issue was decided. Katsura resigned and Yamagata asked Admiral Yamamoto to organize a cabinet in harmony with the expectations of the Seiyūkai.

With the establishment of the Yamamoto cabinet, the genro and the army authorities had, in fact, conceded the imprudence of the army's attempt to bludgeon the government with the regulations governing the service portfolios. The lesson had not been learned easily; and the tactics of Generals Uehara and Katsura had infused the Diet with great confidence. Equally significantly, Ozaki's parliamentary posture had forced the genro into a weaker political position. Following the Diet's rejection of the Imperial rescript, even Yamagata understood the necessity for resolving political dissension by negotiations with the leaders of the political parties. Henceforth, as Professor Scalapino has noted, "personal intervention by the throne in political controversies practically ceased." And, in his opening moves as premier, Admiral Yamamoto assured the Diet that parliamentary appointments would be made in the ministries, that expansion of the army would not be proposed, and that the requirements for the service ministries would be broadened to include retired or inactive general officers. These were, to be sure, modest concessions; and if they marked the beginning of the principle of cabinet responsibility to the majority party, they did not usher in an age of party government. Neither the genro nor the ministries of state were disposed to accept direction in national policies by the political parties.

WALTER MCLAREN*
The Political System in Japan

The equality of the powers of the two houses in legislation, with no provision for breaking the deadlocks that are likely to arise except a conference between delegates appointed by both or the personal interference of the sovereign, combined with the radically different ideas of members of the two houses, has powerfully strengthened the hands of the administration. During the greater part of their history the peers and the representatives have been working at cross-purposes. The former has clung tenaciously to its aristocratic or bureaucratic traditions, while the latter has voiced to a certain extent at least the ambitions of the masses. Against all the efforts of the political parties to secure responsible government the Upper House has backed up the oligarchy, and has stood ready at the request of the genro to block all legislation presented by a government which was too closely allied with any party. Attempts at party government, therefore, have generally given place to government by the oligarchs with the support of the members of the parties, now in one combination, now in another, secured either by bribery or owing to their conviction that opposition was fruitless. . . .

The administration regards the session of the Diet as a constitutional nuisance which has to be endured, but to be made as short as possible. It has become a custom, therefore, to convene the Diet immediately before the New Year holiday. Late in December the houses are organized and formally opened by the emperor, and before any business is transacted an adjournment to about January 20 is moved and carried, almost a month being cut off the session at one stroke. It is further provided by the Law of the

* Walter McLaren, *A Political History of Japan During the Meiji Period* (London: George Allen and Unwin/New York: Charles Scribner's Sons, 1916), pp. 356–357, 364–369, 374–375.

Houses (Article XXXIII) that the government by Imperial order
may suspend the sittings of either house for a period of not more
than fifteen days, and upon numerous occasions this power has
been exercised, especially when the opposition has been particularly offensive in its obstruction. Again, the Lower House meets
ordinarily on Tuesdays, Thursdays, and Saturdays, the sitting
beginning at one o'clock and concluding before nightfall. It is an
unusual session in which the Lower House sits on more than forty
different days, and a day's sitting which lasts until six o'clock is
almost certain to be commented upon by the press as of extraordinary length. . . .

. . . [I]t is obvious that the creation of representative institutions
in 1890 has afforded the advocates of popular government but few
opportunities to influence the course of Japan's subsequent political development. The brief annual sessions, the perfunctory debates, the arbitrary powers of the government, the independence of
the cabinet, and the general constitutional limitations upon the
Diet's powers over legislation, have all combined to render nuga-
tory the sporadic efforts of the opposition to set up responsible
government. Not only have the party politicians failed to make
progress toward popular government—a failure that was inevitable
under the existing constitution—but in yielding to the temptations
placed in their way by successive cabinets since 1898 they have
forfeited the esteem, if not the confidence, of the people. By deserting their party principles, as outlined in 1890, and by selling their
support to the oligarchy, the parties have immensely strengthened
the latter's position, and at the same time postponed the realization
of responsible government for a generation or even longer. . . .

The epidemic of bribery and corruption in the Diet in 1898
and 1899 was the result of the peculiarities of the Japanese political system and the Japanese character. If the representatives of the
people in the Lower House were unable to control the policy of the
government, they could at least, by refusing their consent, prevent
the government from carrying out its measures; therefore the
government was forced to purchase a sufficient number of votes. A
punitive dissolution, while it meant financial embarrassment for
the politicians, did not directly accomplish the administration's
purpose, for it delayed the passage of its measures for a year, while
to the parties it was evident that a general election could not
possibly result in placing them in office. Under these circumstances

it was considered only wise on the part of the cabinet, and prudent on that of the opposition, to compose their differences on the basis of monetary considerations given and received. Hence in 1898 and 1899 Yamagata for the oligarchs and Hoshi Tōru for the Kenseitō arranged terms satisfactory to everyone concerned. In return for the votes of the party and the enactment of its own program of legislation the government handed over valuable considerations in franchises and money. . . .

Few party politicians have made as immense fortunes out of bribes as have the cabinet ministers, and it is only necessary to point to the list of Japanese millionaires to prove the point. A few of them are businessmen—the Mitsuis, the Iwasakis, Ōkura, Shibusawa, Furukawa, Yasuda—others are the descendants of the great daimyō families, who at the beginning of the Meiji era were already in possession of great wealth, and the remainder are the so-called elder statesmen and cabinet ministers. These latter were originally in almost every case either poor samurai or the sons of men of very modest fortune, and have been all their lives in the service of the state, drawing small salaries. Their present immense properties are not the result of savings wisely invested but of peculations and bribes.

The devices by which the members of the administrations, past and present, have made their money are not unknown in other countries, but some of them are so interesting as to be worth recording. The foundations of the Inoue and Ōkuma fortunes were laid in very early days. Inoue during his incumbency of the Department of Public Works had charge of the building of all railroads and telegraphs, and, according to officially compiled reports of the Railway Bureau, the construction expense per mile was cut in half after his resignation. Ōkuma, who while in the Finance Office was called upon to provide the means for carrying on the campaign against Satsuma in 1877, adopted the expedient of an issue of paper money, and it is commonly reported in Japan that he carried off several cartloads of the script which remained in the Treasury after the rebellion had been suppressed. The official careers of both these men had ended about 1881, though they have occupied cabinet offices for short periods since then, and from that time they devoted their energies mainly to serving the interests of the great business houses of Mitsui and Iwasaki respectively. The first issue of the *Japan Year Book,* published in 1905, in a section made up of short biographical sketches of the influential men of the country, refers to Inoue as the Mitsui's representative in the Council of the Elder Statesmen. ...

The venality of the members of the Lower House, when contrasted with the peculations of the official class, appears extremely sordid. The bribes are smaller, and the transactions almost invariably take place in disreputable resorts in an atmosphere of vulgar dissipation. The official reports of the preliminary trial of the members of the Diet implicated in the sugar scandal of 1909 present the revolting details of a debauch lasting through the whole session. ...

It is to this pass that Itō's arrangements, as embodied in the constitution, and the clan oligarchy's tenacity in clinging to power have brought the government of Japan. Two remedies alone seem to be adequate to cure the "disease of government proceeding from multiform centers": either to abolish once and for all the constitution and the Diet and revert to a system of absolute and autocratic monarchy, or to amend the constitution in the sense of placing the control of the affairs of state in the hands of a cabinet responsible to the dominant party or combination of parties in the Lower House. Either of these changes would produce a form of government that could be easily understood and operated. If the time has gone by when the first of the suggested remedies could be safely applied, the present or the immediate future seems a favorable opportunity for the application of the second. Only two or three of the Meiji statesmen remain, and they have all reached an advanced age. The House of Peers could be so reconstructed, or its powers so reduced as part of the project of constitutional revision, as to make it subservient to the cabinet and the Lower House.

Even if responsible government were established in Japan, there would still remain to interest Europeans and Americans the question of the nation's foreign politics. Japan's predominance in Eastern Asia has become the foundation of the national policy. "Nibbling at China" is no longer the propaganda of the military party alone: that policy has come to be universally accepted as leading directly to the realization of the nation's destiny. Korea, Manchuria, Mongolia, and, finally, the Middle Kingdom itself—this is the order of conquest in the minds of the Japanese, not only among the dreamers or the professional militarists, but among the rank and file of the people also.

The passing of the genro, the amendment of the constitution, the establishment of party government—these would probably only accentuate the rampant imperialism of the Japanese nation. As Ōkuma has taken advantage of the present European situation to initiate the most recent as well as the most flagrant attempt to violate China's sovereign rights, vastly more dangerous than Itō's attempt in 1894, so other cabinets in future may be expected to follow his lead. The policy is popular in the country, and opposition from without alone will stop the process. In the event of China's inability to defend herself, what Western power will intervene to save her?

2. *Agriculture*

❀ BY THE END of World War I, Japan was no longer an overwhelmingly rural society, and productivity was higher in industry than in agriculture. Between 1877 and 1921, the percentage of population engaged in agriculture and forestry declined from eighty percent to 51.6 percent. Moreover, the growth of urban areas which accompanied rapid industrialization was not due primarily to rising population, but to migration from the country to the city. Peasants were leaving a life which was still very difficult as well as poor, for productivity gains were lost in low crop prices, rents, and inflation. Industry was successfully built on this traditional base because it allowed for cheap rice and low wages. While its benefits did not significantly reduce rural poverty, living standards overall rose steadily—especially in the burgeoning cities.

FUKUTAKE TADASHI*
Landlords and Village Society

... By the beginning of the Meiji period already more than a quarter of the arable area was tenanted land. And this proportion rapidly increased after the Meiji restoration. ... Too many farmers found themselves unable to adjust to the successive waves of inflation and deflation. ... As the price of rice became inflated

* Fukutake Tadashi, *Japanese Rural Society* (Tokyo: Oxford University Press, 1967), pp. 9–14.

while their taxes remained fixed, their standards of living rose, but when the reverse process set in, in the 1880s, their income fell rapidly. A large number of farmers lost their land in the process. The area under tenancy, estimated to be about twenty-nine percent in 1872 before the new land tax was instituted, approached forty percent only fifteen years later. This percentage continued to increase gradually, and at its peak in 1930 reached 46.7 percent—nearly half of the total area.

This tenanted land was shared between about seventy percent of the total number of farmers, thirty percent of them classified in the official figures . . . as "tenants" (*i.e.*, those who owned less than one tenth of the land they cultivated) and some forty percent as "part-tenants" (those who owned less than ninety percent but more than ten percent of the land they cultivated). In detail the figures show that during the Meiji period there was an increase in the number of tenants, while after about 1920 a bigger increase came in part-tenants; but it remains true for the whole period since the late nineteenth century that owner-farmers made up less than a third of the total. The landlord–tenant relationship was a crucial one for village society, not simply because of the high proportion of tenanted land, but because of the very high proportion of farm households which were involved.

There were, however, among the landlords thus involved with such a large proportion of the farmers, a variety of types. There were the local magnates of long standing, descended from the medieval squires. . . . There were the merchant-moneylender landlords. And then there were the peasant landlords, the owner-farmers who by their own efforts had managed to secure extra land which they leased to tenants. Some among them, particularly the merchant-moneylender type, owned very large estates (by Japanese standards), but for the most part landlords of whatever type held modest holdings. There were no more than about 3000 in the whole of Japan who owned more than fifty hectares of land, and about 50,000 with more than ten. Even the number holding five or more hectares of leased-out land was only about 100,000; which means, if we assume a total number of about 150,000 hamlet settlements, that there was less than one per hamlet. However, if we include the small landlords owning between one and five hectares of tenanted land, the total number of landlords becomes 380,000 of whom more than 160,000 were themselves cultivating farmers. If one takes into account the fact that the owners of very large tracts of territory appointed managers of their land in hamlets in which they did not themselves live—the manager in this case performing much the same kind of social role as the landlord—it is a fairly safe assertion that there was hardly a single hamlet in Japan from which landlord domination was absent.

The concrete nature of this landlord dominance varied, of course, according to the type of landlord, but certain common characteristics were shared in all cases and may be considered typical of Japanese landlord–tenant relations. They are as follows.

In the first place, rents for rice land were usually fixed in kind at so much per unit area and they were fixed at the same high level as the feudal dues of the Tokugawa period. From around 1930 rent rates began to show a slight decline, and since yields were improving there was an additional slight decline in the proportion of the crop paid in rent, but even so it would be no exaggeration to say that rents generally amounted to as much as half the crop.

Secondly, tenancy contracts were for the most part verbal, and written contracts were rare except in the case of very large landlords and in districts where there had been tenancy disputes. Moreover, except for a small number of cases where rights of permanent occupancy were recognized by custom, the term of the contract was rarely specified. This did not mean that the tenant was able to stay indefinitely on the land; it meant rather that his cultivating rights were insecure since the landlord could always evict him at his own convenience. For a tenant family the prospect of being forced off its land meant immediate privation, and in a situation of surplus population with consequent keen competition for tenancy rights, this further strengthened the position of the landlord.

Then, thirdly, the agreed rent rate, though expressed in terms of a fixed amount of rice, was by general custom open to reduction in years of bad harvest. The usual procedure was for the tenant to ask the landlord for a reduction, and for the latter then to inspect the crop and grant relief according to the degree to which it fell below the normal yield. But whether such a reduction was granted or not, and if so by how much, was entirely left to the discretionary benevolence of the landlord.

For these various reasons, the tenant-farmer was in a weak

position *vis-à-vis* the landlord. If he offended his landlord he might be evicted from his land; at the very least it would become difficult for him to ask for a rent reduction if his crop failed. Except for tenants of the local magnates of feudal origin, or of other large landlords who held something like monopoly rights over land in certain districts, it was usual for tenant-farmers to rent parcels of land not from a single landlord but from several. In other words, tenants who depended on a single landlord were in a minority. But despite this diffusion of dependency the tenant was still unable to treat on equal terms with his landlords because of those characteristics of the landlord–tenant relationship outlined above. The patron–client relationships typically found in districts where there were old-style local magnates, with tenants who had only in recent centuries evolved from a more direct form of serfdom, represent only a more exaggerated form of the landlord–tenant relationships typical of the whole of Japan.

However, the pattern of landlord control in the villages changed slowly. The big and medium landlords who accumulated land after the Meiji restoration gradually, around the turn of the century when the foundations of Japanese capitalism were established, reduced the size of their own cultivated holdings or gave up agriculture altogether, thus becoming purely parasitical landlords. Even among those with smaller holdings there were a number whose children were sent away to receive higher education, often coming back to become schoolteachers or village officials and give up farming. These tendencies weakened the authority of the landlords in the villages. As a consequence—and as a result, too, of changing attitudes on the part of tenants caused by the spread of literacy, their military experience as conscripts, and the proselytizing activities of left-wing intellectuals—from around 1920 there were frequent outbreaks of tenancy disputes. There developed an organized tenants' movement which gradually gathered strength as the tenants' demands increased—from rent reductions for a particular bad harvest to permanent reductions in rental rates and the guarantee of secure tenure.

This tenants' movement, however, never succeeded in destroying the landlord system. Even at the peak of its activity it did not extend over the whole country. Even if the larger and medium landlords did come to play a purely parasitical role, and even if a number of the smaller landlords did move out of farming, the majority still continued to be peasant landlords cultivating a holding of their own. They continued to function as the ruling stratum of the village.

Thus, despite changes in the landlord system *pari passu* with the social and economic development of Japanese society after the Meiji restoration, the landlord remained the dominant element in rural society. One should, however, distinguish between those who were responsible for progress in agricultural technology and for the creation of agricultural associations in the Meiji period or who played a major role in developing local self-government after the system was founded in 1888, and, on the other hand, those who, in the 1930s, carried through the remolding and strengthening of the traditional village social order and so prepared a firm basis for putting the country on a war footing—the landlords, that is, who were active in the producers' cooperatives and organized the new farmers' associations. Though both types bear the name landlords, their character was different. As the former ceased to farm and gradually lost their control of the villages, the latter, as farming landlords, came to play the major role in dominating them. These changes over time in the ruling stratum necessarily brought, of course, simultaneous changes among the tenants and part-tenants—the stratum of the ruled. But for these changes to take any conclusive form it was not enough simply for the landlord system to change; it had to be entirely destroyed. This was post-poned until after the war. The landlord system, though changing in character, continued until the defeat in World War II to be the main determinant of the structure of Japanese village society.

❀ ALTHOUGH THE MAJOR CHANGES in society during the Meiji period reached all levels and classes, they undoubtedly had the least effect on the countryside. Landholding continued to be the basis for both economic and political power in the village. Fukutake describes the position of landlords in the hamlets, as well as at the village council level, the governing body made up of hamlet representatives. Thus, despite such important changes in the village as universal literacy, the land-lords' power was not fundamentally challenged. Even after

suffrage was extended in 1925 to include all males, new political patterns were more the result of the ascendant influence of
the new industrial combines than a surge of democratic sentiments in the village. Fukutake shows the shape of rural power
from the village council to the Diet (Japanese parliament).

FUKUTAKE TADASHI*
The Power Structure of the Hamlet

... [T]he Tokugawa village was controlled by the holders of the
"three local offices," those of the headman (*nanushi*), *kumi*
chiefs, ... and farmers' representatives. ... The office of headman
was usually hereditary in a wealthy family at the pinnacle of the
hamlet hierarchy, or, if there was no outstandingly wealthy family,
it might circulate among a number of influential families. The
other offices would be filled by members of the next rank of
farmers. These were collectively known as the "senior farmers" of
the village, ... and, unless there was some drastic decline in their
families' fortunes, membership in this group would be inherited. In
other words, the ruling stratum of the village was more or less
fixed in terms of a small number of families. The rest of the
village ... submitted to their hereditary rule, while at the same
time their lives were circumscribed by the constraining bonds of
the solidary community.

The system continued under different names even after the
beginning of the Meiji period. The former *nanushi* often became
the new *kochō* in the system initially established after the restoration. When, later on, the new local government system was finally
promulgated it was generally a man from a family of the highest
rank who became the hamlet's member of the new village council,
and someone from the next rank of families who became head of
the hamlet. The notion of a group of senior farmer families which
formed the hamlet council and filled the hamlet and village offices
long survived the Tokugawa period. They were known in modern

* Fukutake Tadashi, *Japanese Rural Society* (Tokyo: Oxford University
Press, 1967), pp. 145–148, 175–178, 189–190.

times as the *omodachi*—the "prominent"—and they were usually *oyakata* of the other families in the hamlet.

... [T]he authority of this upper stratum was maintained through their positions as landlords, as *oyakata* and as stem families, through their paternalistic protection of the lower strata of the village, and through their effective control over the common property of the hamlet and the hamlet work organization—a control which was not much affected by the fact that decisions were formally taken at hamlet general meetings, for those who did not belong to the circle customarily observed a compliant silence on these occasions.

Despite considerable changes in this pattern after the creation of the new local government system, it would not have been difficult to find hamlets in the least developed parts of the country which still fitted this description right up to the end of the last war, hamlets where the group of families which made up the hamlet council was fairly rigidly fixed and gaps in their ranks left when families died out or lost their wealth could only be filled by others which had acquired ownership over at least a minimum area of land. Appointments to hamlet and village offices would be decided in such cases by consultation within the group, and the more important offices would be reserved by the group for themselves. The other members of the hamlet put up no resistance to their power, for to resist would be to be cut off from the life of the hamlet. If there was dissension and conflict within such hamlets it was factional conflict arising from a split within the ruling segment itself, for there was no room for conflict between the strata to develop.

However, hamlets in which the traditional patterns showed this degree of stability right up to the recent war made up a minority of the whole. In most hamlets there was a shift in the power structure during the first quarter of this century. This was particularly marked in those villages where the upper landlord families lost their fortune in the sharp economic fluctuations of the first half of the Meiji period. Even where this was not the case the gradual extension of the suffrage removed the formal mark of the hereditary oligarchy's separateness—there was no longer a distinction to be drawn between those who were first-class citizens of the nation and those who were mere residents of the hamlet. The process might begin, for instance, with the demand that the lesser farmers should be represented on the hamlet council, and a kind of "people's tribune" might be formally included as their representative. In hamlets where farmers' unions were formed and the first stirrings of class tension and conflict were heard, the tenancy disputes over rents and security of tenure might be paralleled by a movement to democratize the government of the hamlet. As a final step the whole system of a council of hereditary "prominent men" might be abandoned in favor of an elected body on which the old upper-stratum families no longer had a monopoly but were also joined or replaced by members of the middle groups.

The change in the power structure of the hamlet reflected on the one hand the withdrawal from agriculture of the landlords and the growing economic strength of the owner-farmers and part-tenants which resulted from the development of a capitalist economy. On the other, it was also a reflection of the fact that by the turn of the century the upper strata of villagers no longer had a monopoly of literacy. With the spread of school education even a middle-ranking farmer of ability was perfectly equipped to manage the hamlet's affairs. Nor should one overlook the fact that hamlet residents all became citizens with equal rights in a legal sense. After the enactment of universal manhood suffrage in 1925 it ceased to be possible in a good many hamlets for a small privileged group to maintain its hereditary monopoly over official positions.

For all that, the upper stratum still maintained its predominance. Since these offices were usually honorary or at most carried only a small expense allowance, they were beyond the means of the poorer tenants or part-owners. Even though many of the bigger landlords ceased to farm, or left the villages entirely, the smaller farming landlords, the richer owner-farmers, and the managing agents of the larger landlords retained their authority—by virtue of their greater wealth, of their positions at the top of the traditional status hierarchies, and through their ability to manipulate the community solidarity of the hamlet. Their position was reinforced by the fact that in absolute terms they contributed larger amounts in hamlet dues—though relative to their incomes their burden in this regard might be lighter than it was for the poorer residents. One might say that a man's voice in hamlet affairs continued to be proportionate to his contribution to hamlet finances, and that it was simply the narrowing of the contribution gap between the upper and the middle strata which brought hamlet offices within the reach of the latter. . . .

From the beginning of the local government system it was largely dominated by landlords. The limited suffrage with its division into two classes made it easy for the big landlords to become members of the council, and when hamlets chose their candidates to represent them it was natural that, given the typical hamlet status structure, a landlord—probably someone who was at the same time an *oyakata* and head of a powerful main family—would be chosen. The mayor and vice-mayor chosen by such councillors were likely to be either the most powerful landlords or else lesser landlords who could be relied on to work in the latter's interests. It was not uncommon for the sons of such lesser landlord families to start life early as officials in the village office and to work their way up through the position of treasurer and vice-mayor until they finally achieved the mayoralty, having shown that they were men in whom the powerful landlord members on the council could place complete confidence.

Thus the basis of village politics lay in the landlords' dominance of the hamlets. Its major tasks lay in securing a balance between the hamlets which continued in large measure to look after their own needs. How were the small sums available for public works to be divided among the hamlets? How were the various levies and charitable contributions required from the village to be collected from each hamlet? In setting up standards for the household tax, how was a balance between the hamlets to be preserved? These were the matters in which councillors were expected to protect the interest of their hamlets. The strength of each hamlet's influence in these matters depended not simply on its size and its social and economic power, but also on the strength of its landlords and especially on the landed wealth of the particular landlord who represented it in the council. As a consequence the actual policies which resulted from the council's decisions were not only determined by the interests of the various hamlets but also coincided with the class interests' of the landlords themselves. We have already seen how funds provided for road or irrigation works in the hamlets had to be supplemented by the hamlet's own contributions in cash or in unpaid labor. These projects were spoken of as being for the good of the hamlet, but the actual profit went in larger measure to the landlords than to anybody else. And of course the benefit was all the greater for those with extensive estates which extended into several hamlets.

This coincidence between hamlet interests and landlord interests was not fundamentally altered even after a good proportion of the landlords had withdrawn from farming and even after, with the abolition of suffrage classes and the enactment of universal suffrage, councillors came to be drawn from the owner-farmers and even from the upper strata of part-tenants. The interests of their very own hamlet was an idea which made an immediate appeal to the farmer's mentality, but in this concept of the hamlet interests the real class interests of the lower strata of poor farmers tended to be obliterated. It was a seemingly class-neutral concept, but in effect the interests of the hamlet tended to be equated with the interests of the landlords and richer farmers.

Thus village politics tended to be a matter chiefly of attaining compromise between the interests of different hamlets, in effect between the interests of different landlords. Consequently, if there were in the village a few landlords who were powerful enough to dominate it and enforce such a compromise things tended to go quite smoothly. If there was a single landlord whose property was extensive enough to allow him to dominate the whole village there might even be some positively forward-looking policies adopted. But where such a central pivot of authority was lacking the landlord delegates, backed by their separate hamlets, tended to cling tenaciously to their positions. The maintenance of a mechanical kind of balance was about as much as could be expected. Any new positive departures would threaten to disrupt that balance and consequently a negative attitude of avoiding controversy tended to dominate village politics. There were some villages in which, from the beginning of the local government system, deep-seated rivalries between landlords from different hamlets admitted of no compromise, with the result that factional conflict was continuous and no mayor could ever be secure in his position. Since local government funds were in any case severely limited, in such villages where every policy proposal led to conflict the possibilities of positive developmental policies became even more remote.

Consequently, those who were elected to the village councils were not men qualified by the ability or the breadth of vision necessary to consider the interests of the village as a whole and carry it forward by measures of enlightened reform. They considered themselves to be honorary representatives of their hamlet. And to fulfill their function of ensuring that nothing was done to damage their own hamlet's interests it was necessary only that they should have some social standing in the village backed by sufficient land ownership and a certain amount of experience in hamlet and village affairs. Provided that they maintained their hamlet's relative position, whatever their bargaining activities produced by way of a share-out would be considered by the residents of their hamlet as something to be grateful for. Since the patterns of hamlet self-government were left more or less intact, they considered it as entirely natural that hamlet works should be done by the hamlet, and hence even a small subsidy from village funds was likely to be much appreciated as the result of their representative's efforts. Likewise, if their quotas for village levies and charity contributions were kept at a reasonable level, they would consider this also to be thanks to their representative's efforts in speaking up for his hamlet. In point of fact the business of reaching a reasonable compromise between the interests of various hamlets—or in effect between the interests of different landlords—was generally a matter of fairly simple arithmetical adjustment. Consequently, most business was settled in informal discussions before the council meetings. The minutes of village councils are usually a bland and simple record of a series of motions carried by unanimous approval.

In the twenties, it is true, local government ceased to be government by a handful of landlords. The lower strata of tenants and poor farmers did not succeed in getting their interests reflected in village politics, but, as the bigger landlords became more purely parasitic and as members of the owner-farmer and part-tenant groups were elected to the council, it was no longer possible for the interests of the landlords and the interests of their hamlets to be simply equated. And in the local government units which had a small town as a nucleus, the conflict of interest between town and village became more marked. It consequently became more difficult to preserve a satisfactory balance between districts, and the minutes of council meetings came to record a certain number of decisions carried not unanimously but over the dissent of a minority. This was more especially the case in those towns and villages where farmers' unions were organized and succeeded in getting some of their representatives elected to the council.

⚙ WORLD WAR I had a major social impact on the country-side, even though Japan was not an active belligerent. Conscription, inflation, and other severe economic dislocations resulting from the war spread to all parts of the countryside. This gave a considerable boost to the tenant union movement, which along with the union movement had begun in the 1890s and now began to expand rapidly. The shattering rice riots of 1918, which began in a small village, were perhaps the surest sign that the peasants were not as reliably conservative as had been assumed. Shaken by the extent and violence of the riots, the government suppressed the tenant movement just as it grew to mass proportions. Serious internal splits also created difficulties for the movement, and the peasant unions were driven underground.

WAKUKAWA SEIYEI*
The Tenant Movement

Within the past two and a half decades [before 1946] a tenant movement has grown to proportions disconcerting to the landed class and to the government. The Japanese tenant farmer no longer is meek and servile as he was. He has learned to organize unions and fortify his bargaining power even as his city brothers had begun to do with their labor unions. He is discovering the power of collective action in demanding rent reduction and in refusing to give up the land.

The tenant union is the center of this organized effort. In 1937

* Wakukawa Seiyei, "The Japanese Farm–Tenancy System," in Douglas G. Haring, ed., *Japan's Prospect* (Cambridge, Mass.: Harvard University Press, 1946), pp. 149–155.

there were nearly 4000 such unions with a combined membership of over 220,000. Another 3000 unions with about 250,000 members had been organized and supported jointly by tenants and landowners. While the latter organizations occupy a position somewhat analogous to that of a company union, the former group is founded strictly on a class basis. The tenant movement, in consequence, has centered around the class-conscious unions. In former years they were associated closely with the farmer–labor parties and other more or less militant agrarian groups. With the compulsory dissolution of these affiliated organizations, the tenant unions have become the peasants' only rallying point in the fight for freedom and security.

As a class-conscious movement, the tenant movement is rather recent; it dates from the years immediately following the First World War. Its precursors were the peasant uprisings of the Tokugawa period and the early Meiji years. Nearly 250 peasant uprisings and disturbances occurred in the first seventeen years of the Meiji era; of these 190 occurred in the first ten years. In most of these peasant disturbances tenants participated in one way or another. The uprisings were directed variously—against the new government's monetary policy; against military conscription; against usurious farm debts; or against the new land and taxation measures. Not a few were opposed to abolition of traditional emphyteusis rights, or to continued payment of rents in kind, or simply to high rents.

As early as 1875, in Gifu and Kōchi prefectures, a movement arose to organize tenant farmers into unions. About 1888 the movement spread to Kyoto. The next ten years witnessed sporadic attempts at tenant organization in Nagasaki, Shimane, Tochigi, and Kagawa. Between 1897 and 1907, twenty-two tenant associations were formed. By the time of the First World War the number had increased to about sixty, tokens of a nascent struggle by an overexploited class. Sporadically the associations appeared and disappeared, spontaneous in origin but lacking continuity and clarity of purpose. The war changed the whole perspective.

In that four-year European war Japan enjoyed all the rights and privileges of a belligerent in return for token participation in combat, and her economic activities expanded tremendously. The "modern" industrialists established their monopolies firmly. The landed class amassed abundant capital in consequence of an unprecedented rise in the price of rice and strengthened their hold on the peasantry by expanding their land holdings. In the general deterioration of the position of the peasants, the tenant farmers suffered most from the soaring cost of living. The simultaneous experience of a war boom and a miserable condition of life profoundly altered the minds of even the backward Japanese peasantry. In the cities an organized worker's movement sprang into being, and echoes of the Russian revolution shook the countryside. Then occurred the greatest mass uprising in modern Japanese history: the rice riots of 1918, three weeks of nationwide near-rebellion. Shaken from their stupor the peasants gained consciousness of their latent power; in the voice of the new intelligentsia they heard the expression of their own discontent and rancor. Some of the more intelligent peasants began to talk of class struggle. The hope of self-liberation was beginning to dawn among them.

A surging wave of tenant disputes became nationwide within a few years. The number of disputes rose from eighty-four in 1917—the first year for which data are recorded—to 296 the following year, to 408 in 1920, and leaped to 1680 in 1921. Tenant unions appeared first in Niigata, Yamanashi, Gumma, Nagano, Saitama, and Osaka prefectures, and soon spread to the rest of the nation. In 1922 the Japan Farmers' Union—the first national body—was organized. The havoc wrought by the 1923 earthquake, the financial panic of 1924, and the general economic crisis of 1929 all added impetus to the movement. In the year of the great earthquake tenant disputes rose to 1917; in 1926 they numbered 2751. The number of tenant unions in 1927 was 4582—an increase of nearly sevenfold within six years.

The outstanding event in the history of the Japanese tenant movement probably was the founding in 1922 of the *Nippon Nōmin Kumiai* (Japan Farmers' Union). Tenant unions formed the backbone of the new organization. From that day on the movement ceased to be purely a tenant movement and became part of a larger effort designed to improve the lot of the entire peasant class. Measures advocated included the socialization of land, laws to protect farm tenants, a legal minimum wage for agricultural labor, universal suffrage, revision of the notorious Peace Preservation Law, etc. The peasants responded to the program; by 1924 the union had 508 branches with a total membership of 53,000.

Under the leadership of militant intelligentsia the Japan Farmers' Union took the lead in many tenant disputes, including the famous Kizakimura dispute in Niigata prefecture. In a number of cases it succeeded in abolishing surcharges on rents; in many cases rent rates were reduced permanently or temporarily. The union also participated actively in local political campaigns; in 1925, 339 out of 408 candidates were elected to local assemblies. It was the first mass organization to advocate alliance between the urban proletariat and the rural poor in a farmer–labor party.

The *Nōmin Rōdōtō* (Farmer–Labor party) was formed in December 1925. Within three hours of its birth the new party was dissolved by order of the Home Minister because of suspected radical affiliations. In the following March it was revived as the *Rōdō Nōmintō* (Labor–Farmer party) with four left-wing organizations excluded to insure legality in the eyes of the police. The Farmers' Union continued as a chief supporting organization of the revived party.

The subsequent history of both the Farmers' Union and the Labor–Farmer party, however, was one of the repeated schism, due on the one hand to police suppression and on the other to incessant internal dissension. . . .

Amid these kaleidoscopic changes the movement grew with vigor and enthusiasm. In the prefectural elections of 1927—the first under universal male suffrage—the Labor–Farmer party, supported by the Japan Farmers' Union, elected many candidates to prefectural assemblies in regions where the farmers' movement had been most vigorous—Kagawa, Niigata, Akita, Hyōgo, etc. In the parliamentary election of the following year, the proletarian parties elected eight of their candidates to the Diet—a historic event in the class-liberation movement of Japan.

Alarmed by the phenomenal start of the labor–farmer movement, the government lost no time in applying oppressive measures. On March 15, 1928, one month after the election, the first large-scale arrest of radical leaders occurred. This was followed by forced dissolution of three left-wing organizations, including the Labor–Farmer party. In the general roundup the Japan Farmers' Union lost several hundred of its most aggressive leaders. This prompted a reunion with the center-wing All-Japan Farmers' Union. The merger of these two agrarian organizations—the former with 70,000 members, the latter with 16,000—resulted in organization of the *Zenkoku Nōmin Kumiai* (National Farmers' Union), better known as *Zennō*.

The farmers' movement seemed well on the way to recovery when, on April 16, 1929, another mass arrest netted several thousand more prisoners. Thereafter the story of Japan's agrarian movement was one of hide-and-seek between the police and the underground organizers. Internally the story was split and merger, especially within *Zennō,* within which heated rivalry continued between the communists represented by the *Zennō Zenkoku Kaigi* (*Zennō* All-National Congress Group) and the center- and right-wing social democrats. Politically the latter rallied around the *Zenkoku Rōnō Taishūtō* (All-Nation Labor–Farmer Mass party) formed by the more moderate section of the defunct Labor–Farmer party.

3. Education and the Position
of Women

❀ EDUCATION in late Meiji Japan supported the hierarchical structure of the country. The description below of a school observance of the emperor's birthday illustrates the intensity of feeling about the emperor taught to children. Beyond such overt indoctrination, the schools channeled students into a very competitive system. Passin describes this system, and how it reflected the elitism of Japanese society and politics, as well as affecting it by creating more intellectuals and providing some social mobility. He also assesses the effectiveness of the "moral education" side of education.

SYDNEY GREENBIE*
The Emperor's Birthday

The emperor's birthday is an occasion for more than mere cessation of work or school. Throughout all the institutions the portraits of the emperor and empress and crown prince are set upon the platforms, veiled. At our school the faculty stands before it, in front of the assemblage of students. The director, in full-dress with gilt embroidery and sword, takes his place, half facing the portrait and half the assembly. At a word from one of the faculty the students rise to be welcomed. Then the *Kimigayo* (national anthem) is sung. So sacred is this hymn that singing it has been

* Sydney Greenbie, *Japan—Real and Imaginary* (New York: Harper and Row, 1920), pp. 394–395.

prohibited except on national occasions. Without formal announcement, the director steps solemnly in front of us to where he faces the pictures; then, just upon the sound of *"yo wa"* in the song, he advances, and upon the word *"sazareishi"* he pulls the curtains aside, having at due intervals bowed reverently. The song is sung twice over, a lacquer box is opened and the Imperial Rescript on Education is read. . . . After a short address by one of the faculty and the reading of a slight paper by a student, the ceremony is over—and the curtains are again drawn across the portraits. There is nothing shabby nor affected about it. It is done thoroughly and properly and with reverence.

I had once unwittingly led a class in general discussion from one thing to another until, under current events, I contrasted the freedom of movement of the President of the United States with the King of England. It had been reported that returned soldiers on parade broke ranks and shook hands with the King. I then contrasted the easy simplicity of Prince Arthur with the rigid formalism of Prince Nashimoto, both of whom I had seen while stopping at the Nara Hotel one summer. Then I added that formerly, when their emperor passed, they were not allowed to look at him, anyone caught so doing being in danger of losing his eyes. Even today no one can be on an open balcony but must be on the ground when royalty goes by. I made no comment on this. Up spoke one student, "You must not mention our emperor in the same breath with kings and presidents."

HERBERT PASSIN*
The Japanese Educational System

After the six years of elementary schooling, pupils faced their first, and perhaps most important, streaming out. This separation once accomplished, it became extraordinarily difficult, if not impossible, to transfer from one stream to another. The first major separation was between boys and girls. The middle schools were not coeduca-

* Herbert Passin, *Society and Education in Japan* (New York: Teachers College and East Asian Institute, Columbia University, 1965), pp. 103–108, 122–125, 142–145, 152–155, 157–159.

tional, girls taking their middle school training in special girls' schools (called "girls' high schools") and the boys going on to exclusively male institutions. Among boys, the major separation was between those going on toward higher education (about ten percent) and those either terminating with elementary school or aiming for terminal training at the middle school level. For the former, there were the middle schools; for the latter, a wide variety of institutions, including advanced primary, continuation, vocational, technical, and normal schools. The main-channel middle schools, that is, those leading to higher education, were for five years.

It was at the next step, the transition from middle school to the university-preparatory school, or "higher school" (*kōtōgakkō*), that the student encountered the most radical streaming. Because facilities for higher education were far below demand, competition was ferocious and ruthless. Only one out of thirteen middle school graduates could expect to enter higher school, and only one out of twenty-five was admitted to the prestige higher schools that opened the way into the Imperial universities. Normally, there were about seven times more applicants than openings. The gateway to higher education was therefore a very narrow one. In 1929, for example, there were almost 70,000 middle school graduates; of these, about 5000 were accepted into the thirty-three university-preparatory higher schools. This stage was decisive for the child's future. Without university, he could not expect to enter the higher channels of business or government; his life chances were demonstrably poorer.

The anxiety of parents for their children's future, the anxiety of the pupils themselves, and their feeling of obligation to their parents created an unbearable pressure known to everybody as *shiken jigoku,* the "examination hell." Both students and parents awaited the results with frantic anxiety, and suicide because of failure was not uncommon. "Second-chance" channels were not entirely absent, as, for example, the *kentei-shiken* (licensing examination), through which nonsecondary school graduates could go on to higher school or college; or the normal school course leading to the "higher normal school," and from there (after their establishment in 1929) to the two universities of arts and sciences. But they were limited.

Successful candidates proceeded to the three-year higher school, which was preparatory to the university. The rest had several choices: terminating their education, entering an inferior channel (such as the normal school or military school, which were important outlets for poor but bright boys who could not attend the higher schools or could not leave their home area for one reason or another), or going into the "colleges" (*semmongakkō*) and higher technical schools (*kōtōsemmongakkō*). These latter were junior to the university, even though they provided a wide range of professional and even literary curricula. Through them one could become a doctor, dentist, engineer, architect, or pharmacist, but at a lower level than professionals trained in the universities. Once one had entered the *semmongakkō* channel, it was extremely difficult (although not completely impossible) to transfer to a university. The highest education for girls, who had already been streamed into their own channels after primary school, was in the "women's universities," which ranked at the level of the *semmongakkō*. Therefore, many ambitious young men and women, finding themselves unable to enter the university channel at home, went abroad, and often to the United States, for their higher education. In the prewar period, many of them suffered for this because overseas education was rated inferior to domestic, and American university graduates were often treated in business and government at the same level as *semmongakkō* rather than as university graduates.

What intensified the competition was the hierarchical ranking of schools. Ambitious elementary school graduates aimed not only for middle school, but for the best ones. The competition for the famous higher schools, where hierarchical ranking was explicit in its consequences for the future, was most intense of all. In order to enter a high-ranking university, with all this meant for one's career, it was necessary to come through a high-ranking higher school. The best way, for example, to reach Japan's elite university, Tokyo Imperial, was through the First Higher School. An elite course came to be defined: Tokyo First Middle School–First Higher School–Tokyo Imperial. Among higher schools the state and public ones ranked above the private, and among the state schools the First, Third, and Second (in that order) outranked all the others. The middle school graduate had therefore not only to try for higher school, but preferably for one of the elite state schools. Otherwise he would find himself qualified only for second- and third-ranking institutions, usually private, which meant calculable limitations on his career chances. "[It] is estimated," wrote Keenleyside and Thomas in 1937, "that an Imperial University graduate has at least twice the chance of finding a satisfactory post as has a graduate of equal ability from a less prominent institution." Among the forty-five prewar universities, the "Imperial" universities ranked highest, and among the Imperial universities Tokyo stood unchallengeably first; next in rank came the remaining government universities plus a small number of private schools; well below these came the twenty-three remaining private universities. The result of this elitism was not only the crushing competition for the good schools but a concentration of the best students in the small number of prestige schools. State higher school students were, in fact, better than students of other schools, at least in their academic preparation; and Tokyo University concentrated in its halls the flower of the Japanese university world.

If one passed through higher school, however, entrance into university was almost automatic. The graduate of a government higher school could be sure that he would get into a leading national university. Others had to scramble and content themselves with lesser institutions.

Once in the university, the pressure relaxed. The successful entrant was virtually guaranteed a diploma, the all-important passport into the high-ranking main channels of Japanese society. No matter how the student might slack off in his university years, it was extremely unusual for him to be dropped from school. Thus the rhythm of the Japanese educational system is almost the inverse of the American—and rather like the European, particularly the French. American schools are relatively easy and noncompetitive at the lower levels, gradually becoming more demanding as the school level rises. The Japanese schools, like those of France, were severely competitive in the early stages, and then eased off at the university level.

The rate of attrition from elementary school through university completion was extremely high. Of every 1000 elementary school entrants, about five would finish university. The reason was not, of course, only the ruthless competitiveness of the system, but the economic difficulty many had in trying to carry their education beyond the elementary or secondary level.

... Once universal education came into full operation, the

educational ladder became the skeletal core of the social-achievement ladder. Those with elementary education went into agricultural or manual labor jobs, middle school graduates into lower-ranking white-collar positions, and university graduates into the higher administrative and executive positions. Although it was not entirely impossible for a person with elementary school education to go up in the ranks, the odds were heavily against his going very far. Enterprises were usually divided into two entirely separate channels, a labor, or production, channel, and an administrative channel. Once a worker entered a firm in the production channel, he was able to move up the ranks through seniority and personal merit, but he could not move over into the administrative channel.

In the larger enterprises, a further distinction was usually made between a lower administrative and a higher executive channel. These two were somewhat less impermeable, but someone who started in the lower channel was not likely to go very high in the executive line. The separation worked the other way as well. Companies would not accept persons with higher education in production or other low-grade jobs. No greater tragedy could be imagined than for educated people to be forced by economic conditions to take inferior jobs, as in the 1920s and 1930s, when *"Tōdai* [Tokyo University] policemen" and lower-grade civil servants came to public notice. And this may have had something to do with the alienation of intellectuals from the regime that developed so rapidly in the 1920s and 1930s.

In government as well, schooling was made a decisive consideration, especially in the higher civil service. For these posts one had to come from a proper university. In some cases the university was specified, in other cases the choice was assured by a two-stage system—first, the examination which established an eligibility list, and then a personal interview, which virtually guaranteed that only graduates of the proper schools would be appointed.

The hierarchical distinctions that grew up among the universities and the *semmongakkō* had immediate consequences for career chances. Many companies took their executive-level entrants only from a particular school or schools; others assigned quotas to different schools. Once accepted in a company, salary scales would be found to vary with the school. The Japan Broadcasting Corporation, for example, before the war used to give Imperial university graduates a starting salary of eighty yen per month, private university graduates seventy-five, and *semmongakkō* graduates seventy. In 1927, to take another example, the Mitsubishi enterprises paid new company entrants starting salaries on the following scale:

	Monthly salary (in yen)
GRADUATES OF:	
Imperial university (engineering)	90
Imperial university (law)	80
Tokyo Commercial University	80
Waseda and Keiō universities	75
Other private universities	65–70
Semmongakkō	65–70

The Mitsui Mining Company was equally specific in its starting salaries paid to new employees:

	Monthly salary (in yen)
TECHNICAL EMPLOYEES—GRADUATES OF:	
Imperial universities	75
Waseda (science and engineering)	65
Meiji, Senshū, Mukden universities	60
Higher technical schools	55
Class A engineering schools	1.30 (per day)
CLERICAL AND ADMINISTRATIVE EMPLOYEES— GRADUATES OF:	
Imperial universities	75
Waseda and Keiō universities	65
Other private universities	60
Kobe Higher Commercial School	60
Other higher commercial schools	55
Semmongakkō	55
Class A commercial schools	1.30 (per day)
Middle schools	1.15 (per day)

For the higher and more desirable posts in Japanese life, it was almost essential to have gone to elite schools. The lesser universities provided entrée into the lower levels of government and lesser businesses.

The universities not only provided training and connections, but lifetime identification with a clique. These cliques, or *batsu* as they are called, are intimate, informal groups based on personal loyalties that span many fields from the university into business, the professional world, government, and politics. A person without a *batsu* faces Japanese society unsupported, with no one to sponsor him or to help him in times of crisis. It is one's *batsu* that opens the closed doors. Characteristically, each *batsu* has its own sphere of influence, which it guards jealously against outsiders and opens only to its intimates. Universities form their own *batsu,* and even individual departments within the university may have *batsu* on their own. . . .

The establishment of a modern school system did not . . . in the first instance influence the redistribution of political power. This was already solidly held by an elite formed in the pre-Meiji period. The early products of the schools fit into the systems they created, manning the newly opened bureaucratic posts and institutions, and moving cautiously into the slowly developing modern economic sector. Most of the graduates of the higher schools were immediately drawn in.

But the very existence of a school system and its entrenchment as the main channel for access to government position, business, and power brought about important changes in the composition of the elite. The samurai, as a legally privileged class, had been on a rapid downgrade and, particularly after the abortive revolt of Saigō Takamori in 1877 (the very year Tokyo University was established), had to face increasingly vigorous competition from the other classes. Although persons of samurai origin remained disproportionately high among the elite and among those with higher education (as they do even today), their absolute dominance continued to diminish in tandem with the rise of the former underprivileged classes. The emergence into the national political community of the former lower orders is a process that has been going on slowly throughout the ninety years of modern Japanese history, and in a sense it can still be said to be going on. The first enfranchised electorate in Japan numbered about 400,000 people (the population at that time, 1890, was about 40,000,000). By means of tax and property qualifications it was held down to the well-educated, the people of means, the wealthier farmers, and the growing class of industrialists and entrepreneurs. Only in 1925 did universal manhood suffrage bring the working class and the peasantry into the national political community. (Full universal suffrage, including women, and down to the age of twenty years, came only with the American occupation.)

But in spite of this restriction of the electorate, the growth and differentiation of society, governmental institutions, and the economy went on rapidly. New classes—a modern working class and a modern industrialist class, for example—came into existence, and these expanded in numbers and influence at the expense of the older classes. The rise of military power and the political party system transformed politics from a monopoly of the oligarchy into a three-way struggle, in the course of which there were many compromises and coalitions.

The intellectuals and university graduates of the Meiji period had been essentially a political elite, taking part in the governance of the country. Whether in government itself as members of the bureaucracy, in one of the important national institutions (such as the army or the school system), in politics, or in a private capacity, the educated classes felt themselves committed members of a common national effort. But as the Meiji period began to draw to its close and the great restoration leaders to leave the scene, the products of the new universities and the school system began to enter the marketplace. Where in an earlier day any educated person could feel that he was making his personal contribution to national affairs, whether or not he held an official position, now a gap began to appear between the bureaucratic and civil elites. For the first time there were modern intellectuals who felt themselves outside the national political community, or even hostile to it. The early Meiji leaders had all been "generalists," cultivated men with a strong sense of national dedication, rather than technical specialists in particular fields. The new university products included increasing numbers of technicians, engineers, and even writers and artists who looked on politics as a condition of life rather than as an arena of activity. A Mori Ōgai could still feel that the intellectual must serve the nation (he was an M.D. and novelist), but Shimazaki Tōson and others were already arguing the priority of personal vision and morality as against the state. The educated classes began to divide into two broad streams: a bureaucratic elite taking part in public affairs in one form or another; and a civil element, which again consisted of two parts—the holders of stable, respectable, mainline positions who identified themselves with the "Establishment," and a new intelligentsia, disaffected and inclined toward all the great heresies of individualism, radicalism, liberalism, and Westernism.

Entrance into the Establishment was therefore through the educational channels, but the educational system could not completely channel all of its products. Some of them went into opposition and found arenas of activity in nonmainline channels that were growing up: the trade union and radical movements; Christian institutions (churches, schools, colleges, social work, etc.); foreign-connected institutions; the growing communications and entertainment industries; and freelance creative work. In the more organized political and social movements, they joined with the leaders arising from within these movements to form a new leadership which in itself became a counter-elite to the elite of the Establishment.

To reach high political, as distinct from bureaucratic, position, therefore, there were channels other than those of the school system. Local bosses with their own areas of control could be elected to the Diet, even if they had very little schooling. Leaders of mass movements or wealthy businessmen could also be elected. Thus the grass-roots politicians often had their own independent bastions of support from which to negotiate with the official cliques. But within the framework of the party, the various *batsu* had to compete among themselves and make effective coalitions to carry on the practical work of politics. And here the bureaucratic element, with its school-based *batsu,* played a very important part. Internal party life was essentially a question of struggle, compromise, and coalition among factions. The higher the formal level of political power, the more clearly can clique lines be seen. While the party back-benchers in the Diet might come from many different backgrounds, there is increasing homogeneity as one goes up the scale to, say, party executives and cabinets. . . .

From 1890 on until the American occupation, the inculcation of loyalty and an official version of morality became central to the mission and methods of the school system. The official doctrine taught in the schools was essentially that of the "Japanists" (*Nihon-shugisha*): Japan is a unique family-state, descended from a common ancestor. The emperor, as the direct descendant of the Imperial ancestor, has qualities of divinity and embodies in his person the unity of the state and the people. The unique Japanese family system is based on reverence for ancestors, the power and responsibility of the family head, obedience, and filial piety. Filial piety is the model for the relation of the citizen both to the state and to superiors.

Although both the family and the state ideology preached in the schools were drawn from the Japanese tradition, they represented only a selective adaptation of traditional principles. The divinity of the emperor and the obligation of absolute obedience to him, for example, were essentially revivals of prefeudal concepts. During feudal times, the emperors had been eclipsed and primary loyalty owed to one's personal overlord. What the Meiji leaders did was retain the principle of unquestioning loyalty but transfer it from feudal lord to the emperor. And, since the emperor system was the kingpin of the unified national state, it was all the more important to fix this loyalty firmly. In the same way, the family ethic preached in the schools was essentially the Confucian ethic of the upper classes; it was not that of the lower classes. But the Meiji leaders set out to inculcate the samurai ethic as the national ethic, and the school system played the key role in this transformation.

Family and state ethics were considered, both by supporters and opponents of the doctrine, to reinforce each other. Filial piety was the prototype for loyalty to superiors, the state, and the emperor. The subordination of the self to the needs of the collective family group was concordant with the more generalized notion of subordination of self to the national collectivity. *Kō*—unending obligation to parents—was the basis of loyalty to the father-emperor —*chū*.

> Precious are my parents that gave me birth,
> So that I might serve His Majesty

might serve as a statement of the doctrine in a nutshell. The notion that one owed unlimited obligation and obedience (or *on*) to all superiors, just as one did to one's parents and the emperor, was promoted in many ways, leading to the doctrines of "*on* to the teacher" and "*on* to one's benefactor."

The principal instrument for the inculcation of these ideas was the morals course (*shūshin*). A minimum of one hour per week of morals was mandatory in all classes, from elementary through the secondary school. But apart from the formal morals course, the ideas were woven into the curriculum and into school life in any way the ingenuity of the educators could devise. Wherever subject matter permitted, they were to be worked into the textual material. "The essential aim of teaching Japanese history is to make children comprehend the fundamental character of the empire and to foster in them the national spirit," read the regulations for the teaching of history. "Children should be taught the outlines of the establishment of the empire, the continuity of the Imperial dynasty. . . . It is above all important to keep in touch with the teaching of morals." In geography, "The essential object . . . is to give children a general knowledge of the condition of the earth's surface . . . to make them understand in a general way how our country stands in the world, and to instill into their minds the love of their country." Morals indoctrination even turned up in such unlikely subjects as arithmetic, language, and music.

Outside of class, the official doctrine was promoted in a variety of ways. There were frequent ceremonial assemblies requiring the reading of the Imperial Rescript on Education, the showing of the Imperial portrait, and the raising of the national flag, and these were carried through with the utmost protocol and gravity to make a proper impression on the children. The reading of the Imperial Rescript was more a religious incantation than the recitation of a secular document. The reader had to carry the sacred scroll reverently, hold it in white-gloved hands, and read it impressively and perfectly. So sacred were these symbols that in case of fire they were to be saved before everything else, even at the risk of life. The slightest impropriety led to disgrace and humiliation. There have been dramatic cases where teachers or principals of schools, accidentally responsible for some impropriety—for example, dropping the Imperial Rescript, or making a mistake in its reading— committed suicide. The cult of the state, which has come to be known as state Shinto, was brought into close relation with the school system. Its doctrines were taught, and pupils were required to participate in its rituals and to visit its shrines on ceremonial and national occasions. Schools organized pilgrimages and outings designed to strengthen the pupils' loyalty and devotion to the national cult. . . .

Outside of school, the teaching was reinforced by family life itself. The Japanese family was, as someone has observed, a "training ground in hierarchy." Relations within the family had a strong hierarchical element: The head of the family had superordinate authority, legally enjoined by the civil code, over the family members; females were subordinate to males, juniors were subordinate to seniors; younger brothers were subordinate to the elder brother, the family head's heir-apparent. Where extended family relations were maintained, these too were characteristically hierarchical in character, with the "main house" holding authority over the "branch houses," who in turn owed obedience and often service to the former. It is not without significance that Japan's leading sociologist of law [Kawashima Takeyoshi] has entitled one of his main books *The Family System as Ideology*. In all public institutions the same ethic of hierarchy was insisted upon, and in the army, to which most Japanese men were obligated for a period of service, the indoctrination and its exemplification in military life reached their high point.

How effective this system was is a different matter, and no easy answer can be given. Japanese sociologists, anthropologists, psychologists, and historians are still trying laboriously to piece the whole story together. It is clear, however, that there were strong elements of resistance to the penetration of the official doctrine. In spite of the indoctrination of an official orthodoxy, the suppression of academic freedom, and ultimately the imposition of a system of thought control, there were many products of the school system who opposed the official views. This was particularly the case at the higher levels of education where, as Mori had seen, the necessity for comparison, critical thought, and studying foreign ideas makes the imposition of an official doctrine more difficult. In fact it was in the great Imperial universities, the breeding ground of officialdom, that the greatest intellectual resistance to official ideology was to be found. Ironically, it was here too that Marxism achieved its deepest penetration, not only as a set of political ideas but, more importantly, as a system of thought. In an earlier period it had been the private universities that had led the way in the advocacy of unorthodoxy, but by the end of the First World War this honor had shifted to the high-prestige state schools, the "breeding grounds of bureaucracy." Students in higher institutions were evidently more affected by their general reading and studies than by the official morals course. The schools were so open to outside ideas—through foreign books, libraries, and the inherent conclusions of reading and reflective thought—that no official attempts could completely close them off. Nor was this seriously attempted until the militarists came to power. Until the rise of politically organized mass movements, the universities provided the main centers of resistance to official ideology, and even extreme suppression could not wipe them out.

Similarly there were other deviant channels of Japanese life and thought, sustained by the outside world or by particular life experiences, that resisted orthodoxy: Christian institutions, foreign-linked activities, liberal and radical political movements—even to some extent the private universities—in general, all those for whom the *bummei kaika* (civilization and enlightenment) part of the Meiji consensus was more important than the *fukoku kyōhei* (prosperous country, strong military) part.

Nor is there any evidence that the officially promoted morality penetrated as deeply among the masses as the leaders might have hoped. For many people, the official dogmas were mere formalities, external to themselves and their way of life.

⛊ IN THE 1920s cracks of rebellion occurred in the educational structure of Japan. The turbulent atmosphere was reminiscent of an earlier poem, *"V Narod"* (To the People), by Ishikawa Takuboku (1885–1912). Takuboku was involved in the *Heimin Shimbun* (*Commoners' Newspaper*), which was founded in 1903 and opposed the Russo-Japanese War. The poem, inspired by Russian anarchist students of the 1860s, reflects popular sentiments of the times.

By the post-World War I years, there were contemporary inspirations for radical students—the Russian Revolution, and social discontent in Japan itself. Many students, unsatisfied with mere discussion, did go to the people, taking part in labor organizing and left-wing political party work, giving up respectable careers that would have followed from their university education.

ISHIKAWA TAKUBOKU*
After a Fruitless Argument

What we read and what we argue over
And the light in our eyes
Are not inferior to young Russians fifty years ago.
We argue what's to be done—
Yet, even so, not one of us clenches his fist,
Crashes it on the table
And shouts V NAROD.

We know what it is we want:
We know what the people want
And we know what's to be done.
Yes, we know more than young Russians of fifty years ago.
Yet, even so, not one of us clenches his fist,
Crashes it on the table
And shouts V NAROD.

It is the young who are assembled here—
The young, always building something new for the world.
We knew the old would die before long and we should win.
Look at the light in our eyes, at the savagery of our arguments.
Yet even so, not one of us clenches his fist,
Crashes it on the table
And shouts V NAROD.

Fresh candles three times now:
Dead flies in our empty teacups:
The girls' zest unabated: yet
In their eyes the exhaustion at the end of a fruitless argument.
Yet even so, not one of us clenches his fist,
Crashes it on the table
And shouts V NAROD.

* Ishikawa Takuboku, "After a Fruitless Argument," in Geoffrey Bownas
and Anthony Thwaite, trans. and eds., *The Penguin Book of Japanese Verse*
(Baltimore: Penguin Books, 1964), pp. 182–183.

PETER DUUS*
Student Enthusiasts

There had always been an incipient tradition of student protest in Japan, but until the Taishō period it had been limited by and large to the private universities, particularly Waseda, where the example and early ideas of Ōkuma exercised considerable influence on the students and atmosphere of the university. The novelty of student radicalism at the end of the World War was its appearance at the Imperial universities, particularly at Tokyo University. Then as now, the national universities were geared to recruitment of a national elite. Stress was on high marks and achievement rather than enthusiasm and fervor. To some it seemed almost as though an individual's worth was judged by his examination scores, not by his sincerity or compassion for others. From the beginning of the war, however, there was a growing number of students who chafed in this academic straightjacket and sought to break away from the conventional path to success. They did not wish to become "flunkies of the zaibatsu and the bureaucracy." They were beginning to think for themselves instead of regurgitating lecture notes and were beginning to take more interest in the problems of their own society than in the textbook knowledge necessary to pass the examinations for entry into the bureaucracy or large business firms.

Why these students made their appearance in this period is fascinatingly obscure. Perhaps one reason was that from the end of the Meiji period, opportunities for upward mobility in government and business were declining. In the early and middle years of the Meiji period a university graduate had been almost assured of swift and dramatic success in the world, but now he was less and less a privileged individual with a guaranteed future than a member of an intellectual working force, a learned proletariat. The generation of students emerging in the Taishō period may also have been a more diverse group than those of the Meiji period, fewer and fewer

* Peter Duus, *Party Rivalry and Political Change in Taishō Japan* (Cambridge, Mass.: Harvard University Press, 1968), pp. 118–121.

coming from a *shizoku* background with its traditions of service and separateness, more and more coming from rural hamlets or from the families of city shopkeepers. As such, they may have been less docile in their acceptance of aspirations that reflected the traditional interests of the *shizoku* class in government. Finally, we cannot discount the influence of certain teachers at the Imperial universities, in particular Yoshino Sakuzō at Tokyo and Kawakami Hajime at Kyoto, who by force of personality and by an approach to scholarship that dealt not simply with formalistic theories but with contemporary realities inspired in students interests other than those of conventional success.

Whatever the origins of this discontent with the goals of conventional students and this concern over the social and political status quo in Japan, both were crystalized into activity at the end of 1918, following hard both on the rice riots and on the signing of the armistice. At Tokyo Imperial University several students of Yoshino Sakuzō and a number of recent graduates who had already taken jobs in journalism or the bureaucracy formed the Shinjinkai. At Waseda, the Minjin Dōmei was founded several months later in February 1919. The students who formed these groups did not have an ideology or set of beliefs, no common framework of discourse, only a common mood. Encouraged and excited by the events of 1918, they were in a state of ferment, receptive to new ideas, but uncertain and undiscriminating in their search for answers. The importance of these groups was not so much their intellectual sophistication as their emotional momentum. Theirs was not a reasoned argument, but a cry of rebellion, a yearning for change, an indignation at social wrongs. They were imbued with a vague but confident optimism that the world was on the verge of a great change, an optimism much less tempered than that of the new liberals. Akamatsu Katsumaro, who later moved in and out of the Communist party to become a chauvinist publicist, recalled, "We were stirred by the extraordinary presentiment that, perhaps on the morrow, the curtain would rise on a great transformation of society." What the change would be and how it would come were not so clear, but its advent seemed certain. The whole world was moving "exultantly, at a gallop, without hindrance." "Ahead . . . was only the ideal human society. If one but reached out a hand . . . it would be delivered immediately."

Like the new liberals, the students had lost hope that change would come about voluntarily by the action of the ruling classes. They had a heroic and romantic conception of themselves as an idealistic and youthful elite who could "rise completely above social considerations and connections, and above class conceptions," uniquely equipped to speed the transformation of society through the emancipation of the underprivileged and the downtrodden. As one student proclaimed,

> At this moment of dawning enlightenment who will undertake the task of Japan's reconstruction? What of the privileged classes who are now in the position of leading the country? What of the educated classes, the bureaucrats, the military cliques, the party politicians, the capitalists, and the university professors? Their past and present condition are the most eloquent proof that they are not qualified for the task. In practice, their past is too corrupt, too gross, too wanting of ideals to hold the confidence of the people. We have already lost hope in the ruling class. Those who lead in reconstruction . . . must be the youth themselves with their purity of conscience, their splendid intellect, their enthusiasm of temperament.

It was no longer possible to leave matters to their elders.

For the students, the "mass awakening" probably had a greater psychological than political importance. They were really *shishi* [patriots] in student uniform. Their interest lay in deeds not in words, in action not in thought, in a yearning to move among the common people, to share their aspirations, and to help achieve their hopes. To a much greater degree than the "new liberals" the students were in search of a movement, an opportunity to fulfill the heroic role they saw for themselves in the transition from the old world to the new. The almost revivalistic atmosphere of the student movement can be judged from a passage in Asō Hisashi's autobiographical novel, *Reimei,* where he describes one meeting of the Shinjinkai.

> Agitated, K. suddenly rose to his feet. "Brothers! The masses are waiting for us. We must this moment cast aside everything. We must cast aside every sort of pleasure. Yet in spite of this, what are we doing now? Oh God! Forgive us." Having shouted this, he dropped to his seat like a shot and burst into a flood of tears. Everyone was extraordinarily tense. As though in sympathy they began to shout and cry.

No wonder that Yoshino later commented that the students granted "equal, nay higher esteem, to energy than to truth." For them the new liberals' apparent faith in the efficacy of debate was tepid when compared with the heady opportunities of personal involvement. Many must have found emotional catharsis in the sought-after struggle for "the cooperation of all freely emancipated classes" and the destruction of the "outmoded illusions of the bigoted."

✿ THE SUBSERVIENT POSITION of women in Meiji Japan extended beyond the family and factory to political life. In 1889 women were forbidden even to *attend* political meetings, much less join political parties. After World War I, however, women began organizing to seek the right to vote. Their struggle for basic civil rights continued until dissent was stifled in the late 1930s. Meanwhile, women also formed auxiliaries in the radical political groups of the 1920s, and published works on women's problems.

The poem "Rather Than Cry" by Takuboku reflects poignantly the hopelessness a woman could feel in Japanese society. In contrast, the passages from the autobiography of Baroness Shidzué Ishimoto show a young woman struggling against the oppressive position of women in the Japanese family. She was active in the women's movement in the 1920s, both in Japan and abroad, and had a particular interest in promoting birth control. In 1937, probably because of this stand, she was arrested along with other leftists.

ISHIKAWA TAKUBOKU*
Rather Than Cry

It was in a dream—
What year, what night I do not remember—

* Ishikawa Takuboku, "Rather Than Cry," in Bownas and Thwaite, trans. and eds., *The Penguin Book of Japanese Verse*, pp. 183–184.

That I met her.
She'll be dead and gone by now.

Heavy larding of oil on her black hair,
White as the fur of a rabbit dying in torment
Her thick powder,
Blood-colored lipstick daubed on her mouth,

Among a crowd of girls she sang filthy songs
One after another, to a sprightly samisen.*
Putting down, as if it were water,
Stuff that took the skin off your tongue.
By her side, young sprouts
Of twenty, not drinking.

"Why sing like this?" I asked,
In my dream.
And she replied,
With a drunken, flushed laugh,
"Rather than cry. . . ."

* samisen: a three-stringed instrument which is plucked.

SHIDZUÉ ISHIMOTO*
A Japanese Husband

As I look back even over my short life I see there repeated challenges of the new against the old, the perfect feminine in the old sense trying to put down the struggles of the new feminine aspiring to express itself in a progressive world. It was my own mother who regarded it as her great work to cast her daughter into the mold deemed so admirable by Occidental and Oriental "philosophers." When mother bought a kimono or an obi for me, she was always particular to select one elegantly quiet in color and design. I was not to look younger than I was actually; nor was I to be the focus of all eyes by reason of some splashing decoration in my apparel. If my garments were costly, the fact was not to be strident. My

* Baroness Shidzué Ishimoto, *Facing Two Ways* (New York: Farrar and Rinehart, 1935), pp. 297–305, 317–320.

manner she hoped to make accord with the refined modesty of my dress. A naïve grace was the desired effect. Even my speech was to be free of such assertions as "I think," "I like," "I want," "I, I, I . . ."—the *I* never coming first, unlike the style of free Western girls. My mother warned me that I must listen to others always, smile at whatever they said, and express as little as possible of myself.

While my mother was eager to make a dainty bride of me, the man I married was writing in his diary: "O God! bless my heart! If Thy will is to make me Thy faithful servant and let me work to bring Thy Kingdom on earth, then select for me a wife with whom I shall work to bring glory to Thy Name!" Again he wrote: "I am not hoping that my wife, Shidzué, will be a baroness of the sort depicted in fiction or drama, leading an elaborate life amid luxurious surroundings; what I really hope for her future is that she will concern herself with the great problems of her countrywomen!"

After our marriage and while he found inspiration in working for labor, he watched with interest my growth in social consciousness. As soon as we had settled in a cottage in the coal mine district in western Japan, away from the traditions and complication of the old family system in Tokyo and its guardian mother-in-law, my husband began his constructive task of educating his girl bride into a "real" person. He insisted on my changing my attitude even toward him from a meek feudal wife to an alive, liberal, and understanding companion. He did not permit me to sit on the mat without a cushion as I had done in our Tokyo house—a true Japanese is supposed not to use a cushion in sitting before his elders—but assured me that I could behave as an equal. I must admit that I enjoyed the cushion. When he took a bath, I asked him whether he needed assistance, as is the way of a proper feudal wife, but he replied scornfully that he did not need a slave. His persistent call to me to rise from a stage "too delightful to behold" toward that of the "self-conscious woman" changed even my appearance.

After his long and hard effort to put spirit into a doll-like creature, and just as his labor began to bear fruit—that is to say, just as I learned to express myself, my husband said to me one day that he thought my appearance was losing charm for him.

Now he frankly declared that the beauty of a Japanese woman lay only in her naïveté. He pointed to the delicate feminine figures in the old prints, pronouncing them his ideal. What a contradiction! After having so long admired the sturdy women of Millet and the powerful masterpieces of Rodin! He who once had undertaken to educate his wife with a view to making her as active and independent as any English or American woman was now gloating over Japanese dolls in the old prints as types to emulate! But as my husband had always been ahead of his time, so his reaction against liberalism was a sign of the newest national tendency.

It now seemed foolish in my eyes for a man to take off his hat in the elevator when a woman entered, to rise from his seat in a train if a woman were standing, or to help a woman carry parcels. He reverted to the "good old" ways of his people marked by masculine hauteur. The "inferior sex" could stick to its grace and modesty. He would not lift another finger to change habits and customs.

What brought my husband to this sudden reversion of attitude? What made him move from one extreme to the other—from progressivism to conservatism? He had been such a zealous crusader for human rights! He had been ready to risk everything in an effort to get into Russia regardless of what this implied for his wife and children, and when he was prevented from seeing that great social experiment at first hand his disappointment seemed deep and genuine. He had thrown in his lot with the laborers of Japan, sympathizing intellectually with their class war and aiding them directly in many ways. What had robbed him of conviction and loyalty to the common people? What had transformed him into an antifeminist?

His diagnosis of the movement of history seems to have been the basis of his mental and spiritual change. Having believed in a swift reconstruction of Japanese life from top to bottom, he was unprepared for the slow and tedious march of events toward that goal. As the reactionary forces at home grew bolder, he grew correspondingly discouraged and soon felt that idealism had been irrevocably betrayed. Immediate realities curbed his imaginative flights and eventually he was completely overcome by the influences of his bourgeois environment. There he was at last—a mere man of aristocratic urban culture, captivated by the conventions of his own class!

His second trip to America and Europe had driven him backward instead of forward, and nothing I could say or do or pray had any effect. He lost faith in the downfall of capitalism, within his lifetime at any rate, after he saw the status of the Western countries in 1924. It was disillusioning to the young Marxist, indoctrinated with the idea that capitalism was a frail thing, to discover how stanchly it was, to all appearances, entrenched despite the world war. On returning from his second trip to the West, my husband whitewashed his socialistic internationalistic colors, and repainted them with vigorous nationalism. In this respect, too, he was a pioneer adjusting himself to new conditions. He put aside all his work of a socialistic nature and let the petty profit-seekers gather intimately around him.

Having awakened from his romantic dream of quick social reconstruction, he was hungry for capitalistic enterprise which lured him by its covering names of "national policy" and "the reconstructive project of great Japan." Now he laid a plan for rice-field irrigation in Korea, for the establishment of a financial organ and a railroad business in North Korea and East Manchuria, among other things. His money and his labor went into such schemes as these.

But no enterprise under the sun of capitalism can flourish without profits. And this man, ingenious as he was in the realm of ideas, was less gifted in executive talent. Actual experience was also lacking as a basis of success. Naturally record after record of failure struck fatal blows at the family fortunes. But he refused to admit defeat. He learned to picture himself as a great empire builder—a forerunner of Asiatic statesmen who were to play a new role in the mainland, especially in Manchuria. The more fixedly he bent his head in this direction, the more purely he symbolized Oriental heroics.

In family life in Japan, as it must be everywhere, the husband's mental outlook directly affects the life of his wife. This ancient truth, known to my ancestors of course, I now took to my heart. Hardly had I become conscious of myself when I had to face this reactionary wave at home.

If the ensuing domestic problem and struggle had been but an isolated private affair, my melancholy plight would have been of little moment as a story. But my story is a common one among the present-day Japanese women who are trying to emerge from the condition of nonresistance to events however meaningful and take their place in the shaping of events in their own interests, in the interests of the race and of the nation. So, in talking about myself, I am really talking about countless members of my sex in Japan.

Several courses lay before me in the circumstances I have just described. I could try to forge straight ahead working for the realization of my dreams as a social innovator. I could spurn my husband's protests and remind him bluntly of his own responsibility for my new interests and convictions. I could subside completely and revert, if I tried, to the type of feudal woman beloved of my class. I could battle to restore my husband to the idealism of his youth—make him again the humanistic crusader; the man among men, his handsome aristocratic figure distinguished among copper-colored miners and other laborers as that of a person who owned himself; the strong individual able to work twelve hours a day in the dark pit and find satisfaction as a toiler; the guide and friend of woman in her effort to rise out of slavery. Images of his former power and charm floated before my eyes incessantly.

So I chose the latter course. I attempted to win my husband again to the path he had believed enlightened. I thought that a seat in the House of Peers would enable him to give voice to his appreciation of the facts and problems staring him so starkly in the face and that he could utilize his abundant knowledge of politics and economics in the interests of national progress. At the same time I fancied that if he took his seat among the peers he might give up harmful friends and assume new obligations. So I urged my husband to start a campaign for membership in the House of Peers. Now this plan does not imply that such a campaign for membership in the Upper House of the Japanese Diet is like an English contest for membership in the House of Lords, with English ladies openly and actively taking a hand. For the seats in the Upper House of the Japanese parliament are inherited by princes, marquises, and counts, while viscounts and barons receive this honor only through the unanimous vote of the peers of the same rank, over which the council of powerful elders within each rank has entire control. Naturally a candidate must thus fulfill requirements pleasing to the conservative eyeglasses of the elders. In this situation I had to face a severe inner struggle of my own to advance my husband's status.

When he discussed the proposed entry into the Diet, his friends with one accord insisted that the wife of a candidate for the House of Peers must absolutely conform to the feudal code. She must not talk about women's rights and women's personality; there could be no suffrage campaigning on her part. They scarcely needed to assure him that his wife could not work for birth control. There was clearly no chance for his winning a seat among the peers so long as my "dangerous thoughts" continued to find expression.

To give up all my social interests and maintain a dead silence even within the narrow walls of home was like being sentenced to prison. But my devotion to my husband, my effort to bring him back to his better self, made me pay any price for his sake. However, after paying the heavy costs of this campaign, opportunity for which comes only once in every seven years, he failed to win the seat. It was claimed that his own too-radical years were his handicap. It would be years now before he could live down his past sufficiently to stand again for the House of Peers. To expect membership in any case meant that his wife must hold aloof from social activities in the future. My co-workers in the social movement attempted to draw me out from this status of spiritual imprisonment, but I was determined first to regain domestic happiness. I never thought of sacrificing my husband's career for mine. Gladly I resolved to sacrifice mine for his.

As I spent unhappy days in praying for a bright passage to open for my husband, he proceeded to discover a dark one leading in another direction. His injurious friends led him to shadowy corners. Their first project was to remove him from my watching eyes. Geisha and the teahouses were the fortresses for these men in this gloomy battle—fortresses which the wife could not assault.

My husband has been and still is a very honest man. He has been unable to doubt other people, whom he always takes to be just as honest as himself. This good nature of his is found in many men who have been brought up in the wealthy or well-to-do families of Japan. And this simplicity led Baron Ishimoto more and more into the entanglements of a dishonest and complex society. With the worldwide depression financial difficulties arose and grew until they overwhelmed him. He thought that he must not let his wife know the real state of his finances, and instead of telling everything frankly and counting on a natural approach to the solution of difficulties, he resorted to proud defiance or sullen silence as a way out. In his effort not to lose the honorable husband's dignity, he conducted himself almost like one deprived of reason.

So after all I had a regular feudal lord at home. The only thing that was absent from the picture was the perfect feudal wife. The days and months wore on as if we were traveling over a desert. But my devotion to my husband never changed; I continued to pray that I might be able to rejuvenate idealism along progressive lines. I aspired to conduct myself as far as could be done according to what is taught in the book of great learning for women. . . . It was not because I approved of this blind feudal code as such but only because it seemed to offer the only means of restoring a friendship held so precious and vital.

To my infinite regret, the gentler I tried to be the harsher was my failure in reaching my goal of rehumanizing my husband. Often the image of a grindstone came to my mind during those trying years as if I were set to polish it with patient and unerring labor. But I had other tasks as well as grindstones to think about those days. So many duties dropped upon my shoulders.

My husband's interest in the railroad works in the northern border of Korea and in Manchuria deepened, and most of the time he left me alone except for financial problems while he traveled about bent on elaborate business schemes, dreaming about Cecil Rhodes of Great Britain, writing Chinese poems dedicated to Prince Itō, the man who succeeded in annexing Korea to Japan. It was during his many trips to Korea and Manchuria that he published pamphlets taking for their theme Japan's national policies in relation to Manchuria and Mongolia. With his historical knowledge of the East and the West combined with ideas of Japan's future economy, he looked forward to a national drive toward the huge natural wealth in Manchuria and Mongolia, declaring in his fiery manner like a pioneer and prophet that to exploit this unutilized land and wealth was the true mission for the Japanese nation.

Meanwhile he wrote me no real letter to console my lonely and difficult days at home. Nor did he let me know what he was actually doing. The happiness of wife and children was a trifling matter for a man who was solving great national problems and framing national policy. Tenderness would be a disgrace in an Oriental hero at work on a state issue! There could be no wasting of affection on one who was only a wife! And a woman! I heard from him very seldom, and when I did his letter was written on a long piece of rice paper with India ink and brush, filled with the most exaggerated form of the classical Chinese expressions repre-

senting the stiff formality of the old school. He seemed to have
forgotten that I was his wife. The thorough orientalization of my
husband made me recall the story of a wise emperor in ancient
China, who, during the time when he was a loyal subject entrusted
with the diking of a great river, was so heroically absorbed in the
public work that he passed the front of his own house three times
without once entering it during the three years of his responsibility.
It has often been considered a great virtue or even been taken as a
matter of course for a man to neglect or sacrifice his family for a
noble cause.

When I replied with news of what I had been doing for my
husband and for the family during his absence, mentioning some of
the difficulties and anxieties, the answer was wont to be only a few
lines stating casually that "The Japanese nation will be grateful to
you, as I consider you meritorious in managing the difficult family
affairs, as a good wife should do to help her husband who is
fighting in the front line in behalf of a national policy." Great
Heaven! I never thought of being recognized by the nation. My
dreams soared no higher than acknowledgment by my dear husband. This did not come and my heart was finally broken. . . .

Although my melancholia was somewhat alleviated by the dis-
persal of the gloomy cloud in the performance of my dancing, I did
not regain true mental happiness while my relation with my
husband was dangling in the air. It may have been burdensome to
him to have a wife whose disposition was not meek enough to be
controlled under an absolute despotism. But apparently in his
mind, busily occupied with varied enterprises, with his ancient
Oriental attitude of heroism, with his wild interest in animals, his
kind of wife had no place. She could not slip into his heart again.

During the later years of this unstable situation, I began to take
part in such social activities as the woman suffrage movement, but
my mind was more concerned with family problems than with
public duties. One day I was invited to go to Kobe to speak about
women's enfranchisement, the question being agitated in a lively
fashion. I was glad to go on this occasion, because my husband
was then just coming back from Korea after spending a severe
winter in the heavy snow, struggling with a railroad construction
problem. Not only the weather, which had been severe, but the
whole condition of his business was unfavorable, and he had to
return uncomfortable and humiliated. With the deepest sympathy I
wanted to welcome him at the station; so after I had finished my

talk in Kobe, I waited for his train from the west and met him. An intimate friend of ours, who was then living at Kobe, suggested our going to Arima Hot Springs over the ridge of the Rokkō Mountains to rest. I thought it would be a rare occasion for me to talk quietly and honestly with my husband. Our friend kindly led the way to Arima, about two hours' drive from Kobe, up hills and into the mountains. We stopped at a neat-looking Japanese inn. All of us enjoyed the mountain springs and we spent the afternoon together in a cozy little mat room with a tastefully decorated *tokonoma* [alcove] in the corner. There was a garden in front of the room and a big magnolia tree with its tightly closed buds casting shadows on the white shoji-screens. A nightingale was singing, hopping from branch to branch on the tree without knowing that we were looking at its shadow from behind the closed shoji. A peaceful atmosphere governed the room.

There on the mat was set a *kotatsu* (a firebox resting on and covered with thickly padded silk quilts) to keep our feet warm. A quiet conversation was begun. Our friend surprised me by saying to my husband suddenly:

"Don't you think that Japanese wives are, as a rule, too much neglected by their husbands? I think a man should consider it a duty to open his mind to his wife and consult with her as to what he is going to do in the future or what he is doing at present." My husband was silent. I was killing my breath wondering what this spokesman of my interest was going to say next—the spokesman who voluntarily entered the lists for me without premeditation. "Times have changed," she went on. "No one of us present-day Japanese women will be happy if she is ignored intellectually and expelled from being her husband's mental companion."

"I have a different opinion from yours, my dear madam," my husband replied. "A man likes to keep his ideas and ambitions sacred and solemn in the inner court of his heart. There lies man's heroic conceit. Solitude is the pride of strong men. In the history of our great forefathers, or the ancient Chinese heroes, I have never heard of a single man so despicable as to confide his ambition to his woman! It spoils masculine heroism. It will ruin great enterprises!"

"Oh! no, that's not fair!" The lady was excited. "You treat women without sympathy. You don't understand their problems. You are ignoring woman's intelligence, sensitiveness, and even disturbing her heart! If she were ignorant, if she were uneducated, if she had no sense of right judgment, your philosophy might be justified, but I do not think this is the case, baron!" She pressed her argument. I did not utter a word. "It's man's selfishness! Too much egotism. He expects his wife to stand every phase of hardship, as his partner. Men today count on their wives' being intelligent enough to bring up their children, while they neglect to treat their wives as persons. It is customary for wives to cooperate with their husbands to an extent where, with any mishap occurring, the wife is to be blamed equally with the master of the family. And, if that is the position woman has to take in our society, naturally she should be trusted to look into every corner of her husband's mental life."

"Please go ahead, my dear woman suffragist! I don't care what other men think or do. I won't follow suit. No, madam, never shall I be weak enough to have to consult a woman!" My husband laughed.

"Oh, dear baron, you are being very narrow-minded," he was told.

"I am sorry that you don't understand the psychology of Oriental men. But, madam, I shall never agree with you or follow your advice on my attitude toward my wife!"

The spring sun vanished quickly behind the shadow of the hills and the room was getting dark. The nightingale had flown away while we were arguing around the fire. Gloom settled over us, and my heart was heavy under the pressure of despair. My friend called a maid to bring in a samisen and she tried to create cheer with her music. But my heart only sank into a depth of sorrow with the realization of a broken love. From the early days of my marriage, I had followed my husband's pace. From humanism to liberalism and realism to radicalism, I continued. And now I had to realize that I was unable to follow him any farther on his way to Oriental heroism.

I had to determine to give up trying to follow and let my husband go alone on his way with my prayers to a kind providence. This was indeed a tragic conclusion to my married life as it had started with such happiness and enthusiasm. However, it had to be accepted.

With the sorrow of a broken love but with gratitude to the man who had been my guide toward mental maturity, I set out on a path of thought and action—alone.

4. Labor and Industry

❀ THE RAPID FORCED-DRAFT industrialization program of the Meiji elite was highly successful from various perspectives. It created a modern transportation and banking system, and it established through government subsidies a wide range of heavy industries, including the all-important areas necessary to support a modern military. In the process large cartels and monopolies, based in some cases on the old merchant houses, were created—the zaibatsu (money cliques). William Lockwood, an economic historian, describes how these combines came to control a far greater percentage of industrial production and trade in Japan than similar monopolies did in Western countries. The four largest zaibatsu, in fact, developed into early versions of conglomerates on a vast scale. The resulting concentration of economic power and the intimate connections between business and government have been a characteristic of Japan's economic development.

WILLIAM LOCKWOOD*
The Great Combines

At the other pole from the family farm and workshop were the towering combines which dominated the large-scale industry and commerce of prewar Japan. The one, like the other, was a sign of

* William Lockwood, *The Economic Development of Japan* (Princeton, N.J.: Princeton University Press, 1964), pp. 214–220, 234–235.

Japan's late entry on the path of industrialism; but it also reflected her ambition to acquire the sinews of national power as rapidly as possible. Political pretension thus reinforced economic circumstance to develop in combination such extremes of economic organization as few countries in history have displayed side by side.

The pattern of small enterprise in most fields was dictated by Japan's poverty in capital, as well as in advanced technical and entrepreneurial skills. A national framework of banking and transport could hardly be created on this basis, however. Nor was it adequate for the heavy industries essential to military strength— mining, metallurgy, machinery, and chemicals. From the beginning they required large units of investment in capitalistic establishments operated on a large scale. . . . [S]uch enterprises were launched early in the Meiji period by the state and various financial magnates, acting in conjunction. Although the state soon withdrew from active participation all but a few selected fields, especially banking, railways, and steel, it continued to lavish patronage on the few families and groups able to command the necessary capital and technical experience. Out of this situation grew the great financial aggregations known as the zaibatsu (money cliques). With the advantages gained in the early years, they were able to develop far-flung networks of business enterprise which maintained their predominance in large-scale finance and industry for sixty years.

One can list ten to twenty zaibatsu in prewar Japan, depending on the scope of the definition. Four were outstanding, however, until their preeminence was challenged by the new war-created combines of the thirties. These were Mitsui, Mitsubishi, Sumitomo, and Yasuda. Others were important in restricted fields: Furukawa in copper and electric power; Shibusawa in banking and engineering; Kawasaki in shipbuilding, locomotives, and steel products; Asano in cement and steel; Okura and Kuhara in mining and engineering; etc. The Big Four were distinguished not only by their size but also by the spread of their interests through industry, commerce, and banking. Especially strategic were their powerful banks, which in turn gave them tremendous influence throughout Japanese economic life.

Each of the Big Four combines remained a family enterprise in some degree. The exact pattern of control varied from one to another. The Sumitomo interests were almost entirely owned and directed by the single head of the family. The Mitsubishi combine was controlled by two Iwasaki families, with common policy responsibility vested alternately by custom in the eldest son first of one family, then of the other. The eleven branches of the Mitsui family acted as a unit in accordance with formal household rules, last revised in 1900. They held ninety percent of their wealth collectively. Policies were decided through a family council presided over by the head of the elder son's family. While the zaibatsu families invested largely in equities, and thus retained ownership control over immense properties, their practice increasingly was to vest managerial responsibility in hired executives (*bantō*). These men were carefully selected, trained, and rewarded for their skill and clanlike loyalty to the house.

Internally the devices employed to concentrate control below the family level were the familiar techniques of Western corporate practice, reinforced by the Japanese penchant for disciplined group action. Each combine was dominated by a closely owned holding company. Here the bulk of the house fortune was usually concentrated, though the family might invest directly in operating enterprises as well. Control was then extended through a network of subsidiaries and affiliates by intercorporate stockholdings, interlocking directorates, management agreements, and loans from the combine bank. This gave a degree of cohesion and unity which might extend even to companies only ten to twenty percent of whose stock was actually held by the combine. Supplementing the more formal instruments of control was of course the tremendous financial power latent in the hands of the executives at the top levels.

The House of Mitsui was the largest and most powerful of these financial aggregations. Unlike the Mitsubishi and Yasuda combines, which first gained importance in post-restoration shipping and banking respectively, the Mitsuis were important bankers and traders as early as the seventeenth century. They played a leading role in financing the restoration movement and the governments which followed. Like the other houses, they received numerous privileges in return which enabled them steadily to expand the scope of their activities. From commerce and banking they went into mining and lumbering. In subsequent decades the great family holding company, Mitsui Gōmei, the Mitsui Bank, Mitsui Bussan (trading), and Mitsui Kōzan (mining) extended their interests into textiles, shipping, warehousing, sugar, metals, and machinery, and scores of other branches of industry. Whereas Yasuda remained first and foremost a banking combine, and Mitsubishi and Sumitomo were preeminent especially in the mining and equipment industries, Mitsui branched out in all directions, both at home and abroad. By 1937 the house was said to own properties with a market value of 1635 million yen ($470 million), giving control over a business empire many times this size.

. . . The other combines likewise employed the device of intercorporate stockholding to pyramid business controls on a scale without parallel in the history of Western industrial nations. In this phase of business technology the Japanese were apt students. Yasuda Hozensha, the holding company of the Yasuda combine, valued its assets at only 140 million yen at the end of 1944; its own capital was only thirty million. Yet through its stockholdings in Yasuda subsidiaries, especially financial institutions, it "directly controlled assets in excess of forty billion yen in banking enterprises and two billion yen in other enterprises." Sumitomo Honsha was itself a great mining operator, but in 1945 it also had investments of 326 million yen in 123 other companies and over thirty industries. Its eighteen admitted subsidiaries had assets of 13.9 billion yen. Mitsubishi's importance in the Japanese economy can be illustrated by citing its share in the control of various spheres of activity in 1944: shipping and shipbuilding, twenty-five percent; coal and metals, fifteen percent; warehousing, sixteen percent; bank loans, sixteen percent (March 1945); electrical equipment, twenty-one to thirty-five percent; flour milling, fifty percent; sheet glass, fifty-nine percent; sugar, thirty-five percent; cotton textiles, fifteen percent.

All such estimates of zaibatsu "control" are necessarily partial, and they can be misleading unless one is careful to note the fields to which they are restricted. They show nevertheless the tremendous concentration of entrepreneurial control in major sectors of prewar Japanese industry, finance, and commerce. Even if the seventeen leading combines are defined so as to include only companies in which they held twenty-five percent or more of the stock, their aggregate paid-in capital was nearly one fifth (eighteen percent) of the paid-in capital of all Japanese joint-stock companies in 1935. Even greater was the concentration of control in the banking, insurance, and trust business. This grew steadily with the failure and absorption of hundreds of small banks during the twenties. On the eve of World War II, the seven big private banks of the country—each with assets exceeding 1.5 billion yen ($350 million)—held nearly sixty percent of the total assets and the deposits of "ordinary" (private, commercial) banks. Together with the six leading government banks, they accounted for over half of the capital and deposits of *all* banks. Four of the seven were the Mitsui, Mitsubishi, Sumitomo, and Yasuda banks. In the others the lesser zaibatsu were also prominent: the First (Shibusawa, Furukawa, Kawasaki); the Sanwa (Yamaguchi, Kōnoike); and the One Hundredth (Kawasaki).

Many factors entered into the historic growth of the Japanese combines. Some were social and political, others of a more economic and technical character. In a real sense the zaibatsu carried over into modern times, but with a new tempo of innovation, the traditions of merchant guild organization, and of clan monopoly in trade and manufacture. The spirit of hierarchical organization, of leadership, subordination, and group teamwork, found fresh expression in the new world of corporate finance and industry. The ancient practice of primogeniture, another aspect of family relationship, likewise helped to perpetuate great family fortunes under unified and continuous management, especially as it was sometimes qualified to permit the family headship to pass by the eldest son where he was unfit for responsibility.

. . . Against the technical achievements of the zaibatsu as capitalists and innovators in prewar Japan must be set the more repugnant social and political features of the system. . . . Extreme inequalities of wealth and income characterized Japanese capitalism from the beginning. . . . Under different forms this perpetuated the inequality of status and opportunity which runs so deeply in Japanese history and tradition. The actual concentration of economic power went even beyond the concentration of property ownership, through the wide ramifications of economic and political influence exercised by financial magnates.

Aside from the obvious evils of gross disparity between the wealth of the few and the poverty of the many, there were other social consequences of profound significance.

The existence of great aggregates of financial power, reinforced by political influence, tended from early times to discourage the growth of a sturdy middle class, *i.e.,* a broad class of independent businessmen endowed with sufficient capital and freedom of opportunity so that they could develop medium-size, modern enterprise efficiently and on their own. Equally, the power of the zaibatsu concerns in the labor market, where they were careful to maintain a common front, helped to stifle the growth of a vigorous trade union movement. There were other obstacles to trade unionism, to be sure—the pressure of population, the prevalence of female labor in factory industry, the wide dispersion of small enterprise throughout the countryside, the lack of experience in democratic mass organization. But the weakness of collective bargaining, even at its height in the twenties, and especially Japan's lagging progress in factory and social legislation, must be attributed in large measure to the intense opposition, led by business interests, which greeted every proposal for advance in these fields. Whatever the business rivalries of big firms, here they closed ranks and presented a solid front. In the political realm, as well, the existence of concentrated business power retarded the growth of democratic movements at home, while providing a pliant instrument for military aggression abroad.

☉ THE DEVELOPMENT of heavy industry and the rise of the labor movement were at least partly results of Japan's involvement in wars—the Sino-Japanese War in 1895 and the Russo-Japanese War of 1905. As in most economies, war in Japan led to booms, emphasized by massive government spending in munitions and shipbuilding. Along with the booms and rapid industrialization came labor unrest and attempts to form labor organizations which were not welcomed by business and government leadership. Almost before unions were established, severe government restrictions were instituted, and the subsequent history of Japanese labor unions through World War II was one of repression.

In the passages below Ayusawa and Totten discuss the early history of labor and socialist movements to World War I. They show the dual effects government repression had on the Japanese movements: on the one hand, some radicals resorted to extra-legal, clandestine activities that were suppressed through draconian laws such as the Public Peace Police Act of 1900; and, on the other hand, denied opportunities for open political work, many leftists found themselves extremely isolated. Ultimately government repression was successful in preventing the growth of labor organizations, in separating the leadership from the rank and file, and finally in silencing all forces in Japanese society that might have inhibited the course of Japanese militarism and aggression on the continent of Asia.

AYUSAWA IWAO*
Labor, Repression, and the Public Police Act

IMPACT OF THE SINO-JAPANESE WAR

Every war that Japan had to fight after the restoration, except perhaps Saigō's rebellion in 1878, which was a civil war, had a tremendous effect on the national life. Of all those international wars, the Sino-Japanese War was the first major war, and its impact was startling, particularly in industrial relations.

To what extent that war was a "capitalistic war" in the sense of having been planned by and promoted in the interest of capitalists is of slight interest to us here. But it is of interest to note that the capitalists did help maneuver the war to a successful conclusion, a service for which the Mitsuis and Iwasakis were raised to the peerage. Such captains of industry as Hiranuma Senzō and Ōkura Kihachirō were also decorated and/or raised to the peerage. They learned, through the experience of the war, the advantages of close dealings with the men of power in the government. One morning they awoke to find that they were themselves men of power, though not in the government. Indeed, it was more advantageous not to be in the government, but to control it from outside. The story of the zaibatsu, or financial oligarchy, has its first chapter in the Sino-Japanese War.

* Ayusawa Iwao, *A History of Labor in Modern Japan* (Honolulu: East-West Center Press, University of Hawaii, 1966), pp. 56–58, 69–74, 91, 93–94.

Inevitably, as in any country engaged in a successful war, Japan in the Sino-Japanese War had unscrupulous men speculating in business and profiting heavily from munitions industries under contract with the government. The material gains on the part of those speculators were unfortunately accompanied by suffering and resentment on the part of the masses of workers, on account of the program of arms expansion, higher taxes, mounting prices, and general inflation. The program of arms expansion received a spur when Japan was forced, under pressure from Russia, France, and Germany, to surrender her rights on the Liaotung Peninsula, rights acquired under the Treaty of Shimonoseki. The extent of economic development during the war can be seen in the increases in state revenue, in the numbers of commercial firms and banks, and in the amounts of investment. . . .

[There was] a rapid expansion of state revenue [and] a rapid increase in the per capita burden of the nation. This is only an indirect indication of the hardship inflicted on the people in this period; the response of the workers was shown in the spread of strikes.

Prior to the Sino-Japanese War, spontaneous work stoppages in protest against maltreatment of workers were not unknown. Called *dōmei-hikō* (concerted work stoppage), the practice had gradually spread in Japanese factories since the early years of Meiji. After the English word "strike" was introduced widely by Takano Fusatarō and other leaders of *Shokkō Giyūkai* (the Workers' Volunteer Society), this practice came to be better known by the English word, as were many other useful things introduced from the West. However, it was only after the Sino-Japanese War, during the recession in 1897 and 1898, that strikes became a more or less established institution in industrial relations in Japan.

. . . [T]he effects of the Sino-Japanese War were the emergence of a bourgeoisie and financial oligarchy conscious of its power, on the one hand, and, on the other, wage earners rising in protest against the conditions in which they were placed.

THE PUBLIC PEACE POLICE ACT, 1900

In order to understand the spirit and behavior of Japan in the early decades of Meiji, we have to recall the position of Prussia—and later, Germany—a rising power in that period in the

Western world. . . . Japanese statesmen were led naturally to revere the Bismarckian *Sozialpolitik* type of legislation. When the government of Meiji was first confronted with the opposition of groups of men disgruntled with the new regime, and later with the spread of socialist thought that seemed a menace to the absolutist regime of the Japanese empire, one example of effective legislation that the asute statesmen in the government bureaucracy could think of to follow was the legislation that Bismarck had applied in 1878 to suppress socialism. The German Chancellor had proclaimed in the Reichstag a policy "to help the development of workers' organizations for the maintenance or improvement of working conditions." But thereafter, the law of 1878, originally intended to prohibit public assembly, street demonstrations, pamphleteering, and other socialist activities, was used for effectively restricting the activities of any militant trade unions.

In July 1890, the Japanese government had enacted a law entitled *Shūkai oyobi Kessha Hō* (Law on Assemblies and Associations), the real object of which was simply to regulate assemblies and associations. Considering more stringent legislation necessary, the government in 1900 went ahead to replace this ten-year-old law with a new law, which had the definite aim of restraining the associations of workers. The government's objective in submitting to the Diet the bill for the new legislation is made clear in a statement made by Secretary of the Home Office Arimatsu in the House of Representatives at its session in February 1900. He said: "It is quite likely that the associations of workers will become rampant in the future. How can peace and order be maintained in such an event, if dissolution cannot be ordered until after their assemblies are held?"

. . . It was not until March 1900 that the Japanese government succeeded in having the Diet enact and promulgate the Public Peace Police Act, a law that had baneful effects on social and labor movements in Japan for nearly a quarter of a century. . . . [The] Public Peace Police Act was to restrain the political activities of those opposed to the new regime; the restriction of trade union activities was secondary. Before the enactment of the legislation, there were as yet fewer cases of trade union activity than of the above-mentioned political actions. It was after the promulgation of the law that more cases arose of the activities of trade unions and socialist groups. Obviously, that did not detract in the slightest, in the estimation of the government, from the value of the legislation.

The Public Peace Police Act required, first, the filing with the police of a report on the formation of a political association; there was a fine for failure to do so (Article 1). Political assembly had to be reported at least three hours in advance (Article 2). Public meetings not necessary for maintenance of peace and order had to be reported (Article 3). Outdoor mass meetings and actions had to be reported twelve hours in advance, subject to a fine for offenses (Article 4). A policeman might, if necessary for peace and order, restrict, prohibit, or dissolve an outdoor assembly or mass action or crowds of people (Article 8). If an indoor assembly, he could, for similar cause, dissolve it. Those who refused to obey the order of restriction, prohibition, or dissolution could be fined or sentenced to minor imprisonment (Article 23). When necessary for peace and order, the Home Minister could prohibit an association (Articles 8–11). Offenders against this order were liable to imprisonment of not more than six months (Article 23). A police officer in uniform could visit or request a seat at the assembly and ask questions. Refusal to comply with the request or to reply was punishable by fine (Articles 11, 25). All secret associations were prohibited, offenders being liable to imprisonment of six to twelve months (Articles 14, 28).

The provision that proved to be one of the most obnoxious obstacles to social or labor movements was the article whereby the police officer, on his own authority, could prohibit display, distribution, reading or singing or giving vocal or other expressions to literature, a document, or a song which in his judgment was liable to disturb peace and order (Article 18). However, even worse than this were Articles 17 and 30, which ran as follows:

Article 17: No one shall commit violence or threaten others or publicly slander others for the purposes of the following paragraphs, or seduce or incite others for the purpose of paragraph 2 below:

(1) In order to let others join, or to prevent others from joining an organization which aims at collective action concerning conditions of work or remuneration.

(2) In order to let the employer discharge the workers, or to let him reject an application for work or to let a worker stop his work, or to let him refuse an offer of employment with the view to organizing a lockout or a strike.

(3) In order to compel the other party to agree to the conditions of remuneration.

No one shall commit violence or threaten the other party or slander him publicly in order to compel the other party to certain conditions of rental of land for the purpose of farming. . . .

Article 30: Those who violate Article 17 shall be liable to a heavy imprisonment of one to six months and in addition a fine of from three to thirty yen. The same shall apply to those who commit violence on, threaten, or publicly slander persons who have not joined the employer in a lockout or the workers in a strike.

GOVERNMENT REPRESSION AND ITS REPERCUSSIONS

. . . When we recall the generally antirevolutionary, idealistic, and moderate character of both the trade union movement and the socialist party, the repressive attitude taken by the government does seem to us today somewhat inordinate. Therefore, it is of interest to see what were the final effects of the drastic attitude taken by the government.

The immediate effects and the ultimate results were not the same. The more immediate effect of the legislation and its application was the decline of organized trade unions. But that did not mean any decrease in interest on the part of the workers in trade unions. For, as a matter of fact, the workers of Japan were only beginning to awaken to their new status. There was little "class consciousness" which needed to be stifled or killed. Most writers on the subject seem to agree that the effect indeed was the reverse. The highhanded acts of the police authorities served to stimulate the interest of the workers in trade unionism instead of weakening it. This in turn meant that the ultimate effect of repression of the movement, particularly of the left wing, was to drive the movement underground and to turn it into radicalism. . . .

Strangely enough, as with Christian evangelism, the persecution or awareness of it tended to make the leaders of the movement more heroic and ready to sacrifice themselves. Katayama, Nishikawa, and others began to travel far down to Kyūshū to address meetings of workingmen, and the gospel which these Christians now carried was that of socialism.

. . . Although Japan had received an indemnity of 200 million taels after the Sino-Japanese War, she failed to receive a single ruble from Russia. This great disappointment to the Japanese people led to riots in the streets of Tokyo, but the acquisition of the southern half of Sakhalin and of control over Korea and southern Manchuria, with its railway of high economic and strategic importance, were undeniable gains which gave new life to [the] Japanese economy.

The second stage of the industrial revolution was reached as the result of the war, with an increase in the number of factories. There was an expansion of the iron and steel industry, coal and metal mining, the electrical industry, and so on. A sudden increase in textile manufacturing was noted and this was accompanied by a sudden expansion in exports.

It was after the Russo-Japanese War that Japan embarked upon an aggressive colonial expansionist policy with the full knowledge or recognition of the powers that had read the terms of the Peace of Portsmouth, concluded under the good offices of President Theodore Roosevelt of the United States. For colonial expansion into South Manchuria and later to China proper, full use was made of the rights or powers ceded by Russia. Japan had men to manage the South Manchuria railways to her best political and economic advantage.

There was an expansion in shipbuilding and in the shipping of Japanese-made goods to world markets, which had been monopolized hitherto by the West European nations. It will be seen that expansion along these lines continued in the following years, through World War I, until it began to alarm the Western world: it would not be wrong to consider that the start in this direction was made in the Russo-Japanese War.

Industrial or manufacturing expansion was, as a matter of course, accompanied by an increase in factories and industrial workers. New modes appeared in goods, clothing, and in living conditions as a whole, all of which inevitably entailed a rise in the cost of living. However, the higher cost of living was not accompanied by a corresponding rise in wages or earnings.

There was no decrease in the production of rice, the staple food. In fact, more rice was produced, but there was a constant decrease in the number of farm workers and the price of rice rose constantly. This meant hardship for the industrial workers. As is usually the case in any country at war, the wages of workers had been practically frozen, while the prices of commodities were rising because of shortages. . . .

The year 1900 saw the promulgation of the Public Peace Police

Act, which, as already explained, had a devastating effect on the nascent trade union movement. Writers on the history of trade unionism in Japan refer to the period of a decade or so after 1900 as *Chinsen Ki* (the Period of Submersion). As no normal trade union activity was possible, the workers thereafter resorted to direct-action tactics which involved violence, a course which seemed natural when the door to quiet and orderly negotiation through collective bargaining was closed.

During this period of submersion of trade unionism, labor disputes were apt to take the form of riots, with the wrecking or burning of properties of the companies. From 1899 to 1900 onward, the number of participants in disputes kept diminishing, but there was an increase in destruction. The peak of violence was reached in 1909 when the number of cases of dispute, total number of participants, and the number involved per case were the highest ever recorded. The first of the outbursts occurred in February 1909 at Ashio Copper Mine, where 1200 miners demanded higher wages and better treatment. When the demands were rejected, the men cut off electricity, smashed electric lamps, threw bombs, and burned the company housing. Finally, they seized the company's stores, whereupon three infantry companies were dispatched from Takasaki Regiment Headquarters to suppress violence.

Among the disputes accompanied by violence in the latter part of the Meiji period, one that left a deep impression was the strike of the city tramways of Tokyo. The tramways, which had been a private undertaking until the end of 1911, were bought up by the city, which meant the dissolution of the company. In effecting the dissolution, allowances were given to the entire staff. The lower staff men discovered that the allowances given to higher staff men were far higher than those given out to the lower staff. This discovery ignited the dispute; it took the form of a strike, which began on the last day of 1911 and ran into the following New Year's Day. Depriving the citizens of their transportation on New Year's Day naturally aroused the anger of the population. In order to appease the men, the chiefs of the transportation and the lighting sections distributed all they had received and the dispute came to an end on January 5. Thus, the dispute was finally settled, but the intervention of the authorities was severe: forty-seven men were arrested at work and imprisoned. Of particular significance is

298]IMPERIAL JAPAN: 1800-1945

the fact that this was the first tramway strike in the history of Japan.

GEORGE O. TOTTEN, III*
The Early Socialist Movement

The attempted formation of the Social Democratic party on May 22, 1901, by Katayama and a group of socialist intellectuals with labor union support, especially from the railroad engineers' Society to Correct Abuses, might be considered the point from which the political socialist movement could be dated. The so-called "proletarian parties" that were formed after the franchise was greatly extended in 1925 trace their lineages back to this party, called in Japanese the Shakai Minshutō. As a matter of fact, the men who formed that party later came to represent the major trends in Japanese socialist activity: Denjirō Kōtoku became an anarchist; Sen Katayama a Communist; and Isō Abe a social democrat.

These socialist intellectuals and their comrades, supported briefly by the infant labor movement, were already the products of several diverse influences that had evolved over the preceding two decades. Some of the more radical participants in the people's rights movement had begun to read and help in the translation of Western works that dealt with socialism in one way or another. The transliteration of the term "socialism" as *"soshiaruisume"* by Hiroyuki Katō, an early radical who later became conservative, first appeared in a book of his in 1870. The translation of this term as *"shakaishugi"* first appeared in print in 1878 when the press reported the attempted assassination of Kaiser Wilhelm I by the socialists (giving fuel to police suspicions). But the popularization (among a limited audience to be sure) of the word took place in 1887 when the first number of *Nation's Friend* (*Kokumin no Tomo*) started a serialized translation of one of the writings of Henry George in which he made frequent reference to "socialism." This journal became for a time the mouthpiece of the left wing of the Liberal party, which still carried on the tradition of the "free-

* George O. Totten, III, *The Social Democratic Movement in Prewar Japan* (New Haven, Conn.: Yale University Press, 1966), pp. 23-31.

dom and people's rights movement" and espoused the principles of
the French Revolution. It carried articles by students who were
studying in France or Germany or who had just returned from
abroad.

Being now in possession not only of foreign books and articles
but also firsthand reports, a number of small groups met to discuss
the "advanced" thought of the West regarding various aspects of
the "social question" with a view to discovering what might be
applicable to Japan. Most of these groups were ephemeral, but one
that became permanent was the Social Policy Academic Association (*Shakai Seisaku Gakkai*) formed on April 2, 1896. Drawn to
a study of the contemporary German *Sozialpolitik* school, this
group rejected "socialism" and laissez-faire but urged the state to
work out welfare policies. Composed of government people and
professors at Tokyo Imperial University, it was to become a continuing antagonist to the French-English-American-inspired hu-
manists, on the one hand, and the later class-conscious Marxists,
on the other.

Another influence that had been at work to swell the ranks of
socialists was Christianity, which had reentered the country after
Japan's long period of isolation. It brought with it this time a sense
of social consciousness and concern for the physical as well as
spiritual well-being of others, of which the recent Protestant uplift
movements were a manifestation. Some Japanese who were impressed with this element of Christianity but repelled by the
doctrinal differences among the various Protestant sects welcomed
the Unitarians who appeared to them most tolerant. But again the
very tolerance of the Unitarians led some eventually to abandon
Christianity altogether in favor of various socialist doctrines.

In the midst of this process, which had been hastened by a spate
of translations of Western socialist authors, a group of Christian
socialists began to meet together with members of the left wing of
the Liberal party in the hall of the Unitarian Society in Tokyo.
They formed the Society for the Study of Socialism (*Shakaishugi
Kenkyūkai*) in the fall of 1898 and began a somewhat systematic
discussion of such writers as Saint-Simon, Proudhon, Fourier, and
Marx, with a view to applying socialist theory in Japan. After two
years, some of the members became impatient for action. This
caused those who were lukewarm to the idea to drop out and the
group was reorganized into the Socialist Society (*Shakaishugi*

Kyōkai) in 1900. While the forty or so members left were too few
to do much by themselves, they supplied the nucleus of the attempt
to rally a broader group and win labor support for the formation
of the Social Democratic Party. Five of the six initiators were.
Christians at the time.

The fact that this party had obtained enough backing to be
launched at all was viewed so seriously by the cabinet of Hirobumi
Itō (the supposedly more liberal of the oligarchs) that the Home
Ministry ordered its immediate dissolution. In any case, it is
doubtful that the party could have had much success at the polls,
since only a well-off minority of the propertied class was allowed
to vote. The leaders of the party, such as Katayama, Abe, and
Kōtoku, could have avoided the government's order to disband if
they had compromised the party's platform in certain respects, but
this they refused to do lest such a precedent cripple the socialist
movement from its birth.

In retrospect, the Social Democratic party's platform appears
moderate indeed, and most of its immediate aims were democratic
rather than socialist in nature. The party declared that it did not
champion the interests of the poor only, nor was it hostile to the
rich, but desired to work for the prosperity of the nation as a
whole. Its goals were not socialist, but rather either democratic—
popular referendum and abolition of the House of Peers—or
pacifist—an end to military expenditures. The fact that these
demands were attacked as "seditious" by government-party politicians, some of whom were formerly leaders in the people's rights
movement, shows to what extent the Japanese liberals had abandoned their former demands for political liberties and universal
suffrage.

In the decade after 1900 the authoritarian attitude of the government and the weakness of labor inevitably inclined the socialist
movement toward intellectualism rather than activism. The Public
Peace Police Law crushed the incipient labor union movement, and
the order to disband the Social Democratic party left no room for
even moderate political reformist activities. The socialist movement after 1901, therefore, was confined to educational and
propaganda activities. With the divorce of the socialist and the
labor movements, socialist leadership fell from the hands of the
then more moderate and organizationally minded Sen Katayama
and was taken up by the more anarchistic and intellectually in-

clined Denjirō Kōtoku and his close disciple, Toshihiko Sakai. The resultant tendency toward radical theorizing rather than practical activity became a marked characteristic of the Japanese socialist movement.

If the social movement is thought of in the singular, it contained in the years 1899 to 1902 two aspects: labor and socialist. In 1899 the handful of socialists were discussing and studying the abstract theories of socialism, while the infant labor movement and its leaders were negotiating about concrete working conditions and actually carrying on strikes. By 1901 the socialists who were eager for political activity found the incipient trade unionists receptive to the message that political reforms were a necessary concomitant to purely economic demands if labor's condition were really to be bettered. But by 1902 the trade union movement had been struck down and had collapsed, and the socialists were left no alternative but to confine themselves to education and propaganda.

Despite the severity of its measures against the unions and labor activity, the government continued to tolerate the existence of the Socialist Society. Socialist thought even became a limited intellectual fad around 1902–1903 among the avant-garde, but at the same time the socialists themselves had lost contact with the very working classes whose interests they were supposedly championing.

With the danger of an outbreak of hostilities with Imperial Russia, however, the socialist movement again came to grips with a vital problem: would war benefit or burden the poorer classes in Japan? Traditional socialist thought seemed to brand war as evil. Around this conviction the socialists created an antiwar movement, led by Kōtoku and Sakai who together founded the Commoners' Society (*Heiminsha*) and began publishing the *Commoners' Newspaper* (*Heimin Shimbun*) on November 15, 1903. This journal carried many antiwar articles, the main theses of which were as follows: (1) war is contrary to the way of human love and subverts the just principles of society; (2) war benefits the bourgeoisie but sacrifices the common people; (3) the House of Representatives which approved the war represents the land-owners and the capitalists, not the common people; therefore we are against war and the very existence of our army.

The socialist movement now began to encounter sterner restrictions by the government, especially after the outbreak of the Russo-

Japanese War in 1904. These they resisted for over a year, carrying on their peace campaign by writing, making speeches, and holding meetings. On January 29, 1905, however, the sixty-fourth issue of the *Commoners' Newspaper* was suppressed and the Commoners' Society ordered disbanded on October 9, 1905. This antiwar movement, supported by the Christian pacifists and Christian socialists, who had combined forces with secular socialists, put up a brave fight, but their influence reached little beyond a limited circle of intellectuals and did not penetrate the ranks of labor.

When the more liberal Saionji first succeeded Katsura as prime minister, the socialists immediately formed the Japan Socialist party (*Nihon Shakaitō*) and, on January 28, 1906, received permission to be a legal party inasmuch as they advocated "socialism within the limits of the constitution." The "materialists" published a journal called *Light* (*Hikari*) while the Christian socialists put out *New Century* (*Shinkigen*). Then in 1907 the two groups united for a time and revived the *Commoners' Newspaper,* this time as a daily. Although they broadened their activities, they never succeeded in doing more than defeating a fare raise on the Tokyo municipal trolley system. They were, in effect, the direct successors of the Socialist Society, engaging mainly in education and propaganda while the labor unions had become almost entirely defunct.

Deteriorating labor conditions, however, were having an effect on the workers. The Russo-Japanese War had reduced the low living standard of labor still further and had brought about a great deal of suffering which resulted in a series of spontaneous strikes, numbering 107 between 1903 and 1907 and involving 20,789 workers. The frustration of constant defeat gave rise to anarcho-syndicalism within the ranks of labor.

This radical development was reflected in the socialist movement by the complete conversion of Kōtoku in 1906. Until November 1905, he had been in prison for his antiwar activities during the Russo-Japanese War. When released, he traveled for nearly a year in the United States where he was impressed with the anarcho-syndicalism of the International Workers of the World (IWW). The antiparliamentary bent of anarcho-syndicalism and its emphasis on direct action seemed attuned to the situation in

Japan at the time—the postwar poverty, the social unrest, the severe suppression of socialist thought.

Kōtoku's new turn of thought convinced a number of the intellectuals who made up the small socialist movement. On June 28, 1906, at a Socialist party meeting to welcome him back to Japan, Kōtoku made a speech on "The Tide of the World Revolutionary Movement." In it he rejected parliamentarianism because he found that the victories of the British Independent Labor party and the German Social Democratic party did not immediately usher in the new world of the proletariat. He rejected not only reformism, but also the contemporary "orthodox" Marxism of Bebel and Kautsky. Instead, he called for direct negotiation with employers and the use of the strike if necessary, and argued against involvement in political issues on the grounds that that would divert the energy of labor from its real fight against the capitalists.

At the Socialist Party Conference of February 1907, Kōtoku, excited by the current Ashio Copper Mine disturbance, gave a one-hour speech advocating what he called "direct action." As a result of this, the Saionji cabinet ordered the immediate disbanding of the Socialist party. The movement then split into two main factions: the believers in parliamentary means (Sen Katayama, Tetsuji Tazoe, and Kōjirō Nishikawa) and the believers in "direct action" (Kōtoku, Sakai, and their younger followers, Sakae Ōsugi and Hitoshi Yamakawa).

Kōtoku's brand of anarcho-syndicalism was peculiarly Japanese. European syndicalism was born mainly out of a feeling that the social democratic parties had become compromising and ineffective within the national legislatures, that politics was a set of tricks by which the bourgeoisie distracted the working class, and that, consequently, direct action by well-organized and synchronized labor unions was the only thing that would get results. In contrast to this, Japanese syndicalism expressed the feelings of frustration that arose from the inability to get even a voice in the Diet, the prompt police suppression of any kind of labor activity, the all-pervading ideology of the "emperor system" that restricted any fundamental criticism of the state, and, finally, the prevalence of scattered, spontaneous strikes that resembled small-scale uprisings more than modern, organized action.

At that time Sen Katayama and other socialists criticized this kind of syndicalism, branding it a dangerous tendency. They advocated organizing the workers peacefully without provoking the ruling classes. Nevertheless, the syndicalist trend became more pronounced and brought in its wake first the Red Flag incident in 1908 and finally the High Treason Trial of 1910–1911 in which Kōtoku and eleven other socialists were condemned to death for allegedly plotting against the life of the emperor. This trial now appears to have been a conscious frame-up by the Katsura government.

After the trial, police suppression of the socialist movement intensified. No distinction was made between syndicalists such as Sakae Ōsugi and orthodox socialists such as Sen Katayama, who at that time supported the Second International. Katayama led a strike of workers in the Tokyo municipal trolley system, but that was his last activity in Japan. In complete frustration, he finally left his homeland in 1914, never to return. The socialist movement was at a standstill.

❀ LABOR CONDITIONS were often harsh during Japanese industrialization. Efforts to organize workers faced numerous obstacles, as Orchard points out below. Crucial in his opinion were the factory dormitory system, which held the large number of girl workers virtually prisoners, and the peculiar "dual economic structure" of Japanese industry. Over two thirds of the work force was employed in small-scale and family enterprises, essentially premodern and reminiscent of precapitalist work conditions, while simultaneously the large-scale modern industrial sector was being developed. This resulted in the modern and pre-modern sectors of the economy growing up side by side. Orchard's detailed observations of working conditions were based on visits and research conducted in Japan.

JOHN ORCHARD*
Japan's Economic Position—The Progress of Industrialization

Throughout the process of industrialization in Japan, industry has depended on so-called cheap labor. Wages have been low, working hours long, and labor, for the most part, unorganized. And yet, Japanese labor has not been really cheap, certainly not as cheap as it is considered to be by Western industrialists or even by the Japanese employers.

Labor is dear or cheap to industry according to the labor cost per unit of output, not according to the wage per worker. The output of the worker in Japan is low compared with the output of workers in Western countries. Though the individual worker is cheap, collective labor costs are not particularly low. The element of skill has been neglected for the cheapness of the individual. Efficiency has been sacrificed to low wages.

But it is not at all surprising that Japanese industrialists have failed to question the advantages of cheap labor. They, as individuals, are not primarily concerned with the future development of industry and the economic position of the nation fifty years hence; nor has their industrial background been of a nature likely to start them questioning along these lines. Modern industry, in Japan, exists side by side with domestic workshops. Under the autocratic paternalism of household industry, labor receives little if any reward in wages. The skilled craftsmen are paid a wage, but apprentices earn their board, lodging, and clothing, with perhaps some spending money now and then on holidays, but no daily or weekly wage. The workshop is the home of the master craftsman, and the workers live as members of the family. They work long hours for little pay. The personal equation is very important. . . .

Most Japanese industry, in spite of the development of Western mechanical industry in the past half century, is still organized

* John Orchard, *Japan's Economic Position—The Progress of Industrialization* (New York: McGraw-Hill/Whittlesey House, 1930), pp. 346–348, 351–353, 342–344, 355–358.

on this feudal system. Nearly all products for purely Japanese consumption are made under the family system. Japanese clothing is made in the home of the master tailor who may have twelve to 100 workers living under his roof, to only ten percent of whom he pays any wage. The rest are apprentices. The same is true of the cabinetmaker, the lacquerer, the lantern maker, the mat maker, and the many thousands of small establishments that produce the necessities and luxuries of Japanese life. . . .

The wage system in the modern industries varies with each industry and each factory and according to the operation. The same factory may have some workers on piecework, some on a time basis with a production bonus, some with a monthly wage, and some partially on piecework and partially on time work. Throughout Japanese industry, the wage rates are low whatever the system.

To the daily or monthly money wages of the workers, a bonus must be added, for in all industries and in practically every factory the bonus system prevails, a survival of the feudal paternalism. There are variations in the bonus practice according to the individual plant, but in general an incentive bonus is paid to the workers twice a year, in January and again in July, the amount varying for each individual according to the whim of the management and the state of business. It has been estimated that the semiannual bonus of the average cotton mill hand in the prosperous days of 1919 amounted to fifteen dollars. Generally, there is extreme variation in the individual amounts. . . . The workers themselves had no idea on what basis the distinctions were made.

. . . Japanese wages may be said to range from thirty to eighty cents a day for women, and from fifty cents to two dollars a day for men. The significance of those figures lies, for the workman, in their relation to the cost of living and, for the employer, in their relation to total labor costs. In most Japanese mills, the wage is only a part of the direct labor costs. The workers receive additional reward in the form of free lodging, food at below cost, clothing or other necessities. Even the most modern Japanese factories are not free from the old feudal custom of boarding and lodging the help. . . .

Men are housed or boarded to a much less extent than are women. Some companies provide houses at low rental for married employees, and some provide dormitories for their unmarried male workers; but generally the men and boys are not housed, except in cases where the plant is located away from the centers of population, or in the mining industry. They do, however, in many cases, receive some form of indirect wage or a higher money wage to equalize their compensation. . . .

The country girl who comes to the cotton mill, a raw recruit from the farm, receives thirty cents a day as wage, and in addition, her lodging at the company dormitories, free or partially free. Her food in the mill dining hall costs her about nine cents a day, which, though less than its cost to the company, amounts to about thirty-six percent of her income. The daily wage of thirty cents is paid only for her working days. For the rest days and holidays and sick days, she receives no pay, but food costs are deducted from her pay for each of the 365 days of the year. Thus she has only about sixteen cents a day for the rest of her living expenses, her clothing, the payments on the loan to her parents or on the advance of car-fare, or the accumulation of the marriage dowry. Sixteen cents a day does not provide her with an extravagant living. A large part of the experienced girl workers earn sixty cents a day, but when the cost of food has been deducted from their pay, their income amounts to but forty-one cents a day or $150 a year. It is not much, even to a country girl, especially when she is in debt and must clothe herself and meet sundry other expenses. The men workers in the textile mills get a little higher wage, but they feed and lodge themselves, and often they have a family to support.

In the engineering trades, where the wages are generally higher and less is done for the worker as indirect reward, the individual wage is also low in reference to the cost of living. If fifteen cents is taken as the daily cost of food for one worker—and that is about what the large textile mills allow in their budgets—the man who earns one dollar a day for each day of labor uses seventeen percent of his income just to keep himself in food. A wage of one dollar a day amounts to about eighty-eight cents a day in income, and fifteen cents is not such a trifling sum in such a budget. If he has but a single dependent, there is only fifty-eight cents a day, after both have been fed, to provide lodging and clothing, medicine and amusement, and all the other necessaries of life. The more skilled worker can earn two dollars a day, but the number in this class is not large. The greater part of the labor force of Japan is being paid on the lower level of wages, largely because so much of it is unskilled and untrained—raw agricultural labor with little industrial experience. The low level of the average wages published in the government reports on wages is influenced by this fact. There is no denying the cheapness of the individual worker in Japan. The question at issue is not, "Are wages low," but, "Is the collective cost of labor low?" . . .

It may be said that, after all, the recruiting of raw labor is to be expected in a newly industrialized country. That is true, but Japan is a land overpopulated and industrialization has been in progress for seventy-five years, and yet the problem of securing labor is still acute. The recruited labor does not become permanently industrial. Once introduced into the factory, it does not stay. It comes reluctantly, and the period of service is short. Experience has shown that the girl recruits, and most of the recruits are girls— about eighty-four percent—return to the farm as soon as they have worked out the advance made to their parents, or have saved enough for a marriage dowry, or have completed their contract, or otherwise freed themselves of the obligation that kept them at the mill. Japanese labor not only has to be recruited to establish a mill but it must be recruited over and over, year after year, to keep the mill going.

In the early days of industry in Japan, labor was so scarce and so difficult to obtain for industrial purposes that it was not uncommon for one factory to steal the labor of another. . . . It soon became expedient for all the factories to lock their high gates and keep their girl workers strictly within the compound. This practice of locking in the female labor still continues in most of the textile plants. Once the girl or woman has been recruited for the factory, she is not allowed to leave the grounds without permission from a company official. That the practice is more than the relic of an old policy is evidenced by the fact that permission to leave the factory grounds is difficult to secure and does not come to any one girl more than two or four times a month. . . .

It is generally claimed by employers that the restrictions on the freedom of girl workers are for their own protection, that they are young and inexperienced, and that, since the management has recruited these workers from their farms and brought them to live in an industrial community, they feel a responsibility for the girls in their unfamiliar surroundings. There may be some sincerity in such claims, but the original impetus was the labor pirating of other companies, and even at the present the locked gates serve the management more than they protect the workers. The young country girls get terribly homesick and many of them run away, but under such close supervision it is not so easy for a girl to break her contract and return to the farm before her year is up. For those who remain, close supervision and restricted freedom hinder the growth of unionism. If a strike is called, the dormitory workers are locked in the factory grounds and cut off from all communication with the strikers outside—the men workers and the women who live at home. Of course, the workers manage in devious ways to surmount these obstacles in a serious strike, but the barred gates of the factory compound are a distinct advantage in breaking a good many strikes. . . .

The dormitory system has tremendous advantages for the manufacturer. By this means, he is certain of his labor force from day to day, and absenteeism and lateness are under check. It permits him practically to double his capital by operating the machinery night and day. The leisure as well as the working hours of the employees are under his control. Labor unionism is barred out; strikes are difficult to call. There is opportunity, if he cares to use it, for vast industrial experiments with labor.

But the dormitory system is also a two-edged weapon. It is a breeder of discontent and labor turnover. It smacks of being a prison. The workers chafe under their restricted freedom; they rebel against the institutional food. Every labor union in the country has marked the dormitory system for attack. Every strike among the workers foments about the restrictions of freedom and the poor quality of food.

Some of the dormitories are quite pleasant places, except that they are all under the shadow of their factories. They are clean and airy and they have small gardens about them, careful sanitation according to Japanese standards, and various social features. But some are not well kept. Too many girls are crowded together into one room for sleeping quarters. The night and day shifts share the same quarters, the same bedding. This is not often true, but it does happen. Sanitation is careless. The food is bad or, if not bad, unpalatable. . . .

An investigation into the physical condition of operatives living in factory dormitories in Tokyo City in May 1930, made by the metropolitan police with the assistance of diet experts, disclosed the fact that a large number of the occupants of factory dormitories are badly undernourished. The police and the experts pointed out to the factory management that it was often not so much a question of the quality of the food served as the lack of variety in the menus that led to the undernourishment of the operatives. One large factory dormitory, it was said, served *miso-shiru* (a bean soup) and pickles at breakfast, salted salmon at dinner, and *miso-shiru* and pickles at supper; and the same menu had been served for years.

Labor unionism is gradually getting inside the factory gates, and domiciled workers on strike are a distinct liability. Social agencies besides the labor unions are agitating against the abuses of the dormitory system. The press has given the textile industry unwanted publicity in several food and sanitation scandals. There have been cases of poisoned food, unhealthy sanitation, crowded sleeping quarters. The abuse and the agitation have been sufficient to cause the government to take action. Regulations on sanitation in dormitories, the size and occupancy of bedrooms, separate accommodations for separate shifts, etc., were put in force in May 1927. The labor movement demands complete abolition or radical reform of the dormitory system. It seems likely that the dormitory system will be a problem so long as it exists and that the manufacturers will be forced to make important changes in the housing of employees.

❀ THESE TWO SELECTIONS describe labor conditions as seen by an industrialist, on the one hand, and by a woman observer, on the other. Matsukata, a prominent industrialist and owner of a shipyard and a newspaper, was writing for an American audience in 1914. Somewhat in the vein of "enlightened paternalism," he presents his view of labor conditions and the proper behavior expected of employees.

Baroness Ishimoto, a noted social reformer and feminist, describes the conditions she saw in coal mines in Japan during World War I.

MATSUKATA KŌJIRŌ*
Japanese Laborers

In the organization of labor as well as in the legal guarantee for the labor interest, Japan is still far behind Europe and especially America. In these respects, we have very little to tell you. There are, however, some peculiar features in our labor life that may be of interest to American readers.

To begin with, there is in Japan a social relationship between employer and employee that does not prevail in your country. It is the relationship of lord and retainer. For many centuries, Japan was under a feudal system where the giver of *roku* (or annual pensions) was the lord, while the recipient of them was the retainer. Such feudalistic relations between payer and payee have not yet altogether died away in this country, though they are gradually diminishing with the capitalization of labor. Even today, he who pays wages is allowed to assume something of the mental attitude of the lord—not in a despotic but in a protectoral sense—toward those who receive them. A young man who was earning his school expenses by work in America came into possession of a lengthy letter from his mother left behind in Japan, repeatedly advising him to be loyal to the person of his master; and he looked round to find to his renewed surprise that nobody would claim in the Republic such personal loyalty as his good old mother must have meant. But in Japan there exist many subjects for this quasi-feudalistic virtue.

The relationship between employer and employee in Japan may be good or bad in its consequences. It depends upon the caliber and character of the master—of the president, if a company—whether or not this institution is turned to account. However loyal the Japanese laborers may be to their wage-payer, they would never look upon him as a "master" unless he possessed sufficient weight and sympathy to inspire his men with reverence. If, however, the employer has such qualifications, the relations between

* Matsukata Kōjirō, "Japanese Labourers," in Masaoka Naoichi, ed., *Japan to America* (New York: G. P. Putnam's Sons, 1914), pp. 104–108.

himself and his workmen will be, in Japan, more domestic, more intimate, and more personal than in Europe or America.

The standard of living is very low here. While labor is cheap, the prices of commodities are also cheap. Consequently, the Japanese workmen are, generally speaking, much happier than their American colleagues, so far as material comfort is concerned. In America, they have bread with cheese for the midday meal—rarely furnishing them with potatoes or some other substantial food. As a rule, they live in a tenement house where it is often impossible to enjoy fresh air and warm sunlight. But, in Japan, laborers whose wages are thirty sen (that is, fifteen cents) a day can even afford fish or meat at tiffin, and they live in cottages not so bad from the hygienic point of view.

The more progressive Japanese employers realize that their own interests are in accordance with the interests of their workmen, to whom they give every encouragement that is in their power. In the Kawasaki shipbuilding yard, of which I am now president, the best workhands are from time to time sent to Europe or America in order to study their trade, and those returned from abroad are given comparatively important posts in our works. According to the regulations of our company, an employee who resigns after serving for ten years is entitled to a grant of 1000 yen, but the president is authorized to give more at his discretion. The elasticity of his competence is a strong point in the management of the Kawasaki shipbuilding yard.

As a whole, the Japanese workmen are ambitious and they appreciate the value of learning. Out of 11,500 hands in the employ of the yard, more than 1000 attend a night school which receives a regular subvention from the company. To our thinking, to establish and attach a laborers' school to the company is not advisable, for in that case attendance would become rather compulsory, much to the injury of their self-initiative.

Fortunately, labor disputes are very rare in this country. Strikes are few and far between, while there have been practically no lockouts. I myself have ever been striving to inculcate upon the workmen in our company that I as president am bound to consider the interests not only of the capital but also of the labor; that the harmony between the two elements is essential to the successful management of the whole concern; and that I expect all the workmen, from the foreman down to a shopboy, to cooperate with me in the promotion of the company's interests. My men, it seems to me, have come to be impressed with these ideas, which chiefly accounts for the fact that no strikes have ever occurred among them. Only once, however, there was an attempt at striking. I heard that a bad man was instigating his fellows. One morning, on going around to inspect the works, I found him idle. I demanded, "You don't want to work?" "No, sir," came the sullen answer. "Then," said I, going nearer to him and addressing him in a mild tone, "then, I hope you will get away. Our company doesn't want men who don't work. You can perhaps find some work congenial to you elsewhere." To this he replied that he would leave us after getting his things together. I lent him a hand in putting his kit in a box and sent him away. Thus a strike was nipped in the bud. Well, my American readers may think that the comparative scarcity of strikes in Japan is due to lack of self-assertion on the part of the laborers, but that is not quite right. The chief explanation must be found in their active loyalty to their employer's person, rather than in their passive forbearance.

SHIDZUÉ ISHIMOTO*
Are Miners Human Beings?

I began to look at the people around me in a new way and tried to see their lives and problems more sympathetically. One day while I was at Kattachi I asked my husband to take me down into the pit, descending seven hundred feet into the ground. This old-fashioned mine had only one elevator which was used for carrying up and down both coal and human beings. The cage had just a platform to stand on; no wall or rails around it. So, when this elevator started downward, it ran so fast that I felt as if I were in an instant thrown and dashed against the hell in the bottom of the earth. Pitch darkness, heat, and moisture reigned in this subterranean world. As I groped along the passage guided by my husband and a little dim mining lamp, the ceiling came down lower and lower. I had to bend double and pay constant attention to my steps on the rocky

* Baroness Shidzué Ishimoto, *Facing Two Ways* (New York: Farrar and Rinehart, 1935), pp. 158–164.

path slippery with puddles of water. Rumbling coal trucks dashed through this dark narrow passage constantly but without any warning of approach—a very dangerous proceeding. I saw—I smelled rather—the rows of stables in the darkness. The horses were worn and feeble, their energy lost by their long stay underground. They were used to pull coal wagons in some parts where the path was wide and the roof was high enough for animals to pass back and forth.

As I went farther and farther, the roof of the pit dropped to less than four feet high. Naked men sat on their knees digging coal with their picks. I felt that I could not go any farther, but my husband told me that the miners worked in places narrower and lower than this and that women had to creep into these passages like wiggling worms to pull baskets of coal out to the place where the wagons stood. Perhaps I did not spend more than an hour in the pit, but I felt that I could not stay a minute longer. I looked at my husband, wondering how in the world he dared to select this profession voluntarily! Yet he seemed to me utterly absorbed in it. He treated the miners in the most democratic manner, a reflection of his Christian humanism. With his sensitive heart and his sympathy for and deep insight into the conditions of the Japanese miners, he seemed to me a true hero, or "a prince in disguise" whom, though I could not quite understand him, I was perfectly happy to follow with absolute trust.

About fifty thousand miners and their families were attempting to survive in this Miike mining district. It may be unavoidable in any civilized country that the life of miners is exposed to more danger than that of any other kind of laborers, but Japanese miners are especially subject to risks and these are largely due to poor accommodations in the pit and to the narrow width of the coal beds.

. . . The fact is that the actual loss of miners per one million tons of coal mined in England is about ten persons, while in Japan thirty human lives are actually sacrificed for every million tons. Moreover, the rate of injury by accident in this industry is as high as two and a half to every three miners. If we add the cases of disease directly caused by poor sanitary conditions in the mines and wretched living accommodations, the percentage is even greater.

While we were in Manda or Kattachi pit, no day passed without its accident. Every three or four days I heard the news of a miner's death and occasionally that of an engineer, mostly the result of their being crushed by falling rocks. While carrying coal in baskets from pit to wagons, the girls were often crushed by the sudden overturn of the heavy coal trucks, caught under the big wagons. This happened too often because of careless excessive speed.

I used to stand at the front of our house at Kattachi of an evening when the five o'clock whistle blew and the shifting to the night work began, waiting anxiously for my husband's safe return, while I watched men and women plodding uphill to their homes and downhill to their work, each with a lunch box and pickax.

"Up safely?"

"With the mercy of the gods!"

They exchanged greetings in this fashion. They were very superstitious, fearing almost any phenomenon as a fatal omen.

> Don't become the sweetheart of a miner, my girl,
> When a gas explosion comes in just one moment,
> Then good-bye, forever, to your man!

They chant songs of sorrow. Nevertheless, widows with children soon marry other men of the same trade, as there is no choice but to continue sharing this human tragedy.

A strange logic of social life can be seen in the rewards of miners, whose labor is strenuous, whose life is threatened by constant danger and disease. They are paid very little compared with less arduous labor in Japan. During our stay at the mines, I often saw a squad of prisoners from Miike Prison in their ugly red uniforms, with heavy chains on their hips, sent down to the mining pit to work as forced laborers. Often miners had to compete for pay with these groups of chained prisoners. Other wage competitors are the women and children of their own families who are given various tasks because they are so much cheaper.

It was only recently that Japan adopted prohibitive measures against the employment of women miners and against midnight labor in general for women, both regarded as evils in Western countries long ago. While I was at the Miike mines, wives and daughters of miners went down in a half-naked condition, mingling with the naked men laborers. They followed the men and carried out the coal as the men loosened it with their picks. It was ridiculous to expect morality in such circumstances. Women who worked in the darkness had a pale complexion like the skin of a silkworm; they spoke and acted shamelessly, the last sign of feminine dignity sloughing off. Often pregnant women, working until the last moment, gave birth to children in the dark pit.

It would be hard to tell the difference between the life of pigs and the life of these miners. Certainly the human beings were living like animals in barns. Their barns were built on the bare hill in rows, barrack fashion, out of poor rough boards roofed with thin sheets of zinc. One barrack was usually divided so as to house from five to seven families. Each one of these booths was about twelve feet square, separated from the adjoining booth by thin boards. The average size of one family was five or six members, and there was only one lavatory for a whole row of barracks. There was neither gas nor water service. It might be bearable in winter to live in a booth crowded with five or six people, but how could one stand the summer heat of south Japan in such conditions?

I felt especially sorry for those who worked at night and had no place to rest their tired bodies by day against another night's work. They just lay down on their mats, while the women were chattering in groups washing and cooking, and the children making noises everywhere. My husband often told me that when their bodies were weary the men became more careless and hardly had energy enough to avoid injury even when they were aware of danger. The people who lived in these barns were strictly watched and loyalty to their employers was enforced. It was impossible for them to run away; nor could labor organizers get among the miners, for labor unions were severely banned in the coal field. Even today [the 1930s] the miners are unorganized and exhibit only meek feudalistic submission. However, perhaps owing to their meekness, the Japanese miners are fortunate enough to be protected as citizens, and they have never been attacked by machine guns as has happened in some so-called civilized countries!

The miners I knew were usually desperate. They saw no hope in the future and sought merely momentary pleasures. Men and their wives quarreled a great deal. Men beat women and children. The quarrels were more frequent on their wage-paying days which came twice a month. Many men literally drank nearly all their pay before they brought any pennies to their families. But it would be rash to blame them! Who would dare preach family obligations to men who got only twenty dollars for a month's work? The average wage for men in those days was about forty yen (twenty dollars), and twenty-four yen (twelve dollars) was the maximum pay for women for their monthly labor. Now this pay has been raised a little. The low rate of workers' wages was not only due to the low social status of laborers, but must be largely attributed to the lack of efficiency in their working power. They could go to their work only sixteen days a month on the average, for their physical strength was unequal to greater strain, owing to conditions in the pits and to the low quality of their food and housing. The women usually went down with their husbands, sometimes taking their babies on their backs, as there were no nursery provisions. As soon as children were old enough, both boys and girls went to work, competing for wages with adults. But there was no other way for the population to keep alive unless it could manage to control the overflooded market of cheap labor by exercising birth control.

I often wondered whether the Japanese capitalists were true to their consciences in saying that the beautiful family system in Japan made men, women, and children work harmoniously and pleasantly at their tasks, when they claimed Japanese exemption for women, on such grounds, in the international labor regulations drawn up at the Labor Conference in Geneva.

Where is the harmony in fact? Where is the joy of labor in truth? Women who were already fully tired from their long day's labor in the mines returned home to carry pails of water from a distant well to their kitchens. They cooked, washed, and nursed like other women whose energies are spent only on such domestic tasks. Naturally they were abnormally nervous and exhausted. They often beat their impatiently hungry children who could not wait for their mothers to cook the meals. Nothing could be compared to the sight of these crowded nests of ignorance, poverty, and misery. It is the very picture of Hades! Children were born without love and reared without proper care, receiving even little affection from their parents. Westerners often say that Japan is a paradise for children. I wish this were true, but my impression of the children in mining camps is so vivid that I can never forget the horror of the dirty little creatures who haunted the garbage box at my door. My heart ached when I saw babies coughing badly and left without medical attention till they died. I shuddered to see youngsters screaming and running away from home pursued by peevish mothers with big pieces of firewood in their hands.

"Why must women work outside the home like men?"

"Why must the mother breed and nurse while she works for wages?"

As I watched the lives of these laborers and their women and children, these questions rose in my mind, but I myself did not realize then that they were the seeds that were to grow and revolutionize my own life.

⊛ THE TEMPORARY BOOM produced by World War I pulled Japan out of a serious economic crisis. It also paved the way for a vast expansion of Japan's steel and munitions industries, as Orchard shows, even though Japan was not itself directly involved in the war. The boom was short-lived, however, and the first years after the war's end saw a severe depression as European industry reasserted a competitive pressure in world markets. An unexpected result of the raging inflation in food prices was a nationwide series of riots in 1918 over the price of rice, begun by housewives in a small fishing town. The first massive expression of popular discontent in industrial Japan, the rice riots shook the government and led to the first party cabinet in Japanese history.

JOHN ORCHARD*
The Effects of the World War on Industrialization

The World War was especially effective in its encouragement of industrialization. It involved Japan only to a limited extent in the actual hostilities, but it created a huge home market for munitions

* John Orchard, *Japan's Economic Position—The Progress of Industrialization* (New York: McGraw-Hill/Whittlesey House, 1930), pp. 231–235.

and uniforms, and, through the disruption of European industries and world shipping, it freed Japan, for the time being, from the competition of European goods in her domestic markets and opened to Japanese trade the markets of the countries of the Asiatic mainland previously served by European manufacturers. There was even an increase in the export of Japanese goods to Europe, to North and South America, and to Australia.

The first reaction to the war was a severe business and industrial depression that continued through the last half of 1914 and into 1915. Stock prices were demoralized, there were many failures, and in almost every industry the curtailment of output was necessary. Finally, the full effect of the war upon the demand for goods and upon the trade of countries outside the zone of conflict became evident and then the recovery began. It was rapid and by the time of the armistice, practically every Japanese factory industry had had a substantial growth and many new industries had been established. Within a period of three or four years, greater progress in industrialization had been made than in the previous decade. . . .

Between 1914 and 1919, the number of workers in factories employing more than five increased from 1,086,000 to 1,777,000, or by sixty-three percent. A period of ten years had been required between 1904 and 1914 to accomplish a similar percentage increase on a much smaller base. The power developed by prime movers for industrial purposes increased by thirty-four percent and the capacity of electric motors by 206 percent, an increase due in part to the expansion of manufacturing and in part to the electrification of existing industries. The increase in capital invested is often cited as a measure of growth, but it is an especially unsatisfactory index both because of the inaccuracies in the collection of the data and because a large part of the increase is due to the inflation of prices and the depreciated purchasing power of the yen. The real increase between 1915 and 1919 in the paid-up capital in joint-stock companies engaged in manufacturing, though undoubtedly great, was therefore something less than the apparent increase of 160 percent shown in the official government reports.

The consumption of coal, though its use is not confined to manufacturing, may be taken as an index of industrial activity. The Japanese coal reserves are not large, and new mines cannot be opened in response to demand as readily as they can in the United States, but between 1913 and 1918 the consumption of coal increased by forty-seven percent, partly through a curtailment of exports, but more largely through an increase in the output of the Japanese mines.

For the measurement of the expansion of specific industries, the data are more complete and more accurate. In the cotton spinning industry, there was an increase between 1913 and 1918 of forty-four percent in the number of spindles and of twenty-three percent in yarn output. The output of raw silk increased by fifty-five percent. Other industries showed a similar growth, but the most spectacular expansion occurred in the iron and steel industry. In textiles, Japan was practically self-sufficient before the outbreak of the war, and produced a surplus for export, but in iron and steel the country was completely dependent upon imports for many products and partially dependent for others. About one half of the total consumption of pig iron and three fourths of the consumption of steel were imported. Germany and England were two of the principal sources of supply and both were quickly and effectively cut off, the one by blockade and the other by the huge demand for iron and steel at home and by the Allies, and by the scarcity of shipping. At the outbreak of the World War, Great Britain placed an embargo on the export of iron and iron manufactures. Japan was suddenly thrown upon her own inadequate industries for her requirements of iron and steel. After the depression of the early months of the war, there was a great increase in the demand for iron and steel in the making of munitions, in shipbuilding, and in the expansion of industries. Prices mounted rapidly. The price of pig iron rose from an average of less than twenty-four dollars per ton for 1915 to $250 per ton in September 1918. There was a similar increase in the price of steel. In the meantime, there had been but little change in wages, and, since a large part of the raw materials was being delivered on long term contracts, the cost of production remained substantially at the prewar level. Profits were accordingly very high and in an industry that had always had a most precarious existence and had depended upon the government for subsidies and other forms of assistance, fabulous dividends were paid. . . . The profits of the Imperial Steel Works for the four years 1915 to 1918 were sufficient to cover the initial construction costs though the plant had had to depend upon the national treasury to meet its annual deficit in almost every year since it started operations in 1901.

To stimulate further the establishment of the steel industry and perhaps in response to the American war embargo on the export of iron and munitions, a law was promulgated by the Japanese government in July 1917 exempting newly constructed iron or steel plants from business and income taxes for a period of ten years and permitting plants with a capacity of 35,000 tons or more per year to import ores and construction materials free of duty. The existing steel plants were pushed to the very limit of their capacity and new plants were quickly built with no regard to costs of construction. In some instances, old plants were purchased in America and reerected in Japan [in the 1920s].

The Japanese steel industry of the present day is a product of the World War. Before the war, there were in Japan only eight iron and steel plants with a capacity of over 5000 tons per year and forty-two plants with a capacity of less than 5000 tons. Of the larger plants, the Imperial Steel Works, built and operated by the government, was by far the most important. It produced seventy-four percent of the pig iron output and eighty-five percent of the steel products output of the country in 1913. Many of the other plants owed their existence to government contracts for the army, navy, or railroads. By 1918, the number of the larger plants had increased to fourteen and of the smaller plants to 166, and three plants with capacities of more than 5000 tons a year had been built in Korea and Manchuria. The output of pig iron increased from 240,000 metric tons in 1913 to 583,000 tons in 1918, or by 143 percent, and the output of rolled steel, forgings, and steel castings from 255,000 tons to 550,000 tons, or by 116 percent. Though there had been an expansion of the Imperial Steel Works, the greater part of the increase in production was due to the building of private plants. The government plant in 1918 contributed only forty-six percent of the output of pig iron in Japan proper and fifty-seven percent of the output of steel products.

The expansion of industry was not checked immediately with the signing of the armistice. The impetus furnished by the World War spent itself slowly and, though a few industries fell into difficulties within a few months, the number of factory workers continued to increase through 1921, and for a time there was no interruption to the general prosperity. But the blow, though delayed, was severe when it fell. With the rehabilitation of the European industries on a peace basis and the recovery of world trade from the chaos of the war years, Asia could not remain a closed market, and Japan was forced once again to meet severe competition both in her own markets and in the Asiatic countries. It was soon evident that the recently won export markets could not be retained undiminished and that manufacturing capacity had been extended far beyond the possible demand for manufactured goods. There was a general industrial depression, and the downward trend of business was almost as precipitate as had been the rise during the war. Prosperity and generous dividends gave way to diminished output and the contraction of industry. The number of factory workers declined and did not return to the 1921 level until 1926. The output of cotton yarn remained below its high point of 1918 until 1925, and the 1919 consumption of coal was not equaled again until 1924. There were numerous failures, and other concerns were able to weather the period of distress only by resort to the most drastic measures. Appeals were made to the government for subsidies or for loans. Output was curtailed, and agreements were made for the fixing of prices. Dividends were reduced or passed, and many companies attempted to solve their financial difficulties by writing off a part of their capital cr by mergers.

ARTHUR YOUNG*
The Rice Riots of 1918

It was in little fishing villages in the province of Toyama, away from the beaten track of modern industry and commerce, that the first signs of the storm appeared, almost at once assuming their most characteristic form, raiding the shop of a rice dealer. The first raid recorded was on August fourth.

In Kobe and some lesser localities, the authorities took immediate steps to forestall "rioting," by establishing special sales of cheap rice. But there was no checking the storm which the profiteers had raised about themselves, at least until it had spent some of its fury. Printed appeals were already appearing in Kobe,

* Arthur Young, *The Socialist and Labour Movement in Japan* (Kobe, Japan: "The Japan Chronicle," 1921), pp. 25–30, 34–36.

Tokyo, and other places, composed and printed by no one knew whom, calling for militant action against the high prices, against "plutocratic despotism."

On the night of the tenth of August the big-scale outbreaks began, in Kyoto. The following night they spread to Nagoya, and on the twelfth to Osaka and Kobe. They took much the same course, the common characteristics being raids on rice shops. Dealers who agreed to dispose of their rice at more normal prices, *i.e.,* about half of those existing, were left in peace or found immediate purchasers. (The price of rice three years before had been less than twenty sen per *shō*. It had now risen to around sixty sen. As the "staff of life" of the Japanese people, its rise affected them far more than that of any other commodity.) The more obstinate merchants were sometimes beaten or stoned, and their shops usually wrecked and stocks thrown out or destroyed. Police efforts to stop the raiders were everywhere unavailing, and troops were sent for. In Osaka, Nagoya, and Kyoto there were fights with the soldiers, the mobs being armed with bamboo pikes (the traditional weapon of the Japanese mob) and with stones. Many were injured on both sides and some killed, but the trained and disciplined soldiery in all cases gained the upper hand, although at Nagoya the raiding and fighting continued night after night until early in the morning of the fourteenth.

In Kobe the damage was greatest, a mob setting fire to the offices of Suzuki & Company, the great rice wholesalers and importers, to the same company's camphor factory, to the branches of a large and intensely unpopular house agency, to the homes of two moneylenders regarded as usurers, and to the building of a local newspaper, the *Kōbe Shimbun*.

Raids and riots were reported on the twelfth, thirteenth, and fourteenth from scores of smaller cities and towns, and it was necessary to call out troops in over twenty places.

Throughout the great factory district of the Kansai, the attention of the mobs, so far as it extended beyond the rice shops, was directed to profiteers of other types, as well as to restaurants, exclusive shops, brothels, and other places guilty of catering to the expensive tastes of the *narikin* [nouveaux riches]. Little interest was shown in police boxes and government buildings. In Tokyo, however, where things began to "move" on the fourteenth, the last-named institutions came in for their share of attention, and both

324]   IMPERIAL JAPAN: 1800–1945

the Department of Agriculture and Commerce, and the Department of Communications, had their offices stoned and badly battered, while police boxes were everywhere destroyed. The riots here subsided after the sixteenth.

The gravity of the situation induced the Home Department, early on the fifteenth, to forbid any news whatever being printed about the disturbances. The united protest of the newspapers, however, brought a modification of the order the following day, when the Department agreed to issue regular official reports for publication, and the newspapers had to rest content with this.

On the sixteenth, there was a meeting of the Privy Council, which determined to take some measures to try—or at least to give the impression of trying—to bring down the price of rice, as well as of other cereals. The measures decided upon, however, which principally consisted of the commissioning of private merchants to buy rice and sell it for the government, had little or no effect on prices. . . .

In the meantime, strikes were beginning to break out. It was after the rice raids had begun to subside that strikes became almost epidemic.

Though many classes of workers were involved, the miners' strikes attracted most attention, owing to the violence involved in the struggles. They usually began with demands for wage increases, running from thirty to fifty percent, and were frequently coupled with demands for reduction in price of the commodities— usually including foodstuffs—sold them by the mining companies. Sometimes there were more radical demands including a measure of industrial control.

Mine strikes started in Fukuoka and Yamaguchi provinces on the seventeenth of August, and, upon the mine officials' declining to accede to the demands of the men, the offices were raided, as well as the residences of some of the officials, and smashed or burned. These were the characteristics of the miners' strikes throughout the epidemic.

Almost daily new strikes were reported, principally in Kyūshū. Dynamite was sometimes brought into play, and when troops were brought in there were pitched battles, with many casualties. In most cases a settlement was effected at an early date, satisfactory to the strikers, but it was well into September before the strike-wave could be said to have subsided.

Throughout the country the number of killed on both sides in the fighting, both in the "rice riots" proper and in the strike battles, reached three figures, and the injured numbered thousands. That the mobs had occasionally given a good account of themselves is shown by the Osaka police report of casualties, which claimed to be by no means complete as regards civilians (giving only ninety-two), but which mentioned 162 police and firemen, and thirty soldiers, injured in the fights.

The "transcendental" ministry of Count Terauchi, holding itself above any responsibility to the political parties, fell on September seventeenth. Ten days later Hara Takashi, the chief of the Seiyū-kai—the strongest party in the Parliament—a commoner by birth (every Japanese premier down to this time had been a nobleman), was called upon to take office as premier and organize a government.

. . . The crude methods of the raiders had, of course, succeeded immediately in getting cheap rice, and though obviously this could not have continued, the interference of the authorities on behalf of the merchants simply convinced the people that the government was in league with the profiteers, and the ineffectual attempts made by the government to bring down prices strengthened the conviction. Feeling was in no way bettered by the fact that relief funds largely found their way into the pockets of corrupt local officials and dishonest merchants, or were used for bettering the conditions of policemen.

The thousands of prosecutions, and the severe sentences served out (life imprisonment in many cases), also did much to increase feeling against the government, especially in regard to the cases of individuals whose only crime was buying rice at the forcibly reduced prices, and whose sentences sometimes ran into years.

It was made clear, however, though no intelligent person had doubted it, that the government was strong enough promptly to crush any popular revolt, and that the soldiers could be depended upon to be loyal. The police, indeed, had frequently shown themselves very half-hearted in the work of suppressing the raiders, which may be explained quite as much by hesitation to offend the populace as by secret sympathy (though the latter is explicable enough, in view of their miserable wages and bitter struggle for existence with the advancing prices). Also, thousands of the raiders and rioters were men who had served in the army or navy.

But the army itself could be depended upon. More than once during the fighting appeals had been made to the soldiers "not to fire on the people," but with no visible influence. . . .

From a practical viewpoint, the raids had failed, as far as any permanent change in conditions was concerned. It was seen that other methods must be adopted to gain any real relief. There was a greatly increased receptivity to new ideas which tried to show a way out of the difficulty, and this psychology worked in favor of the labor unionists and their movements, as well as of the radicals generally.

§ THE RICE RIOTS of 1918 and the labor unrest that followed seemed to offer a new opportunity for political organizing. Labor and socialist groups flourished together. Shaken by the rice riots, and fearful of the influence of the Russian Revolution, the government took strong action. Groups it considered dangerous were suppressed: socialists, anarcho-syndicalists, the incipient communist movement, and other farmer and labor groups. Even as the oligarchs yielded some responsibilities in the Diet to party cabinets, violent repression continued. During the 1923 Tokyo earthquake, for example, police used the pretext of maintaining order to imprison and murder numerous militants. Racial incidents against the Koreans were also particularly ugly during this period.

Moreover, the most significant reform since the constitution itself, the establishment of universal male suffrage in 1926, failed to place the Diet under truly democratic rule. Perhaps a better indication of the direction Japan was moving, the Peace Preservation Act of 1925 served to reinforce the government's repressive powers and laid the groundwork for the total suppression in the 1930s of labor and left-wing groups. Totten and Orchard explore the effects the laws and continued repression had on the still-growing labor movement.

GEORGE O. TOTTEN, III*
The New Labor and the Japanese Communists

Subjected to continuous suppression, labor remained almost completely unorganized until the time of the First World War. The one important exception was the Friendly Society (*Yūaikai*), headed by Bunji Suzuki. The society was organized by well-wishers on the outside as a mutual aid society for workers and had no pretensions of being a trade union federation until shortly after the close of the First World War.

... The war-produced spiral in prices, the work speedups, and the influence of the Russian Revolution drove labor to greater activity and self-awareness. The rice riots of 1918 dramatically revealed deep and widespread unrest, and in this setting labor's demands for higher wages increased rapidly; in 1918, 417 disputes occurred in which 66,457 workers were involved; in 1919, 497 disputes involved 63,137 workers. Though still technically illegal, labor unions increased from a scant forty in 1911 to 107 in 1918, to 187 in 1919, and to 273 in 1920. In 1919 the Friendly Society, which had started out in 1912 as a moderate welfare association based on the principle of harmony between capital and labor, transformed itself openly into a trade union federation dedicated to the fight against capital in the interests of labor. It soon adopted a name more in accord with its new outlook: the Friendly Society Greater Japan General Federation of Labor. Two years later it dropped the first three words from its (English) title.

In terms of numbers the Friendly Society had grown rapidly until it reached a plateau in 1917, hovering around 30,000 workers. In 1920 it began to grow again. Even before the change in name its goal had become industrial unionism, but since the majority of members were employed in small industry, mixed or general locals were most common. Regionalism also characterized the General Federation. A brisk rivalry developed between the Kantō and Kansai area federations; within these geographical

* George O. Totten, III, *The Social Democratic Movement in Prewar Japan* (New Haven, Conn.: Yale University Press, 1966), pp. 31–34, 42–45.

groupings and elsewhere subregional localism prevailed over industrial or craft ties. Activities included welfare, recreation, education, savings, employment exchanges, and organizing consumers'
unions, as well as negotiating or disputing with management when
warranted.

At this time the movement for universal suffrage was gaining
more support than ever and by 1919 labor was taking part in it on
a national scale. However, when the government dissolved the Diet
rather than allow a vote on the suffrage bill presented in February
1920, labor's interest cooled. The postwar depression had set in,
weakening labor's bargaining power and forcing its strategy to
change from offense to defense. After May 1920, with the defeat
of labor's campaign to obtain the right to organize, revolutionary
syndicalism, most successfully advocated by Ōsugi, pervaded the
labor movement and reached its peak in the period 1921–1923.

Although this postwar syndicalism was not essentially different
from the principles of direct action advocated by Kōtoku after the
Russo-Japanese War, it was more influential in the labor movement. Some anarcho-syndicalists were actually leading strikes
against management and struggles against police interference. The
general disillusionment with the Diet and the inability to secure
recognition of the right to organize were conducive to radicalism.

In these circumstances socialists again began to organize. The
fact that the labor movement had become more active could not
help but stimulate the surviving socialists, who again began to
make contact with one another through articles in magazines and
through meetings. In December 1920 they formed the Japan
Socialist Federation (*Nihon Shakaishugi Dōmei*), composed of all
sorts of socialists, ranging from anarchists to "Bolsheviks" and
from parliamentarians to state socialists. It included the old socialists and the new ones whose experience had begun in the World
War period. As a result, it led a stormy life, before being dissolved
by the government in May 1921.

The federation had nevertheless served to bring the veteran
socialists into close touch with the labor movement. The dominant
controversy between anarcho-syndicalism and Bolshevism took on
a new importance. The former meant the use of nonpolitical,
economic direct action by way of spontaneous strikes, building up
eventually to the "general strike" which would achieve workers'
control over production. It deemphasized organization in favor of

courageous action by leaders even in the face of violence. In opposition to this, what was known as Bolshevism in the Japanese labor movement at that time meant an emphasis on building strong labor organizations, uniting them with close ties, appealing for public support in labor disputes, and linking up labor demands with political issues. The Japan General Federation of Labor (the former Friendly Society) championed this type of Bolshevism since it was in line with the General Federation's aspiration to rally all the other unions to its ranks.

The conflict between anarcho-syndicalism and Bolshevism came to a head on September 30, 1922, when the syndicalists failed in their attempt to organize a loose general alliance of all the important unions on the basis of independent union autonomy. The failure was due to the opposition of the General Federation which held out for its alternative proposal for a strong federation of disciplined unions operating under centralized direction. After that the tide of anarcho-syndicalism began to recede rapidly.

It had been a grave blunder for the anarchists to adopt tactics of the offensive during a period of recession when the workers were at a disadvantage. Many syndicalist unions had thus been utterly wiped out and workers had turned away from them. The police hounded and harassed the anarchist leaders to such an extent, because of their involvement with violence, that their effectiveness was greatly impaired. Abroad, especially in Italy where it had been an important force, anarchism had met serious setbacks, convincing Japanese anarchists that they were on the wrong track. In the meanwhile, the Russian Bolsheviks appeared to be successfully defending their revolution in the largest nation on earth.

. . . Yamakawa elaborated on the slogan of the 1921 Third Comintern Congress, "to the masses," which implicitly called for utilizing all the bourgeois freedoms and institutions, however limited they might be, in order to reach the masses. What Yamakawa said to his Japanese audience, in effect, was that up to now the Japanese proletarian movement had been characterized by a small group of "advanced" activists who spent their efforts defining their goals and refining their theories but in so doing had left the main contingents of the working class behind. The time had now come for the minority of socialists to return to the masses armed with their advanced theoretical formulations. Only if the movement discovered what the immediate demands of the masses were and helped to secure them could it hope to win their strong support. "We must represent the present interests of the masses, improve their livelihood, and proceed with partial victories," urged Yamakawa. "The boycotting of politics is a negative tactic, while resistance through the political process is a positive one."

Although the communists at this time remained a small group, unable to implement the slogan, the appeal was well timed for it verbalized what many in the socialist movement were already thinking. Despite official censorship, this "change of direction" statement became widely known and had far-reaching repercussions.

Behind it lay the extremism that had characterized the various social movements during the preceding three years. The growing number of strikes in 1918 and 1919 were generally mildly successful, especially the "ca'canny" (go-slow) strikes at the Kawasaki and Osaka ironworks, but they gradually became more and more defensive in 1920 and 1921. Perhaps the most symbolic was the tense dispute at the Kawasaki dockyards in Kobe, led by Toyohiko Kagawa from June to August 1921. Kagawa worked out a plan for workers' control of the yards based on the idea that it was a shame and a waste to stop production when a strike occurred. But the more radical elements saw this as a step toward abolition of the capitalist system and felt that the revolution in Japan was at hand. Alarmed, the government called in troops to break the system of workers' control. The strike ended in a crushing defeat for the workers with Kagawa and other leaders under arrest. . . .

The government's stepping in portended both a change in the government's tactics from a somewhat neutralist position with regard to strikes to an aggressive policy for crushing the leftists. The strong action by the government also raised doubts in the minds of those who believed the revolution would soon occur. The failure of this strike helped to convince many that direct action alone was ineffective and that political means must also be adopted. Liberals had long been pressing for universal suffrage, but now those who had come to think of themselves as Marxists took the lead in calling for the creation of a centralized, unified, political movement to press for and take advantage of the vote.

Before the newly formed Communist party could make itself known within the labor and agrarian movements on its own terms, most of its leaders were rounded up in a surprise mass arrest of about a hundred people on June 5, 1923. Since the authorities gave out little information regarding the background of the action, some newspapers played up sensational stories alleging that the Special Higher Police had stumbled upon a plot to assassinate the whole Japanese government and set up a communist dictatorship by *coup d'état*. It is difficult to know what was the precise effect on the public of this sudden exposure of the fact that a communist party had been formed. But the lack of details given out by the authorities probably induced both the sympathetic and the horrified to exaggerate the strength of the newly organized communist movement. The long-range results were both a tightening of police surveillance and an increase in the number of people who came forward to dedicate themselves to the direct or indirect service of the communist movement, as evidenced in its rapid subsequent growth.

The immediate results of the arrests of the communists in May and the ensuing newspaper publicity given to radical activities were the terroristic attacks against radicals and minority groups in the confusion and disorder following the disastrous earthquake of September 1, 1923, which wrought havoc in the industrial centers of Tokyo and Kanagawa prefectures. Amid the smoke, fire, and ruin, hysterical mobs, incensed with racial hatred and whipped up by the recent newspaper campaigns against "subversion," massacred possibly as many as several thousand Koreans and hundreds of Chinese. Scores of socialists, anarchists, communists, and radical labor leaders were locked up by the police "as a security measure." Some were tortured, some expelled from the Tokyo area, which had been placed under martial law. At the Kamedo police station eight alleged communist leaders of the Nankatsu labor union and one from another union were shot to death, while in another police cell in Tokyo the anarcho-syndicalist leader, Sakae Ōsugi, his wife, Noe Itō, who was a well-known advocate of women's rights, and his seven-year-old nephew were all strangled to death by Captain Amakasu of the gendarmerie.

JOHN ORCHARD*
Government Suppression of the Labor Movement

. . . So persistent have been the efforts of the government to suppress the movement that the antagonism of the employing class and their methods of combating unionism have taken second place in considerations of union policy. The government has been the chief opponent of the movement. From the very beginning, it has opposed the development of labor unions, and, whenever a union has become at all powerful or radical or in any way troublesome, it has been dissolved by the government forthwith.

The police of Japan are national, not local, and are employed as a national body to keep constant watch for "dangerous thought," for the government of Japan is very autocratic. The police attend all labor meetings. They watch the movements of labor leaders. Disguised as students, they attend the classes of liberal professors of economic thought. They report to the Home Minister on the activities of anyone and everyone who shows any interest in Japanese labor and Japanese labor unions.

The police of Japan are national, not local, and are employed as the offices of labor unions and search for radical literature. They frequently prevent meetings where it is thought the speeches will be "dangerous thought" and break up those that do not conform to their thought standards. At May Day celebrations in the large cities, police officers sit on the platforms at the mass meetings, not as honored guests, but in order that they may censor each speaker as he speaks. When the discourse verges on "dangerous thought," the speaker is silenced and his address brought to a sudden close. Some speakers are allowed to proceed to the end of their talks, but others are stopped in the midst of their opening sentences. Many thousands of arrests of workers and leaders are made every year for sundry activities in the cause of unionism. Constant police

* John Orchard, *Japan's Economic Position—The Progress of Industrialization* (New York: McGraw-Hill/Whittlesey House, 1930), pp. 390–392.

supervision and government suppression attend the labor movement of Japan.

In the fall of 1926, thirty-seven students of the leading universities and colleges were indicted and arrested for "dangerous thought." It was said that they were involved in a nationwide plot for the study and propagation of social theories. Chief among the charges against the students was an alleged attempt to transmit a message to a Russian workers' delegate when he passed through Kyoto on his way home from Tokyo. This action was regarded by the police as the first attempt to internationalize the movement. It was never brought out that the students had done anything more than organize clubs for the study of social sciences on a national scale and collect some radical literature on changing the social system, educating the proletariat, and opposing military training in the schools. The arrests were made in December 1925 and preliminary trials given, but the whole affair was kept from the public by an official ban on the news until the formal indictment in September 1926. The thirty-seven boy students were dismissed from their universities and were under arrest for nearly ten months before they came to public trial for their offenses.

Following the first general election under the Universal Manhood Suffrage Act in February 1928, 1000 workers and intellectuals were arrested as communists. News of these arrests was banned until April. It was then declared that the police had uncovered a nationwide communist plot. The evidence of the plot was based largely on literature distributed during the election campaign and found in raids upon political labor and union headquarters. The Japanese press openly inferred that it was less of a communist plot than a political maneuver on the part of the Seiyūkai, the governing party, to turn public attention from certain autocratic acts by its leaders at the time of the election. The press refused to take seriously the charge of any national danger from the activities of a handful of powerless communist agitators. Many of the arrested persons were later released for lack of evidence, but hundreds were committed for further trial. In April 1930, two years after their arrest, thirty-five of the 1000 alleged communists were notified to prepare themselves for public trial. Of the thirty-five, thirteen had been released on bail, but the remaining twenty-two had spent their two years of waiting in prison.

These are two spectacular instances of the government's active opposition to the development of social movements, but in their ordinary day-to-day activities the labor unions are in almost continuous conflict with the police. Arrests of union members, student agitators, and labor leaders are almost daily occurrences.

Following the spectacular round-up of April 9, 1928, the Home Office decided to appropriate 2,300,000 yen ($1,150,000) to provide a special bureau not only to deal with radical activities in Japan itself, but to study the methods of and cooperate with those engaged in the suppression of communism in other countries. For this purpose, special commissioners were dispatched to Peking, Harbin, London, and Berlin. Within the country, extremist organizations were suppressed; social study groups were abolished or forced to curtail their activities; liberal and radical university professors were dismissed from their posts; and scores of girl and boy students were arrested for belonging to social science clubs. The Labor–Farmer party of the left, the Council of Japanese Labor which was the left wing of the labor movement, and the League of Proletariat Youth were dissolved by government order.

Finally, on June 29, 1928, a special edition of the *Official Gazette* promulgated an emergency Imperial ordinance in order to provide heavier penalties, including capital punishment, for radical plotting against the constitution and the political system of Japan. The Imperial ordinance revised the Peace Preservation Act of 1925, which fixed the maximum penalty at ten years imprisonment, and provided in its stead punishment ranging from confinement for not less than five years, with or without grace, to capital punishment for those who organize secret associations with the aim of changing the fundamental national constitution, or for leaders of such organizations. The lesser punishments are for those who form or even join secret associations with the aim of destroying the system of individual property ownership. It is specifically provided that the punishment apply also to the attempted cases of the offenses specified.

The Imperial ordinance raised a storm of protest, not alone from labor and farmer unions, but from all liberal bodies and from the Japanese press in general. As it was promulgated when the Diet was not in session, it required the approval of the Diet when it reconvened in order to become a permanent law. It was generally hoped that this approval would not be granted, but that hope was

soon dissipated when the revised law received *de facto* recognition
at the next session of the Diet. Immediately following the Imperial
ordinance, many arrests were made secretly under the provisions
of the new law.

5. *The Twenties and Beyond*

⊛ THE TWENTIES in Japan began inauspiciously with the collapse of the World War I economic boom. If one accepts the "Roaring Twenties" as a label for the American economy in this period, the "Sputtering Twenties" fits Japan.

Initially, the Japanese yen was undervalued in the world money market, causing an unfavorable balance of payments. Inflation, exacerbated by easy credit policies of banks, continued. The 1923 Tokyo earthquake worsened all these situations. Furthermore, since the economy—both the urban *and* rural sectors—was progressively more integrated into the world market, price fluctuations were felt painfully at all levels. Finally, in 1929 a poorly timed deflationary policy was compounded by the effects of the American 1929 crash. In the countryside, real rural income fell one third between 1925 and 1930, worsening already difficult rural conditions. William Lockwood discusses the financial disorder of the period, especially as it affected and was affected by the zaibatsu—the gigantic conglomerates of Japan.

WILLIAM LOCKWOOD*
Japan's Economy in Transition

The armistice of November 1918 signaled the approaching end of Japan's war boom. As in other countries, economic activity was

* William Lockwood, *The Economic Development of Japan* (Princeton, N.J.: Princeton University Press, 1954), pp. 42–43, 59–63.

maintained at a high level for another year under the influence of a continuing spiral of inflation. The break in Japan came in March 1920, heralding the worldwide collapse a few months later. There followed a period of deflation and readjustment. From this financial crisis Japan recovered rather more quickly than most countries, owing to the liberal credit and subsidy policies of the government. With the return to "normalcy," however, she now faced again the problem of finding peacetime economic opportunities for her rapidly growing millions, a problem temporarily obscured in the flush of war prosperity.

The postwar decade registered only modest progress toward this long-term goal, though it did witness the consolidation and extension of the industrial advance of the war period. It was, first of all, a decade of marked financial instability. The inflated cost structure of the war years remained to complicate postwar adjustment, in Japan as elsewhere. Before much headway had been made in this direction the great earthquake of 1923 dealt a shattering blow. Some 100,000 lives were lost in the fires which swept great cities like Tokyo and Yokohama. Property destruction was estimated at 3.1 to 5.5 billion yen. A reconstruction boom developed in the wake of the catastrophe, but this led into a banking crisis in 1927. Certain sectors of the economy—notably the silk industry—shared in world prosperity induced by boom conditions in the United States. Others failed to do so. The gains were spotty and irregular, and economic opportunity hardly kept pace with the large number of new job seekers pouring into the labor market each year as the population grew. Japan was now reaping some of the disadvantages as well as the advantages of industrialism—dependence upon an unstable world economy, growing class conflicts and social strains, and all the difficulties that go with the maintenance of growth and equilibrium in an industrializing economy. . . .

Confronted with major decisions in the field of economic policy, however, the party governments of the twenties were inclined to vacillate and compromise. Perhaps it was for the very reason that national politics now represented more adequately the diversity of interests and classes in Japan. In this respect the situation in Japan was not unique. But here the issues were peculiarly urgent, as subsequent events showed all too clearly. When the great depression descended in 1930–1931, an acute crisis set in. The history of the thirties, in both its military and economic aspects, was in some degree a delayed response to the pressures building up in the preceding decade. . . .

Concentration of Controls. The financial disorder of this period appears to have been traceable in some degree to the power and independence of Japan's great business combines, the zaibatsu. At the same time it tended to concentrate economic control still further in their hands. The zaibatsu held an important position in Japanese banking and finance, but their interests in early postwar years were still predominantly industrial. G. C. Allen, a close student of this period, concludes that these interests led them to resist the deflationary policy which seems to have been called for on technical, financial grounds. Their opposition was the more effective because of their influence with the Diet and the bureaucracy, and their comparative independence from central bank control. Yet the government authorities, with few exceptions, appear to have shared with business circles a persistent bias in favor of cheap money and liberal lending through most of the period after 1868. . . .

These great family combines grew steadily in size and power during the war and postwar years. Already dominant in the more modern sectors of the Japanese economy, they now extended their control indirectly over an increasing share of small-scale commerce and manufacturing. Through an intricate, pyramided structure of intercorporate, personal, and political ties, the larger combines, notably Mitsui and Mitsubishi, developed into huge agglomerations of heterogeneous enterprise—trading, shipping, banking, insurance, real estate, mining, manufacturing, and colonial undertakings. . . . [T]his concentration of control had been facilitated from the beginning by close association with the military oligarchy and the civil bureaucracy, and also by the complete absence of antitrust laws and other public restraints on the exercise and perpetuation of monopolistic power such as developed in the United States and England with the growth of the corporate device. Now it was accelerated by postwar financial difficulties like the bank crisis of 1927. These eliminated thousands of smaller and weaker concerns which were less well equipped than the zaibatsu companies to take losses, cut costs, and readjust to the new situation.

The decade of the twenties witnessed a large reduction in the number of small banks. While aggregate bank deposits increased by one quarter from 1920 to 1929, the number of banks declined from 2041 to 1008. Financial power came to be centered increasingly in a handful of great private banks and trust companies, along with semiofficial institutions like the Bank of Japan, Industrial Bank, and Yokohama Specie Bank, in which the former also had influential representation. These private banks with their numerous branches were largely owned or controlled by the zaibatsu. Their key position in the Japanese economy was enhanced by the typically close relations between commercial banks and industrial concerns in Japan. The absence of a capital market for public issues made the banks the chief external source of private capital for business firms. The zaibatsu banks were also relatively free from bank inspection and other forms of government regulation. Tied in as they were with all sorts of affiliated concerns, they were powerful instruments for eliminating and absorbing their smaller competitors and those of their sister companies. Thus they served steadily to extend the dominion of the family partnerships or holding companies at the top of the combines.

Probably no other modern industrial society organized on the basis of private property has offered a comparable display of the unrestrained "power of bigness," employing all the devices of monopolistic control. The single qualification—and an important one—would seem to be the comparative rarity of actual market monopolies in individual products. Usually two or more of the giant combines were found in more or less active rivalry with each other and sometimes with a host of small producers. The same combines, however, tended to dominate a number of fields of industry and trade. This situation of oligopoly probably encouraged the maintenance of prices and profits above the level to which they would have been reduced by a more atomistic type of competition. As a group, in any case, the zaibatsu and their satellites dominated the more modern sector of the Japanese economy. With controls ramifying outwards from their nuclei of great financial, industrial, and trading concerns, they presented the most extreme contrast to the small-scale pattern of organization which persisted in agriculture and even in a large proportion of Japanese manufacturing and commerce. . . .

The institution of the zaibatsu contributed greatly to the rapid accumulation of capital and modernization of technology which underlay Japan's industrial development. It enabled Japan to reap certain economies of large-scale organization, even where the production unit remained small; it placed the direction of large sectors of the economy in the hands of able technicians and executives employed by the combines; it afforded a device by which industrial investment was accelerated through the plowing back of huge profits accruing to the owners.

On the other hand, if the concentration of control in Japanese industry and finance was progressive in these technical aspects, its social aspects were less admirable. It was one of the factors perpetuating inequalities of income and opportunity in modern Japan almost as wide as those of feudal times. It carried over into modern industry the tradition of hierarchical status and authoritarian control which was inimical to political and social democracy. By hampering the pervasive growth of independence and individual initiative in economic life it reinforced other circumstances militating against the emergence of a broad and sturdy middle class, or a vigorous trade union movement. And in politics the plutocratic alliance of the zaibatsu and the political parties contributed eventually to the defeat and discrediting of parliamentary government after 1930.

It is widely assumed today that the introduction of modern technology to raise the productive power of "backward" peoples will itself bring democracy and peace. Japan's experience hardly supports this thesis—even over a span of fifty years. For she acquired modern industrialism without a corresponding growth of liberal movements such as have emerged in countries with a more democratic tradition to harness this power in pursuit of welfare goals. The latter trend was by no means absent in the prewar years, to be sure. In the twenties especially, Japanese liberalism asserted itself with increasing vigor despite the heritage of authoritarian government so firmly entrenched in the Constitution of 1889. However, its power base remained essentially weak, and its programs compromised by the interests of the business oligarchy. In the end it proved inadequate to withstand the resurgence of the military after 1931. For this there are many reasons, including the impact of the forces let loose in the outside world by the Great Depression. But one major explanation is to be found in the realm of economic organization. Here both tradition and circumstance combined to concentrate controls over wide sectors of industry, commerce, and finance, and prevented the creation of a firm economic foundation for political and social democracy.

Collapse of the Yen. In concluding this narrative of the twenties, it remains only to record the events which brought the decade to a dramatic close. With the advantage of hindsight it is possible to see the onset, as far back as 1926, of the deflationary pressures which were to reach a climax in the world depression of 1929–1932. Following the bank crisis of 1927, however, the Japanese economy seemed financially in a sounder position than before. Manufacturing and trading activity was buoyed up in the two succeeding years by easy money conditions and by prosperity abroad, especially in the United States. Industrial production rose twenty-three percent from 1926 to 1929, and exports almost in proportion.

The Minseitō government which assumed office in 1929 thereupon determined, under the leadership of its finance minister, the vigorous Mr. J. Inoue, that greater exchange stability and prestige should be sought through returning to the gold standard at the old parity. It prepared itself to undertake whatever measures of retrenchment were necessary to this end. Accordingly, government expenditures were cut, and industry was encouraged to cut costs through rationalization measures. In January 1930 the gold embargo was lifted.

The moment could hardly have been more inopportune for stabilization along orthodox lines. The return to gold would doubtless have called for some deflation in any event, as Japanese domestic prices were still relatively high. But now world commodity prices had already begun their steep descent from postwar levels. This greatly intensified the deflationary strain in Japan. Wholesale prices, having already declined twenty percent from the end of 1925 to the end of 1929, proceeded to drop another twenty percent in the next twelve months. Agricultural staples, notably rice and silk, fell even more precipitately under the influences of shrinking monetary demand and a series of bumper crops.

As previously observed, the impact upon the rural population was calamitous. From 1925 to 1930, according to surveys of the Department of Agriculture and Forestry, gross income per agricultural household declined forty to forty-five percent. Net income after deducting working expenses shrank by one half or more. The farmer's cost of living meantime declined only twenty-six percent. Thus his real income, meager in the best of times, was reduced by something like one third.

In Japan's balance of payments the repercussions were also serious. With the removal of the gold embargo early in 1930 gold exports were resumed. They far exceeded Mr. Inoue's expectations. The bottom dropped out of the export market as the value of exports declined fifty percent from 1929 to 1931, again mainly as a result of the collapse of prices.

❀ DURING THE 1920s, four groups were involved in governmental decision-making: the bureaucrats, the parties, the zaibatsu, and the military. Although protest movements from the left forced a few reforms, such as expanded suffrage, the elite nature of decision-making continued behind a democratic façade. Further, the policies of the shifting cabinets failed to ameliorate the mounting economic distress. By the end of the decade, as depression deepened at home and "moderate" policies on the continent were not safeguarding the privileges the Japanese elite felt to be essential, criticism of the government increased from all sides.

T. A. BISSON*
Japan as a Political Organism

The Japanese political system, as it has existed since the Constitution of 1889, defies any simple or easy characterization. Its complexity derives primarily from the fact that it is an amalgam of feudal, theocratic, and democratic elements. While each element possesses an institutional structure and mode of operation of its own, the whole system or the net political outcome at any given time is constituted by the interaction of all three. Perhaps the most basic—and most disastrous—error of appraisal in the past has been the failure to recognize that the feudal and theocratic elements, rather than the democratic, have represented the determining motivation and source of authority for the total system.

* T. A. Bisson, "Japan as a Political Organism," *Pacific Affairs* 17 (December 1944), pp. 393–398, 400–401.

Democratic forces that were attempting to express themselves in the twenties, and for a time seemed to be succeeding, were in reality held in careful leading strings by the dominant groups. . . .

. . . The controlling force in modern Japanese politics has never expressed itself exclusively through a single group. No one political vehicle through which power is solely conducted exists in Japan or can exist there under the present system. . . . Not the dominance of one group interest but the accommodation of several, all within a single dictatorial coalition, is the typical expression of the Japanese system.

Political decisions are reached and effectuated through a consensus which takes into account the opinions and reflects the immediate and continuing shifts in power of four main groups: the bureaucrats (including those surrounding the emperor), the military services, the business interests, and the party leaders. Normally, each of these four groups occupies a well-defined sphere within the cabinet or the administration as a whole. When the coalition is "in balance," the distribution of cabinet portfolios follows a conventional pattern. The military leaders hold the army and navy ministries, and no others. This is in addition, of course, to the general staffs and other organs of the supreme command. The business interests will occupy one or more of the economic portfolios, typically the Finance and the Commerce and Industry ministries. The party leaders are likely to hold at least two of the following four: Railways, Communications, Agriculture and Forestry, and Interior. . . . Except for the Foreign Ministry, the cabinet posts held by the bureaucrats are not so clearly defined, being scattered among the economic portfolios and occasionally including the Home Ministry. Outside the cabinet, however, the important offices in the Imperial household, as well as the presidency of the Privy Council, form a normal preserve of the bureaucrats.

An access of strength to one group enables it to assume greater power and thus to encroach on the administrative spheres customarily held by the others. . . .

So closely are the shifts in relative strength among the several groups reflected in the administration that it becomes possible to trace the interaction even within a single cabinet, especially if it holds office for a long term. . . . While this "style" of operation gives rise to oscillations of political influence, with continual shifts in favor of one group or another, the underlying tendency is always for the correction of extreme deviations. The political pendulum, in other words, tends basically to swing back into the balance which represents for each group its generally accepted sphere of administrative control. Extremes are avoided. Neither the absolute supremacy nor the final liquidation of any one group is tolerated. The coalition strives as a whole to buttress its dictatorship at home and to press Japan's "manifest destiny" overseas. The political norm, toward which it always reverts, is a "golden mean" under which each group is allotted its appropriate field of authority.

. . . No one of these Japanese groups is inherently moderate or extremist. Moderates and extremists are found in all four groups. Japan's interests, or the interests of the ruling coalition, can be better preserved at one time under an alignment essentially moderate or at another essentially extremist. . . .

Disagreements do arise within the coalition, and these disagreements lead to sharp controversy. The point to be stressed is that the political mechanism is effectively adjusted to absorb the shocks of the competing groups. A pronounced feature of the system . . . is its flexibility, enabling shifts in the equilibrium of the ruling groups to be easily and quickly registered in the cabinet alignment or in other agencies of the Imperial regime.

. . . Each group is intent on increasing its power within the coalition, on maximizing its economic advantages, on limiting the cost which it must bear of any common effort. These are conflicts incident to any coalition of diverse groups. Under conditions of extreme stress, the strife might become so intense as to disrupt the coalition and destroy its political effectiveness. Thus far in Japan's modern history, even in cases of such extreme friction as to lead to assassination and armed uprising, there has been no break in political continuity. After each crisis the ruling coalition has immediately reformed on a new basis and continued to operate in the old way. . . .

Up to the present, disagreements leading to crisis in Japan have as a rule been intra-coalition disagreements. The single exception that comes to mind is that of the "rice riots" of 1918. In this case the dictatorial position of the coalition was temporarily shaken by a threat coming from a force wholly outside it—that is, the Japanese people. Here, of course, is one of the main centripetal influences acting upon the coalition. The four groups are unitedly determined that their ruling position at home should not be overthrown by popular forces striving to attain genuine democratic rights. Their system is intrinsically authoritarian and undemocratic. All decisions that matter are made by a relatively small group operating behind the scenes and not amenable to popular control. Even an overwhelming popular mandate can be disregarded and swept into the ashcan by the groups in control, as has happened more than once. Intra-coalition struggles must obviously be subordinated to the overriding necessity of maintaining the dictatorial system as a whole.

... A Japanese "moderate" is not a pacifist, nor a good internationalist, nor is he opposed to Japanese aggrandizement. He is rather more cautious than the "extremist" and may differ over the incidentals of timing and tactic, yet he is thoroughly willing to move his pins forward on the map when additional territory has been occupied. In the past his most useful role has been in the Foreign Office when the army was running amok, since he could then act as polite screen, apologist, and general scapegoat. It may yet be shown that he can perform an even more effective job when it comes to obtaining the best possible peace after a disastrous war. . . .

In its flexibility and tensile strength Japan's political system is akin to a living organism. Its intrinsic authoritarianism is the product of continually repeated adjustments made by businessmen and the militarists, bureaucrats and the party leaders. In this group dictatorship, no one man can set himself up as the undisputed and all powerful dictator. The leader at any given moment registers the net group adjustment and functions as the temporary representative of the existing balance of power within the coalition. His position is as impermanent as the shifting basis of the successive intra-coalition adjustments, in response to the declining strength of one group or the growing power of another. The emperor, not the premier, is the center of the system. As a real functionary, and as an ideological symbol of overpowering importance, the emperor occupies the key position in the regime. He is the crucial element in the whole apparatus of rule through which the coalition maintains the unity and permanence of its group dictatorship. Beside him even a Tōjō fades into relative insignificance and can be hustled off the political stage without ceremony. The system makes a new adjustment, places another temporary leader in power, and continues to operate in its accustomed manner.

IV.

*Depression, Militarism,
and War
1929–1945*

✿ DURING THE 1930s the increasing tensions in the newly industrialized Japanese state were subsumed in military adventures abroad which culminated in war with China and the United States. "Fascism," "ultranationalism," and "militarism" are terms often used to contrast this period with the 1920s. Yet behind the emotionally charged words lies a debate central to understanding these years. Were the late teens and 1920s a time of rapidly emerging democratic forces which were thwarted in the 1930s? Was the increased diversification of Japanese society in the 1920s—the modern intelligentsia, industrial workers, a salaried white-collar class—reflected in progressive reforms and the growing strength of the Populist party? Or did the reforms represent little change in the essentially authoritarian political system established in the Constitution of 1889, and no fundamental move toward genuinely democratic institutions?

By and large, there is little evidence of a trend in the 1920s toward the extension of political and economic power to the Japanese people themselves or to a truly representative Diet. Although the political parties increased their power, they acted in support of zaibatsu interests, not as representatives of any popular movements. Universal male suffrage was granted in 1925, but in the same year the government passed the notorious Peace Preservation Law which it used to repress groups it regarded as too far to the left. General prosperity was marred by the catastrophic Tokyo earthquake of 1923 and growing rural poverty.

The worldwide depression beginning in 1929 was intensified in Japan by low rice prices following a series of bumper crops and the collapse of the international silk market. But after the initial shock during 1930–1932, big business recovered rapidly, largely because of a government-sponsored export campaign. Japanese leaders were sensitive to the threatened collapse of the world economic system, on which Japan depended for both customers and raw materials. Like other nations, however, Japan sought to protect its own interests, even though this led to increased economic protectionism and political competition among the principal industrial powers.

Under the impact of the Depression and Japan's growing military involvement on the Asian mainland, government repression of dissenting groups and political parties increased. The relative tolerance of the early 1920s gave way by the mid-1930s to attacks on labor unions and peasant tenant unions and harsh restrictions on political activities. Moreover, the stability of the political system was threatened throughout the mid-thirties by assassinations of prominent politicians and business leaders, and the military seemed to be gaining control. These are the events frequently characterized as the beginning of Japanese fascism.

The decline of parliamentary institutions and the suppression of labor and the left in the late 1930s, after the war with China was well underway, did represent a step away from the political climate of the previous decade. But to use the term "fascist" would imply a radical change in policy, a shift of power into the hands of an extreme rightist element, as in Germany or Italy. Yet Japan never had a popular rightist movement, and even the military cabinets, which took power after the assassination of Prime Minister Inukai in 1932, and embarked on military adventures abroad, instituted few policies at home that broke sharply with the past.

Indeed, the Japanese invasion of China was a plausible outcome of the imperialist ideas about foreign policy held by the Meiji oligarchy. Since Japan began to industrialize, its leaders had believed that economic expansion beyond its borders for markets and raw materials was the necessary companion to industrialization at home. This consensus on the need for empire, a consensus with deep historical roots, defined the framework of Japanese policy-making until the end of World War II.

Northern China, Manchuria, and Korea had a prominent role in plans for the economic and military security of this empire. Physically close to Japan and a barrier between it and the Soviet Union, the area had the raw materials essential for heavy industry, which Japan lacked. Japan's interest in this area was evident even before the 1930s. Both the Sino-Japanese War of 1894–1895 and the Russo-Japanese War of 1904–1905 were fought to secure and protect a special position there.

As the decade of the 1920s drew to a close, Japan's efforts to expand its position in northern China conflicted sharply with the rise in Chinese nationalism and the gradual unification of China under the leadership of Chiang Kai-shek. While Chinese resistance was making a more active role in China difficult, the Depression, coupled with reluctant Japanese acquiescence in armament agreements and the 1930 London Conference, created pressures for a more aggressive stance. Economic anxieties emphasized the importance of Japanese interests in Manchuria and northern China, and military incidents in 1931 provoked the Japanese occupation of Manchuria, followed by the setting up of the puppet state of Manchukuo. This move into an area that had long been a part of China forced a direct confrontation with the Chinese and led to a continuing series of military clashes and diplomatic maneuvers culminating in the outbreak of full-scale war between China and Japan in 1937.

Yet in the opinion of historians today and Japanese leaders at the time, it was the decision to enter war with the United States that ultimately doomed Japan to defeat. A large part of the Japanese army was bogged down in an exhausting land war with China, where guerrilla warfare made any kind of clear military victory virtually impossible, and Japan's strategic position was weak because it was partly or wholly dependent on Western nations for many important natural resources. The need for fuel oil, for example, became critical after the American ban on export of war matériel to Japan in 1941. Finally, isolated politically and economically and forced to decide between war and probable defeat or surrender of its empire, Japan went to war.

The war was a catastrophe for Japan, but it did not affect all segments of society equally. The influence of military leaders declined after the battlefield situation deteriorated, but the bureaucracy and the zaibatsu remained active during the war, and business in particular consolidated its position. In one respect, however, all Japanese suffered alike: at the end of the war industry was in flames, the cities were bombed, and the people were on the verge of starvation.

1. Political Economy, 1929–1936

JAPAN IN 1929 faced the onset of the depression as one of the leading powers of Asia. She had entered World War I on the side of the Allies, taking the opportunity to seize German concessions in China. Japan also joined the Allied intervention in Siberia, thus taking an early anti-Bolshevik position. In the 1920s Japan's pursuit of her economic and political interests was carried out without resorting to war. She made agreements restricting naval strength with the Western powers and cooperated with them on matters relating to China. Meanwhile, Japan's economic interests in Manchuria were growing, and the Kwantung Army—the Japanese army stationed there to protect Japanese investments and railroads—felt that a more aggressive or "positive" policy should be undertaken. The goal was to obtain a guarantee for Japan's special position in Manchuria. Those for and those against a more aggressive policy were, however, agreed that Japan should have imperialist privileges on the continent that infringed on Chinese sovereignty; they differed only on the appropriate means to secure these concessions from the unwilling Chinese.

The men making foreign policy in Japan accepted imperialism as a basic assumption, and this fact gives continuity to the shift toward "fascism" in the early 1930s. It is often argued that extreme militarists took over the government during this period, dragging Japan into a disastrous war. The empirical basis for this view lies in the Manchurian Incident of 1931 and in a succession of extreme rightist coup attempts and assassinations culminating in the rebellion of February 26, 1936.

On September 18, 1931, officers of the Kwantung Army in Manchuria escalated a small incident into a large expansion of the territory they controlled. The following March, the cabinet approved the establishment of a puppet state there, called Manchukuo. Under attack for this policy in the League of Nations, Japan pulled out of the League, an act which symbolized her break with the policy of cooperation with the other imperialist nations such as Britain and the United States.

During early 1932, immediately after the Manchurian Incident, there was a string of assassinations by a rightist group of young officers which came to a head in May when Prime Minister Inukai . . . was killed. These incidents were followed by others, including the February 1936 rebellion in Tokyo during which a military unit in the Japanese capital seized various government buildings in the city, hoping to take over the government; but after killing several government officials the rebels surrendered on request of the emperor. This was the sign for a wholesale purge of such troublesome radicals inside the military services, and the often violent politics of rightist military groups died down.

Even before the Japanese military rose to prominence in the 1930s, other groups, mostly on the political right, were advocating with equal vigor an expansionist role for Japan on the Asian mainland. Among the most famous of these right-wing, nationalistic societies were the Genyōsha, named for the strait separating Korea and Japan, and the Kokuryūkai, which took its name from the Amur River dividing Manchuria from the Soviet Far East. The history of the Genyōsha, whose roots go back to the early Meiji era, and the career of its famous leader Tōyama Mitsuru are discussed here by E. H. Norman, writing in 1944. Such societies not only had considerable influence inside the government and the military, but were themselves actively involved in expansionist activities in China and Korea: the Genyōsha and other such groups thus were important components both of imperialism and of the domestic movements to the right during the 1930s.

E. H. NORMAN*
The Genyōsha: A Study in the Origins of Japanese Imperialism

MODERN JAPANESE politics conform to categories different from those of the West. This does not mean that Japanese politics are so incomparable or opaque that they can resist the analytical scrutiny of a political scientist. But social and economic forces which run parallel to those in Western countries have expressed themselves in Japan in different political forms, whether it be the constitutional development or the role and activities of political parties. One of the most elusive yet characteristic features of political life in Japan since the restoration of 1868 has been the activities of the so-called patriotic societies, the prototypes of which are the Genyōsha (Dark Ocean Society) and its offshoot, the Kokuryūkai (Black Dragon Society). It is difficult to find an adjective or phrase which accurately describes them. They are sometimes termed "secret societies," but this is misleading since secret societies scarcely publish their own official histories or the biographies of their leading members. "Reactionary" is at once too broad and negative a term for such dynamic groups as the Genyōsha or the Kokuryūkai, which in the past half century or more have spawned numerous societies concerned primarily with advancing the cause of Japanese imperialism. In order not to be drawn into a too elaborate and perhaps barren theoretical discussion, and for the sake of convenience, these societies will simply be described as "extreme nationalist" or "reactionary," although it should be understood that such terms are merely convenient labels and by no means adequate. . . .

The city of Fukuoka in Kyūshū is separated from the Asiatic mainland by narrow seas known in Japanese as the *genkainada*. Fukuoka is the closest Japanese approach to the Continent. Today it is the center of a huge munitions industry, the terminal for air lines linking Japan to the Continent, and an embarkation point for

  * E. H. Norman, "The Genyōsha: A Study in the Origins of Japanese Imperialism," *Pacific Affairs* XVII (Sept. 1944), pp. 261–284.

troops en route to China. It is a city where in recent years few foreigners have been permitted even to alight from the train.

But Fukuoka is more than a strategic center for the Japanese
war machine; it is the spiritual home of the most rabid brand of
Japanese nationalism and imperialism. Because of its history and
geographical location Fukuoka has been the starting point for all
Japanese efforts to secure foothold on the Continent, beginning
with the semilegendary invasion of Korea by the Empress Jingū.
The district about Fukuoka was the chief target of the Mongol
invasions of 1274 and 1281, and it was the main base for Hideyoshi's armadas in his invasions of Korea in 1592 and following
years; finally it was the chief base of naval operations during the
Russo-Japanese War. In comparatively modern times it has produced more men who have concerned themselves with an aggressive foreign policy than perhaps any other center. The roster of
Fukuoka leaders of expansionist and chauvinist societies is imposing; it includes Tōyama Mitsuru, Uchida Ryōhei, Hiraoka Kotarō, Akashi Motojirō, Hirota Koki, Nakano Seigō, and a host of
lesser patrioteers.

In the early Meiji years Fukuoka was a castle-town swarming
with declassed and embittered samurai. The first overt act of violence aimed at the government, an attempt on the life of Iwakura
on January 14, 1874, was organized by Fukuoka men who were
inflamed over the defeat of the *seikanron* (the advocacy of a campaign against Korea). Every center of conspiracy in Kyūshū, every
armed attempt at uprising in that island, found accomplices and
eager volunteers from Fukuoka. In no city outside of Satsuma was
the defeat of Saigō so deeply mourned as in Fukuoka, where his
admirers were numerous and devoted.

In those years small bands of intransigents gathered together in
the hostels and tea-houses of the old city, declaiming against the
government, foreigners, Korea, pension commutation, and other
targets of reactionary abuse. Some of these groups formed ephemeral societies with such characteristic names as the Kyōshisha
(Purpose-Rectifying Society), the Kyōninsha (Stubbornly Enduring Society), the Kenshisha (Purpose-Hardening Society). There
was one called the Kōyōsha (Facing the Sun Society), which
showed some influence of that liberalism which was a dominant
trend in Tosa and so, in contrast to the other societies, paid lip
service to such phrases as people's rights, and wider representation

in government. It also launched an unsuccessful scheme for the relief of impoverished samurai through settling them on the land.

In February 1881 these societies of Fukuoka banded together and formed the Genyōsha, with Hiraoka Kotarō as its president. The first headquarters of the society as revealed in a photograph was a modest one-story frame house fronted by an entranceway with two wooden posts so typical of the lower-middle-class Japanese residence. On one of the wooden pillars there is a plaque on which is written in bold Chinese characters GENYŌSHA. The articles of its policy were vague and disclosed nothing of its later history or real nature. Its three principles were to revere the emperor, to love and respect the nation, to defend the people's rights. In the official history of the Genyōsha, it is stated that these broad principles were interpreted to mean that the society would consider itself the guardian of the nation's prestige, ever watchful for slights and insults by the foreign powers. Rather than summarize this philosophy of nationalism it will be better to let the society's activities speak for themselves.

The leaders in the Genyōsha had learned one lesson from the defeat of Saigō. The raising of armed revolt as a means to achieve their goal of a reactionary government at home and expansion abroad was foredoomed to failure. It was not unlike the lesson learned by Hitler from the Munich Putsch of 1923, after which he chose a policy of winning over the key leaders of army, bureaucracy, and big business to his program. Henceforth the role of these ex-samurai opposition elements would be primarily to work within the constitutional framework. This did not exclude the use of terror, political blackmail, backstairs intrigue, and other similar favored devices. It simply meant that they would capitalize on a great natural advantage—the profoundly reactionary nature of the bureaucratic personnel, particularly in the General Staff. Thus the Genyōsha from the first enjoyed and won many active sympathizers within the state apparatus itself. These sympathizers in the government served as the transmission belt conveying the threats or demands of the reactionary societies to the proper authorities in the government, or, at times of great crisis, they would act as go-betweens, personally introducing Tōyama or Uchida to some cabinet minister, general, or high bureaucrat. In the reverse direction, these contacts in the government kept the leaders of the Genyōsha closely informed of government trends and policy.

One of the peculiar characteristics of the Genyōsha and its lesser contemporaries was its organization on a local basis with headquarters in a city of rich historical traditions where intense local patriotism or clannishness gave it an inner cohesiveness which later broadening by the inclusion of members from other centers never completely shattered. In the literature on the subject the Genyōsha is almost always referred to as the Genyōsha of Fukuoka; its leaders have been without exception men from Fukuoka.

Another feature of these societies is the tendency to build them around some strong or colorful personality, whether Saigō, Tōyama, or Uchida, after the fashion of a school with its master and his disciples. The Japanese have shown a marked preference for indirection and anonymity in government. It frequently happens that the formal head of an organization is not so important in policy-making as some dynamic personality who makes the decisions from "behind the screen." This has been true to a certain extent of the Genyōsha, where from its early days till the present the most forceful leader in it has been Tōyama Mitsuru, although he has never formally been named as head of the society. It is appropriate to sketch the character of Tōyama, the only surviving and most notorious disciple of Saigō Takamori.

In his early years Tōyama appears to have been a feckless youth who despite his poverty was utterly indifferent to learning a trade or profession. He preferred the turbulent and dissolute atmosphere of the Fukuoka tea-houses and brothels where embittered samurai combined dissipation with sedition. Tōyama has retained throughout his life some of the more boorish qualities of the rōnin without any of that intellectual curiosity and hunger for learning which made some of the rōnin (masterless samurai) in the late Tokugawa period the first pioneers of Western learning. Tōyama never writes for publication but occasionally narrates an incident in his life or some reminiscence of his contemporaries; this memoir is then written up for him by a disciple. His sense of humor, judged even by the most loutish manifestation of Japanese rusticity, is crudely scatological; in his tastes and manners he bears a striking similarity to the "best" Nazi type.

Unlike his boyhood hero, Saigō Takamori, whom he still reveres, Tōyama has never displayed that fatalistic disregard for his own life which is popularly believed to be one of the essential ingredients for a leader of rōnin or "patriots." Perhaps early in his career he came to regard himself as a general who must not lightly risk his life in battle. However that may be, he has been most lavish in sacrificing the lives of his more fanatic disciples, not to mention those of his opponents. As Morgan Young once aptly pointed out, there seems to be some curious legerdemain which transfers the bravado recklessness of his followers to the personal credit of Tōyama. Like Saigō, however, he has proved a cunning conspirator. In his early career he was often subject to police suspicion for plotting acts of terror in which Genyōsha members were implicated, but he was careful never to be found with incriminating evidence. In later years, of course, he has become a law unto himself, far removed from the vulgar considerations of police inquiry. Once secure in his position as "genro of the rōnin," Tōyama's home became a sanctuary for foreign exiles or native terrorists wanted by the police; once within that sanctum anyone is immune against the attentions of the otherwise ubiquitous Japanese police. . . .

Another of Tōyama's chief activities has been his sedulous cultivation of Asiatic nationalists and leaders of dissident groups who might be of service in Japanese continental ambitions. It would take us too far afield to relate here the vicissitudes of Tōyama's efforts to exploit political exiles, some of whom have been genuine patriots but many again nothing more than potential puppets. Suffice it to give a brief list of the more outstanding figures whom Tōyama has befriended. This list begins with Kim Ok-kiun, the Korean revolutionary whose assassination in 1894 in Shanghai spurred Japan's aggressive designs against China; it includes anti-Manchu revolutionaries such as Sun Yat-sen, Huang Hsing, Sung Chiao-jen; prominent Chinese contemporaries such as Generalissimo Chiang Kai-shek and Wang Ching-wei; the Philippine rebel Aguinaldo; the Indian terrorist and present puppet Ras Behari Bose (to be distinguished from Subhas Chandra Bose, Japan's leading India puppet); the former Russian Moslem leader Kourbangalieff; the White Russian leader the Ataman Semyonov; the Afghan Mahendra Pratap.

Tōyama's purpose in extending hospitality to anti-Manchu revolutionaries such as Dr. Sun Yat-sen and his followers was obvious. He hoped that, should they ever take power, they would look to Japan for financial help and advice in the reform and modernization of China, in return granting Japan special privileges, and finally accepting Japanese leadership in all vital matters of domestic and foreign policy. From the others he expected and in many cases received political intelligence; through them the Japanese army and Foreign Office have obtained valuable contacts in such parts of the world as the Philippines, China, and Central Asia. . . .

According to Tōyama's own story he has always been frank in telling his foreign guests what he would expect from them, namely, cooperation with Japan (a euphemism for accepting Japanese leadership), especially in driving Western interests and influence out of Asia, and secondly, support in an uncompromising struggle against communism in any shape or form. Other features of Tōyama's political tactics and methods will appear in the further description of the Genyōsha, to which we now return at the point where we left it, just after it had entered upon its career as an organization center of Japanese imperialism, or as it was called, "the Mecca of the nationalist movement."

The first head of the Genyōsha was Hiraoka Kotarō (died 1906) who became one of the most important liaison men with senior government officials in the army and Foreign Office. In the months preceding the Russo-Japanese War he made frequent trips through North China meeting important Chinese officials, threatening those whom he regarded as pro-Russian, and attempting to cajole and win over to the Japanese side those who were of the opposite tendency. His activity was of so important a nature that he and an associate, Komuchi Chijo, were called the "unofficial ambassadors" of Japan in Korea and China. He was a man of wealth who owned some of the richest coal mines in Kyūshū. He drew heavily on his private means to subsidize various enterprises of the Genyōsha. Although shortly after the founding of the Genyōsha he resigned in order to travel in China, he remained one of the closest associates to Tōyama and the inner circle of the Genyōsha. . . .

The first clear evidence of the Genyōsha's support of militarism and reaction in domestic politics was the agreement it reached with the Matsukata cabinet promising support in the coming general elections of January 1892. In return Tōyama, who negotiated the agreement, was assured that the government would pursue a strong foreign policy with an enormous increase in military and naval expenditure. In the Genyōsha account of this agreement the government is described as divided into two factions, the "soft" (*nanron-ha*) and the "tough" (*kōron-ha*). The latter included the home minister, Shinagawa Yajirō, the minister of war, Takashima Tomonosuke, and the navy minister, Kabayama Sukenori. They succeeded in compelling the whole cabinet to agree to the use of the police force in the coming election to ensure victory for government-supported candidates at the polls. The election was the bloodiest in Japan's history, with scores dead and hundreds wounded.

The Genyōsha campaigned for the government candidates in their bailiwick of Fukuoka, where they organized bands of ruffians to terrorize supporters of antigovernment or popular candidates. It is an interesting indication of the obstinacy of the opposition even in Fukuoka that one popular candidate, Okada Koka, was returned. The Genyōsha, feeling that the forces mobilized might not be adequate, called for aid from Sasa Tomofusa, leader of the Kokken-tō in Kumamoto, who sent three hundred *sōshi* ("toughs") to Fukuoka as reinforcements. A band of former samurai also came from the neighboring clan of Akizuki. These gangs were aided in every way by the local police. The Genyōsha in its official account states quite frankly that the purpose of this campaign of terror was to uproot all democratic or liberal organizations in Fukuoka.

This incident is of special interest since it established the practice in Japanese politics of the secret or unofficial agreement between the Home Ministry and the most powerful right-wing organizations to spread a campaign of terror at times of internal crisis, cowing and beating up popular leaders, particularly those of democratic or labor organizations. At such times the police force is considered inadequate for a real mass attack on the people; it is obviously more convenient if the government can rely on ruffians who are not wearing uniforms to spearpoint the attack. The police can then arrive to restore law and order, taking care only to arrest the victims of the attack. Such organizations as the Genyōsha, and in more recent times the Kokuryūkai, have always maintained close contact with the gangster elements who swarm in the slums of the great cities. In recent times Adachi Kenzō, for many years minister of the interior, worked closely with Tōyama and Uchida in organizing such terroristic campaigns.

There are two or three features of this incident which call for some special comment. First was the inner unity of the "tough" faction within the cabinet of the Ministries of Interior, War, and

Navy, the three posts which in Japanese politics have always acted as the chief organizers of reaction in domestic affairs. Even before they succeeded in forcing other members of the cabinet to agree to their policy, they had already made their pact with the Genyōsha. This was also the first occasion in domestic politics that the *Kempeitai* [riot police] were turned loose on the people, a foretaste of their future role in Japanese politics. It is characteristic of this use of gangsters that the largest numbers are often imported from other centers, a guarantee that they will be even more ruthless than the local variety, who might be somewhat inhibited by the fear of later retribution from their outraged fellow citizens.

Finally Tōyama and his associates were well aware of the close connection between repression at home and aggression abroad. The stifling of free expression, the smashing of all organizations potentially dangerous to a militaristic government, were the basic prerequisite for unbridled attacks upon peaceful and helpless neighbors. One of the chief purposes of the Fukuoka Genyōsha was the establishment of an unofficial intelligence service by sending young men to China, Central Asia, Siberia, and Southeast Asia to collect information on a wide range of subjects. Much of this information would be of value to the army, while commercial and economic intelligence would be of use to the Foreign Office and business houses. Contacts with anti-Manchu secret societies, nationalist groups in colonial territories, and dissident Moslems in Central Asia were established and developed. In 1882, Tōyama, with the help of the Kumamoto Sōai-sha (Mutual Love Society), sent over one hundred young men to China to gather information. The most remarkable of these "pioneer patriots in Eastern Asia" was Arao Kiyoshi.

After graduating from the Military Academy, Arao was attached to the General Staff, where he became a specialist in Chinese affairs. At his suggestion a special bureau was set up for the study of secret intelligence relating to China; in time it grew into branch bureaus covering all parts of the Far East and Central Asia. Under the instructions of the General Staff he left for Shanghai in 1886, where he set up a branch of the Rakuzendō (Hall of Pleasurable Delights) and in the following year moved up to Hankow, where he opened another branch.

The Rakuzendō was the creation of one of the most enterprising figures of the late Tokugawa and early Meiji eras, Kishida Ginkō.

He studied English under Hepburn, the pioneer American missionary, took the manuscript of the famous Hepburn Japanese-English dictionary to Shanghai for publishing, and later was a pioneer in the field of journalism. In 1864 he jointly founded with the better-known Joseph Hiko the first Japanese newspaper, the *Shimbunshi.* After a few years in journalism and dabbling in business enterprises with varying success, he entered the pharmaceutical business, not as some petty retail merchant but on a lavish scale, importing not only the medicines and luxury toiletries of the West but also stocking the nostrums, salves, and perfumes of the East. His main store on the Ginza was given the happy name of Raku-zendō. Anxious to enter the same field of business in China before it was pre-empted by others, he set up branches in Shanghai and Hankow. Kishida had always been interested in the Far Eastern question and was in close touch with societies such as the Genyōsha which specialized in the study of China. Shrewdly combining business and "patriotism," he chose his branch managers and salesmen from young men who were either anxious to get a start in the commercial world, or who were pioneers in Japanese intelligence work in China and who could be quite conveniently supported in their work through the proceeds of the Rakuzendō. Arao was one of these.

Arao gathered around him in the Hankow Rakuzendō a group of young men who made tours into remote parts of Central Asia or China dressed as Chinese with queue and appropriate clothes, speaking the language fluently and supporting themselves by peddling medicines and literature, which consisted chiefly of aphrodisiacs and obscene pictures. Their trips into Sinkiang, Central Asia, Mongolia, and Yunnan are described in some detail in their biographies in the last volume of *Tōa Senkaku Shishi Kiden* (*Biographical Memoirs of Pioneer Patriots in Eastern Asia*). The hazards of travel amongst a distant and often hostile people were many. Some were apprehended and detained by Russian police in Turkestan, and the leader of one expedition disappeared in Sinkiang without leaving any trace. But all who returned brought with them what must have been the first detailed information available to the Japanese intelligence services on those parts of the world. The chief subjects of investigation included economic and agricultural development; financial conditions and tax grievances; personalities, particularly those likely to be sympathetic to Japan;

roads and communications; the Russian, Chinese, Burmese, and Indian defenses in Asia; the prospects of utilizing Moslem and Buddhist clergy for Japanese intrigue.

After his work in Hankow, Arao conceived a more ambitious enterprise to push Japanese penetration of China. Returning to Japan in 1889 he resigned his commission as captain, and with the encouragement of Premier Kuroda and Finance Minister Matsukata, toured the country, speaking before chambers of commerce in the larger cities, urging business leaders to enter the China trade. He completed his tour in 1891 and, on the basis of widely circulated applications, he chose one hundred and fifty prospective teachers who were to go to Shanghai to study Chinese language, geography, commerce, finance, and related subjects. This school for Japanese agents was known as the Nisshin Bōeki Kenkyūjo (Sino-Japanese Commercial Research). At first this project was impeded by financial difficulties, since promised government subsidies were not forthcoming, but eventually Arao secured adequate financial support chiefly from interested business firms and through Tōyama's help. In later years, the number of students increased.

At the end of their course, the graduates of this school were divided into teams of about twenty to make trips into all parts of China, Manchuria, Siam, India, the Philippines, and the South Seas. Later, some would be employed as the local agents of the more enterprising Japanese trading firms; others would enter the Japanese consular service as specialists in Far Eastern trade; many became scouts and official interpreters during the Sino-Japanese War; others again disappeared into the nebulous and ever-growing army of Japanese adventurers whose exact function is hard to define but who have in the course of a half century performed unsavory tasks for the Japanese army, Foreign Office, or expansionist societies.

Arao died in Formosa shortly after the Sino-Japanese War, having performed valuable services for Japanese imperialism. He exemplified in his career the intimate tie-up between Japanese military intelligence, the extreme nationalist societies, and business interests, especially those seeking foreign markets.

Finally, a page from the Genyōsha history illustrates how even at an early stage the Genyōsha both established intimate connections with the General Staff and under its encouragement acted as a firebrand in the war against China in 1894-1895. From the very start the Genyōsha always closely followed events in Korea. Many of its agents or sympathizers whose business took them to Korea, whether merchants establishing trade connections in Korea, or Buddhist priests (usually from Honganji, which had a branch temple in Fusan) who sought to maintain friendly relations with fellow Buddhists in Korea, built up a detailed and rich store of varied information concerning the peninsula. During the eighties, clashes and incidents in Korea multiplied and tension between China and Japan increased. The members of the Genyōsha were in a state of frenzy over the anticipation of war. Events appeared to be moving too slowly for them. The assassination in 1894 in Shanghai of the Korean revolutionary Kim Ok-kiun, who was in close touch with the Genyōsha, created a considerable stir since the assassin was an agent of the Chinese government and was officially rewarded for his deed. This seemed to the Genyōsha a providential incident which could be made a *casus belli*.

Matono Hansuke, one of the chief figures in the Genyōsha, interviewed the foreign minister, Mutsu Munemitsu, asking him to make war at once on China. Mutsu was evasive and suggested that Matono consult General Kawakami Sōroku, vice-chief of General Staff, giving him a letter of introduction. Matono at once went to Kawakami who, after listening intently to Matono's arguments in favor of war against China, finally said, "What you say is full of good sense, but with a prime minister such as Itō we cannot entertain the hope of opening hostilities. According to reports, I have heard of some distinguished men of the Fukuoka Genyōsha, which is the heart and soul of the movement in favor of a military expedition. If there were only some who would cross to Korea and start a conflagration, it would then be my duty, which I would not hesitate for a moment to fulfill, to go and extinguish the fire." This oracular statement allowed of little ambiguity and Matono returned overjoyed to his companions of the Genyōsha. Under the leadership of Uchida Ryōhei, Suzuki Tengan, and Matono, a subsidiary society of the Genyōsha was created to operate in Korea, with the pretentious name *Tenyukyo* (Society of Heavenly Salvation for the Oppressed). At once a band of conspirators and ronin crossed to Korea, committing various acts of terrorism. . . .

Meanwhile, before the outbreak of war itself, the activities of the *Tenyukyo* became so notorious that, goaded by the protests of the Korean government, the Japanese authorities could no longer ignore it, and so promised to make an official investigation. The Japanese army, however, promptly intervened, designating the *Tenyukyo* a "volunteer corps"; all plans for the investigation were dropped. In the ensuing war the *Tenyukyo* continued to operate under its title of "volunteer corps," enjoying the full confidence of the Japanese command as scouts and local intelligence agents.

While the implications of this incident are obvious, some of the details are particularly noteworthy and have a strangely contemporary character. First, the noncommittal attitude of the foreign minister who, rather than oppose the Genyōsha, sends its representative to the General Staff. The General Staff in turn expresses quite openly its contempt even for the prime minister and proceeds to encourage the Genyōsha to stir up incidents likely to start a war. With the organization in 1901 of the Kokuryūkai, primarily an anti-Russian society, the liaison between it and the General Staff became much closer; in fact almost all the preparatory intelligence work in Siberia and Russia for the war of 1904–1905 was carried out by Uchida Ryōhei and his agents in the Kokuryūkai.

In this description of the origins and development of the Genyōsha an attempt has been made to choose for illustration those activities which were most typical and, by drawing the moral from each, to suggest that the scope of these extreme nationalist societies has enormously increased, keeping step with the ever bolder and more aggressive plans of Japanese imperialism. A student of Japanese politics who devotes some time to an investigation of these societies must guard, however, against the myopia which comes from scrutinizing at too close range some aspect of Japanese political life, thus exaggerating the importance of one institution or trend at the expense of the totality of Japanese political forces. Thus it would give the reader a false impression if it were implied that Uchida, Tōyama, and their cohorts were, exclusively and uniquely, the basic driving force behind Japanese fascism. But this would be nearer the truth, perhaps, than the opposite extreme which sees these societies only as the lunatic fringe of Japanese political life, to be dismissed in any serious discussion with a few ironical phrases.

The Genyōsha and Kokuryūkai (both of which are still active today) and their numerous offshoots have been, for the last sixty years, the advance guard of Japanese imperialism. They have charted the course of aggression and have even thrust themselves into the position of an uninvited pilot who at times of great danger or uncertainty has played a decisive role in guiding Japanese policy along that charted course. It is these societies rather than any political party or succession of parties which have molded public opinion in favor of aggression. They have provided continuity from one stage to the other in the unfolding strategy of Japanese expansionism. All this has been politically possible only through the unique position which these societies enjoy with regard to the bureaucracy, but more important, the army.

As pointed out above, this position was secured in the early Meiji years because of the strength of the samurai opposition to the government, an opposition which abandoned the policy of armed insurrection and instead worked within the constitutional framework of the government. But the purely samurai character of this opposition soon evaporated in its later political evolutions. Utilizing to the full their favored position with regard to the army and bureaucracy, the Genyōsha and Kokuryūkai succeeded in establishing and maintaining a close but informal alliance with the most ambitious houses, including the zaibatsu (big capitalists), which were interested in expansion as a means of acquiring lucrative overseas markets and a cheap source of raw material. These societies thus are the cement which holds together the whole edifice of Japanese aggression—the army, big business, and the key sections of the bureaucracy. . . .

☘ DURING THE TOKYO WAR CRIMES TRIALS after World War II, civilian leaders as well as some military men were anxious to blame the war on the radical young officers' conspiracies and the incidents they provoked. This was, of course, self-serving, since they thereby abdicated their own responsibilities. James Crowley here assesses the impact of the incidents, disputing the theories giving them credit for starting World War II. Rather, he stresses the *lack* of real influence of the radical soldiers, the increasing influence of higher ranking officers, and the way in which every radical officer eventually found his career jeopardized.

JAMES CROWLEY*
Japan's Quest for Autonomy

The outbreak of a major diplomatic or military crisis unavoidably affects the foreign and security policies of a country. Japan was no exception to this rule, and the clashes at Mukden and the Marco Polo Bridge thrust the empire in bold new directions of foreign policy. To affirm this truism, however, is not to claim that, in both incidents, one witnessed a common pattern of decision-making in which the field armies, in conjunction with the assistance of the general staff, exercised ultimate control over the determination of national policy. In fact, common denominators are difficult to locate in these diplomatic, military, and political crises. In 1931, the Kwantung army willfully provoked an incident at Mukden; but, in 1937, the North China army neither sought nor organized the confrontation at the Marco Polo Bridge. In September 1931, the general staff sanctioned the seizure of South Manchuria by its interpretation of the "supreme command" prerogative; but, in July 1937, the general staff forestalled operations in North China. In the fall of 1931, the inability of the Wakatsuki cabinet to effect a diplomatic settlement satisfactory to the demands of the chief of staff caused the formation of a new government; but, in the fall of 1937, the lack of a diplomatic accord in harmony with the dictates of the general staff yielded no change of cabinets.

Granting these divergent patterns, there were still two traits common to both crises: (1) the operational orders of the general staff were not technically flaunted by the field armies; and (2) basic policies were formulated in the cabinet. During the Wakatsuki cabinet, for example, although the commands of General Kanaya precluded the conquest of North Manchuria, his orders were reluctantly obeyed by the Kwantung army; and, during the fall of 1937, the field armies of generals Matsui and Terauchi disdainfully complied with the commands of General Tada. In the winter of 1931–1932, the seizure of North Manchuria and the

* James Crowley, *Japan's Quest for Autonomy* (Princeton, N.J.: Princeton University Press, 1966), pp. 379–384.

establishment of a new Manchurian regime were sanctioned by the Inukai cabinet; and, in 1937–1938, the organization of new regimes in North and Central China were authorized by the Konoe cabinet. In both crises, moreover, the cabinet was subjected to powerful political currents which pushed the government into programs of expansion and imperialism; and, in both crises, one of these currents was the pervasive domestic endorsement of the endeavors proposed by the field armies. Even so, the peculiar cluster of circumstances in 1931 and 1937 which produced major alterations in foreign policy cannot be compressed into one maxim, to the effect that the control and determination of national policy were exercised by field armies who manipulated army headquarters and the cabinet. . . .

Throughout the 1930s, the threat and actual occurrence of military clashes on the China mainland accentuated the authority of military personnel in matters of foreign policy. A less vivid but almost equally decisive manifestation of political influence by army and naval officers centered on the utilization of the communications media in order to assail, alter, or propound national policies. . . .

This inclination to condone and encourage open discussion of national defense policy by military and naval personnel was tantamount to opening Pandora's box. Among the more unsavory results, of course, was the rebellion of February 26, 1936. Setting aside its effects on the members of the National Principle group, it is noteworthy that the public rhetoric and publications of the two service ministries were mainly linked with responsible and official policies. For this reason, the evolving political and economic programs of both services were far more influential than the political opinions and deeds of staff officers who conspired to alter or promote policies by means of political schemes or *coups d'état*. . . .

Regardless of the passionate quarrels being waged over the Manchurian problem and the encompassing scope of the "total war" philosophy, there was no apparent tendency in army central headquarters to regard the "right of supreme command" as a political vehicle by which the army could overturn "Shidehara diplomacy" or impress its economic and political plans on cabinet policies. Historically, the "right of supreme command" had invested each service with complete control over all its internal administrative affairs; and it had confirmed complete control of the conduct of military operations in time of hostilities. It had not, however, been viewed as empowering the service ministers or general staffs with the right to set national policy, as witness the conduct and determination of policy during the Sino- and Russo-Japanese Wars, World War I, and the Siberian intervention.

. . . There is no compelling reason to consider the March and October incidents, the 1932 murders, and the February twenty-sixth rebellion as a sequence of events which a Control Faction adroitly engineered in order to acquire a position of leadership and to impose a policy of war with China. Actually, rather than regard army central headquarters as a hothouse which nurtured a brand of political radicalism, it would seem more pertinent to concentrate on the process by which every staff officer who articulated a program of domestic violence or military coups found his professional career seriously, often fatally, jeopardized. The Imperial army was not a praetorian institution; its leadership did not aspire to garner political power via mutinies, coups, or threats of army rebellion. . . .

☃ IN THE EARLY 1930s most of the world was in the throes of the Great Depression. By contrast, beginning in 1932, the economy of Japan was undergoing a boom, and the devaluation of the yen encouraged exports. The organizational support and initiative for the boom came from the zaibatsu, the great industrial and trading conglomerates: Mitsui, Mitsubishi, Sumitomo, Yasuda. From the Depression of the late 1920s they rose in full strength, as Lockwood and Allen show.

Japanese exports received hostile reactions, however, from other nations reeling under the impact of the Depression, and this in turn stimulated economic nationalism at home. Yet there was also within Japan widespread resentment of the power of the zaibatsu, often expressed as criticism of the corruption thought to be typical among the Japanese elite.

Antizaibatsu feelings were also held by groups within the military. Thus, at the time the zaibatsu had achieved unparalleled power and influence, the military gave control of industrial enterprises in Japan's colony of Manchukuo (Manchuria) to a new zaibatsu, Nissan. Despite the prevalence of such anticapitalist feelings, the position of the zaibatsu remained unassailable through World War II.

WILLIAM LOCKWOOD*
Trade, Armament, Industrial Expansion, 1930–1938

Invasion of World Markets. The most conspicuous feature of the early thirties in Japan, so far as the rest of the world was concerned, was the boom in Japanese exports after 1931. The immediate stimulus came from the swift depreciation of the currency. From U.S. $0.494 in November 1931 the value of the yen plummeted to $0.207 a year later. With the devaluation of the dollar in 1933, it recovered to the neighborhood of $0.30 (or ls. 2d.). Here it remained until 1939.

The bounty thus conferred upon Japanese exports—in part a correction of the previous overvaluation—brought a soaring advance in shipments of Japanese goods all over the world. From 1930 to 1936 exports to foreign countries increased from 1435 to 2641 million yen. Their physical volume increased even more rapidly than their value. For export prices (in yen) dropped twenty-four percent in 1931, and despite currency depreciation had failed to return to their 1930 level by 1936. The volume of exports nearly doubled in six years. Meanwhile sales to the colonies (Korea and Formosa) advanced even more rapidly, so that total overseas exports, valued at 1930 prices, rose by 104 percent.

Textile manufactures, long dominant in Japan's export trade, again led the way in this new penetration of world markets. But there were conspicuous shifts within this category, as well as a decline in its relative importance. Raw silk failed notably to share in the recovery. Hard times in the United States, coupled with rising competition from synthetic fibers, exerted a severe drag on any revival of silk prices. Shipments continued at a high level, but their yen value was only half what it had been a decade earlier.

* William Lockwood, *The Economic Growth of Japan* (Princeton, N.J.: Princeton University Press, 1954), pp. 64–68, 70–75.

By contrast, Japanese cotton goods spread rapidly through foreign markets; the production and exports of rayon textiles both mounted steeply for the first time; and Japanese woolens also won a substantial foothold abroad. By 1936 Japan had become the world's premier exporter of cotton piece goods. . . .

Certain countries, particularly the United Kingdom, felt keenly the pressure of Japanese competition. Others found new markets for raw materials and equipment in Japan which could only in part be said to have replaced former markets elsewhere. This was especially true of the United States. She now supplied large quantities of cotton, petroleum products, iron and steel, machinery, copper, and lumber to Japanese industries engaged in the manufacture of consumer goods, munitions, and plant equipment. By 1936, in fact, Japan was absorbing half of all United States exports to Asia—or as much as the whole continent of South America.

The balance of trade with the United States, long heavily in Japan's favor, now reversed itself. A credit balance of 167 million yen in 1927 was converted into a deficit of 244 million yen in 1936.

. . . The flooding of Japanese goods into foreign markets after 1931 brought frantic outcries in the West. Most other countries, including Japan's major industrial competitors, were struggling in the slough of depression. This was, indeed, one of the reasons for the ready appeal of Japanese manufactures. Their cheapness enabled them in some degree to tap levels of consumer demand below the reach of higher-priced European and American goods. But they also cut deeply into established markets, especially those of Lancashire. And elsewhere, as in the United States, though they remained small in volume, their unsettling effects spread uncertainty and alarm just when governments were attempting to put a floor under prices and wages, or at least to reserve shrunken markets for home producers. Antagonism was further increased by the political reaction to the Japanese army's concurrent invasion of China. Only in China itself, however, did popular boycotts reach substantial proportions. This was countered by steady Japanese encroachments upon China's territorial and administrative integrity in the north.

Almost everywhere else, after 1932, tariffs were raised or quotas established against Japanese goods. Probably they were most effective, and least justified, in the colonial markets of Asia and Africa controlled by the other industrial powers. . . . Despite the spectacular expansion of trade actually achieved, and Japan's obvious economic interest in supporting the kind of world trading system which would permit its continuation, her militarists were quick to make propaganda out of the situation. It was now easier to summon economic arguments to support a drive toward the illusory goal of self-sufficient empire.

In retrospect, the near hysteria aroused abroad by the Japanese "trade menace" seems to have had little justification. At its peak Japan's total export trade was less than four percent of world exports. Moreover, the expansion of the thirties did not represent some new and unlimited competitive power suddenly acquired by Japanese industry. Nor could it be attributed simply to low-wage Oriental labor, against which the higher-standard countries were helpless to compete. Japanese labor had always been miserably paid, judged by Western standards. The new circumstances which now strengthened its competitive ability in certain lines were the marked gains in technical efficiency and business organization achieved through the decade 1926–1936 and the violent dislocation of costs, prices, and exchange rates precipitated by the Great Depression. It was the concentrated impact of Japan's export drive, both in time and in particular types of manufactures, which created the problem.

. . . Meanwhile, at home, other policies reinforced the expansion of industry. No country, in fact, pursued a more successful policy of rapid industrial recovery after 1931—or one which ultimately ended in greater disaster.

The ill-timed retrenchment program of Mr. Inoue was now abandoned in favor of monetary expansion. Under the direction of the veteran finance minister, Korekiyo Takahashi, rising armament expenditures were met by deficit financing—"red ink bonds," as they were called. . . . Interest rates declined, while the national debt nearly doubled. It rose from six billion to over ten billion yen. This was still a relatively modest sum, however, absorbed by the banking system without undue strain. Wholesale prices at the end of 1936 stood only thirty-three percent above 1930. The cost of living had advanced even less. Although the note issue of the Bank of Japan had risen thirty percent, bank loans and discounts outstanding remained at about the same level.

Reflation at home thus reinforced the stimulus of yen depreciation abroad, without canceling its effects. Under this double impetus Japanese industry forged rapidly ahead. Mining output rose thirty-four percent from 1930 to 1936; manufacturing, sixty-three percent. Meanwhile wage rates recovered only slowly from their depression lows in most industries. Average real wage rates, which had risen as much as fifty percent from 1914 to 1926, showed little net advance over the next decade. . . . The gain which came from the fall in living costs during the depression was largely canceled by the upward drift of prices from 1932 to 1936. Such benefits as accrued to workers from the industrial boom thus came largely in the form of wider employment opportunities, particularly for males in industry. Business profits reached peak levels, however. They provided huge sums for the expansion and reequipment of Japan's major industries.

The progress of different sectors of Japanese industry was nevertheless uneven. All of the textile trades except raw silk made substantial advances in their scale of production, equipment, and organization. . . .

It was chiefly the metallurgical, machinery, and chemical industries, however, which mushroomed under the stimulus of armament spending and industrial construction. Consumer goods production in Japanese industry advanced only thirty-three percent from 1930 to 1936. By contrast, the output of producer goods jumped eighty-three percent. In the machinery trades, where production was valued at 1609 million yen in the latter year, Japan could now supply virtually all her own requirements except in the more specialized and advanced types of machinery, power plant, and metalworking equipment. The expanding output of fuel and basic materials—coal, steel, cement, and electricity, for example—likewise reflected her growing industrial capacity. Soda ash, caustic soda, dyestuffs, and other basic chemicals advanced two- and threefold in production, some items even more.

The structure of Japanese industry continued through this period to exhibit the evolutionary tendencies observable in the previous decade. Throughout manufacturing there was a growth in the scale and efficiency of factory production, despite the persistence of the small plant of less than 100 workers as the typical establishment in all but a few lines. The great firms and combines which had always dominated heavy industry increased their preponderance. They were joined now by several newer financial groups which rose to prominence through association with the army and navy in the expansion of munitions production. In foreign trade, the closer integration of the processes of importing, exporting, production, shipping, and finance contributed to Japan's commercial successes, especially in cotton goods markets.

At home the depression of 1930–1931 gave a marked impetus to the formation of cartels. These were now legally sanctioned and encouraged by the government under the Major Industries Control Law and Industrial Association Law of 1931. Government intervention and control was also extended in several key industries, notably iron and steel, electric power, and shipping. In the main, however, the cartel movement proved largely ineffectual until after 1936, when the state began to foster it more actively as an instrument of national policy in the transition to war economy. Except in Manchuria, where industrial development under the aegis of the army followed the pattern of state capitalism from the beginning, Japanese industry preserved its predominantly private and uncontrolled character until the eve of World War II.

In marked contrast to the flush of industrial prosperity was the situation which prevailed in Japanese agriculture. Here, as previously observed, the Depression fell with crushing impact. At prices prevailing in 1930–1931 a large section of the Japanese farming class was insolvent, burdened as it was with heavy taxes, high rents, and a farm debt of five to six billion yen. Agricultural output increased comparatively little in the years which followed. And it was 1935 before farm prices climbed back to their pre-Depression parity with the prices of industrial goods purchased by the peasant. In the meantime agricultural distress bred social unrest through the countryside, affecting also the army, which drew most of its recruits from farm families. This failed, however, to induce large-scale relief expenditures, in preference to armament, despite the ascendancy of military leadership in Tokyo. The government did appropriate considerable sums in the effort to stabilize rice and silk prices. It also experimented with the readjustment of farm debts, the relief of tenancy, the control of fertilizer prices, and even the encouragement of emigration to Manchukuo. But these were all makeshifts which hardly touched the fundamentals of the problem. . . .

More significant was the acceleration of the long-term drift from agriculture into industrial and urban occupations. As before, this failed to reduce the farm population. But it did take care of the increased numbers seeking gainful employment. Factory employment alone increased from 1,886,000 in 1930 to 2,876,000 in 1936. By the latter date one in every three Japanese lived in a city of 30,000 or more; one in four in a city of over 100,000. Mining, manufacturing, and construction taken together now afforded the chief occupation for about a quarter of the entire working population, and a considerably larger fraction of all able-bodied males. They provided as much as forty percent of the national net product, at price levels prevailing in 1936.

Manufacturing alone, including handicraft as well as factory industry, accounted for five billion yen, nearly a third of the total national income. In factory industry, net product was valued at 3.6 billion yen. Here the traditional supremacy of the textile trades was now challenged by the chemical and machinery industries. At the comparatively high prices and rates of earnings prevailing in 1936, these newer groups each far surpassed the textile industries in net value of output.... The most rapid growth thus took place in heavy industries which, while serving civilian uses, were also crucial in the military realm. Significant for the latter purpose, too, was the fact that another large complex, that of iron and steel and other basic industries, was now being established under Japanese political control in Manchuria.

The net growth of the Japanese economy during this period may be summarized as follows: From 1930 to 1936 Japan's net national product, at 1930 prices, increased from 10.2 billion to 15.8 billion yen. Real net *income* rose less substantially, however, as a result of the adverse shift in the barter terms of trade following the depreciation of the yen in 1931. From 1930 to 1936 the average price of exports to foreign countries and colonies dropped five percent, while import prices rose twenty-nine percent.... Japan thus had to ship larger amounts of goods abroad to pay for her 1936 imports than would have been required had the terms of trade remained unchanged. These additional exports absorbed about one fifth of the gain in real national product. Net income therefore increased only about 4.3 billion yen at 1930 prices—still an impressive advance.

Part of the forty percent gain in real income from 1930 to 1936 represented increased civilian consumption. But the greater share probably took the form of additions to capital assets and military supply, especially the former. In 1930 military expenditure was still relatively small. Net investment, including changes in stocks of goods as well as in durable assets, may well have been negative. By 1936 direct military expenditures were running close to one billion yen (1930 prices). Net private and governmental investment was on the order of two billion yen. Thus at least twenty percent of the national income was now being withheld from civilian consumption for one purpose or the other. The greater part of this three billion yen, however, was still being plowed back into plants, equipment, and business inventories in Japan proper, most of them civilian or civilian-military in character. Net investment in Manchuria, North China, and elsewhere abroad probably did not yet exceed 250–350 million yen.

Meanwhile real civilian consumption in Japan rose about twenty percent from 1930 to 1936. The total output of consumer goods actually increased more than this. But part of it went into exports, where it was exchanged against imports on less favorable terms than before. At the same time the population grew from 64.5 million to 70.2 million, or nine percent. Consumption of goods and services per capita therefore advanced only ten percent or so.

Food standards remained more or less unchanged in the aggregate. Imports of foodstuffs for domestic use actually increased one third, but this was little more than enough to support the growing population at existing levels of diet. The principal gains came in other types of consumption, which now comprised over half of consumer expenditures. Per capita use of clothing materials increased one third. Other basic materials going into civilian consumption show a somewhat similar growth. Most of this advance came from more effective utilization of home resources, rather than greater per capita imports for domestic use. The latter continued, however, to play a vital role in sustaining the whole Japanese economy.

In the light of the above summary, this dramatic period in Japan's economic growth can be seen in its true perspective. Essentially it continued the trends observable in previous decades. It did not signify merely a boom in armaments and zaibatsu profits without gains to the general civilian economy, as some critics have alleged. Nor, on the other hand, did it bring sweeping advances in the material well-being of the population as a whole. Such gains as were achieved were distributed unevenly through the country.

They accrued largely to the urban population, thus accelerating the drift to the city so long in evidence. Being heavily concentrated among well-to-do groups who owned and managed the great industries, banks, and trading houses, they probably increased somewhat the gross inequalities of income and wealth which characterized the whole course of Japan's prewar development. From these higher income classes, and the corporations they controlled, came much of the savings which permitted large investments in the creation of new productive capacity as well as rising military expenditure.

Since the period bridged a great world depression, it was no small achievement even to maintain the country's living standards, especially as the population was now growing at the rate of a million a year. These standards were now the highest in the Far East, and well above those of the previous generation in Japan. Rising employment opportunities had only been sustained, it is true, by accepting less favorable terms of exchange on world markets. These terms had deteriorated with the decline of the silk trade, and their improvement was now hampered by spreading restrictions on Japanese goods. The Japanese could nevertheless look with satisfaction on the progress of the decade ending in 1936. It had witnessed a substantial growth in the scale and maturity of industry and trade through a period in which many other countries, particularly those more abundantly blessed with raw materials, were mired in depression.

G. C. ALLEN*
The Concentration of Economic Control

Of late years the zaibatsu have been subjected to much public criticism, and this has led them to modify considerably their business methods. The reasons for these attacks deserve notice. As long as the zaibatsu confined their interests to large-scale industry, the financing of new enterprises, colonial development, and the

* G. C. Allen, "Japanese Industry," in E. B. Schumpeter, ed., *The Industrialization of Japan and Manchukuo 1930–1940* (New York: Macmillan, 1940), pp. 640–646.

administration of concerns of national importance, they did not come into serious conflict with that part of Japan's economy which is associated with small-scale manufacture and trade and with agriculture. But partly through the ambitions of able officials who wished to extend their sphere of control and partly through certain developments in Japan's economic situation, the activities of the zaibatsu began to encroach on fields hitherto outside their scope. In the postwar period there was a pronounced movement toward the consolidation of banking. This is to be attributed in some measure to the deliberate policy of the government, which was anxious to eliminate the recurrent financial panics—the concomitant of a system composed of numerous small and recklessly managed banks—and also to the gradual disappearance of the minor banks by amalgamation or bankruptcy. As a result, a banking system has been created which is much less prone than formerly to succumb to panic, but the smaller merchants and manufacturers who were the chief customers of the minor banks have suffered from this change. To an increasing extent they have been forced within the financial orbit of the zaibatsu, and they have resented this. The trading activities of the great concerns, moreover, have increased during the last decade, Mitsui Bussan having enlarged its range of products to a remarkable degree. Small merchants have found themselves driven out of markets and small manufacturers have been reduced to dependence on the great trading companies. It is said that groups of small merchants originally opened up the trade with the South Seas countries, but that this trade has since been absorbed by Mitsui Bussan. A few years ago this concern also began to trade in agricultural and marine products like eggs and seaweed, formerly conducted entirely by small local merchants. The intense depression of the period 1929–1932 drove many of these small concerns out of business, leaving Mitsui Bussan supreme. There can be little doubt that Japan's foreign trade benefited by the intrusion of the zaibatsu into these new lines; but this did not prevent the rise of a strong feeling of resentment against them. At the same time the growing influence of the political parties was objected to not merely by the army and navy, but also by the peasants and small traders, who saw in that development a further extension of the power of the great concerns that were known to control the parties. Frequent political scandals fomented this discontent; while the economic distress, the consequence of the deflationary policy of the Minseitō government in 1930–1931 and of the fall in raw silk prices, was attributed to the zaibatsu also. When Japan was driven off gold at the end of 1931, the Mitsui Bank and Mitsui Bussan were charged with having made large profits from speculating in the dollar exchange. . . .

Mitsui and the other zaibatsu have also tried to divert public attention from their business interests. At one time it was customary for new enterprises, when launched by Mitsui, to bear the name of the house; but an attempt is now being made to confer anonymity upon many of their enterprises. For instance, the Mitsui Tea Company has come to be known as the Nittō Tea Company. After the February Incident of 1936, which was to a large extent the outcome of anticapitalist feeling, the family members announced their intention of withdrawing from directorates and from all active participation in the business. A compulsory retiring age has also been instituted which will lead to the removal of several of the leading *bantō* in the course of a few years. To placate the army by showing that they are devoted to the national interests the zaibatsu have established new enterprises that are considered to have political importance, such as plants for hydrogenation and for staple-fiber production. They have recently provided most of the capital for a newly instituted bank which is intended to finance small traders and industrialists who are members of manufacturers' and exporters' guilds or associations. They all exert themselves to prevent references to their families from appearing in the press.

The public has scarcely been placated. The new policy is commonly known as the "Camouflage Policy." It is pointed out that the selling of blocks of shares in certain firms does not mean the elimination of the zaibatsu's control of them. The donations to the social services are held to demonstrate, not their change of heart, but their capacity to pay. Indeed, it is doubtful if the zaibatsu have done more than *"reculer pour mieux sauter"* ["gather themselves for a renewed assault"]. The smaller industrialists and the raw silk producers and merchants who have to find export markets for their goods cannot dispense with the huge resources and world-wide organization of Mitsui Bussan. The public may hate these great concerns, but its savings will still be entrusted to their efficient financial institutions rather than to the less secure minor banks. Whatever government is in office must depend upon the zaibatsu for the resources and expert knowledge needed to carry out its programs of political and economic expansion. The Kwantung army cannot develop Manchukuo without their help. The admiralty and the war office can only extend armaments by utilizing the resources of the zaibatsu's factories, and these orders serve to increase their profits. In a time of crisis the government must turn to them to furnish officials to act as heads of the semi-official banks and other public enterprises. It is significant that only recently, at a time when the army has achieved a still further measure of control over the political machine, Mr. S. Ikeda, formerly president of the Mitsui Bank, and one of the *bantō* who were held responsible for the aggressive policy of Mitsui, should be called to the position of governor of the Bank of Japan. A recently appointed head of the Yokohama Specie Bank is a relative of Iwasaki. No doubt the appearance of a more liberal regime in economics and politics and the reduction of expenditure on arma-ments and colonial development might weaken the grip which the zaibatsu have upon the economic life of Japan; but this cannot reasonably be expected for many years to come. As long as Japan persists in the course of development upon which she has been set ever since the restoration, the zaibatsu's power is not likely to diminish.

During the last year or two much attention has been attracted to the so-called "younger" business groups, which have risen in importance along with the growth of the war industries. Of these the chief is the Nissan (Nippon Sangyō Kaisha) group managed by Mr. Y. Aikawa. Mr. Aikawa, who was a protégé of Marquis Kaoru Inoue, first became prominent about ten years ago when he took over the Kuhara Mining Company, and since 1931 he has greatly extended the range of his interests, largely, though not entirely, in connection with supplying the demand for armament materials. Apart from its great mining properties, Nissan is espe-cially important in the engineering industry—it owns the famous Hitachi Works—and it has large subsidiaries engaged in the match and aquatic products trades. Toward the end of 1937 it entered upon a new phase in its career as a result of a change in the government's industrial policy with regard to Manchukuo. Up to that time investments by Japanese in the new state had fallen far short of what was necessary to carry out the industrial develop-ment which had been planned for it. This was partly because the great capitalists were skeptical of the profitability of many of the Manchurian enterprises, especially in view of the rigid system of industrial control which had been deliberately set up by the Manchukuo government on the initiative of the army leaders there. The state-controlled South Manchuria Railway Company, in whose hands most of the large-scale undertakings were concentrated, for this reason found difficulty in raising adequate capital for the firms which it wished to establish or to extend. The outbreak of the war with China and the deterioration in the international situation as a whole during 1937 made the full exploitation of Manchukuo's resources all the more essential in the opinion of the army leaders, and a change of policy was therefore decided upon. In October 1937, the Japanese government announced that in future the South Manchuria Railway Company would confine its activities to the development and administration of the railway system, while its industrial undertakings would be transferred to a new company, the Manchukuo Heavy Industries Development Company, in which the Nissan group would hold half of the capital, the remainder being in the ownership of the Manchukuo government.

The reason why Nissan rather than the great zaibatsu was chosen as the agency for the industrial development of Manchukuo was purely political. The army in Manchukuo has been bitterly opposed to the great family businesses and has objected to their profiting from the exploitation of the new state. But it has now been realized that the country cannot be fully developed without the capital which huge concerns alone can provide, and that the capital will not be forthcoming under the old system of rigid state control. So the army has been willing to compromise to the extent of admitting a capital group ostensibly outside the great families to a share in the development and control of Manchurian resources. Moreover, the capital of the Nissan holding company, unlike that of the zaibatsu's holding companies, has been subscribed by many thousands of shareholders, and in this respect it apparently possesses a very different financial foundation from that of the other large capital groups. The army has thus been persuaded that the profits of Nissan will be widely distributed and will not be confined to a few families. This alleged contrast between Nissan and the other capital groups, however, may well prove to be more apparent than real. The holders of shares in Nissan's subsidiaries include members of the older family businesses, and it is not likely that Nissan will be able to raise the additional capital needed to exploit Manchukuo (unless foreign capitalists fill the gap) without resort to the financial institutions of the zaibatsu. The semi-official banks are supporting Nissan; but in the present financial situation they have many other preoccupations and can scarcely supply sufficient funds for long-term investment outside Japan proper. Furthermore, Mr. Aikawa has family connections with leading persons in the Mitsubishi group, and these connections count for much in Japan. Indeed, it may well be that most of these "younger" financial groups already have connections of one kind or another with the zaibatsu; for instance, Mori, a "young" financial group in the chemical and electrical industries, has affiliations with Yasuda. Unless there is a rapid growth of a class of investor in industrial securities from among the general public, then most of these "young" groups may ultimately become subservient to the great families.

This tendency would become pronounced if Japan entered upon a serious depression or if Manchurian enterprises failed to provide the profits that are expected under the new regime. The "young" capital groups are heavily involved in the war industries and in risky enterprises on the Continent, and they would be the first to feel the effects of a fall in the demand for munitions and a check to Japanese schemes of industrial development in eastern Asia. In these circumstances the older and more cautious groups would be provided with an opportunity, such as has often come to them in the past, of acquiring the industrial properties of the "younger" groups at low prices. This chance may well come at the end of the present war when the Japanese economy will be subjected to the strain of adjusting itself to peacetime conditions. . . .

2. Labor, Peasants, Women, Conscription, Repression

❀ IN 1931 the Manchurian Incident and the beginning of economic recovery presented left-wing groups and labor organizations with crucial decisions. How would they stand on Japanese imperialism? How much would they band together to protect the existence of an independent labor movement? The selections from Totten detail the gradual transformation of the left and the unions as events, as well as shaky leadership, pulled them to the right.

The Manchurian Incident evoked "national socialist," as opposed to "international socialist," sentiments in some leftist leaders. They were recruited by extreme right groups, which sought to gain followings within their parties as well as outside. However, neither they nor other Japanese rightists succeeded in creating mass organizations supporting imperialism abroad and reaction at home. Militarism in Japan was sometimes helped by extreme right movements, but it was primarily a gradual imposition of control from above. It had little room for mass-oriented "national socialists," who persisted in trying to be anticapitalist too.

Pressures on the left were exacerbated by popular support for the war and economic imperialism in Asia. In both the Manchurian Incident of 1931 and the Marco Polo Bridge Incident of 1937 (the beginning of the second Sino-Japanese War), union leadership neglected to hold to strong anti-imperialist positions, giving way by degrees to support of the government. They realized that they were threatened, so various mergers followed, and a popular front against fascism was set up. But the inches they kept surrendering—voting for war financing, agreeing to industrial peace, combined with intermittent repression of communists and other leftists— led to the demise of the left-wing parties and labor groups, which dissolved themselves into government-organized groups. The final tragedy was the war itself and what it did to Japan and the rest of Asia.

GEORGE O. TOTTEN, III*
Social Democratic Reactions To War and Totalitarianism

SOCIAL DEMOCRATIC REACTIONS TO THE MANCHURIAN INCIDENT

What was the role played by the social democrats in this process? Did they prove effective in resisting the radical fascist trends in Japan, did they compromise, or did they even to an extent get in step with them?

The occupation of Manchuria by Japan's Kwantung army after September 18, 1931, shocked and initially bewildered the Japanese social democratic parties. Despite clear-cut antiwar planks in their platforms, they found it difficult to take an unequivocal stand on the issue. Already factions were rising within the parties ready to support national socialism at home and expansion abroad.

In the Social Democratic party at this time such a faction was led by Katsumaro Akamatsu. He soon proved to be an inveterate opportunist who ran the gamut of the political scale from communism to fascism within a decade. In 1922 he had been one of the supporters of the Japan Communist party, when it appeared that communism was the wave of the future. By accident he was not arrested along with the other communist leaders, and, as the possibility of a revolution occurring in Japan appeared increasingly

* George O. Totten, III, *The Social Democratic Movement in Prewar Japan* (New Haven, Conn.: Yale University Press, 1966), pp. 69–72, 74–78, 87–91, 95–103, 105–106.

remote, he was soon counted among the conservative right-wingers of the General Federation leadership. . . .

The majority opinion within the Social Democratic party was less radical and somewhat closer to that of the bourgeois parties. Yet despite some theoretical differences between them, both factions were in fundamental agreement on the justice of Japan's actions in Manchuria. The heightened patriotism resulting from the victories of Japanese arms in Manchuria, combined with the increasingly frequent acts of violence perpetrated against "unpatriotic" individuals or groups in the semi-wartime atmosphere, certainly formed the background in which these decisions of the Social Democratic party were reached.

But in order to understand why the party reacted to the situation as it did, a more detailed sociological analysis of its support is necessary. . . . [M]ost of the party's organized labor support was drawn from two groups: (1) the comparatively well-off segments of labor (sometimes called the "labor aristocracy," if that term can be applied to Japanese labor at all), composed of the merchant marine unions, and the army, navy, and government workers' unions; and (2) the comparatively backward sections of labor that worked in relatively large factories such as textiles, and formed what were virtually company unions or at least ones which fully supported the principle of labor-capital "harmony."

At the head of these sections of labor, many of the Social Democratic leaders were able to strengthen their position as a result of the Manchurian affair. Their advocacy of class harmony had greater relevance and their bureaucratic control over their unions seemed more justified than in the slough of the Depression before the outbreak of hostilities. They emphasized labor peace in the following statement at the twenty-first national conference of the General Federation held November 15–17, 1931, shortly after the outbreak of hostilities in Manchuria: "The policy of the General Federation has always been to keep the number of strikes down to the lowest possible limit. The General Federation is dead set against turning strikes into political struggles or provoking them recklessly." Mild as this statement was, taken in the context of the post-Manchurian crisis it could easily be interpreted as betraying a desire on the part of the General Federation's leaders to share in the prosperity about to be created by increased orders for military goods and by the new economic expansion in China. . . .

All the proletarian political groupings to the left of the Social Democratic party had united into one party just before the Manchurian incident. Officially set up on July 5, 1931, it was called the National Labor–Farmer Masses' party (*Zenkoku Rōnō Taishūtō*). The leaders of the former Japan Labor–Farmer party or the Japan–Labor clique, together with some Labor–Farmer factionists, formed the backbone of the new party. They had been joined by the remnants of the reorganized Labor–Farmer party which had moved to the right with the continued arrests and defections of communists and communist sympathizers. The party had also attracted several smaller parties which had been largely influenced by the Labor–Farmer faction, another left-wing group. . . .

With the outbreak of Japanese aggression in Manchuria, this party was quick to condemn the "imperialistic" policy being pursued by the government and the military. It demanded the withdrawal of all Japanese troops from China and set up a committee to work out tactics to effectuate this demand and struggle against the spread of the fighting.

At its annual convention held on December 5–6, 1931, the National Labor–Farmer party attacked its rival in the following terms:

> The Social Democratic party's social democracy (in practice, class collaboration) . . . is quickly becoming bankrupt in the present conditions of capitalism. It can be said that socialism has already become the generally accepted goal within the proletarian class movement, but in the end it can only degenerate into social fascism (or national socialism) if it tries to avoid a head-on clash with bourgeois imperialism. The sight of the Social Democratic party excitedly pandering to the recent trend toward fascism unmercifully exposes its corrupt nature to the masses. For the sake of the liberation of the workers and peasants, such supporters of bourgeois reaction must be completely obliterated.

A proposal was made at the convention to "oppose the imperialistic war," and a stirring message supporting it which had been written by Toshihiko Sakai, one of the "grand old men" of the party who was ill and near death, was read. But Chief Takeuchi of the Atago Police Station, present at the convention in accordance with the law, would not allow any other speakers to be heard on behalf of this proposal. When the convention, chaired by Asō, unanimously adopted the proposal, the police chief ordered that the word "adopted" be excised from the minutes and closed the convention.

In these circumstances, the party's antiwar campaign appears to have been limited to one rally at the Honjo Public Hall in Tokyo. Although this policy had the full backing of the delegates at the open convention, behind the scenes a clash of opinion among the leaders further stymied the campaign. A few of the Japan–Labor clique leaders had begun to get in touch with civilian fascists and young officers soon after the March 1931 plot, and apparently contact men from the military actually visited the majority of National Labor–Farmer Masses' party leaders after the outbreak of war in Manchuria and attempted to persuade them to support the army's actions. . . .

As the Manchurian affair dragged on and as the crisis atmosphere pervaded the country, a number of party leaders began to feel that the party was not moving to the right fast enough, that is, was not going along with the times, and a series of fascist-oriented deviations began to take place. . . .

The severest shock to the party's already fainthearted opposition to the war in Manchuria, however, came from a statement issued by Yojirō Matsutani, one of the party's two representatives in the Diet, when he returned to Japan from an inspection tour in Manchuria with several other Diet members. He unequivocally supported Japan's actions there, saying that it was not "imperialistic" to dispatch troops to protect Japanese interests, but he went on to argue that these interests should be taken from the capitalists and given to the peasants and workers and that the two million unemployed in Japan should be sent as settlers to Manchuria. It was rumored that he was pressured by the army to take this stand. A movement for Matsutani's expulsion from the party immediately got underway, but it was not successful. . . .

Furthermore, Matsutani's position appeared to be vindicated by the general election of February 20, 1932. He was reelected to the Diet from his constituency in Tokyo. . . . But worst of all, the party's popular vote melted away. It received only some 135,000 votes compared to the aggregate of almost 269,000 garnered by its predecessors in the election of 1930. . . .

Even among labor unions which had officially espoused national socialism, Nipponism, or some other variety of fascist dogma, the older trade union philosophy still retained an underlying vitality. The workers in such unions often opposed the "industrial peace during foreign crisis" philosophy of their leaders by demanding wage increases, protesting against job controls, or making various political demands. An example of this was the unprecedented wildcat strike at the Toshima Post Office in May 1933 by members of the Postmen's Brotherhood, which by this time had long since switched its political support from social democracy and now supposedly eschewed such "disruptive activities" as strikes. In other cases, some union leaders who had been converted to Nipponism were still forced to maintain a policy of "trade union-ism" with regard to their own unions. Organized labor, like the intelligentsia, appeared unable to provide the mass basis for a fascist movement that was seen in Germany or Italy.

The situation was somewhat different with regard to the organized agrarian movement in Japan. The first farmers' group to be converted from the social democratic camp to a brand of fascism was led by Rikizō Hirano. In January 1931 his farmers' union had merged with that of the Socio-Democrats to form the Japan Farmers' Union. . . . When he was converted to national socialism . . . the minority led by the Socio-Democrats bolted the Japan Farmers' Union; but otherwise only two local sections of the union, those of Kanagawa and Saitama, protested the farmers' union's conversion to fascism.

Hirano also succeeded in taking with him a substantial following when he later switched his support to the Imperial Way Associa-tion (*Kōdōkai*) in 1933. Even in the period of decline of the radical fascist organizations he did not lose his organized mass support among small landlords and well-to-do farmers, although their political demands had to be phrased in terms that relegated agrarian class lines to the background. During the agricultural crisis of 1931–1932, when tenant-farmer disputes were breaking out all over Japan and when tenant farmers were turning against their landlords with demands for full possession of the lands they tilled, Hirano's demands were as follows: "Return to the agricul-tural villages the exploitation taken by the big cities; lend money to agriculture without collateral; and overthrow capitalism which is selfishly exploiting the agricultural villages." The attempt here was to deflect the anger of the tenant farmers at their distress away from the landlords and direct it toward the cities.

UNIFICATION OF THE SOCIAL DEMOCRATS AND SUBSEQUENT REACTIONS TO FASCISM AND WAR

With defections to national socialism from the ranks of both the National Labor–Farmer Masses' party and the Social Democratic party, pressure for their unification mounted. Both parties had made a poor showing in the 1932 Diet election, and this was attributable partly to their attacks on each other. The National Labor–Farmer Masses' party was no longer much to the left of the Social Democratic party inasmuch as some of its leftists, such as Kenzō Asahara, had embraced fascism while others, notably Kanjū Katō and his following, had withdrawn from the party and had been expelled from National Labor. Both parties were almost equally targets for the attacks from the illegal leftist National Conference of Japanese Labor Unions in its last burst of energy in 1932. . . .

The merger ceremony of the two parties took place on July 24, 1932, at the *Kyōchō Kaikan* (Harmonization Hall) in Shiba Park in Tokyo. The new party was called the Socialist Masses' party (*Shakai Taishūtō*) and in its "Terms of the Merger" it took a clearly antifascist stand, "opposing imperialistic wars" and "strengthening the antifascist front." As a socialist party it was also dedicated to "the overthrow of the declining capitalist system" and still spoke in the radical phrases of opposition to "class collaborationism" and "parliamentarianism"—by which term they meant "elections as the only form of political activity." The party was obviously not opposed to campaigning for office but wanted to supplement this with street demonstrations that would gradually build up the militancy of the masses. It aspired to be the single proletarian party and to promote cooperation between labor and the farmers. . . .

In the beginning the Socialist Masses' party clearly opposed fascism, but it gradually came to support a war policy and then the whole structure of military fascism or totalitarianism in Japan. The first step seemed almost innocuous: it reversed its stand in 1933 on the question of "military orders inflation" which was one of the government's methods of getting out of the 1931 Depression and consisted of expanding military orders and of large-scale deficit spending for military purposes, a policy that made necessary the "dumping" of goods abroad to secure imports. . . .

With regard to labor policy, the Socialist Masses' party (particularly the Social Democratic clique within it) called for industrial peace and greater cooperation between labor and management. The government and the military were very much interested in this campaign, and through it the party's labor leaders increased their contacts with the authorities and began to advocate governmental control over industry and labor. The Congress of Japanese Labor Unions on December 16, 1933, met with representatives from the government, from proletarian and bourgeois political parties, from business, and from the academic world to consider the problem. This trend was eventually to develop, some six years later, into what was called the Industrial Patriotic Movement (*Sampō Undō*) in which labor was brought under governmental control for the purpose of prosecuting the total war effort. . . .

In sum, it may be said that this whole trend toward social democratic unity meant a consolidation of power in the right wing with the formerly somewhat more leftist Japan-Laborites taking at times an ultra-rightist position, advocating closer ties with the military in order to strengthen the proletarian movement *vis-à-vis* the main established political parties and the government (specifically the Home Ministry and the police)—and to strengthen their own position relative to the more entrenched Social Democrats. Nevertheless, in maintaining various principles of social democracy and in drawing a line between themselves and converts to national socialism, social democratic unity continued to have strong antifascist connotations which cannot be overlooked in the electoral successes for the Socialist Masses' party in 1936 and 1937. That they remained "connotations" rather than an open stand will become clearer from an examination of what was called the "popular front." . . .

The intelligentsia were undoubtedly the Japanese most sensitive to developments abroad. The European popular front movements were reported in detail and polemically praised in the journal literature they read (and wrote) during this period.

Through the channels of journalism the idea of the popular front infiltrated to a certain extent into the socialist and labor movements.

Communist influence in promoting a popular front appears to have been slight. Although the Japanese communists had been able to revamp their strategy after the clarification of their position in the so-called 1932 Thesis, their membership was gradually dispersed by continuous police oppression. By the end of 1933 ... most of the top leaders had been tried and imprisoned, and a number had recanted. With the arrest of Satomi Hakamada, the last of the Central Committee members who remained loyal, the communist organ *Red Flag* (*Akahata*) ceased underground publication and all party organization was crushed. Thereafter, scattered communist groups tried to rebuild the party, but they were always arrested before they could accomplish anything substantial.

This was the state of affairs in Japan when the tactic of the united front against fascism was adopted at the Seventh Comintern Congress in July and August 1935. In February 1936 Sanzō Nozaka, who had escaped from arrest in Japan in 1931 and had just been elected at the Congress to the Presidium of the Comintern, wrote in collaboration with Kenzō Yamamoto, the Japanese representative to the Profintern, what they called "A Letter to the Communists of Japan," explaining the new tactic, and sent it to Japan via the United States. Since this was almost a directive, it must have been read by many of the remaining communists as a guide for their activities.

Among other things, it proposed infiltrating the Socialist Masses' party and other social democratic labor and farmer organizations. But it is not clear what effect this and the report of the Seventh Comintern Congress had in Japan, as they were circulated clandestinely. ...

The Japan Proletarian party claimed to be the driving force behind the antifascist popular front in Japan, and yet it encountered considerable opposition based on the counterclaim that, instead of uniting the proletarian front, with its own small and more radical following it was disruptive. ...

The Socialist Masses' party ... [in the election of April 1937] leapt from twenty-four to thirty-eight members in Diet representation and thereby became the third largest parliamentary party. Much speculation appeared in the press concerning this advance.

Noting the tenseness of the situation in North China, some observers argued that this was a protest reflecting dissatisfaction with the lack of party cabinets since 1932, the increasing number of scandals associated with the main, established political parties, and opposition to the possible outbreak of hostilities. In this sense the vote constituted implicit support for the popular front idea.

While conceding that the people were worried by the war clouds, others argued that the mass of manual and white-collar workers and tenant and small farmers who had voted for the Socialist Masses' party accepted the necessity for defending Japanese interests on the continent but voted for the Socialist Masses' party because they were convinced that it might be able to do something for them within the context of a politics of weak and greedy parties and of an economy in many ways preparing for war. The party appeared to have exhibited unprecedented stability for the last five years, and to have representatives in the Diet who interpellated the government on increasingly specific issues rather than roundly denouncing it in a dogmatic manner.

When headlines of the China incident splashed across the front pages of the daily papers following the exchange of fire on the night of July 7 at the Marco Polo Bridge (Lukouch'iao) in North China, the proletarian party leaders were faced with the necessity of taking a stand. Behind closed doors a peculiar reversal took place. The Social Democratic leaders who had been so quick to support Japan's actions in the Manchurian Incident of 1931 were now worried about foreign reactions against Japan that could lead to international isolation, and they were wary of the increasing power of the military. In contrast, the Japan Laborite leaders, who had braved the police and flouted dominant public opinion in criticizing the military moves in Manchuria as "imperialistic," this time demanded that the party pledge all-out support for the cabinet in promoting national unity. While Asō and others had had contacts with elements of the military . . . what convinced the majority of the party's leadership to support this stand was consideration of the sharp electoral reverses suffered in 1932 by those opposed to the army's actions in Manchuria. At that time the proletarian popular vote fell to less than half that of 1930.

As the self-avowed champion of the popular front against fascism and war, the Japan Proletarian party could hardly condone the army's advance into China, but in the tense atmosphere it did not dare to make a public condemnation. Its position was one of eloquent silence. The party did, however, express concern for the welfare of families deprived of their breadwinners and for the morale of troops in the field.

As war fever heightened, however, more positive "patriotic" support was demanded of all Japanese subjects. The Home Ministry decided to move resolutely against opinion-makers suspected of possible "disloyalty," especially all those involved in the "plot" of the popular front. On December 15, the police arrested hundreds of leftist labor leaders and even nonparty intellectuals. . . .

Obviously the trend of events in Japan made practically impossible an effective antiwar campaign. There were, nevertheless, certain subjective factors within the Japan Proletarian party itself that abetted the defeat of the antifascist popular front.

First, its numerical weakness was of crucial importance. . . .

Besides being weak, the Japan Proletarian party and the force it led had no well-worked-out program. The police had forbidden publication of its campaign policy. In its other statements, it did not even hint at measures that went beyond the pale of the very restricted sphere of "legal" activities at that time. In addition, its partisan political stand alienated a number of organizations that might otherwise have favored a popular front. Furthermore, its electoral competition with the Socialist Masses' party automatically cut off collaboration with the antifascists within that party, such as Kiyoomi Taman. Finally, the party's quick cessation of all activity as soon as the hostilities started in China deprived of leadership whatever latent antiwar protest existed.

Even before the Japan Proletarian party was ordered to disband, the Socialist Masses' party, like Peter before the cock crowed thrice, disowned its founding principles. This came in a Diet speech by Kanichirō Kamei who stated categorically: "Our party is neither social democratic nor socialist." While the denial did not actually represent the truth, the political social democratic movement had reached a crisis. Its formal termination awaited the decision by party leaders to initiate the campaign to dissolve all political parties.

The first move in this direction would be for the Socialist Masses' party to demonstrate its willingness to dissolve itself. Such a policy was actually proposed as early as December 1937 by Diet Representative Suejirō Yoshikawa, a Social Democratic member of the party's Central Executive Committee. He reasoned that since national unity was needed to carry out Japan's mission in Asia, "politics" should be abandoned, and this could begin with the party's own dissolution. The membership, however, was not yet ready for such a move. . . .

The idea of a totalitarian "reorganization" of the people was nevertheless gradually gaining adherents. Public opinion turned more and more against the "corrupt politicians." The idea in the beginning was that the Diet should be done away with entirely, but, since its existence was sanctioned by the constitution which had been given to the people by the Meiji emperor himself, the proposition of a single totalitarian party came to supersede it.

Prince Konoe, who had become Prime Minister a month before the Lukouch'iao incident on July 7, 1937, early indicated that he was favorably inclined toward this solution. . . .

On the first anniversary of the Lukouch'iao incident, July 7, 1938, the Socialist Masses' party proposed forming a "national party" (*kokumin no tō*) as the means for achieving "national unification" (*kyokoku itchi*), overcoming class conflict, factional strife, and mutual misunderstandings. To this end the party itself was taking an attitude of "self-effacement" (*onore o munashū shite*), as all other special interests should, to help prosecute the "holy war." . . .

When it became clear that Prince Konoe considered the time ripe for his becoming the leader of a "new structure," the Socialist Masses' party formally made its decision, on July 6, 1940, at the *Kyōchō Kaikan* in Tokyo, to dissolve. Asō, having arisen from his sickbed to address the party, attempted, as chairman of the Central Committee, to make it appear that the totalitarianization of the nation was what the social democratic movement had striven for all along, saying, "Now our call for the organization of the people has become the call of the nation and our advocacy of dedication has become the advocacy of the race. I rejoice that the day has come when our simple wishes have spread abroad and our sacrifice has opened the road to renovation."

Two days later the General Federation, with twenty-eight years of activity behind it, dissolved voluntarily rather than be ordered to disband, as had been feared ever since the abortive Nationalist Labor party had been prohibited on May 7, 1940. The General Federation had promised its support to the formation of that party.

On July 16, Premier Yonai submitted the resignation of his cabinet so that the second Konoe cabinet might be formed, and almost simultaneously the Seiyūkai, the Minseitō, and the Kokumin Dōmei, as well as the remaining smaller parties, all dissolved themselves. The agrarian movement soon came to an end with the dissolution of the Japan Farmers' Union and the General Federation of Japanese Farmers' Unions.

☖ AT A TIME when the political parties and labor unions had been dissolved into a national patriotic front, John K. Emmerson argues that only the Japan Communist party (JCP), operating clandestinely in the face of harsh police repression, continued to oppose radically Japanese militarism and overseas expansion. Emmerson, an American foreign service officer, was writing in the last year of World War II. His report provides a concise history of the Japanese Communist party. In this document Okano Susumu is a pseudonym for Nozaka Sanzō, the famous postwar JCP leader who lived in Yenan during the 1940s.

Emmerson's report includes a translation of the 1932 Thesis by the Communist International on "The Japanese Situation and the Duty of the Japanese Communist Party." The document is one of the few at the time that set forth a political program of opposing within Japan the continuing militarization of society and overseas expansion. It alone called for the abolition of the emperor system and complete withdrawal from Japan's overseas colonies.

JOHN K. EMMERSON*
The Japanese Communist Party

INTRODUCTION

Japanese fascism has so totally eclipsed opposition that the existence of dissenting elements within the country is frequently doubted. Or, government and ex-government personalities popularly tagged as "moderates" are thought to be the only hope of a Japan to rise out of the ruins. Our political responsibility for Japan, which we cannot evade, makes it imperative that we begin to evaluate the forces on our side. One of these forces is the Communist party.

More than twenty years of dogged persecution by the indefatigable Japanese police have failed to destroy the Communist underground in Japan. While most liberals and moderates have actively participated in war activities, only the communists have consistently denounced Japanese aggression. In 1931 and again in 1937 they scattered handbills condemning Japan's attacks on Manchuria and China. Successive waves of arrests have crippled but not killed them. Theirs now is a potential rather than an active force but one likely to grow and one to be recognized for what it can and may do first to defeat and later to revive Japan.

HISTORY

The Industrial Revolution came to Japan, not as to Great Britain, in a long sequence of social shocks set off by the inventions of the cotton gin and the steam engine, but as a sudden encounter between a static feudalism and a full-blown, going industrial mechanism. As a proletarian consciousness began to develop, the police power, well known and well used in Tokugawa times, soon asserted itself to check the rapid growth of a popular

* U.S., Congress, Senate, Committee on the Judiciary, *The Amerasia Papers: A Clue to the Catastrophe of China,* 91st Cong., 1st sess., January 26, 1970, pp. 1219–1225.

mass movement. It is therefore the more noteworthy that without a socially conscious populace and in spite of constant obstacles and suppression, liberal and proletarian movements did arise in Japan and to a degree flourish. Defeat in this war could be the cataclysm out of which these elements crystalize to bring into being a genuine people's government. This will be their unique historical opportunity.

Socialist thought entered Japan with the machines she imported from abroad. The first industrial strike occurred in 1886. The first socialist party was formed in 1901 and the first socialist newspaper published in 1903. The Communist Manifesto was translated in 1904 and its appearance in the newspaper *Heimin Shimbun* resulted in the immediate suppression of both newspaper and document.

In 1910 occurred the famous "Kōtoku Incident." Kōtoku Shūsui, who had translated the Communist Manifesto and was the leader of an anarchistic group, was arrested with twenty-three of his followers. The charge was plotting to assassinate the emperor. Kōtoku and eleven others were executed. The government took occasion to dissolve all socialist and labor groups and to ban all leftist publications.

Japan's proletariat movement received its next impetus from the Russian Revolution and the First World War. In 1917 prices had risen ninety-five percent over the prewar level while wages had increased only twenty-two percent. Strikes jumped by eighty-five percent over the prewar total.

The rice riots of 1918 stand out as a landmark in the history of the Japanese proletarian. Started by fishwives in a tiny village on the Japan Sea on August 3, 1918, this popular protest against exorbitant rice prices spread like a tidal wave over the entire country. In Kobe rioters attacked rice stores, set fire to newspaper establishments, wrecked the homes of wealthy officials, and finally advanced upon the police stations, armed with an array of home-made weapons. Troops finally quelled the disturbances after several days. As the riots multiplied throughout the countryside and in all the large cities, they became a mass national uprising participated in by laborers, farmers, merchants, clerks, students, and unemployed. As a final result, approximately 8000 persons were convicted and imprisoned.

The extent of the rice riots suggests how quickly and with what force a popular movement can gain momentum among the Japanese people.

The Communist party has never been legal in Japan. It was organized secretly in Tokyo in July [1922]. Meetings of leaders were held clandestinely under various guises. In March of 1923 the party platform was drawn up and it was decided to send a delegate to the Third International in Moscow. Police discovered the existence of the party and the names of the thirty delegates attending the March meeting. These were arrested on June 5, 1923; among them was Okano Susumu. They had, however, been warned of their impending arrest and were able to appoint a committee of other members to carry on the work of the party in the strictest secrecy.

In September of 1926 instructions were received from the Comintern to reorganize the Communist party in Japan and on December 4 in an inn in Yamagata prefecture, an assembly met to undertake this work.

In 1926 the Rōdō Nōmintō (Workers and Peasants party) was founded with the support of the Communist party. Leftist movements were gaining sympathizers among the intellectuals; students became organized and many of them were arrested. Before its suppression in 1928, the *Musansha Shimbun,* a legal newspaper supported by the Communists, had a circulation of 35,000.

In Japan's first election under restricted manhood suffrage in 1923, the Rōdō Nōmintō polled 200,000 votes and won two Diet seats. The Communists called this their first real victory in Japan.

During 1928 and 1929 over a thousand members of the Communist party were arrested in Japan. Public trials were held in an effort thoroughly to discredit communism as a poisonous menace threatening the Japanese state. Party members, both in and out of prison, took advantage of the opportunity to write about communist doctrines and have these aired in court. Although minutes of court proceedings were strictly secret, stenographers found their way into the courtrooms and reports of proceedings were clandestinely printed and circulated.

Cases were still being tried when the Manchurian Incident broke out on September 18, 1931. On the following day the Communist party published a statement denouncing Japan's action as an imperialist war. Leaflets carrying this statement were circulated throughout Japan's major cities. On July 26, 1932, the last day of the Communist trials, more than 1500 laborers staged demonstrations in Tokyo, waving red flags and shouting such slogans as: "Down with the War of Aggression! Withdraw from Manchuria! Release the Communists at once! Long Live the Communist Party!"

Ideological differences divided the party. In 1927 an ultra-left movement had been started within the party by Fukumoto Kazuo and the Comintern had issued a "thesis" disapproving of this tendency. Now again a division arose between those who favored an immediate proletarian revolution and those who subscribed to the original Comintern dictum that the revolution in Japan would come about in two stages, first, a period of bourgeois democracy and finally, the communist revolution.

In May 1932, the Comintern issued a second "thesis" entitled "The Situation in Japan and the Duty of the Japanese Communist Party." The thesis attacked the emperor system, the arbitrary police power, the landlord system, and monopolistic capitalism. It prescribed for Japan a "bourgeois democratic revolution with a strong tendency toward progression into the social devolution." It demanded the liberation of Korea and the return to China of all occupied territory including Formosa and Manchuria.

From 1932 on, government suppression of communist activities became progressively more severe. Nevertheless the party continued to operate underground and was successful in fomenting strikes, unrest among the students, and agitation against the forced buying of government bonds. In Tokyo alone, forty branches of an illegal metal workers union were organized. Agitation spread among railroad employees, mine workers, department store employees, primary school teachers, and the unemployed. Police records reported 1700 arrests of members of illegal labor unions during the first seven months of 1933.

Communist literature has had wide circulation in Japan. In 1931 and 1932 the complete works of Marx, Engels, and Lenin were translated into Japanese and sold by a commercial publishing house. The fact that such a venture was profitable testifies to a large reading public in Japan. During those same years at least 100,000 copies of legal magazines of communist color were being printed and sold. According to statistics compiled in Moscow, Japan was surpassed only by the Soviet Union and Germany in the number of communist books published.

On the day following the outbreak of the China Incident on July 7, 1937, the Communist party scattered leaflets in Tokyo, Osaka, and Hokkaido denouncing Japan's attack as an "unjust robbers' war" which every Japanese should oppose. Using the slogan "people's front," the party continued to obstruct the war in every way, by campaigning for aid for soldiers' families, payment of soldiers' wages during their service, and encouraging demonstrations and incidents. It is estimated that an average of one arrest per day for activity against the war occurred during the two years following the outbreak of the China Incident.

Suggesting that the Japanese government was still apprehensive of the strength and activity of the Communist party, the Home Minister stated in the Diet session of February, 1943: "It is regrettable that although the communist movement has gradually diminished since the China Incident, it has still not been completely obliterated."

RELATIONS WITH THE U.S.S.R.

The Japanese Communist party has looked to the Communist International for guidance and policy direction. In 1921, before the party was founded in Japan, Katayama Sen, called the "father of Japanese communism," was a member of the Presidium of the Comintern in Moscow. Upon his death there in 1933, Okano Susumu took his place. . . .

According to Okano, the party's relations with Moscow have been loose from the beginning. Police vigilance in Japan and geographical considerations made communication between the Comintern and the Japanese party difficult. Messages were sent only when absolutely necessary. . . .

In 1932 the Japanese Communist party clandestinely published the Thesis issued by the Comintern. Professor Kawakami Hajime, at that time professor in Kyoto Imperial University, was arrested for implication in its publication. He was later released.

Okano states that the Japanese party, underground from its inception, carried on of necessity a fairly independent existence. In fact he welcomed the dissolution of the Comintern as releasing the Japanese party from certain restrictions and as encouraging adherents to the party's struggle against fascism who were formerly frightened away by the Moscow connection.

PRESENT STRENGTH AND ORGANIZATION

The communists in Japan have had more than twenty years of underground experience. In spite of ruthless persecution by the government an organization has been maintained throughout this time. Since 1940 all leftist political groups in Japan have been dissolved, including the Nihon Musantō (Japan Proletarian party), Rōdō Kumiai (Labor Unions), Nōmin Kumiai (Farmers Unions), and Shakai Taishūtō (Social Mass party). Leaders of these groups may be counted as sympathizers and may be carrying on some underground activities although they are not organized as are the communists.

Okano estimates the number of Communist party members now in Japan to be between 3000 and 4000. He has been unable to maintain regular contact with Japan since Pearl Harbor but he believes this to be a conservative estimate. Approximately 3000 persons were arrested in Japan on December 9, 1941. Okano estimates at least 2000 party members and sympathizers are now serving prison terms. . . .

LOCATION

The party's greatest strength is in Osaka where the Central Committee is located. There are cells in Tokyo, Yokohama, Nagoya, Kobe, Sendai, and in Kyushu (Yukibashi) and Hokkaido. Outside Japan proper there are affiliates in Peking, Tientsin, Shanghai, and Keijō [Seoul]. Party members are found in munitions industries, in Nagoya aircraft factories, and in Kobe shipyards. There are quite a few among radio operators and among seamen.

ACTIVITIES

Before the outbreak of the China Incident in 1937 the party engaged in propaganda, staged demonstrations, and published newspapers. Until 1940 a clandestine monthly magazine was published in Osaka entitled *Arashi o Tsuite* ("Against the Storm"). A second publication appeared for a time under the name *Jimmin no Koe* ("Voice of the People").

Since that time, however, the policy has been to conserve strength and avoid unnecessary sacrifices. In an effort to maintain existence, open activities have virtually ceased. The hand of the Communist party can be seen in strikes which occurred in Nagoya and Kawasaki in 1941.

In 1941 Okano received a letter from Japan which he believes to be authentic. It stated: "Communist party activities are going on normally. The spirit of the working people is rising. We are trying to maintain our organization and strength and are preparing for the future."

THE COMMUNIST POTENTIAL IN JAPAN

(1) The Japanese Communist party is relatively small. It does not represent an underground movement sufficiently strong or well enough organized to carry out extensive sabotage or make a decisive military contribution at the time of landings on Japan. However, as the only known underground now in the country, its military and political potentialities must not be ignored.

(2) As Japan nears defeat the chain of events both inside and outside Japan will strengthen communist elements and communist sympathizers within the country.

(3) When defeat becomes certain the prestige of the Communist party will rise for having been the sole group in Japan to have consistently opposed the policy of military aggression since 1931.

(4) It will become increasingly practicable, as the war develops, to send agents to Japan to contact the communist underground, foment defeatist sentiment among the people, prepare assistance for Allied landings, and to send back intelligence.

(5) To a limited degree the communists may commit acts of sabotage and organize industrial strikes. They could be encouraged in such activities as Japan's military situation becomes more precarious.

(6) The Communist party may become the nucleus of a people's front to include all democratic and antifascist elements upon whom we must depend for a postwar government. A "Free Japan" movement organized abroad and including Japanese communists would stimulate sympathetic elements within the country and become a powerful weapon of psychological warfare before defeat and a unifying political force after defeat.

THE COMMUNIST PROGRAM FOR JAPAN

Okano Susumu, in so far as he speaks for the Japanese Communist party, proposes a moderate, democratic system of government for postwar Japan. His program for Japan is similar to that of the Chinese communists for China: a period of democracy which will eventually lead to the downfall of capitalism and the establishment of a socialist state. Okano's proposals modify the 1932 Comintern Thesis for Japan. For example, the Thesis opposes the Diet, Okano only the House of Peers. The Thesis calls for abolition of the landlord system and monopolistic capitalism; Okano advocates the purchase by the government of the holdings of absentee landlords as a first step toward liquidation of the landlord system and control by the government of large-scale capitalist enterprises. He, as do the Chinese communists, opposes confiscation of property as impractical and undesirable.

The Thesis, written in Moscow, proclaims close affinity for the Soviet Union and Communist China. Whether or not Russia enters the war against Japan, Soviet Far Eastern policy would axiomatically welcome a communist Japan and a communist China. Soviet dominance in the Far East would thereby become a fact.

The United States has within its power the exertion of decisive influence in the political orientation of postwar Japan. If we fail to adopt a positive attitude, some other country, such as the U.S.S.R., may take the lead and boldly carry out a policy in the long run inimical to our interests.

If we desire a democratic Japan we should encourage all elements which might unite in its construction, including the communists. American aid to communists within and without Japan will not surrender the Japanese to the Russians; on the contrary it will give an American direction to Japanese political developments which will advantageously affect our future Pacific relations.

The communists will not be strong enough to seize control in Japan. Realistically they will be content to receive legal recognition for the first time in their history. We may expect them to seek power in the future and Japan may be fertile ground for their growth. We can, however, best prevent Japan's political system from again becoming a danger to us by adopting and activating a positive policy. In spite of war-whipped hate, the Japanese fundamentally like us more than they do the Russians. It is for us to make the most of our opportunity.

THE 1932 THESIS APPROVED BY THE COMMUNIST INTERNATIONAL*
The Japanese Situation and the Duty of the Japanese Communist Party

1. The present war for territorial expansion undertaken by Japanese imperialism bears a direct relationship to the stages occurring before the development of this imperialism. Thirst for aggression is a special quality of Japan's plunderous imperialism which has risen out of a policy of strengthening the nation by piling up capital, acquiring war materials, and grasping colonies. . . .

3. Bourgeois landlord Japan has assumed the role of leadership in war. This is characteristic of Japanese imperialism. The present aggression is caused by a combination of monopolistic capitalism, absolutist militarism, and feudalistic imperialism.

4. Japanese communists must understand the inseparable relationship between Japan's imperialistic aggression abroad and the country's internal politics, between its imperialistic war of plunder and enslavement of colonies on the one hand and internal reaction on the other. Japanese imperialism, as it follows its course of war, continues and even strengthens the oppressive control of laborers through the military-police-emperor system. It plans ever increasing oppression of the farmers and lowering of the standard of living of the masses.

5. The Japanese Communist party must understand clearly and correctly the strength and relations of the various classes within Japan, the immediate significance of the Japanese revolution, and the party's duties with regard to it.

(a) In a concrete analysis of the Japanese situation the starting point must always be the essence of the emperor system.

* U.S., Congress, Senate, Committee on the Judiciary, *The Amerasia Papers: A Clue to the Catastrophe of China,* 91st Cong., 1st sess., January 26, 1970, pp. 1225–1228, 1230.

(b) The second important controlling element is the landlord system. This is the feudal control which prevents development of agricultural production, keeps agriculture in a backward state, and impoverishes the farmers.

(c) The third controlling factor is monopolistic capitalism.

6. The obvious conclusion from the above analysis is that the totality of the country's economy and politics must first and foremost turn the revolutionary movement against the imperialist war, against the authoritarian police-emperor system, against the low, colonial standard of living of the workers, and against their lack of political rights. Furthermore we must fight against the bonds of feudalism and usury which strangle our farm villages.

The following are our objectives at the present stage of the revolution:

(a) Destroy the emperor system.

(b) Wipe out the parasitic landlord system.

(c) Establish a seven-hour working day.

Bring all banks under the control of one government-controlled bank. Place this bank and capitalistic enterprises, especially the production of all cartels and trusts, under the management of workers' and farmers' soviets. Thus the character of the immediate revolution in Japan will be a bourgeois democratic revolution with a strong tendency toward progression into the social revolution.

At present the most important, urgent, action slogans should be the following:

(a) Down with the imperialist war! Change the imperialist war into a domestic war!

(b) Down with the bourgeois emperor-landlord system! Build a farmers' and workers' soviet government!

(c) For the sake of the farmers, confiscate without compensation all lands belonging to landlords, the emperor, and shrines and temples. Cancel all debts owed by farmers to the landlords, usurers, and banks.

(d) Establish the seven-hour day and improve fundamentally the conditions of the workers. Permit labor unions to organize and act freely.

(e) Free the colonies (Chōsen [Korea], Manchuria, Taiwan, etc.) from Japanese imperialism.

(f) Support the Soviet Union and the Chinese Revolution.

The Communist party, for the sake of the struggle represented by these slogans, must call upon all the revolutionary and democratic power within Japan, namely, the laborers, farmers, and poor people of the cities. The Communist party's most important slogan is, "Down with the imperialist war and the police-emperor system! A People's revolution for the freedom of rice and land, and for the establishment of a workers' and peasants' government!"

The Communist party must ally its struggle for a soviet republic of workers and farmers closely to a systematic socialist propaganda. For this purpose the party must make wide use of the success and experience of the Soviet Union.

7. The great strength for the revolution will come from the proletariat and the poor and middle-class farmers.

8. The workers' and peasants' revolution will succeed only when it establishes the power of workers' and peasants' soviets.

With relation to the progress of the revolution, the duties which the communists must not neglect are as follows: When the revolution comes, especially the moment when the emperor system is overthrown, farmers' and peasants' soviets must be set up in every part of the country. The national structure of bourgeois landowner dictatorship must be broken. (Police, gendarmes, army and navy officers will be disarmed; workers and peasants will be armed; a proletarian Red Army will be organized; the Diet and central and provincial organs of power will be abolished; a system of elections of officials by the workers and peasants will be set up, etc.)

9. The proletariat's economic warfare and the struggle of the peasants against the landlords will become intensified as the economic situation becomes grave with outbreak of war and as the pressure of the capitalists and landlords increases against the workers and peasants. . . .

12. The party's duties in the fight against war are as follows:

(a) Unrelenting agitation and propaganda by the written and spoken word against the imperialistic, antirevolutionary war.

(b) Expose the antidemocratic, imperialistic, and counter-revolutionary nature of the slogans issued by the ruling classes and the social democrats: "Rights of the People," "Protection of the Lives and Property of the Japanese Subjects," "Preserve the National Polity of the Japanese Empire."

(c) Vigorous struggle against the policy of the social democrats and supporters of the bourgeois landlord-emperor system who propose to establish peace among the classes within the nation.

Patiently overcoming the obstinate, fanatical antiforeignism of the working masses by enlightening them that all the suffering and hardships they have had to bear are the result of a succession of wars.

(d) Propagandizing of the achievements of the Soviet Union's social construction, of its treatment of peasants and workers, and of its peace policy. Propagandizing of the aims and achievements of the Chinese Soviet movement.

(e) With its objective the changing of the imperialist war into a domestic war, the Japanese Communist party must present appropriate slogans and carry out its activities against the war. On the occasion of this imperialist war, it is our duty to demand the immediate withdrawal of Japanese troops from China and to call upon the Japanese soldiers to refuse to fight, to throw away or turn over their arms, to leave the front and to form a soldiers' organization. In the event of war against the Soviet Union or against revolutionary Soviet China, we must urge the Japanese soldiers to join the Red Armies.

(f) In the case of a counterrevolutionary war the revolutionary classes must not content themselves with hoping for the defeat of their own country. Defeat of the government's armies will weaken the emperor's government and will facilitate an internal war against the ruling class. In the present war which has as its aim reduction of China to a colony, the Japanese communists' action slogan must be: "Struggle for the complete independence of China." Under the conditions of an imperialistic war against China or the Soviet Union, Japanese communists are not merely defeatists but must fight positively for the victory of the Soviet Union and the freedom of the Chinese people.

(g) All-out efforts must be made to carry out strikes on railroads, steamships, and in munitions factories. Mass action and the revolutionary antiwar movement must grow and extend constantly. In such a case a general strike should be proclaimed and efforts exerted to turn it into an armed uprising.

(h) In order to enlist the masses into the antiwar struggle on as wide a scale as possible, the party should carry on special work among young people, disabled veterans, women, and particularly the wives and mothers of soldiers.

(i) Every effort should be exerted to strengthen activities

within the armed forces. It is the duty of the communists to support the local demands of the soldiers and sailors. For example, improvement of material conditions and treatment, guarantees of families' support, increase of furloughs, election system for superior officers, organization of soldiers' committees, political rights, etc. Communists should do everything possible to increase discontent within the armed forces, to encourage dispute between officers and men, and to set up soldiers' committees to deal with the disputes. Efforts should be exerted to break up organizations of veterans, youths, and other popular patriotic elements.

(j) The communists must completely and clearly understand that the principal element of the antiwar struggle is inevitably found within the mass movement and within the mass struggle. Only activity among the masses within the administration, within the armed forces, within labor unions, and among the people in villages can direct the imperialist war into a domestic struggle. . . .

By extending the struggle for local demands and by winning over the masses to the Communist party, the party will bring nearer the opening of a decisive struggle. The war and economic unrest are bringing the clash between the classes within the country to an extremely serious stage. The revolutionary struggle of the workers and peasants led by the Communist party is bringing on a greater revolutionary crisis. Through it the emperor system will receive a mortal blow, the workers' and peasants' soviet will be established, and the Japanese Communist party under this soviet flag will lead the laboring classes and all the workers to the final victory.

❋ THE JAPAN GENERAL FEDERATION OF LABOR dissolved itself in July 1940, an event that was quickly followed by a calamitous plunge in union membership. In 1939, membership was still about 350,000; by the end of 1940 it had dropped to less than 10,000. The government's opposition to independent labor groups had accelerated with the beginning of war with China in 1937, and this tendency was underlined by Japan's withdrawal from the International Labor Organization (ILO) in 1938. The ILO was the labor division of the League of Nations, and in its meetings Japan's labor practices had been criticized.

The solution for labor's reorganization chosen by the government was the Sampō, the Industrial Patriotic Society, set up in 1938. Sampō was in effect a nationwide company union covering all industrial fields. The purpose, not entirely realized, was to draw membership from independent unions and to unite labor to make sacrifices for the war effort.

AYUSAWA IWAO*
Labor's Lot in the War Period

Japan withdrew from the League of Nations in 1933 and from the ILO in 1938. . . . Strangely, at the general elections in 1936 and 1937 the parties of the working class registered a remarkable advance, but this was a passing phenomenon. In 1938 the General Mobilization Law was promulgated, which was the signal for preparation for a headlong plunge into total war. . . .

For a brief period after the "success" of the Manchurian Incident, when, because of its apparent impotence in dealing with the new state of Manchukuo, the League of Nations had become a laughing-stock among cynical critics throughout the world, Japan's war industries were enjoying illusory gains and the workmen employed by them were living in a fool's paradise. Unemployment was disappearing. Wages were on the increase; industries were expanding. A drop in the exchange rate of yen as a result of the inflation occasioned by the sudden expansion of the munitions industries meant an increase in exports. The result was that trade unions gained strength through increased membership. In fact, Japanese trade unions reached the highest peak of the prewar period in 1936, with a total of 420,589 members.

As a result of the favorable economic situation, the number of dispute cases decreased from the outbreak of the Manchurian

* Ayusawa Iwao, *A History of Labor in Modern Japan* (Honolulu: East-West Center Press, University of Hawaii, 1966), pp. 226–227, 229, 230–231.

Incident up to 1935; also, there were fewer strikes and the number of participants in disputes decreased from year to year. . . .

However, the illusions of the fool's paradise could not last much longer. The China Incident became a contest in which every move Japan's war leaders made only dragged the mikado's loyal troops farther into a muddy river from which there was no return. Munitions works were kept busy, employment increased, nominal wages kept rising, but peace industries were all condemned and shrinking. Sickness and accident cases multiplied. Deterioration of working conditions led to an increase in labor disputes. To cope with this situation, the government, which was under military control, only tightened economic controls. In Japan, as in any country at war, it was the working class that bore the heaviest burden of sacrifice. Under wartime control the workers had lost the freedom to choose their occupations. Prices were rising at the same time that wages were under strict control. The inevitable consequences were lower efficiency, more disputes, and widespread unrest.

In this situation it was only natural for the workers to show signs of resistance. It has been noted that trade union membership in prewar Japan reached its peak in 1936. . . .

Sampō is the abbreviation of the longer Japanese title Sangyō Hōkoku Kai (Industrial Patriotic Society). It was designed to ensure the cooperation of management and labor in all plants throughout the nation for the effective prosecution of war. People are apt to equate it with the *Arbeitsfront* in Nazi Germany, but this is inaccurate, since, although the basic ideas of Sampō and *Arbeitsfront* are largely identical, the movement in Japan started at the suggestion of local police officers who had been engaged in labor relations control work. The sporadic trials of the local police impressed the central authority, especially since Kyōchō Kai [Conciliation Society] assumed sponsorship in turning this into a national organization in response to the National General Mobilization Law in March 1938. In August of that year an official memorandum issued jointly by the vice-ministers of Welfare and of the Interior suggested to the prefectural governors that they promote the organization of the Sampō. Another joint communication of the two vice-ministers directed the governors to establish the Sampō in their respective prefectures; it also directed that each governor become the president of his prefectural organization.

How did organized labor react to this? As already intimated, the pressure was too great. Reluctantly but steadily it succumbed. . . .

The philosophy on which the Sampō was predicated was that of the old traditional family system. *Jigyō Ikka* ("Enterprise Family") was its slogan. The head of the enterprise or of management was the father of the family and all the employees represented his children. All were to work together in harmony for higher productivity and ultimate victory in the war. In the years around 1940–1941, the movement seemed to thrive, with more than 19,060 organizations throughout Japan with a total membership exceeding three million supporting it. It apparently succeeded in reducing membership in trade unions, but it did not succeed in reducing the number of labor disputes. . . .

Ordinarily one does not—indeed, one must not—expect a normal development of labor laws in any country at war. It is a delightful surprise, therefore, to find in Japan some instances of progress in labor legislation during this period, though in no case could it be considered substantial progress.

Generally speaking, labor laws of a liberal nature were at a standstill during the fourteen war years. The attempt to enact a trade union law came to an end in 1931. The laws designed primarily to "protect" labor, such as the Factory Act and the Mining Workers' Regulations, underwent major improvements for the last time in 1929. The legal benefits of workmen's compensation, hitherto confined to factory and mining workers, were extended in 1931 to such outdoor workers as those engaged in construction and transportation works. Another remarkable development was the *Shōten Hō* (Commercial Shops Act), enacted in 1938, which placed workers in commercial shops under the protection of law. This was not strictly a "war necessity" but it was done nonetheless.

In 1938 a new department of the government called the Welfare Ministry was created. The government was awakening to the necessity of safeguarding the health and well-being of the nation and of establishing for that purpose a new ministry. One might say that in this instance war necessity was a major motivation. As a matter of fact, innumerable modifications were made in the rules regulating conditions of work as *senji tokurei* (wartime exceptions). There was, for instance, a rule made in 1938 to limit working hours to twelve hours per day. This measure was enforced to prevent the exhaustion of manpower. In other words, it was war necessity rather than liberal or humanistic ideas which prompted the government to take this measure. The idea of protection of labor was only incidental or secondary—prosecution of the war was the paramount need.

☘ THE WORKING CONDITIONS of factory girls were investigated by Helen Mears, who visited Japan in 1935. Assisted by a Japanese woman translator (Akiko in this selection), Mears went to a textile plant. Here she retells one girl's story. She also talked with both a union official at this "model" factory, and with one of the managers, who suggests that, if labor agitators had been able to reach the factory girls, ninety percent of them would have grown unhappy with their lot. This offhand assessment underscores the way the dormitory system hampered labor organizing.

HELEN MEARS*
The Way of the Gods

My inspection of the textile industry started with a cotton mill, the Dai Nippon Tokyo factory. The Dai Nippon is one of the largest of the textile companies, and the Tokyo factory which Akiko and I visited was the prize factory—the factory which was shown to all interested foreigners as a demonstration of Japanese paternalism and organization as its best. I was sent there by Mr. Toko, an official in the Home Office to whom I had a letter of introduction. . . .

In preparation for my visit, Mr. Toko had given me a descriptive booklet, text, and excellent photographs, showing the small girl workers leading an ideal life.

"Of course," he had said with a man-to-man twinkle, "this

* Helen Mears, *Year of the Wild Boar* (Philadelphia: Lippincott, 1942), pp. 272–289.

pamphlet was gotten up to show at the International Labor Congress."

. . . Japanese like Mr. Toko have traveled enough in the West to observe conditions that convince them that Western management's expressed concern for labor is a game. They try to play it; they have learned the rules; they can issue statements and prepare reports expressing the sentiments they feel are expected of them; but—in unmythological terms, the hypocrisy is too apparent. So they give one the knowing elbow in the ribs. I understood that I was expected to realize that the Dai Nippon was a model institution which it was a pleasure to show to foreigners.

To reach the factory, Akiko and I rode in a taxi for better than an hour, and came to a stop in a muddy road outside a high stone wall that suggested a penitentiary. The entrance was guarded by a watchman who expected us. Beside him waited a little girl in a white middy blouse and black pleated skirt who led us to an office where we were served tea. We were joined at once by a man in foreign clothes whose hollow cheeks gave him a saturnine appearance, but whose manner was cordial. He led us on a swift tour of the plant, which took an hour from the time we passed into the mill, beginning where the piles of raw cotton stood waiting, through various processes, room after room, until we followed the finished product, packed in burlap in the form of cotton cloth and white thread, out to the narrow-gauge track that would take it to the main line and the markets of the world. . . .

. . . We next viewed the dormitories. Leaving our shoes at the door and putting on felt slippers, we entered a narrow corridor along which came a procession of girls, from the morning shift, on their way to the bath-house. They all stopped dead, and with expressionless faces, bowed low, long braids bobbing down their backs. Suddenly I was reminded of the mechanical Japanese dolls who bob their heads back and forth at the tap of a finger that used to fascinate me when I was a child. We passed rooms where classes in sewing were conducted. We saw also classes in ethics and history under the aegis of an elderly gentleman in a gray silk kimono. The wall of the history classroom was papered with pictures of the Meiji shrine which the professor told us were used to illustrate his history lessons. In the auditorium, a group of girls, in their cotton everyday kimonos and bare feet, were being taught etiquette. We saw the dining room, the swimming pool. The kitchen was large and clean and the food smelled delicious. We saw the clinic, a doctor (in action), a dentist (in action), the pharmacy, the infirmary. The mill was a walled town, self-sufficient, oblivious of and indifferent to the rest of the world.

After we had seen everything, we asked if we might talk to some of the girls. *"Dōzo."* (Please.) We were escorted back to the office and joined by another saturnine gentleman and, after an interval, by two girls, pretty and dignified in formal kimono. We all sat about the table and were served tea, which the girls did not touch. They sat very straight, flanked by the two gentlemen. I was urged to ask them anything I wanted to. Akiko put the questions for me and translated the answers. It was my impression that everything the girls said was verified by the management. Through our exchange of question and answer, they lived their daily life for us. The story of one was, with minor variations, the story of the other—and the story of all.

Let us take the girl called Tsuki.

Tsuki-san was the daughter of a small farmer from a village an hour's journey north of Tokyo. She was eighteen years old and had worked in the Dai Nippon for nearly three years. She lived in the dormitory, a two-storied barracks adjoining the mill, separated from another by a small garden with a lawn of turf and a large swimming pool. Tsuki's sister, Tama, lived in the neighboring dormitory, but they seldom saw each other. The sixteen hundred girl workers were divided into morning and afternoon shifts, and the routine of their lives kept them apart.

Tsuki-san shared a fifteen-mat room (fifteen feet by eighteen feet) with nine other girls, one of a long row of rooms under the supervision of a matron. When she was on the early shift, the rising gong sounded at 4 A.M. By 4:05, Tsuki was jostling her roommates as they rolled up their bedding and packed it away in the cupboards behind the sliding panels. Working swiftly, the girls swept and scrubbed the white matting of the room and the corridor outside. The head girl made sure that they were all up in time, and the room left in order—that is, clean and empty except for the low table with perhaps a mirror, an alarm clock, a vase of flowers. The room tidy, Tsuki washed quickly at the gray cement trough at the end of the corridor, and, slipping into her work uniform, scurried to the auditorium for setting-up exercises under the direction of a health instructor attached to the mill staff. Breakfast, of fermented bean soup, fish, rice, and radish pickle, came at 4:30. At 5 A.M. she was at her machine.

Tsuki-san's job was to watch for defects in the finished cloth. Miles of white cotton shirting, in a monotonous flow, climbed up her machine, passed through the roller, and, beyond her, ascended to the high roof, then descended into the folder. She watched with a practiced eye for any irregularity, an extra thread, a smudge of oil. With a quick movement of the lever, she stopped the machine, picked out the extra thread with a sharp comb, rubbed the spot smooth. She did not think. In the beginning the work was difficult, and it was three months before she felt at ease, but now her movements were as automatic as those of the machine. She became tired, of course, but with the fatigue of young muscles which spring back very quickly. She could not leave her machine, but at 10:30 there was a half-hour for a wash and lunch. At eleven, she was back at her machine, where she watched the endless flow of white cloth until 2 P.M. when the other shift came on.

Work over, a long afternoon ahead, what did Tsuki-san do with it? She wasted no time in deciding . . . it was all planned for her. From two until 3:30, her time was all her own. She hurried to change her work uniform for a kimono, and then, her hair down her back in a bobbing braid, carrying her *tenugui,* her soap bag, and perhaps a pail of clothes to launder, she pattered down the corridor on *tabi*'d feet to the huge bathroom for a general cleaning-up and social half-hour with her friends. Here, as she washed her hair, or laundered her clothes, standing with the others at the low cement basins, she could make up in chatter for her silent hours at the machine. It was now nearly 3 P.M. If it was summer, she could go for a swim in the outdoor pool, or sit on the grass in the garden. Or she might rush to buy a brace for her obi, or some sewing silk, from the branch of the large Tokyo department store situated conveniently for her within the mill walls. In winter, she would carry from the kitchen the redhot charcoal for the brazier which was the only heat in the dormitory, and then she and her friends could sit huddled around it, chatting until 3:30.

At 3:30, she had to be in the classroom. She might have a class in arithmetic, writing, composition, geography, history, sewing, ethics, knowledge of national life, international topics. There was a definite schedule and each day had its special subject. Sometimes she gathered with a group of fifty in the large auditorium and was taught deportment. Sometimes she was even instructed in tea ceremony and flower arrangement. This was a rare privilege, for usually a farmer's daughter had no opportunity to learn these rituals. Tsuki-san liked her sewing classes best, for in them she made kimonos for her trousseau, and other articles of clothing, and perhaps dresses for her small sister. Every Japanese woman must be a competent seamstress, for no self-respecting Japanese man would marry a girl who could not sew, and, if she did not learn at the mill, she would have to go to a sewing school for a term before marriage.

At 4:30, the class was over and Tsuki-san, carrying her chopsticks, went to supper in a large dining room decorated with posters showing muscular young men doing gymnastics and cherry trees blossoming in Kyoto. She sat at a Western-style table with seven of her friends and there was no time for ceremony. She helped herself to rice and *tempura* vegetables (fried in a pastry-batter) and radish sauce—which were piled in wooden tubs in the center of the room—eating from a small, individual tub, and washing it all down with tea. The meals had the proper number of calories and were passed by the inspector of the police department. After supper she took a bath, parboiling with her friends for ten minutes in a large cement tank at a temperature of 112° Fahrenheit.

Then she was ready for more classes. She was at her desk at six, and stayed there until nine, learning sewing, history, ethics, etcetera. Dismissed from class, she went to her room in the dormitory, took her mattress and quilt from the cupboard, arranged them on the matting, allowing a foot of space on all sides between hers and the mattresses of her neighbors. Usually she slept very soundly. Whirrrrr! Four A.M.

The shift was changed every week, with Sunday a holiday. When Tsuki was on the late shift, she got up at 8 A.M. and had the advantage of a Buddhist religious service in the auditorium. She attended classes during the morning, went to her machine at two, and worked till 11 P.M. By 1 A.M., she was in bed. She liked the early shift better.

Once or twice a year, classes were suspended and a movie was shown in the auditorium. Sometimes on a national holiday some respected great men came and told them about the Nippon Spirit. Occasionally she might go out for a half-day's picnic with the other girls of her shift, otherwise there was no reason for her to leave the mill grounds, as everything she wanted was supplied to her there.

Tsuki began at a wage of thirty-five sen a day but had been raised to forty-five sen. At New Year's, she received a bonus of five yen. She paid the mill fifteen sen a day for board, and two percent of her wages went for government health insurance. She was not paid for Sunday or holidays. Except for an allowance of one yen a month, her money was sent by the management to her parents. . . .

Akiko was slowly translating. The girl said that she came to the mill to help her family and to save money for her trousseau. She had not realized that she could not leave the mill and was sorry not to see the beauties of Tokyo, but she was busy and had no time to think about it, or to go out. She expected to send her money to her parents anyway and it was convenient that the mill did it for her. She did not need much money for herself.

Had Tsuki known of profits and dividends, what meaning would they have had to her? She was housed and fed. She was receiving an education. And all she had to do was to work at a machine for eight hours. Her hours at her farm home were longer, the work harder, the food not so good. When had a farmer had *tempura* vegetables? She was accustomed to obedience, and had never had so much as a sen to spend on herself. A yen a month was a fortune.

Tsuki would work in the mill, perhaps, for four years, although most of the girls stayed only three. Then she would return to her farm home, and, if her family had been able to save some of her money for a trousseau, they would find her a husband, a neighbor-farmer. She would marry him, and he might well consider that her years of mill discipline had served as a finishing school in the educational process that had shaped her for the Japanese ideal of "good wife and wise mother."

The Japanese could well point with pride to the perfection of their system. It had every advantage of conscript labor and none of the disadvantages. Here was a young girl who was self-supporting;

who was helping her family during hard times; was helping her country; who was, meanwhile, housed and fed luxuriously; sheltered from any harm; educated beyond the possibilities of her farm home; who would be released after a few years to an assured marriage. It behooved those European countries that believed in a controlled society to look to Japan for guidance; for how amateurish and inadequate did the Nazi "Strength Through Joy" labor service seem when contrasted with the integrated Japanese way that functioned from childhood on, and touched every part of life. Tsuki-san was prepared for her mill job by her home conditioning, her education, her economic dependence. There was no ambition to make her restless. Her "ambition" was to perform her duty, to marry the man whom her family should select, to have children in her turn, preferably boy children to carry on the family name and serve the ancestors and the country. This was not coercion—it was *shūkan*. Here was another paradox of Japan. Part of the dynamic force behind her powerful advance was inertia—the steady unthinking pressure of a mass—unvolatile and irresistible.

Like Akiko, Tsuki had been caught by the upsurge of the new Japan. Tsuki, however, had been carried along in the current without even feeling the motion. Her sleep had never been disturbed. Not one of her fundamental truths had been shaken. For Tsuki there was no conflict. She was completely insulated against "dangerous thoughts." She was living in two worlds, but she did not know it.

There remained the problem of what would happen to Japanese industry should Tsuki awake from this sleep to learn about a society where the woman received the wages she earned, earning enough to live independently; marrying, if she chose to marry, the man of her own choosing, whose equal she would be before the law. Was it possible to guess from the reaction of Akiko, whose disapproving, "These girls are not awake yet," was obviously based on her own experience of certainly questionable independence? Mr. Toko had said to me, "Now, ninety percent of these girl workers are happy and contented, and ten percent discontented. But if propaganda and agitators got in among them, within six months, ninety percent would be discontented and ten percent contented." Certainly it would be impossible for an "agitator" to reach behind these walls to these girls. Moreover, the classes kept them too busy to leave time for "dangerous thoughts." But how typical was this mill? And how average was Tsuki? Like all answers in Japan, this led only to more questions.

For the next month or two, my life was a series of false trails and blind alleys, as I went about attempting to discover if there was a labor movement among the women workers. I was told innumerable times, by people who should have known, that there was not. I persisted in my search, however, because I found along the way so many things of interest. . . .

Finally, however, an indirect trail led me to Miss Nara, who had the distinction of being one of the half-dozen women labor organizers in Japan. She was little, and very Japanese in appearance and dress, an extraordinary surprise even in a country that became daily more surprising. With Miss Nara and Miss Hayashi, an American-born, handsome young woman with a Phi Beta Kappa key from a Midwestern university, I visited a group of girl textile workers in their union headquarters. While we sat in a circle on the mats, and they served tea with great ceremony, they told me about their lives at the mill, and the history of their union. This mill was not one of the show institutions. It was the average large factory. The life of the girls was like that of the Dai Nippon in the routine of the working day, the dormitory life, the communal meals, the lack of freedom, the small wages. It was unlike it in the girls' leisure. They were not pampered with swimming pools; there were no classes except sewing, and occasionally a lecture on ethics, or a lesson in flower arrangement. There was no health program and the union took care of the sick. The wages ranged from thirty-five sen a day for the beginners, to one yen fifty sen for the most skilled. . . .

The mill employed 700 girls, of whom 400 belonged to the union; and 130 men, of whom ninety belonged. The history of the union—though not typical—was interesting as illustrating the difficulties in the way of union organization in Japan. The union owed its existence to a tactical blunder on the part of management. As a substitute for "welfare activities" the management had organized a company union which met occasionally to hear pep talks, or to go on an infrequent outing. Through the energetic efforts of one of the men employees, the union began to take itself seriously and demanded payment of wages to individuals (instead of retaining them, or sending them to parents) and permission for the girls to leave the mill when not working. The management at once disbanded the union. In the meantime, another worker had begun a "self-help" group to give mutual aid in case of sickness, accidents, and so on. This group had grown, and when the company disbanded its union, the entire organization en masse joined the "self-help" club. Then they applied to the national organization for a charter. This was an extremely unusual situation. It meant that practically the entire body of workers was demanding a union. To enforce the demand, they went out on a strike that lasted for fifty days, during which time Miss Nara was arrested. They won the strike, however. At least, management promised them a raise of two sen a day; and promised that the girls should be allowed to leave the mill in their free time, and receive their wages. They had gone back to work. The raise had not yet gone into effect, though the strike was a month past; and in order to leave the mill, they had to have permission from their dormitory matron, which still could be, and usually was, refused.

Conditions at this factory, however, according to Miss Nara, were really very good, for the industry. The worst conditions were in the smaller mills—where the food was likely to be bad; and where the different shifts had to share the same mattresses and bedding; and where there was no union provision for sick care—and so no provision. Moreover, the statistics on wages were very misleading. For actually it was usual for the mill to advance the family of the girl some small sum; to pay her transportation to the mill; to supply a uniform. These expenses were charged against the girl's wages, and it was not unusual, for the first six months, to have no wages at all. Moreover, these girls had no schooling beyond the primary grades. Most of them had not learned to read or write, or even to do the simplest sum in arithmetic. Therefore, they could not keep track of what was due them, were wholly dependent on the management; so that, if the management wished to take advantage, it was extremely easy to do so.

These girls, almost without exception, came from farms, largely from the northern prefectures. They seemed indifferent to whether they worked at the mill or at home, though several said that they preferred the mill. They did not understand my question, "Are you happy?" They took their lives and their work for granted, and belonging to a union and getting certain problematic privileges was a great adventure—a break in the routine. They were young girls, and the union was a sort of club. They had no sense of insecurity. They all expected to marry, and were rather resentful of my question, "Where will you meet your husbands?" They explained that, although they might belong to a union, they were not *moga*s [modern girls]. Their parents would find them husbands at the proper time.

I had a number of meetings with Miss Nara, who finally took me to the headquarters of the Japan Federation of Labor. There she gave me a sketch of the labor movement in Japan, and outlined the difficulties in the way of unionizing women workers. Like everything else Western in Japan, unions did not arise spontaneously, but were first imported from some Western nation—in this case, America. The first union was formed in Japan as an importation from San Francisco, and was part of the international socialist movement. Both the Japanese government and the industrialists objected strongly to the idea of the workers forming organizations and asking for rights. The Japanese way was paternalism, with the workers accepting gratefully whatever was given, and the notion of mass action against industry was revolutionary. Therefore, from the beginning, union activity was directly and indirectly fought both by industry and government—the two, in any case, very closely connected when not synonymous.

The first unions were, therefore, disbanded by the government, and the labor movement was quiescent until begun again by accident by an American missionary—a Mr. MacCauley, a Unitarian minister. Mr. MacCauley started a small settlement in Tokyo where his activities among the people attracted the attention of Bunji Suzuki, known as the Samuel Gompers of Japan. Suzuki was a Christian and he associated himself with Mr. MacCauley, and together they formed a group of workers to study Christianity and arrange mutual aid. This group became the Yūaikai ("Friendly Love Society"), which—by hewing close to the Japanese way, and purging any sign of radicalism—grew into the General Federation of Labor of Japan, the A.F. of L. of the Japanese labor movement.

... The reasons for the weakness of the labor movement, Miss Nara explained, were four: first, the "theory of the state," which could always be used to stir up patriotism; second, the active interference of the government; third, the prevailingly small-shop organization of industry that prevented concentrations of workers

—except in a few industries; and fourth, the extreme importance of women in industrial Japan.

The Japanese woman, Miss Nara pointed out, was very far from being confined to her home in her role of good wife and wise mother. Around eighty-five percent of all women between the ages of fifteen and fifty-nine were engaged in some sort of remunerative work, and could be found in all occupations. Women shared farm work equally with their men, and had entire charge of the silkworms; they worked on the fishing beaches, in the mines, in manufacturing, in commerce. There were, Miss Nara said, smiling, only around 80,000 geisha, while there were around two million women in large-scale industry, and around 400,000 employed as common laborers—working on roads, or on construction jobs.

To organize such workers was, obviously, almost impossible. They were psychologically not ripe for it. They were not "workers" in a class-conscious sense; they were members of a family, contributing their strength to the communal toil to make ends meet. In the large-scale textile industry they were segregated within the mill walls, where organizers could not reach them. Moreover, their terms of contract were for three or four years, which in itself greatly decreased their interest in union activity. With such a constant turnover and such workers, continuity of union interest was almost impossible. As Miss Nara commented, the girls who did join a union did so as they would join any social club, for a break in the routine. Those few who took the union seriously thought of it in terms of getting such privileges as permission to leave the mill grounds; and to receive their wages. No Japanese woman ever thought in terms of "rights."

The union of girl workers I met with was so exceptional as to be almost unique. At the highest estimate there were never more than around 21,000 women organized into unions in Japan. Although women made up two thirds of the industrial workers, they represented only .05 percent of the organized workers. Therefore, they exerted a drag on the whole labor movement; and strongly tended to keep wages in general at a low level. For the women workers, everywhere, received consistently only half of the rate of wages paid to men for similar work.

Those young girls, who looked so helpless as they sat on the mats in their union room, in their best kimono in honor of visitors, were representatives of the most important class in their country.

For women were the vast majority of the workers in all the export industries. Today they were even taking on such jobs as oiling of machines, and making minor repairs. They were almost half of the workers even in the explosive industry. Their importance was enormous. For not only did they hold down the general wage level; not only did they hold down the labor movement; but they released the men workers for heavy industry, for armaments, for the army. Unconscious, unaware, fitting sleekly into the Japanese way for which they had been so thoroughly conditioned, these little girls were creating the "modern nation" Japan.

☃ THE MARRIED LIFE that the factory girl saw in her future was not necessarily easier or less strenuous than the assembly line and dormitory. After World War II ended, Hani Setsuko prepared the article excerpted here for "A Symposium on Democratization in Japan." The position of the woman in the family was almost a helpless one. She was legally incompetent, economically dependent, and even lacked the right to keep her children if widowed. Hani discusses the inequalities of the Meiji civil code, and provides typical examples of how it enforced the subservience of women.

HANI SETSUKO*
*The Japanese Family System as Seen by
a Japanese Woman*

The feudalistic character of the existing civil code is mainly attributed to the overemphasis placed on the "house," which constitutes a feature of Japan's family system. A "house" in the family system is in itself a world, which essentially hinges on the moral idea that places the foremost value on the vertical relations between the members of the family. In other words, it is a world where the primary importance is attached to the continuation of the lineage

* Hani Setsuko, *The Japanese Family System* (Tokyo: The Japan Institute of Foreign Studies, 1948), pp. 9, 13–19, 26–28.

or the family tradition, where its successor is required to be a male, and where the whole family is placed under the control of the head of the house of paternal rights. It is no wonder that in such a "house" the freedom and development of its individual members, especially of the female sex, should be regarded as of only secondary importance, rarely being considered a matter of any account. Since the "house" thus stands for a family community, where vertical relations predominate over all the other relations, it is essentially exclusive and isolated in character, which is contrary to the idea of modern society. . . .

Characterized by such feudalistic family community, it is only natural that there has grown in Japan a concept of women peculiar to itself. Submission being considered the foremost feminine virtue, women in this country have long been deprived of the freedom of criticism in the name of obedience, gracefulness, or the womanly gentleness to hush up a matter. Especially during the late war, this noncritical attitude was brought to the fore as "the non-arguing mind" which constitutes an attribute of the Japanese spirit. It was imposed not only on the fair sex but also on the young people in general. Under the circumstances, resignation has offered a place of refuge to Japanese women, and in resignation have they found their only life-philosophy.

As in the case of all the other phases of woman's life, a "house" has supreme authority over marriage which practically means the starting-point for women. In Japan, the number of families each composed of a couple and children represents only thirty percent of the whole number; in the majority of cases, several couples of married people live together in the same house under its head. In most cases, marriage is not considered as a union of man and woman, but a bride is regarded as a newly admitted member of a "house." Professor Zennosuke Nakagawa illustrated the point as follows:

> A certain girl whom I knew was married some time ago to a man belonging to a farmer family in a rural village. Before one week had passed since their wedding ceremony took place, she was ordered by her family people to pay a visit to her parents' house, according to the custom pertaining to marriage. When the innocent bride, however, was visiting her parents and other dear ones, she unexpectedly found her trousseau, which she had brought with her to her new home, being sent back to her parents' house. Following it a messenger came to her parents' house from

the bridegroom's house, informing that she had been divorced. The reason for her divorce was explained by the messenger: she was not in harmony with the family tradition. This story was told to me nearly one month after the incident. To my question of how the bride's family had negotiated with the bridegroom's family on this matter, I was informed that, although they asked the go-between several times to negotiate with the other party, the matter was still standing unsettled. She was twenty-three or twenty-four, and was still of marriageable age, and this was her first marriage. But finding that she was half resigning herself to fate, with her qualification for marriage mercilessly negated in only ten days or so after her marriage, I felt strange, rather than provoked. It was one of many incidents taking place among the uncultured farmers in northeastern Japan. But it is preposterous to divorce a bride, simply for the reason that she was found unsatisfactory, so lightly, like casting away a kitten. The same may be said of the bride, who is so easily divorced. It is, indeed, no exaggeration to say that there is not a bit of recognition given to the personality of the woman in this case.

A similar case has been obtained in the field study conducted in Oshikiri Village in the Shōnai district of Yamagata prefecture. The report says in part: "As first consideration is given to the 'house' in marriage, there are many instances of unreasonable or forced marriages in this village. Many men and women get married against their intentions solely 'for the sake of their houses.' " However, this is not only a problem in the backwood villages in northeastern Japan, but also in big cities as well, where even intellectual people often divorce their wives not intrinsically for personal reasons but for reasons relative to their "houses."

In a "house" it is found that its headship is so strongly protected that the head of the house, being vested with the right to designate the domiciles of the family members and also the right to consent to the entry of a nonfamily member's name in the family register, is enabled to refuse the entry of the bride's name on the family register and further to have the names of the newly married couple removed from it, in case the girl, whom one of the male members of his family married, is not liked by him, even when both parties have already reached maturity legally. I myself know a case of a young man and a girl who experienced similar difficulties. Although they both eagerly desired to be united, on a sincere understanding formed between themselves, with the approval of the girl's parents and the sincere encouragement of their friends, the man's father, who was the head of the house, stubbornly refused to give his consent to their marriage for the reason that she was against the family tradition as she was a Christian and, besides, an office clerk. But, thinking that it would be against nature to wait for years to obtain the old man's consent, since they had already reached the age which legally authorizes free marriage, they were finally united as man and wife in the church, at their friends' recommendation. Even after that, they made every effort to persuade the father to give his formal consent to the marriage, but all in vain. Adamant in his attitude, the father finally disinherited the man, who was his eldest son, and had his name removed from the family register, justifying this drastic measure as "the only possible means to take for the family member who acts against the family rules."

This father was by no means a bad person. He is simply a victim of the family system. Indignant at seeing his authority as the head of the house, of which he is unshakably convinced, disregarded, he has failed to appreciate the real character of the girl who is to be his daughter-in-law. A certain old census officer in a village office near Morioka City once told me: "It is impossible to get the actual number of cases of marriages and divorces in this district, because brides are married to 'houses,' and therefore they are very often divorced, when they are not found satisfactory to the houses, before their names are even entered in the family registers. It is usual that their names are left unregistered for one or two years, and so the village office is quite unaware of the actual number of divorces of such nature which take place during that period."

The status of women is said to be the measure of the development of civilization of a society. In fact, it becomes clear that Japanese women are still under the yoke of feudalistic influences, if we consult the marriage and divorce laws in the existing civil code. So far as the position of women is concerned, marriage, which should mean their lifelong happiness, is necessarily considered on the basis of a "house" but never keynoted by the personality of their husbands. Even if a "house" or "lineage" may be taken up for consideration, respect for the personality of wives is utterly disregarded. The civil code provides that a wife does not enjoy freedom of conduct, whether it be personal, of property, or concerning business, these requiring her husband's permission. The wife's conduct without her husband's permission may be canceled by the latter. Let me cite an extreme case in this connection. When a wife borrows money from some person on her own responsibility in her husband's absence, the husband, on returning from the journey, can be authorized to take back the money she has paid back, even if it was loaned her as relief money by the kindness of the lender, so long as it is not proved that the husband's whereabouts was unknown during his absence. However, nothing is more outrageous than the stipulation in the civil code that a wife cannot even "accept or refuse a donation" without her husband's permission. This means that a wife must remain a puppet without her own volition. According to the civil code, an unmarried woman of over twenty years of age is a competent person just as a man is, although marriage turns her into an incompetent person. This stipulation can be interpreted only in the light that marriage produces as its effect the incompetency of a wife as a means to impose upon her complete submission to her husband.

Adultery is taken up as the cause of divorce only against a wife. In justification of this unfair and partial treatment, it is explained that, although adultery committed by a husband does not directly affect his lineage, that committed by his wife does generally stain the family line. Earlier in the Meiji era there were some progressive scholars, like Dr. Shigejirō Ōgawa, who bravely insisted on the legal equality between man and wife in this regard against swaying public opinion. When, in 1919, the Temporary Legislative Deliberative Council was formed for reviewing the provisions of the civil code which may not conform to good morals and wholesome manners traditional to this country, Dr. Tatsukichi Minobe censured the system to charge wives only with illicit intercourse. Opposing him, Dr. Yoshirō Sakatani said that, in view of the traditional practice in this country, which hinges on the family system, to allow a husband to keep a concubine very often with his wife's understanding, in order to maintain his lineage unbroken, it was problematical to denounce this custom as an act of conjugal infidelity. When in the same Deliberative Council an article in the civil code regarding the causes of divorce was taken up for discussion, the majority opinion was in favor of removing the passage saying: "When a wife has received an extremely unreasonable treatment from her consort's lineal ascendants," for the reason that it implied the parents-in-law's cruelty to her. Yet they insisted on retaining the passage which says: "When his consort has given an extremely unreasonable treatment to his lineal ascendants" as one of the principal causes of divorce in favor of a husband. In this way, an act of cruelty committed by a wife to her husband's parents was sufficient cause for divorcing the wife, while the opposite case was removed from among the causes of divorce. The conclusion reached by the Deliberative Council proved only to reinforce the family system, failing to contribute anything to the improvement of the position of a married woman.

Later Professor Takigawa of the Kyoto Imperial University asserted the equality of man and wife in regard to their responsibility for illicit intercourse, but pressure by the government authorities finally banished him from the university. In this country, still beset with feudal customs, as a marriage contract is concluded with only secondary importance given to the intentions of the young man and the girl, so is divorce, as they cannot divorce each other without their parents' consent, when they are under twenty-five years of age. This is justified as the means to protect a young couple from resorting to a reckless divorce, but in reality they are divorced very often at the whim of the wife's parents-in-law, even against their intentions. In the worst case, a young wife finds her divorce registered without her knowledge. It is generally admitted by jurists in this country that conjugal separation has seldom been effected as a divorce by mutual consent based on the free will of both parties, but usually in the form of "casting off of a wife" for the convenience of the "house." . . .

Not very rarely is it found in rural villages that, along with the head of a house, the eldest son, even if still under age, is left to indulge in selfishness and arrogance due to his privileged consciousness, which comes from his right to inherit the headship of the house. In this connection, I want to quote a letter sent me from a rural girl, who is a primary school teacher, complaining of a similar situation in her own house. . . .

This girl has five sisters and one brother, who is the youngest of them all but the heir to the house. Since the days when this boy was still very young, his grandfather, who is the head of the house, has lavished his love on him, professing that, as a son is essential to the Japanese family system, it was natural that the house should depend on the grandson. Under such circumstances, the brother was gradually brought up into a man outrageously out of control.

The mother, who is a woman coming from another house and not primarily belonging to this house, had no voice at all in family matters, and found herself quite helpless at the outrageous attitude of her son, who was acting under the shelter of the influence of his grandfather and the head of the house. In the meantime, he married a girl, which fact seemed to promise an improvement in this situation. But, contrary to expectations of his mother and sisters, a disagreement arising between the young wife and her mother-in-law proved only to worsen it. This family trouble drove the helpless mother and the sisters into an increasingly difficult position. Pressed by the shortage of food, some of the sisters who had been married to houses in nearby towns would visit their parents' house for some vegetables or greens; the brother would treat them harshly, saying that, as even a particle of dust in his house belonged to him, they could not get anything without his permission. Being placed in a dilemma between the grandfather and his son, her father was comforting himself with the thought that a bad elder son was a misfortune of the house to which one must submit. "My house may be one of the rare cases. But I believe that there exists no small number of houses in rural villages, where one of their male members is lording over them like a tyrant under the feudalistic family system," closes this letter.

As a result of the practice that only the eldest son is given the predominant position in succession to a house, almost all the property under the management of the preceding head of the house is inherited by him, preferential to his younger brothers. What is mainly intended under this system is to prevent the property for inheritance from being scattered, on the basis of such contingents as sex, the order of birth, etc. But no consideration is paid at all to the basic rights of individual members of the house. Especially in the case of a wife, who is entirely excluded from the list of inheritors of property. As mention was already made, marriage robs a woman of her right as its legal effect in regard to property. The most unreasonable case would be when a husband has been survived by his wife, leaving a child born by another woman which he had legally recognized as his child by having its name entered in his family register without her knowledge. The death of her husband entitles this child to succeed to his property, while on the other hand imposing on it the responsibility to take care of its father's legitimate wife. Thus, she finds herself in a position ex-

tremely unreasonable and hard. Since, however, a wife must fall
back on some person or other for sustenance for lack of any
property to possess or to inherit, whether or not she can inherit
property left by her deceased husband really means a question of
her subsistence.

⚙ SOME ANALYSTS, in exploring the reasons for Japanese
imperialism in the thirties, looked to the Japanese countryside.
They hypothesized various links between agrarian distress and
repression at home, and aggression overseas. The assumption of
this link underpinned the support given to land reform during
the postwar American occupation, which sought to eradicate the
problem of rural poverty. There is still little consensus on
the agrarian arguments, which R. P. Dore summarizes below.

R. P. DORE*
Tenancy and Aggression

What then of the possible links between agrarian distress—including tenancy as one component element—and the rise of totalitarianism at home accompanied by expansion abroad? A few
hypotheses will be enumerated and discussed in turn.

1. *That a powerful motive for expansion was to secure opportunities for emigration in order to relieve the pressure of population at home. Whereas by suitably adjusting the system of land
tenure the worst distresses of the tenants could have been relieved,
exclusive emphasis on the shortage of land as the cause of rural
poverty by those who were unwilling to touch the vested interests
of the landlords made emigration seem the only solution. As a
report issued by the Natural Resources Section of the Occupation
Army states, "Repulsed in their demands for remedial legislation,
farmers, during the decade preceding World War II, consciously*

* Ronald Dore, *Land Reform in Japan* (London: Oxford University Press,
1959), pp. 116–125.

and unconsciously gave strong support to the military group which
held out the promise of new lands and prosperity to be won
through aggressive war."

There may well be something in this. The possibility of continental emigration as a solution to the land problem was already
being discussed before the First World War, and by the late 1930s
the importance of Manchuria as an outlet for Japan's surplus rural
population was accepted as axiomatic. Count Arima, for instance,
speaking as Minister of Agriculture in the Diet in 1937 on the
prospects for the Owner-Farmer Establishment Scheme he was
introducing, mentioned the current plan to transfer a million families to Manchuria in the next twenty years as providing a possible
means of "getting round" the problem of establishing owner-
farmers. But this is not to say that this was a powerful motive
among those who engineered the Manchurian Incident or those
who condoned and supported their action at home. It was only in
the late 1930s that such plans came to be widely talked of, and
that it was hardly uppermost in men's minds at the beginning of
the decade seems a fair inference from the lengthy interview,
considered to be of somewhat sensational frankness, given by Mori
Kaku, one of the most powerful politician supporters of the army's
expansionist policies, some months after the Manchurian Incident.
He mentioned, in the course of this interview, the possibilities of
solving Japan's population problems by expansion in Asia. But he
saw the means of solution as lying in the development of Japanese
industry which would be assured if Japan were able to "act freely"
in Asia. He made no mention of emigration except to say that such
a development of industry would be a better solution of the population problem than emigration to the Americas. Though not
necessarily relevant to the question of how far the need for
emigration provided a motive for expansion, it is worth remarking
that the opportunity offered by Manchuria was never fully utilized.

2. *That the maldistribution of income kept at a low level the*
purchasing power of the mass of the peasants. Rural poverty, at
the same time, implied an extremely low "floor" for industrial
wages, the merest pittance being enough to recruit labor from
depressed peasant families. Hence, the home market for consump-
tion goods was extremely constricted, while at the same time the

*high profits of the landlords helped to swell the flow of savings
available for industrial investment. Hence an expanding Japanese
industry was obliged to look for external markets and, where they
could only be effectively secured by force, force was used.*

This argument makes sense. . . . And there is evidence . . . that
this was a conscious preoccupation of those who planned and
aided the expansionist policies. It needs to be modified, however,
by the reminder that although there were some industrialists whose
fortunes were from the very first linked with the army—the so-
called New Zaibatsu men typified by Kuhara Fusanosuke—the big
industrial concerns like Mitsui and Mitsubishi were lukewarm
towards the Manchurian adventure and supported Shidehara's
"peaceful diplomacy." For them at that time the prospects of
advantage to be derived from monopolizing and developing the
Manchurian market were outweighed by the prospect of reprisals
from Britain and America against Japanese trade in other areas.
They jumped on the band wagon later on, but still probably the
most important connection between industrialists and the army's
expansion policies was the usual one—that development of the
armament industries offered them, directly and indirectly, higher
profits.

3. *That the ruling groups—of army leaders, elder statesmen,
politicians, industrialists, and bureaucrats in a position to influence
policy—though at loggerheads in many respects, were at one in
being alarmed at the growing signs of disaffection evident in the
tenancy disputes and industrial disputes of the 1920s. As a means
of countering the threat to their own power they deliberately
adopted a policy of overseas expansion hoping thereby to (a)
divert attention from distress at home, and (b) heal rifts in the
social structure by fostering a sense of national unity in the face of
a common danger.*

. . . The need for national unity is certainly a common theme in
the speeches of those concerned with the furthering of expansion
policies. There are, too, good precedents in recent Japanese history
which must have occurred to Japanese statesmen. The opportunity
which the Sino-Japanese War offered of quelling a recalcitrant Diet
is generally thought to have been one of the war's major attrac-

tions in the eyes of the oligarchy at the time. But, perhaps in the nature of the case, it is difficult to find any direct evidence that the sort of calculation outlined above went on in the mind of anyone in control of policy. In any case it is hardly likely to have been more than a subsidiary contributing motive on the part of the army leaders and right-wing nationalists who provided the main driving force for expansion. Their chauvinism has a much too genuinely ideological ring to be merely expediential, and their heart-felt disapproval of social disunity is as likely to have been a consequence of their concern for national military strength and of their military ambitions as vice versa.

It may well be, however, that considerations such as these made those who were temperamentally moderates in foreign policy matters but concerned at threats to their interests at home less anxious to restrain the hotheads, and that in order to suppress possible threats to their interests they committed themselves to propaganda slogans and to factions which were bent on foreign expansion. It is no accident, for instance, that Hiranuma's *Koku-honsha*—the right-wing group formed in the early 1920s—contained prominent industrialists as well as generals and admirals among its leaders, was specifically a countermovement against the growth of left-wing movements at the time, and proclaimed as its objective the harmonization of the interests of capital and labor, as well as "nourishing and developing the national spirit."

Post hoc does not argue *propter hoc,* but, at any rate, if overseas expansion was adopted as a cure for internal conflicts the remedy may be said to have worked. Class tensions in the villages did decrease with the growing emergency, as the decline in the number of tenancy disputes after 1935 shows.

4. *That the right-wing nationalists and the army—in particular the Young Officers—succeeded, by their advocacy of internal reform, in tapping the latent demand for a reform of the land tenure system on the part of the distressed tenants and so both prevented the development of a genuine reform movement and won the support of the peasants which carried over to support for their external policies as well.*

. . . In the first place, neither the Young Officers nor the army leaders placed much emphasis on creating a mass movement or seeking the support of the peasants as a means of gaining power. It is true that in the abortive October rising of 1931 Ōkawa Shūmei was to provide a mass demonstration of rightist trade unionists, and that some branches of the radical right-wing movement sought to create mass organizations in such bodies as the Japanese National Socialist party, the Great Japan Production party, and in the federated organization of the Patriotic United Action Association of 1930. But these never formed the mainstream of the right-wing revolutionary movement which was throughout directed by small groups of scheming revolutionaries who saw themselves as an elite destined to seize power by a top-level coup and having no need of mass followers. After the February 1936 incident one of the Young Officers writes in his diary that this neglect to tap the revolutionary energies of the masses was one of the causes of their failure.

Secondly, what mass support was organized for these ultra-nationalist parties by such organizations as the National Socialist party was mostly urban.

Thirdly, such promises of internal reform as these movements held out were extremely vague. Their appeal to the masses (in so far as they did appeal, at the time, for instance, of the trials of the May 1932 revolutionaries) lay in their formulation of a general resentment against the capitalists and the political parties. ("Fierce Attack on Decadence of the Ruling Class," said the headlines of a national newspaper at the time.) They did not specifically advocate a reform of the land system to benefit the tenants.

. . . [N]evertheless, the Depression and the events of the 1930s did help to make the peasants as a whole—as distinct from just the tenants—favorably disposed toward the army and by extension to the ideals and policies it stood for. . . . It is also clear that the army was at pains to cultivate mass support by its championship of relief measures and its direct publication of propaganda pamphlets in large editions. It is doubtful, however, how far such support was *necessary* to the army in seizing control of the state. Organized opposition might have made its task more difficult, but, given the authoritarian structure of Japanese society, it was enough to gain control at the center: the rest followed.

These arguments are, however, intended only to qualify the assertion of a direct causal connection between the army's rise to power and the desire for reform on the part of the *mass* of the peasants. There are, at the same time, good reasons for thinking that the land problem and agrarian distress, and the fact that the army and the right-wing radical movements associated with it seemed to offer the best hopes of reform, did help to gain the latter sympathy among some elements of what might be called the informed public opinion of the time—among, that is to say, the sort of people in universities and newspaper offices and government departments whose temperament and outlook were such that had they been Americans they would have been supporters of the New Deal and had they been British they would have been counted among the middle-class intellectuals in the ranks of the Labor party.

At the very least the existence of these agrarian problems and the unwillingness of successive governments to tackle them served to alienate these bodies of opinion from the political parties—the only potential focus of effective opposition to the military power. The sense of disillusionment with the fruits of "party government" is well expressed in a book published in 1931 entitled *How to Save the Villages*. The author, who makes sweeping proposals for a land reform, devotes a good deal of space to attacks on the ruling politicians whose factional squabbles and corrupt favoritism of their capitalist friends prevented any action to save the countryside. He speaks with nostalgia of the days of Meiji absolutism when the ruling oligarchy did, at least, have the interests of the nation at heart. It was attitudes such as these which created a favorable climate for the army to make its bid for power, for it too attacked the political parties and claimed to speak, like the Meiji oligarchs, not for sectional interests, but for the nation. It was no accident that some of the active intellectual left-wingers of the 1920s should have swung round to whole-hearted support of the military radicals in the 1930s. . . . The hundred-and-eighty-degree implications of the terms "a switch from the 'left' to the 'right' " certainly exaggerate the nature of this conversion. Hostility toward the political parties and the capitalists remained a consistent theme throughout the intellectual history of these men.

5. *That it was concern for the distress of the peasants which inspired the Young Officers in their revolts which paved the way for the army to gain power.*

... It might ... be misleading to carry this argument to the extent of suggesting that had the peasants been well-fed and contented there would have been no Young Officer revolts. Men with the backgrounds and ideas of Kita Ikki and Ōkawa Shūmei could hardly have lived without revolutionary intrigue, distressed peasants or no distressed peasants, and given the nature of army education it would have been odd if there had not been some young officers ready to be influenced by them. And in the early incidents of 1931 which set the pattern for the later bigger ones resentment against disarmament and pay cuts seems to have provided an important motive. Nevertheless, there is plenty of evidence of the stimulus provided by rural poverty.

6. *That the structure of social relations in the villages which the landlord system preserved provided a natural base for totalitarianism.*

This argument can take a number of forms all of which have considerable plausibility. First, the paternalistic authoritarianism of the relations between landlord and tenant and the strict observance of status distinctions which they involved formed the dominant element in the whole social structure of villages where landlordism was common. People born into, and trained to survive in, such an atmosphere inevitably had an inbred susceptibility to authoritarian leadership of any sort, whether it came from their immediate master, the landlord, or from their remoter masters, "the authorities" and the emperor. It simply did not pertain to the tenant's situation in life to consider the actions of his superiors in a critical spirit. According to this argument the actual direction in which the ruling class led the nation was irrelevant. It was enough that the disposition to be led was there.

Secondly, it might be argued that the system of values which was supported by the landlord class ... were, with their simple emphasis on hard work and the loyal performance of duty without selfish regard for personal profit, an eminently suitable base for the kind of ideology with which the authorities attempted to bring the peasants into the "spiritual mobilization" campaign of the 1930s. ...

Thirdly, the all-inclusive and self-contained nature of the geographically concentrated hamlet community, together with the traditional emphasis on a complete harmony of neighbor relations, produced strong pressures for social conformity. This made it difficult for clashes of economic interest to be brought into the open, or for interest groups formalizing conflict to be created. At the same time any deviant individuals who did not have the psychological "disposition to be led" and showed tendencies to react against authority were easily made to toe the line. It was always much more difficult to harbor slightly dangerous thoughts in the villages than in the towns.

7. *Finally, there are the usual psychological arguments relating the frustrations of poverty with aggressiveness.*

The argument would run thus: in the state of economic hardship in which the peasants found themselves, war and overseas expansion, and the sense that they were members of a nation which was achieving glory in which they themselves shared, provided a sort of psychological compensation for which, had they been better off, they would have had less need. Again, however, even if the psychological assumptions of this argument are correct, it still remains a question how far the wishes or the psychological needs of the mass of the people had a direct bearing on the course of events.

Speculation concerning the "causes" of historical events is fraught with many pitfalls and must in the nature of the case, the experimental reproduction of situations being impossible, remain mere speculation. The "ifs" will always remain to tantalize. Supposing the governments of the early 1920s had carried out a radical adjustment of the distribution of land ownership, would the subsequent history of Japan have been entirely different? It is impossible to say more than that there are some fairly plausible reasons for thinking that it might have been.

❧ FROM AUGUST 1935 to December 1936 John Embree, an American anthropologist, spent a year and a half in Suye Mura, a Japanese village on the island of Kyushu. Japan was not yet plunged into the midst of World War II, and life went on according to the rhythm of rice-growing. Yet young

Japanese children in the village elementary school were inculcated with discipline, hardship, nationalism, and loyalty to the emperor. The emphasis was not on intellectual training, but on morals—responsibilities to others and to the nation. This education was especially relevant for the young men who were drafted. Service at this time was likely to be a year in a barrack, but it was treated more seriously. The passages from Embree describe first the elementary school training, then army experience, as seen from the village.

JOHN EMBREE*
Suye Mura—The Life History of the Individual

At full six years the child goes with all the other little six-year-olds and their fathers or mothers in April to the village shrine of Suwasan. Here, with teachers and other older school children, a short Shinto ritual is performed. The priest gives the young a little talk on the virtues and greatness of Japan, the emperor, and the gods and then hands to each of the neophytes a copy of the first-year book of ethics published by the department of education. This is a child's first introduction to a world beyond his *buraku* and *mura* [hamlet and village]. After the shrine service he attends school for the first time as a student, dressed up in a new black uniform and cap. (He has been here often before with his mother when she came to some meeting or party held in the school auditorium, or with his nurse to play in the schoolyard.) The trip to the shrine did not mean much to him, but it was significant of the close association of official Shinto and the public-school system.

At school he meets for the first time children from all over the village. His constant association with them for the next six years is an important one both for him and for the unity of the village. The ties of men who were classmates in school are very close.

The school building, a long one- or two-storied wooden structure, is partly paid for by village taxes, partly by prefectural and central government funds. As there are no heating facilities, chil-

* John Embree, *Suye Mura—A Japanese Village* (Chicago: University of Chicago Press, 1939), pp. 185–190, 195–197, 200–202.

dren shiver and sniffle their way through the winter months. There is a confirmed belief that cold and discomfort are good for learning and mental discipline. If any child complains of the cold, the teacher tells him to think of the brave soldiers in Manchukuo [Manchuria], where it is *really* cold. Every day after school hours pupils clean up the yard with straw brooms, while girls get on their hands and knees to wipe up the floors. A school servant exists but chiefly for the purpose of running errands and making tea for the teachers to drink between classes.

Every morning now the child gets up about five and washes; he need not dress as he probably slept in his school uniform. After bowing to the household gods, he has a breakfast of bean soup and rice and runs out of the house and off to school. If he lives far from school, this trip by foot may be as long as two or three miles; if close by, it may be only a few yards. On the way he plays games, chiefly a kind of cops and robbers. These games are played with boys and girls alike amid shouts and shrieks as someone is captured. On entering the school grounds, he bows toward the closet in the main auditorium where the emperor's portrait is housed. (More well-to-do schools have a special concrete house costing a thousand yen or more to house the sacred photograph.)

At school shortly before eight all the children from first grade to sixth line up in the schoolyard for radio exercises. From 7:50 to 8:00 the entire youth of the nation under the leadership of hundreds of teachers goes through the same daily dozen to the shrill directions of the same government radio announcer.

After this, the schoolchildren break ranks and file into their various classrooms. Here the boys or girls find their places, small fixed cramped wooden benches and desks, each sex on a different side of the room. The teacher in black uniform comes in—all children rise and bow to him, receiving a slight bow in return—and class begins, with singing perhaps. Many of the songs are simple little nursery rhymes about birds and insects, but the first one the children learn describes the "beautiful national flag with the red sun on it" and the next one is called *The Soldier* ("With the gun over his shoulder the soldier marches, to the sound of the bugle he marches; the beautiful soldier, I love the soldier"). Then they learn to read and write. In their first-year reader they again read of the soldier and the flag.

The older children are expected to help the newcomers find their way around school. From now on for six years the child goes to school from April to July and from August to April again. School is from nine to twelve noon for first-year children, 8:30 to 3:30 after that. Most of the time is taken up with singing, reading, and athletics—all three with a leaven of nationalism. No attempt is made to teach children to think critically either in primary school or in high school. The schoolmaster of the primary school sets as his aim the rules for primary-school education of the department of education in Tokyo, the schoolmaster of the middle school sets as his aim the rules of middle-school education of the department of education, and so also for the agricultural school, girls' high school, etc. The schoolmasters vary from the sacred word of the department only on the side of greater nationalism. In the agricultural school in Menda, for instance, boys are given many lectures on Japanese spirit, and second sons are encouraged to emigrate to Manchukuo.

The great difficulty of learning two or three thousand characters in the first six years, in addition to two sets of fifty-syllable characters, gives but little chance for a student to do much original composition. Geography, arithmetic, and drawing are taught. The drawing is European style, but in arithmetic emphasis is on the use of the *soroban* (abacus)—so much so that many a man can scarcely add two and three without the aid of this device. In Suye boys and girls are also given some practical lessons in farming on a few *chō* of paddy and upland fields belonging to the school.

In higher grades some geography, history, and general science find their way into the curriculum, but the major part of the child's time is still taken up with reading and writing, singing, and ethics. The reading lessons are performed by the deafening method of the whole class reading aloud at once.

In rural schools practically all children are promoted every year, the emphasis in teaching being more moral than intellectual. Teachers feel that, if they left some child behind his class, he would feel very badly about it and that the resulting psychological effect and family chagrin would not be compensated for by any good the child might receive mentally by repeating a school grade. Similarly, at school athletic contests all entrants, not only first, second, and third, receive prizes. By giving prizes thus generously, no one feels unduly slighted. While occasionally people are shown the virtues of initiative and leadership, they are more often shown the virtues of cooperation, and the good but mediocre child is held out to be superior to the bad but brilliant one.

Unquestioning acceptance of everything the teacher says at school is the rule. Occasionally, this causes trouble at home when the father says something to the boy and he replies that the teacher did not say so. The more a child is educated, the wider becomes the gap between the old people's folkways and the young people's ideas. By the time they reach university the gap is too wide to bridge; hence, college graduates from villages almost never return to their homes.

To solve this and other behavior problems that arise, there is an annual parents' day on which old people, many of whom went to no school at all or to only a four-year elementary course, come to the school, see classes in action, and later have discussions with the teachers. With a touching faith in the rightness of their children's teachers, the parents discuss their parental troubles.

At frequent intervals during the school year there are other special days. Some are national holidays, such as the Emperor Meiji's death day, when there is a general assembly with a solemn reading of the Imperial Rescript on Education while all present bow their heads, followed by an uplifting lecture by the schoolmaster and by the singing of the national anthem. On other occasions the students have more fun, for instance, at the annual athletic meet, for which they train for weeks ahead. This is attended by practically everyone in the village, the families coming with lunch baskets to stay all day. People of a *buraku* sit together. Another big day is the old students' day, when the graduates come to watch the present students perform skits and dances.

After six years a boy or girl has learned enough to read simple things. He has also imbibed a good deal of nationalism and martial Japanese spirit by means of games of war and the watching of young men drilling in the schoolyard four times a month. If he leaves school at this point, he will probably forget much of his reading ability and his nationalism will lie dormant in a life whose primary object is to raise good rice and get along amicably with his neighbors. . . .

Every year the army holds physical and mental examinations for men twenty years old. The so-called mental test is largely a civics and patriotic attitude test. In Kuma the examinations are held in Hitoyoshi about June. Fifteen or twenty young men of Suye are called each year for this. As one must report from the village in which one's *koseki* [census registration] is kept, this often means a return home from some other region where one is working as a servant at the time examination comes up. From Suye in 1936 about half the boys examined were working in other villages as menservants.

The examination is a routine medical one accompanied by a long talk on patriotism and the duties of a soldier. That some boys do not care to be conscripted can be seen from the warning given by the colonel in charge not to tell lies.

Even before this official medical examination all men to come up in a given year are first examined in the village by a doctor hired by the village office. This preliminary examination is chiefly concerned with trachoma and venereal diseases.

About a third of the young men pass the examination. Families of boys who do not pass, while somewhat sorry to miss the honor and glory of sending a son to serve the country, actually are rather glad to keep him at home. When an able-bodied young man is suddenly taken away from a farming family, its productivity is reduced. Often a family must hire a manservant to replace the conscripted son, and farmers always complain that such a hired man is not so good as their own son. For a poor family there is nothing to be done but grin and bear it.

Though it is actually only to the training barracks that a young man goes, the whole attitude on his departure and return is as if he had been in active service in defense of the country. It is probable that much of this attitude has been instilled into the people by the authorities. The conscript army only began under Meiji with the dissolving of the old hereditary soldier class (samurai). The very allowing of a common man to be a defender of the godly emperor and his country is made to appear a great honor. When the time comes for the soldier to leave, usually in January, preparations are made by the family for a big send-off party. . . .

A year or more is spent in the barracks. Here are hundreds of similar boys living under the same conditions of military training. Fathers sometimes visit sons in the barracks, and sons occasionally come home on leave but in such an event there is no special party.

At the end of the barracks term the young man makes a triumphal return. He is met at the train by his father and friends.

Schoolchildren, the Young Men's Association, and reservists all come to meet him at the train. His father and his age group will often go to Hitoyoshi to meet him. The women of his *buraku* dress up in outlandish costumes, often as soldiers or tramps, and meet the returning procession by the bridge in the next *mura*. The women make obscene jokes as if they were men, try to rape the young schoolgirls, and in general cause bursts of laughter and gaiety. They are always well disguised, and it is not always possible to tell the identity of a given masquerader.

At the soldier's home the front gate now, as at his departure, is specially decorated with branches of evergreen and flags. A welcome party is held there. Again the guests are all men; but, after the party is begun, older *buraku* women come to drink and to dance, one or two younger ones to play the samisen. The party ends in song and dance many hours later.

The soldier, like any returned traveler, brings back with him some small gift for everyone who attended his farewell party and brought him money as *sembetsu*.

When a young man comes back from the barracks, he is no longer a rustic farmer but a chauvinistic Japanese subject. He finds it difficult to readjust himself to the unexciting routine of farm work and local custom. The occasional soldier who has been sent to Tokyo as an Imperial guard or to Manchukuo to fight what he really believes to be bandits feels the ennui more strongly than others. After a few months, however, he drops back into village patterns, and it is not long before he is married to some girl selected by his parents.

🔳 WHEN FULL-SCALE WAR finally came, in both city and country the mobilization of men was accompanied by the general mobilization of the economy and society. The changes in local government that Steiner describes tightened the already centralized system of Japanese government. Sometimes building on traditional structures, sometimes not, the central government reached down to every neighborhood to ensure complete solidarity in the war effort. However, because the system evoked hostility, its effectiveness was in doubt.

KURT STEINER*
Wartime Local Government

As Japan prepared for war and faced the problems of large-scale planning in the organization of industrial and agricultural production, the allocation of manpower and matériel, and the rationing of food and consumer goods, the government had to mobilize the masses and channel all their energies into the war effort. This meant integration on a new scale and of a new and modern type.

The establishment of neighborhood associations in 1940 was the capstone of several earlier measures to tighten government control over the economic and social life of the nation. Economic and social organizations had been increasingly regulated from the top even before the war in China, but now, with a bigger war approaching, they were integrated into the governmental structure. In due time, local public entities assumed a new role: they became, in the language of Japanese observers, "collective entities." The strands that connected the individual with a variety of associations—the local entity as an inhabitant, the agricultural association as a producer, the *buraku* as a participant in the "cooperative life"—were all gathered together and linked with the big strand that connected him with the government as a subject of the emperor. This "gathering" was one of the two chief trends in government during the period.

The other trend was toward application of the executive leadership principle on all levels. The revisions of the local government laws of the twenties had tended to increase the power of the assemblies, but now the trend was sharply reversed. In addition, the executive was given the authority to direct the various associations, which had been integrated into the local entity. He was thus much more of a "leader" than his predecessor. This trend reached its climax in the creation of the position of superintendent-general, who headed the newly created regions until the end of the war.

A "reformation of the local government system" was demanded

* Kurt Steiner, *Local Government in Japan* (Stanford, Calif.: Stanford University Press, 1965), pp. 55–60.

by Japan's military leaders as early as 1936, when a "Plan for the Renovation of the National Government" was submitted by the war and navy ministers to Prime Minister Hirota. The announced purpose was to free the government from "individualistic institutions and liberalistic policies" and to establish a totalitarian country "in accordance with the needs of national defense and the spirit of Japan." In 1937 the first Konoe cabinet established a Local Institutions Research Institute. Later, the National Spiritual Mobilization Movement proposed plans to "bridge the gap between the people and the government." A number of drafts resulted from all these projects, but none was submitted to the Diet, because it was feared that there was not enough political backing for them. It was not until 1940 that any measures affecting local government were actually put into effect.

The political parties, which had supplied most of the prime ministers of the twenties, gradually lost their feeble hold on the government of the country to the exponents of militarism and totalitarianism. In the summer of 1940 they meekly submitted to the demands for a "new political structure" and disbanded. The new look in Japanese politics was the Imperial Rule Assistance Association, a pet project of Prince Konoe, who formed his second cabinet at the time. This association was to be organized at the lowest level on the basis of the *buraku* and the *chō* (town precincts).

In September 1940, a month before the inauguration of the Imperial Rule Assistance Association, Home Ministry Ordinance No. 17 called for the establishment of a net of neighborhood associations. These associations had both a political and an administrative *raison d'être,* and it is thus not surprising that there was some rivalry over leadership of them between the Imperial Rule Assistance Association and the Home Ministry. The Association saw them primarily as cells for political integration, whereas the ministry considered them primarily as small-scale local agencies for such administrative purposes as rationing, civil air defense, and fire-fighting. The declared political aim was to provide channels for transmitting government policies down to the people and popular feeling up to the government, which was to unify the nation spiritually. The emphasis was definitely on the channel that led from the top to the bottom, rather than on the one leading the other way. Government control was to be strengthened and extended to cover all phases of the life of the people, including their "spiritual life." The neighborhood associations were to cultivate conservative sentiments and to stem the inroads of new forces wherever they existed.

The government's scheme was to graft the new associations onto existing groupings. . . .

Sometimes the areas of the economic and social groups, which had come under government regulation, coincided with those of one or the other natural community, but this was not always the case.

Most important, the natural communities did not exist everywhere. Especially in the cities, *chō* and *tonarigumi* covered only part of the urban areas, being most prevalent in the districts of small shopkeepers. In the past, there had been occasional attempts to keep them alive or even to revive them, especially at such times of stress as after the Russo-Japanese War, after the First World War, and during the Depression of 1930–1932. Sometimes they had sprung up more or less spontaneously after a calamity, as after the great earthquake in Tokyo and Yokohama in 1923. But this had always been a temporary phenomenon. Whereas the *buraku*—in the wider meaning of the larger natural unit below the village level—could look back on a more or less continuous and widespread existence, small units of a size comparable to the *goningumi* could be found only in about a third of the towns and villages. Sweeping generalizations regarding the traditional and indigenous character of the entire neighborhood association system and the social needs that it fulfilled are thus somewhat misleading. . . .

. . . [S]uch existence as they had at the time was utilized in 1940 to create new echelons of local government below the city, town, and village level. These echelons were the *tonarigumi,* the rural *burakukai,* and the urban *chōnaikai.*

In general, about ten households formed a *tonarigumi* and ten to twenty *tonarigumi* a block association (*burakukai* or *chōnaikai*). In cities, or in the wards of the larger cities, federations of *tonarigumi* were sometimes set up. Where such groupings did not exist, they were artifically created without any semblance of support by social or economic need or any traditional community spirit. Nevertheless, the job was speedily accomplished; in April 1941, only seven months after the initial ordinance, the Home

Ministry announced that the system was in complete operation throughout Japan. A total of 199,700 block associations and 1,120,000 *tonarigumi* had been created.

The *tonarigumi* disseminated official instructions, usually by means of a *kairamban,* or "circulating bulletin board," reported on compliance with them, distributed rations, collected taxes and contributions, and performed a number of similar services. The block associations served as channels for the distribution of orders and such essential papers as ration books, and directed agricultural and welfare work. Heads of block associations met at regular intervals to receive instructions from municipal, prefectural, and national officials.

Control from above was rigid. The leaders of the block associations were appointed by the mayor, although "nomination or other suitable ways of recommendation" by the associations were permitted. Regular monthly meetings, called *jōkai,* had to be attended by all members on the day and hour prescribed by instructions. These meetings served as much for indoctrination as for the conduct of any business of immediate practicality, and the participation of the membership consisted almost exclusively of being present.

The leadership of these groups often fell to the most conservative and nationalistic elements within them, who gladly used their position to suppress all criticism of the existing regime and to berate any lukewarm attitude toward it. In many instances, the local "boss" or his henchmen achieved official recognition in this way, and submission to them thus became unavoidable, because they could easily deny food, fuel, and other necessities to a recalcitrant individual or family. Often the block association heads became petty tyrants and the position they held was resented, especially where it had no roots in tradition or in acknowledged local needs. In the urban centers, in particular, where artificial face-to-face group patterns had to be superimposed on the natural anonymity of city life, the *tonarigumi* often created more friction than neighborliness and there was a good deal of hostility against the system.

◒ ALTHOUGH the landlord class enthusiastically supported Japanese imperialism, the war that resulted eventually threatened landlord privileges. The government's aims were increased production, political stability, and price stability. Thus stable land prices and rent control were introduced, and subsidies were established to benefit the actual cultivator, especially the owner-cultivator. Landlords had the political power to weaken some of these measures but not enough to prevent them, since the government saw them as important for maintaining rural peace.

LAWRENCE HEWES*
Japan—Land and Men

After 1937, several agrarian war measures of considerable severity were put in effect. Arbitration of tenant–landlord disputes became mandatory. Eviction of tenants except in extreme cases was prohibited. Farm rentals were frozen, as were land prices. These and similar measures remained in effect throughout the entire war period. Together with the legislation of the twenties and thirties, they represented in 1945 the body of law developed by the Japanese people for meeting the problems of the tiny farms and the toiling peasants.

By now Japan was at war, and as the war deepened the simple life of the Japanese rural villages was caught up in the grinding grim machinery of a war economy. Everything was rationed and almost all aspects of life were strictly regimented. Village authorities were in effect agents of the Imperial government. Crops were planted on order as to amount and kind. Quotas established for delivery of the crops to the authorities had to be met. Distribution of seed, fertilizer, and other items of production was geared to production quotas. Autonomous village cooperatives were succeeded by a government-run Village Association (*Nōgyō Kai*), which served as a delivery and receiving point of all production goods and crop collection quotas. Payments for crops to individual farmers were set up as credits on the association books, and these were automatically drawn against by the authorities to meet all

* Lawrence Hewes, *Japan—Land and Men* (Ames, Ia.: Iowa State College Press, 1955), pp. 38–39.

sorts of new war taxes and assessments with little or no consultation of depositors. Surplus balances, which were actually conscripted peasant savings, were forwarded to central banking agencies to meet mounting war expenses. Farmers were permitted to draw against their balances only in accord with strict regulations. In effect, the individual family lost almost completely any control whatever over its own economic life.

These measures were supplemented by continual exhortation to further sacrifices by the village bureaucracy. The mayor, the schoolmaster, the agricultural agent, the stationmaster, the postmaster, and the policeman all became explicitly and definitively the masters of Tanaka-san [the average Joe]. Police surveillance was meticulous. The dread *Kempeitai* (thought police) revived the old *gonin-kumiai* (association of five families) for mutual surveillance and responsibility, with each family head responsible for the carrying out of their duties by the other four. Military needs for land, to be used for training purposes, airfields, artillery ranges, and maneuver areas, were met by ruthless expropriation of owners and cultivators with payment to be made at the end of the war. Thousands and thousands of acres of sorely needed land went for these purposes. Villages were expected to accept and shelter the large number of refugees from the war-torn cities. In addition, men needed for the army and for employment in the war industries were drafted with little or no notice and without reducing village quotas for production.

R. P. DORE*
War and the Rural Areas

In 1941 forty-six percent of the cultivated land was tenanted and only thirty percent of the peasants owned all the land they tilled. The war, however, brought considerable changes. For the first time surplus population was siphoned off the farms into the services and war industries. There were even complaints of a shortage of agricultural labor for the first time in modern Japa-

* Ronald Dore, *Land Reform in Japan* (London: Oxford University Press, 1959), pp. 22, 114.

nese history. Subsidiary part-time occupations and the employment of family members in industry increased the income of farm families. Moreover, the overwhelming need to ensure the maximum deliveries of food by the peasants led to a series of measures which considerably benefited the tenants at the expense of the landlords. Rents were controlled and a double-price system was introduced for rice, a much higher price being paid for rice delivered by an owner-cultivator than for rice delivered by a landlord. Many landlords under these conditions were glad to sell out their land to tenants now able to buy it. Later, in the closing stages of, and immediately after, the war, tenancy further decreased with the return of formerly absent landlords from the starving cities to the rice-producing security of their villages where they took back into their own cultivation land which had been leased out to tenants. Even so this did not amount to more than a five percent decrease in tenancy. . . .

Landlords were, however, given every incentive to sell by their differential treatment in the matter of government rice deliveries. As the war progressed it became more and more important to the government to secure the maximum deliveries of rice from the peasants—and more and more difficult. Despite the need to check inflation a gradual increase in the price of rice became a necessary incentive. However, such incentives could only be effective if they were paid to the actual producer. Hence the system adopted was to raise the basic price of rice—paid to landlords, tenants, and owner-farmers alike—only slightly, but to make the biggest increases in the additional subsidies and bonus payments which were paid only to owner-farmers marketing their own rice, or, in the case of rice marketed by a landlord, to the tenant who had actually grown it. The gap between the price paid to landlords and the price paid to cultivators . . . increased as the war progressed. The effect of these measures was, in fact, to change the rents in kind, hitherto almost universal, into money rents and, moreover, to peg those rents in a period of considerable inflation. By the end of the war there was no great profit to be derived from being a landlord.

3. Political Economy, 1936-1945

❀ THE WARTIME YEARS saw continued conflict between the military and business elites. Eleanor Hadley and T. A. Bisson argue that the military had no choice except to share power with the zaibatsu, and that the military leaders were *not* able to control these powerful corporations. Furthermore, the zaibatsu took advantage of the war to move into heavy industry; they assumed control of industrial regulation; and they even managed to get insurance against any losses from bombing. Wartime Japan was thus not simply a military dictatorship but a nation led by representatives of business and the government bureaucracy, as well as soldiers.

ELEANOR HADLEY*
The Zaibatsu and the War

It frequently happened that the Japanese army and navy turned industrial and mining installations in areas coming under Japanese jurisdiction over to Mitsui, Mitsubishi, or Sumitomo to operate. Thus, for example, as the Mitsubishi group wrote of itself: "The [Mitsubishi Heavy Industries] Company was entrusted by the Japanese navy with the management and operation of the Kiang-Nan shipyard and engine works in Shanghai in 1938 and with the Shonan shipyard and engine works in Singapore in 1942."

* Eleanor Hadley, *Antitrust in Japan* (Princeton, N.J.: Princeton University Press, 1970), pp. 41–45.

Further . . . the Big Four doubled their position in the economy in the years 1941 to 1945. They increased their position from twelve percent of total corporate and partnership capital to twenty-four percent in that four-year period. And in addition, the Big Four made comparable gains in their position outside Japan. While at the outbreak of the Pacific War Nissan with its enormous investments in Manchuria represented three quarters of overseas investments among the eight largest combines, it was down to six percent by war's end and Mitsui and Mitsubishi were up to sixty percent. It is customary to describe the Japanese government during World War II as being under the control of the militarists. What kind of cleavage between militarists and "liberal" business elements can there be when the "liberal" business elements fared so handsomely? Rewards don't follow cleavages; they follow fundamental similarity. There were no real cleavages between the military and the views of the older combines. Other bits of information corroborating the similarity of zaibatsu-gumbatsu [military clique] interests lie scattered about.

From conversations in Paris after the war, I learned that Mitsui Trading's French affiliate, S. A. Française Bussan, had been highly commended for the intelligence activities it had been carrying on up to the fall of the Vichy government. In fact, Française Bussan was in receipt of a memorandum from the Imperial Japanese War Ministry informing . . . [it] that the reporting job it was doing was superior even to that of the Japanese Embassy in Paris.

One sees political indication in appointments. Under the zaibatsu system, all political work was handled from the top holding company. There was no such thing as a subsidiary making direct political contributions, as one sees today, or engaging in political dialogue on its own. In the Mitsui combine the political work was carried on in the "research department" of the top holding company. The research of this department was political maneuvering—with cabinet ministers, army and navy officials, bureaucrats, Diet members. Who did the House of Mitsui pick for its last appointment to this most sensitive post?—an ardent admirer of Nazi Germany. Elsewhere I remarked,

> The finances of the research department were handled on a cash basis for which no records were kept. The department was headed for a number of years by Sasaki Shirō, a favorite of Takakimi [head of the eleven-family House of Mitsui], who in

1941 became concurrently president of real estate. Sasaki, who was an enthusiastic collaborator of Hitler Germany under the Berlin–Rome–Tokyo Axis, managed all political arrangements of the entire Mitsui combine. Under "normal" conditions the post was peculiarly important because of the extremely close relations between the major combines and government in Japan; under the war economy where informal combine–government collaboration gave way to legalized forms, the position was of even greater significance.

When I interviewed Mitsui Takakimi in August 1947, at a time when severe inflation was threatening the economy and output in the second postwar year was little above the preceding year, Takakimi's concerns were not with these problems but with communism and international Jewry. He was fearful of domestic communists spreading communism within Japan. But it is not clear what he imagined about Jews. It is worth noting that at the time practically the only Jews in Japan were members of the Allied occupation forces.

To suppose that the older combines represented liberalism of the Western type is to misread Japanese history. Nothing in their origins, in their structure, in their operations would suggest bourgeois thinking. Yet naturally such a supposition appealed to the conservative political groups who took over the government of Japan following its surrender. Mr. Yoshida, four-time prime minister of postwar Japan and a master politician, wrote in his *Memoirs* of a press conference he held shortly after the start of the occupation:

> As was the case within GHQ, foreigners . . . in Japan in those days entertained feelings of animosity toward our financial leaders and there was already much talk among them of the coming disintegration of the trading "empires" which had been built up. So it came as no surprise when, at a press conference with foreign correspondents held shortly after the formation of the Shidehara cabinet in October 1945 with myself as foreign minister, I was confronted with the kind of questions one might expect. The general purport was that, since the financiers had been behind the war, the strictest measures should be taken against them. I answered that it would be a great mistake to regard Japan's financial leaders as a bunch of criminals, that the nation's economic structure had been built by such old established and major financial concerns as Mitsui and Mitsubishi, and that modern Japan owed her prosperity to their endeavors, so that it was most doubtful

whether the Japanese people would benefit from the disintegration
of these concerns.

I explained further that the so-called zaibatsu had never
worked solely for their own profit, but often at a loss, as for instance during the war when they continued to produce ships and
planes on government orders regardless of the sacrifices involved;
that the people who had actually joined hands with the militarists
and profited from the war were not the established financial
groups, but the new rich who were alone permitted by the military
to conduct business in Manchuria and other occupied territories
to the detriment of the old established concerns; and that those
who had most heartily welcomed the termination of the Pacific
conflict were the leaders of these old established concerns that had
laid the foundations of their prosperity in time of peace and had
never felt at ease in their relations with the military clique who
had become the masters of the nation for the duration of the
war.

It is colorful and lively to equate criticism of a system of
enterprise which gave great opportunity and great wealth to a
handful of families with "Japan's financial leaders as a bunch of
criminals," but it is scarcely descriptive. Obviously neither the
zaibatsu families nor their hand-picked officers were a bunch of
criminals. They were for the most part talented and able persons
whom the political-economic system favored in enterprise and
income to the disregard of all other Japanese persons. As quoted
at the outset of this study, President Roosevelt, in his 1938
message to Congress, calling for an investigation of concentrated
economic power in the United States, observed: "Governments
can deal and should deal with blindly selfish men. But that is a
comparatively small part—the easier part—of our problem. The
larger, more important, and more difficult part of our problem is to
deal with men who are not selfish and who are good citizens, but
who cannot see the social and economic consequences of their
actions in a modern economically interdependent community."
The sin of the zaibatsu was that they and their political spokes-
men, such as Prime Minister Yoshida, could not see the social and
economic consequences of a system of enterprise which did not
permit Japan to outgrow the duality of its economy, which denied
it a viable labor movement, failed to provide any real labor-
standards legislation, and which stunted the consumer market. To
their minds what was good for the zaibatsu was good for Japan,

but of course the interests of fifty-six persons and the interests of seventy-two million persons are likely to be different.

T. A. BISSON*
Increase of Zaibatsu Predominance in Wartime Japan

The most obvious as well as the most far-reaching change has occurred in the composition of Japanese industry. For more than a decade light industry has played a declining role in Japan's production. The depression of 1929–1932 marks the watershed. Measured by value of output, the textile industry alone still surpassed heavy industry in 1931. Out of a total industrial production valued at 5,178,130,000 yen in that year, the textile industries accounted for 1,926,800,000 yen, or 37.2 percent. The metallic, machine and tool, and chemical industries took 1,745,990,000 yen or 33.7 percent. Thereafter, with Japan's assumption of new imperial responsibilities in "Manchukuo" [Manchuria] and with the beginning of efforts to reequip the armed forces in preparation for further aggression, the growth of the heavy industries was accelerated. By 1935 total industrial production had risen to 10,836,-890,000 yen. Of this amount, however, the same heavy industries took 5,158,140,000 yen, or 47.2 percent, while textiles took only 3,352,560,000 yen, or 30.9 percent. The absolute increase for the heavy industries, from 1,745,990,000 yen to 5,158,140,000 yen, or nearly 200 percent, is the striking aspect of these figures. While some qualification must be made for price increases, there can be no doubt that the figures represented a substantial growth in the output of heavy industry.

For several years after 1935, until the outbreak of the European war, the output of the textile and other light industries, spurred by the need for foreign exchange, continued to increase. The proceeds of these exports, however, supported by a lavish expenditure of Japan's gold reserve and gold production, were largely diverted to the construction of a war economy. After 1937 the flow of investment capital was channeled ever more rigorously into the muni-

* T. A. Bisson, "Increase of Zaibatsu Predominance in Wartime Japan," *Pacific Affairs*, XVIII (March 1945), pp. 55–59.

tions and strategic industries. In the 1931–1935 period the value output of the heavy industries had trebled. The second period, from 1937 to 1941, witnessed a more urgent development, with a differentiation between light and heavy industries undertaken as a deliberate policy. Curtailment was first applied to the consumption industries. Between 1939 and 1941, however, export markets were progressively limited by the spread of war, including the spread of Japan's aggressive activities. This process culminated in the Anglo-American-Dutch freezing regulations of July 1941. Textile and other light industrial exports thus declined steadily in the later years of the 1937–1941 period. Production shifted to the heavy industries, which were undergoing a planned expansion and supplying the armed services with increasing amounts of finished munitions. . . .

By the close of 1944 the output of light industry had been reduced to a minor segment of total industrial production. Only the barest minimum, devoted to essential civilian requirements, was retained. War production, centered in the basic steel and light metals industries, the munitions and aircraft factories, and the shipbuilding yards, had become the overwhelmingly predominant feature of Japan's economy.

An indirect measure of the scope of this transformation exists in the form of periodic Japanese statements on the distribution of national income, usually made when the new budgets are under consideration. In the 1941–1942 fiscal year, out of a total national income of approximately forty billion yen, seventeen billion were allotted to civilian consumption. Since then the corresponding figures have been fifteen billion out of forty-five in 1942–1943, thirteen billion out of fifty in 1943–1944, and eleven billion out of sixty-five in 1944–1945. The civilian economy, which absorbed 42.5 percent of the national income in 1941–1942, thus took but 18.5 percent in 1944–1945. In one aspect, this sharp decline reflects the extent of the tribute exacted from the Japanese people, and rendered even greater by price rises, commodity shortages, and deterioration in the quality of consumer goods. Equally obvious, however, is another aspect: the degree to which the industrial structure of Japan has been modified over the past four years. It must be assumed that war industry, which means heavy industry, today accounts for more than four-fifths of Japan's total industrial output. In the course of the war years, and the preceding decade of war preparations, the ruling groups of Japan have succeeded in transforming their country into a major industrial power.

. . . In the crucial struggle, beginning with Tōjō's request for special powers in January 1943 and ending with the final agreement which enabled the munitions ministry to inaugurate its activities on January 15, 1944, the zaibatsu held out for an unconditional victory and won it. During the latter part of this period, which lasted for a full year, the zaibatsu were engaged in a maneuver that can be characterized, without unduly stretching the facts, as a sitdown strike. If the Army-Navy-Air Force General Headquarters were to insist on retaining administrative control over an expanded aircraft production program, involving complete mobilization of the industrial giants of the Japanese economy, the monopolists were simply not interested. They became willing to play ball when the administrative authority was vested in a munitions ministry controlled by their men and operating within the framework of a Munitions Company Act to which they subscribed. . . .

T. A. BISSON*
The Zaibatsu's Wartime Role

During the course of the Pacific War American official propaganda placed such emphasis on the "military dictatorship" which allegedly ruled Japan as to distort beyond recognition the role which the zaibatsu monopolies were playing, both in the politics and economy of the country. On the political side, it is sufficient to note that Japan's last two wartime cabinets, under premiers Koiso and Suzuki, were thoroughly dominated by a coalition of the Imperial palace guard and representatives of the zaibatsu monopolies, aided by a number of bureaucrats. The military and naval men in these cabinets played second fiddle to the nominees of the conservative zaibatsu-monarchist combination within the Japanese oligarchy, while the bureaucrats accommodated themselves to the stronger force. This situation already prevailed *de facto* during the

* T. A. Bisson, "The Zaibatsu's Wartime Role," *Pacific Affairs* XVIII (Dec. 1945), pp. 355-364.

last half of Tōjō's long term of office, as an examination of his ministerial appointments and domestic policies in 1942–1943 clearly indicates. Two years later the Suzuki cabinet was so constituted that it could effect total and ignominious military surrender with not the slightest effective opposition from the supposedly all-powerful military. From the standpoint of Japanese politics, here lies the point which requires explanation. How did the "military dictatorship" crumble so rapidly? The true answer is that it never existed, save as a figment of imaginative official and nonofficial American propaganda.

A similar misapprehension exists with respect to the Japanese economy. Since the military were all-powerful, the propaganda line runs, they dictated to the zaibatsu the terms on which the national economy worked—in effect, they "nationalized" industry. Nothing could be further from the truth. Full domination of Japan's war economy by representatives of the zaibatsu was expressed on two levels: first, in their control of the direction and scope of the government's wartime economic policy and, second, in the vast increases effected in the plant and capital expansion of the monopoly concerns. . . .

The Major Industries Association Ordinance, under which the Industrial Control Associations were established, was promulgated on September 1, 1941, three months before Pearl Harbor. Debate and struggle over this measure had proceeded for more than a year, during the period of the second and third Konoe cabinets. At one stage in the struggle, in November–December 1940, the more extreme program of the Japanese military had been presented in the Hoshino Plan, which would have subjected industry to direct bureaucratic control. The zaibatsu reacted strongly and the cabinet quickly dropped this program of industrial control, despite a joint statement by the army and navy ministers supporting it. In its place, eight months later, the cabinet finally sanctioned an Imperial ordinance which embodied a wholly different control policy.

In the terms of the Major Industries Association Ordinance, the zaibatsu had forced complete acceptance of the technique of wartime industrial control which their powerful national organizations, such as the Japan Economic Federation, had been vigorously advocating in 1940–1941. Its essence was of an extreme simplicity: the existing cartels of the private industrialists in each field of industry were transformed into control associations vested with official powers over materials and labor and capital supply. Even more to their liking, cartel leaders who headed the control associations were supplied with official sanction to "rationalize" their industries, *i.e.*, to force all smaller enterprises to accept the dictates of the zaibatsu houses.

The control associations experienced their heyday during the first year of the war. Japan's business leaders reveled in the process of rounding out their cartels in industry, finance, and trade, and moving into the larger economic empire which the military were conquering in the southern regions. All groups in the oligarchy were thus busied with congenial tasks. The zaibatsu, too, were able to bask in a reflected glory, since theirs had been the economic achievements which produced the Zeros that swept the skies and the bombers that humbled Anglo-American naval pride. Their major attention, however, was claimed by the more prosaic task of streamlining the cartelization of Japan's economy with the backing of state authority. General Tōjō Hideki, the new premier, naturally assisted them in this task since, as war minister in the preceding cabinet, he had approved the Imperial ordinance which brought the control associations into being. . . .

By the end of 1942, when the demand for more planes and ships was becoming insistent, the shortcomings of the control associations as agencies of wartime economic mobilization had been made fully evident. Adequate enforcement of priorities could not be achieved through a set of so-called control associations which were in reality competing among themselves and hoarding scarce commodities. The cartels grew bigger and the zaibatsu's profits mounted higher, but controls were lax and the war economy bogged down. To complicate matters still further the cabinet ministries, which supposedly exerted supervisory direction over the control associations, were themselves divided as to areas of jurisdiction. One handled industry and commerce, another railways, and still others labor, agriculture, finance, and communications. Each ministry jealously guarded its prerogatives, while the prime minister did not possess the authority requisite to coordinate these overlapping ministerial jurisdictions.

Through 1943 and into early 1944, Japan stumbled along with little improvement in this painfully inadequate system of wartime economic administration. The zaibatsu, responsible in considerable measure for the difficult situation due to their original insistence on the formation of the control associations, nevertheless fought vigorously against any reform which did not satisfy their requirements. Premier Tōjō had secured from the Diet "special powers" adequate to coordinate ministerial administration of the war economy by the spring of 1943, but only at the cost of revamping his cabinet and associating with the cabinet an advisory council of seven leading zaibatsu representatives to advise with him on the use of his new powers.

With these business advisers largely dictating the measures adopted, Tōjō eventually accomplished the cabinet reorganization of November 1, 1943, which centralized administrative control of war production in the munitions ministry. . . .

Two major compromises, both on Tōjō's part, marked the establishment of the new ministry. In the first place, the zaibatsu stood out for and won control of the munitions ministry's administration. The initial stage of their control over the new agency was accomplished through a peculiar compromise designed to save the face of Tōjō, whose political power was rapidly declining. Tōjō himself became the first munitions minister. A Japanese broadcast, however, disclosed that this was but a titular post, with the actual executive powers falling to the vice-minister, Nobusuke Kishi. Even Kishi was not wholly acceptable to the zaibatsu, although he was by this time sloughing off the effects of his previous background as a Manchukuo bureaucrat. Thus, a third step was taken by the introduction of Ginjirō Fujihara into the cabinet on November 17, 1943, as minister of state without portfolio. Fujihara was a Mitsui executive, and a veteran industrialist of great prestige. As one of the members of the advisory council, he had "advised" Tōjō on the nature of the administrative reform which centered in the munitions ministry. As state minister, he was slated to keep a fatherly eye on Vice-Minister Kishi as the new ministry began its operations. And then, in July 1944, when Tōjō fell and the Koiso cabinet was formed, Fujihara himself took over the munitions ministry portfolio.*

The second compromise by Tōjō, *i.e.,* by the military, dealt with the procedures under which the new ministry would function. As

---

* In December 1944 Shigeru Yoshida, a bureaucrat, replaced Fujihara; in April 1945 Admiral Teijirō Toyada, related to the Mitsui family by marriage, became the fourth munitions minister.

might be surmised, the zaibatsu did not leave this highly important matter to chance. Procedural limits were carefully defined in a Munitions Company Act, the terms of which were applied to all "munitions companies" designated by the ministry. Since the Munitions Company Act determined the extent to which the interests of the designated industrialists were affected, either for good or ill, the nature of its provisions was of some considerable importance.

As always, the decisive factor in respect to the real center of control lay in the choice of the executive. In this matter, the terms of the act were explicit. Under Article 5, the designated munitions company was "to select a person responsible for production from among the officials of the company." Only in case the munitions company could not make the selection might the government "appoint a person," in which case the person appointed would "become an official of the company." . . .

With the top officials of the munitions ministry safely under zaibatsu control, and with a Munitions Company Act of this sort on the books, there were substantial reasons impelling the industrialists to enter the list of designated munitions companies. The industrial sphere in which these companies would operate was the expanding one. Priorities, the factor of life and death for enterprises in a controlled economy, would be available in largest measure for industries engaged in this sector of the national economy. Raw materials, machine tools, labor, motive power, and capital—all were being channeled into this field. Here, moreover, the door was wide open to the big companies for the most drastic program of absorption of smaller competing or subsidiary firms. The larger the concern, the greater would be the possibility for such action. The fact that such an industrial giant as Mitsubishi Heavy Industries became a designated munitions company is an eloquent indication of the extent to which the "privileges" of the Munitions Company Act outweighed its "responsibilities." . . .

The third major act of zaibatsu policy was played as the shadow of defeat spread over Japan in 1945. Taking precedence over all else, in the minds of Japan's business leaders, was the growing threat of the B29 raids. They anticipated two results: extensive destruction to their plants and serious unrest among the workers. Against the background of these two simple fears, the zaibatsu and their political henchmen in the parties set up a clamor for "nationalization" of industry and the enrolling of the workers in an "industrial army" subject to military discipline. The first steps to these ends were taken by the Koiso cabinet; the complete program was fulfilled by the Suzuki cabinet before the military surrender.

Under the "nationalization" scheme, the Japanese government instituted a temporary receivership for the zaibatsu's industrial plants. Through a state treasury guarantee, the private concerns were assured fixed dividend rates for the receivership period. In addition, they were absolved of responsibility for payment of repairs for damages, also assumed by the state treasury. Finally, they were assured that title of ownership still remained in their hands. After the war, in other words, the receivership would terminate and the zaibatsu would reassume full ownership of their plants.

Operative control of the industrial plants, moreover, continued to be vested in zaibatsu hands even during the receivership term. Initially, an effort was made to vest control of the "nationalized" industry in a so-called munitions arsenal, constituting an "economic general staff" dominated by the zaibatsu's representatives. By the late spring, however, the rapid increase of bombed-out plants and the disruption of transport had nullified the possibility of an effective centralized direction of industrial operations. At this point the Industrial Control Associations, which had continued to function as auxiliaries of the munitions ministry, once more assumed a leading role. On July 4 a revision of the Major Industries Association Ordinance vested two new powers of far-reaching scope in the Control Associations: (1) the function of "operating the [major] industries," and (2) the responsibility for disposition of "profits and losses incurred by the major industries."

This solution to the management problem was a notable tribute to zaibatsu power and a stark reflection of the destructive results of the Allied bombing raids. The munitions ministry was no longer in a position to exert supervisory direction of the nation's industrial economy. Only the executives of the business concerns were on the spot as bombing raids occurred and so able to make the emergency decisions and adjustments required. In its political aspects, the move put the crowning touch to the zaibatsu role in Japan's war economy. The state treasury had first assumed the losses and guaranteed the profits of "nationalized" industries. It had then turned over to the zaibatsu the management of these industries and disposition of the profits and losses incurred.

On the security side, this development was rounded out by the Suzuki cabinet's swift campaign for establishment of the "Civilian Volunteer Corps" during the spring of 1945. Ostensibly directed toward mobilization of the people into a *Volkssturm* for "home defense," the corps was in fact designed to snuff out any possibility of a popular outbreak during the period of defeat and surrender. By the summer of 1945 the Suzuki cabinet had achieved its goal. Both workers and farmers were enrolled in militia detachments largely subject to the control of army officers. Under these conditions, they represented no threat to either the zaibatsu or the landlords when the time came for the Suzuki cabinet to move decisively toward the military surrender for which it had been constituted. The "people's army" ensured the Japanese oligarchy against the dangers of a revolt during the period before the Allied forces of occupation entered the country.

During 1941–1945 the zaibatsu's successful effort to bend governmental controls to their requirements represented but one aspect of the complex economic process taking place in Japan. Preoccupation with official control procedures should not becloud the fact that the overwhelming proportion of Japan's wartime industrial activity was still essentially private activity. Under the Munitions Company Control Act, the industrialists had in effect agreed to abide by certain rules in exchange for great advantages. They were further assured that the interpretation and application of the rules by the munitions ministry, as it was set up, would tend in their favor and not against them. But the industrial economy remained in zaibatsu hands, profits and losses were reckoned in normal fashion, and all the usual private corporate manipulations continued to take place. The "nationalization" of industry was merely a demagogic phrase, in no sense expressing the realities of the Japanese economic scene.

4. The Japanese People and the War

✿ THE END OF THE WAR in Japan brought many people to the edge of starvation, with the average Japanese consuming about 1500 calories a day. Gwen Terasaki, the wife of a Japanese diplomat, was in Washington, D.C., with her husband and child when Pearl Harbor was bombed. After a period of internment, they were sent back to Japan, where they spent the rest of the war. In this memoir she describes the last months of the war, after the Terasakis moved to a house in the country. The food situation was critical and was accentuated by the flow of refugees from the bombed-out cities.

GWEN TERASAKI*
Hunger in the Mountains

One of our friends from the Shanghai days wrote us that he was coming to visit. When he arrived he told us of his little *bessō* (summer house) in the mountains of Nagano prefecture above Suwa City. Yes, we could have it; he wanted us to enjoy it and to take care of it for him during his absence.

Again we began to pack, this time under the pressure of making an immediate move. Mako's teacher stayed with me three days and we hired a Mr. Katō, a fisherman from the nearby village, to help with the heavy work. He was an able fellow and took charge of the

* Gwen Terasaki, *Bridge to the Sun* (Chapel Hill, N.C.: University of North Carolina Press, 1957), pp. 157–161, 163–165, 168–172, 178–180.

whole moving operation, managing to send our belongings by rail on the last car allowed to carry nonmilitary freight. Our furniture and several trunks of household goods were left with friends for storage. Seeing the train depart so laden filled me with a wistful sense of abandonment and of last ditch desperation.

Everyone helped us. The Germans stayed up the entire last night before we left helping with odds and ends. Our Japanese neighbors cooked an *o-bentō* (boxed lunch) for each of us, packing them with rice balls, roast dried fish, and pickled radish. We were up at dawn to breakfast at the Brasches', and then we shouldered our packs, Mako carrying her two birds, I with the *o-bentō* and all the neighbors trailing behind—the clack-clack of their wooden clogs echoing through the hills and across the waters of Sagami Bay. We turned around and looked once more at our little house nestled among the spring blossoms. Our eyes again beheld the majesty of Nangoyama, serene and aloof in the background, and we whispered *sayōnara* to the Seven Jewels of Izu. I have never known a more beautiful spot.

Our train coughed and sputtered, and with a mighty effort we were off. Our friends waved good-bye, running along beside the train a little way. . . .

The wailing of the sirens began and I thought at last we were caught in a bombing. Kōfu was a railway terminal of importance and was bound to be attacked sooner or later. Mako's anxious eyes pleaded with me not to let the planes come. Her long pigtails were swaying to and fro, and in each hand she carried a birdcage. We walked in silence to where Terry stood guard over our luggage, heard the planes throbbing by, and saw them cast a shadow across the sun.

An unutterable sadness encompassed me that we should die so near our refuge. A prayer escaped me, "God, don't let it happen."

The planes flew on. My knees went weak and I had to sit down. Two weeks later the bombers struck Kōfu and devastated it.

Our *densha* came along and we hastened aboard amid shovings and pushings. Many of the people had been on foraging trips and had large rucksacks on their backs full of food. Often police boarded the trains and confiscated the food carried by the people; this was especially resented because one had to exchange some treasured possession for the food which the farmers would not sell for money. The farmers were tired of the refugees that poured from the broken cities, dirty, ragged, and hungry, and the city people thought the farmers were turning the war into a profit-making scheme, exacting exorbitant prices for their produce.

Our station was Chino, where the *densha* stopped for only a few minutes. It was a scramble for us to get off and unload our luggage onto the platform before the whistle blew. Terry had engaged a charcoal-burning taxi for the climb up the mountain, a trip that took two and one-half hours on foot. We had written ahead to the resort hotel at the village of Tateshina for a room until we could get settled at the summer house.

Our taxi emitted a volume of smoke and fumes but slowly climbed the mountain. I felt sick from the fumes and realized our birds would die if we did not hold them out of the windows.

We must have looked strange on our arrival at the hotel, grim, covered with soot from the train and the charcoal-burning taxi, with two birdcages swinging crazily from the windows. The villagers, astonished enough at this, immediately remarked at the foreigner. I knew I would remain the *gaijin* [foreigner] for the duration of my sojourn in their community. They were tolerant and rather patronizing, thinking I was a little "off," but they treated me kindly. . . .

After we had rested we went up the road to our little house. Perched on the side of the mountain, it overlooked the valley toward the snow-capped peaks beyond. It was built in the Western style except for two Japanese rooms, and it was light and airy and convenient. There were six built-in bunks and a tiny bathroom— but it was completely unfurnished and we did not know whether our things would reach us or not. We had only our clothes and what we could carry with us. Wondering whether any furniture would reach us, we began cleaning the house, going up every day to clean and scrub and then returning to the hotel for the night. In less than a week the caretaker brought us the welcome news that our things had arrived at Chino after all; and we immediately asked him to have them brought to the house. . . .

We had not been in our new home a week before we realized our biggest problem would be food. The farming district of Tateshina was more than two hours and a half on foot down the mountain. A day or two after moving in, we heard voices in our garden and there were eight young men of the group who had helped us move in, busily spading up our small garden. Terry went out and they told him there was still time to put in vegetables. We planted turnips, *daikon* (radishes), and beans. With much bargaining and two pairs of Terry's socks, we were able to procure potatoes for planting. We needed help and advice, never having raised anything in our lives except flowers. The soil was rocky and the stones we had to remove formed a huge pile. We worked furiously, having to stop often and rest because of our undernourished condition.

The bread that I had brought with me from Manazuru had been used up. We had no flour and were on a rice diet. We had dried soy beans, *shōyu* sauce, and butter, part of the supply I had gotten through the Germans. We had a box full of canned goods, but we were saving this against the approaching winter. Our rations consisted only of rice and sauce, and now and then some dried fish. The fish had such a hideous smell that I could not endure the thought of our eating it, hungry as we were. I threw it out to the voracious little field mice who scampered across our yard, their lean bodies showing every rib. Our rice ration was delayed each month so that there were as many as ten days to two weeks when every family had to forage for something to fill in. We learned to chop carrots, potatoes, or turnip tops to boil with the rice. The Japanese called this gruel-like stew *zōsui* and ate it with much complaint.

For breakfast we had boiled rice mixed with soy beans fried in butter, and we drank black tea without milk or sugar. I had about a cup of sugar and one one-pound can of Klim powdered milk that I had been saving to use in case of further illness. Breakfast was the meal that I minded most. The only food I used to long for was cornflakes. I had never been particularly fond of cornflakes but breakfast had always been my favorite meal and the thought of a cereal came repeatedly to mind. Enough toilet soap was another thing I missed. In my dreams I was always in a large department store with shelves and shelves of toilet soap and cornflakes.

Before our little garden began to yield anything green to eat we used to search for wild edible greens. Our neighbors showed us the ones we could eat safely. We found that the wild onions, a cross between garlic and our garden variety, were very tasty, but they were so small that they could only serve as seasoning. As I am very susceptible to insect bites, I always wore long-sleeved shirts and slacks, or *mompe,* and a scarf over my head when we went searching for mountain vegetables. I seemed to have a talent for putting my hands on crawling things and half of the time I was crashing down the mountain, fleeing in terror from centipedes or snakes. . . .

The only vegetable that seemed to thrive on our mountain ledge was the turnip. We ate not only the turnip but the leafy top. The Japanese are very fond of simply cooked greens and, having no supplies, I could cook only in their manner. They wash them and cook them in a pot with the lid fastened tightly, using only the water that clings to the leaves. Afterwards the vegetable is cooled, drained, chopped into intricate shapes, and usually garnished with shredded bonito. We saved our butter for breakfast and there was never enough *shōyu* sauce for seasoning.

The three of us were growing much weaker. I had lost my physical energy and suffered from a mental lethargy which made me very forgetful. When one starves slowly, it is not a spectacular thing, a great yearning for food and craving to eat. One is content to sit in the sun and do nothing; one even forgets that there is anything to do. One loses control of tears and lets them roll unheeded down one's cheek. It took me at least forty minutes to an hour every morning to comb my hair. My arms ached if I kept them up to my head for more than a minute or so. I had to stop and rest several times before I was finished. Mako's hair was another chore. Her long pigtails reached almost to her waist, and, since she could not do them herself and I was unable to do them for her, we finally had to cut them off.

A very fine doctor, who was suffering from high blood pressure, lived in the village. When he evacuated from Tokyo, he had brought his supply of medicines with him, keeping it buried against the day when our mountain retreat might be bombed. In Japan one often receives one's medicines from the doctor. He usually has a large supply on hand and has his own dispensary connected with his office. We found that the doctor had Vitamin B Complex shots and I began taking them every day. . . .

More and more the authorities called on the people to give time to the war effort. Someone had found that fuel for airplanes could be manufactured from the resin of pine trees, and each family in the countryside was required to extract a certain amount of it to be turned over to the local *chōkai* (town assembly). Terry and Mako were called to that duty but their efforts resulted in the smallest amount of resin collected by any family in our neighborhood association.

Terry had always been opposed to the whole idea of a *kamikaze* corps, saying that if a country had to use such methods to continue, it should give up. The pine-tree tapping for fuel also depressed him, and he kept muttering, "How long, how long?"

Our little garden had started to yield green beans and a few *daikon*. We were especially proud of one perfect *daikon,* and gave it a place of honor in our living room. We admired it until it became too shriveled to eat.

The air-raid sirens let us know that American planes now flew over Nagano more frequently. One day we heard that Matsumoto, a city in our prefecture, had been bombed. We also heard by the grapevine that the Japanese army had planned its last stand in the foothills of Nagano. One discounted three fourths of what one heard, as a fresh rumor skipped about every day. Our newspapers came irregularly and the static in our mountains made it almost impossible to hear news broadcasts. But we knew that the cities of Japan were being bombed steadily and even in our remote village what at first was a trickle of refugees became a flood. . . .

The refugees were called *sokaijin* (escaped to the country). A friend of Terry's furnished a remarkable example of someone very much *sokaijin*. He was a wealthy person who had collected Chinese art for many years and had a fine home furnished with beautiful carved furniture which he had painstakingly collected during a long sojourn on the mainland. His library contained many ancient scrolls of the T'ang dynasty in China, a period which the Japanese had regarded with awe for centuries. This gentleman had been forced to move repeatedly, and each time he was forced to pack away his delicate curios, his scrolls, and his carved furniture. They were not easily packed, and much care was required to ship them from one place to another without doing considerable damage. As it was, exercising every precaution that money and love could afford, a few mishaps occurred each time a change was made. On the first move this connoisseur had transported his possessions out of Tokyo and to a small suburb, then in a few months farther inland, then again, and yet again. In the early summer of 1945 he came to visit us at Tateshina in high spirits and announced happily to Terry,

"Terasaki-san, I have very good news. You know all my things that I have been moving and moving all over Japan? Well, they are all gone. A bomb hit my house and burned them all. I don't have to worry with them any more. Only this small vase is left, and I have brought it to you so I can move freely once more!"

There is, I guess, such a thing as a spiritual "second wind."

I was getting weaker steadily, and the symptoms of malnutrition were becoming more evident day by day. Mako was thin to the point of emaciation, and the ribs stood out pitifully on Terry's once stocky chest. We had no energy beyond that needed to prepare our rice and keep our house and ourselves clean. My fingernails were almost gone, and I had to bandage my fingers to keep blood from getting on everything I touched. . . .

All our spare time was taken up in searching for food, or for people who had food to sell. How happy we were one morning to see Mr. Okura, an old friend from Karuizawa, arrive suddenly with a rucksack on his back! He had been walking for more than three hours and had been on a train that was bombed and machinegunned. He had lost the way back to the train, and when the attack was over it had gone on without him. He had stumbled into a barracks for evacuated children and in the darkness had blandly climbed into bed with a little boy. He told us of their mutual astonishment upon awakening the next morning.

Our guest brought bread, flour, butter, and jam—and news of the outside world. We sat up most of the night as he talked of Karuizawa and our friends there. He told us for the first time of the persistent rumor that Japan had sent out peace feelers.

Adoringly I held the loaf of bread in my hands, poor little loaf of black bread that it was, and we felt joy again. Not only did Mr. Okura bring news and food but he delivered a fat letter from my dear friend Hélène who had moved to Karuizawa. She told of life there where most of the foreign refugees had gone to escape the intensified bombings of Tokyo. Food was getting scarcer at Karuizawa also, but, since the government gave special rations to foreign nationals, Hélène had fared better than we. However, they had not fared so well that she had not written, "Our children are healthier now as we have *daikon* again."

Mr. Okura had been on Terry's staff years before when he was chargé d'affaires in Havana, and we spent a second evening talking of Cuba and our life there. We spoke with warmth of the Cuban people, of their music, gay but with an undertone of sadness, their optimism and gusto. We saw Mr. Okura off next day with the hope that he would get home safely.

We had alerts very often, and now and then we could hear vague rumblings in the distance. The war was getting closer. More and more people were toiling up our mountain, heavily laden, searching for relatives or friends to give them shelter. Some of them had large burns on their faces and arms, and others, more severely injured, were carried on the backs of the men.

The rice ration was being held up more frequently, and we heard the devastating news that a large warehouse full of rice had burned and in its place we were to be rationed *kabocha* (pumpkin). It was like being told to eat squash instead of bread. . . .

Mako one day brought a letter to her father on her return from the daily trip to the village post office that told of the strange bombing of Hiroshima. The letter was from a newspaperman, an old friend of many years. Of course, he did not know that it was an atomic bomb but he did know it was something extraordinary. He added as a postscript, "As yet we know of no defense against this new and terribly destructive weapon." We discussed this all day and remembered that years before in Shanghai a European Buddhist monk had told us one evening that he foresaw a bomb so powerful that it could wipe out an entire city—a bomb that would change the course of history, that would create an era of fear of total destruction of civilization. At the time we had thought the monk was mad, but on this August day in 1945 we remembered his predictions and were afraid.

Terry and I were constantly talking it over. Believing much of the talk of the *Yamato* spirit, I thought that Japan would fight until the entire country was destroyed, the Japanese people broken and almost extinct. Terry disagreed and insisted that among Japanese statesmen there were realists who had a true love of country and the welfare of the people at heart. I remember asking him once how he thought the Japanese government should approach the Allies, through Russia or Switzerland. His reply was quick.

"Never! Go to the United States directly, and lay our cards on the table. Americans are good sports, and if we are direct and sincere it saves time. The Russians should have no part in it."

The very next day when Mako returned breathless from the village, panting from her run up the hill, with the news that Russia had gone into the war against Japan, Terry looked at me and said, "Now the change in world politics will be swift and ruthless. Japan is beaten already. Russia has only come in for the kill; the Four Horsemen will ride across the night." Underneath their despair the Japanese felt a smoldering resentment against the Russians.

We learned that the Americans were dropping leaflets that were masterpieces of insight and knowledge of the Japanese, of their poetry and psychology, their love of nature. Few Japanese got to read them for the military had given orders to turn them over at once to the nearest police box and not to repeat what was written on them. Yet the contents of the leaflets were passed by word of mouth and even far up in the hills we had learned of the messages. It had been reported that the emperor himself picked up one of the leaflets in the palace garden.

It was August 15, 1945. We struggled through breakfast, a bowl of rough cereal (a kind of oatmeal) with salt to season it. While we were drinking our tea an excited, urgent call came from the entrance, "Terasaki-san, Terasaki-san, *ohayō gozaimasu!* [Good morning.]" Terry and Mako rushed to the door and were told that orders were for members of the entire *tonarigumi* to assemble at the home of the *kumichō* because the emperor, for the first time in history, was to speak over the radio. The speech was scheduled at 10 A.M. I heard the clack, clack of the messenger's wooden *geta* as he went on to the next house.

Terry dropped into a chair. Mako and I went up to him. Clasped tightly in our three-way embrace, he sobbed, "It is over; no more bloodshed, at last, at last, my poor country!"

I told him, "I'm sure it is not surrender. His Majesty will only tell us to fight on to the last man and die."

Mako spoke up, "I don't want to die."

Terry, looking gently on her, said, "The emperor will not waste his time to reiterate what others have said. He will say something different."

As Terry was still weak from his illness, I told Mako to accompany him to the house of the *kumichō* which was farther up the mountain. Feeling that I, the *gaijin*, had no place there, I announced that I would remain at home. I told Terry that, if it was really surrender, on returning he should lift his hand as he came around the corner on the high crest where I could first see him. Otherwise there would be no sign. I watched them as they walked slowly across the garden, around the bend, and up until they were out of sight. Alone, I wanted to cry out. There was no sound but the "dree, dree, dree" of the *semi* (cicada) and then the "coo, coo" of the mourning doves. All my thoughts were with Terry. His bitterness was twofold. His country was defeated in a war that he had never believed in. A needless war. He had not been himself these past four years. His previous life had been one of hard work, contributing steadily to the cause of Japanese statesmanship with ability, energy, and optimism, always without display. Pearl Harbor had shaken him radically and for these four years he had been a sick man. His wretchedness was the measure of his quality; he felt boredom at this enforced leisure to the extent of his fine intellect and his frustration was fed by nobility of spirit. Now, perhaps, he could return to his work.

I looked across the beautiful valley, watched the sun playing with the shadows, and hoped that if we had to die it would be here on a mountain in Nagano.

After a timeless wait I moved out onto our little porch where I could see the high crest in the bend of the road. Our two birds kept up a smart conversation from their swinging cages, responding to the chant of the *semi*. A snake, startled for a moment, made his way across a large flat rock and lost himself in the tall autumn grasses nearby. First to the horizon and then up to the bend in the road went my anxious gaze.

Terry appeared and raised his hand, little Mako silent beside him. It was peace.

❀ THE AMERICAN DECISION to firebomb and destroy Japanese cities was made almost a year before the first atomic bomb was dropped on Hiroshima. In late November 1944, the first incendiary bombs were dropped on Tokyo, and the raids mounted as the months passed, with hundreds of planes bombing at once. On March 9, 1945, waves of planes dropped incendiary bombs containing an early form of napalm on Tokyo. Aided by gale-force winds, fires raged through the city built of wood and paper in a huge fire storm that burned almost two days. This single saturation bombing raid killed over 125,000

people. Raids extended to practically all Japanese cities, and by
the end of the war 668,000 civilians had died, a greater
number than Japan's military casualties; fifty percent of the
housing in sixty-six cities and towns had been destroyed. Robert
Guillain, a French correspondent assigned to Japan during the
war (the Vichy regime in France was not at war with Japan),
describes the raids as he saw them while living in Tokyo.

ROBERT GUILLAIN*
Tokyo Burns†

Nothing more had been done since the summer of 1943 to improve
the condition of the bomb shelters which had already been built in
the city—shelters which consisted of holes in the ground covered
with a few pieces of wood (torn from houses already destroyed by
fire) and then hastily topped with soil. The neighborhood groups
had barely finished preparing a few hand pumps which were
attached to troughs or cisterns and which created a pressureless
stream of water no thicker than a finger. To fight the ultra-modern
firebombs, the essential weapons are a straw mat which can be
soaked in water; sand in little paper bags which can be thrown; but
principally a bucket of water which can be filled at the house's
regulation trough and which is then passed along a chain of fire-
fighters—the servants, the housekeepers, the old people, and the
pensioners of the neighborhood. According to the propaganda,
which circulates rapidly and efficiently, these tools will suffice in
case of even the most violent of conflagrations. The alerts are still
looked upon as an opportunity to influence the people, to bolster
the general morale—rather than as a sign of any actual danger.
The newspapers speak incessantly of government plans for mass
evacuation of useless civilians. But, apart from sending children to
schools in the country or the mountains, nothing has been done as
yet. The instructions given by the neighborhood groups request
that people not stray in case of an air raid, and that each indi-

* Robert Guillain, *Le peuple japonais et la guerre* (Paris: René Juillard,
1947), pp. 198–211.
† Translated by Jean Schiffman.

vidual home have a nearby shelter. Tokyo will be saved, they say, if each family remains to defend its own home. The police systematically discourage public bomb shelters: if people gather in large groups, homes will be left empty and defenseless; since it takes only a few minutes for a Japanese home to burn up, people would not be able to get back to their homes after the attack in enough time to save them.

In general, during these first raids, everything goes on as if the government refuses to believe in the potential danger of it all. Or, if the government does believe in the danger it is as if its policy is to keep the people in the city and leave them there, exposed, so that there will be immediate action on the part of a great number of defenders to master the fires—even if this method is costly in terms of human life. . . .

During the night of November 29–30, 1944: Alert! The first nighttime raid! Millions are learning for the first time to do what they will be doing every night, and soon several times nightly: to leap out from between mat and quilt, to bolt outdoors into the icy downpour, and to jump into primitive holes already filled to the brim with water. Everywhere, pressed together like stacks of dry wood in a timber yard, the wooden houses . . . Planes pass by, flying low: so begins the hunting game on a Japanese night. The earth trembles; bombs burst. Then, suddenly, a strange rhythmic humming fills the night with its thunderous pulse and makes my whole house shake: the incredible sound of B29s passing invisibly in a nearby corner of the sky, followed by the buzzing of the antiaircraft guns and fire. The radio announces that half the bombs have been released. I climb onto the roof of my terrace where I will spend so many of the coming winter nights, for in order to fight the bombs, if they land on the house, one must be above ground and see them land, since the flame must be instantly quelled before it turns into a fiery geyser. Above, the B29s, in formation, peacefully continue on their way, followed by the red explosions of antiaircraft shells which fail to reach them. On the horizon, a pink light rising behind a nearby hill grows larger, bloodying the sky. More red stains spread mistily across the sky: the sight will soon be familiar. In ancient Tokyo (then called Edo), terror reigned when frequent accidental fires, euphemistically called "the flowers of Edo," lit up the skies. This night, Tokyo has begun to blossom. . . .

January is fairly calm, the Americans being busy with their attack on the Philippines. However, before the end of the month, there is a terrible raid. The clouds are very low, and the people fear this above all, for there is a strange myth about radar. The people say that radar enables the enemy to see through clouds or in the dark. The raid takes place at one P.M., on a Saturday. The all-clear had been sounded, crowds from the downtown districts, believing the raid to be over, left their shelters at the exact moment when fifteen superfortresses, flying in formation, dropped explosive bombs on Nihombashi and the Ginza. There are several thousand victims, mostly in Owari-chō—the very heart of Tokyo—where a bomb destroyed the subway station which was still packed with refugees; and also near the *Asahi* newspaper office, where hundreds, beneath the arches of the elevated railway, were massacred by explosions or their aftereffects. I visit these sites two days later, when police barricades have been lifted—only a horrifying wreckage remains. The Ginza: a noisy, colorful district in the center of the capital, a paradise of restaurants and bars, theaters and geishas, streets lined with weeping willow trees, thousands of boutiques selling jade, silk, seashells, and pearls. The Ginza is in ruins and ashes. A large, curious crowd comes from every corner of the city to gaze at the wreckage, stupified. It is at this moment that the people of Tokyo know that the war is lost.

Now the alerts are becoming more frequent, by day and by night, the biggest raids coming every eight to fifteen days. The alert system is remarkably efficient in contrast to the general disorder. Well before the alarm sounds, the people are warned by the radio, whose voice, sometimes calm, but urgent if danger is near, announces that the enemy planes have been spotted over the "South Sea" and are heading for Japan. The attack is traced and described as long as it lasts, the speaker announcing the arrival and departure of waves of bombardiers in the areas of the defense line. The network of islands which stretch from Tokyo to the Marianas appears to be of great help in the defense of the capital, and the alert is usually given a good half-hour in advance. On the other hand, the Japanese accuse Mount Fuji of betraying them, for her white peak, always visible above the clouds, serves as a guide and a meeting point for small squadrons heading for the nearby city. . . .

Four days pass. It is March 9 . . . March 9, 1945: a date which Tokyo will remember just as she remembers September 1, 1923, the date of the great earthquake. On this day, springtime erupted suddenly, as the seasons do in Japan. But the beautiful weather, in these days of air raids, brings anxiety instead of joy. Still more unsettling is the wind—a wind which has been blowing since morning, blowing more gustily in the afternoon, bringing clouds in the night—a wind which, in the evening, became as violent as a springtime typhoon. The drama about to unfold will be due to this storm. All over the city there is but one thought: if *they* come with such a wind, it could be disastrous. Now *they* know what the weather is like in Tokyo, for a single B29, flying at an altitude of 11,000 meters, surveyed the capital during the day, apparently on a reconnaissance mission. And at eleven P.M., here they come indeed: sirens announce their arrival, the radio warns of their approach.

Before midnight, *they* are there and immediately they begin their fertilization of the sky. Bright flashes illumine the shadows, Christmas trees blossoming with flame in the depths of the night, then hurtling downward in zigzagging bouquets of flame, whistling as they fall. Barely fifteen minutes after the beginning of the attack, the fire, whipped by the wind, starts to rake through the depths of the wooden city.

Once more, luckily (or rather due to the methodical plans of the American command) my district is not directly hit. An immense dawn brought forth by the bombs has been rising above the center of the city, brightening from raid to raid. Now the dawn is apparently winning the battle—the great light chases away the darkness, and here and there a B29 appears in the sky. For the first time, they are flying at a low or medium altitude, at varying levels. Among the oblique columns of smoke which are now starting to rise from the city, one can see their long metal wings, razor sharp, shining harshly in the reflected glow of the flames, casting black silhouettes on the fiery sky, reappearing, golden, in a distant stretch of dark sky, or blue like meteors in the gleam of the searchlights whose compasses open and shut on the horizon. In such a raid, it is no good to remain underground, without seeing anything, for one could be roasted alive before having had the time to understand what was happening. The Japanese people in the gardens near mine are all outside, or at the mouth of their holes, and I hear their cries of admiration (how typically Japanese!) as they view this grandiose, this almost theatrical spectacle.

In the distance, beyond the hill which is my horizon, the bombing continues. But the wind, as violent as ever, has begun to carry with it the burnt debris which the flaming sky spills forth. More and more burning embers—then bits of wood and paper ignite and soon there is a raging fire. One must make continual rounds of the terrace, the garden, the house, in order to keep track of the danger and extinguish the flames. In the distant sky, torches explode and drop, vibrating, onto the city. The bombs sometimes look like flaming locks of hair—probably the effect of the burning liquid. Here and there the red petals of the antiaircraft fire pursue each other across the sky in harsh explosions of light; but the defense lines are not strong, and the huge B29s, flying in disarray, seem unhampered. Occasionally they disappear and the sky is empty. But the hoarse yet confident voice of the radio announces that new formations have come to fill the night. And the terrifying Holocaust begins once more. Flames gush forth, apparently fairly close to the heights of my district. We see them twisting and turning beneath the wind at the shadowy low rooftops, dark debris whirls beneath us in the tempest. The word has already spread that the conflagration is approaching and soon it takes control of the neighboring district of Sarumachi, a word meaning "Village of Monkeys." People are running down the nearby road; now the crackling of the flames is close by, apparently it is the sound of houses collapsing. Above us, a wide boulevard stretches across the pathway of the flames, which will be blocked, nearer still, by the parks and gardens. The Village of Monkeys will be partially burned, but once more the flank of my hill is spared. The anxiously flaming trail moves on, while, gradually, night makes way for a red and black daybreak, with the whole city smoking upward to the sky.

However, all this was but a terrifying illustration of a drama which was actually taking place further away, in the northeast and eastern sections of the capital. I will tell the stories such as I found them, in those days that followed, and later on; and I can vouch for their accuracy. The target area was the flat countryside of Tokyo, that indefinite stretch of land which constitutes the Tokyo of the worker and the factory. Here one finds not only huge factories, and factory workers' homes, but also countless attics where artisans and their families live and do work for the national defense. This area is called "the plain," as opposed to "the mountain" and the residential districts scattered among the hills of the

west and south. It is indeed a plain, and the districts are pressed
together like a jungle, the overcrowded neighborhoods heaped
together in a compact mass, mobs glued together in the tiny,
narrow streets. Across a few rectilinear avenues and a lacework of
stagnant canals, the Sumida River traces a solitary pathway
through this mass, past thousands of wooden houses. On the left
bank: Fukagawa, with her docks facing the Bay of Tokyo, and
Honjo and Mukojima, filled with factories. On the right bank:
Asakusa, Shitaya, and the suburbs of Kanda and Nihombashi.
These are the main target areas, destined for the holocaust.
Around midnight the first superfortresses release hundreds of
incendiaries in order to demarcate, by four or five large fires, the
target zone. The people nickname the incendiaries "Molotov
flower-baskets." The planes that follow, flying still lower, zigzag
and crisscross their way through the area, leaving in their wake
huge flaming rings. Soon more planes arrive to plant incendiaries
within these flaming circles. So hell begins.

The people hold their ground beneath the explosion of bombs,
faithful to the edict which decrees that each family shall defend its
own home. But how does one quell a fire in such a wind? and when
a single house receives ten bombs, or even more? For these bombs
weigh no more than three kilos apiece and fall by the thousands in
a veritable downpour. In addition, in full flight, the metal cylinders
release a rosy incendiary which slides along the rooftops, igniting
wherever it splashes, spreading a stream of dancing flames everywhere. The poor weapons, the thousands of amateur firemen, the
feeble jets of water from hand pumps, the soaked straw mats, the
sand thrown on the bomb when one can get close enough to the
terrible heat—all are revealed to be totally useless. Rooftops
collapse under the impact of the bombs, and in a matter of minutes
the fragile wood and straw houses flare up, the interior glowing
like a paper lantern. The stormy wind still expels its fiery breath,
sending flaming boards flying, wounding people, igniting things
everywhere. Flames move quickly from one group of houses to
another, with all the rapidity of a forest fire. Screaming families
decide to evacuate; sometimes the women have already left, carrying their babies, dragging along boxes or mattresses. Too late: at
the foot of the road, a circle of fire has blocked the path. Everywhere, sooner or later: no exit.

The police and the helpless firemen attempt momentarily to

control the fleeing mobs, to direct them toward the blackened holes where previous fires have preserved an occasional outlet. In the rare places where the fire hoses are functioning (for water is scarce or pressureless in most of the canal areas) the firemen hose down the refugees so that they may safely escape through fiery passages. Elsewhere, people douse themselves in the trough that sits in front of each house before continuing their flight. But the flight is an obstacle course: the electric poles and wires which spin a thick web around Tokyo have fallen across the road. In the thick smoke, with a wind so fiery that it burns the lungs, the fugitives collapse before burning up in place. The wind beats the flaming currents to the ground and often it is the feet that catch fire first: the leggings of the men and the trousers of the women ignite and the rest follows suit. The air-raid clothing distributed by the government consists of thickly padded hoods which cover the head and shoulders. These hoods are especially designed to protect the ears from the noise of explosives—for Tokyo has been under bomb attack for many months. The hoods ignite under the downpour of sparks, and those whose feet do not catch fire burn first at their heads. Mothers, carrying babies strapped to their backs in the Japanese style, suddenly notice (often too late) that their infants' blankets have caught fire. In the rare open spaces—the crossroads, the gardens, the parks—the fugitives are packed together. But bundles catch fire even more quickly than clothing; and the crowd smoulders from within. Hundreds, refusing to flee, disappear into the holes which serve as shelters, with or without their precious belongings. They will be found, later, carbonized. Whole families die in holes beneath their homes—so limited is the available space for building even the tiniest shelter under the wooden houses of these poor, overcrowded, beehivelike districts. The houses shrivel and burn above them, charring them in their holes, choking them to death.

The burning front lines advance so rapidly that, in many places, the police, having assumed an escape route to be available, suddenly have no time to evacuate an area. And the wind gives birth to flames in unexpected places, seeded over great distances by flying debris. In the other half of the city, firemen try to penetrate the pyre or attack the boundary points, but the wind carries the fire off too quickly. The firemen are left in a destroyed area; the boundary point has moved. One sees once again a phenomenon which terrorized Tokyo during the fire of 1923: the combination of wind and flame creates several huge, fierce cyclones which whirl about in a frenzy, sucking whole housing complexes into their fiery vortexes.

Wherever there are canals, crowds jump in; in the shallow areas, people wait, half-submerged in the dirty pools, their mouths above the water. They will be found dead, thousands of them—not drowned, but choked by the burning air and the smoke. In other areas, the temperature of the water quickly rises, becomes intolerable, and the unlucky bathers perish; they will be found with their bodies boiled. Some of the canals connect directly to the Sumida River: at high tide, many people slip and drown. At Asakusa and Honjo, crowds seek refuge on the bridges. But the bridges are made of metal and gradually they heat up: the masses, huddled at the now-scorching railings, let go and fall into the river which sweeps them away. On both banks of the Sumida, thousands of refugees escape to the riverside parks and gardens. Panic pulses through the mob, so tightly pressed together in this narrow strip of land. The shoving, crowding masses are gradually inching in the direction of the river, and the outermost fringes of the screaming mob are thrown into the deep water and swallowed up. Thousands of drowned bodies will be found in the estuary of the Sumida River.

At Asakusa, the crowd seeks refuge around an old Buddhist temple, one of the most beautiful temples in Tokyo. It is the sanctuary of Kannon, Goddess of Pity, and it attracts fifty to sixty thousand visitors in peacetime. This temple is a sure asylum, for it dates back to the seventeenth century, and has survived all the great fires of Tokyo, including the earthquake of 1923, mainly because the priests will only admit people without packages into the surrounding park. However, the people believe that the temple's salvation is due to protection by the goddess. Alas! this time Kannon did not save her people: lit by firebrands and bombs, the huge wooden framework catches fire, and the immense gray tile roof collapses. The enormous ginko trees in the parks are aflame and so are the gardens and the people. Wherever a rare oasis occurs in the midst of the city, a grotesque scene is revealed: refugees dying by the hundreds—in the Garden of Hyakkaen, so dear to the hearts of Japanese poets, in the Kiyozumi Park in Fukagawa, and so on. In the inner hallways of the Temple of

Kameido, well known for its glycin plants, the people find themselves surrounded by flaming buildings. It is there, or in the little nearby houses, that the whores of the neighboring district perish. In the famous Yoshiwara, near Asakusa, a drama is recreated which has become more or less a classic among the great fires of Tokyo's past. Those who remained before the bombing reached its peak hastened to shut the high metal doors which close off this district. Their aim: to prevent their valuable collection of women of the night from escaping. On this early springtime evening, the houses were raking in money. Many clients were not aware of the danger; when they wanted to escape, it was too late. Most of the women died in the flames—with their lover of the evening.

At Nihombashi, the police direct the refugees toward a high, sturdily constructed building, the Meijiza, or Meiji Theater. The encroaching fire fills the air with smoke, the choking refugees lower the huge, electrically controlled fire curtains of the theater. But—the neighboring district catches fire and in turn ignites the inside of the theater; and the occupants, wanting to flee, try to raise the curtain, but it is blocked and they roast to death . . . but what is the point of continuing this horror story?

Around five A.M., the all-clear sounds. The sirens that are still working in the half of the city that has been spared announce the end of the raid. But the other half will burn for twelve hours more. I joined forces with someone who passed through the destroyed areas during the day of March 11. This witness told me that the most distressing thing was the necessity of getting off his bicycle every few steps in order to avoid the countless bodies lying in the road. There was still a light wind, and since some of the carbonized bodies had been reduced to ash, they now crumbled into dust and the wind blew them away like sand. In many places, burnt corpses barricaded the road.

Some time later I saw the first official list of the victims. It was supposedly top secret, but rumor spread it throughout Japan: 120,000 dead. After the war, I learned that, according to official Japanese documents seized by the American command (secret documents which belonged to the Japanese government during the war and which were not drawn to the attention of the Americans), the definitive total was 197,000 dead or missing. The enormity of that holocaust, so much greater than that of the atomic bomb (about 130,000 in Hiroshima—half dying immediately, the other half later, as a result of their injuries) was due to the terrible wind the night of March 9–10. Tokyo was to suffer through raids even more violent in terms of number of planes and the quantity of bombs dropped; but it appears that none of the subsequent raids killed more than 20,000 at the most.

According to information published by the Americans, 300 superfortresses (of which only two did not return) participated in that March 9 raid. Each one carried a load of seven to eight tons of untested bombing equipment; this was a new type of bomb, an M29, which contained in its cylinder a mixture of incendiary jelly and oil [an early form of napalm]. On that single night, between midnight and about three A.M., 700,000 bombs were dropped on the city. The total load was ten times greater than the bombs dropped by the Luftwaffe during the "Great Fire of London" in September 1940; and the area of Tokyo razed on March 9 is fifteen times greater than the surface destruction of the English capital four and a half years earlier.

Finally, need I add that, if I wanted to give all these details (which I believe have never before been published), that it has not been with the afterthought of condemning the creators of the punishment—nor has it been to absolve those who were responsible—but only to publish the facts, which bring further testimony to the trial and condemnation of the war . . . and this happened five months before the atomic bomb.

❀ FOR THE SOLDIERS as well as for the civilians the war became increasingly devastating. The authors of the two novels excerpted here both served in the Philippines, and Ōoka Shōhei was a POW at the end of the war. Noma Hiroshi in his work attempts to portray the wartime army with all its backbiting and corruption. Ōoka, writing about the close of the war in the Philippines, concentrates more on the breakdown of civilized behavior among men struggling to stay alive. Both passages illustrate the harsh realities of the honor of fighting for the emperor.

NOMA HIROSHI*
Zone of Emptiness

It was already late when Soda returned to the company. Night was falling, but the buildings were not yet lit up. The sinister walls of the post loomed vaguely against the somber sky. The first sergeant was sitting at his desk, looking very important. Soda went up to him.

"Sergeant, I'm returning from an official mission."

"All right," said the sergeant, who seemed nervous and pre-occupied.

Soda began his report. Kitani's brother would come as soon as he could. He was going to ask for leave from the factory where he was mobilized and had requested Soda to pay his respects to the first sergeant.

"All right," repeated the sergeant. "You'll give me full details later. For the time being, I've got other things on my mind. . . . Here, read that," he said abruptly, handing Soda a paper with a headquarters stamp. "I'm fed up. It's impossible to work under such conditions. The captain plans to cancel all leaves for privates and noncoms."

"What's he doing that for?"

"Read the paper and you'll see. They're going to send fifteen men to the front. The captain doesn't want wind of the matter to get around town. He may be right, but I don't want any part of it. Starting tomorrow, I'm going to go in for rifle exercise. That's the best way of keeping out of trouble. Good exercise all year round."

Each of the sergeant's words seemed to be bristling with hostility toward the captain. Without quite knowing why, Soda felt vaguely hopeful. Opposite him, Private First Class Komuro winked at him as if signaling something.

"Who's going to be sent," asked Soda, "the replacements or those on active duty? I imagine it'll be the replacements, don't you?"

* Noma Hiroshi, *Zone of Emptiness* (Cleveland and New York: World, 1956), pp. 172–176.

The news that men were to be shipped out spread like wildfire. The office staff, the attachés in the quartermaster's department, the telephone operators, the men in the supply room, and the medical personnel all added the rumors that were circulating in their own departments, with the result that the entire post was seething with excitement. The men stood around in groups discussing the latest news. The more reasonable among them tried to calm the others by pointing out that similar rumors had made the rounds a number of times but that nothing had come of them.

However, three men had actually been sent out a month earlier, and their fate had seemed a particularly bad break as all three had been just about due for discharge. Instead of the long-awaited release, they were given combat equipment. The other soldiers often spoke of the raw deal they had been given and of the long faces they had pulled. The three soldiers had been so depressed that they had not even stood their bunkmates a drink, as was the custom on such occasions. Then, life at the post resumed its monotony. The number of soldiers increased daily owing to the return of convalescents from the hospital. But the impression left by the departure of the three men remained vivid in the minds of the entire company and set them on edge whenever a new rumor arose.

That day, Soda kept going back and forth between the office and the barrack room. The men were on the lookout for him and whenever they caught sight of him bombarded him with questions.

"Who's going to be picked? Are they going to draw on the replacements or those on active service?"

Soda loathed being regarded as a source of information. He kept telling them that he was not in on any secrets, but they crowded round him nevertheless. They dragged him to the stove and sat him down so that he would be warm and comfortable and then pumped him with questions. All he could tell them was that fifteen soldiers had been requisitioned for the expeditionary corps. Headquarters was to issue an order in two days indicating how the men were to be chosen and the exact date of their departure. The old-timers shuddered. They had hoped that only the replacements would be picked, but it now seemed to them just as likely that they themselves might be.

"When will the list be out?"

"I haven't the slightest idea," said Soda. "Maybe the first sergeant knows, though I doubt it."

He looked about for Kitani and was surprised not to see him among the others. He would have liked to talk about his visit to the hatter and to let him know that his brother had promised to come as soon as possible. The first sergeant would then get in touch with the right authority and would certainly be able to arrange a leave for Kitani's brother.

Some second- and third-year soldiers had joined the group, and Soda now found himself the center of a noisy circle. Among them were men over thirty years of age and fathers of families.

"What do you want me to tell you?" continued Soda. "I have a feeling that most of those picked will be replacements, though there'll probably also be a few older soldiers."

"That's just what I've been saying," said one of the men. "Veterans who've already been at the front and who are up for discharge. That's justice for you."

"It's outrageous . . . outrageous," muttered several others.

"And it's the first sergeant who makes the decisions," said Hashimoto, a third-year man. "If he has me shipped out, I'm capable of killing him before I go."

"Some deal . . . a man's life and death in the hands of a first sergeant," said Tsuchiya.

"To think that when we were mobilized as replacements we were told that it was just a matter of three months. Then they kept adding on more and more months, and now they're ending by sending us overseas."

"I want to clear out and go home . . . I'm fed up . . . fed up."

"And to make matters worse, all leaves are being canceled. We're all going to have to stick around next Sunday."

"That's to keep the news from spreading," said Soda.

"Still and all, they're not going to be sent to the southern front. You said that it's for the expeditionary corps. That means China."

"You don't believe that, do you? They wouldn't cancel leaves if it were for China."

"Of course it's for the south. Don't you think so, Soda?"

Soda merely made a vague gesture. He left the group and went to look for Kitani. But no sooner had he reached the corridor than he was surrounded by a group of replacements who had just heard the news and wanted details from a member of the office staff. They clung to Soda as to a life preserver. Several of them were undersized and narrow-chested. Some had bad eyes. Their uniforms were too big for them, and they looked cold and pathetic.

"Third-Year Soldier, it's said that men are going to be sent to the front. Who's going to be taken? The replacements, aren't they?" asked Private First Class Tode, speaking for the others. He had an angular, corpselike face, with eyes that seemed to be popping out of his head.

"Nothing's been decided yet," said Soda.

They were joined by another group. Soda felt pity for the anxious faces and puny bodies.

"There's nothing I can tell you. I don't know a thing."

Several of the men felt there was no point standing around and shuffled off.

"Has any one of you seen Kitani?" asked Soda.

"Kitani? The fellow who got back the other day? I saw him over there a while ago," said Tode, pointing with his dirty hand in the direction of the washrooms.

Soda thought of the poplars. Perhaps Kitani was keeping an eye on the spot where he had hid his money.

"I'll go see whether I can find him there," he thought. "But he'll be furious if he thinks I'm spying on him."

"Third-Year Soldier," continued Tode, in a pleading voice, "a soldier in the kitchen told us that the entire contingent is going to be made up of replacements, except for two old-timers."

Tode, who was a carpenter in civilian life, was a familiar figure at the post because of the odd jobs he did in the various departments. His face was dark and wrinkled. Soda could see in the eyes that were scanning his face an anxiety that Tode was unable to conceal. Soda turned his head away, unable to bear the sadness of the soldier's gaze.

"It's impossible for me to give you any more exact information," he said, in an effort to break the painful tension. "No official statement has been issued yet."

"But they told us in the kitchen . . ."

Tode turned to the others as if calling them to witness.

"Why do you think a man in the kitchen is in on official secrets?" asked Soda.

He knew, as did everyone else, that the kitchen was always the first to be informed because of the food distribution, but he was so disturbed by the look of terror on Tode's face that he wanted to reassure him.

"So you're sure that nobody knows anything?"

"Of course. Stop tormenting yourself before anything's definite. You know as well as I do that the rumors that circulate are rarely confirmed."

As the group broke up, the phrase "nobody knows anything" was repeated like an echo.

"Can anyone lend me a cap and shoes?" asked Soda. "I've got to go outside for a moment."

One of the replacements took off his shoes and cap and gave them to Soda. As Soda left, he heard one of the men say to another, "It's good-bye for good for anyone who's sent to the front. There's no chance of getting back alive. Everyone says so."

ŌOKA SHŌHEI*
Fires on the Plain

My squad leader slapped me in the face.

"You damned fool!" he said. "D'you mean to say you let them send you back here? If you'd told them at the hospital you had nowhere to go, they'd have had to take care of you. You know perfectly well there's no room in this company for consumptives like you!"

My eyes were riveted to his lips, which became more and more moist as he babbled away. Why he should be so excited I could not understand, seeing that it was I, not he, who was receiving the fatal sentence. No doubt it was just an instance of the military tendency to raise one's temper automatically as one raised one's voice. I had noticed that as our condition had deteriorated the officers had begun to let loose on us soldiers the nervousness lying beneath their mask of military impassivity. Food was our squad leader's chief preoccupation (as it was indeed of the entire Japanese army

* Ōoka Shōhei, *Fires on the Plain* (New York: Alfred A. Knopf, 1957), pp. 3–12.

in the Philippines) and accordingly the theme of food underlay his present screed.

"Look here, Private Tamura," he continued, "almost all our men are out foraging for food. Don't you understand? We're fighting for our lives! We've no place for anyone who can't pull his own weight." His voice grew louder. "You've damned well got to go back to that hospital! If they won't let you in, just plant yourself by the front door and wait till they do! They'll take care of you in the end. And if they still refuse, then—well, you'd better put your hand grenade to good use and make an end to it all. At least you'll be carrying out your final duty to your country."

I knew perfectly well that, however long I "planted" myself in front of the hospital, I would not be admitted unless I was equipped with an adequate supply of food. The army doctors and medical orderlies depended entirely on the patients for their provisions. The ever-increasing group of men "planted" outside the hospital bespoke the futility of seeking admission without this vital commodity. Like me, these men had all been thrown out of their companies and left to their fates.

I had suffered a slight hemorrhage shortly after we landed on the west coast of Leyte in the latter part of November. While I was stationed in Luzon I had constantly feared a recurrence of my illness, and this in fact had come about in the course of our forced march into the interior of the island following the landing on Leyte. I was promptly given a five-day ration of food and sent to a field hospital in the mountains.

In the hospital wounded soldiers were lying about on rough wooden beds that had been requisitioned from civilian houses. The men were covered with blood and dirt, but no one seemed to be doing anything for them. When the doctor saw me, he first lectured me severely for having come to a field hospital suffering from consumption; but when he realized that I had brought my own food he gave instructions for me to be admitted.

After I had spent three days in bed, the doctor pronounced me cured and I left the hospital. My squad leader, however, did not agree with the doctor's verdict; he further contended that, since I had brought five days' rations with me, I should have stuck it out in the hospital for the full five days. I was ordered to return. When I reappeared at the hospital, the doctor indignantly denied that my rations had been sufficient for five days and added that in any case they had already been used up. And so this morning I had once more found myself shuttling back to my unit. I was fully aware that I would not be taken back and was really only curious whether my company would completely abandon one of its men to his fate.

"Yes, sir," I said, my eyes still fixed on the squad leader's humid lips, "I understand perfectly. I am to report back to the hospital. And if I am not admitted, I am to kill myself."

Normally, the squad leader would have objected to the suggestion of individual judgment implied in the words "I understand perfectly," a terse repetition of orders being considered adequate; this time he chose to overlook the peccadillo.

"That's right. And look here, Private Tamura, try to cheer up! Remember—it's all for the fatherland. To the very end I expect you to act like a true soldier of the emperor."

"Yes, sir."

In the corner of the room, by the window, the quartermaster sergeant was busy filling out some document. He was sitting with his back turned, in front of the old wooden crate that served as desk. I did not think he was listening, but when I had repeated my orders he got to his feet, and screwing up his eyes so that they became even narrower than usual, said: "That's right, Tamura. I'm sorry we seem to be throwing you out like this, but you must try and look at it from the squad leader's point of view as well. Now don't go and kill yourself unless you absolutely have to," the sergeant added, as if by an afterthought. "Here, I'm going to give you some provisions."

He went to the opposite corner and from a pile of potatoes picked up a few at random in both hands. They were the small Philippine potatoes known as *kamote,* which taste rather like our own sweet potatoes. I thanked him politely, but as I put the potatoes into my haversack my hands were trembling. Six small potatoes—to this extent and no further was my country prepared to guarantee my survival: this country of mine to which I was offering my life. There was a terrifying mathematical exactness about this number six.

I saluted, made a right about-face, and opened the door. As I left the room the squad leader's voice followed me into the passage. "Don't bother to report to the company commander!" he shouted.

In the back of my mind had lurked a hope—a hope that if I

spoke to the company commander he might possibly intercede on
my behalf. I suppose that even at this stage I vaguely thought that
I might contrive to remain with my unit. At the other end of the
short passage I could see the company commander's room. A
straw mat hanging over the entrance gave it an air of utter calm.
But now the squad leader's last words had expunged my final
hope. Obviously the company commander had already settled my
case when he sent me back to the hospital the day before. My
return this afternoon had in effect changed nothing: all that had
remained was for the squad leader to pronounce sentence.

As I descended the half-rotted stairs I noticed how the sun
shone down through the cracks in the wood, making neat patterns
on the ground below. In front of the building stood rows of bushes,
interspersed with faded tropical plants; beyond these was a clump
of trees where a group of soldiers busied themselves digging an
antiaircraft trench. They were using sticks and old pans (requisitioned from civilian houses) by way of shovels. Our company had
in fact become no more than a broken group of stragglers skulking
in a small mountain village; for some time the Americans had no
longer even bothered to bomb us. Yet the antiaircraft trench
somehow gave us a sense of security, and, besides, there was no
other work to be done at the camp.

In the shade of the trees, the soldiers' faces were dark and
expressionless; one of the men looked up in my direction but
immediately turned aside and continued his digging. Most of these
soldiers were conscripts who had come here from Japan at the
same time as myself. The boredom of life on the troopship had
brought us together and given us a certain sense of kinship; but
when we arrived in the Philippines and were assigned to units with
veteran troops, we soon began to sink back into our normal
egotism. Then we landed on Leyte Island and our real difficulties
began.

Before long any comradeship that we had once felt for each
other had virtually disappeared. When I felt ill and was on the way
to becoming a burden to the other men, I noticed a growing chill in
their attitude toward me. For people like us, living day and night
on the brink of danger, the normal instinct of survival seems to
strike inward, like a disease, distorting the personality and removing all motives other than those of sheer self-interest. That is why
this afternoon I did not wait to go and tell my former comrades-in-

arms what had happened to me. For one thing, they probably already knew; besides, it seemed unfair to risk awakening their dormant sense of humanity.

Beside a roadside tree was gathered a group of sentries—all that remained of our company's effective military strength. We had landed on the west coast of Leyte as part of a mixed brigade, which in turn belonged to one of several army corps that had been sent to relieve the desperate position of the Japanese forces in the Tacloban area. At the beach we had been met by a massive American air attack; half of our men had been killed, and all heavy equipment sunk together with the transports. The surviving half of our corps was then ordered to proceed eastward, according to plan, along the narrow path that crossed the island's central mountain range. Our objective was Burauen airfield, but we had only just reached the foot of the mountains when we ran into the scattered remnants of another army corps, which had set out ahead of us. It appeared that they had been turned back by an American flying column armed with trench mortars.

We now tried to cross the mountains farther south where there was no path at all, but as soon as we started to climb we were subjected to a fierce trench mortar attack from three directions. We returned on the double to the foot of the mountains and deployed. The various companies spread out over the valley and pitched camp; a liaison officer was dispatched to the base at Ormoc for further instructions. When he returned, the rumor spread among the soldiers that headquarters had sent us orders to force our way across the mountains, but that our C.O. had torn them up in disgust.

Be that as it may, our company, which by now had been decimated to the size of a platoon, remained in a small village in the valley. The rations, brought with us from Ormoc, were soon exhausted, nor was it long before we had finished the corn and other cereals that the Filipino inhabitants had left behind when they abandoned their houses. Our activities became concentrated on searching for potatoes, bananas, and any other food that we could lay our hands on in the nearby fields and hills.

For the purpose of these foraging expeditions our company was divided into three groups. One group would go and live off the land for a few days; when they returned, they would bring enough food for themselves and for the third group to live on while the second group went out in its turn. Often on these expeditions they would run into members from other units and fierce arguments would ensue as to which company had the preferential rights in such and such an area. Inevitably the distance and duration of the foraging trips became longer as the weeks went by.

After my hemorrhage I was not fit to carry heavy loads and therefore could not take part in the foraging. Fom this stemmed the ineluctable order to go and kill myself.

As I made my way between the trees toward the sentries they looked up at me in silent greeting. I dreaded having to repeat my formal report to the N.C.O. in charge; even more, I hated exposing myself to their apathetic sympathy. I felt that they were all waiting for the fateful words, "I've been thrown out," and it seemed ages before I reached the tree trunk around which they were gathered.

The lance corporal's pale face was impassive while he listened to my report. Yet, when I had finished, I could see that he was moved, as if my fate had reminded him of his own uneasiness about the future.

"I really don't know who's better off," he muttered, "you or we. It won't be long now before they'll be ordering us to mass for a final breakthrough. At least you'll be getting out of that!"

"I don't suppose they'll let you into the hospital, though," said one of the soldiers.

I smiled.

"If they don't let me in, I've just got to wait till they do," I said, repeating the squad leader's words. But all this time I was wondering how to bring the scene to an end as quickly as possible.

When I said good-bye, I noticed that one of the soldiers with whom I exchanged glances had a twisted look on his face. I wondered if the twisted look that I felt on my own face was catching, like a yawn.

Thus I left my company.

Chronology: 1600–1945

1600: Tokugawa hegemony established following battle of Sekigahara

1639–40: Portuguese expelled; persecution of Christians continues

1641: Exclusion Policy (*sakoku*) begun

1688–1703: Genroku era of literary-cultural opulence

1791–92: American and Russian ships try to enter Japan

1804: Russian envoy arrives at Nagasaki

1837: Urban riots led by Ōshio Heihachirō at Osaka

1853: Commodore Perry arrives at Uraga

1854: Perry returns, Treaty of Kanagawa is concluded between Japan and US

1858: Three ports—Kanagawa, Nagasaki, Hakodate—opened to foreign trade

1860: First foreign mission sent to the United States

1863: British ships bombard Kagoshima

1864: Chōshū rebellion

1867: Revolt leads to end of feudal Tokugawa shogunate

1868: Meiji restoration; Imperial rule formally proclaimed

1871: Feudal domains abolished

1873: Conscription begun

1877: Satsuma rebellion put down; establishment of Tokyo University

1881: Constitution promised

1885: First cabinet

1889: Meiji Constitution

1890: First Diet convened; Imperial Rescript on Education issued

1894–95: Sino-Japanese War; Japan receives Taiwan and rights in Korea

1899: Extraterritoriality ended for foreigners

1900: Participation in suppression of Boxer Rebellion

1902: Anglo-Japanese alliance

1904–5: Russo-Japanese War

1910: Korea annexed

1912: Taishō era begins

1915: Twenty-One Demands made by Japan on China

1918: Rice riots begin in Tōyama, spread rapidly throughout Japan

1919: Versailles Treaty gives Japan former German concessions in China's Shantung province

1921: Washington Conference; Hara Kei assassinated

1923: Great Kantō Earthquake; socialists murdered in Tokyo jail; mob attacks Koreans

1925: Peace Preservation Law; Universal Manhood Suffrage Law

1926: Shōwa era begins (reign of Emperor Hirohito)

1930: London Naval Treaty

1931: Manchurian Incident

1932: Puppet state of Manchukuo established as Japanese colony; Prime Minister Inukai assassinated

1933: Japan withdraws from League of Nations

1936: Attempted *coup d'état* known as February 26th Incident

1937: China Incident provokes Japan to invade China (Marco Polo Bridge)

1940: Rome-Berlin-Tokyo Axis established; political parties and labor unions dissolved; Imperial Rule Assistance Association set up

1941: Neutrality agreement with Soviet Union; Anglo-Dutch oil embargo; Japan attacks the United States at Pearl Harbor

1941–45: Greater East Asia War (Daitōa Sensō)

1945: Japan accepts Potsdam Proclamation and surrenders to the Allies

Further Reading

Books listed here are useful for more detailed information in several areas; some literature is included. Books used in *The Japan Reader* are not included.

1. Japan's Feudal Origins, 1800–1868

John W. Hall, "Feudalism in Japan—a Reassessment", in John W. Hall and Marius B. Jansen, eds., *Studies in the Institutional History of Early Modern Japan*, Princeton University Press, Princeton, N.J., 1968

Barrington Moore, Jr, *Social Origins of Dictatorship and Democracy*, Allen Lane The Penguin Press, 1973

G. B. Sansom, *The Western World and Japan*, Barrie & Jenkins, 1966

Bradley Smith, Marius Jansen and Nagatake Asano, *Japan: A History in Art*, Simon & Schuster, New York, 1964

Thomas C. Smith, *The Agrarian Origins of Modern Japan*, Stanford University Press, Stanford, Calif., 1959

Oliver Statler, *Japanese Inn*, Random House, New York, 1961

2. Meiji Japan–Foundations for Empire, 1868–1890

W. G. Beasley, *The Meiji Restoration*, Oxford University Press, 1973

Fukuzawa Yukichi, *The Autobiography of Fukuzawa Yukichi*, Columbia University Press, New York, 1966

Marius B. Jansen, "The Meiji State: 1868–1912", in James B. Crowley, ed., *Modern East Asia: Essays in Interpretation*, Harcourt Brace Jovanovich, New York, 1970

3. Industrialization and Imperialism, 1890–1929

Hilary Conroy, *The Japanese Seizure of Korea*, University of Pennsylvania Press, Philadelphia, 1960

Hyman Kublin, *Katayama Sen: The Making of a Bolshevik*, Princeton University Press, Princeton, N.J., 1964

Mishima Yukio, *Spring Snow*, Secker & Warburg, 1972

Marlene J. Mayo, ed., *The Emergence of Imperial Japan: Self-Defense or Calculated Aggression?*, D. C. Heath & Co., Lexington, Mass., 1970

Robert A. Scalapino, *Democracy and the Party Movement in Prewar Japan* University of California Press, Berkeley and Los Angeles, 1953

4. Depression, Militarism and War, 1929–1945

David Bergamini, *Japan's Imperial Conspiracy*, Heinemann, 1971

Hugh Byas, *Government by Assassination*, Alfred A. Knopf, New York, 1942

Noam Chomsky, "The Revolutionary Pacifism of A. J. Muste: On the Backgrounds of the Pacific War", *American Power and the New Manderins*, Penguin Books, Harmondsworth, 1969

Hilary Conroy, "Japan's War in China: Historical Parallel to Vietnam?" *Pacific Affairs*, XLIII:I, Spring, 1970

James B. Crowley, "A New Deal for Japan and Asia: One Road to Pearl Harbor", in James B. Crowley, ed., *Modern East Asia: Essays in Interpretation*, Harcourt Brace Jovanovich, New York, 1970

Mishima Yukio, "Patriotism", *Death in Midsummer, and other Stories*, Penguin Books, Harmondsworth, 1971

Mishima Yukio, *Runaway Horses*, Alfred A. Knopf, New York, 1973

Ivan Morris, ed., *Japan 1931–1945: Militarism, Fascism, Japanism?*, D. C. Heath & Co., Boston, 1963

George O. Totten, ed., *Democracy in Prewar Japan: Groundwork or Facade?*, D. C. Heath & Co., Boston, 1967

Tanizaki Junichirō, *The Makioka Sisters*, Alfred A. Knopf, New York, 1956

Yoshie Sugihara and David W. Plath, *Sensei and his People: The Building of a Japanese Commune*, University of California Press, Berkeley and Los Angeles, 1969

Notes on Contributors

G. C. ALLEN is a specialist on Japanese economic history at the University of London.

AYUSAWA IWAO is a professor at the International Christian University in Tokyo.

W. G. BEASLEY is Professor of History at the School of Oriental and African Studies, University of London.

HARUMI BEFU teaches anthropology at Stanford University.

T. A. BISSON taught at Yenching University in Peking in the late 1920s, published *America's Far Eastern Policy,* and worked during the Occupation of Japan with the U.S. Strategic Bombing Survey and the Government Section, SCAP. He taught at the University of California, Berkeley, from 1948 to 1953. He was a major figure in the controversy over the Institute of Pacific Relations in the early 1950s, and is currently preparing a memoir of the Occupation period.

HUGH BORTON is Professor of History at the East Asian Institute, Columbia University.

JAMES CROWLEY teaches history at Yale University.

R. P. DORE teaches sociology at the Institute of Development Studies, University of Sussex, England.

PETER DUUS teaches history at the University of California, Berkeley.

JOHN EMBREE was a pioneer in researching Japanese society. His *Suye Mura,* published in 1939, is still a standard work on the Japanese village.

JOHN K. EMMERSON was a career foreign service officer. He served as U.S. Minister to Japan from 1962 to 1966.

FUKUTAKE TADASHI is Professor of Sociology at the University of Tokyo.

FUTABATEI SHIMEI was one of the first Western-style novelists in Japan.

CAPTAIN VASILII GALOWNIN was captain of a ship in the Russian Imperial Navy captured by the Japanese off Hokkaido during a foraging raid in 1811.

ROBERT GUILLAIN, who spent part of World War II in Japan, is the Tokyo correspondent for the French newspaper *Le Monde*.

IHARA SAIKAKU was the most famous novelist of the Tokugawa period and wrote such classics as *Five Women Who Loved Love* and *The Life of an Amorous Woman*.

JIPPENSHA IKKU, author of *Shank's Mare* (*Hizakurige*), was a famous satirist of the late Tokugawa period and his novel-travelogue is a classic of ribald Japanese humor.

ISHIKAWA TAKUBOKU was a poet in the late Meiji period, and was one of the few Japanese to actively oppose the Russo-Japanese War of 1904–05.

BARONESS SHIDZUÉ ISHIMOTO was a noted early Japanese feminist and advocate of birth control. As a result of her activities (she brought Margaret Sanger to Japan for a speaking tour), she was imprisoned by the militarist government in the 1930s. After World War II, she and her husband entered politics as socialists.

JOSEPH M. KITAGAWA is Professor of Religion at the University of Chicago.

WILLIAM W. LOCKWOOD teaches economics at Princeton University.

WALTER MCLAREN was a journalist/observer of the early Japanese political scene from the 1890s onward, when he lived in Japan.

NOBUTAKE IKE taught political science at Stanford University.

MAKI IZUMI was a dissident samurai and political activist in the Bakumatsu period at the end of the Tokugawa feudal regime.

MATSUKATA KŌJIRŌ, a prominent industrialist during the Meiji period, owned shipyards and other enterprises.

MARLENE MAYO teaches Japanese history at the University of Maryland.

HELEN MEARS is the author of several books about her travels in Japan.

NOMA HIROSHI is a well-known postwar Japanese novelist.

E. HERBERT NORMAN, one of the first Western scholars of Japan to use Japanese-language sources, was a Canadian diplomat by profession. He is the author of *Japan's Emergence as a Modern State* and *Andō Shōeki*.

OOKA SHŌHEI is a famous postwar Japanese novelist.

JOHN E. ORCHARD, a specialist on Japanese economics, did field work in Japan before World War II.

HERBERT PASSIN is Professor of Sociology at Columbia University.

J. W. ROBERTSON SCOTT was a British agronomist.

GEORGE B. SANSOM, who taught at Stanford and Columbia universities, is the author of the standard history of premodern Japan (to 1867): *A History of Japan,* in three volumes.

T. C. SMITH is Professor of History at the University of California, Berkeley.

KURT STEINER is Professor of Political Science at Stanford University.

RICHARD STORRY is a British historian at Oxford University who has written several books on modern Japan.

GWEN TERASAKI, originally an American citizen, married a Japanese diplomat just before the beginning of World War II and spent the war years in Japan.

GEORGE OAKLEY TOTTEN, III, is Professor of Political Science at the University of Southern California.

YANAGIDA KUNIO is the author of many books about the Meiji era.

YAZAKI TAKEO is Professor of Sociology at Keiō University in Tokyo.

ARTHUR MORGAN YOUNG was a journalist who lived in Japan and wrote about the Taishō period.

Index

Abe, Isō, 298, 300
abortion, 24
Adachi, Kenzō, 362
adoption, 9, 163
adultery, 428–9
Against the Storm (journal), 402
age-grade system, 40–1
agriculture: depression and, 375;
    fascism and, 389–90; imperialism
    and, 431–8; Meiji period, 111,
    129–32; Tokugawa shogunate,
    22–5; World War II and, 449–51.
    See also peasants; rice; tenant
    farmers
Aichi cotton mill, 111–12, 119
Aikawa, Yoshisuke, 381, 383
Akamatsu, Katsumaro, 272, 385
Akashi, Motojirō, 356
All-Japan Farmers' Union, 254–5
Allen, G. C., 338, 378–83
alternate attendance, 15, 18, 50
Amakasu, Captain, 331
anarcho-syndicalism, 302–4, 328–9
"Ancient on Account and Modern
    Cash Down" (Saikaku), 72–5
Anglo-Japanese Alliance (1902),
    199, 225–6, 227, 231
Arao, Kiyoshi, 362–5
Arashi o Tsuite (journal), 402
Arima, Count, 432
Arimatsu (Secretary of Home Of-
    fice), 293
army: bushidō in, 229; colonial gov-
    ernment and, 224–5; develop-

ment, 165–71; in fiction, 485–94;
    increase, 225, 227, 232; right of
    supreme command, 228, 229–30,
    368, 369–70; samurai and, 167,
    168–70. *See also* conscription;
    Kwantung Army; military
artisans, 11, 96–7
Asahara, Kenzō, 390
Asano Company, 120, 121, 286
Ashio Copper Mine, 297, 303
Asia, emancipation of, 359. *See also*
    imperialism
Asō, Hisashi, 273, 388, 393, 395
assembly, elective, 194–5; Itagaki
    and, 178–81; in local govern-
    ment, 204–6. *See also* Diet
Ayusawa, Iwao, 291–8, 410–13

banishment, 39
bank of Japan, 339, 373, 381
banking: 1927 crisis in, 337, 338–9,
    341; zaibatsu and, 287–8, 289,
    338–9, 379, 380–1
batsu (cliques), 262–3, 265
Beasley, W. G., 15–19, 63
Befu, Harumi, 34–42
Bismarck, Otto von, 293
Bisson, T. A., 342–5, 456–64
Black Dragon Society. *See* Kokury-
    ūkai
blood taxes, 125. *See also* taxation
Bolshevism, 328–9
Borton, Hugh, 49–55, 157

Brotherhood of the New Life, The
    (U.S. utopian colony), 151
Buddhism, 156, 158; in fiction, 62,
    67–71
burakukai (block association),
    447–8
bureaucrats: as political bloc, 343–5;
    samurai as, 3, 93, 97–8
bushidō (warrior code), 17–18, 229

cabinets: balance of power in, 343;
    colonial government and, 224–5;
    Diet and, 207–8; rivalry in, 229,
    232–5. See also names of specific
    cabinets, e.g. Konoe cabinet
Canadian Pacific Railway, 214
capitalism, 19–21, 117–18, 247, 289
careers, education and, 260–1
cartels, 375, 459–60
caste system, 3, 7–12, 13, 96–8. See
    also social classes
Chiang Kai-shek, 351
Chichibu uprising, 183–4
Chikamatsu, Monzaemon, 20
children: education of, 439–42; laws
    concerning, 163–4; of miners,
    317–18; as slaves, 11, 24. See
    also family structure, daughters
    in, . . . sons in
China, 215, 219–21, 238–9, 350–1,
    368–9. See also Sino-Japanese
    War
China Incident, 393, 395, 401, 411.
    See also Marco Polo Bridge
    Incident; Sino-Japanese War
    (1937)
chōnaikai (block association), 447–8
Chōshū (province), 87–90
Christian socialists, 299, 302
Christianity, 156, 157, 158
Chu Hsi, 16, 59
civil service, 261
Civilian Volunteer Corps, 464
Class. See caste system; middle
    class; social classes

coalition politics, 208–10, 343–5
colonial governments, 223–5, 227
combines. See zaibatsu
Comintern, 392, 399, 400, 401
commerce. See foreign trade
Commercial Shops Act, 412
Commoners' Newspaper, 269, 301–2,
    398
Commoners' Society, 301–2
Communist party: history, 397–401;
    1932 Thesis of, 405–9; repression
    of, 330–1, 333, 392, 399, 400
Conciliation Society, 411
Conference of the Three Religions
    (1912), 158
Confucianism: education and, 150,
    152, 154–8; family structure and,
    160; organizations of, 156–7
conglomerates. See zaibatsu
Congress of Japanese Labor Unions,
    391
Conroy, Hilary, 216, 226
conscription, 105, 125, 169; efficacy
    of, 171–5; exemption from,
    173–4; nationalism and, 229;
    peasants and, 173, 442–4. See
    also army; military; navy
Conscription Act of 1872–1873, 172,
    173, 174–5
Constitution of 1889, 106–7, 157,
    202; Diet and, 188, 193, 194–5,
    207–8; Emperor and, 187–8, 190;
    formulation of, 186–94; Gneist
    on 189; opposition to, 208; pro-
    mulgation of, 206–7; Stein on,
    189–90
Control Faction, 370
corruption, political, 210–11, 236–8
Council of Japanese Labor, 334
Cromwell, Oliver, 88
Crowley, James, 166–71, 225–30,
    231–5, 368–70
culture, 20, 62–3, 99
currency depreciation, 109, 371,
    373–4

Dai Nippon factory, 413–20
Daikyō ("Great Teaching or Doctrine"), 156
daimyō (lords), 3, 7–8
Dajōkan (Council of State), 175, 191, 203
Dark Ocean Society. *See* Genyōsha
Darwinism, imperialism and, 217, 221
daughters. *See* children; family structure, daughters in; women
democracy: failure of, 195–6; industrialization and, 340; Meiji period, 175, 185–6, 194–5, 205–6; memorial on, 178–80
Depression, Great, 322, 337–8, 341–2; agriculture and, 375. *See also* economic conditions
Diet (Parliament): budget approval and, 188, 189, 193, 202, 207, 209–10, 231–5; constitutional power, 188, 193, 194–5, 207–8; convening of, 235–6; corruption in, 210–11, 236–8; Sino-Japanese War (1894) and, 221, 223. *See also* assembly, elective
divorce, 59, 426–7, 428–9
Dore, R. P., 431–8, 450–1
dormitory system, 133–4, 306–7, 308–10, 413–22
"Dose of What the Doctor Never Orders, A" (Saikaku), 75–9
du Bousquet, Albert Charles, 168
Duus, Peter, 271–4

earthquakes, *1891*, 209–10; *1923*, 210, 331, 337
Echigo (province), 50–1
economic conditions: Meiji preiod, 108–16, 127–8, 129–32; *1919–1929*, 336–42; *1930–1940*, 349, 371–8, 456–7; Russo-Japanese War, 296; Sino-Japanese War (1894), 222, 292; Tokugawa shogunate, 4, 13–14, 19–25; World War I, 252–3, 319, 321–2; World War II, 457. *See also* Depression, Great

Edo, 18, 20; cultural life, 63, 71; population, 19, 92. *See also* Tokyo
education: career and, 260–1; competitive nature of, 258–60; Confucianism and, 150, 152, 154–8; conscription and, 172; elementary, 152–3, 439–42; family structure and, 265–8; Imperial Rescripts on, 151–4, 157–8; Meiji period, 147–58; modernist movement in, 155–6; morality and, 150, 152–4, 155, 157–8, 265–9, 439; nationalism and, 148, 149–51; politics and, 263–5; salary scales and, 261–2; Shinto and, 154–5, 156, 158, 267; Taishō period, 257–69; Tokugawa shogunate, 59; Westernization of, 155–6; of women, 259, 416–17. *See also* schools
elections: local, 204–5; *1890*, 208; *1928*, 254, 333; *1930*, 388; *1932*, 390
Elementary School Decree (1886), 149
Embree, John, 439–44
Emmerson, John K., 397–405
emperor: constitutional power, 187–8, 190; genro and, 208; as institution, 186, 195–6; loyalty to, 265, 266; political role, 345; restoration of, 194; reverence for, 256–7
England: alliance with (1902), 199, 225–6, 227, 231
ethics. *See* Morality
Etō, Shimpei, 170

factories, 296; dormitory system in, 133–4, 306–7, 308–10, 413–22; sale of 118–21. *See also* industries
Factory Act, 412

family structure, 107; daughters in, 133-4, 161; education and, 265-8; "house" concept in, 424-7; ideology of, 267-8; of merchants, 136; of peasants, 159-61; of samurai, 57-9, 158-60, 162-4; sons in, 58, 161-2, 163-4, 429-30; urbanization and, 160-2; wives in, 58, 59, 162-4, 275-84, 424-31

Family System as Ideology, The (Kawashima), 268

Farmer-Labor party, 254

farmers' unions, 244, 251, 396; fascism and, 389-90. *See also* tenants' unions; names of specific unions

fascism, 389-90, 391-2; political parties and, 390, 392-6. *See also* right-wing movements; totalitarianism

fashion, 72-5, 136

February 26 Incident, 369, 370, 435

feudalism, 3-6; caste system of, 7-12, 13; restoration attempts, 177; samurai and, 56-62. *See also* Tokugawa shogunate

filial piety, 266. *See also* morality

Fires on the Plain (Ōoka), 489-94

First Bank, 289

First Higher School, 259

five-man groups, 35, 37, 39, 450

foreign trade, 200; imperialism and, 432-3; Meiji period, 108-11; *1930-1940*, 371-3; World War II and, 457; zaibatsu and, 379. *See also* tariffs

Formosa, 213; colonial government of, 223-4; strategic importance of, 214, 216, 225; trade with, 371

Française Bussan (company), 453

Friendly Society, 327, 422

Fujihara, Ginjirō, 461 and n.

Fukagawa Cement Factory, 120

fukoku kyōhei (rich country, strong army), 165, 179, 202, 269

Fukudome, Admiral, 227

Fukumoto, Kazuo, 400

Fukuoka (city), 355-8

Fukuoka silk mill, 118, 120

Fukutake, Tadashi, 240-4, 245-51

Fukuzawa, Yukichi, 150, 155-6, 183, 217-21

Furukawa (zaibatsu), 121, 237, 286, 289

Furuzawa, Shigeru, 178

Futabatei, Shimei, 138-46

Galownin, Vasilii, 7-12

General Federation of Japanese Farmers' Union, 396

General Federation of Labor, 327-8, 329, 386, 395, 409, 422

General Mobilization Law, 410, 411

genro (council of elder statesmen), 208, 234

Genyōsha (Dark Ocean Society), 354, 355, 357-67

George, Henry, 298

Gneist, Rudolf von, 189, 190

gold standard, 341, 380

Gotō, Shōjirō, 130, 170, 178, 181

Great Japan Production party, 435

"Great Teaching or Doctrine," 156

Greenbie, Sydney, 256-7

Guillan, Robert, 475-84

Hadley, Eleanor, 452-6

Hakamada, Satomi, 392

Hani, Setsuko, 424-31

Hara, Takashi, 325

Harris, Thomas Lake, 151

Hayashi, Miss (union organizer), 420

Heimin Shimbun (*Commoners' Newspaper*), 269, 301-2, 398

Heiminsha (Commoners' Society), 301-2

Hewes, Lawrence, 449-50

Hideyoshi, Toyotomi, 44

High Treason Trial (1910-1911), 304. *See also* Kōtoku, Denjirō

Hiko, Joseph, 363
Hirano, Rikizō, 389–90
Hiranuma, Senzō, 291, 434
Hiraoka, Kotarō, 356, 357, 360
Hiroshima, 483–4
Hirota, Koki, 356, 446
Hitachi Works, 381
Hizen uprising, 170
Holding companies, 287–8, 453–4
Home Affairs, Ministry of, 203–4, 206
Hoshi, Tōru, 237
Hoshino Plan, 459
"house," as family community, 424–7
house laws, 114–15, 287
housing, westernization of, 135–6

Ieyasu. *See* Tokugawa, Ieyasu
Ihara, Saikaku, 20, 72–9
Ike, Nobutaka, 159–62, 176–81, 186–96
Ikeda, Seihin, 381
Ikku, Jippensha, 64–71
Imperial House Law, 191, 192
Imperial Household, 157
Imperial Rescript (1879), 150, 151–3
Imperial Rescript (1881), 186
Imperial Rescript on Education (1890), 107, 153–4, 157–8; ceremonial readings of, 257, 267, 442
Imperial Rule Assistance Association, 446
Imperial Steel Works, 320, 321
Imperial University Decree (1886), 149
Imperial Way Association, 389
imperialism, 199, 212–19, 225–30; agriculture and, 431–8; in China, 219–21, 238–9, 350–1, 368–9; Darwinism and, 217, 221; foreign trade and, 432–3; in Formosa, 213, 214, 216, 223–4, 225, 371; in Korea, 199, 213, 215–16, 219, 225–8, 231, 371; in Liao-

tung Peninsula, 119, 213, 214, 216, 223, 225, 227; liberalism and, 218; in Manchukuo, 351, 369, 375–6, 381–3, 385, 431–2; in Manchuria, 217, 225, 227–8, 231, 296, 353, 368; military and, 368; in Russia, 214–15, 225, 227, 228, 296; Western, 83–4, 85–6. *See also* national security; Russo-Japanese War; Sino-Japanese War; World War II
Industrial Bank, 339
industrial control, World War II and, 458–64
Industrial Control Associations, 459, 463
Industrial Patriotic Society, 391, 410, 411–12
industrialization: democracy and, 340; Meiji period, 106, 114–22, 131–2, 286; merchants and, 114–15, 117; motivations for, 108–13; *1930–1940*, 373, 456–7; Russo-Japanese War and, 199–200, 296; Sino-Japanese War (1894) and, 199–200, 291–2, 296; taxation and, 105; World War I and, 318–22; World War II and, 457–8; zaibatsu and, 339–40
industries: cottage, 21, 110–12, 200, 305–6; dormitory system in, 133–4, 306–7, 308–10, 413–22; government and, 118–21, 200, 286, 375; heavy, 296, 320–1, 374–5, 376, 456–8; investment in, 115–16, 117, 286; mass production in, 136; Meiji period, 106, 114–22, 131–2; military, 118, 121–2; "nationalization" of, 462–4; *1930–1940*, 411; silk, 111, 118, 320, 337, 371, 374; textile, 118–20, 296, 320, 371–2, 374, 376, 456–7. *See also* factories
infanticide, 24
Inoue, Junnosuke, 341, 373
Inoue, Kaoru, 187, 188, 191–2, 210–11, 237, 238, 381

Inoue, Tetsujirō, 157
intelligentsia, fascism and, 391–2
International Labor Organization
    (ILO), 409–10
International Workers of the World
    (IWW), 302
Inukai, Ki Tsuyoshi, 350, 354
Inukai cabinet, 369
Ishimoto, General, 232
Ishimoto, Shidzué, 274, 275–84,
    313–18
Ishimura Company, 120
Itagaki, Taisuke, 170, 175, 177–81,
    192, 208
Itō, Chūbei, 98
Itō, Hirobumi, 148, 176, 209, 226;
    constitution of 1889 and, 187–94
Itō, Myōji, 191
Itō, Noe, 331
Iwakura, Tomomi, 112, 113, 176,
    187–8, 356
Iwasaki (zaibatsu), 211, 237, 287,
    291
Iwasaki, Yatarō, 120
Izumo uprising, 53–5

Japan Broadcasting Corporation,
    261–2
Japan Economic Federation, 459
Japan Farmers' Union, 253–5, 389,
    396, 402
Japan General Federation of Labor,
    327–8, 329, 386, 395, 409, 422
Japan-Labor clique, 387, 388
Japan Proletarian party, 392, 393–4,
    402
Japan Socialist Federation, 328
Japan Socialist party, 302
Japan Year Book (1905), 237–8
Japanese National Socialist party,
    435
"Japanese Situation and the Duty of
    the Japanese Communist Party,
    The." See 1932 Thesis
Japanist doctrine, 265–6

Jimmin no Koe (journal), 402
Jiyūtō (Liberal party), 174, 182–5,
    195, 202, 208, 298–9

Kabuki theater, 20
Kagawa, Toyohiko, 330
Kagoshima mill, 118
Kaibara, Ekken, 58
Kaishintō (Progressive party), 184,
    202
Kamei, Kanichirō, 394
Kanagawa (union leader), 389
Kanaya, General, 368
Kaneko, Kentarō, 190, 191–2, 193
K'ang Yu-wei, 220
Katayama, Sen, 295, 298, 300, 303,
    304, 401
Katō, Hiroyuki, 180–1, 298, 300
Katō, Kanjū, 390
Katsura, Taro, 229, 233–4
Kawakami, Hajime, 229, 272, 401
Kawasaki (zaibatsu), 121, 286, 289
Kawasaki shipyard, 312–13, 330
Kawashima, Takeyoshi, 268
Kenseitō (Constitutionalist party),
    237
Kido, Kōin, 90, 174, 176
Kimigayō (national anthem), 256–7
Kishi, Nobusuke, 461
Kishida, Ginkō, 363
Kita, Ikki, 437
Kitagawa, Joseph, 14–15, 154–8
Kizakimura dispute, 254
Kobe (city), 322, 323, 330, 398
Kōdōkai (Imperial Way Associa-
    tion), 389
Koiso cabinet, 458, 461, 463
Kokoro (Natsume), 161–2
Kokuhonsha (right-wing group), 434
Kokumin Dōmei (political party),
    396
Kokumin no Tomo (journal), 298
Kokuryūkai (Black Dragon So-
    ciety), 354, 355, 365, 367
Kokushō, Iwao, 124, 126
Komuchi, Chijo, 360

Komuro, Nobuo, 178
Konoe, Fumimaro, 395
Konoe cabinet, 369, 396, 446, 459
Kōnoike (zaibatsu), 289
Korea, 199, 213, 225–8, 231, 371;
strategic importance of, 215, 216,
219. See also *seikanron*
Kōtoku, Denjirō, 298, 300, 302–3,
304, 328
Kōtoku, Shūsui, 398
Kuhara, Fusanosuke, 433
Kuhara Mining Company, 381
Kuroda (Minister President), 209
Kwantung Army, 353, 368, 385. See
also army; military
Kyōchō Kai (Conciliation Society),
411
Kyōdo Un'yu Kaisha (company),
120
Kyogaku Taishi. See Imperial Re-
script (1879)

labor. *See* workers
labor disputes, 410–11. *See also*
strikes
Labor-Farmer party, 254, 255, 334,
387, 399
labor laws, 412
labor movement, 253; fascism and,
391; *1919–1929*, 327–31; *1930–
1940*, 410–13; repression of, 201,
292–7, 300, 327, 330, 332–5,
350; Sino-Japanese War (1894)
and, 292; socialism and, 301;
weakness of, 422–3; zaibatsu
and, 290
labor unions: fascism and, 389;
membership, 410; miners and,
316; right-wing groups and, 361;
riots and, 297; Sampō and, 412;
statistics, 327; women workers
and, 310, 419–23. *See also* names
of specific unions
land: cultivated, 27, 51, 129; sale of,
129, 130

land registers, 42–3
land tax, 109, 127–9, 129–32. *See
also* taxation
landlord system: local government
and, 240–4, 247–51; totalitarianism and, 437–8; World War II
and, 449–51. *See also* tenancy;
tenant farmers
landowners, 42–5, 61; absentee,
50–1; politics and, 182–5; taxation of, 128–9; tenants and, 45–8,
53; types of, 241–2; weakened
authority of, 243
League of Nations, 410
League of Proletariat Youth, 334
Lebon, Major, 167
Liaotung Peninsula, 199, 213; colonial government of, 223, 227;
strategic importance of, 214, 216,
225
Liberal party, 174, 182–5, 195, 202,
208, 298–9
liberalism, 175, 181–5; imperialism
and, 218; of students, 271–4;
Taishō period, 340; of zaibatsu,
454–6
Light (journal), 302
literacy, 99, 168, 247. *See also* education
literature: autobiography, 275–84;
465–74; communist, 400; fiction,
64–71, 72–9, 138–46, 161–2,
485–94; poetry, 270, 274–5;
satire, 64–71
local government, 204–6, 245–51,
445–8. *See also* villages, administration of
Local Institutions Research Institute,
446
Lockwood, William, 285–90, 336–
42, 371–8
London Conference (1930), 351
lords. *See* daimyō
loyalty, 229; to emperor, 265, 266.
See also morality; nationalism

MacCauley, Mr. (missionary), 422

McLaren, Walter, 177, 203–11, 221–5, 235–9

Maebashi filatures, 118

Mahan, Alfred Thayer, 225, 226, 228

Major Industries Association Ordinance, 459, 463

Maki, Izumi, 85–6

Makino family, 50–1

Manchukuo, 351, 369, 385; emigration to, 375, 431–2, 441; industrialization, 375, 376, 381–3, 433

Manchukuo Heavy Industries Development Company, 382

Manchuria, 225, 227–8, 231, 296, 368; importance, 217, 353

Manchurian Incident (1931), 353, 385–8, 393, 399–400

March Incident, 370

Marco Polo Bridge Incident (1937), 368, 384, 393, 395. *See also* China Incident

Marriage, 58–9, 163, 275–84, 425–7. *See also* divorce

Marxism, 268

Matsudaira (Lord of Hōki), 89

Matsudaira, Harusato, 53

Matsui, General, 368

Matsukata, Kojirō, 311–13

Matsukata, Masayoshi, 110, 111, 119, 209

Matsutani, Yojirō, 388

Mayet, Paul, 129

Mayo, Marlene, 212–21

Mears, Helen, 413–24

Meckel (historian), 225, 226, 228, 229

Meiji period (1868–1912): agriculture, 111, 129–32; centralized government of, 95–6, 203–4; democracy in, 175, 185–6, 194–5, 205–6; economic conditions, 108–16, 127–8, 129–32; education in, 147–58; foreign trade, 108–11; industrialization in, 106,

114–22, 131–2, 286; politics in, 175, 176–81, 194–6, 203–11, 235–9, 342–5; social reforms of, 125–6, 135–7

Meiji restoration, 90–101, 194

merchants: culture end, 71; employees of 137; family structure of, 136; in fiction, 72–9; house laws of, 114–15, 287; industrialization and, 114–15, 117; as moneylenders, 18, 21; samurai and, 3, 13–14, 18, 19–20, 93; as social class, 10–11, 20, 96–7, 136

middle class, zaibatsu and, 289–90

Middle School Decree (1886), 149

military, 9–10; in fiction, 485–94; influences on, 228–9; peasants and, 434–7; politics and, 343–5; right of supreme command, 228, 229–30, 368, 369–70; zaibatsu and, 382–3, 452–3, 458–64. *See also* army; conscription; Kwantung Army

military expenditures, 231–5

military techniques, Western, 87–90

Mill, John Stuart, 195

millionaires, 237–8

miners, 313–18, 324

Mining Workers' Regulations, 412

Minjin Dōmei (student group), 272

Minobe, Tatsukichi, 428

Minseitō (political party), 341, 396

missionaries, 6, 84

Mitsubishi (zaibatsu), 120–1, 200, 211, 286–9 passim, 338, 383, 453; salaries at, 262

Mitsubishi Heavy Industries Company, 452, 462

Mitsui (zaibatsu), 21, 120, 121, 200, 286–91 passim, 338, 453; camouflage policy of, 380; Inoue and, 210–11; politics and, 237, 238, 453–4

Mitsui, Kurōemon, 74–5

Mitsui, Takakimi, 453–4

Mitsui Bank, 287, 380, 381

Mitsui Bussan (company), 287, 379, 380
Mitsui Gōmei (company), 287
Mitsui Kōzan (company), 288
Mitsui Mining Company, 262
Mitsui Tea Company, 380
miyaza (shrine association), 39–40
mob appeal. *See* riots
Mombetsu sugar refinery, 111
money economy. *See* economic conditions, Tokugawa shogunate
morality, 150, 152–4, 155, 157–8, 265–9, 439. *See also* loyalty
Mori (zaibatsu), 382
Mori, Arinori, 147, 148–51
Mori, Kaku, 432
Mori, Ōgai, 264
Mori, Takachika, 87–8
Morihiro, Ikuta, 54
Morihiroya, Gampei, 54
Motoda, Eifu, 147, 148, 150, 152–3
Mukden Incident. *See* Manchurian Incident
Municipal Code, 204
Munitions Company Act, 458, 462, 464
Munitions Ministry, 458, 461–4
mura hachibu (ostracism), 39, 41
Musansha Shimbun (newspaper), 399
Mutsu, Munemitsu, 213

Nakagawa, Zennosuke, 160, 425
Nakajima (politician), 209
Nakano, Seigō, 356
Nankatsu labor union, 331
Nara, Miss (union organizer), 420
Nashimoto, Prince, 257
National Conference of Japanese Labor Unions, 390
National Farmers' Union, 255
National General Mobilization Law, 410, 411
National Labor-Farmer Masses' party, 255, 387–8, 390
National Principle group, 369

national security, 166–71, 215–17, 225, 227–8. *See also* imperialism
National Spiritual Mobilization Movement, 446
nationalism, 148, 149–51, 196, 229, 354–67. *See also* loyalty
Nationalist Labor party, 395
Nation's Friend (journal), 298
Natsume, Sōseki, 161–2
navy, 224–7, 231, 232; right of supreme command, 228, 229–30, 368, 369–70. *See also* conscription
neighborhood associations, local government and, 446–8
New Century (journal), 302
Nihon Musantō (Japan Proletarian party), 392, 393–4, 402
Nihon Shakaishugi Dōmei (Japan Socialist Federation), 328
Nihon Shakaitō (Japan Socialist party), 302
Nihon Yūsen Kaisha (company), 120
1932 Thesis, 392, 400, 401, 404; text of, 405–9
Nippon Nōmin Kumiai (Japan Farmers' Union), 253–5, 389, 396, 402
Nippon Railroad Company, 120
Nippon Sangyō Kaisha. *See* Nissan
Nishikawa, Kōjirō, 295, 303
Nissan (zaibatsu), 381–3, 453
Nisshin Boeki Kenkyūjo (Sino-Japanese Commercial Research), 364
Nitto Tea Company, 380
nobility, 8; restoration of, 190–1
nōhei (peasant armies), 86–90
Noma, Hiroshi, 485–9
Nōmin Rōdōtō (Farmer-Labor party), 254
Norman, E. H., 87–90, 116–22, 124–9, 171–5, 181–5, 354–67
Nozaka, Sanzō, 392

Obata, Kōan, 89
October Incident, 370, 435
Ōgawa, Shigejirō, 428
Okano, Susumu, 399, 401, 402, 404
Ōkawa, Shūmei, 435, 437
Ōkubo, Toshimichi, 115, 170, 174, 176, 204
Ōkuma, Shigenobu, 176, 192–3, 208, 223, 239, 271; corruption of, 210–11, 237
Ōkura (zaibatsu), 237, 286
Ōkura, Kihachirō, 291
Ōmura, Masujirō, 89–90, 166–7
"On Armaments" (Fukuzawa), 219
One Hundredth Bank, 289
Ōoka, Shōhei, 489–94
Orchard, John, 305–10, 318–22, 332–5
Osaka, 18, 63; Communist party in, 402; population, 19, 92; riots in, 81–2, 323
Ōshio, Heihachirō, 81–2
ostracism, 39, 41
Ōsugi, Sakae, 303, 304, 328, 331
Owner-Farmer Establishment Scheme, 432
Ōyama, General, 227
Ozaki, Yukio, 209, 233–4

paddy farming, wet, 26–33
Parliament. See Diet
Parliamentary Rescript (1881), 206
Passin, Herbert, 148–51, 257–69
Patriotic United Action Association, 435
Peace Preservation Act (1925), 253, 334–5, 349
peasant armies, 86–90
peasant uprisings, 49–55; Meiji period, 105–6, 111, 124–7, 131, 173, 183–4, 252. See also rice riots; riots
peasants: conscription and, 173, 442–4; economic conditions of, 129–32, 341; family structure of, 159–61; landowners and 45–8,

53; military and, 434–7; politics and, 182–5; as social class, 3, 11, 22–5, 46–8, 96–7; social control of, 36–41, 48; social reforms and, 125–6; village life of, 35–41, 439–44. See also agriculture; tenant farmers
political parties, 200–1, 233–6, 349; dissolution of, 394–6, 402, 446; fascism and, 390, 392–6; Meiji period, 107, 175–85, 194–6; repression of, 254, 255; socialist, 298–302; zaibatsu and, 379–80. See also names of specific parties
politicians, as political bloc, 343–5
politics: of coalition, 208–10, 343–5; corruption in, 210–11, 236–8; education and, 263–5; emperor and, 345; landowners and, 182–5; Meiji period, 175, 176–81, 194–6, 203–11, 235–9, 342–5; military and, 343–5; Mitsui and, 453–4; peasants and, 182–5; Russo-Japanese War and, 231–5; Sino-Japanese War (1894) and, 221–2, 223; tenants' unions and, 254–5; zaibatsu and, 343–5, 379–80, 453–4
Popular Rights movement, 175, 185–6
population, 19, 92, 160–1
Portsmouth, Peace of, 296
Postmen's Brotherhood, 389
priests, 8–9
primogeniture, 160–1, 162–4, 289
princes. See daimyō
prisoners: as miners, 315; as slaves, 11–12
Privy Council, 224, 324; constitution and, 192–3
producers' cooperatives, 244. See also farmers' unions
Prussia, 180–1, 292–3
Public Peace Police Act (1900), 293–5, 296–7, 300

Quigley, Professor, 193

racism, 331
railroads, 120
Red Flag (newspaper), 392
Red Flag Incident, 304
Reimei (Asō), 273
religion. *See* Buddhism; Christianity; Confucianism; Shinto
repression: of communism, 330–1, 333, 392, 399, 400; in labor movement, 201, 292–7, 300, 327, 330, 332–5, 350; of political parties, 254, 255; of socialism, 300, 301–2, 304; of students, 333
Rezanov, Nikolai, 6
rice, 19, 22; cultivation of, 26–33; price of, 109, 296, 323, 451
rice riots, 51, 80, 398–9; of 1918, 201, 253, 322–6, 327, 344–5. *See also* peasant uprisings; riots
right-wing movements, 354–67, 391, 434–7; *See also* fascism; totalitarianism
riots, 49–50, 53, 54–5, 80–2, 297. *See also* peasant uprisings; rice riots
Robertson Scott, J. W., 26–33
Rōdō Nōmintō (Labor-Farmer party), 254, 255, 344, 387, 399
Roessler, Dr. Carl Friedrich Hermann, 191–2
rōnin (lordless warriors), 52–3, 87, 358–9
Roosevelt, Franklin D., 455
Roosevelt, Theodore, 231, 296
Root-Takahira agreement, 231
Rousseau, Jean Jacques, 195
Russia, 214–15, 227, 228, 231; Japanese Communist party and, 401; Manchuria and, 225
Russo-Japanese War (1904), 199–200, 296, 301–2, 351, 356

Saigō, Takamori, 165, 169–70, 174, 177, 199, 263, 356, 357, 358, 359
Saikaku. *See* Ihara, Saikaku
Saionji, Kimmochi, 189, 232–3, 302
Saitama (union leader), 389
Saitō cabinet, 364
Sakai, Toshihiko, 301, 303, 387
Sakatani, Yoshirō, 428
salary. *See* wages
Sampō (Industrial Patriotic Society), 391, 410, 411–12
samurai: army and, 167, 168–70; as bureaucrats, 3, 93, 97–8; family structure of, 57–9, 158–60, 162–4; fashion and, 73–4; feudalism and, 56–62; in fiction, 62, 64–7; Meiji restoration and, 90–101, 106, 113; merchants and, 3, 13–14, 18, 19–20, 93, 109, 112; role change of, 15–18, 56, 95; as social class, 3, 9–10, 57–60, 92–3, 96–7, 263; tradition of, 16–17, 95–6; uprisings of, 109, 112–13, 170, 172–3, 177, 237. *See also* rōnin; Satsuma Rebellion
Sansom, G. B., 21–5
Sangyō Hōkoku Kai. *See* Sampō
Sanwa Bank, 289
Sasaki, Shirō, 453–5
Sat-Cho faction, 176–7, 210. *See also* Meiji period, politics in
Satsuma Rebellion, 113, 172–3, 177, 237
schools, 97, 177, 257–60; elementary, 439–42. *See also* education; names of specific schools
sea transportation, 120–1
seikanron (1873 Korean controversy), 169–70, 182, 356. *See also* Korea
Seinan War, 170
Seiyūkai (Landlords' party), 182, 185, 233, 234, 333, 396
servants, 47
Shakai Minshutō (Social Democratic party), 298, 300, 385–8, 390, 393

Shakai Taishūtō (Socialist Masses party), 390–1, 392–3, 394–5, 402
Shakkintō (Debtors' party), 183
Shanghai Incident, 356
Shank's Mare (Ikku), 62, 64–71
Shibun Gakkai (Society for the Cause of Truth), 156–7
Shibusawa (zaibatsu), 237, 286, 289
Shidehara cabinet, 369, 433, 454
Shimada (politician), 209
Shimazaki, Tōson, 264
Shimmachi mill, 120
Shimonoseki, Treaty of (1895), 217, 292
Shinagawa Glass Factory, 120
Shinjinkai (student group), 272
Shinoda Company, 120
Shinto, 154–5, 156, 158, 267
Shiseikai (Association of Equality of Ideas), 156
shogun, 194
shogunate, 13, 36. *See also* Tokugawa shogunate
Shōheizaka Gakumonjo (college), 156
Shokkō Giyūkai (Workers' Volunteer Society), 292
Shōwa period (1926–): economic conditions, 349, 371–8, 456–7; foreign trade, 371–3; industrialization, 373, 456–7; labor movement, 410–13
shrine association, 39–40
shushigaku (Neo-Confucianist philosophy), 59
Siberia, 353
Sino-Japanese War: *1894–1895*, 199–200, 214, 219–23, 225, 291–2, 296, 351; *1937–1945*, 351, 433–4. *See also* China
slaves, 11–12
Smith, T. C., 42–8, 91–101, 108–16, 129–32
social classes, 135. *See also* caste system

Social Democratic party, 298, 300, 385–8, 390, 393
Social Policy Academic Association, 299
Socialist Masses' party, 390–1, 392–3, 394–5, 402
Socialist movement, 298–304, 328–9
Socialist Party Conference (1907), 303
Socialist Society, 299–300, 301, 302
Society for the Study of Socialism, 299
Society to Correct Abuses, 298
Soejima (constitutionalist), 181
soldiers. *See* army; rōnin; samurai
sons. *See* children; family structure, sons in
South Manchuria Railway Company, 382
Spencer, Herbert, 190, 195
Stein, Lorenz von, 189–90
Steiner, Kurt, 445–8
Storry, Richard, 19–21
strikes, 292, 302, 309, 312–13, 330, 398, 403; Ashio Copper Mine, 297, 303; of miners, 324; Toshima Post Office, 389; tramway workers, 297–8, 304
students, 269–74; repression of, 333
succession, family. *See* primogeniture
suffrage, 129–30, 181, 328; universal, 263–4; universal manhood, 201, 247, 263
Sumitomo (zaibatsu), 121, 200, 286, 287, 288, 289, 453
Sumitomo Honsha (company), 288
sumptuary regulations, 71, 76–7
Sun Yat-sen, 359
supreme command, right of, 228, 229–30, 368, 369–70
Suye Mura (village), 439–44
Suzuki, Bunji, 327, 422
Suzuki and Company, 323
Suzuki cabinet, 458–9, 463, 464
syndicalism, 302–4, 328–9

Tada, General, 368
Taft-Katsura Agreement, 231
Taishō period (1912–1926), 234;
economic conditions, 252–3, 319,
321–2, 336–42; educational sys-
tem, 257–69; industrialization,
318–22; labor movement, 327–
31; liberalism of, 340; local government, 250–1
Taiwan. *See* Formosa
Takahashi, Korekiyo, 373
Takano, Fusatarō, 292
Takasugi, Shinsaku, 83–4, 87–8
Takeuchi, Chief, 387
Takigawa, Professor, 429
Takuboku, Ishikawa, 274–5
Taman, Kiyoomi, 394
Tanaka (zaibatsu), 121
Tani, Takeki, 173
tariffs, 108–9, 110, 372–3. *See also*
foreign trade
taxation, 50, 51–2, 53, 105, 126–9,
131. *See also* land tax
Tazoe, Tetsuji, 303
tenancy, 242–3. *See also* landlord
system
tenancy disputes, 243, 253, 254, 449
tenant farmers, 129; contracts of,
242–3; emigration of, 431–2;
statistics on, 240–1; Tokugawa
shogunate, 25, 45–8, 53, 61;
World War I and, 252–3; World
War II and, 449–51. *See also*
agriculture; landlord system;
peasants
tenants' movement, 243–4, 251–5
tenants' unions, 201; politics and,
254–5; statistics on, 251–2. *See
also* farmers' unions; names of
specific unions
Terasaki, Gwen, 465–74
Terauchi, Seiki, 325
Third International, 399
Tientsin Treaty (1885), 215
"To the People" (Takuboku), 269,
270

Tōjō, Hideki, 458, 459, 460, 461
Tokugawa, Ieyasu, 3, 13, 14, 60
Tokugawa shogunate (1603–1867),
4–5, 13; economic conditions,
4, 13–14, 19–25; education during, 59; government of, 14–15,
34–42, 52, 60–2, 245. *See also*
feudalism
Tokyo: 1923 earthquake, 337; firebombing of, 475–84; population,
160–1; riots in, 323–4; tramway
strike in, 297–8, 304. *See also*
Edo
Tokyo First Middle School, 259
Tokyo Higher Normal School, 150
Tokyo Imperial University, 149,
259, 260, 299; student movement
at, 271–2
Tomioka silk mill, 111, 113, 118
tonarigumi (neighborhood groups),
447–8
Torio, Koyata, 168–9, 180, 193
Toshima Post Office strike, 389
totalitarianism, 395–6, 437–8, 445–8.
See also fascism; right-wing
movements
Totten, George, 298–304, 327–31,
385–96
Toyada, Teijirō, 461 n.
Tōyama, Mitsuru, 354, 356, 358,
359–63, 366
trade unions. *See* labor unions
trans-Siberian railway, 214, 226
Tripartite Intervention (1895), 199,
225, 292
Twenty-One Demands (1915), 199

Uchida, Ryōhei, 356, 358, 366
Ueda, Professor, 160–1
Uehara, General, 232, 233, 234
Ueki, Emori, 174
Ukigumo (Futabatei), 138–46
Ukiyo (floating world), 63, 71
Unions. *See* farmers' unions; labor
unions; tenants' unions

United States, 227, 228, 231, 372; Japanese Communist party and, 404–5. *See also* World War II

urbanization, 160–2, 375–6

U.S.S.R. *See* Russia

"V Narod" (Takuboku), 269, 270

Versailles Conference, 199

Village Associations, 449

village codes, 36–9

village elders, 35, 60

village headman, 34, 40, 44, 60–1, 204, 245

village life, 35–41, 439–44

village youth groups, 40–1

villages: administration of, 34–42, 52, 60–62, 245, 249–51; landlord system in, 240–4, 247–51; totalitarianism and, 437–8; World War II and, 449–51. *See also* local government

Voice of the People (journal), 402

voting. *See* suffrage

wages, 132–3, 137, 305–6, 374; education and, 261–2; of government ministers, 135; for men, 306, 307, 317; of miners, 317; for women, 306, 307, 317, 418, 423

Wakatsuki cabinet, 368

Wakukawa, Seiyei, 251–5

warriors. *See* rōnin; samurai

Welfare Ministry, 412

westernization, 135–6, 155–6

wives. *See* family structure, wives in; women

women, 164; in autobiography, 275–84; education of, 259, 416–17; as factory workers, 133–4, 308–10, 413–24; as miners, 315–16, 317–18; in poetry, 274–5; status of, 164, 424–31; wages of, 306, 307, 317, 418, 423. *See also* family structure, daughters in, . . . wives in

workers, 132–4, 137, 305, 311–13, 376; in literature, 138–46; women as, 133–4, 308–10, 413–24; World War I and, 319, 321, 322. *See also* labor movement

Workers' Volunteer Society, 292

working conditions: dormitory system, 133–4, 306–7, 308–10, 413–22; legislation on, 412–13; of miners, 313–18; *1930–1940*, 411, 412; Taishō period, 305–10, 311–13

World War I, 252–3, 318–22, 353

World War II, 351–2; agriculture and, 449–51; in autobiography, 465–74; economic conditions, 457; in fiction, 485–94; firebombing of Tokyo, 475–84; foreign trade and, 457; industrial control during, 458–64; industrialization in, 457–8; local government and, 445–8; zaibatsu and, 452–6, 458–64

Yamada, Kengi, 90, 168, 169

Yamaga, Sokō, 16

Yamagata, Aritomo, 90, 169, 176, 209, 232, 233, 234; corruption of, 237; military strategy of, 172–3, 174, 213–17

Yamaguchi (zaibatsu), 289

Yamakawa, Colonel, 150

Yamakawa, Hitoshi, 303, 329–30

Yamamoto, Gombei, 234

Yamamoto, Kenzō, 392

Yamamoto cabinet, 234–5

Yanagida, Kunio, 132–4

Yasuda (zaibatsu), 121, 200, 237, 286, 383, 453; as bankers, 287, 288, 289

Yasuda Hozensha (company), 288

Yazaki, Takeo, 57–62, 80–2, 135–7, 162–4

Yokohama Specie Bank, 339, 381

Yonai, Mitsumasa, 396

Yoshida, Shigeru, 454–5, 461 n.

Yoshida, Shōin, 222
Yoshikawa, Suejirō, 394–5
Yoshino, Sakuzō, 272, 273
Young, Arthur, 322–6
Yūaikai (Friendly Society), 327, 422
Yūbin, Jōkisen Kaisha (company),
120

zaibatsu (financial oligarchs), 121,
200, 285–90; banking and, 287–8,
289, 338–9, 379, 380–1; camouflage policy of, 380; as family
enterprises, 286–7, 289; foreign
trade and, 379; holding companies of, 287–8, 453–4; house
laws of, 114–15, 287; industrialization and, 339–40; labor movement and, 290; liberalism of,
454–6; Manchukuo and, 381;
middle class and, 289–90; military and, 382–3, 452–3, 458–64;
Munitions Ministry and, 458,
461–2; "nationalization" of industry and, 462–4; *1930–1940*,
378–83; politics and, 343–5, 379–
80, 453–4; Sino-Japanese War
(1894) and, 291; World War II
and, 452–6, 458–64. *See also*
Mitsubishi; Mitsui; Sumitomo;
Yasuda
Zenkoku Nōmin Kumiai (National
Farmers' Union), 255
Zenkoku Rōnō Taishūtō (National
Labor-Farmer Masses' party),
255, 387–8, 390
Zennō. *See* Zenkoku Nōmin Kumiai
Zennō Zenkoku Kaigi (Zennō All-
National Congress group), 255
Zone of Emptiness (Noma), 485–9

More about Penguins and Pelicans

The Emerging Japanese Superstate

Herman Kahn

Herman Kahn, whom Bernard Levin described as "the man who contemplates calmly what other men are reluctant or even afraid to contemplate", marshals his enormous erudition and expertise in this Pelican to predict the future of the Japanese nation.

Resilience, spectacular growth and an "unbelievable display of social solidarity and community responsibility" have resulted in Japan becoming the third greatest economic force in the world, after the U.S.A. and the U.S.S.R. So far this strength has arisen from a highly developed domestic industrial base and has had the minimum of international political effect.

But, the author asks, could this economic miracle result in a Japanese economic imperialism? In view of the paradoxical character of the Japanese, might they challenge the nuclear giants in a bid for military superpower? If they did so successfully, Kahn prognosticates, the core of civilization would shift from the Atlantic to the Pacific.

The Emerging Japanese Superstate is a gripping, chilling and thoughtful book; and the author, by airing his theories, has performed a valuable service both for the Japanese and the rest of the world.

Japanese Imperialism Today

"CO-PROSPERITY IN GREATER EAST ASIA"

Jon Halliday and Gavan McCormack

One Japanese design for "co-prosperity with its Asian neighbours" ended in disaster in the 1940s. Since then, with solid backing from its old enemy, the United States, Japan has achieved a remarkable recovery.

Jon Halliday and Gavan McCormack have written a lively and convincing Marxist study of Japan's new economic empire in Asia, detailing the new forms of dependency and control built into its relations with the region. They argue that Japan, having established during the 1960s a powerful grip on South-East Asia's markets, is now tightening its fist on the supply of raw materials: by 1980 it plans to monopolize 30 per cent of the entire world's raw-material exports.

While concentrating on East and South-East Asia, the authors set their analysis firmly in the context of Japan's changing relations with the United States and China, adding appendices on the Soviet Union and Australasia. To complete the picture, they describe the internal restructuring of Japan's society and economy that has accompanied overseas expansion, and in particular they pinpoint the speed and extent of Japan's rearmament.